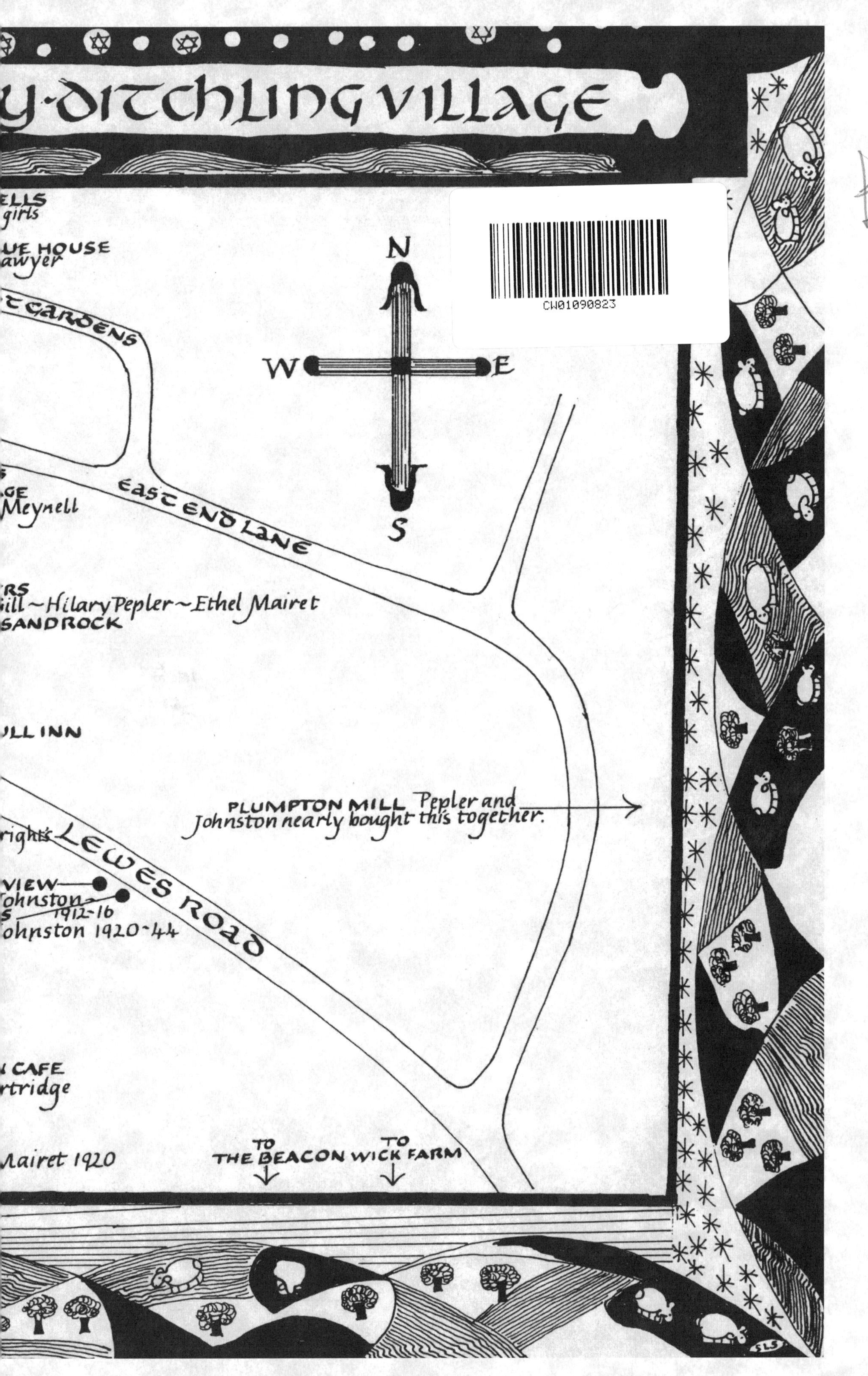

CW01090823
E4

Edward Johnston
Master Calligrapher

PETER HOLLIDAY

Edward Johnston 1902

Edward Johnston

Master Calligrapher

Peter Holliday

'We shall remember thy great water, O Silver River,
Oh river, grey or golden, or crimson dyed by
the sun, you in all your moods have life.'

EDWARD JOHNSTON 1911

The British Library
&
Oak Knoll Press
2007

First published 2007 by
The British Library
96 Euston Road
London NW1 2DB
and
Oak Knoll Press
310 Delaware Street
New Castle
DE 19720

© The Estate of Peter Holliday 2007

Cataloguing-in-Publication data
available from the publishers

ISBN 978 07123 4927 7 (British Library)
ISBN 978 1 58456 198 9 (Oak Knoll)

Designed by Peter Holliday, Sam Mullen and Susan Skinner
Typeset in Adobe Caslon

THIS STUDY IS OFFERED TO MY TEACHERS
AND MY COLLEAGUES, MY STUDENTS
AND MY FRIENDS

Note

Peter Holliday had almost completed his book: EDWARD JOHNSTON: MASTER CALLIGRAPHER when he tragically died on the 4th of November 2003. He knew that I, his sister, as a calligrapher and writer, recognized the importance of what he was doing, so the day before his death he asked me to see the book on its way as soon as possible and to seek whatever help I could. I soon realized that the job of putting his erudite chapters, full of footnotes and illustrations and subheadings, into book form would be impossible on my own. There were various print-outs of individual chapters but nothing had been finalized. In other words, the book was still in the computer. With this in mind I sought the help of Sam Mullen, Peter's 'computer angel'. I couldn't have made a better decision. It is true to say that without Sam's expertise, patience, tenacity and sense of artistry this book could never have seen the light of day. I myself have lightly edited the chapters but rarely changed the writing itself. Peter's research was impeccable, and has left the reader with an option of reading the book right through, or studying it in conjunction with endnotes and the three appendices.

He wrote the preface in 2002, and on his behalf I would like to extend his gratitude to all who helped him in 2003 and to add my own thanks to Patricia Lovett and Jenny Moulton and acknowledgement to anyone I have been unable to contact or have unwittingly missed.

Susan Skinner

Preface

This study is intended to place Edward Johnston in the context of the ideas and people who helped shape his thought and work. In no sense is it a biography, for the good reason that the account of Johnston's life written by his daughter Priscilla Johnston in 1959 has such intimate knowledge and warmth that it is unlikely to be superseded. Nevertheless, the chronology of Johnston's life is one of the structures of this study as is the pattern of his life among his fellow artist-craftsmen, first in London and then in Ditchling.

The project germinated during the time I was teaching in the School of Graphic Design at Ravensbourne College of Design. It seems odd now that the name Edward Johnston was not especially dear to the students, nor even to the staff, during the period from the mid-1970s to 1990. Attention was focused elsewhere, on ostensibly more relevant developments for graphic design such as the Russian Constructivist movement, Bauhaus theory, Swiss modernist graphics, or Californian post-modernist departures.

My realisation of Johnston's role in the formation of twentieth-century letter design and typography came gradually. It was prompted (as Johnston himself was) by an interest in that period of transition from the handwritten manuscript to the printed page which took place from the mid-fifteenth to early sixteenth centuries.

My interest was quickened by the calligraphy exhibition, *Sharpness Unity & Freedom*, occasioned by the fiftieth anniversary of Johnston's death, which was held at Ditchling Museum in April, 1994. The question then arose: given Johnston's dates (1872–1944), what part did he himself play in the development of modernist design thinking in Britain? And what was his impact on others? His followers, many of whose work was shown in the Ditchling exhibition, formed a Johnston tradition that became predominant in Britain. Its calligraphers do not appear remotely to have been connected to modernism. Yet Johnston's typographic legacy clearly does. Is this because of Johnston, or was it in spite of him?

Answers would emerge only by understanding Johnston within the broad context of the ideas of his time. A project presented itself: to examine Johnston's philosophical roots. His voice needed to be heard within three interconnected but implicitly rival systems of thought. One was the the Arts and Crafts movement, to which Johnston himself was a brother born. The second was the more diffuse modern movement itself, of which Johnston's block letter alphabet used for the London Underground is a clear affirmation. The third was the nineteenth-century resurgence of Roman Catholicism, of which the craft-based Guild of St. Joseph and St. Dominic in Ditchling, was an important offshoot. For the Guild was begun by Johnston's two closest friends and colleagues, Eric Gill and Hilary Pepler, and located on the common of his home village. These movements were further intertwined by virtue of having developed during the same period of time. Furthermore, Johnston's place in twentieth-century design history, already elusive on account of the complexity of these movements, is made more so because he himself was largely reticent about the matter. There is no autobiography and few public utterances or personal statements of belief from Johnston's own hand. There can only be certain illuminations.

The project was fostered by the most promising circumstances. Johnston, it seemed, was to be celebrated as one of a group of craftsmen to be shown in a much expanded Ditchling Museum, to be funded by the Heritage Lottery Fund. The Museum would be able to show and explain more fully the communality of Ditchling's twentieth-century artist-craftsmen within the wider history of the handmade artefact – an aesthetic of 'manufacture' – first acclaimed by Johnston's mentors, John Ruskin, William Morris, and William Richard Lethaby. Recognition, it seemed, would come not only to Johnston, who is anyway firmly on the map, but to the village of Ditchling. As home to other pre-eminent artist-craftsmen, including Eric Gill, Ethel Mairet, Frank Brangwyn, Hilary Pepler, David Jones, Joseph Cribb, Dunstan Pruden, and Philip Hagreen, Ditchling is quite as significant a place as, say, St. Ives in the history of English artistic craft and design. Sadly, this project did not materialise.

To return to Johnston. Good decisions were made by those who have secured many of Johnston's papers for public collections. And there are compensations, perhaps, for the fact that they are shared between scattered institutions in Los Angeles, Texas, New York, Chicago, Edinburgh, Oxford, Cambridge, Farnham, London, and Ditchling itself. For it is remarkable how views can be inspired according to the location in which one studies – by the enveloping Gothic brown of Dr. Williams' Theological Library in Bloomsbury, by the spacious clarity of the new British Library, by the rambling, makeshift cellars of the Dominican archives in Edinburgh. But how fitting it is that a significant portion of Johnston's papers have found their way back to Ditchling, where he worked and thought for thirty-two years in his modest workshops in his three Ditchling homes – Downsview, Halletts, and Cleves.

ACKNOWLEDGEMENTS

Directly and indirectly many people helped me in this project. Firstly thanks go to Susan Skinner, who designed the maps and did much else besides; to Hermann Zapf, James Mosley, Gerry Cinamon, Michelle Brown, Alan Crawford, Nicolas Barker, Gillian Naylor, Justin Howes, Ray Watkinson, Godfrey Rubens, Peter Cormack, John Nash, and Peter Faulkner who each surveyed aspects of the lettering and design history; to Father Bede Bailey and Hilary Bourne who gave advice about Roman Catholic and local history; to Colin Maitland, Colin Maugham, and Patrick Burke, who gave editorial advice; to Diana de Vere Cole, Ivor Davies, Gustav Metzger, Rosslyn Cole, Geoff White, and Joan Denvir who read drafts; to Ron Saunders who undertook proofreading; and to Zita Drew who, at the outset, did much word-processing.

A second line of support, upon which I have been entirely dependent, has come from libraries and museums and their staffs, notably: the V&A's National Art Library, National Archive of Art and Design, and Picture Library; the St. Bride Printing Library; the Crafts Study Centre, now at Farnham; Ditchling Museum; The British Library, its Oriental and India Office Collections and its Manuscripts Department; Cambridge University Library; the Bodleian Library; Dr. Williams's Library; the Brighton and Hove Public Libraries; St. Peter's House, Brighton University; the Local History Archives of Hammersmith Library, and Chiswick Library; the Record Office for East Sussex at Lewes and for West Sussex at Chichester; the Palaeography Room at Senate House, London University; the William Morris Society; Heythrop Theological College; the School of Oriental and African Studies; the Royal Society of Arts; the Tate Gallery; and the Royal College of Art – all in London; the Edward Clark Library at Napier University, and the Archives of the English Province of the Order of Preachers, both in Edinburgh.

More distant support has come from the librarians of the Harry Ransom Humanities Research Center at the University of Texas at Austin, Texas; the Newberry Library, Chicago; the William Andrews Clark Foundation, at UCLA; and the Pierpont Morgan Library, New York City.

Information, advice, help, and encouragement have been given to me by John Scruby, John Dreyfus, Heather Child, Rupert Otten, George Ramsden, Graham Forbes, Geoff Green, Eva White, Lucy Myers, Bernie Blackmore, Philip Poole, Jeremy Carden, Barbara Muir, Bridget Wilkins, Rivka Sinclair, Roger and Ginny and Clare Broadbent, Ann Phillips, Nicki Jarvis, Katie Wilmshurst, Barry Marks, Gillian Jason, Maire McQueeney, Winifride Denyer, Cleo Witt, Maria Dorigato, Winefride Pruden, Zoë Lubowieska, Yoshiko Yasumura, Michiyo Mori, Yuko Kikuchi, Yoshie Nakayama, Yoko Fukuda, Alix and Juliette Wheeler, Marjorie Kenny, Ewan Clayton, Michael Renton, Oliver Clark, Colin Banks, Malcolm Smith, Rosemary Voaden, Keith Hogg, Dr. Milo Keynes, Dorothy Keats, Lynne Aldcotte, Nigel Roche, Jo Wallace, Bernard Horrocks, Cornelia

Thiels, Tim McCann, Eugene Rae, Mark Walker, Margaret Payne, Dorothy Carr, and George Breeze.

Material help was given by David Glews and Nola Fontaine. Importantly, Winnie Wamaitha Thuo and Jon Aistui listened and so, in her own way, did Amélie Muller who – *une fille à l'oeil de faucon* – spotted many a hidden typo. Through Enfys Roberts, serendipity played a hand.

Acknowledgement for the inclusion of quotations is due to Andrew Johnston for the Edward Johnston material, to Rosalind Hague for entries from the Gill diaries, to Christopher and Lawrence Pepler for the use of Hilary Pepler's letters, and to John Nash, William Gardner, Felicity Ashbee, Susan Falkner, Hilary Bourne, and David Leach for other quotations.

Acknowledgement is due to the following for the inclusion of quotations from their titles (itemised in the text): Faber and Faber; Carcanet Press; Lund Humphries; Whittington Press; Iceni Press; Kodansha International; Burns and Oates; Longmans Green & Co; Sir Isaac Pitman & Sons; Brighton and Hove Museums (for a detail of the endpapers map); the archives of the English Province of the Order of Preachers at Edinburgh. Similarly, acknowledgement is due to the following journals: *The Chesterton Review*; *Blackfriars*; *Print Collectors' Quarterly*; *The Register*; *The Times Literary Supplement*; *The Dublin Review*; *Craft History One*; *The Scribe* (the journal of the Society of Scribes & Illuminators).

For quotations from other letters, documents and the reproduction of illustrations acknowledgement is also due to Clare Broadbent and to Roger and Ginny Broadbent; to the Syndics of Cambridge University Library; to the Trustees of the Royal Society of Arts (for the reproduction of the Johnston/Graily Hewitt lecture to the RSA [Royal Society of Arts]); to the William Andrews Clark Memorial Library, UCLA; to the Crafts Study Centre, Farnham; to the Trustees of Ditchling Museum; to the Trustees of the Victoria and Albert Museum (for the facsimile printing of the Johnston manuscripts and other illustrations); and to the Trustees of the National Portrait Gallery for reproductions of portraits of Johnston.

All copyright omissions will be settled in good faith.

CONTENTS

ILLUSTRATIONS

CHAPTER ONE

CHAPTER THREE

CHAPTER FOUR

CHAPTER FIVE

CHAPTER SIX

CHAPTER TEN

CHAPTER ELEVEN

APPENDIX ONE

APPENDIX TWO

sincerely
Edward Johnston
14.4.mcmxxx.A.D.

Edward Johnston

Edward Johnston

it. E. J. 13.4.19-
28. A.D.

it. E. J. 13.4.19-
28. A.D.

it. E. J. 13.4.19-
28. A.D.

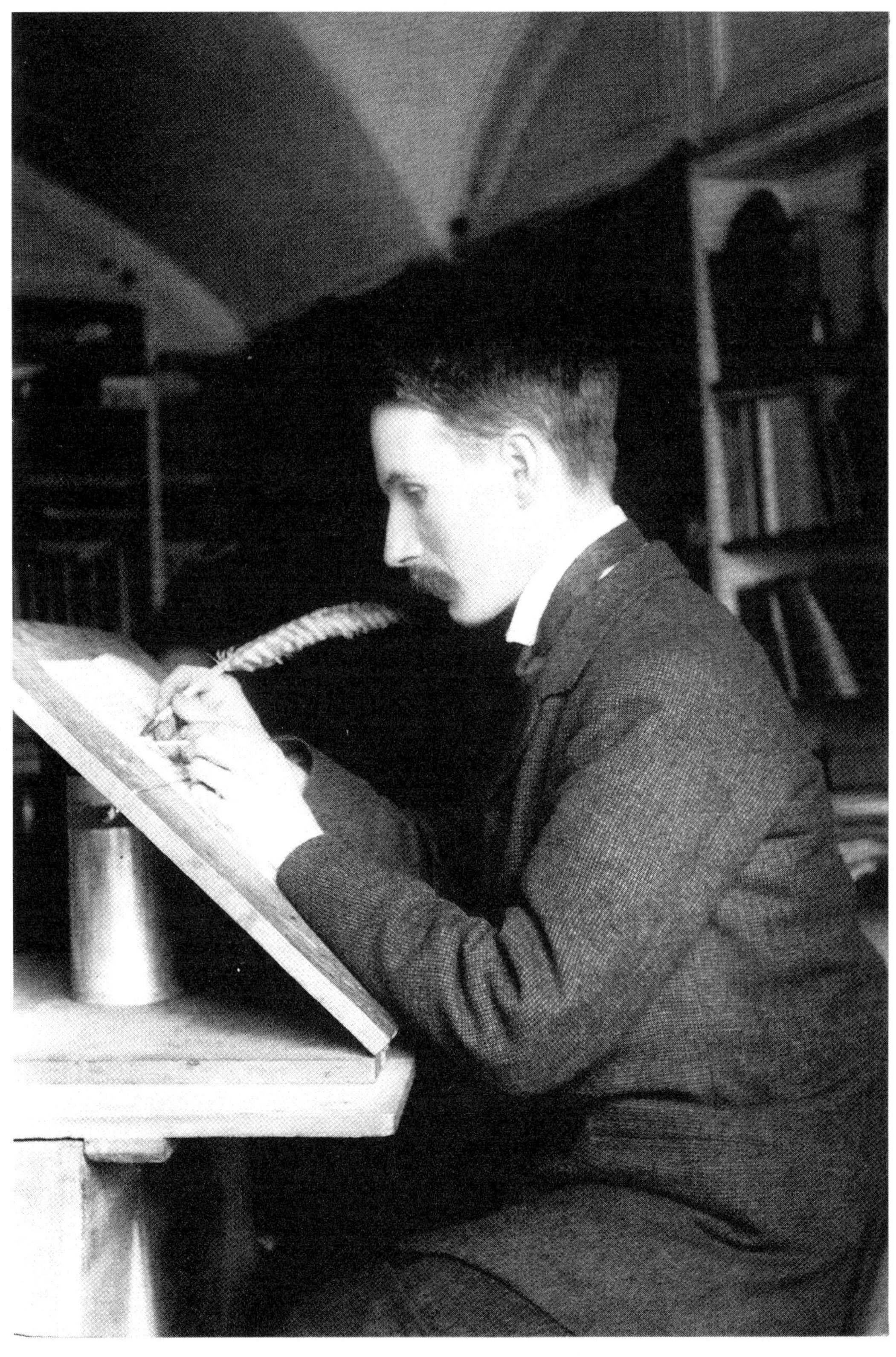

Johnston working at his desk in his apartment in Old Buildings, Lincoln's Inn, Holborn. 1902.
(Courtesy of the Edward Johnston estate).

CHAPTER ONE

EDWARD JOHNSTON
A BIRD'S EYE VIEW

Edward Johnston

The making of things was Edward Johnston's life force. Johnston's 'things' were informed by clear beliefs and made more vital by the like-minded views of his friends and associates who not infrequently helped engender them. Between these elements a mutuality flourished. To name Johnston's skills is not so straightforward, however. At the outset of his career in 1898–9 he said he was: 'only a letterist or "Scribe" '.[1] Towards its end, in 1939, on becoming a CBE (Commander of the British Empire) he said what he did was:

> ... difficult to define but the least unsatisfactory term for it seems to be calligrapher.[2]

Johnston was involved in calligraphing and illuminating texts on paper or on vellum to create documents such as rolls of honour and addresses. However, he also designed alphabets and, in one exceptional commission, typefaces for books. So, additionally, he can be described as a penman, as an illuminator and as a type designer. A wider description is Johnston's own phrase – a 'letter-craftsman'. More fundamentally he was an artist-craftsman doing jobbing work. These overlapping terms describe different facets of Johnston as a maker.

But Johnston was equally a thinker, a writer and a teacher. He set out to formulate a philosophy of the lettering arts. His aim was to restore letters to their essential forms. He pointed to historical exemplars, though these were to be 'weeded of archaisms' as he put it. His concern from the outset was to take:

> ... the best letters we can find and acquire them *and make them our own.*[3]

Johnston, however, was forward-looking rather than historicist. He wanted letters to meet the needs of the contemporary, even urban, world. His reforming zeal was

CALLIGRAPHY & ILLUMINATION
A paper read before the Society of Arts on the 31st January 1905, with additional matter & illustrations by the Author. 29. Novr. 1905.
The development of the book-hands from the Roman alphabet, shewing the growth of varied letter forms for use or ornament, is the key to the practical study of calligraphy & illumination. Doubtless the forms of the letters of the fine inscriptions in stone and the forms used in writing, acted and reacted upon each other, so that the pen, the chisel, and the brush all con-

Fig. 1. Johnston's first lecture, 1905, 'Calligraphy & Illumination', title page from Johnston's calligraphed transcript.

WRITING & ILLUMINATING, & LETTERING
BY EDWARD JOHNSTON. WITH DIAGRAMS & ILLUSTRATIONS BY THE AUTHOR & NOEL ROOKE
8 pp. EXAMPLES IN RED & BLACK AND 24 pp. OF COLLOTYPES

PUBLISHED BY JOHN HOGG
13 PATERNOSTER ROW
LONDON 1906

Fig. 2. Johnston's handbook, *Writing & Illuminating, & Lettering* ('The Artistic Craft Series of Technical Handbooks'. John Hogg, 1906).

charged with a social as well as an aesthetic purpose. Such restored letters would be 'useful' to people, as well as being imbued with artistic 'life' – two further words which Johnston made especially his own – and so bring fulfilment to those who might write or read them. Johnston's purpose remained constant:

> We aim at readableness or making the written words easy-and-pleasant-to-read. This then is the scribe's direct purpose –*The making of useful things legibly beautiful.*[4]

Johnston's earliest public utterance was his little-known lecture, 'Calligraphy and Illumination' (Fig. 1), given to the Society of Arts in 1905.[5] The achievements for which he is best known occurred in the period following this lecture up to the end of the First World War. His 'guide' for 'Letter-craftsmen and Students', called *Writing & Illuminating, & Lettering* (Fig. 2), was published in 1906. The second volume in the 'Artistic Craft Series of Technical Handbooks', it is justly regarded as a classic manual of craft practice and, with Johnston's revisions, has remained in use and even in print ever since. His basic teaching script, which was modelled on tenth-century English Carolingian writing and named by him Foundational hand, had its starting point in that book. Johnston begins with remarks about the general aptness of the Carolingian script as a model.

The manuscript he finally settled on was the late tenth-century British Library *Harley MS. 2904* (or the *Ramsey Psalter*)[6] – see Fig. 35:

Manuscript &
Inscription Letters

FOR SCHOOLS & CLASSES
& for the use of CRAFTSMEN
By
EDWARD JOHNSTON
With 5 Plates by A. E. R. GILL
(Portfolio No. 2, "School Copies & Examples")

Fig. 3. Johnston's *Manuscript & Inscription Letters.*

Decoration and its Uses

to get or to cut for himself a very broad nibbed pen—made from a quill, a bamboo cane, or a reed—and, with that in his hand, to follow the argument practically. I subjoin an illustration of the pens with which the following examples were written (fig. 1).

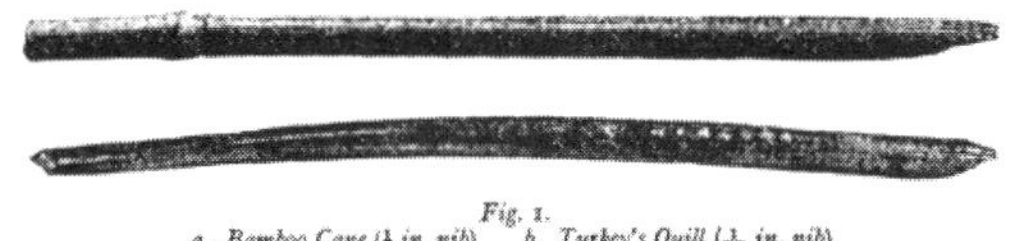

Fig. 1.
a. Bamboo Cane (⅛ in. nib). b. Turkey's Quill (1/16 in. nib).

CHAPTER I. Formal Writing & the Broad-nibbed Pen

Fig. 4. Illustration from *Decoration and its Uses.*

DEFGI

αβγλεηθι

Fig. 5A. Johnston's quasi-Black Letter type, for the Cranach Presse, *Hamlet*, 1914.

Fig. 5B. Johnston's Greek typeface for the Cranach Presse.

> An extremely good, formal, 'slanted-pen' writing, having great freedom (note the very slight slope forward) and simplicity. This extremely legible MANUSCRIPT would form an almost perfect model for a modern formal hand....

His teaching portfolio, *Manuscript and Inscription Letters,*[7] which appeared in 1909, extended the range of the handbook for lettering artists but it was intended equally for school pupils (Fig. 3). Johnston was especially concerned about the teaching of handwriting in schools.[8] He also wrote a series of seven articles called 'Decoration and its Uses' (Fig. 4). These appeared in 1913 in *The Imprint,* a newly conceived journal intended largely for trade printers of which Johnston was a founding-editor.[9] These articles had a seminal influence in raising standards in the printing industry.

From 1911 Johnston agreed to design a set of three typefaces: a quasi-Black Letter (Fig. 5A), an Italic (Fig. 5B) and a Greek face (Fig 5C). These were for Count Harry Kessler, the Anglophile and wealthy founder of the private Cranach Presse, in Weimar. (Johnston, with Gill and others, had already drawn titling letters via Kessler for books for the Insel publishers). This work lasted many years and, as it turned out, the types were used just for single book titles.

In 1915 Johnston was commissioned to design his sanserif block letter alphabet (Fig 6). Intended for the posters and then the signing system of the London Underground, it was put into use from 1916 onwards. It has become Johnston's best known monument and a key exemplar of twentieth-century lettering.[10]

A B C
F G H I
L M N
Q R S
V W X
1 2 3
6 7 8

Fig. 6. Detail from the block letter (sanserif) alphabet for the London Electric Railways (later the London Underground), 1915–16.

Fig. 7. The title page for the manuscript *The House of David, his Inheritance: A book of sample scripts, 1914. A.D.*.

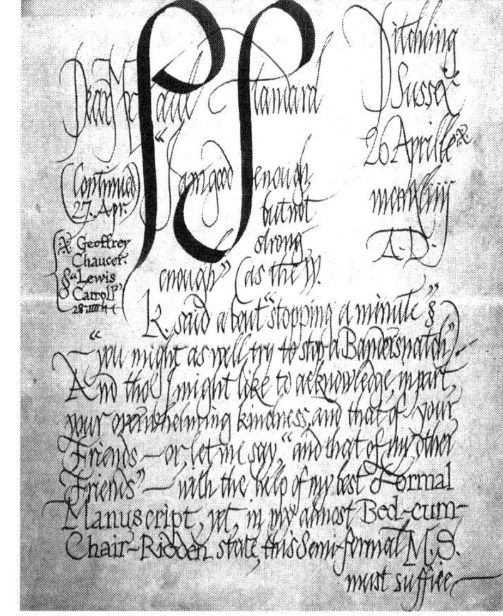

FIG. 8. Johnston's 'cypher' letter written to Paul Standard. 26th April–5th May 1944.

The piece of calligraphy which Johnston thought his most outstanding was, characteristically, a considerable time in the making. He called it *The House of David, his Inheritance: A book of sample scripts 1914. A.D.* (Fig. 7)[11]

Johnston's later achievements are less well-known, perhaps, but equally important. From 1929 onwards, he was preoccupied with thinking further about the writing of scripts. He reformulated his ideas in his unfinished book project, *Formal Penmanship*.[12] Its fragments were the distillation of a lifetime's work.

Underlying these more public projects, however, was Johnston's private calligraphy. He worked on his commissions in a small workshop (hardly a scriptorium) at home. To date there is no *catalogue raisonné* of this work.[13] In the last three years of his life, from 1941 to 1944, Johnston calligraphed some sixteen letters to friends and benefactors. He incorporated the initial letters of their names written in large format with a reed pen. These intertwined or 'cypher' letters are highly expressive works of art (Fig. 8). Taken as a group they constitute an elegiac swan song.

Johnston's outstanding gifts were cultivated not just by dedicated work or by self-discipline, alone. Self-taught and ever alert, the stimulation of discourse was vital to him. Enquiry progressed through exacting discussion with like-minded friends and fellow-craftsmen. Furthermore, these friendships often arose out of, or led to, creative collaborations on the various commissions he engaged in. These factors help to explain how Johnston came to be associated with communities of craftsmen, albeit loosely clustered ones. He was drawn to such groups and, in turn, invariably became one of their focal points. This need even helped determine Johnston's choice of the locations of his successive homes.

In 1898, aged twenty-six, Johnston experienced a change of heart – and of direction.[14] He gave up his medical studies in Edinburgh 'on account of health' and left for London to 'go in for art'. He lodged with three Scottish artist-friends, the MacRae sisters, at 2 Vernon Place, Holborn, near the British Museum. Of immediate help was their architect-friend from Edinburgh, an amateur calligrapher, William Cowlishaw. He introduced Johnston, first, to Emery Walker, a typographic expert who had assisted William Morris, and secondly, to William Lethaby. Lethaby was an architect, historian and educationist who became Johnston's mentor and employer. Lethaby, in turn, introduced him to Sir Sydney Cockerell, who had been the secretary to William Morris. Having a scholarly knowledge of medieval manuscripts, Cockerell guided Johnston in his researches. By 1900, Johnston's talent attracted the interest of Robert Bridges (later the Poet Laureate), with whom Johnston collaborated to design a new phonetic alphabet to simplify English spelling. Johnston gained insights into the history of scripts, especially the Half-Uncial, through Bridges and his wife, Mary Monica, who was pioneering the teaching of writing in schools.[15] In this company Johnston found his home university – nurturing, inviting, instructing and even flattering, perhaps. Such encouragement was the taper Johnston needed to ignite his artistry.

A second circle of contacts was associated with the Central School of Arts and Crafts, newly established – largely through Lethaby. From 1899 Johnston was persuaded by Lethaby to teach calligraphy there. This institution embodied the values of the Arts and Crafts movement, values which Johnston now espoused. Its teachers became his colleagues and friends. Nearby, in Queen Square, was the movement's mother institution, the Art Workers' Guild. Johnston became a member of the Guild in 1901. By attending meetings there he further enlarged his circle of associates. This process continued in 1901, when he began teaching at the newly reorganised Royal College of Art, again at Lethaby's instigation.

From 1900 Johnston lodged in a tiny flat in Lincoln's Inn (16, Old Buildings), Holborn, where he was joined by his pupil, the lettering artist Eric Gill (and a cat). On his marriage on the 20th August 1903 to Greta Kathleen Greig, an Oxford graduate, he moved to 4 Gray's Inn. Lethaby had his offices next door. Lethaby's fellow architect, Philip Webb, also had his offices in Gray's Inn. Webb had designed the Red House for William Morris. Crucial to Johnston, too, at this period was John Hogg, an enigmatic figure who undertook the publishing of *Writing & Illuminating, & Lettering*. Another partnership was with his pupil, Noel Rooke, later a teacher at the Central School. Johnston encouraged him to revive wood engraving and asked him to illustrate the diagrams for his calligraphy handbook. Noel Rooke recalled a discussion of this project with Johnston lasting into the early morning. In this period, in Holborn, such discourse would take place in a restaurant formerly much patronised by William Morris – Gatti's in the Strand.

While Johnston may have thrived on the cut and thrust of conversation, he was well known for his monologues. His youngest daughter, Priscilla, whose biography of her father is rich in vignettes of his life, described his manner of: '... speaking very slowly with long pauses but with never an actual break'.[16] His friends, absorbed but tantalised, would hang on his words waiting to get in.

9

10

11

12

13

Figs. 9–13.

9. Emery Walker
10. William Lethaby
11. Sydney Cockerell
12. Robert Bridges
13. Mary Monica Bridges

From 1905 Johnston lived at 3 Hammersmith Terrace in West London. This gracious eighteenth-century street was home to several accomplished artist-craftsmen. Moreover, the Terrace was adjacent to Upper Mall where Morris had lived, in Kelmscott House, until his death in 1896. This quarter, like Holborn, was a centre of the Arts and Crafts movement. Emery Walker was one such resident. He was Johnston's landlord as well as friend. Another was Thomas James Cobden-Sanderson. His wife had inherited the wealth of her father, Richard Cobden of the free trade movement, which enabled Cobden-Sanderson to set up his private Doves Press in 1900. Johnston calligraphed for him initial letters for some of his Doves Press books. Later in 1903 Eric Gill arrived to live nearby, much in the spell of Johnston. Another resident was Douglas H. Pepler, a Quaker, a Fabian and pioneer social worker with whom Johnston had a close working association. Count Harry Kessler was a frequent visitor.

In late September 1912 Johnston, now aged forty, followed in the wake of Gill and settled in Ditchling in East Sussex. Gill had moved there in 1907 because at that time the village was secluded, even remote. At Ditchling Johnston enjoyed one of his most creative periods. In 1912 he gave a seminal lecture on the teaching of lettering in Dresden. The same year he met Gerard Tuke Meynell, one of the 'Clan Meynell' of writers, publishers, booksellers and printers – the poet Alice Meynell being at its apex. Gerard Meynell helped initiate *The Imprint* and printed it at his Westminster Press.[17] He also exerted an influence on Frank Pick, the commercial manager at the London Electric Railways Co., to improve the design of the company's public face. In 1913 he introduced Pick to Johnston, whose block letter sanserif alphabet ensued. Gill was briefly involved. Johnston was also in touch with Gerard's cousin, Francis Meynell, whose first venture in printing was his tiny Romney Street Press. Johnston rubricated the initials of a volume of Alice Meynell's poems printed at the Romney Street Press in 1915.

A working partnership developed with Gill and Hilary Pepler until about 1918. It was cemented by friendship. An ever-growing craft community now began to develop around them. His two companions, having converted to Roman Catholicism, then became lay members of the order of St. Dominic under the guidance of Father Vincent McNabb. By 1920 they had formed the craft-based Guild of St. Joseph and St. Dominic, from which Johnston emphatically excluded himself. Johnston, it appears, was the philosophical antithesis to Father McNabb. As an Anglican his convictions precluded him from accepting the dogma of absolute papal authority. In this he was much prompted by his wife.

Henceforth Johnston became more reclusive. His life in Ditchling was a largely uneventful one spent in work and thought and in weekly trips to London to teach at the Royal College of Art. (From 1912 he stopped teaching at the Central School.) In 1934 he became the president of the Arts and Crafts Exhibition Society. In 1939 he was awarded the CBE. Aside from his work, Johnston was occupied in tending his garden (and chickens), enjoying the countryside, devising ingenious gadgets and, in their childhood days, making toys for his three daughters, Bridget, Barbara and Priscilla. Never very robust, his health and eyesight progressively failed

14

15

16

17

18

Figs. 14–18.

14. Eric Gill
15. Philip Webb
16. Noel Rooke
17. Thomas James Cobden-Sanderson
18. Douglas (Hilary) Pepler

him. In 1943 he suffered seriously from pneumonia. He died on the 26th November 1944. His headstone, shared with Greta's, is in the churchyard of St. Margaret's, Ditchling. Inscribed by Joseph Cribb, who came to Ditchling as Gill's assistant at the outset in 1908, it conveys the couple's Christian devotion:

EDWARD JOHNSTON
1872–1944
GRETA JOHNSTON
1872–1936
THE PEACE OF GOD
WHICH PASSETH ALL
UNDERSTANDING
BE WITH YOU ALWAYS

19

20

21

22

Figs. 19–22.

19. Count Harry Kessler
20. Gerard Meynell
21. Frank Pick
22. Vincent McNabb

Johnston's friends and colleagues mentioned here were the more prominent among many other such kindred spirits. They made up the conjunctions of his life by which new meanings – social, artistic, philosophical – were construed and new projects were realised. That such associations worked out so well was largely due to a quality of steadfastness in Johnston's character and to the value he set on artistic truthfulness. In her biography of her father Priscilla Johnston discussed his single-minded and painstaking dedication to truth. She spoke of him as:

> … thinking intensely, penetratingly about things, about ideas, about problems in mathematics, or problems in life; what is time, what is reality, what is truth? [18]

In the lifelong process of clarifying his ideas Johnston was inevitably affected by contemporary currents of thought concerned with art and craft. Another focus of this study, therefore, is on the intellectual milieu in which Johnston lived and how it helped formulate his points of view. While disparate in their aims, each of these movements had as its mainspring a profound disquiet with industrialised society. In their development, they became closely intertwined. Strands of their thinking were shared, others were hotly disputed.

The Arts and Crafts movement provided the bedrock of Johnston's beliefs. Fundamental to the movement were the writings of the nineteenth-century social critics, John Ruskin and William Morris. Each, in turn, attempted to give a purpose to art and design in society. They wished to restore the primacy of the handmade artefact, made according to the natural propensity of the craftsman's tools. Following them, Johnston saw clearly that the activity of making – he eschewed the word 'designing' – was part of life itself, that one was contained within the other. But as changing circumstances shaped the society, so the successive prescriptions offered by Ruskin and Morris were seen to have shortcomings. But Johnston took much from their systems of thought. His links back to the two great thinkers will be examined later.

The Roman Catholic revival was equally alarmed – felt threatened, indeed – by the unrest in industrialised society. The Catholic view of craft as integral with life itself was, at heart, also Morrisian. More specifically, its social policy (with its off-shoot, Distributism) encouraged the Catholic family to return to small-scale rural

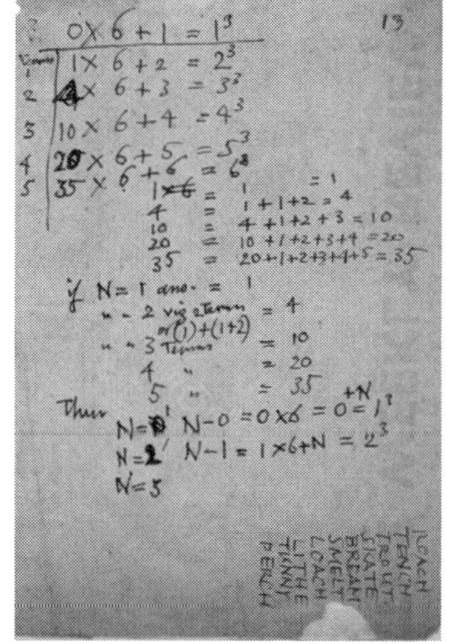

23A

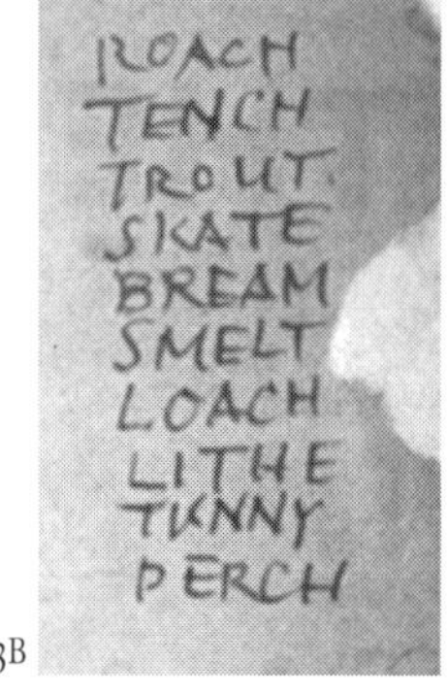

23B

Figs. 23A–B.
Page from manuscripts of mathematical jottings by Edward Johnston, with a detail showing his list of ten names of fish, each with five letters. (See endnote 18.)

subsistence. Johnston spent the years 1917–19 in such a Distributist experiment in living. His response to Catholicism provides clues to his make-up.

Thirdly, Modernism was an emerging force to which Johnston related, though less consciously, given that its ideas were still in flux at that time, and with a certain reluctance. The new outlook urged a *rapprochement* between craft and industrial methods. Craft was replaced by the concept of 'design'. While Johnston never became, remotely, a self-proclaiming radical of the *avant-garde*, he responded ambiguously to this rising ground swell of ideas. Lethaby's developing views, influencing those of Gerard Meynell and Frank Pick, took Johnston into the twentieth century. Johnston devised, for example, the 'bull's eye' logo of the London Underground, now claimed as a quintessential image of British modernism (Fig. 24). The theme of British 'conservative' modernism and Johnston's tentative connections to it is an elusive one, to be explored in a later chapter.

Johnston related to ideologies with a tolerant but independent cast of mind. In the preface of *Writing & Illuminating, & Lettering* he incorporated three quotations, one from Plato, a second from the French sixteenth-century potter, Palissy, a third from the American nineteenth-century philosopher, Ralph Waldo Emerson. His choice of a passage of Emerson's resounding prose is telling. It must have chimed with Johnston, struggling with his handbook.[19] A section reads:

> ... much is to say on both sides, and, while the fight waxes hot, thou, dearest scholar stick to thy foolish task, add a line every hour, and between whiles add a line. Right to hold land, right of property is disputed, and the conventions convene, and before the vote is taken, dig away in your garden, and spend your earnings as a waif or godsend to all serene and beautiful purposes. Life itself is a bubble and a scepticism, and a sleep within a sleep. Grant it, and as much more as they will, ... but thou, God's darling! heed thy private dream; thou will not be missed in scorning and scepticism: there are enough of them: stay there in thy closet, and toil, until the rest are agreed what to do about it ... know that thy life is a flitting state, a tent for the night, and do thou, sick or well, finish that stint. Thou art sick, but shalt not be worse, and the universe, which holds thee dear, shall be the better. (Fig. 25)

Throughout his life Johnston was in accord with Emerson's philosophical scepticism. His detachment, based on reason, exemplified Emerson's appeal to individuality – 'dig away in your garden'. This, clearly, was a source of the strength he drew on to uproot the entrenched habits of nineteenth-century lettering arts.

Johnston is now venerated as the ancestor of an extended family of lettering artists and designers nurtured in the purist tradition he revived. The more prominent of these undoubtedly included Eric Gill. Others were Johnston's former pupils, Graily Hewitt, Percy Smith, Anna Simons and Irene Wellington. To these should be added two of Gill's early assistants in inscriptional lettering, Joseph and Laurie Cribb, as well as the pioneer of the Italic script revival, Alfred Fairbank. In later years homage was paid to him by the type designers Stanley Morison, Jan Tschichold, Victor Hammer and Hermann Zapf as well as by the inscriptional lettering artists Reynolds Stone and David Kindersley. As a counterpart, the inscriptional artist and writer, David Jones, should also be mentioned. While these figures enjoy renown as creators of letter-forms in their own right, they regarded

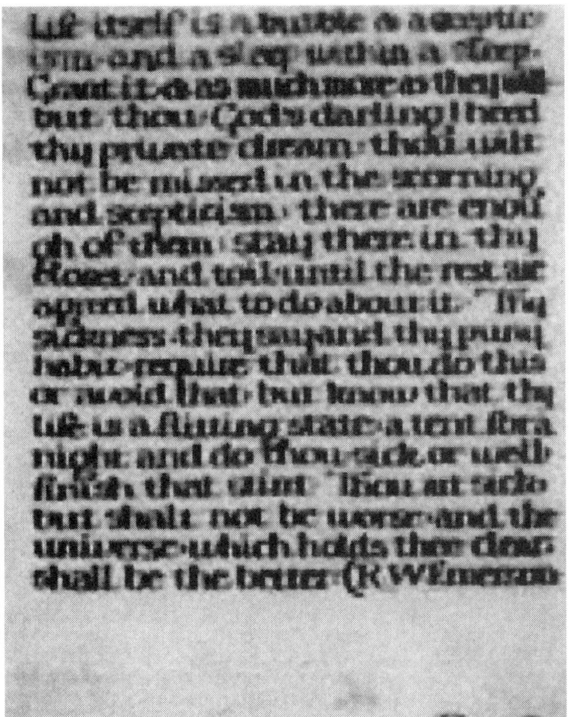

Life itself is a bubble & a scepticism and a sleep within a sleep. Grant it & as much more as they will but thou God's darling! heed thy private dream: thou wilt not be missed in the scorning and scepticism: there are enough of them: stay there in thy closet and toil until the rest are agreed what to do about it. Thy sickness they say and thy puny habit require that thou do this or avoid that but know that thy life is a flitting state a tent for a night and do thou sick or well finish that stint. Thou art sick but shalt not be worse and the universe which holds thee dear shall be the better (R W Emerson

Fig. 24. (FAR LEFT) The logo Johnston devised in 1919 for the London Electric Railways Company. (It was later renamed the London Passenger Transport Board which was then shortened to the London Underground).

FIG. 25. (LEFT) Emerson Manuscript, 1899. (See endnote 19.)

Johnston's ideas as their source. Through them, and subsequent generations of lettering artists, the tradition that Johnston started has enriched the broad stream of twentieth-century calligraphy and lettering more generally. He remains to this day calligraphy's single most important teacher.[20]

For such admirers Johnston's stature was one of quiet authority. In a series of posthumous tributes paid to him in 1945 at the Art Workers' Guild in Queen Square, Bloomsbury, Sir Sydney Cockerell, spoke of:

> … his gentle bearing, his quality of unconscious saintliness, his unworldly outlook, his whimsicality.[21]

During the same commemoration, another friend (and former pupil and teaching assistant), Irene Wellington, said of him:

> I learnt from what he *was*. We scribes of today, directly or indirectly, look upon him as *Master*.

Yet another pupil and teaching assistant was Violet Hawkes. Her admiration reached alarming proportions given that she would address Johnston in her letters as 'Dear Father Scribe'. Another insight is offered by one of Johnston's private pupils, Margaret Alexander. In her letter to him dated the 5th September 1940, she remarked:

> Your practical help is invaluable, but what I especially appreciate is the way in which you have 'illuminated' the work for me, and given me a new vision about it. It must seem strange to you, and I am rather ashamed to admit it, but it had not seriously occurred to me before to raise the question 'why'.[22]

Fig. 26. An alphabet designed as display letters by the architect, C. F. A Voysey, undated.

Aside from these devotees, Johnston was esteemed simply as a person who conveyed with wit and joy his enchantment with day-to-day life. He was admired and revered for his knowledge and seen as a font of inspiration, wonder, and amusement by his students, his colleagues, his friends and family, alike. In Johnston's family mythology, his wife, Greta, once exclaimed:

> My husband is a saint; but saints are not always easy to live with.[23]

One further detail of Johnston's life is characteristically endearing. Calligraphers visiting the museum at Ditchling to see the Johnston memorabilia there sometimes comment how easily his writing desk, dilapidated even beyond its years, might pass for a relic from a medieval scriptorium. With an adjustable lid, it was made by Johnston as a novice at the beginning of his career, in 1898, and used by him throughout his writing life.

From that beginning, at the turn of the century, Johnston saw the need to re-establish a sense of order in the lettering arts. They were caught up in the confusion which affected the entire gamut of design in the nineteenth century. Artefacts were increasingly mass-produced and in a profusion of styles – Greek, Roman, Islamic, Gothic, and Renaissance among them – echoing the Victorian imperial quest to document, catalogue and appropriate the historic cultures of the world. Owen Jones's *The Grammar of Ornament* of 1856 is one instance of such compendia – albeit a highly accomplished one by a versatile architect-designer.[24] Richard Glazier's *Historic Ornament*, which appeared in 1899, is another. Once such repertoires of styles were compiled, it followed that they would be applied commercially, laying designers open to the dangers of visual solecism.

Moreover, factory-made artefacts were impersonal, devoid of human warmth and touch. That manufacture – literally the 'making by hand' – was taken over by machine production was an irony not lost on Johnston. He was affected by Ruskin's notion of the alienation of the factory worker from a creative involvement in making artefacts – the malaise, as Ruskin perceived, of industrialisation.

Nineteenth-century lettering artists were eclectic in the use of scripts. Their work tended to be overwhelmed with decoration. Calligraphers were particularly in thrall to the Gothic Black Letter, and frequently applied themselves to it with an antiquarian zeal. Characteristic are the manuscripts written by Owen Jones between the 1840s and 1860s. One is the title and contents pages of his *Flowers and their Kindred Thoughts* of 1848.[25] Another is doubtless his most accomplished manuscript, *The Victoria Psalter*, of 1861,[26] dedicated to Queen Victoria. Symptomatic of the unbridled nature of calligraphy in the nineteenth century were the two thousand-odd addresses of congratulations which were sent to Queen Victoria by a wide range of societies and institutions in Britain and the Empire to celebrate her Golden Jubilee of 1887. The two scripts which predominate in these documents are the Gothic Black Letter and the Copperplate.[27] A similar set of addresses, to the Duke and Duchess of Cornwall, was seen by Johnston in 1902. He returned from the show 'depressed by the ... lamentable bad taste shown'.[28]

W. CASLON,

ABCD
EGHK

Fig. 27. Sample of Caslon 'Old Style' typeface, from the Caslon type specimen sheet of 1734 (W. Caslon) and 1766.

A further measure of nineteenth-century eclecticism is the scope of many of its handwriting manuals. Their title pages were largely written with the assurance characteristic of the professional penman. Two examples are William Shinton's *Beauties of Ancient and Modern*, of 1815, and William Thompson's *The Writing Master's Assistant*, of 1820. Their lettering repertoires could be mixed and matched with little regard for their purpose. From the 1880s, the teaching copy-books of the Irish educationalist, De Vere H. L. Foster, became widely used and officially recognised by School Boards. De Vere's *Lettering Plain and Ornamental, Copy Book No 10,* gave a wide repertoire to be learnt by repetition, a practice not so dissimilar, perhaps, from the learning of Latin verbs, by rote.

Commercial display lettering was of equal concern to Johnston. Among these were the fat-faces, the Egyptians and the sanserifs, which were set to work by printers to convey nineteenth-century commercial values. The legibility of their robust but often maverick forms was questionable. Johnston remarked of them:

> If it were necessary to show horrid examples, how many of our display types could be refused a dishonourable place?'[29]

With some notable exceptions, book-printers in the nineteenth century were seen to have lost sight of those principles which guided the Renaissance printers, among whom Nicholas Jenson and Aldus Manutius in Venice were pre-eminent.[30] Their type designs were modelled on humanist calligraphic forms made with the broad-edged pen, giving a gently swelling diagonal stress to the letters. Jenson's type is still known as 'Venetian' and the Aldus as 'Old Style'.[31] The 'Old Style' (Fig. 27) evolved in a continuous arc right up into the eighteenth century, strengthened *en route* by the design of William Caslon in the late 1720s. It was broken only by the fashion adopted by printers of the so-called 'Modern' roman typefaces. These were begun by Firmin Didot (Fig. 28) in the 1780s and then by Giambattista Bodoni. The extreme contrast between the thicks and thins of the strokes of the 'Moderns' and their vertical stress and narrower proportions was regarded by Johnston as a 'degraded' form.

DICTION
NAIRE
PARIS
1865

Fig. 28. Example of the Didot typeface, used for the title page of a French dictionary, dated 1865.

Additionally, the word spacing and page layout of nineteenth-century books were often the victims of commercial expediency. Frequently cramped or ill-conceived, they were all too often unkind on the eye. (Illustrations, too, could be badly printed, the explanation for which lay in part with the newly mechanised, though not yet perfected, half-tone processes for picture-printing.) Another factor of some importance was paper, the higher demand for which led to poorer quality.

However, a fine example of the restitution of traditional book typography was close at hand for Johnston to see. The hand-printed and hand-bound books of

OFFICINA COLUM
Cobden-Sanderson et E
it J.W. Mackail typos co
exercuit H. Gage-Cole

Medicin.

Figs. 29(A–C)
29A–B. Two details of the letter-forms of the Doves Press type, designed by Emery Walker, 1900, and based on Jenson's type, 1470.

Mithrida

29C. Detail of letter-forms of the Jenson type, from his edition of Pliny's *Historia Naturalis*, 1476.

Cobden-Sanderson's newly established Doves Press persuaded him of a belief held by historians of the book at that time. For scholars such as Emery Walker a seamless transition had taken place from the handwritten, or manuscript, book to the printed one (Figs. 29A–C). The *mise en page* of the early printed books fitted exactly the templates of scribal manuscripts. Cobden-Sanderson's tract, *The Ideal Book or Book Beautiful* (Figs. 30A–B), treating 'calligraphy, printing, and illustration and on the book beautiful as a whole', advocated that printers should return to these first principles. His own Doves Press type, designed by Emery Walker in 1900, was modelled on Jenson's type – as, before him, was Morris's 'Golden' type design for his Kelmscott Press. In 1901, Johnston made two transcriptions of *Ideal Book*. In the synopsis of his teaching course of 1901 Johnston, echoing Cobden-Sanderson, stated:

> Writing [calligraphy and lettering] and Illumination form the *necessary foundation* of good Typography and Book Decoration.[32]

The creative purpose of Johnston's lettering was sustained by an understanding of the history of manuscripts. The continuum of the crafts of calligraphy, illumination and printing was a crucial principle in his teaching.

Johnston also rejected another tradition. In the nineteenth century, writing masters continued to teach the predominant Roundhand, or Copperplate, script. Generically this was a hybrid script – and in Johnston's eyes even a corrupted one. Its distant ancestor was the Italian Humanist Cursive, or Italic script (ironically, perhaps, given that Johnston was much inspired by the Humanist Italic). It

30A. Title page of Cobden-Sanderson's tract, *The Ideal Book or Book Beautiful*, 1900. (Reprinted by Cadenza Press in 1987).

30B. The second page from Johnston's transcription of *The Ideal Book or Book Beautiful*, 1900.

THE IDEAL BOOK OR BOOK BEAUTIFUL
A TRACT ON CALLIGRAPHY PRINTING
AND ILLUSTRATION & ON THE BOOK
BEAUTIFUL AS A WHOLE

THE DOVES PRESS
Nº I THE TERRACE HAMMERSMITH
MDCCCC

CALLI-
GRAPHY
& HANDWRITING
and handecoration of letter & page
are at the root of the Book Beautiful / are at the root of Typography
and of woodcut or engraved decoration / and every printer / & indeed
everyone having to do with the making of books should / I think / ground
himself in the practice and knowledge of the Art of Beautiful Writing or Calligraphy / and let both
hand & soul luxuriate & rejoice
for a while in the art of illumination: Such practice would keep
Type alive under the influence of
an ever living & fluent prototype:
It would supply a stock of exemplars and suggestions from which

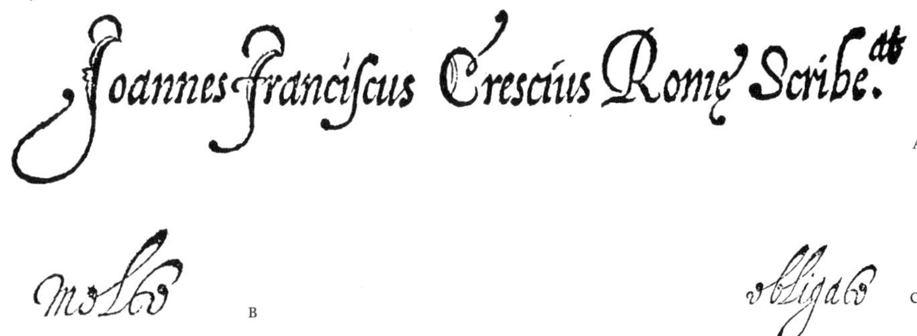

B

C

Fig 31A. A detail from G. F. Cresci's *Essemplare di piu sorti lettere,* Rome, 1560.

31B–C. Two details from Cresci's *Il perfetto cancelleresco corsivo*, Rome, 1579.

developed in the mid-seventeenth century from a French variant of that Italic script, called *lettre italienne bâtarde,* to meet the practical needs of English commerce.[33] Its *raison d'être* was business legibility and efficiency. The Roundhand is demonstrated in the writing masters' specimen copy-books, notably the alphabets shown in George Shelley's *Natural Writing in all the Hands, with a Variety of Ornament* of 1709 and in George Bickham's *The Universal Penman* of 1743.

One of Johnston's dissatisfactions concerned the tool with which the penman made his sensual strokes. The pointed, rather than the broad-edged, pen had first come into use in the sixteenth century, recommended by a Roman penman, the flamboyant Giovan Francesco Cresci for the faster writing of the chancery Italic script. His writing book, *Essemplare di piu sorti lettere*, was published in 1560 (Figs 31A-C). Cresci condemned Arrighi and Palatino because '... they employ a pen which is too broad and square at the tip ....' By Cresci's method, the stress of the letter-forms – the varying thicks and thins – is created by altering the pressure on its flexible pointed nib. A marked contrast can thus be achieved between hairline upward strokes (made with the nib's slit closed and pushed up away from the calligrapher) and swelling downward strokes (made with the nib splayed open and pulled down towards the calligrapher). Thicker strokes still had to be 'built up'.[34]

These effects were much enhanced by the, then, new Copperplate engraving process which was used to print the writing masters' specimen copy-books.[35] The engraver's pointed burin, which was well-suited to incise into the receptive copper,

Fig 32. Details from Thomas Tomkins's *The Beauties of Writing Exemplified in a Variety of Plain and Ornamental Penmanship Designed to excite Emulation in this valuable Art.* 1777. (Republished by T. Varty at 31 Strand. 1844. Engraved by Ashby, Woodthorpe, *et al.*)

enlarged

enlarged

Figs. 33–35. Details of plates from *Writing & Illuminating, & Lettering*:
33. The Trajan Column inscription. (Plate II).

34. *Book of Kells.* (Plate VI).

35. *Harley MS. 2904*, or the *Ramsey Psalter.* (Plate VIII).

encouraged the vogue. Being first written with a pointed pen and then transcribed by the engraver, this script did not meet with Johnston's approval.

Another feature made it anathema to his canon. The eighteenth-century rococo style imported its typical embellishments into lettering generally and into the Roundhand in particular. To its skeletal simplicity was added the penman's flourishes and exaggerated loops. An example is *The Beauties of Writing* by Thomas Tomkins, printed in London in 1777 (Fig. 32). In the nineteenth century the tendency continued – Tomkins was reprinted in 1844. Penmen demonstrated their virtuoso 'command of hand' with a panache which Johnston decried as 'foolish affectations'.

During the nineteenth century the pointed steel-nibbed pen, introduced by James Perry in 1830, complemented the burin. It lent itself perfectly to the penman's 'sleight of hand'. The widespread use of the steel nib profoundly affected handwriting in schools and homes, reinforcing the tendencies of the pointed quill.

Additionally, the standards of writing of clerks in the legal profession and the civil service were threatened by the advent of the typewriter. Both inventions were well suited to factory production, a development which remained deeply suspect to the generation of artist-craftsmen who influenced Johnston's ideas.

Supporting his disquiet, too, was a quasi-moral consideration. That the Gothic Black Letter was associated with bibles and prayer books was a long and accepted tradition. But in the mind of the Arts and Crafts movement the Roundhand Copperplate script bore the stigma of bank-ledgers and with commerce. It was held in disdain for being at the service of Mammon

Johnston translated these strictures into a programme of action. It cannot be said of many crafts that their revival is traceable back to a single individual, as it can for formal calligraphy at the turn of the twentieth century. In the face of the apparent 'degeneration' all around him, Johnston returned to medieval practices. He

E gli è manifesto Egregio lettore, che le lettere Can:
cellaresche sono de uarie sorti, si come poi ueder
nelle scritte tabelle, le quali io scritto con mesura
e arte, Et per satisfatione de chi apitisse una
sorte, et chi unaltra, Io to scritto questa altra
uariatione de lettere la qual uolendo imparare
osserua la regula del sottoscritto Alphabeto :
A a.b.c.d.e e.ff.g.h.i.k.l.m.n.o.p p.
.q.q.r.s.f.t.u.x.y.z.&.

a.a b.c.d.e e.f.g.

enlarged

Fig. 36. Page from G. A. Tagliente's *Opera che insegna a scrivere*, 1524 edition, with detail of letter-forms.

HAST thou longed through weary days
For the sight of one loved face,
Hast thou cried aloud for rest,
Mid the pain of sundering hours
Cried aloud for sleep and death
Since the sweet unhoped for best
Was a shadow and a breath —
O long now for no fear lowers
O'er these faint feet-kissing flowers
O rest now; and yet in sleep

Uncontent and waste and
Thou shalt wake, and thin

enlarged

Fig. 37. Page from Morris's manuscript *A Book of Verse*, 1870, with detail showing Morris's idiosyncratic 'hairline' strokes. (V&A.)

had a special love of early medieval manuscripts, inculcated by Bridges and Cockerell. This was deepened by study of manuscripts; uppermost were the eighth-century *Book of Kells* and the late tenth-century *Harley MS. 2904* (the *Ramsey Psalter*) (Figs. 33–35). Importantly, though, he also studied ancient Roman lettering such as the Trajan Column inscription and the Roman-based alphabet designed by the Italian Renaissance writing master, Tagliente. In these he found his models.

The appreciation of scripts other than Gothic ones had begun in earnest with William Morris.[36] He focused particularly on Italian Renaissance Humanist and Italic scripts. He owned copies of each of the manuals of the principal Italian sixteenth-century writing-masters – Arrighi, Tagliente, Ugo da Carpi. He knew about the use of the broad-edged pen (Fig. 36). However, Morris cultivated a 'flattened Italic script' of his own, with hairline mannerisms (Fig. 37).[37] He was a highly skilled calligrapher and had a refined sense of historical exactitude towards the works he transcribed. He paid much attention to *mise en page*, considering margins, illumination, and written text in terms of double page openings. His calligraphic masterpiece is the transcription of Virgil's *Aeneid*, 1874–75, but left incomplete.[38]

Johnston was well aware of Morris's calligraphy and speaks of 'honour due' to him in his handbook.[39] He built on what Morris had begun. But, whereas Morris's approach was passionate but individualistic, Johnston's was passionate and analytical. His interest was in the anatomy of letters. The word 'anatomy' was important to Johnston and he focuses on it in the preface to his handbook. His own

38A

38B

38C

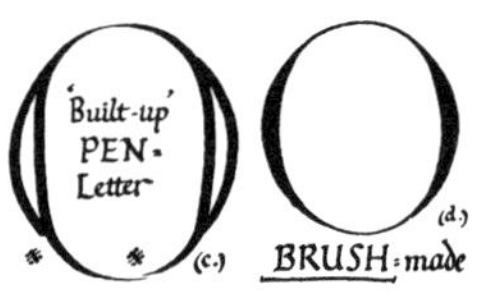

38D

Figs. 38A–D.
Four diagrams from *Writing & Illuminating, & Lettering*, 1906, demonstrating the letter-forms made by the broad-edged pen, (a quill, reed or cane) and by brush. At this time, 1906, Johnston was still recommending the Half-Uncial as the model for formal writing.

calligraphy was based on knowledge of the structure of letters and thus it superseded Morris's enthusiastic evocations. In Morris's calligraphy he saw a:

> … sweetness and naturalness … the absence of strain and the beauty…[40]

The key to meaningful reform lay with techniques and tools – a way of thinking generic to the Arts and Crafts movement. In this matter Johnston, in a sense, developed far further than Morris. Like him, Johnston understood the traditional preparation of vellum and parchment, and the methods of making ink. But, critically, he also recovered the scribe's preparation of the broad-edged (or chisel-edged) quill (or reed pen or cane) and so achieved the more evenly balanced stress of the letter-forms that he so admired (Fig 38A–D). To this method he returned again and again in *Writing & Illuminating, & Lettering*:

> Letting the nib glide about with the least possible pressure … lets the pen do the writing.
>
> A broad-edged pen actually controls the hand of the writer and will create alphabets out of their skeletons giving harmony and proportion and character to the different letters….
>
> … generally, the more simply and naturally a *tool-made* form is the better.[41]

Additionally, Johnston did away with the sensual effects of the pointed pen and so, in effect, banished Giovan Francesco Cresci. There was little room for uncalled-for frills (or, indeed, for curlicues) in his approach to his craft. The priority was to work truthfully with the materials and to the purpose 'without empty mimicry and foolish affectations'. Johnston invited his readers to take to their hearts 'a little allegory … sufficiently apt to permit of its quotation' in a draft preface of *circa* 1902 to *Writing & Illuminating, & Lettering*:

> Straight is the line of duty
> Curved is the line of beauty
> Follow the first and thou shalt see
> The second, it shall follow thee.

His enlisting a child's *aide-mémoire* to convey his fundamental idea about lettering was characteristic of his teaching. Of actual practice, he wrote in the sixth of his articles *Decoration and its Uses*:

> I would attempt to plead with decorators who desire something finer than the riot of 'display' decoration – as we may call it – of the modern world, to seek for simplicity in their intentions together with clearness: then, if our methods are right, the work will grow by nature beautiful.[42]

Johnston's gift as a teacher was his lucidity. He had the ability to analyse by close reasoning. The complex aspects of the evolution of the forms of letters were reduced to their essential elements. Hilary Pepler experienced the inexorable logic of Johnston's thinking, having first engaged in lengthy discussions with him in Hammersmith. In his memoir, 'Forty Years Back' – back, that is, to the year 1909, or thereabouts – he recalled:

Figs. 39 A–C.
Diagrams from *Formal Penmanship* showing:

A. The 'weight' of the script achieved by the breadth of the pen's nib or edge: three variations – 'wide, medium, & narrow for the same height of letter'.

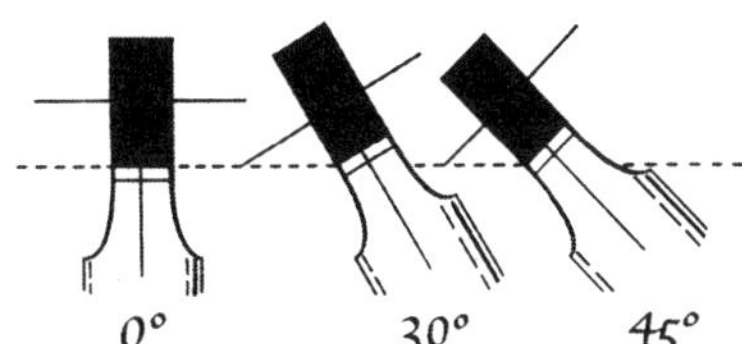

B. The 'angle' of nib's edge to the horizontal line of the writing.

C. 'The position (and lengths) of the strokes', or the "form" of the manuscript, or the letter-form.' (*Formal Penmanship*: page 90 figs. 19A–C)

> It was not so much that Johnston was a born teacher as a born thinker, greatly assisted in that gift by the presence of a sympathetic audience. His thinking was synthetic rather than speculative, as he thought aloud the hearer seemed to be able to watch an arrangement of things taking their appointed place in an inevitable order.[43]

Another witness of Johnston's discourses – a hapless, embroiled one, it seems – was William Rothenstein, the Director of the Royal College of Art and the artist of a portrait drawing of Johnston. He spoke of Johnston as having a 'whole philosophy of writing', but was struck, too, by his way of thinking:

> To him handwriting has ever been a moral, almost a religious thing. As a writer of script he is a master. No one, to my mind, gives to script such masculine beauty, so vigorous a style; but to become involved in talk about him on this, indeed on any subject, is to find oneself in a close field of logic, from which one can only escape by physical departure; so tense, so tenacious his grip.[44]

Lethaby had recognised Johnston's ability at the very outset by suggesting that he might extend his teaching to the writing of a handbook. Johnston gave it a deceptively simple – even an alluring and poetic – title with three parts: *Writing & Illuminating, & Lettering*. Expressing his thoughts in this way, in terms of a triad, runs through Johnston's writings. While teaching in his preface the need 'To make good letters and to arrange them well', he also stipulated that they should aspire to certain 'qualities'. He categorised these under the rubric of 'Readableness, Beauty and Character'.[45]

The 'Readableness' of a given piece of lettering, he claimed, depends upon the 'distinguishing characteristics' being 'strongly marked', with 'no unnecessary parts' and 'no part of a letter wrongly exaggerated or dwarfed'. Each letter should be 'simply' and 'proportionally arranged'.

By 'Beauty' Johnston meant that: '... each letter is an individual and living whole (not merely a collection of parts)', suited to its purpose. This extended to the 'placing, connecting and spacing of letters, words, and lines' on the page, 'in the proportion of every part of the lettering and its margins': in effect, the layout (Figs. 39 A–C).

By 'Character' Johnston referred to the correct technique – 'the rightly made and rightly handled pen' – and to the individual expression – '... the skilled and unaffected boldness' which flows from the confidence of the scribe in his co-ordination of pen with hand. 'Character' is the personality – those 'characteristics which distinguish one person's hand from another's'. These broad categories were then subdivided into further triads, making nine in all.

During the fifteen years or more that Johnston worked on *Formal Penmanship* he continued to formulate the '... right form, the right arrangement, [and] the right expression' of good lettering. His three categories came to be redefined as 'Sharpness, Unity, and Freedom'.[46]

'Sharpness' is concerned with the preparation of the tools – especially with the 'clean-cut, sharp-cornered' nib, and with the surface of the vellum or parchment, and with the correct consistency of the ink. 'Unity' is to do with the consistency of the pen's strokes:

> ... giving a characteristic uniformity to the writing, while at the same time producing a characteristic (and, often, striking) contrast between the thick and the thin strokes'.

And 'Freedom' is a reworking of 'Character'. It is concerned with the 'sureness-and-freedom of direction-and-movement' of the calligrapher's pen. Johnston also says such strokes are 'Swift'. The 'scribe' is:

> ready to spring at a chance:
> *Metaphorically*, his penmanship – which is as swift and as free as he can make it –
> Runs with the freedom of a channelled stream.
> But there comes a fall or a bend in the stream,
> And the stream leaps the fall, scours and widens the bend, and then runs on again
> Care-free (like the spirit of the stream) the happy scribe writes ...

In attaining this 'natural or controlled freedom' the calligrapher becomes, in Johnston's eyes, the artist-craftsman.

Like its predecessor, *Formal Penmanship* shows Johnston's propensity to rationalise a problem into sets of categories. One of the most frequently used graphic devices in his notebooks is the bracket, coupling items together.

There are many other instances of Johnston's analyses in the form of triads (Fig. 40). The whole of man's discovery of truth was, in his view, contained in the scholastic-sounding trivium: 'Religion, Science and Art'. In the tributes of 1945, his daughter, Bridget, spoke of her father's ideas of artistic creation. Three stages of creativity were involved. On 16th July 1944, in a note associated with *Formal Penmanship,* he settled on the terms 'Embodying, Animating, and Inspiring'.

The acuity of Johnston's analyses shows in yet another way. His belief in the value of explaining the craft process led him to read a paper in 1933 on the seemingly peripheral topic, 'The Labelling of Exhibits'. He gave it to the Arts and Crafts Exhibition Society, on the occasion of an exhibition, in his capacity as the society's president (Figs. 41A–B).[47] Johnston's starting point was that the craftsman might usefully reflect on the processes of his craft and his intentions in making the 'Thing' to be exhibited. While reducing these reflections to a concise explanatory label would help the visitor to a better understanding of the craftsman, it would also, he claimed, help the craftsmen to a better understanding of each other. Firstly, Johnston suggested that they be aware of sharing a unifying activity:

THE QUALITIES OF GOOD WRITING

Good Lettering—Some Methods of Construction & Arrangement

READABLENESS

RIGHT FORM

1. *Simplicity:* As having no unnecessary parts (and as being *simply* arranged: see 6).
2. *Distinctiveness:* As having the distinguishing characteristics of each letter strongly marked (and the words *distinctly* arranged: see 6).
3. *Proportion:* As having no part of a letter wrongly exaggerated or dwarfed (and as the lettering being *proportionally* arranged: see 6).

BEAUTY

4. *Beauty of Form:* As having beautiful shapes and constructions, so that each letter is an individual and living whole (not a mere collection of parts) fitted for the position, office, and material of the object bearing the inscription.
5. *Beauty of Uniformity:* As the assimilation of the corresponding parts — "bodies," "limbs," "heads"—and as the "family likeness" of the different letters, so that they go well together.

RIGHT ARRANGEMENT

6. *Beauty of Arrangement:* As having a general fitness in the placing, connecting, and spacing of letters, words, and lines, in the disposal of the lettering in the given space, and in the proportioning of every part of the lettering and its margins.

CHARACTER

RIGHT EXPRESSION

7. *Essential qualities of (Hand and Pen) work:* As being genuine calligraphy, the direct outcome of a rightly made and rightly handled *pen*. (*See* p. 278.)
8. *Freedom:* As having skilled and unaffected boldness. (*See* pp. 122, 327, 323, 369.)
9. *Personality:* As having the characteristics which distinguish one person's hand from another's. (*See also* pp. 278, 323.)

239

Fig. 40. Page 239 of *Writing & Illuminating, & Lettering*, 1906, in which Johnston set out his concept of the nature of letters in terms of a triad ('Readableness, Beauty and Character'), which is then subdivided into further sets of triads.

Four Papers

READ BY MEMBERS OF
THE ARTS AND CRAFTS EXHIBITION
SOCIETY

Published for the
ARTS & CRAFTS EXHIBITION SOCIETY
BY LONGMANS, GREEN, & CO., LTD.
39 PATERNOSTER ROW, LONDON, E.C.4
1935

A PAPER ON THE LABELLING OF EXHIBITS read by the President EDWARD JOHNSTON at the general meeting of the Society, 13 June, 1933, and an addendum with an example of MS. work.

THREE PAPERS read by members of the Society at the symposium, 12 December, 1933:

JOHN FARLEIGH: Welcome! Machinery.

J. H. MASON: The Place of Hand-work in modern Civilisation.

N. ROOKE: The Craftsman and Education for Industry.

Figs. 41 A–B. Title pages from Johnston's address read to the Arts and Crafts Exhibition Society on the 13th June 1933.

> … the different tongues of the different Crafts are branches of one language of Creation, the workers in the different Crafts understand each others' words to a great extent.…

The second notion was then explored:

> Each one of us Craftsmen speaks by *Signs* in his own special accent, yet – even to those who are technically ignorant of both – our Works can, and do, speak; and further, *and this is my principal claim*, that we can give a partial *Translation of our Works into Words* which will assist understanding.
> Each of us can, however, be sure of one thing – that to try to explain his Craftsmanship in words, or to put his Intentions in words, will assist his *own* understanding.

Johnston's eldest daughter, Bridget, spoke of this in a different way. In her letter to Sydney Cockerell, written very shortly after Johnston's death, she described how exhaustively he undertook commissions:

> He was saying to me quite recently how deeply impressed he was by the wording of the oath 'The truth the whole truth and nothing but the truth, so help me God'. That, he thought, was the duty and purpose of the artist and every commission which he accepted imposed the need for a new search for the Truth far more exhaustive than most of those who gave the commission would ever have imagined.[48]

In 1943 Johnston wrote to Sydney Cockerell a letter in which he movingly recalled his youthful awakening to a sense of 'a high ideal'. He realised that:

> ... there was something fascinating about lettering ... letters were intended primarily to be read ... the forms of the written letters would somehow depend upon the pen that wrote them.[49]

In the same letter he explained further. Out of this, and the encouragement first given to him by Lethaby, Cockerell and Bridges:

> ... the ideal came – to make living letters with a formal pen.

This was the essential theme of his life-work. He had already enunciated it in a lecture given in Dresden, in 1912. He began by quoting Goethe:

> Das wir uns in ihr zerstreuen. Darum ist die Welt so gross.[50]
>
> This expresses my sentiments not only in regard to writing, but to life itself. Life is a thing we all want and it is the desire for life that is behind all religion and all art. I do not care what nation the art belongs to, or what 'school' as long as it is alive. I think I can claim that, poor as they are, the letters on the blackboard are alive; this is not due to myself – I am only a superior kind of motor or engine – it is due to the pen which brings life to letters and to all the life and the spirit of men that were before this. Our aim should be, I think, to make letters live that we can bring to life our poor letters – not merely for the sake of art, not to make advertisements for them, not for the sake of their beauty, but that men, themselves, may have more life.[51]

Yet, letters are worth perfecting only in so far as they are used to serve the text. Calligraphy that is well executed can still fall short by ignoring the meaning of the text. When illness once prevented Johnston from lecturing at the Royal College of Art, he asked his assistant, Madelyn Walker, to do no more for his students than to: '... tell them to think of the words'. The meaning of the text is the proper template for the calligrapher's design.

Johnston made unflinching criticism of his students' work. 'There is a great strain of firmness in my nature', he wrote in his short story, *Tranquil*.[52] In his Notebook for the years 1899–1904 appears a hastily written enigmatic jotting, an exhortation perhaps. It is followed by a quotation remembered from Plato:

> (for end L. B.) [Lettering Book – *Writing & Illuminating, & Lettering*] You must frankly face the impossibility of final attainment. 'Beautiful possessions' (Ruskin). You will only understand the infinitude of that worth & see how transcendental is that beauty when still straining with all your might you know that THIS IS NOT YOUR REST. (E J 20 Mar. '02). I believe Plato said: 'Nothing ever is but is always becoming.'[53]

But Johnston was also legendary for the humour which ran through his ideas, for amusing his students in his lectures with *bons mots* and wry asides. He was fond of quoting from *Alice in Wonderland.*

Johnston was also proverbially slow in his work. His *Writing & Illuminating, & Lettering* took much devoted concentration over a period of four years. Priscilla Johnston reports that there was great excitement and relief when, in 1905, the draft was finally sent off to the printers.[54] In its preface, he writes of:

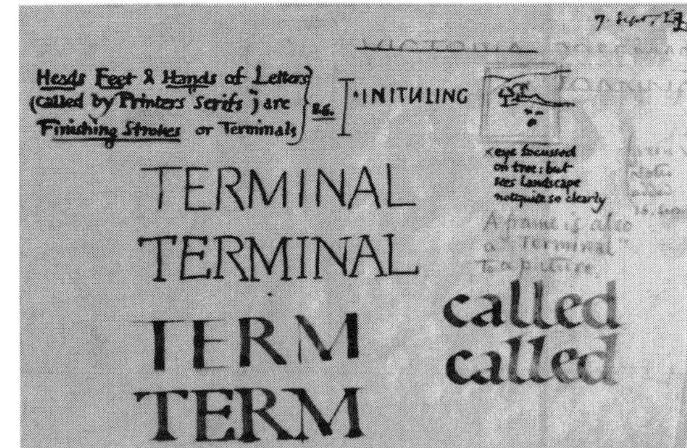

Figs. 42A–B. Johnston's manuscript 'Lettering Illustrating the Formation of the Roman alphabet for Mrs. Meynell's children'. September 1926.
V&A. (E 220–24 –1946.)

> '... achieving beauty by taking pains'.

His was an integrity that gave rise to a spiritual regard for truthfulness. In the tributes of 1945 Bridget Johnston added her own insight into his approach.

> Johnston held that Beauty is an ultimate Grace which will be conferred on the craftsman's work if it has been well done. If Truth, in fact, has been well served, the result will be beauty. [55]

Simplicity, Johnston believed, is born of clarity. The need to be clear extended to other aspects of his life. Towards children it combined with his delightful and eccentric sense of fun. In his memoir, *Forty Years Back*, Hilary Pepler also wrote:

> Children were very fond of Johnston, he could do and did things with magnets, magnesium, wax, wire, pens ... explaining the whys and wherefores of what he was doing with a simplicity and an exactness that they may not have understood but nevertheless appreciated because his language to them was precisely the same as it was to their elders; they knew they were being taken seriously.[56]

In a letter written to Johnston dated the 29th March 1914, Pepler spoke of wanting his son, David, to stay with Johnston in order for him:

> ... to be instructed in the art of pen-cutting – he is nearly ready to begin his apprenticeship. Noel Rooke was here yesterday and saw your 'David was Seven Yesterday' verses which naturally he had to copy down. It obviously made him see David in a new light; I always feel that you have partially adopted our eldest son. Rooke had a queer twist in his face as though he would share a fragment of your artistic parentage. [57]

In another letter to Johnston, written probably between 1912 and 1914, he described the impact which Johnston had on David:

> It was good to have you for that hour or so [*sic*] that we would love to know when you can come again so as to look forward. David said that if flying machines had not been invented Mr. Johnston would probably have made one. The day after you left he made about 20 paper kinds entirely on his own account, many of them flew passing well.[58]

The affection that Johnston felt for Gerard Meynell's daughter, Rosemary, was evidently much the same. (Figs. 42A-B). Her recollections of her childhood in the late 1920s include the writing lessons she had with him at his home in Ditchling. Her description conveys Johnston's coupling of playfulness with explanation:

> On a particularly hot summer afternoon I watched him burning patterns on leaves and bits of paper with the sun caught in a glass. I had several lessons from him in writing with quill pens, but he had to draw elaborate little crutches to hold most of my letters up.[59]

Priscilla Johnston's reminiscences of her father's story telling – they included stories such as *Ula and the Rabbit*, the *Pukwudjies*, *Under the Weight of the Soup Tureen* – best remain where they have been most sensitively described, in her biography. But another child entranced by Johnston was Hilary Bourne, a playmate of Johnston's daughters and a long-standing resident of Ditchling. She remembers particular details about Johnston, for instance, his hands:[60]

> He used to make his own cigarettes, dripping the tobacco with studied care onto the paper before rolling it and licking its gummed edge. He would press the tobacco into the paper and smoothe it out gently. They were beautifully made cigarettes. Everything he did with his hands, he did delicately. They were craftsman's hands. On the occasion of my sister Margery's birthday we were with Johnston's daughters at his home. She was given a book by them as a present. Johnston came downstairs. He had some pens in his top pocket. On being pressed by Bridget, he laid the book onto his knee and wrote out straightaway a most beautifully written greeting.
>
> Mr. Johnston, as I called him, was like a father to me. He loved children and we loved him and played exciting games with him. As we were often singing, he called us the 'song birds'. He taught us a form of Morse code [using torch flashes and semaphore flags] and sometimes we used to go up on the Downs for him to signal to us. And there was always a discussion about everything – that's why meals would never get finished. We would sit on the verandah, it getting darker and darker, with the Downs in front of us. The talk went on and on because he was interested and we were interested. If we used the wrong word he would get out his dictionary from his pocket and point out it wasn't the right word, and what, then, the right word was.[61]

She recalls one Hallowe'en evening when she was perhaps fifteen years old:

> We children spent it making masks, though not from pumpkins but from mangel-wurzels. We were busy fixing them on the barred wooden gate at the entrance to Cleves, as we would for passers-by to see. It was very misty. Suddenly a tall ghost came round the corner of the house. I was terrified and ran in to Mrs Johnston who said to me: 'Oh, don't worry, that's only Edward'. He had placed a white bedsheet on top of a yard-broom, held it aloft over his head, and emerged from out of the mist.

Johnston's 'gorgeous sense of humour' would show through. She remembers:

> … he would give a light twitch on the side of his face, like a half-smile, so that you never knew whether he was having you on or not. You could never be quite sure; he kept you guessing.

Of his wry sense of humour, Noel Rooke wrote:

> Johnston could not discuss serious matters, or even plain things, without leaving … some unobtrusive bit of fun with tail peeping out.… [62]

Others observed a whimsicality in Johnston's make-up. It was touched on by

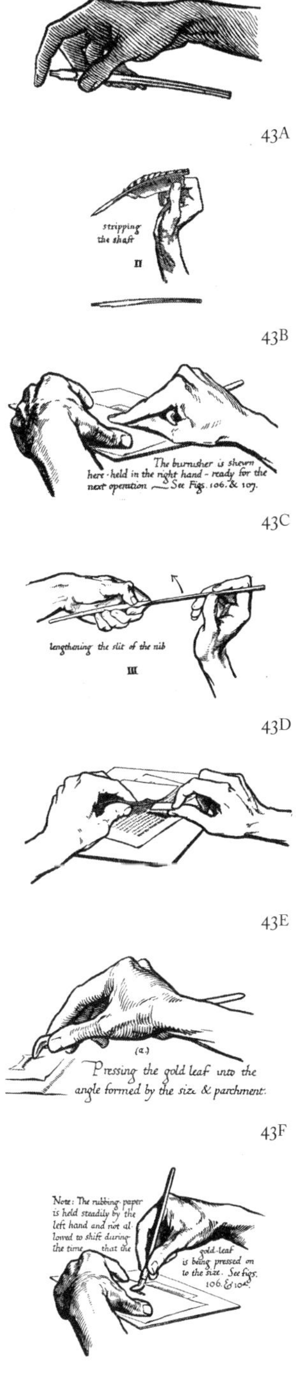

Figs. 43 A–G. Noel Rooke's portraits of Johnston's hands, used for diagrams in *Writing & Illuminating, & Lettering.*

Sydney Cockerell. An 'occasional Magazine', which Johnston compiled with Eric Gill and Hilary Pepler at Ditchling from 1916 to air their ideas, was called, in fact, *The Game*. Johnston's whimsical nature also runs through his imaginative writings. He wrote such short pieces only occasionally. They include two short stories, *The Roothing* and *Tranquil*, both of which were published in the periodical *The Chapbook (A Miscellany)* in 1922 and 1924.[63] Johnston could conceivably have pursued a vocation as an imaginative writer. *Tranquil* is the account of a walk he takes out into the countryside (in all probability up over the Ditchling Beacon, past the Jack and Jill windmills, down to Moulsecoomb in the valley), one sunny autumn morning, a 'gastronome' in search of lunch. His writing shares in both the tranquillity of Richard Jefferies's pastoral descriptions and the inventive fun of Edward Lear. And he brings to it those qualities of clarity, of freshness, and of surprise which enlivened other aspects of his life – his teaching, his friendships, his calligraphy and his handwriting.

It must have been a love of paradox which on one occasion prompted Johnston to reason about the nature of superstition. In 1927 he submitted the winning entry to a competition organised by *The Observer* newspaper which invited its readers to write on the theme of 'A Defence of Superstition'. His entry reads, in part:

> Beliefs, hopes, instincts, imaginations, apprehensions, even fears (though fears may be liars) strike their roots in undiscovered truth. And tradition, legend, proverbs, and sometimes even rumour, are all pillars of smoke that come from ancient fires. When Belief follows Tradition it is wisdom to respect it.
>
> Without the superstition of Astrology and Alchemy, we should be without modern Astronomy and Chemistry. We are satisfied that the pioneers were right in much: we have not proved their superstitions false – we are even beginning again to believe in some of them: as the Transmutation of Gold.
>
> We are dust of the stars, and the stars rule our lives. Who will venture to deny that our destiny is written in them! [64]

Johnston's stature as the pioneer who restated the fundamentals of 'letter-craft' was well appraised by his friend, Alfred Fairbank, a devotee of Johnston whose interest in the Italic script was first inspired by illustrations he saw in *Writing & Illuminating, & Lettering*. As a tribute to him he wrote an article in 1932 intended for publication in Germany. Alluding to Johnston's affirmation of the Book of Kells, one paragraph, somewhat effusive in tone, reads:

> We are helped to understand the product of his genius if we understand something of the man: he has the concentration, profundity, logic, accuracy, and the analytical and synthetical ability of the true philosopher; the detached and unworldly independence, and the sensitive eye of the artist; the interest in tools, materials and design, and the assured skill, and the ready invention of the craftsman; and the masterly, clear, inspiring, and convincing style of the teacher. His practice is founded on tradition adapted to modern conditions, and on sweetreasonableness that allows action on the impulse of the moment. Always he aims at perfection: he is ... the only calligrapher who believes in the *Book of Kells*.[65]

END NOTES

1. Letter to Mr. Kates, a prospective private pupil, 1899. Crafts Study Centre Collection and Archive, Farnham, Surrey. Johnston archive. (Letters 2/107.)

2. Letter to the Prime Minister's Office in 1938. Crafts Study Centre Collection and Archive, Farnham, Surrey. Johnston archive.(Letter-copies book. 2–11.)

3. Edward Johnston. *Writing & Illuminating, & Lettering.* (London. John Hogg, 1906).

4. Edward Johnston. *Formal Penmanship* and other papers, edited by Heather Child. (London: Lund Humphries, 1971): page 144.

5. Edward Johnston (with Graily Hewitt). 'Calligraphy and Illumination', given to the Society of Arts. January 31st, 1905. *Journal of the Society of Arts.* Vol. 53 (17th February 1905). Two transcripts were written out by Johnston. One is in the National Art Library (NAL) at the Victoria & Albert Museum (V&A). (MS. L. 2482–1952).

6. *Writing & Illuminating, & Lettering*: pages 305 and 416. The term 'Foundational Hand' first appeared in print on a duplicated sheet of model alphabets in 1908 given out to his students stating: 'Slanted-Pen Hands. 1. Foundational Hand'. It then occurred as a title on Plate No. 6 of Johnston's *Manuscript and Inscription Letters* in 1909. He discussed the Foundational Hand further in *The Imprint* Vol. 1 No. 5 Ch. 5 (17th May 1913): pages 346–47.

7. *Manuscript and Inscription Letters.* (13 Paternoster Row, London: John Hogg, 1909).

8. It was to this end that Johnston wrote occasional papers as well as devising a print script for school children. He was an adviser to the handwriting educationist, Marion Richardson, and a consultant to the Education Committee of the London County Council. He addressed the London County Council Conference of Teachers in 1913.

9. *The Imprint.* (11 Henrietta Street, Covent Garden, London: Westminster Press) 1913.

10. See Justin Howes. *Johnston's Underground Type.* (38 Long Elmes, Harrow Weald, Middlesex: Capital Transport Publishing, 2000).

11. This manuscript is in the NAL in the V&A (L 4391–1959). Facsimile edition: V&A Museum. J. Harthan. *Edward Johnston The House of David, his Inheritance: A book of sample scripts 1914 A.D.*(London: Her Majesty's Stationery Office, 1966).

12. It was published posthumously as *Formal Penmanship and other papers.* Edited by Heather Child. (London: Lund Humphries, 1971).

13. The manuscripts are dispersed in museums, libraries and private collections. However, a pioneering basis for such a catalogue raisonné is *Edward Johnston, a Catalogue of the Crafts Study Collections and Archive*, compiled and annotated by Justin Howes. (Bath, 1987).
14. Johnston's ancestral background is discussed further in Appendix One, with a genealogy.
15. This portfolio of manuscripts is in the NAL at the V&A. (MS L.24–1982). Mary Monica Bridges. *A New Handwriting for Teachers*. (sl., sn., nd. 1898). P. Holliday. 'Edward Johnston and Robert Bridges 1901–26: A Phonetic Alphabet in the Half-Uncial Script'. See: *Printing History* (2004).
16. Priscilla Johnston. 'So Completely Himself'. A talk to the Society of Scribes and Illuminators. October 1979. *Journal of The Society of Scribes & Illuminators* (Winter 1986). In the same talk she recalled Johnston's interlocutors:
... leaning forward in a pause ... and then sinking back defeated as my father went serenely on. Johnston's friend, Montague Weekly, an art critic and librarian at the V&A who wrote his obituary in 1945, described his voice in a review of the commemorative exhibition to Johnston at the V&A, published in The Times Literary Supplement. (3rd November 1945): Johnston had a fine head, a frail body, and a strange, chanting voice – imagine a minor canon who forgot to shed his liturgical voice on leaving the cathedral choir. (cont...)

The suggestion that Johnston had a 'liturgical voice' prompted Noel Rooke to respond with a different observation. Part of his letter to Bridget Johnston, dated 12th August 1945, reads: 'A 'liturgical voice', to most people, would suggest a voice by which the meaning was slightly arrested by the enunciation – the hearer's attention is demanded by the manner and the matter gets across later, if it can. With E. J. it was the opposite. One was arrested and held by the idea of what was being conveyed – the chanting seemed the result of holding in, and refraining until the precise word had been found, not by the desire to give fine expression to words that had been selected centuries ago. It is a family voice, as you say. But the weight of slow accurate statement ....'
Crafts Study Centre Collection. Farnham, Surrey. Johnston archive. (Letters. 2/256.)
17. See: John Dreyfus. 'Gerard Meynell and the Westminster Press'. *Matrix* Vol. 10 (1990).
18. Priscilla Johnston: *Edward Johnston*. (Faber and Faber, 1959). Johnston seemed especially taken up by the symmetry of number relationships, of algebraic formulae and of Euclidian geometry. Among his papers at the Bodleian Library, Oxford, are sheets of mathematical jottings. Dating from 1937 they show him to be intensely absorbed in patterns of mathematical thought. One sheet has written on it a sequence of the names of ten fish, each name having five letters. (Bodleian Library. MS. Eng. Misc. c 340 fol: 13e.). (Figs. 23 A–B).
19. Johnston had calligraphed this quotation as early as 13–14th January 1899. See Crafts Study Collection. C 86.27.i. Another, 'Life itself is a mixture of power and form' is in the Pierpont Morgan Library, New York (MA 1720 N-2 13 D).
20. See also Peter Holliday. 'The Tradition and Study of Johnston in Britain and the USA'. Unpublished typescript, 2001, lodged with Ditchling Museum (Johnston archive).
21. These tributes were edited by Charles Pickering and printed in book form as *Tributes to Edward Johnston*. (The School of Printing. Maidstone College of Art, 1948).
22. Crafts Study Centre Collection and Archive, Farnham, Surrey. Johnston archive. (Notebook 2/Loan 12.)
23. Priscilla Johnston. *Edward Johnston*. (London: Faber and Faber, 1959).
24. In this project Owen Jones received the help of other major mid-Victorian designers, including Matthew Digby Wyatt, John Burley Waring, John Westwood, Joseph Bonomi, Charles Richardson, and Christopher Dresser, most of whom published books and articles on various aspects of what was called historic ornamentation.
25. This example of Owen Jones's work was printed by the new chromolithographic process by Day & Co. A copy is in the NAL at the V&A.
26. 'The Original Drawings for the Victoria Psalter'. National Art Library at the V&A (Special Collections. RCKK 31).
27. The Royal Librarian, Sir John Fortescue, remarked in 1905 of these manuscripts: 'The contemplation of them always makes me rather sad ... all follow an evil tradition, as I guess, from the earlier decades of the nineteenth century.' Cited from his *Memoirs*, 1933, by William Gardner in: 'High Victorian Taste in Calligraphy & Illumination: The Loyal Addresses

Presented to Queen Victoria in 1887'. *Journal of the Royal Society of Arts* Vol. 135. (July. 1987). William Gardner, a calligrapher in the Johnston tradition, summarises the illumination of the addresses by saying: 'High Victorian Illumination, the decoration that accompanies the inscriptional work ranges very widely and includes pseudo Anglo-French borders ... through a welter of symbolic, heraldic and natural depictions of every kind – flowers, foliage, geometric patterns,and so forth.' He also observes that while the Blackletter forms are easily and quickly written with a broad-edged pen, those in the addresses were 'meticulously drawn in outline and then filled in, a painfully time-consuming thing.'

28. Priscilla Johnston. *Edward Johnston* (London: Faber & Faber, 1959): page 71.

29. Edward Johnston. 'Decoration and Its Uses'. *The Imprint* Vol. 1 No. 5 Ch. 5 (1913): p. 349.

30. Among these exceptions was the Daniel Press, run by Dr. Charles Henry Olive Daniel at Oxford, who pioneered the revival of the 'Old Style' Fell types that had fallen into disuse by the Oxford University Press. Another was the Chiswick Press, in London, run by William Pickering, by Charles Whittingham and then by Charles Jacobi. (William Morris's writings were printed there prior to his own Kelmscott Press.) Both continued to use Caslon, the traditional 'Old Style' Roman type design used in Britain since the late 1720s.

31. The question of the categorisation of type designs is quite outside the scope of this study.

32. Edward Johnston. 'Syllabus for Writing and Illuminating Course. Royal College of Art'. *Lessons in Formal Writing*. Edited by Heather Child & Justin Howes. (Lund Humphries, 1986): page 83.

33. The fact that this writing style, written properly, took time and care probably did not aid business efficiency as much as legibility.

34. In *Writing & Illumination, &Lettering* (page 256) Johnston wrote: 'other tools [than the pen], such as the stylus, needle, graver etc., produce various scratches, stitches, or cuts, generally of the nature of rather varying thin strokes, and to produce thick strokes a building-up process is required.'

35. To reproduce tiny cursive letters by woodcut was difficult. The first writing book printed by the Copperplate process was Giulantonio Hercolani's *Essemplare utile*. (Rome, 1571).

36. The Prime Minister, Lord Palmerston, made adverse criticism of the Roundhand script of his day. See: L. Hector. *The Handwriting of English Documents*. (Edward Arnold, 1960.)

37. See: John Nash. 'Calligraphy', in 'William Morris', being the catalogue of the exhibition *William Morris 1834–96*, edited by Linda Parry. (V&A/Philip Wilson, 1996.)

38. William Morris's manuscript, written in Latin, is entitled *Virgil's Aeneid*. It was completed by Fairfax Murray and two of Johnston's pupils, Graily Hewitt and Louise Powell.

39. Johnston's indebtedness to Morris is signalled in his chapter 'The Development of Illumination' in *Writing & Illuminating, & Lettering*: page 170.

40. Johnston's diary for 31st October 1898, Crafts Study Centre Collection and Archive, Farnham, Surrey. Johnston archive. (diary 2/Loan 2).

41. Edward Johnston. *Writing & Illuminating, & Lettering*: pages 63, 85, and 293.

42. 'Decoration and its Uses'. *The Imprint* Vol. 1 No. 6 Ch. 6 (17th June 1913): page 429. Johnston had already touched on this notion in 1906 in *Writing & Illuminating, & Lettering* (page 232): 'A good craftsman seeks out the commonplace and tries to master it, knowing that originality comes of necessity and not of searching'. There is a broader sense, too, in which Johnston's concerns relate to other developments which were taking place in the visual arts at much the same time. His notion of structure, for example, corresponds to Cézanne's notion of the 'architecture' of landscape and still life, which informed his paintings in the 1880s, challenging Impressionism which was based on subjective retinal sense perception. Respect for the natural qualities of the tools and materials is paralleled in the photography of Paul Strand in the 1910s. He proposed an objective portrayal of form through 'chiaroscuro' – natural light and dark – alone. Strand held this to be the truthful use of the photographer's tool, the camera lens, in contrast to the painterly techniques of the Pictorial photographers, then much in vogue.

43. Hilary Pepler. 'Forty Years Back'. *The Register* (1949).

44. William Rothenstein. *Since Fifty. Men and Memories*. (Faber and Faber, 1939).

45. Edward Johnston. *Writing & Illuminating, & Lettering*. (13 Paternoster Row, London:

John Hogg, 1906): page 238–99. Also in 'The Leicester Lectures 1906–1907. "Sign Writing", September 1906' in Edward Johnston. *Lessons in Formal Writing*. Edited by Heather Child and Justin Howes. (Lund Humphries, 1986): page 91.

In 1900, Edward Strange gave a lecture entitled 'The Practice of Lettering' to the Royal Society of Arts in which he also uses the term 'character'. He intended it to mean a 'certain personal singularity in the making of letters which gives distinction – or individuality anyway – to the accepted and still easily understood letter.' Might this be a source for Johnston's own use of the term 'character'? 'The Practice of Lettering'. *Journal of the Royal Society of Arts*. Vol. 48. (June 1905).

46. *Formal Penmanship and other papers*. Edited by Heather Child. (Lund Humphries, 1971): Part i, Chapter 6, pages 117–18 and Part iii, page 142. Unfinished and unprepared for publication *Formal Penmanship* is fragmentary. The triad Sharpness, Unity and Freedom co-exists within an over-arching triad. Thus, formal penmanship is described in Part i by its 'Tools', in Part ii by its 'Traditions', in Part iii by its 'Things'. Then there are subdivisions. For example, Part i, Chapter 3, begins with Johnston discerning that: 'Three primary conditions determine the special character of any manuscript made with the formal pen'. These are 'the weight of the stroke, the angle which gives the stress, and the form of the letter'. (Weight concerns the thickness of the letter's strokes in relation to its height. Angle concerns how the broad-edged pen is held in relation to the horizontal line of writing, thereby achieving a different stress to the curves of the letters. Form, or shape, concerns the overall design of the letters to form a script, e.g., the Roman script, or the Italic, or Gothic Black Letter ones.)

47. 'Paper on the Labelling of Exhibits read ... at the General Meeting of the Society, 13th June 1933'. Published in *Four Papers, Read by Members of the Arts and Crafts Exhibition Society*. (Longmans, Green & Co., Ltd, for the Society, 1933).

48. Crafts Study Centre Collection and Archive, Farnham, Surrey. Johnston archive. (Letters 2/15).

49. Edward Johnston. Letter to Sir Sydney Cockerell. (NAL at the V&A. Manuscripts, England 1943–49 AAT.)

50. A quotation from Goethe and freely translated as: 'Only in reaching for life within it, therefore is the world so large'. Rendered with the help of Dr. Cornelia Thiels. Berlin. The responsibility of the translation is the author's. A poetic rendering is: 'Only through our freely faring Is the world so truly great.' Cited from Priscilla Johnston. *Edward Johnston* (London: Faber & Faber, 1959): page 186.

51. Edward Johnston. Lecture/Demonstration to the Fourth International Congress for Art Education. Dresden 1912. This, arguably the key statement of all Johnston's writings, is preserved on a mere scrap of paper. Crafts Study Centre Collection and Archive, Farnham, Surrey. Johnston archive. (2/333).

52. 'Tranquil' appeared in *The Chapbook* (A Miscellany). Vol. 39 (1924).

53. Edward Johnston: 2 Ams Notebooks 1899–1904 held at the Harry Ransom Humanities Research Center at the University of Texas at Austin, Texas.

54. The portfolio of the draft contains all the folios of the handbook, typed in parts and handwritten in others, Noel Rooke's illustrations and Johnston's instructions to the printers. It is now in the National Art Library at the V&A. (Box II. 86.ee).

55. Printed in *Tributes to Edward Johnston*. Edited by Charles Pickering. (The School of Printing: Maidstone College of Art, 1948).

56. Hilary Pepler. 'Forty Years Back'. *The Register* 1949.

57. Crafts Study Centre Collection and Archive, Farnham, Surrey. Johnston archive. (Letters 2/Loan 42).

58. Crafts Study Centre Collection and Archive, Farnham, Surrey. Johnston archive. (Letters 2/Loan 40).

59. Rosemary Pepler. *Guide to Ditchling* (1965). Local history archive. Brighton Library. (She married Pepler's son, Mark, who later ran the S. Dominic's Press, renamed the Ditchling Press, which is now run by his son, Lawrence.) See Johnston's manuscript: 'Lettering Illustrating the Formation of the Roman alphabet for Mrs. Meynell's children'. V&A. (E 220–24–1946.)

60. Noel Rooke, too, was struck by Johnston's hands. Aside from his portraits of his hands (see Figs. 43A–G) he commented in a letter to Bridget Johnston dated 29th October 1945: '... his hands were at first glance seen to be capable and very sensitive ....' Crafts Study Centre Collection and Archive, Farnham, Surrey. Johnston archive. (Letters 2/255.)
61. Recorded in conversation with Hilary Bourne in 1998, on the 4th November 1999 and on 27th April 2003. See also Hilary Bourne's memoirs, *Spinning the Thread*, edited by Susan Skinner. (Hurstpierpoint: Bruno and Lucy Press, 1999). James Wardrop also spoke of Johnston's 'powerful and expressive hands'. See: *Tributes to Edward Johnston*. Ed. Charles Pickering. (Maidstone College of Art, 1948). It was Johnston's hands that Noel Rooke depicted holding quill and reed in his wood-engraved diagrams for *Writing & Illuminating, & Lettering*. Surely no book contains more portraits of its author's hands.
62. Noel Rooke. Cited in Priscilla Johnston. *Edward Johnston*. (London: Faber & Faber, 1959).
63. *The Chapbook. A Miscellany* [fomerly Poetry and Drama] No. 31 (1922) and No. 39 (1924) Published by The Poetry Bookshop, 35 Devonshire Street, Theobalds Road. London WC. I. '*The Roothing*' was written with Johnston's nephew, A. Gunnar D. Johnston.
64. Competition. The Observer. (16th October. 1927).
65. Alfred Fairbank. 'Edward Johnston and English Calligraphy'. Typescript in the Crafts Study Centre Collection and Archive, Farnham, Surrey. Johnston archive. (Letters 2/70).

Edward Johnston, portrait by William Rothenstein,
drawn in pencil at the Royal College of Art, London, 1922.
(Courtesy of the National Portrait Gallery)

CHAPTER TWO

JOHNSTON FROM 1898: MENTORS AND MODELS

Johnston is rightly regarded as a pioneer, but pioneers rarely work in total isolation. During the course of 1898, the year in which Johnston arrived in London, he had the good fortune to fall in with an extraordinary group of lettering connoisseurs, comprising William H. Cowlishaw, William Lethaby, Sir Sydney Cockerell and the poet Robert Bridges. Initially, Johnston's interest in lettering was little more than a hobby. Gradually, it took an increasing hold on him so that, with his poor health and his waning interest in his medical studies in Edinburgh early in that year, it became a dominant enthusiasm. He proved to be very receptive to his new mentors.

As a prelude to these friendships, Johnston appears to have been artistically inspired by a gently romantic encounter. Early in 1898, he enjoyed a short but emotionally charged stay in London with two Scottish sisters, Georgina and Mollie MacRae, whom he had known for the past two years through his cousins in Edinburgh. Propitiously, it was in their home at 2 Vernon Place, off Bloomsbury Square and close by the British Museum, that Johnston was first struck by the allure of artistic freedom. Both sisters were painters and had lived in Paris where Georgina had run a small boarding house for artists. To Johnston, Georgina was known affectionately as 'Hearthmaker', whilst he, in his letters from Scotland, signed himself as 'Mist-lifter'. His feelings come through in a series of letters beautifully decorated with a youthful zeal. One, written to Georgina in 1898, reads in part:

> Thank you again for the very happy time I had at Vernon Place. I would have a tooth out every day for such happiness ... then blossomed the first buds of my art's hope and time was the golden sand that sped by me so befriended – such dear friends are hard to find. I pray I may never lose them ... Bon soir a [*sic*] tout le monde. Goodbye dear Hearthmaker, your friend, Edward Johnston. If either of you can drop me a few lines ever (or a few words) they will be like sweet dew on thirsty ground, God be with you dear folk. Your friend, Edward Johnston.[1]

Some years later, on 31st October 1906, when *Writing & Illuminating, & Lettering*, was published, Johnston remembered Georgina and sent her a copy. He wrote:

> Hearthmaker must have one if no one else has one. So you see it was not your letter that made me think of you, but it was largely gratitude for your care and kindness, when I set out to face my fortune; and a natural affection for my dear Hearthmaker (which persists, believe me, in spite of my seeming neglect of her and of absorption in my own business worries).[2]

However Johnston's more tender attachment was to Mollie, whom he fondly nicknamed 'Wing-seeker'. In return, she called him 'Marcus Aurelius'. The friendship began in 1886 when Mollie had taught him some dancing – he preferred to call it 'tune-stepping'. Johnston sent her a 'parchment' expressing his affection. Johnston's letters to Mollie, while displaying all his customary love of word play, also show the apprehension of a young man anxious to please. One, dated 20th January 1898, reads:

> Dear Miss Mollie MacRae,
>
> … As for nicknames, I like them in reason. 'Marcus' – I agree with you – is a rather nice name. I felt much flattered and touched by it. I am fond of anything that begins with an M ('such as the Moon and Memory and Muchness, you know Much of a Muchness. Have you ever seen a drawing of a Muchness' Alice. I have – some of my parchments and a few other things.)
>
> Thanks for your letter – it was very kind of you to write. I don't think the people who think them 'disjointed or vague' can be at all nice. They seem to be just like yourself speaking, and how could they be nicer at all ….[3]

Another letter dated the 22nd April 1898, becomes more dispirited, however:

> Thank you very much for 'returning' my call and greatly relieving my mind thereby. Tho' very pleased to see your handwriting again I was quite scared at the thought of the criticism of my eccentricities that it might convey and I opened it with much nervousness and quivering [*sic*] finding, as they say, that you evidently look on those eccentricities as amicable in character and proceeding from the heart (head) rather than the heart (I don't quite know which I mean). My own opinion is that my head is rather weak but that on the whole my 'heart is good' as the saying is.
>
> Relieved as I am, notwithstanding, I am desolated by your statement that I 'don't know you at all'. I am [*sic*] desoleé and inconsoleé (I think that is French wh I never learnt tho'), and the only thing that keeps my spirits up is that your letter is so much more cheerful than the last one …[4]

A further letter of late April, 1898 reads, in part:

> You will think me a tiresome preacher, no doubt, but dear Wing-seeker I do so long for wings myself. I'll do anything to help you in your seeking – even to go the lengths of preaching tiresomely … So please forgive the priggishness (or what you will) that comes from a great longing, as you liked that rede [the name Johnston gave to his parchments] and called it 'sweet' read into it that meaning that your own sweet self would fain by finding. Good Bye. Yr Friend, Edward Johnston.

Johnston sent Mollie a Valentine card from Edinburgh in 1898. While reserved in her correspondence with him – she married her husband, J. N. White, late in 1898 – she actively encouraged his artistic interests and arranged for the lettering artist and architect, Harry Cowlishaw, to appraise his 'parchments'. Cowlishaw, who was an instructor in typography at the St. Bride Institute (a technical school established by the London County Council), was duly impressed by Johnston's work. The letter he wrote to Johnston was endorsed by the artist friend he had in Edinburgh, James Cadenhead. Spurred on by such praise, Johnston abandoned his idea of studying the craft of book production at the College of Art in Liverpool, where he had been in touch with Anning Bell R.A., its Head of the School of Painting[5]

Instead, Johnston came to London in April 1898. He was aged twenty-six. He lodged with the MacRae sisters under whose spell he was resolved to 'go in for art', although he had in mind a training in the book arts, in illustration, illumination, and even bookbinding. His more urgent desire, however, was to learn to draw. He enrolled, briefly, in drawing classes at Westminster School of Art and then at the Slade, under Professor Tonks. Cowlishaw's own calligraphy attracted Johnston. He read an article on Cowlishaw by Ford Maddox Hueffer, published in the *The Artist* for 1898, which illustrated details of six pieces of his illuminated manuscript of Edward Garnett's *Imaged World.* (Garnett was a client.)[6] Johnston was to reproduce a detail from Cowlishaw's manuscript, *The Story of Aucassin and Nicolette*, of 1898, as Plate No. XXXIII in *Writing & Illuminating, & Lettering.* He wrote that it 'reminded one of a country hedgerow and showed a vital beauty which is the essence of true illumination'.

It was through Cowlishaw that Johnston was put in touch with the influential William Lethaby, who was well-established as an architect, an architectural historian, and a design educationalist.[7] It was Lethaby who was the moving force in setting up the London County Council's Central School of Arts and Crafts, in 1896. Soon, Johnston's purely artistic attachment to lettering was to be enriched by more intellectual involvements. Among Lethaby's many gifts was his insight into students' potentialities. He instilled in these protégés a sense of confidence and inquiry. Johnston was to say of him: 'He was the perfect man to have met'. He recalled that the meeting was: 'The miracle of my life ... nothing but divine providence'.[8]

Additionally, Lethaby enlightened Johnston on the philosophical as well as practical value of a craft-based training. The thrust of his own convictions, as an educationist, was to be rid of the prevailing dogma that designing was a theoretical skill acquired on the drawing board, which was then to be applied as in a vacuum. Lethaby's approach was to revitalise craft skills, '... based on the reasonable and pleasant solution of present wants'. Authentic designs should happen organically through the practice of craft. The study of historical designs would then fall into place as a critical, rather than an imitative activity. His inaugural lecture, circa 1901, at the RCA – only three years after Johnston first met him – ended with a new message for the students.

> Learn a craft practically. Beware of fashions and shams in design but try to be serious and reasonable in your work. Study old work but from a critical and craft point of view rather than historically.[9]

Lethaby expressed this poetically in his choice of the quotation which opens his book , *Mediæval Art:*[10]

> Are we then to be strong by following the natural fact? Yes, assuredly. (Val d'Arno.)

This policy was reflected in the staff appointments that Lethaby made at the Central School of Arts and Crafts. Craft expertise, rather than academic qualification, counted for Lethaby. For example, William Dodds, who was a registered plumber and R. Hook, a stoneworker, were engaged to teach. By the same criterion, craft apprentices were admitted as students.

Lethaby's views, deriving from Morris, were absorbed by Johnston and crystallised in his practice of calligraphy. They centred round a number of shibboleths: the importance to the design of the tools and the materials used; the necessity for the designer to be also the maker; the re-establishment of work as a way of living; art as 'the well doing of what needs doing'; 'the humanity put into workmanship'; 'thoughtful workmanship'.[11] Their first meeting took place at Lethaby's architectural practice, at 2 Gray's Inn Square, in April, 1898, and subsequently at the Central School of Arts and Crafts, the institution to which Lethaby had been appointed co-Director. This was the starting point of Johnston's decision to take up calligraphy professionally. Lethaby had been one of the first to appreciate the Roman capitals at the base of the Trajan Column, a full scale plaster cast of which had recently been put on view at the V&A Museum.[12] Reinforced by his knowledge of the wide spectrum of the crafts, he offered Johnston his insights into the neglected craft of lettering:

> ... the form of the letter cannot be properly 'drawn' or 'designed': it must be written. The forms first make themselves with a pen and proper development can only be made in the same way.[13]

In order to underpin critical knowledge with practice, Johnston realised the need to understand the connection between the structure of the formal letters used in medieval manuscripts and the techniques of penmanship by which the scribes wrote them. Again, he had Lethaby's encouragement.

The realisation that the tools and materials are integral to the resulting design was acknowledged by a widening circle of people, however. For example, in 1892, J. H. Middleton, the director of the Fitzwilliam Museum in Cambridge, published a detailed book entitled *Illuminated Manuscripts in Classical and Mediæval Times, their Art and Technique*, in which he discusses writing in relation to the reeds and quills used. The idea was also well established as an article of faith for the Arts and Crafts movement. In 1893, the theorist and historian, Lewis F. Day had already written in his book, *The Application of Ornament:*

> ... style is not so much a thing of dates and countries, but of materials and tools .... There was never a tool or a process but it wrote its character on the work done. It was so in a simple practical matter like lettering .... The use of the thick and thin lines (the down stroke and the up stroke) comes from the use of the pen, and so does the characteristic thickening of the backs of certain Gothic capitals such as the G.

In an essay of 1896 entitled 'Mediæval Calligraphy' the pioneer palæographer, E. Maunde Thompson, had stressed that: 'The accident of material has often changed the entire character of an alphabet.'

But Johnston did make the important connection, little appreciated in the nineteenth century, between the actual preparation of the pen used – he was speaking of the quill (turkey, goose, crow) and the reed – and the resulting form. 'The nib must shape the letters', he wrote with characteristic precision. Up to Johnston's time, lettering artists would tend to follow the 'crow-quill-and-fill-in' method by making an outline contour of the letter's shape – especially a capital letter – and then fill in, with ink or colouring.

In place of this practice, Johnston substituted the use of the 'broad-nibbed' pen, which, as he explained in *Writing & Illuminating, & Lettering*: '... naturally writes regular thick and thin and graduated strokes according to its direction (not its pressure)'. It thus creates, said Johnston, 'simple written' forms. To achieve this Johnston stresses that the quill should be cut very sharp, and either square or at an oblique angle. The quill is then to be held in a constant position with its writing edge either parallel to the horizontal line of writing (a 'straight pen'), or at an angle – usually 30 degrees – to it (a 'slanting pen').[14] This gives four basic combinations (square-cut/oblique-edged nib; and parallel/angled pen position), enabling other permutations. Furthermore, Johnston stressed that it was the pen, essentially of itself, which does the work. Of his own manuscript version of his lecture to the [Royal] Society of Arts he wrote:

> This hand is written with a properly cut pen, which is used with the slightest pressure. The shape and proportions of the pen nib, and the direction in which it moves, together produce the thicks and thins and graduated curves, and the graceful forms of proper penmanship.[15]

This study of technique, undertaken by scrutiny of manuscripts in the British Museum, was the basis for his entire life-work.

It is possible that Johnston was prompted to consider the importance of the pen nib in the formation of the letters by his reading of a seminal volume called *Alphabets*, which had been recently published, in 1895, by Edward Strange, a Keeper at the Victoria & Albert Museum. In his chapter, *The Making of Letters*, Strange wrote with considerable prescience ' ... the quill remains to us, although the art of cutting it is well-nigh lost.' Notwithstanding Strange's comments, Johnston's achievement was to refocus attention on a technique which had become neglected in the nineteenth century rather than entirely lost.[16] In formulating this aim Johnston was influenced by another study of letter-forms, namely Lewis F. Day's *Alphabets Old and New*, published in 1898. Johnston's own copy is very heavily annotated. While referring to printed types, two passages (on pages 25–26, and 36–37) nevertheless provided him with key ideas:

> We in our day have arrived by a process of copying the copies of copies, from which all the virtue of vitality and freshness has died out, of a Victorian type (look at the newspapers) which compares most unfavourably with the early printing. There is no need to revive mediæval lettering, no need to invent new lettering out of our heads, if that were possible; any new departure of ours must be very much on old lines but at least we might found ourselves upon the best that has been done, and go straight to that for inspiration.

> It is no use trying to evolve brand new alphabets out of our inner consciousness. No one would understand us and we want to be read.... Practically, what we have to do is take an alphabet and modify it according to our wants and inclinations, without, as a rule, interferring much with its legibility.... An alphabet, however, should not look hybrid. The artist is free to do what he can but the test of success is that his creation should look as if it must be so, and could not have been otherwise.[17]

As a scribe, Johnston became immersed in the history of letter-forms. As a reformer and teacher, his growing concern was to activate that history and revive scripts of proven excellence as models with which to practise in the present. At no point did Johnston wish to invent a new script, as did Robert Bridges, for example, whose new phonetic alphabet Johnston helped to design, at the turn of the nineteenth century.[18] On the opening page of *Writing & Illuminating, & Lettering* he affirmed the value of history:

> ... in trying to revive good Lettering, we cannot do better than make a practical study of the best pen forms and learn at the same time to appreciate the forms of their magnificent archetypes as preserved in the monumental Roman inscriptions.

Johnston found it important, therefore, to trace the historical development of letter-forms and understand the 'skeleton' of the letters. In this work he referred to the scholar of Latin inscriptions, E. Hübner, whose compilation, *Exempla Scripturæ Epigraphicæ Latinæ*, published in Berlin in 1885, he consulted in the Reading Room of the British Museum.[19] The line drawings in E. Hübner's work provided Johnston with the models for the illustrations in his own handbook. Three of Hübner's illustrations are reproduced by Johnston. Drawn in outline (rather than blocked-in, solid) these may have led him to the concept of the 'skeleton' of a letterform. A significant proportion of *Writing & Illuminating, & Lettering* is devoted to the history of lettering. A short introductory chapter is called *The Development of Writing*. It points out the technique of the pen. Chapter XV, entitled *The Roman Alphabet & Its Derivatives*, is a detailed description extending through some seventy pages.[20] A more thorough investigation, still, was made in his later study, *Formal Penmanship*.[21]

In the earliest stage of his investigations, Johnston favoured the Half-Uncial scripts as a model that could be developed as a formal 'copy book' hand. It was, he said, an 'upright Round Hand', written with a 'straight pen', giving the 'finest training to the penman'. He recognised, however, that 'their thin strokes, and their general elegance unfit [*sic*] them for many practical purposes.'[22]

In due course, therefore, he came to focus attention on what amounted to a generic script called the Caroline Minuscule, so-named after Charlemagne. This script had developed in France from as early as the second-half of the eighth century and had then become prevalent in much of Europe, up into the twelfth century, when it was gradually superseded by the Gothic script. Unlike the Half-Uncials, Johnston observed, it was written with the pen held at an angle ('slanting-pen' position), which produces 'thick horizontals' [strokes], giving the script 'greater strength and legibility'. It was 'easily and freely written' and 'for practical purposes ... superior to the straight-pen letter.[23] Johnston saw its potential. He added to his description:

> Carlovingian MSS. may be said to represent a sort of mediæval copy books, and their far-reaching influence on writing makes them of great interest to the modern penman, who would, moreover, find one of these hands an excellent model for a free 'formal hand'. The real importance to us lies, I think, in their relation to the Roman Small Letter, and their great possibilities of development into modern formal hands approaching the 'Roman' type.[24]

By 'type' Johnston is referring to printing types. In the section 'Roman Small Letters', which follows immediately, he goes on to say:

> The Roman Small Letter is the universally recognised type in which the majority of books and newspapers are printed.... And it is the object of the scribe or letter-maker gradually to attain a fine, personal, formal hand, assimilating to the Roman Small Letter ... of which no allegations of unreadableness can be raised, and a hand having a beauty and character now absent or unfamiliar.[25]

In addition to it being practicable, Johnston also favoured the script of the 'Carlovingian manuscripts.' because it approximated modern printing types. At the time of his writing his handbook he was also working with Cobden-Sanderson on some of the Doves Press books. He therefore had an intimate knowledge of the finest example of a revived Roman Old Face type design, modelled on Johnston's Roman Small Letter. For Cobden-Sanderson's 'Doves Press' type had been designed for him by Emery Walker, from 1900.[26] Johnston was therefore making the same kind of reforms for calligraphy that Cobden-Sanderson and Walker, and Morris before them, had made for printing.

Rather than adopt a fifteenth or a sixteenth-century Italian Humanist script (or the 'Roman Small Letter', in Johnston's terminology) as a model for a formal hand, Johnston looked further back to the Caroline Minuscule script. Apart from his preference for the beauty of the medieval manuscripts, the Caroline Minuscule was the fountainhead which displays most clearly the use of the broad-nibbed pen. In his commentary on the plates which he included in *Writing & Illuminating, & Lettering*, Johnston points out that the fifteenth-century humanist script of Plate XX is '... written with a very narrow nib, hence the pen forms are not so obvious as in some early formal hands; and for this reason alone it would be better to practise such a hand as the tenth-century MS. (Plate VIII) before seriously attempting to model a hand on the above.'[27]

Johnston's interest in the Caroline Minuscule script and the pinpointing of the *Ramsey Psalter* as a model was due, in large measure, to the inspiration of one of the Arts and Crafts movement's more distinguished members, the antiquary Sir Sydney Cockerell. One of Cockerell's special interests was the study and the collection of medieval manuscripts. Johnston was introduced to him by William Lethaby. The mentor and the student met for the first time, at the British Museum, in 1898. Recalling that occasion, Johnston wrote in a letter to Cockerell, dated the 15th September, 1904:

> You may have forgotten meeting me at the British Museum, on 28th October 1898 and giving me criticism and advice (for abt half an hour) wh, were and have been of gt value to me. The example of an Italian MSS wh you showed me as a model was the book in question (XCC Italian MSS). A better page is shown in the case, but the writing (minuscule) is precisely the same. I copied it most carefully but did not perpetuate its blobby serifs as I left finish to my pen. PS. I don't mean that that writing formed my hand but it helped me and a glance at some Morris writing soon after did more.[28]

Of that meeting, Cockerell himself wrote:

> On this occasion we did not go behind the scenes. I merely took Johnston from case to case pointing out the finest pieces of handwriting, and laying special stress on the Winchester scripts of the tenth and eleventh centuries, which he soon after took as his models.[29]

Further contact with Cockerell followed on quickly. On the 31st October Johnston recorded in his work diary: '5 pm. met Cockerell at BM. Walked together to Waterloo. Spent evening at Richmond (17 Rosemont Road). Dinner. Afterward Kates (American) came and we looked at Morris things. C. gave us several proofs....' The contact with Cockerell continued. In his diary for 8th August, 1904, Cockerell noted: 'Count Harry Kessler, Edward Johnston, and Treglown came up to my rooms at Richmond and looked at books.'[30] On the 31st October, 1904, Cockerell again noted that 'Johnston came up to Richmond for the evening'.[31] Cockerell gave Johnston good constructive criticism of his studies of medieval manuscripts. An entry in Johnston's diary for 2nd November 1898 reads: 'Cockerell's word final greatest authority.' In 1913, Johnston wrote as a dedication in a presentation copy of his handbook: '... to S.C. Cockerell who (very kindly) always tore me to pieces.'[32] The wider experience that Cockerell passed on to Johnston was equally invaluable.

One of Johnston's most devoted students at the Royal College of Art was Violet Hawkes. In later life she attempted to have *Formal Penmanship* published by Francis Meynell at the Nonesuch Press.[33] In 1945, she wrote to Sydney Cockerell remembering his protégé. Part of her eulogy to Johnston recognises also the importance of Lethaby.

> If I can succeed in placing before the world all that I can gather out of his notes and drafts at Ditchling and the kernel of his teaching at the RCA, future generations will thus honour your name and that of Professor Lethaby for recognising and encouraging (while yet in embryo) a genius more profound than even William Morris or Ruskin ....[34]

Sydney Cockerell maintained contact with Johnston throughout his working life. One of Johnston's most important manuscripts, *The House of David, his Inheritance: a book of sample scripts*, was the outcome of this long friendship.[35] Cockerell was the source of inspiration for the commemorative exhibition to Johnston held at the Victoria & Albert Museum in 1945, following his death.

The specific model on which Johnston focused his attention was an English variant of the Caroline Minuscule, which he studied from an impressive Anglo-Saxon manuscript held at the British Museum. (See Fig. 35). In Johnston's day this book was referred to by its catalogue tag, *Harley MS. 2904* only. Today, it is also known as the *Ramsey Psalter*, having possibly been written at the Abbey of Ramsey, in East Anglia, for Oswald, Bishop of Worcester. Alternative theories, however, attribute it to the Winchester School, under Bishop Æthelwold. On both counts it is dated to the very late tenth century, probably 998. At first glance it appears to be a lengthy book, its continuous text running through two hundred and forty folios (four hundred and eighty pages). But there are only eighteen lines to each page and the letters, which probably number as many as one hundred and fifty thousand, are written in a large size, approximating to the typopgrapher's 18 point. Each is flawlessly penned in rich black ink, with the capitals at the beginning of the lines written in gold. Chapter summaries are in red, and now somewhat faded. Johnston tended to favour this large size of letter. He wrote in *Writing & Illuminating, & Lettering* of his plain and rather austere model:

> This extremely legible manuscript would form an almost perfect model for a modern formal hand (s being substituted for the long s, and the straight t for the curved t) ...[36]

On the strength of these findings Johnston worked out a basic teaching script which would also lend itself to his ultimate goal of individual scribal 'Freedom'. He began showing it in his lecture-demonstrations at the Royal College of Art, possibly from about 1906. It was sometime later that he termed it the Foundational Hand.[37]

Although Johnston adjusted some details of the *Harley MS. 2904* script so as to meet contemporary reading practice, he adhered to the overall conventions of the use of scripts in manuscripts. One in particular stands out in this context. A polarity exists between, on the one hand, the cursive and formal scripts and, on the other, between the minuscule and majuscule letter-forms.

In the first pairing – cursive/formal – there is a distinction between two separate functions. A cursive script, as the name implies, is essentially speedwriting and relates to ordinary handwriting. The scribe's pen scarcely leaves the page in the need to write the letters with a minimum number of strokes and to join them up in a continuous flow. The cursives have traditionally met everyday needs, such as letter-writing, commercial transactions, administrative and legal documents and even books. They are sometimes called Cursive Documentary Scripts.

The formal scripts, on the other hand, were written with a greater deliberation. E. Maunde Thompson referred to them as 'set hands', while another pioneer palaeographer, E. A. Lowe, called them 'calligraphic'. Johnston described them as 'literary'. The letters were written with more pen lifts, or strokes, which are thus separated. Their appearance on the page therefore has a certain dignity appropriate to manuscripts of enduring importance. Religious service books and bibles were the prime reason for the formal scripts to flourish.

In the second pairing – minuscule/majuscule – the key distinction is not between function but between different letter-forms. The minuscules, or small letters, correspond to present-day lower-case printed forms, in which the ascenders and descenders of the consonants extend above and below the body of the letter. They developed in Roman times as abbreviated variations of the capital letters (For example, h from H; or b from B). The majuscules correspond, of course, to our capital letters.

The dynamic that is set up by the conjunction of the two pairs – the minuscule/majuscule and the cursive/formal – appears, on first sight, to be straightforward enough. By and large, the minuscule has been the vehicle of the cursive scripts and the majuscule the vehicle of the formal ones. An early example of the former is the Roman wax tablet, hastily written in a form of minuscule script. An example of the latter is Trajan's Column, in Rome (circa A.D.114), on the base of which monumental capital letters were carved into marble to create a formal inscription, celebrating the Emperor's military triumphs. (The pen-written derivatives from the monumental capitals are known as quadrata and rustica.) In more recent times the entries in a commercial ledger are likely to have been made in haste in a cursive minuscule script such as Roundhand or Copperplate. Likewise, an inscription on a headstone – as cut by Eric Gill, for example, following the Roman tradition – is likely to be carved in separately spaced capital, or majuscule, letters.

However, crossovers between these two axes have also occurred throughout the history of writing. There have been instances where the minuscule letter switched, as it were, from the cursives to the formals. Likewise, majuscules have served cursive scripts. Richly expressive variants have thereby been created.

In these more complex permutations a further principle is discernible, which Johnston also acknowledged. Over periods of time the cursive forms, that is the vernacular, or 'vulgar' forms, have tended to be promoted 'upwards', to serve more elevated functions. Touching on this phenomenon, E. A. Lowe wrote: 'Scripts, like populations, recruit chiefly from below.'[38] Earlier still than Lowe, Sir E. Maunde Thompson also generalised: 'A particular form of writing is gradually developed, takes on a finished calligraphic form and becomes the hand of the day.'[39]

One instance of this process is the Half-Uncial script which Johnston initially considered as a possible model. It developed from cursive origins in late Roman times, from the third to fifth centuries, when it was first used for the lowly task of annotating manuscripts written in the grander Uncial scripts. In time, however, it became more 'calligraphic', more majuscule-like. It developed into a script of great formality and refinement in Ireland, following her Christianisation, and attained lasting glory as the style in which the precious *Book of Kells* was written, in the late eighth or early ninth century. Johnston considered it as a likely model for a 'beautiful ornamental hand'.

The Caroline Minuscule is by far the most significant example, however. Strictly speaking a family of scripts, the Caroline Minuscule also developed from cursive origins, in part at least, and was used from the late eighth century onwards as a formal book script, for both state and religious purposes, including bibles. The prestigious *Winchester Bible*, written in a twelfth-century English variant that relates to the *Harley MS. 2904*, is such an example.

Johnston considered his own version of the Caroline Minuscule to be a 'Foundational Hand', suited to formal writing. It was a basis, he thought, for modern-day usage. Furthermore, it was capable of further and individual development, and was a bridge to an understanding of other scripts.

William Morris died in 1896, two years before Johnston's arrival in London. But it was as if Sydney Cockerell had acted as their spiritual go-between. As Morris's private secretary, librarian and then his literary executor, Cockerell played a key role in the affairs of one of the most influential of all nineteenth-century British designers and critics. Through him Johnston was able to handle books which had been transcribed and illuminated by Morris. The *Rubaiyat of Omar Khayyám*, of 1872, was one. *Horace's Odes*, of 1874, was another. Johnston also inspected some of the book designs that Morris had made for his Kelmscott Press. One can only speculate at his excitement.

A colleague and a friend of all three was the photo-engraver, Emery Walker. In his Sandars bibliographical lectures to the University of Cambridge, in 1924, Walker recalled the seminal meeting of Cockerell and Johnston. Speaking of Morris's part in the annual shows of the Arts and Crafts Exhibition Society, he wrote:

> ... in one of the subsequent annual shows, some small books which Morris had transcribed in a beautiful book hand of an Italianate character and illuminated himself. These attracted the attention of many artists, particularly those who had leanings in a calligraphic direction. Among them was Mr. Edward Johnston, now well known as a leader in the revival of fine writing. Mr. Cockerell, who was then Secretary of the Exhibition, instigated Mr Johnston to take up the subject seriously, and later his services were secured by Professor Lethaby to teach writing in the County Council's Central School of Arts and Crafts ... newly established.[40]

Johnston's sense of a renaissance in lettering in England was further awakened by his friendship with the poet and essayist Robert Bridges and his wife, Mary Monica Bridges. He met them in the summer of 1899 through his uncle, Miles McInnes, himself interested in handwriting. Based in Yattendon, near Newbury, and from 1907 at 'Chilswell', at Boar's Hill, Oxford, the couple had a discerning interest in handwriting, lettering, and typography. It has been said that Bridges, who became Poet Laureate in 1913, had a role in the revival of fine printing comparable to that played by William Morris.

Robert Bridges designed the typography of many of his own publications. In this pursuit he was closely involved with the Daniel Press, the private press cultivated by C. H. O. Daniel, the Provost of Worcester College, Oxford. In 1876 Daniel printed a volume, *New Sermon,* in an entirely novel Roman type which belonged to the Fell types. These were a collection of types, matrices, and punches that had languished at the Oxford University Press unused and virtually forgotten throughout the nineteenth century.[41] Bridges supervised the printing of fifteen volumes of his poems and plays at the Daniel Press in the Fell types, mostly Romans, starting with a poem that was included in the volume, 'A Garland for Rachael', given by Daniel to his daughter as a birthday present in 1882. They continued with *Prometheus the Firegiver* in 1883, *Early Poems* in 1898, *Milton's Prosody* in 1901, and the poem *Now in Wintry Delights* in 1903.

A key work in the second phase of the rehabilitation of the Fell types, however, was Bridges's *Yattendon Hymnal*, of 1895–99. This was a collection of one hundred early hymns compiled by Bridges (with his friends Henry Woolridge and Henry C. Beeching), some of which he translated from German and Latin. They were printed in a small pica size Roman from the Fell types. This time, however, the printer was Horace Hart of the Oxford University Press. As the university's printer Hart took up what Daniel had started. In 1893 he had the Fell types recast and properly organised for use.[42] Furthermore, since Bridges' interest in singing and in speech patterns prompted him to include the music to the hymns, Hart printed it in the types of Peter de Walpergen. These were also taken from the Fell types, Peter de Walpergen having been Dr. Fell's punch-cutter in Oxford. The *Yattendon Hymnal* can now be seen as the origin of the restrained book design which so characterised the Arts and Crafts movement.

Significantly for this account, Johnston owned a copy of the *Yattendon Hymnal.* It is very possible that it was given to him by Bridges.[43] He also owned *Chants for the Psalter* compiled by Bridges and Lionel Muirhead in 1896. Another of Johnston's books was Gordon Duff's *Early English Printing* of 1896. It was printed by Hart in the larger Great Primer Roman, again from the Fell types. There seems little doubt therefore that at the outset of his career Johnston imbibed Bridges' sensibility towards typography.

Robert Bridges' interest in the book arts was shared by Mary Monica Bridges who made an early and singular contribution to the reform of handwriting in schools. Taking up the cause of Italic scripts, she issued some writing sheets in 1897 and then compiled a handwriting manual, *A New Handwriting for Teachers,* 1898.[44] (Johnston's signed copy of the manual is now in the Newberry Library in Chicago.) Mary Monica Bridges was arguably the more important influence on Johnston in encouraging his interest in scripts. Her own interest was atavistic for although her father was the architect Alfred Waterhouse, her great-grandfather was John Hodgkin (1766–1845), a writing master in the eighteenth-century tradition who wrote a manual on Greek lettering with a preface written by the Egyptologist, Thomas Young.[45] Indirectly, through this link, Johnston also become a writing master, creating a twentieth-century tradition.

The Bridges took a caring interest in Johnston during his first period of learning and in his teaching at the Central School and the RCA. Entries in Johnston's work diary for June 1899 notes: 'R. Bridges invit'; 'p.c. Bridges'; 'Mrs Bridges comg. Sat. 1st July'; 'wire Bridges'; 'letter Mrs Bridges & telling of new forms'. Johnston, for his part, sent the couple specimens of his calligraphy written in his Half-Uncial script. They recognised immediately the extent of his talent. The earliest surviving letter is from Mary Monica and is dated 6th August 1899. It discusses amendments to the draft of his article that Johnston was writing, to be published in the 'magazine' – it was probably the *Parents Review* – in which her book on the teaching of handwriting had been reviewed:

> Your card has arrived so I can now write to you and return the article, wh. seems to us to require very little alteration, except to the first page.
>
> 1). The first thing marked is the close proximity of the 2 'quires' wh. perhaps you may like to get rid of.
>
> 2). Then we suggest that from 'Now' to 'carelessness' shd. be taken out & something else substituted. On the other sheet you will find an outline of the sense wh. might come instead of your page 1, if you like it, but please remember this is only an outline, for you to rewrite and fill in, in your style, that it might match with the sequel, wh. seems to us to be just the right kind of thing.
>
> 3). We suggest a curtailment of the next paragraph on page 2, as shown by the brackets.
>
> 4). I think that we might cut out all mention of my little book – as I believe all who have read the 'Parents Review' (or nearly all) have been advised by Miss Mason to use it, further mention is unnecessary.
>
> I like what you say about the qualities of good handwriting & this should be useful – I wish your capital letters on that page were going to be reproduced – I think you have been meditating on the new cursive script.
>
> I am really grateful to you for writing this essay for me. I don't think I should ever have done it. I hope it did not give you much trouble. When you have altered it at your leisure, will you return it to me here & I will forward it to the magazine editors. Please address 'to be forwarded' as we may be away – I hope you will enjoy your Scotch holiday thoroughly. Excuse this untidy letter written under difficulties.
>
> Yours very sincerely M. M. Bridges.[46]

Although the article did not materialise a draft of it has survived.[47]

In the following year, in a letter dated the 5th July 1900, Robert Bridges showed keen interest in Johnston's 'graph' (presumably his depiction of the history of scripts in the form of charts), in a 'script', and in his teaching sheets:

> Very much obliged for the graph. I congratulate you. Z is better. All is as good as can be. Hope to be at home in August – & after – if you are in town try to get a visit to us in before winter. I want very much to know what practical success the business has and whether the script is likely to be used. Also whether you have done anything [?] reproducible smaller than the specimens which I saw. I am at present very busy.
>
> July 5th. I hope you will hear from Professor S at Oxford. The numeration sheet x makes me very curious. I shd. like to buy these sheets if they are for sale. Let me know if I can have them. RB.[48]

One year on again Mary Monica Bridges' letter of the 30th August 1901 struck an almost parental note:

> Many thanks for the beautiful script which I shall treasure with your others sheets – we are delighted to hear about your work, that the students are doing well and that you have a new class. You have not yet paid us your promised visit …[49]

The friendship led Johnston to collaborate with Robert Bridges from 1901 in his 'scheme' to create new phonetic characters. Initially at least the letter-forms were to be based on the Half-Uncial. Bridges' interest was in a system which would enable the poetry he was writing in classical hexameters to scan properly, a pursuit which grew out of his book on *Milton's Prosody*, of 1901. Beyond this, however, he hoped his scheme would remedy the falling standards – as he perceived them – of the pronunciation of English.

It was the Bridges who recommended that Johnston study Sir Edward Maunde Thompson's *Handbook to Greek and Latin Palæography,* of 1893 which at the time was a definitive work on the evolution of Western European scripts. In a letter to Robert Bridges written in 1926 Johnston recalled that:

> You and Mrs Bridges put me on the track of the Half-Uncial, as you may remember, long ago when you gave me a copy of Maunde Thompson's Greek and Latin Palæography. I have always been most grateful for that assistance and it made a sound foundation for my own work, and for about ten years I used it as the foundation for my students work …[50]

Maunde Thompson's book was significant for the added reason that it included fine collotype illustrations, giving exact facsimiles. This was a relatively new printing process in the 1890s and clearly an asset to the student wishing to examine such minute shapes as written letters on the page. It was indispensable to the historical understanding of letter-forms. As Keeper of Manuscripts at the British Museum, Maunde Thompson founded the Palæographical Society in 1873, and issued a series of *Publications*, the illustrations of which were also in collotype.[51] He was the author of the first comprehensive article on old writing, appearing in the 1885 edition of *Encyclopædia Britannica.*

Furthermore, the Bibliographical Society was established in 1892. Its transactions carried articles on calligraphy, illumination, and early printing, as did other journals, such as *Bibliographica* and the *Journal of the (Royal) Society of Arts.* Morris's essay *The Ideal Book*, for example, which had such an impact on Cobden-Sanderson – Johnston's colleague – was published by the Bibliographical Society in 1893.

Thus, much groundwork had been done by 1898–99, the year of Johnston's realisation of his career path. It fostered his interest in reviving the techniques of formal writing with the broad-nibbed pen on an authentic basis. The book by Maunde Thompson and those by other enquirers such as Alfred Pollard (*Early Illustrated Books*, 1893), Edward Strange (*Alphabets*, 1895), Edward Clodd (*The Story of the Alphabet,* 1900), and John Bradley (*Illuminated Letters and Borders*, 1901), are included in Johnston's bibliography. Another was Falconer Madan's

Books in Manuscript, of 1893. It was from this study that Johnston borrowed the illustration of a fifteenth-century French scriptorium which he placed as the frontispiece to his handbook.

END NOTES

1. National Art Library. V&A. Ref: MSS. English Letters & Calligraphy. 86 TT 17.
2. Ibid.
3. N A L at the V&A. Ref: MSS. English. Letters and Calligraphy. E. Johnston. 86.TT.17.
4. Ibid.
5. C. M. Weekley. 'Edward Johnston' in *Art Work*. No. 27. Autumn 1931.
6. Ford Maddox Hueffer. 'The Work of William Harrison Cowleshaw' [sic] in *The Artist*. Vol 19. (Pages 432–436). 1898. Cowlishaw built a house for Edward Garnett in Limpsfield, Surrey.
7. Lethaby's writings covered a wide range of subjects, but its central core was architecture and craft. His early books included *Architecture, Myth and Magic*, of 1892. There followed detailed studies of medieval buildings including *Santa Sophia, Constantinople* of 1894 and *Westminster Abbey and the King's Craftsmen*, of 1906. There also appeared *Leadwork*, 1893, and *Mediæval Art*, 1904. His inaugural lecture, 'Modern Design', to the RCA was probably given in 1901. His two lectures: 'Morris as Work-Master', and 'The Study and Practice of Artistic Crafts', of 1901, were given at the Birmingham School of Art.
8. Cited: Priscilla Johnston's essay: 'Edward Johnston and W. R. Lethaby' in: *Lessons in Formal Writing*, Edited by Heather Child and Justin Howes. (Lund Humphries) 1986. A touching instance of Lethaby's impact is Johnston's entry in his work diary for 7th November 1899, when he recorded 'picking up Lethaby's "Leadwork" 4/6 for 2/6' (Craft Study Centre at Farnham. Ref: 2/Loan 2.)
9. W. R. Lethaby's lecture, 'Modern Design', Edited Godfrey Rubens. In *Craft History One*. 1988, 'Form in Civilisation', in 1922, and his biography, 'Philip Webb and his Work', reprinted from *The Builder*, (1925) in 1935. Godfrey Rubens' study, 'William Richard Lethaby', appeared in 1986.
10. W. R. Lethaby. *Mediæval Art from the Peace of the Church to the eve of The Renaissance.* (Duckworth) 1904.
11. William Lethaby's essay 'Art and Workmanship'. In *The Imprint*. 1913.
12. Details of Lethaby's insight into the Trajan Column are given by M. C. Oliver in John Farleigh's *Fifteen Craftsmen on their Crafts*. (Sylvan Press) 1945. Lethaby writes of the lettering on the Trajan Column in his preface to Johnston's *Writing & Illuminating, & Lettering*.

13. W. R.Lethaby. Preface to Edward Johnston, *Writing & Illuminating, & Lettering.* (J. Hogg) 1906.
14. Johnston also considered using a fountain pen fitted with a broad-edged nib at this early date. The transcript of the discussion which followed the Royal Society of Arts lecture, of 1905, reports: 'He went to the Swan Fountain Pen Company, who said they would make a nib for him, only it would have to be made in New York, and he would have to pay 9s. [shillings] for each nib, and he must take a dozen of them, and it would take four months to get them over, so he went back to the humble quill.'
15. Edward Johnston. 'Calligraphy and Illumination – The Development of Writing'. Lecture to the RSA, January 1905. *Journal of the Royal Society of Arts.* Vol. 53. 1905.
16. For example, the widely used Vere Foster Copy Book No 10 (*Lettering Plain and Ornamental*), offered instructions to school pupils about the nib which show an awareness of the effect of the nib's profile: 'The characteristic tool for lettering is the quill, with its point cut to a chisel-shaped tip .... Of the styles shown in this book the quill is especially suited for those on pages 5–11, inclusive .... All these should be written freely, without pressure on the pen; the width of the nib should be equal to that of the letter at its widest point. Other alphabets, such as the Roman, in its different forms, are best drawn in outline to begin with, the heavy downstrokes being afterwards filled in.' Vere Foster Copy Books. 1880s. NAL at the V&A. (Ref: G 29. FF Box 1.)
17. From Johnston's own copy of Lewis F. Day's *Alphabets Old and New*, 1898, which is held in the Edward Johnston collection in the Edward Clark Library at Napier University, Edinburgh.
18. See Robert Bridges. 'On the Present State of English Pronunciation'. In *Essays and Studies by Members of the English Association.* Collected by A. C. Bradley. (OUP) 1910.
19. Now in the British Library. E. Hübner is cited in the bibliography of *Writing & Illuminating, & Lettering.* For the connection between Johnston and Hübner, I am indebted to James Mosley. It is likely that Johnston knew of Hübner through Cockerell, since he recommended the book to Gill. See Robert Harding. *The Letterforms and Type Designs of Eric Gill.* (Eva Svennson) 1976.
20. Edward Johnston. *Writing & Illuminating, & Lettering.* Chap. XV. 'The Roman Alphabet and its Derivatives'. 'Slanted-Pen Small Letters'. (Pages 232–300)
21. Edward Johnston. Chapter 1 'The Formal Pen and its Stroke Shapes'. *In Formal Penmanship and other papers.* (Pages 71–82.) Ed. Heather Child & Justin Howes. (Lund Humphries) 1971.
22. *Writing & Illuminating, & Lettering.* Op. cit. (Page 268)
23. *Writing & Illuminating, & Lettering.* Op. cit. (Page 269)
24. *Writing & Illuminating, & Lettering.* Op. cit. (Page 269)
25. *Writing & Illuminating, & Lettering.* Op. cit. (Page 269) 'The 'Roman Small Letter', as Johnston called the Humanist script, is important to his development. This discussion is taken up in the Appendix Three.
26. Details of this development are outside the scope of this present study. They belong to that period Johnston spent at Hammersmith, between 1903 and 1912.
27. This Plate illustrated the Harley MS. 2904 (Fig. 35).
28. Letters of Edward Johnston to Sir S. Cockerell. 1900–1924. NAL at V&A (MSS. English. 78.)
29. Letters of Edward Johnston. NAL at the V&A. Op. cit.
30. Cited in a letter from Cockerell to Priscilla Johnston. Crafts Study Collection and Archive, Farnham, Surrey. Johnston archive. (Ref: 2/59.)
31. Stanley Morison. 'Notes on the Development of Latin Script'. (Note 290.) In his *Selected Essays on the History of Letter-Forms in Manuscript and Print.* Ed. by D. McKitterick. (C.U.P) 1981.
32. Cited: Priscilla Johnston. *Edward Johnston.* (Faber and Faber) 1959.
33. V. Hawkes. Letter to F. Meynell. Rare Books Room (Stanley Morison Collection.) Cambridge University Library.
34. NAL at the V&A Museum (Ref: MSS. English. '20 Letters about E. Johnston addressed to Sir S. Cockerell.' Pressmark: 86. QQ 25.)
35. This manuscript is now in the NAL at the V&A Museum. (Ref: KRPA 35.)

36. Edward Johnston. *Writing & Illuminating, & Lettering*. (Page 378.) Op. cit.
37. There is uncertainty about when exactly the term, Foundational Hand, was first used. It does not appear in *Writing & Illuminating, & Lettering*, of 1906, nor in the amended edition of 1911. It does appear, however, in Johnston's teaching portfolio, *Manuscript & Inscription Letters*, of 1909. (Plate 6.)
38. E. A. Lowe. *Writing in the Middle Ages*. (OUP) 1926.
39. *Encyclopaedia Britannica*. 9th edition.
40. Emery Walker. 'Three Lectures for the Sandars Readership in Bibliography'. 1924. Typescript in the Cambridge University Library. (Manuscripts Room).
41. These types had been acquired by Dr. John Fell (1625–85) through his agent Marshall in Holland for the university, which had given him a licence to print. (Dr. Fell set up his presses in the Sheldonian Theatre in 1671.) Some of the types dated back to the 'Old Style' Romans designed by Claude Garamont and Jean Grandjon in sixteenth century France. It was a development that anticipated Johnston's own interest in the revival of Roman letter-forms, although it can be argued that Bridges and Daniel were following an historicist or antiquarian approach in contrast to Johnston's modern practical one. For example they had also an interest in the Black Letter scripts. Bridges' poem *The Growth of Love* of 1890 was printed in a Black Letter type on the basis that it slowed down the reader and thereby helped the comprehension of the poems. It has to be said, though, that Johnston put forward this very reason for writing his manuscript of Shakespeare's *Sonnet No. 116* in his 'Black Letter' script in 1927.
42. Horace Hart. *Notes on a Century of Typography at the University Press. Oxford*. 1693–1794. Edited by Harry Carter. (O.U.P at the Clarendon Press) 1970.
43. Elkin Mathews catalogue. Bodleian Library. Fairbank papers. MSS. Eng Lett b 6. fol. 39–40. Another shorter edition of the *Yattendon Hymnal*, without the music, entitled *Hymns* was printed by the Daniel Press, also in 1899. For this edition Bridges chose a Black Letter type again taken from the Fell Types collection.
44. Just as Johnston initiated the revival of scribal penmanship based upon a formal script, so Mary Monica Bridges initiated a revival of handwriting based on Italic cursive scripts. Although the two lines of development remained separate, there are connections. The Italic scripts were taken up by Marion Richardson, Alfred Fairbank, and James Wardrop. Marion Richardson devised the *Dudley Writing Cards*, which were a basis for the teaching of handwriting in schools from the 1930s. Johnston gave his considered advice and approval of the *Dudley Writing Cards*. (In the 1920s, Stanley Morison undertook historical research into Humanistic Italic scripts of the Renaissance period, which were a basis for the Italic type designs by the Monotype Corporation for whom he was a consultant. Further studies into the Italic were undertaken by Alfred Fairbank and James Wardrop.)
45. *The Calligraphia Græca et Pœcilographia Græca* of 1794, a text book on Greek letter-forms. The edition of 1807 was dedicated to Thomas Young who collaborated on the work by providing a preface which included directions as to how to use the (broad-edged) pen – 'Directions for Writing the Greek Characters' – and a specimen (translated by him into Greek from Shakespeare's King Lear). John Hodgkin also wrote a second manual, *An Introduction to Writing Exhibiting Clear and Concise Rules for the Formation and Combination of Letters,* published in 1811. A third work was called *Specimens of Greek Penmanship*, of 1804. It seems unlikely that Johnston was aware of his connection, via Mary Monica Bridges, to the eighteenth-century writing master tradition. Curiously, it parallels another link, via his Quaker ancestry, to the early nineteenth-century reforming family, the Frys.
46. Bodleian Library. MSS. Eng. Lett. Dep. Bridges. 111. Album 2. Folio 44.
47. An entry in Johnston's work diary for Sunday 16th July 1899 notes: 'Writing article on "Good Writing".' The draft, undated, is among the Johnston papers at the Crafts Study Collection and Archive, Farnham, Surrey. Johnston archive, (Ref: 2/847). Written out on lined paper in his still immature handwriting, it is Johnston's very first theoretical utterance. It should be quoted: "Handwriting and Lettering", written and illustrated by Edward Johnston. In these days of cheap printing and universal promiscuous "Lettering", the art of making beautiful letters seems to have been lost. The traditions which guided the scribes of the Middle Ages and the printers of the XV century have disappeared and the wonderful

beauty of their writing and the magnificence of their printing have been enjoyed only by antiquarians. In the present revival of printing and Book Decoration chiefly set on foot by the work and influence of William Morris there is an evident desire among craftsmen and Artists to restore to our Alphabet some of its past dignity and to revive the lost beauty of our Books. But the study of lettercraft has hitherto been confined to a few specialists and the majority of those who attempt to make lettering decorative (or to decorate lettering) do so in ignorance of its design and reason. There is scarcely an artist in pen or ink who can add a title to, or include a poem or other piece of lettering in his design, without spoiling his work.

As there is no Typography or Calligraphy in common use which is in form or arrangement a suitable guide & model for the Designer some practical suggestions as to models & materials will, it is hoped, help those who are desirous of acquiring a fine handwriting or becoming Letter-Craftsmen.

MODELS The Alphabet, as we know it, began with the magnificent "Roman" Capitals, used at first for Latin inscriptions in stone. Their characteristic & 'monumental' forms were probably evolved by the use of the chisel. When books were written in these letters (til the close of the V cent.) their forms grew out of, and ceased to be chisel-forms (they are known as "square capitals" and "Rustic capitals") and, probably abt. the IV cent. were developed the true pen-forms having the characteristic thick and thin strokes, and beautiful shapes which flow from the rightly handled reed or quill. These were called Uncial letters.

We must all admit the pity of this and its impracticalities when even the "man in the street" shows such keenness about decorated books. But the pity of it is all the more when we know that it is as easy to make letters good as to make them bad to make our books beautiful as to make them commercially "Artistic".'

It seems unlikely, however, that this unfinished draft is the one which was returned by Mary Monica Bridges to Johnston and mentioned in her letter of the 6th August 1899.

48. Bodleian Library. MSS. Eng. Lett. Dep. Bridges III. Album 2. Folio 45.

49. Bodleian Library. MSS. Eng. Lett. Dep. Bridges III. Album 2. Folio 46. The rest of the letter is quoted in Chapter Fifteen, 'Johnston and the Bridges 1901–1926'.

50. 18th January 1926. Bodleian Library. MSS. Eng. Lett. Dep. Bridges III. Folio 70. Alfred Fairbank reported that it was Monica Mary Bridges who actually sent the copy to Johnston. He added that he became the owner of this particular copy. See 'A Scholar Penman' by J. A. Cole in *Calligraphy and Palæography Essays* Presented to Alfred Fairbank. (Faber and Faber) 1965.

51. The publications of the Palæographical Society are mentioned by Johnston in the bibliography of his *Writing & Illuminating, & Lettering*.

Portrait of Edward Johnston in his apartment in Lincoln's Inn, Holborn, with his cat, Pounce.
Circa 1902. Photographer unknown.
(Courtesy of Justin Howes)

CHAPTER THREE

JOHNSTON & THE ARTS & CRAFTS MOVEMENT – SHARED BELIEFS

The excitement of discovery which Johnston evidently felt at first seeing William Morris's calligraphy brought him close in spirit to the great mentor. His work diary entry recording his first visit to Sydney Cockerell's home in Richmond on the 31st October 1898 has already been mentioned. There he saw Morris's manuscripts and 'was impressed more than ever by the sweetness and naturalness of [Morris's] work the absence of strain and the beauty of it. His writing became *v. beautiful.* (founded on Italic scripts) – (beautiful work & interesting practice work)'. Evidently Cockerell recalled that Morris 'worked quickly and often talked while he worked'. Johnston returned home that evening with 'several proofs', including 'p[age] from Golden Legend, p[age] from Golden Fleece, London County Council (L.C.C.) certificate, specimen paper, Kelmscott circular, Morris signature cheque.' Johnston saw more of Morris's calligraphy at the Arts and Crafts Exhibition Society in Bond Street in 1899.[1] The memorial show to Morris there would have included manuscripts such as the *Odes of Horace*, written in Italic and Roman Minuscule scripts based on Renaissance lettering manuals he owned. Soon Johnston acquired some of Morris's books. His Kelmscott Press copy of *The Sundering Flood* is inscribed '4th April 1900'. He also had a copy of Buxton Forman's *The Books of William Morris Explained*, of 1897, and of R. Steele's *Medieval Lore, Classified Gleanings from the Encyclopaedia of Bartholmew Angelicus*, of 1893, for which Morris wrote a preface.[2] In the draft of the very first article he wrote in July 1899 Johnston referred to the 'work and influence set afoot by William Morris'. In 1904 he mentioned in a letter to Sydney Cockerell his continuing interest in Morris's calligraphy.[3]

From beginnings such as this Johnston became engaged in the Arts and Crafts movement. The writings of its foremost thinkers, notably Morris and Lethaby, were the foundation for its development. But the ideas of other craftsmen were in the air, too, including those of Walter Crane, Cobden-Sanderson, Emery Walker, C. R. Ashbee, Reginald Blomfield, May Morris, and John Sedding, all of whom had contributed to a volume called *Arts and Crafts Essays*. Thirty-five essays in all, they were commissioned by Cobden-Sanderson for the Arts and Crafts Exhibition Society in 1893, with a preface by Morris. Johnston was familiar with this all-important collection and included it in the bibliography of his handbook. Clearly, Morris's ideas, spreading through a generation of craftsmen and writers, were the substance of Johnston's own thought.

Morris, in turn, was influenced by Ruskin. Soon after he went up to Oxford in 1853, a fellow-student in the 'Set', Richard Watson Dixon, recalled him reading

Ruskin aloud: 'He had a mighty singing voice and chanted rather than read those weltering oceans of eloquence'. In his article, 'How I became a Socialist' written for the magazine *Justice* in 1894, Morris said of Ruskin:

> ... before my days of practical socialism, he was my master towards the ideal.... It was through him that I learned to give form to my discontent, which I must say was not by any means vague. Apart from the desire to produce beautiful things, the leading passion of my life has been and is hatred of modern civilisation.

Although Morris developed lines of thought distinctly his own he always held Ruskin in reverence. In 1892, one of the first items he printed at his Kelmscott Press was Ruskin's celebrated chapter, 'On the Nature of the Gothic'. It was taken from Book II of *The Stones of Venice*, of 1853. In his preface Morris reminisced:

> To some of us, when we read it, now many years ago, it seemed to point out a new road on which the world would travel. ... It is one of the very few necessary and inevitable utterances of this century.

Morris's 'hatred' of industrialism was fuelled by Ruskin's writings. Ruskin discerned a causal link between medieval society and its architecture, of which he wrote: a 'truly Christian and perfect system' had resulted in the 'freedom of thought' and the 'life and liberty of every workman who struck the stone' in the making of a cathedral and its ornamentation. The breaking of this link, Morris believed, had impoverished present-day architecture and craft. Morris's moral indignation about the present and his concern for the welfare of medieval buildings led him in 1877 to become a founder member of the Society for the Protection of Ancient Buildings (SPAB) the aim of which was to replace ill-considered Victorian restoration with a strategy for their proper protection. His passion for 'mediævalism' (Ruskin's word) was worked into an outpouring of lectures and articles in which he was engaged from the late 1870s onwards. But it was especially manifest in a key book, *News from Nowhere – A Utopian Romance*, written comparatively late, in 1890. It describes a society of federated communes sustained by handicrafts. While it was an unattainable goal, it was nevertheless an inspiration to that new generation of craftsmen known as the Arts and Crafts movement.

The Arts and Crafts movement is readily assumed to have been intellectually static, delivered of the mind of Morris and Ruskin with its values endorsed by followers such as Lethaby who, as a younger man in the 1880–90s, was their most ardent disciple. In fact many of its adherents wrote influential tracts of their own. The Arts and Crafts movement was exactly that, a movement rather then a tightly organised 'front'. Large in number, co-existing over a period of more than thirty years, and professing as many ideas as members, inevitably it existed in a state of flux. Not unlike birds massing on the wing its adherents cohered sufficiently to form a recognisable whole while maintaining individual motion. These two elements – the one converging, the other diverging – relate to quite different issues. They were to affect Johnston in different degrees.

The exemplar of medieval art and an aversion to the Industrial Revolution gave the movement its cohesion, as did an attachment to the handmade artefact and a sense of a craft community or brotherhood. On the other hand, issues which were largely questioned by Morris as to the role of the machine and the necessity of Socialism were divisive. The shared beliefs are best treated in this present chapter.

Johnston entered into discussion about most of these issues. The position he took can be deduced from his (all-too-scarce) writings and from his (all-too-infrequent) public declarations. Additionally there are wisps of evidence recorded by friends such as Emery Walker, Noel Rooke, and Eric Gill, whose diary contains factual notes detailing their lives together. For example, on the 21st August 1911 Johnston attended the lecture Gill gave at the Art Workers' Guild, the very bastion of the Arts and Crafts movement.

> A. W. G. [Art Workers' Guild] lecture in noon (writing) ... lecture after. Very interesting ... W. R. Lethaby in Chair. W[alter] Crane and others spoke. E[dward] J[ohnston] made an excellent speech. Home with E. J. for the night. E. J. very good & jolly.[4]

The classic statement of the empathy that was felt for medieval art is Morris's lecture, *Gothic Architecture* of 1889. But equally masterful is a description by William Lethaby. A practicing architect and designer, Lethaby was involved in his earlier years in developing a general theory of the cultural history of art and architecture. His book *Architecture, Mysticism and Myth* was published in 1891. There, he focused on the ancient and medieval periods. In 1911, he published his short historical survey, *Architecture. An Introduction to the History and Theory of the Art of Building.* The chapter entitled *Gothic Building in France – The Architecture of Energy* describes the spiritual force with which, he claimed, thirteenth-century French cathedrals are imbued. While he had learned from Morris, the unbridled nature of his prose style brought him close to Ruskin:

> The school of the Ile-de-France first took place about 1125, and Paris soon became the centre of medieval thought and art – the culture capital of Europe. Out of the intense furnace of ideas was to run the pure gold of a new style which is probably the most original of all theories of building. It is impossible to explain in words the content of perfect Gothic art. It is frank, clear, gay; it is passionate, mystical and tender; it is energetic, sharp, strong and healthy. It would be a mistake to try to define it in terms of form alone; it embodied a spirit, an aspiration, an age. The ideals of the time of energy and order produced a manner of building of high intensity, all waste tissue was thrown off, and the stonework was gathered up into energetic functional members. These ribs and bars and shafts are all at bowstring tension. A mason will tap a pillar to make its stress audible; we may think of a cathedral as so 'high strung' that if struck it would give a musical note.'[5]

For Lethaby the exemplar of medieval art led not to the faithful recompilation of styles, creative though that kind of medievalism may on occasions have been, but to a sense of new possibilities.[6] As he shows, the aspiration was to emulate rather than relive the medieval state of mind. Another craftsman, John Sedding, epitomised this change of mood. His essay 'Design' was included in the collection of *Arts and Crafts Essays*. Taking embroidery as his example, he pointed out that:

> Fair English hands can copy every trick of ancient artistry ... yet our work hangs fire. It fails in design. Why? .... No more museum-inspired work. No more dry-as-dust stock patterns .... But instead we shall have design *by* living men *for* living men .... We must clothe modern ideas in modern dress.

From a more mystical viewpoint, Cobden-Sanderson spoke of the 'inner vision' of medieval art. Yet, he regarded the Arts and Crafts movement as '...being to do with [a] new world' rather than 'the old world' of the fifteenth-century Gothic.[7]

The emulation of the past was an issue which was important to Johnston. He, too, was anxious to avoid the trap of mere imitation. In his preface to *Writing & Illuminating, & Lettering* Johnston worded his thoughts with careful deliberation:

> Developing, or rather re-developing, an art involves the tracing in one's own experience of a process resembling its past development.

The precision of this statement is wholly characteristic of his thinking. Unlike the Gothic Revival antiquarians of an earlier generation, Johnston found practical guidance in the medieval manuscripts which he considered to be relevant without simply being in thrall to them. His starting point was the 'usefulness' of letters for a modern situation.

This mood was born of respect for the integrity of medieval art, appreciated through historical knowledge. Morris's scholarship, for example, was recognised at the Bodleian Library, at Oxford – he could identify and date medieval manuscripts with astonishing accuracy – just as Sydney Cockerell's and, after him, Johnston's expertise were acknowledged at the British Museum.

However, this medievalism did not arise in isolation. The counterpart to the anxiety Morris felt about the social shortcomings of the Industrial Revolution was his disaffection with the spiritual shortcomings of classical 'pagan' culture, particularly in its revived forms. Greek and Roman architecture, Morris believed, was limited by its failure to develop the arch. While the gain in knowledge achieved by the Renaissance was an advance to be welcomed, its preoccupation with antique classical forms was a paradox. In his lecture *Gothic Architecture* of 1889 he puzzled over what he considered to be a contradiction at its heart: 'Henceforth the past was to be our present, and the blankness of its dead walls was to shut out the future from us.... To this body of social, political, scientific New Birth was bound the dead corpse of a past art.' Furthermore it was not an art of the people, an art of 'co-operation'. In what Morris preferred to call the the 'Age of Commercialism, ... a few individual artists were truly great but artists were no longer the masters of art because the people had ceased to be artists: its masters were pedants.' Especially irksome to Morris was the art and thought of the English eighteenth century. In his preface to the collection of *Arts and Crafts Essays*, of 1893, he claimed that the:

> Art of the eighteenth century, like all intellectual movements of that century, was negative and destructive.[8]

A case was Morris's aversion to Christopher Wren. He was at his most vituperative about St Paul's Cathedral, dismissing it in *Gothic Architecture* as '... the taste of a man who should prefer his lady-love bald, ... built not to be beautiful ...

for the citizens ... but to be proper, respectable ... showing cultivation, and knowledge'. In 1883 Morris attempted to dissuade the designer Arthur Mackmurdo from publishing his book, *Wren's City Churches.* Morris also had an aversion to the puritan classsicism of Milton.[9]

Morris's disapproval of the classical world was generally shared by his devotees. Lethaby, for instance, built on this interpretation. His book *Architecture* argued that, unlike Gothic art, the classically-inspired art of the Renaissance periods(in England as well as in Italy and France) was patronised by courtly circles and, as a consequence, it was 'divorced from the people'. He continued with an illustration on a grand scale:

> As another consequence of its remoteness from the people Renaissance art came to be thought of as a matter of pride and pretty shapes, of taste and appearance. It was not generally seen that great art like great science is the discovery of necessity. It must, I think, be admitted by those who have in part understood the great primary styles, Greek or Gothic, that the Renaissance is a style of boredom. However beautiful single works may be, it tends to be blind, puffy, and big-wiggy; Louis Quatorze might have said of the art of his court as he did of the State, 'It is myself'. Its highest inspiration was good taste, it was architect's architecture. Splendid works were wrought even in the age of its gloomy maturity by Peruzzi, Michelangelo, and Wren, but as a whole it seems to be that art of an age of indigestion. There are things in Nature – a dewy morning, a snowy peak, a clear stream – which are ever and again more wonderful than we had remembered. A true work of art always has something of this surprising freshness; but the Renaissance as a whole lacked the spirit of life. Gothic art witnesses to a nation in training, hunters, craftsmen, athletes; the Renaissance is the art of scholars, courtiers, and the connoisseurship of middlemen.[10]

In due course this historical bias was to pervade the Arts and Crafts movement as a whole. For one thing Classicism was associated with the Royal Academy, an institution which fostered the notion that artistic genius was bestowed by Providence, an elitism deriving ultimately from the Neo-Platonic thought which ran through the art of the Italian Renaissance period. The Royal Academy was therefore discredited philosophically. The English tendency to quarry the classical periods in the name of taste gave way to an appreciation of the English vernacular, including the ruder values of late medieval English design. Morris was a strong protagonist of this fresh attitude where the English cottage was as important as the castle. Furthermore, the cultivation of style or taste gave way to an interest in the process of art. The essay on 'The English Tradition' by the architect, Reginald Blomfield, included in *Arts and Crafts Essays* of 1893, stressed the 'living force' of English design as being 'steadfast of purpose, reserved in design, and thorough in workmanship'. In this sense, strictly speaking, the Arts and Crafts movement was without a prescribed style. This openness implied a distinct eclecticism of design.[11]

And classicism was also associated, emotively, with continental Europe, with an overwrought rococo sophistication that did not always go well with English sensibilities. These reservations were in tune with particular strains of native Englishness already in place, as in the work of William Hogarth and William Blake. That tradition was still potent in Johnston's day. Blake's work was a powerful magnet for Johnston. For example, the image of *Glad Dawn* – for Blake, it was the 'glad dawn' of instinct as opposed to scientific rationalism – was used as a frontispiece for the first issue of *The Imprint*. It was Johnston, as one of its editors,[12] who calligraphed Blake's title beneath the image.

The rationale behind this view of history, whereby the Gothic world was upheld and the Classical world demoted, was essentially a moral one. It connected with the view that human happiness could be enhanced through a renewed spiritual well-being, to which handicraft makes an essential contribution. For the creating of artefacts by hand was, in itself, a source of lasting fulfilment. Morris had said of Ruskin:

> The lesson he taught us was that art is the expression of man's pleasure in labour.[13]

Two other aspects of Morris's and Lethaby's thoughts relate to the Arts and Crafts movement. The first, though less important, was the medieval guilds. The second was the notion of handicraft, the practitioners of which were esteemed as 'designer-craftsmen'. Handicraft was seen to have flourished organically, hand-in-hand with the guild system. The concept of craftsman as designer was at the very heart of Johnston's thought.

Morris identified the medieval guilds as having flourished especially in the reign of Edward III (d. 1377). In his (and Bax's) study 'Socialism from the Root Upwards', of 1886, and in his three lectures, 'Feudal England', (1887), 'Art and Industry in the Fourteenth Century', (1890), and 'The Development of Modern Society', (1890), he outlined a specific historical interpretation.[14] It was based on work by the historians E. A. Freeman and J. Thorold Rogers, who taught at Oxford, and by J. R. Green who studied there.[15]

In 'Art and Industry in the Fourteenth Century' Morris argues that the guilds were of Teutonic (in England, Anglo-Saxon) origin, a form, he said, of present-day 'benefit societies'. They then provided the impetus behind the development of the government of medieval towns in a society dominated by Norman feudal power. Ultimately they evolved into two kinds. One, the merchant guild, was for the defence of trade, creating a 'middle-class nobility', such as the Hanseatic League. The other, at first less powerful but by about 1350 'triumphant', was the 'federated craft-guild' such as the London livery companies. 'Handicraftmen' were 'free in their work except for such regulation they imposed on themselves.' Furthermore the craft guilds ensured high standards:

> In those times there was no such thing as a piece of handicraft being ugly; that everything made had a due and befitting form; that most commonly, however ordinary its use might be, it was elaborately ornamented; such ornament was always both beautiful and inventive, the mind of the workman was allowed full play and freedom in producing it.... That this condition of the ordinary handicrafts ... was the foundation of all that nobility of beauty ... in a building like Peterborough Cathedral.

Additionally, Morris adumbrated the notion that the craft guilds received support from royal power as a 'make-weight' against the Norman fiefdoms. Serfs were attracted into the towns, becoming journeymen, or freemen, thus prompting the 'break-up of serfdom'. (This is the time of John Ball.) Infused by a 'spirit of association' the guilds had made '... the life of the worker better than ever before'. Morris's account reinforced his historical bias. For the craft guilds were also portrayed as part of Teutonic (Anglo-Saxon) culture, as opposed to the classical one of Rome, based, Morris said, on slavery. He used the phrase 'Romanised feudalism' to refer to the Norman settlement.

The word 'guild' enjoyed widespread currency in late nineteenth-century Britain to refer to many different kinds of groupings of like-minded people, a usage which had little to do, in fact, with historical knowledge of medieval guilds.[16] For the Arts and Crafts movement the impulse to band together into 'useful associations' was, on one level, a response to practical requirements. There was a pressing need by craftsmen, as well as artists, for a more appreciative recognition. Equally, there was a need for a more effective integration of their skills with those of architects. Recognition was needed because the alternative institutions, the Royal Academy and the Royal Institute of British Architects represented them not at all. The Royal Academy was regarded by those whose *métier* precluded their admission as little more than an inbred club for painters, sculptors and for what Cobden-Sanderson referred to in his *Arts and Crafts movement* essay of 1905 as 'abstract architecture', or draughtsmanship. Integration was needed because of a dual anxiety that making had become distinct from designing and that the different crafts had become detached from each other. Architecture, for example, was divorced from the crafts in so much that in the building of a church, for example, craftsmen were used merely to embellish its surfaces rather than to integrate the decoration into its fundamental design.

A more interrelated and co-operative process was implicit in the organisational set up of Morris's company (known as 'the Firm'), and of Cobden-Sanderson's bookbinding company (The Doves Bindery), as well as of the two main groupings of the Arts and Crafts movement – the Art Workers' Guild and the Arts and Crafts Exhibition Society. Johnston was involved in all of these, except the Firm.

Its full title was: 'Morris, Marshall, Faulkner & Co., Fine Art Workmen in Painting, Carving, Furniture and the Metals'. Morris set it up in 1861 at the age of twenty-seven, long before he put his mind to write about guilds. It emerged in the wake of his aim to design a 'beautiful house', achieved at the Red House in Bexleyheath. In 1865 he moved the Firm into the ground floor of 26 Queen Square, Holborn, above which he lived. In 1881, he moved it again, though in modified form, to the former site of Merton Abbey, in Wimbledon. (It was chosen for its supply of suitable water needed for the dyeing of textiles.) His partners, Marshall (an architect-engineer) and Faulkner (a mathematician who looked after the accounts), are lesser-known figures who by that date were less prominent. His co-designers were the artists Burne-Jones, Rossetti, and Ford Madox Brown, the architect and furniture designer, Philip Webb, and, from 1880, his assistant, George Jack. Another was the glass and tapestry designer, J. H. Dearle. Throughout, Morris's aim was the integration of management, design and craftsmanship. Part profit-sharing was envisaged. However, divisions of labour also operated. For example, George Wardle became Morris's manager at Merton Abbey, freeing him to extend his interests. In the making of stained glass, Burne-Jones and Rossetti designed the figures, Philip Webb integrated the windows into the architecture, and Morris purchased the glass and supervised the choice of colours, the leading, and the backgrounds for the figure designs.

A precedent of the Arts and Crafts movement's 'spirit of association' was to be found not in history but in a living example created by Ruskin. Not so involved as Morris in practical ventures, Ruskin did set up his Guild of St. George in 1878. Confronted with the news of the Paris Commune, in *Letter VII* of his *Flors Clavigera. Letters to the Workmen and Labourers of Great Britain,* of 1871, Ruskin saw himself '... as a communist of the old school' wishing '... to do good work'. Ruskin's was a 'commune' based on the economic equality of its members. Its primary aim was independent craftsmanship. Thus an attempt was also made to restart the hand-spinning and weaving of linen by Albert Fleming in Westmorland in the 1880s and later by Ruskin himself on the Isle of Man.[17]

Of all those in the Arts and Crafts movement, William Lethaby was its embodiment at this point in his development. In 1884 he helped set up the significantly named Art Workers' Guild. This was the union of two seemingly disparate societies. One was the St. George's Art Society (called after the church in Bloomsbury) consisting of a number of architects, including Lethaby and Gerald Horsley, who were partners in the sizable architectural practice of Norman Shaw. The other, called 'The Fifteen', consisted of prominent figures including the painter, writer and designer, Walter Crane (1845–1915), the designer Lewis F. Day (1845–1910), and the metalworker, William Benson (1854–1924). The aim of the Art Workers' Guild's twenty-five founder members was:

> ... for the purpose of bringing into closer union all classes of Art Workman, and for the furtherance of practical knowledge of various Crafts.

In short, '... each member learns from each'. To that end, lectures and demonstrations were organised on a wide range of craft topics. It was non-competitive and non-campaigning, yet it exercised a profound influence. In 1914 its headquarters were moved from Clifford's Inn to the premises which it still uses at 6 Queen Square, Holborn, across from where Morris had had his workshops. Its architecture and furnishings were designed in part by Lethaby in the idiom of the Arts and Crafts movement.

In 1901 Johnston was elected to the Art Workers' Guild, by which time Emery Walker, Cobden-Sanderson, and his former pupil the book-binder Douglas Cockerell, were already among its members. An endearing feature of the hall was first suggested by Cobden-Sanderson in his essay 'The Arts and Crafts Movement' of 1905. It was decided that the names of the masters and members of the Guild were to be written in chronological order around the walls and the names of deceased members were to be gilded. The formal lettering was designed by Emery Walker. (In 1945 The hall was the venue for the commemorative tributes to Johnston, in which many insights into his life and working practices were expressed.)

Largely due to Lethaby, together with Walter Crane, Cobden-Sanderson, and William Benson, an umbrella organisation was set up in 1888 to co-ordinate the exhibiting of the work produced by the Art Workers' Guild as well as by individual artists and designers outside it. In effect, it was a 'secession' movement offering an alternative 'shop window' to the exclusive practices of the Royal Academy. Implied in its name was the objective pursued by the Arts and Crafts movement as a whole to establish unity across the arts. Significantly, the first name to be proposed was the Combined Arts. Ultimately the name Arts and Crafts Exhibition Society was chosen, both titles being coined by Cobden-Sanderson.

The intention, at least, of the Arts and Crafts Exhibition Society was to be egalitarian in spirit. It rejected, for example, outside offers to award prizes for individual merit. Some three-hundred-and-ninety-nine people accepted the invitation to contribute to the first annual show at the New Gallery in Bond Street. They attracted notice internationally and it was largely on their account that English design came to have such a distinctive reputation on the Continent, notably in Germany through the anglophile Hermann Muthesius, and in Belgium through Henry Van de Velde, (a founder member of the Deutsche Werkbund, in 1907). Walter Crane was its first president. Additionally, Lethaby and Cobden-Sanderson organised the 'essential adjunct' of lectures which were then published in 1893 as the *Arts and Crafts Essays.* One of the more seminal of these, 'Printing', was co-authored by Morris and Emery Walker.[18]

In 1893, William Morris accepted to be president of the Arts and Crafts Exhibition Society, even though he had previously stood aloof from it for reasons to do with his beliefs in the running of his design business. He remained its president until his death in 1896. Between 1932–36, Edward Johnston held the same prestigious office. It was in this capacity that in 1933 he read his paper, 'On the Labelling of Exhibits'.[19]

Like Morris, Cobden-Sanderson was a proprietor as well as a craftsman who attempted to put into practice a guild-like concept in the management of his own Doves Bindery which he set up in 1893. It was run on the lines of a communal workshop, a form of craft socialism. In his article 'Book Binding: its Processes and Ideals', he wrote:

> .... The important thing is that there shall be a common and well understood notion of what the work is or should be ... the transformation of the workplace from a place in which to earn a wage or make a profit, into a place in which the greatest pleasure and the greatest honour in life are to be arrived at, pleasure in the intelligent work of the hand, and honour in the formation and maintenance of great historic tradition.[20]

The 'pleasure', 'honour', and 'intelligent work' in the workplace spoken of by Cobden-Sanderson must have touched Johnston, for he was Cobden-Sanderson's neighbour in Hammersmith Terrace and was commissioned by him to calligraph the initial letters for the chapter openings of some of the Doves Press books. The most prestigious of these was the edition of Milton's *Paradise Lost.*

However, Johnston's temperament and his need for privacy in his work precluded him from an assertive association in any such band, or brotherhood, or guild. He was never a campaigner in the sense of Morris or Lethaby or Walter Crane, nor an organiser such as Mackmurdo or C. R. Ashbee, so it seems that he did not have need of the solidarity which comes from propagating a cause within a group.

Johnston's was a quieter though no less strongly felt need for fellowship. It was in character that as the teacher of a calligraphy class at the Central School of Arts and Crafts from 1899 he wished simply to be an individual among a group of equals who together were pursuing an enquiry. The class was not a guild, of course, but, rather '… a little band of explorers in unknown country. He [Johnston] was the leader of the expedition but as much an explorer as the rest'. So wrote Priscilla Johnston in her biography. Similarly, Johnston welcomed the contributions of others in the making of *Writing & Illuminating, & Lettering* – Gill on inscriptional lettering, Graily Hewitt on gilding, Noel Rooke for the woodcut illustrations, Emery Walker for the collotypes. Johnston shared in the spirit with which Lethaby had set up the Central School. His sympathetic though spasmodic association with the Art Workers' Guild and the Arts and Crafts Exhibition Society were also in keeping. Characteristically, he enjoyed the fellowship-in-craft of Gill and Pepler in Ditchling but stopped short of joining their Guild of St. Joseph and St. Dominic in Ditchling, though his immediate reason was its Roman Catholic precepts rather than its artistic aims.

Johnston's more unequivocal identification, however, was with that other aspect of the Arts and Crafts movement, the practice of handicraft, or the 'designer-craftsman'.

Outside the organised groups there were other craftsmen who, like Johnston himself, worked independently or in small commercial enterprises. Romney Green, the furniture designer and a close friend of Johnston at Hammersmith, is one example. Christopher Whall, the stained-glass artist and teacher with Johnston at the Central School, is another. A third is the Barnsley brothers who had their furniture workshops in the Cotswolds. Their aim was focused less on Morris's 'spirit of association' and more on his notion of handicraft. Two principles central to the Arts and Crafts movement were involved. In his article, 'Cabinet Making', written in 1892, Lethaby argued both that the designing and the making of artefacts are integrated activities and that the materials and tools used are crucial – and organic – determinants of design.[21] Theoretically, at least, the form of an artefact was to emerge as the synthesis of the needs to be fulfilled, the potentiality of the materials, and the capabilities of the craftsman in conjunction with the tools used. It amounted, in effect, to a form of functionalism *avant la lettre*. In his essay, 'The Arts and Crafts Movement', Cobden-Sanderson stressed the message of Morris:

> Never forget the material you are working with, and try always to use it for doing what it can do best … a designer should always understand the processes of the special manufacture he is dealing with, or the result will be merely a *tour de force*.

Cobden-Sanderson added to this : '… the pleasure in understanding the capabilities of a special material … gives the *raison d'être* of decorative art.'[22]

Along with those of Lethaby, it is in the writings of another leading voice within the Arts and Crafts movement that the importance of handicraft, or the 'designer-craftsman', is most fully expressed. Walter Crane was the director of the

Manchester Municipal School of Art between 1893–97 and principal of the Royal College of Art for one year, 1898. His more notable books, all Morrisian in outlook, are *The Claims of Decorative Art*, of 1893, and *Ideals in Art*, of 1895. His essay 'On the Revival of Design and Handicraft' of 1893, was the first contribution in the collection of *Arts and Crafts Essays*. It can be read as a putative manifesto of the Arts and Crafts movement. Having deplored the decline of design and the handicrafts in the earlier part of the nineteenth century, Walter Crane then turned to their contemporary renewal:

> Of late years, however, a kind of revival has been going on, as a protest against the conviction that with our modern mechanical achievements life is growing uglier every day, as Mr Morris puts it .... The effort to unite – or rather to reunite – the artist and the craftsman, so sundered by the industrial conditions of our century, has been growing and gathering force for some time past .... At all events, I think it may be said that the principle of the essential unity and interdependence of the arts has been again asserted – the brotherhood of designer and craftsman; that goes for something with whatever imperfections or disadvantages may have been obscured.[23]

Johnston embodied Crane's notion of the 'brotherhood of designer and craftsman'. It is of significance, too, that he joined the staff of the Royal College of Art in 1901, only two years after Walter Crane's principalship. Thus, a tradition of 'designer-craftsmanship' prevailed there continuously from Crane's presence in 1898 through into the late 1930s. Among Johnston's colleagues at the RCA were others of the same convictions, largely recruited from the Art Workers' Guild. Foremost was Lethaby himself, as the professor of the Department of Design and Ornament. He, in turn, appointed others, including Johnston, Cobden-Sanderson, and Morris's furniture designer, George Jack.

In so far as Johnston was a calligrapher the aesthetic of handicraft was relatively straightforward. In the intimate process of making a manuscript it hardly made sense for Johnston – or any other scribe – to delegate tasks. And, clearly, a decisive influence was exerted over the manuscript by the quality of the vellum and the implements used to prepare it, and by the quills and inks. Many other crafts, however, lent themselves more necessarily to a division of labour. Printing – even hand-printing – and type designing are instances. When Johnston was commissioned to design an Italic typeface for Count Kessler's Cranach Presse, in 1912–13, his beliefs were put to the test. He had grave misgivings in undertaking the designs. The sticking point was that the engraving of the letter-forms on to steel punches – the punch-cutting – was a necessarily separate activity from the initial drawing of the letter-forms onto paper. He would have preferred to defer the responsibility for the entire design to the punch-cutter.[24] In this, and other cases, Johnston regarded his design not as his inviolate creation but rather a 'character sketch'. Starting with enlarged working drawings, the punch-cutter – Johnston and Kessler employed the widely respected craftsmen, George Friend and Edward Prince – would then be able to find the 'necessity', to use Johnston's word, of his own design.[25]

Johnston's instincts remained within this compass: making and designing were one process. In a letter to Sydney Cockerell dating from 1944, the last year of his life, but never posted or even finished, Johnston speaks of handicraft as a natural practice, the outcome of tradition now lost. His voice is that of Morris, who believed art to have formerly belonged to the common man. In one paragraph Johnston conveys the wonder with which he saw a Sussex wagon in Ditchling, some thirty-two years earlier:

> Dear Cockerell .... The ladder was made by an old wheelwright, one of the few real Craftsmen or 'Tradesmen' left. When we came here just 42 years ago – less one month, he could have – with a little help from a Smith – made the whole of a great 'Sussex Wagon' – a kind of Fairy Ship for Beauty – with all its little stop chamfered and painted bannisters and beautiful pine and craft shaped 'parts' (I dare say it had a vocabulary of its own of anything from 50 to a 100 words or more). Once, in that abysm of time, I had the luck to see one: it was empty (but would have carried a whole hayrick); it was drawn by six horses, in pairs. They were slightly decked with coloured ribbons and wore their historic shiny brass ornaments. A Sussex friend of mine who knows much local lore told us the right technical name for each horse according to its position in the team. Three carters shouldering long whips walked at their heads – and the glorious procession passed.[26]

The trend set in motion by the Arts and Crafts movement continued its momentum in the craft practices of the community which grew up in Ditchling. Eric Gill's insistence on total responsibility for all aspects of his work as a stone lettering artist, sculptor and wood engraver set a *modus operandi* for those who followed him to Ditchling, after his arrival there in 1907. One of these was the hand-printer, Douglas (baptised Hilary) Pepler. Although he employed a pressman at his S. Dominic's Press, Pepler insisted on the use of hand-set Caslon Old Face type (so-called after William Caslon, who designed it in the 1730s) and Batchelor hand-made papers. He printed with a 'silent but still active Stanhope and its small retinue of Albions'. Of his Stanhope press, Pepler wrote with undisguised pride:

> ... it is the oldest iron press in the world. I have used it daily for over sixteen years and, except for the wooden handle it is in the same condition not only as when it was when I bought it but as when it was made over 125 years ago.[27]

In a publisher's note with which Pepler prefaced the very first book he printed he expressed his belief in the hand-made. In part it reads:

> ... when Man first discovers how to make anything, that thing which he makes is good. For example: this book is printed upon one of the first iron presses to be made in this country. The press is a good press; it would be difficult to make a press which would enable the printer to print more clearly. The wooden press was a good press and the printing from it has not been surpassed.
>
> Further, this quality of goodness of a first discovery may persist for many years. But there is a tendency to avoid Quality Street. We are choosing rather Quantity Street and the byepaths of Facility and Cleverness; we have become accustomed to the hum of the Time and labour saving machinery; and we are in danger of forgetting the use of good things: indeed the tradition and practice of goodness has been lost in a considerable number of trades.

> For instance: a carpenter has become so used to buying his timber in planks from a yard that he has nearly forgotten its relation to the tree. The man who works to designs conceived by somebody else with wood sawn by another man's machine must be deprived of the natural strength of the tree.
>
> IN VIEW OF THE BEGINNING it is desirable to record what still survives of the traditions of making good things; and I shall endeavour to publish the instructions and advice of men and women who still follow these good traditions. Douglas Pepler[28]

That first achievement in hand-printing is called *A Book of Vegetable Dyes.* Its author was Ethel Mairet who, by 1920, was also working in Ditchling.[29] Ethel Mairet was remarkable for her work as a hand-loom weaver and dyer. Her commitment to undertake the whole weaving processes led her to gather many of the plants needed for the dyeing of fabrics. Like Pepler or Morris, though, she also had a team of assistants.

In asserting that 'designer-craftsmanship' was undergoing a revival, Walter Crane touched on a further issue which bound the Arts and Crafts movement together into a set of common beliefs: the discreet use of ornament, the theme that had been developed by Ruskin and Morris and was to become a central plank in Johnston's own teaching. Walter Crane in his *The Revival of Design and Handicraft*, wrote:

> Plain materials and surfaces are infinitely more preferable to inorganic and inappropriate ornament, yet there is not the simplest article of common use made by the hand of man that is not capable of receiving some touch of art – whether it lies in the planning or proportions, or in the final decorative adornment; whether it is the work of the smith, the carpenter, the carver, the weaver, or the potter, and other indispensable crafts.[30]

Further into the article, Crane maintained that 'true ornamented objects' should grow naturally 'out of organic necessities'. By 'true ornamented objects' he was referring to designed artefacts in general. By 'organic necessities' he meant the natural potential of the materials used. Conversely, badly designed artefacts, vulgarised by what he called '... the ill-considered bedizenment of meaningless and unrelated ornament' occurred because of '... the enormous application of machinery in the interests of competitive production for profit'. Clearly, in Crane's view, design does not exist in a vacuum. It is conditioned by the society for which it was created. Design is produced in an economic, political and even religious context.

In proposing this concept, Crane was reaching up from the foundations which Morris, and Ruskin before him, had been at pains to build during the past twenty years or more. The very phrases 'ornamented objects' and 'organic necessities' are entirely Ruskinian in origin. In Crane's view ornamentation was an essential but subtle matter and propriety in its use was the measure of good design. However, such reasonableness was unattainable in an industrialised society which was itself out of joint. It was through such writers as Crane and Lethaby that Ruskin's plea for restraint became one of the most revered principles of the Arts and Crafts movement.

Johnston shared Crane's notion of 'organic necessity', and its implied view of the moral health of a society. The inclusion of the word 'Illumination' in the title of his handbook *Writing & Illumination, & Lettering* indicates the importance Johnston attached to the role of ornamentation (or decorative illumination) in books and manuscripts. The crux of the matter for him was thoughtful restraint. In *Writing & Illuminating, & Lettering,* Johnston summed up his position in terms almost identical to those used by Walter Crane:

> In fact the qualities of good illumination are the same as the qualities of good writing – Simplicity, Distinctiveness and Proportion. The convention (here, literally a coming together) required is only that the drawing and colouring of the illumination and the drawing and colouring of the writing go well together.

The sparse clarity of this view of the illumination of books and manuscripts in relation to their handwritten texts is echoed in Johnston's recommendations for the letter-forms themselves. In the draft preface that he penned in 1902 for *Writing & Illuminating, & Lettering*, he advised:

> The student should have nothing to do with 'Artistic Lettering' or 'Quaint Lettering' or the novel misarrangements of 'display' lettering. Letters are useful things. We must not degrade them from their high office of usefulness to serve the ends of Affectation or vulgarity: but we must choose good letters and build up fine inscriptions or books with them, precisely as a Builder chooses good bricks and builds good walls or houses with them.

Earlier, the Arts and Crafts movement was described as having experienced divergent as well as cohesive forces. The divergence amounted, in effect, to quiet dissent. This can be attributed to the developing ideas of Morris and, following him, of William Lethaby. The period between the publication of Ruskin's *The Stones of Venice* in 1851 and Morris's early lectures 'The Decorative Arts' in 1877–78 saw the rise of Marxism. *The Communist Manifesto* appeared in 1848. It was followed in 1863 by *Das Kapital.* Morris took this path. Yet his development from liberalism to radicalism was a measured one. He retained something of Ruskin's antipathy to rationalism, showing little interest, for instance, in nineteenth-century science. And vestiges of a romantic outlook were left intact, still potent in an otherwise new form of thinking. Yet, Morris applied socialist ideas to build a new philosophy of design. In the intellectual journey now beginning to separate him from Ruskin, the issues of the alienation of labour and the role of the machine became ever more pertinent. And, for the first time, his thinking about art was informed by the concept of class division. As a consequence, critical doubt became a stimulant for thought within the Arts and Crafts movement.

Johnston's response was mixed. The issue of the machine drew from him some of his most carefully thought out, most concise, and therefore most eloquent statements. In the case of socialism (and Fabianism), he quite evidently distanced himself. But it was a distancing rather than an indifference, which showed an independence of mind. However, in making Johnston's position clear, it is as well to begin with Morris himself.

It was only in 1882 that Morris, well into middle age, was prompted to get down to reading *Das Kapital.* Using a French translation, the work was engaging but difficult. With the help of the economist Belfort Bax he attempted to understand Marxist economics.[31] The book restructured his own experience of English society, for example, his witnessing the slums of the East End and child prostitution. And soon he was caught up in Bloody Sunday.[32] Class was of overriding concern to Morris. He abhorred the class system of eighteenth- and nineteenth-century England, a social structure which had been so reassuring to Ruskin. (Ruskin's *Praeterita* began: 'I am, and my father was before me, a violent Tory of the old school.') Looking back to the early 1880s, Morris realised that the injustices of class had awakened him to the underlying fact that:

> … the seeds of a great change, a Social Revolution, were beginning to germinate … thus I became a practical socialist.[33]

In 1883, Morris joined the moderate Social Democratic Federation, established by Hyndeman in the previous year, in search of information. But, by 1885, his mind was more set. He became a founder member of the activist Socialist League, whose manifesto he wrote in outright Marxist terms and whose weekly paper, *Commonweal*, he edited.

While an active propagandist at street level, Morris fell well short of outright revolutionary militancy. Rather, he was a 'reconstructive socialist' and in the manifesto of 1885 advocated a policy of 'education towards revolution'. G. B. Shaw said of him: 'He was on the side of Marx, *contra mundum*'. By 1890, the increasingly anarchistic Socialist League was reconvened into the more restrained Hammersmith Socialist Society, which continued to meet at Morris's Kelmscott House. Emery Walker, his companion at the Kelmscott Press (and later Edward Johnston's neighbour), was its secretary.

Against this background, the issue which Morris saw as critical was the alienation of labour in the workplace. He identified the 'utilitarian brutality' which he wrote about in *The Socialist Ideal* of 1891 to be the outcome of an industrial system in which man, trapped in a factory system of specialist functions, was merely 'part of the machine'. He described the condition as an 'absence of joy in labour'. Work which is worth doing, Morris believed, is a source of pleasure. Its product can be called art. By art, Morris meant man's creative activities in the widest sense. It encompassed all of man's handicrafts, from architecture to gardening, from painting to the domestic crafts. It was this wider sense of art that was absorbed into the Arts and Crafts movement. From as early as 1884, in his lecture 'Art and Socialism', Morris staked out the claim:

> It is right and necessary that all men should have work to do which shall be worth doing, and be of itself pleasant to do …[34]

By 1891 in a second lecture, 'Art' – one of the series entitled 'The Socialist Ideal' – he linked the concept to Socialism. He claims art as a necessity of human life:

> …. the pleasurable exercise of our energies is at once the source of all art and the cause of all happiness; that is to say, it is the end of life.[35]

In yet another article, published in the *Manchester Examiner* in 1892, Morris reasoned from his own experience:

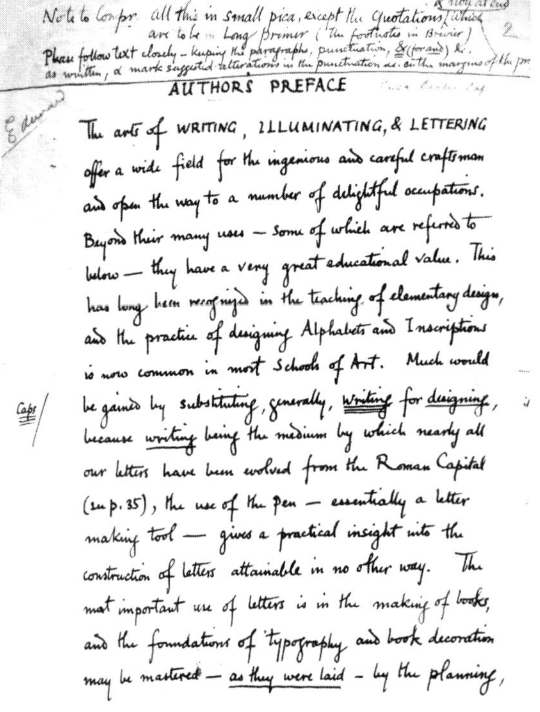

Note to Compr. all this in small pica, except the Quotations (which are to be in Long Primer) (the footnotes in Brevier) & not at end

Please follow text closely – keeping the paragraphs, punctuation, & (for and) &c. as written, & mark suggested alterations in the punctuation &c. on the margins of the proof

AUTHORS PREFACE

The arts of WRITING, ILLUMINATING, & LETTERING offer a wide field for the ingenious and careful craftsman and open the way to a number of delightful occupations. Beyond their many uses – some of which are referred to below – they have a very great educational value. This has long been recognized in the teaching of elementary design, and the practice of designing Alphabets and Inscriptions is now common in most Schools of Art. Much would be gained by substituting, generally, writing for designing, because writing being the medium by which nearly all our letters have been evolved from the Roman Capital (see p. 35), the use of the pen – essentially a letter making tool – gives a practical insight into the construction of letters attainable in no other way. The most important use of letters is in the making of books, and the foundations of typography and book decoration may be mastered – as they were laid – by the planning,

Fig. 44. Draft version of the author's preface to *Writing & Illumination, & Lettering*

> I could never forget thinking ... that my work is little more than pleasure to me; under no circumstances would I give it up. Over and over again I have asked myself why should my lot not be the common lot?[36]

In the late article, 'How I Became a Socialist', of 1894, he affirmed that:

> ... the leading passion of my life is hatred of modern civilisation ... its contempt of simple pleasures ... its eyeless vulgarity which has destroyed art, the one certain solace of labour.'[37]

While the alienation of labour was the principal cause for the malfunction of art, it also exacerbated the class divisions in society. In the manifesto of the Socialist League, of 1885, Morris wrote of:

> ... the one [class] possessing wealth and the instruments of its production, the other [class] producing the wealth by means of those instruments.[38]

These elements were inextricably intertwined. The class divisions, the alienation of labour in the workplace, and the collapse of art as a 'joy to the maker' formed a knot of immorality, a stranglehold on Victorian society. Morris went on to develop a political strategy with which to untie it.

The central question was the alienation of labour. In Morris's view it could be eliminated in two ways. Either manufacturing practices in factories and elsewhere could be gradually humanised. With the right inducements these practices could be returned, in a piecemeal fashion, to smaller-scale operations and so integrate again the process of making and designing. Alternatively, a total reform of the class divisions in society – and therefore in the workplace – could be brought about in order to rebuild society anew. Either way offered the possibility for society to satisfy again its spiritual needs.

Needless to say, Morris rejected the pragmatic approach in favour of radical change. His approach was to reform society from the top down. The first aim was to effect political change by eliminating class divisions. An amelioration of working conditions would then follow thereby reinstating the morally wholesome practice of art as making and designing. The three elements of the problem would unlock. By the early 1890s he had became politically active. His letter to the *News Chronicle* in 1893 said:

> The first steps towards the new birth of art would be a definite rise in the conditions of the people.[39]

At this stage Morris's radicalism was such that he even preferred 'the death of all art' rather than to see it half-reformed as a social democratic compromise within existing class divisions.

On account of his socialist vision, Morris had increasing reservations about the effectiveness of the Arts and Crafts movement in bringing about change, although he did continue to support it. He was still looked to for leadership, and he continued to describe himself as 'designer' on his Socialist League membership card. But the thrust of his energies was now political. His model was no longer solely an evocation of the past, as in *The Dream of John Ball*, but was a Marxist blueprint of a classless society, set in the future. Nevertheless, his vision was still somewhat redolent of an ideal medieval world. The summation was his socialist Utopian writing. *News from Nowhere*, was written in 1890.

Morris's new political stance provoked a range of reactions within the Arts and Crafts movement fraternity. The pragmatic approach – treating the problem from the bottom of society upward – was followed in a random way, and even unwittingly, by a variety of craftsmen. Their underlying aim was to revitalise local and vernacular skills within an egalitarian framework. A patchwork of reformist cells developed. Some, like Ernest Gimson's, were very small-scale organisations. He moved out of London into Gloucestershire. Others, like C. R. Ashbee's, were more aware of Morris's political aims. At his Guild of Handicraft, first in London's East End and then in Gloucestershire, Ashbee attempted to reawaken craft life for a local urban and a rural community.

For a spell Cobden-Sanderson was close to Morris's radical position and he joined the Socialist League. But he came to realise that it jarred with his earlier convictions and he therefore left. Nevertheless, in two later essays, 'Ecce Mundus: Industrial Ideals', of 1902, and 'The Arts and Crafts Movement', of 1905, he still took a strong reformist line. Art, in its wide Morrisian sense, was to be regarded as an agent rather than a mere consequence of social change. 'A general impulse must precede and, itself, bring about a transformation', he wrote in 'The Arts and Crafts Movement'. The same essay continued:

> In the intention of the founders of the Arts and Crafts Exhibition Society, art is, or should be, an agent in the production of noble life, and not merely an executant dependent upon and presupposing its existence.[40]

Emery Walker, who was Morris's consultant at the Kelmscott Press, was a staunch supporter with Morris of the Hammersmith Branch of the League and became its secretary. Morris's engraver-assistant, R. Catterson-Smith, was also a member, as were other of his colleagues, such as Sir Sydney Cockerell, William Lethaby, Henry Halliday Sparling (Morris's son-in-law), and Walter Crane. Another associate of the League was Lucien Pissarro, the son of Camille Pissarro and the founder, in 1894, of the Eragny Press, in Chiswick.

By the time Eric Gill arrived in Hammersmith, in 1905, The Socialist League and the Hammersmith Socialist Society had given ground somewhat to the Fabian Society, with which he was associated. But Gill then became disenchanted. He came to realise that art was of no priority at all to the Fabians. For inspiration, he turned away from Morris and looked back to Ruskin, of whom he wrote in his *Autobiography*:

> He is to be remembered as one of the few men of the nineteenth century who saw clearly that the roots of human action, and therefore of human art, are moral roots.[41]

In his *Autobiography* Eric Gill also reflected:

> My Socialism was from the beginning a rejection of the intellectual degradation of the factory hands and the damned ugliness of all that capitalist industrialism produced, and it was not primarily a revolt against the cruelty and injustice of the possessing classes or against the misery of the poor. It was not so much the working class that concerned me as the working man – not so much what he got from working as what he did by working.[42]

The extent to which Johnston was involved in socialist and Fabian thinking remains ill-defined. Being conversant with Morris's writings, and close to his colleagues, Eric Gill, Emery Walker, and Cobden-Sanderson, he undoubtedly discussed the tenets of Socialism. But there is no clear indication in Johnston's writings about the development of the position which he took. It can be inferred, though, that it amounted to a distancing. It is characteristic of Johnston to have remained aloof from an organised ideology. It seems clear that the strength of his personal religious convictions, based upon his Quaker background and his essential independence of mind, were a bulwark against intellectual intoxication or conversion to socialism or, for that matter, to Catholicism.

The second issue in Morris's mind concerned the role of the machine in a reformed society. As the counterpart to handicraft, it would seem axiomatic that the Arts and Crafts movement would be hostile to a machine-based culture. The respect for the vernacular tradition and the trust placed in the use of hand-held tools had become entrenched, as habits of thought which were not to be dislodged lightly. Yet, over time, into the 1890s, the traditional views were challenged, minds began to waver, and new sympathies were aroused. The issue was confused by what actually constituted a machine. Was the potter's wheel or the Albion printing press, unchanged almost since the fifteenth century, a machine? Or was its definition to be determined by its complexity, and confined to, say, energy-generators, or factory weaving looms, or industrial lathes?

Morris's own position remained circumscribed. While he was among the first to focus on the issue, he did not devote a specific book or even a paper to the subject. His traditional sympathies were naturally with the handicrafts, by which every artefact would be 'a joy to the maker and a joy to the user'. In the early 1890s, he started his hand-operated and private Kelmscott Press as the relaxation and passion of a wealthy man.[43]

But Morris also saw, with common sense, that the solution to the problem of the machine lay with good management rather than with its elimination. It was the system that needed reform. In his lecture, 'Art, Wealth, and Riches', of 1883, the role for the machine was clear. Still, though, Morris's stance was tied to his medievalism.

> I want the invention of machines ... for performing such labour as is revolting and destructive of self-respect to the men who have to do it by hand.

Again, in his lecture published in *Commonweal*, in 1887, he said:

> ... it is allowing machines to be our masters and not our servants that so injures the beauty of life nowadays. It is the token of the terrible crime ... of using our Control of nature for the purpose of enslaving people.[44]

But this is only to say that machines can be labour-saving. Morris fell short of an overall aesthetic of the machine as the craftsman's and the industrialist's tool. Whereas his Marxist analysis accommodated his vision of labour as a source of spiritual fulfilment, he was more circumspect about the machine. His vision was closed to a reality which was beginning to be welcomed by others, just as the class-ridden Ruskin had blocked an earlier reality. It was Lethaby, rather than Morris, who was to loosen the impasse.

The debate fanned out into a spectrum of opinion, each valid within the terms of its own reasoning. A range of craftsmen, each known to Johnston either as a friend or craftsman or writer, held different views according to their individual outlooks or vested interests. At one extreme were the reactionaries – the 'intellectual Luddites', as C. R. Ashbee dismissively called them – who remained loyal to the traditon of a handicraft rooted in the English medieval vernacular. Ruskin was the arch-enemy of the machine. In his St. George's Guild even the steam engine was prohibited. He called the invention 'the toy of the insane and the paralytic'. Less hysterical, though equally purist, was the craftsman Ernest Gimson. The design and quiet authenticity of his furniture relied upon its being handmade.

At the other extreme were the progressive realists such as William Lethaby, who came round to recognise that the future could only lie with the inclusion of the machine into a newly conceived philosophy of design. Lethaby's view of the role of machinery in the making of artefacts was sane, considered and prophetic. A crucial paragraph in his essay, 'The Art of Workmanship', published in *The Imprint* in 1913, shows the progress of his rethinking a design philosophy for the twentieth century. One passage reads:

> Although a machine-made thing can never be a work of art in the proper sense, there is no reason why it should not be good in a secondary order – shapely, strong, well–fitting, useful; in fact, like a machine itself. Machine-work should show frankly that it is the child of the machine; it is the pretence and subterfuge of most machine-made things that makes them disgusting.[45]

Between these extremes were others whose attitude was generally more relaxed. Walter Crane changed his mind completely in this matter. By 1905, he had taken a sympathetic view towards the use of the machine.

Emery Walker's position was more equivocal. Given that he ran a commercial photogravure business which was dependent on photographic apparatus he accepted the necessity for the machine. In another sense, he was all too aware of his antiquarian interests and the craft values implicit in the Kelmscott and Doves Presses to which he was a consultant. Aesthetically, he was more convinced of the high standing of the late-medieval printed book, which, as at the Kelmscott and Doves Presses, was made by hand-operated presses and by the human skill of the punch-cutter. (It is telling, perhaps, that although Walker was involved in the design of typefaces, he was not interested in the pantograph punch-cutting machine invented by Benton in the USA, in 1884.)

Cobden-Sanderson took firm though respectful issue with Morris. As a starting-point he quoted one of Morris's earlier but more outspoken judgements: 'As a condition of life, production by machinery is wholly evil.' In his article, 'On the Revival of Handicraft', of 1888, Cobden-Sanderson argued for the aesthetic value of certain features of modern industrial life (for example the water-pumping station).

> But surely, this is altogether questionable; surely things there are, the production of which by machinery may be wholly right, which when so produced ... maybe ... even works of art. Machinery may be redeemed by Imagination and made to enter even into his [Morris's] restored world adding to the potency of good, and to its power over evil.[46]

Ashbee's position was perhaps more deeply considered than Morris's. He made the vital distinction between machinery, as such, and an engulfing system of mechanisation. Like Morris, he accepted the usefulness of machines to do labour-saving work but, unlike him, he recognised that there should be scope for an aesthetic of the machine. Firmly anchored in the Arts and Crafts movement – he was inspired by seeing a craft-based society *in situ* during a stay in Cairo from 1916–17 – his book, *Where the Great City Stands*, of 1917, admits that: 'Modern civilisation rests on machinery ... no system of the teaching of the arts can be sound if it does not recognise this.' Yet it cautions:

> We know that beautiful things can be made by mechanical power. It is the system as a whole that we have to consider .... We must free the human spirit again .... We have to free it from the incubus of mechanism ... of power misunderstood, misapplied, miscontrolled.[47]

The Arts and Crafts movement designer who most openly welcomed the machine was the metal craftsman, William Benson. An admirer of William Morris and a designer for his Firm, he aspired to become an engineer but instead he established a foundry in Hammersmith for the production mainly of metal hollow-ware such as light-fittings. His views are expressed in his book, *Elements of Handicraft and Design*, of 1893. He also contributed the article 'Metal Work' to the volume of *Arts and Crafts Essays.*[48] A measure of the extent to which Benson incorporated the machine into his design thinking – his products were produced on a large scale and were not expensive – is indicated by his developing affiliations. Initially a founder member of the Art Workers' Guild, in 1884, and of the Arts and Crafts Exhibition Society, in 1886, by 1917 he was a member of the industrially orientated Design and Industries Association (the DIA).

Given Bernard Leach's connections with Johnston in Ditchling and his natural affinities with the Arts and Crafts movement, it is not inappropriate to record his views on the role of the machine in design even though they date from the 1920s. A studio potter who was inspired by English medieval and Japanese traditional hand-thrown pots, Leach's views are expressed in *A Potter's Outlook*. This pamphlet was written at the suggestion of Philip Mairet for the *New Handworker's Gallery Pamphlets* (No 3) and was printed by Pepler in Ditchling in 1928. In discussing the need for a revival of a standard aesthetic for pottery, in England, Leach wrote:

> The next step is to get rid of the idea of the machine as an enemy. The machine is an extension of the tool; the tool of the hand; the hand of the brain; and it is only the unfaithful use of the machine which we can attack. It is here that industry is to blame - just where it is unfaithful to Life in putting money values first. Science which has invented machinery in the XIX century is no enemy of life, but 'business first' has turned it into a bully, a slave driver, a cheat. Art, which is the outcome and proof of life must come into the firm again in the XX Century as an equal partner, or there will be a disaster.[49]

Finally, there is the position of Johnston himself. Like Morris, Johnston did not write a tract, as such, devoted to the question of mechanisation and design, either in regard to his own work in type designing or more generally. As a calligrapher he clearly had no need for machinery. In his work diary for 1911–13 Johnston jotted down:

> Writing and Sewing Machines. Such positive significance as might be claimed for them from the educationist's point of view cannot compare with that of handwriting and hand-sewing.[50]

His *métier* naturally inclined him towards the kind of misgivings which were shared by many craftsmen within the broad fraternity of the Arts & Crafts movement.

He broached the issue from another viewpoint in the articles he wrote in 1919 on the unusual subject of picture frames. 'Notes on Picture Framing, Frames, and Borders (I & II)', was written for the magazine *Illustration,* which was edited by his friend Gerard Meynell.[51] In it Johnston laments the demise of the 'good Tradition' of the handmade:

> … I know an admirable and charming man, a country picture frame maker: he told me that his father had possessed a great number of wonderful moulding planes – many

> of which he himself could not use – but, he explained, it is now customary to buy or use machine-made mouldings. The many moulding planes belong to the good Tradition.... Now, to be guided by standard patterns is a good thing, but to be bound by stock patterns is bad. To be bound by stock patterns ... is, in fact, one of the most demoralising kinds of slavery.

The articles were the occasion for Johnston to set out a case – a moral case – for hand-work as opposed to the machine-made. He associates the latter with 'sham-superiority, sham-culture, sham-art'. Not unlike the playing out of a music score, Johnston's thoughts then unfold to reveal a centre theme, an utterance of startling simplicity:

> Honest is *unscornable.*

His analysis isolates two considerations, 'Humanness and Fitness':

> The qualities which chiefly give attractiveness to human works are Humanness and Fitness. The human touch in a thing gives us a fellow feeling or sympathy, and it makes it recognisable and intelligible or, as I should prefer to call it, *legible;* its fitness satisfies our feeling for that which is harmonious or appropriate. Both the qualities of humanness and fitness appeal to our common, unconscious logic: both qualities may be found in Man's works in the humblest or in the highest degree: they are aspects of Beauty (or Truth) which we can most conveniently contemplate....
>
> Let us consider what makes our work human and fit.... The essential thing is that our feeling and fancies should be true – actual not imaginary. Similarly, passing fashions, followed within limits, may be helpful and stimulating: it is only essential that they be practised in true admiration – actual not simulated.

Yet Johnston was spared the kind of blind intolerance which possessed Ruskin. His interest in science, his personal fascination with gadgetry and electrical apparatus, and his involvement in printing by hand may have contributed to this balance. His joint editorship of *The Imprint*, a journal dedicated to improving standards in the highly mechanised printing industry, tends to bear this out.

Johnston returned to the issue in his capacity as president of the Arts and Crafts Exhibition Society. His letter to *The Times* printed on November 19th 1934,[52] brought him closer to the position adopted by Lethaby. For him, the danger of using mechanical processes lay in their likely exclusion from the designing process of an artefact. His discourse started by saying:

> Without the craftsman there can be no design, in the sense of that word which connotes aesthetic value.

Yet, by this very reasoning, he recognised that:

> In this connection the engineer may be regarded as a craftsman, and the aesthetic value of his work is likely to be in proportion to its fitness for purpose.

In this situation the engineer (or designer) is in the same relation to the machine as a craftsman to his hand-held tools – the design arises out of their use. The essential point for Johnston was that designing must be inherent to the process of making. His letter pursues this line of thought:

> Unless design arises out of the construction of a thing, it is reduced to the level of extraneous ornamentation.

Rather than openly condemning the designer's or craftsman's use of the machine, Johnston cautioned that:

> Design in fact is inherent rather than applied, and the 'application of design' to mechanical processes suggests an attempt to get the best of both worlds by trying to secure the appearance of craftsmanship without its substance.

Johnston's viewpoint was not an intolerant one, nor was it retrograde. Rather, he was simply cautious of mechanical processes being an integral part of designing. But wherever this was possible, wherever 'the engineer may be regarded as a craftsman', it followed that machines are acceptable. These thoughts are further endorsed in a letter to Alfred Fairbank which Johnston wrote in March 1935 concerning the catalogue of a planned exhibition by the Arts and Crafts Exhibition Society, in which Noel Rooke (as the Society's chairman), Alfred Fairbank, and Noel Carrington were involved. (It took place at Dorland House in Lower Regents Street, in November 1935.)[53]

> [Noel] Carrington's excellent suggestion to get one definite aim in view and answer the question – What does civilisation need that the machine cannot do? is clearly the first step for our society's further progress. I should suggest, however, altering 'the machine' to 'machinery' wh[ich] conveys in a fuller sense what we are up against. We have no objection to the machine as such. Any external instrument or tool may be so defined. And, of course, I sh[oul]d prefer the question reduced to the positive statement: Civilisation needs certain things that machinery cannot give followed by what these things are. We all have an idea. I have long been trying to find out and put it in words and that enthusiasm still flares up in me every now and again. E. J.[54]

The issue rumbled on in Johnston's mind. On the 18th October 1935 he wrote to Fairbank: 'I am trying to write an answer to the question: "What can the Hand do that the Machine cannot?" You'll remember that Carrington raised it.'[55] In a follow-up letter of the 21st October he concluded: 'I have decided to give up my Note on Man and Machine this time (your first claim sufficiently covers the main point) – my note is not sufficiently digested, and there is now not time for digestion.'[56] Yet, two days later he again wrote to Fairbank: 'Only few moments before post available. The handwork thing is "more expressive" for obvious reasons & I think at present that sentence will pass tho' "obviously had to" might improve it.'[57]

Johnston's apprehension translated into the dramatic and 'reluctant' rejection, in 1936, of his nomination for the prestigious Royal Designer for Industry Award, newly instituted by the Royal Society for the Encouragement of the Arts, Manufactures & Commerce (the RSA). Johnston outlined his position:

> I am really sorry that I feel unable to accept the honour again offered by the Royal Society of Arts. I should be very sorry if the Society thought that I doubted them or meant to take up a 'superior' position. I believe in their integrity and their philanthropic activities and I regard the R.D.I. as an honour not to be disdained by anyone – let alone by me – and yet, by me, to be conscientiously (and somewhat reluctantly) refused, because 'INDUSTRY' does not appear to be based on good

principles, to be aimed at a good purpose. In other words I doubt the integrity (and philanthropy) of typical industrialism and regard it as opposed, even actively inimical, to the Arts and Crafts and those who practise them.

That is no attack on persons or politics ... but *on a system*, to which the good word 'Industry' has become attached.[58]

These ideas were associated in Johnston's mind with comparable problems relating to his own calligraphic designs being used for reproduction, by print or photography or engraving. Hence, he worried about the Diploma of Fellowship which Noel Rooke asked him to design for the London County Council Central School of Arts and Crafts in 1930. The proposal that it would be photographically reproduced did not appeal to Johnston who then carefully negotiated with George Friend that it be engraved and then printed off. Johnston's position was made plain in a series of letters to George Friend. One, dated 21st August 1931, reads in part: 'The point is this – 1. My original MS is a *Rough Sketch*. 2. It is intended as a guide to the engraver (*not* an exact copy in any way). 3. And for the engraver to translate the pen forms into (comfortable) Engraving forms.'[59] In a later letter to George Friend (29th February 1932) he reiterated:

> When I undertook ... to design a Diploma form for the LCC I insisted that it shd. not be reproduced by a facsimile 'process' – because all such imitations of another craft tend to falsify & are not in themselves works of Art – but insisted that my 'Design' should be '*translated*' into an *Engraving* which is in itself a Work of Art. I also insisted that my 'Design' shd. take the form of a *Rough sketch* to be used by the engraver as a guide rather than a 'Copy' ... Now I wanted something much more a crystallised *Friend*, not *Johnston*, an *Engraving* after Johnston's pen style, rather than a copy.[60]

Johnston took an identical stance in two similar situations involving engraving from his lettering designs. One was the design he undertook in 1936 of the Royal and Imperial cyphers to be used for the medal commemorating the coronation of Edward VIII. To the Crown official concerned Johnston wrote of 'the risk of a Craftsman in metal or other material slavishly copying a sketch – such as one in my formal penmanship – instead of adapting it to his own proper methods.' In his accompanying 'Notes on the Use of Formal Pen Sketches for E.R. & E. VIIIR. & the 'Translation' of Pen Forms into Metal Forms.' Johnston affirmed that: 'the Sketches ... are properly to be regarded as *Authoritative and suggestive PLANS* for another Craftsman – in this case a Worker in Metal – *which his special Tools & skilled Methods will suitably adopt & alter*.'[61] The other occasion, which began in 1912 and continued into the 1930s, concerned his drawn designs for the italic typeface for the Cranach Presse. There, too, he felt 'conscientious objections' about the difficulties faced by the punch-cutters, Edward Prince and George Friend, in the cutting of the punches for his typeface.

In this respect, Johnston's concerns about transcriptions of one artist's work into another medium accorded with those of Morris for he, too, had come up against the same problem when designing his Golden type and Troy type. Morris had made 'sketches' – the term is properly Johnston's – from enlarged photographs printed by Emery Walker. Morris had then arranged for their transcription onto steel punches by the punch-cutter, Edward Prince. In his instructions regarding the royal cyphers for the Edward VIII medal Johnston had raised the spectre of photographic changes of scale:

> In dealing with such photographic Reductions, or any reduction, therefore, it is necessary to alter the reduction & exaggerate, *suitably in relation to the Craft (of the Worker in metal), all its important features – generally increasing the proportional Weight (ie., Thickness) OF EVERY PART.*[62]

However, Johnston does not appear to have had such qualms over the illustrations of lettering in *Writing & Illuminating, & Lettering*. The wood-engravings by Noel Rooke apart, these were presumably photographed from his own calligraphed versions and printed off as zincographs, though no doubt at the same scale.

END NOTES

1. The encounter is referred to by Priscilla Johnston and by Emery Walker, a friend of Morris and Johnston in turn. Ref. Emery Walker. 'Three Lectures for the Sandars Readership in Bibliography', 1947, a typescript copy is in the Manuscripts Room of Cambridge University Library.
2. Elkins Mathews Catalogue. *Books from the Library of Edward Johnston*. Bodleian Library. MSS. Eng. Lett. b/6. Fol. 39–40. The copy of *Medieval Lore* is at Napier University, Edinburgh.
3. The letter is dated the 15th September 1904. See the catalogue of the Edward Johnston Memorial Exhibition at the V&A, 1945. Case G. Item 6.
4. Eric Gill. Diary. W. A. Clark Library. UCLA. California. Microfiche copy. Tate Gallery archives.
5. W. R. Lethaby. *Architecture. An Introduction to the History and Theory of the Art of Building*. (Home University Library) 1911.
6. The term 'mediævalism' was first used by Ruskin (as was 'modernism'). The term 'historicism' – was used by N. Pevsner in his *Pioneers of the Modern Movement*, of 1936. There are distinctions to be made between these complex and imprecise terms. Historicism is a wider concept which refers to nineteenth-century revivalist movements and denotes an imitative, though not necessarily a literal, reproduction of past styles. The Gothic Revivalist designs commissioned by Horace Walpole for his Strawberry Hill House in the 1780–90s, or the early work of Augustus W. Pugin (illustrated in his books *Gothic Furniture of the 15th Century*, of 1835 and *Glossary of Ecclesiastical Ornament and Costume*, of 1844) or the architecture of Gilbert Scott in the 1830–40s are usefully termed 'historicist', as is the furniture of Edward Godwin. His catalogue, *Art Furniture*, 1877, offered clients an eclectic range of styles designed with impressive facility.
7. T. Cobden-Sanderson. *The Arts and Crafts Movement*. (Doves Press) 1905.
8. Wiliam Morris. In *Arts and Crafts Essays*. (Rivington, Percival & Co. Chiswick Press) 1893.
9. The origins of the disapproval of the classicism of the eighteenth century, however, lie much further back, in the writings of the Romantics from the late eighteenth century onwards – of William Blake (1757–1827), of William Cobbett (1763–1835), of Coleridge (1772–1834), of Carlyle (1795–1881), all of whom built on an intuitive distrust of scientific rationalism. It was Blake who so berated Newtonian science. His stance was symbolised in a print of 1795 which depicted

Newton seated on the seabed, looking downwards at his compasses. A later variant of the Romantic attitude is the æsthetic of the architect and decorator, Augustus W. Pugin, whose writings of the 1830–40s extolled the virtues of Catholic, medieval architecture. Produced in the wake of the revival of Roman Catholicism in England, Pugin's *True Principles of Pointed or Christian Architecture* was published in 1841. The Gothic Revivalism of Pugin remained a still active, though historicist, element in the aesthetic ideals of the Arts and Crafts movement from the 1880s onwards. A social study of considerable influence on Morris was Cobbett's writings, including *The History of the Protestant 'Reformation', in England and Ireland, showing how that Event has Impoverished and Degraded the Main Body of People in those Countries*, published in 1827.

10. W. R. Lethaby. *Architecture. A Study in the History and Theory of the Art of Building.* (Home University Library) 1911.

11. Thus it was possible for the furniture designed by George Jack for Morris to be inspired by the English eighteenth century. Similarly, the woodcut book illustrations of the enigmatic, but classically-inspired book, *Hypnerotomachia Poliphili*, first printed in Venice in 1499, had a special fascination for the Arts and Crafts movement book illustrators Charles Ricketts and Charles Shannon.This can be partially explained, however, by those artists' interest in the medium of wood-engraving, which had Gothic origins.

12. *The Imprint.* (Westminster Press) 1913.

13. Edward Johnston. *Writing & Illuminating, & Lettering.* Op. cit.4.

14. William Morris. 'The Development of Modern Society' in *Commonweal.* 1890. Also 'Feudal England' and 'Art and Industry in the Fourteenth Century' (1890). These were two of a trilogy of lectures: 'England As It Was, As It Is, and As It May Be', first published in *Commonweal.* Also in *Collected Works of William Morris.* Vol. XXIII (Pages 39–58) and Vol. XXII (Pages 325–90), edited by May Morris. (Longmans) 1910–15. (The first lecture in the series is 'Early England', 1886.)

15. E. A. Freeman. *The History of the Norman Conquest.* 1867–79. J. R. Green. *A Short History of the English People.* (London) 1878–80. J. E. Thorold Rogers. *Six Centuries of Work and Wages. The History of English Labour.* 1886. They belonged to the Oxford Society for the Promotion of the Study of Gothic Architecture, founded *circa* 1840. Their writings also inspired Ruskin.

16. The guild groupings of the Arts and Crafts movement were not directly inspired by notions of medieval guilds. Morris's historical knowledge was developed later. His books and lectures were to influence Lethaby. Lethaby's article of 1896, entitled 'Art and the Function of the Guilds', published in *The Quest* in 1896, invokes Morris. It argues for the trade unions to take on the responsibility once held by the medieval guilds in ensuring high standards of work.

17. Following Ruskin's lead and then Morris's at the Firm, the concept of co-operative unity characterised other Arts and Crafts guilds which were established during the 1880s. Foremost among these was Arthur Mackmurdo's Century Guild, of 1883. It was formed by the union of two parties which, on the face of it, appeared quite incongruous. On the one hand was the stained-glass artist, Selwyn Image (1849–1930). On the other were the two architects Herbert Horne (1864–1916) and Arthur Mackmurdo (1851–1942). Both had been pupils of Ruskin at his drawing school in Oxford. Mackmurdo had then travelled to Italy with Ruskin, in 1874. The Century Guild published its own journal, *The Hobby Horse*, which became a seminal mouthpiece for Arts and Crafts movement opinion. It declared that the main aim of The Century Guild was:

> To restore building, decorating, pottery, woodcarving, and metalworks to their rightful place beside painting and sculpture. In other words, 'The Century Guild' seeks to emphasise the 'Unity of Art', and by thus dignifying Art in all its forms it hopes to make it living, a thing of our own century, and of the People.

The Hobby Horse. Prospectus. (Chiswick Press) Undated. And in a single issue, No. 1. April 1884.

The Century Guild also ran a showroom. In a sense it can be seen as the forerunner of the modern design practice. (Herbert Horne later lived in Florence, where he collected artworks and wrote a study of Botticelli. His house and collection, named the Museo Horne, exists in Florence.)

One other guild is of central importance to the Arts and Crafts movement. In 1888, Charles Ashbee (1863–1942) established his Guild and School of Handicrafts whose craftsmen practised metalwork, jewellery, woodwork, furniture, and leatherwork. Ashbee himself was especially gifted in jewellery design. A Cambridge history graduate, he trained first as an architect and then become a socialist. He lived at Toynbee Hall, in East London, where he taught classes on the writings of Ruskin. In 1891, he moved his Guild from Commercial Street into Essex House, in the Mile End Road (also in the East End), where it was run co-operatively by its members. In 1902 he again moved the Guild and School of Handicrafts – along with some 120 people, including dependants – out of London to the then remote township of Chipping Campden in rural Gloucestershire. Two of his close friends there were Ethel and Ananda Coomaraswamy. (See endnote 29.) Ashbee's community was a precursor of the one in Ditchling.

A particular interest of Ashbee was his Essex House Press. He acquired the two Albion presses available from Morris's defunct Kelmscott Press and employed Morris's pressmen. His first book was a reprint of Cellini's *Treatises on Goldsmithing and Sculpture*, which he translated from the Italian. A later work was his *Modern English Silverware*, of 1909, the illustrations for which were drawn by his assistant, Philippe Mairet. The Essex House Press has bearing on Pepler's S. Dominic's Press, in Ditchling. Philippe Mairet married the divorced Ethel Coomaraswamy and eventually lived with her in Ditchling where he became a close friend of Johnston. Ashbee was one of the progressive elements in the Arts and Crafts movement. In 1900 he visited Chicago where he met the pioneering modernist architect Frank Lloyd Wright.

18. This essay was a version of Emery Walker's influential lecture, 'Letter-Press Printing and Illustration', originally given in 1888, on account of which, as Cobden-Sanderson put it: 'Morris was induced to turn his attention once again to printing' – and so to his Kelmscott Press.

19. Reproduced in Edward Johnston. *Lessons in Formal Writing*. Edited by Heather Child & Justin Howes (Lund Humphries) 1978.

20. T. Cobden-Sanderson. 'Book Binding: its Processes and Ideals'. In *Fortnightly Review*. Vol. 56. 1894. (Pages 214–224)

21. W. Lethaby. 'Cabinet Making'. Included in A. H. MacMurdo. *Plain Handicraft* (Dryad Handicraft) Leaflet No. 5. Leicester. 1910. Reprinted in 1984.

22. T. Cobden-Sanderson. *The Arts and Crafts Movement*. (Doves Press) 1905.

23. In *Arts and Crafts Essays by Members of the Arts and Crafts Exhibition Society*. With a preface by William Morris. (Longmans, Green.) 1893.

24. Clearly, practical considerations came into play. The practice of handicraft was not adopted universally by Arts and Crafts movement craftsmen. Morris himself learnt the techniques of crafts in order to design, rather than make. His company was so organised that the manufacture of the designs was left to others. In Lethaby's own case, too, theory did not entirely determine practice for his furniture designs were actually made up by a firm of cabinet-makers. The same shortfall characterised the cabinet-making firm with which Lethaby was first associated. In 1890, Sidney and Ernest Barnsley together with Ernest Gimson, William Lethaby, Reginald Blomfield, and others, had set up the short-lived cabinet-making firm of Kenton & Co. It was moved out to the Cotswolds, partly in response to the skills of cabinet-makers they realised were still available there, and partly to use locally grown timber. In the case of Walter Crane, there was also a divergence between theory and practice. He was involved in designing wallpapers, fabrics, embroidery, mosaics, stained glass, although he did not make them. Crane also drew the illustrations for William Morris's *The Story of the Glittering Plain*, which was then printed at the Kelmscott Press in 1894.

25. In letterpress printing the individual letters, or types, are cast in lead alloy from brass moulds, or 'matrices' which are therefore designated 'female'. These, in turn, are made, or 'struck', by steel punches, on to which the letter-forms have been engraved in relief ('male'). Since the printed page is the right way round, the types need to be in mirror image. Consequently, the matrices are the right way round, and the punches, in turn, are in mirror image. Engraving the punches in reverse places added demands on the punch-cutter's skill. The story of this work in Johnston's case is treated by John Dreyfus in *Italic Quartet*. (Cambridge University Press) 1966.

26. Cited from Priscilla Johnston. *Edward Johnston*. (Faber & Faber) 1959.

27. Cited from H. D. C. Pepler. *The Hand Press*. S. Dominic's Press. 1934.

28. H. D. C. Pepler in Ethel Mairet. *A Book of Vegetable Dyes*. S. Dominic's Press. 1915.

29. Ethel Mairet was married to Ananda Coomaraswamy, the pioneer scholar of Indian and Singalese crafts, with whom she gained insights into an aesthetic of handicraft while working and

travelling in what was then Ceylon. A fuller discussion of this development and the links with Johnston are given in Chapter Seven, ('Johnston and the Craft Communities in Ditchling').
30. Walter Crane. 'The Revival of Design and Handicraft'. In *Arts and Crafts Essays by Members of the Arts and Crafts Exhibition Society*. (Rivington, Percival and Co) 1893.
31. See William Morris & B. Bax. *Socialism. Its Growth and Outcome.* (Swan & Sonnensheim) 1893.
32. Bloody Sunday occurred on the 13th November 1887, in Trafalgar Square. Unemployed and socialist demonstrators were repressed by the police and troops. Three people died.
33. From 'How I became a Socialist'. In *Justice,* the paper of the Social Democratic Federation 1894.
34. William Morris. 'Art and Socialism'. Lecture to the Leicester Secular Society. & Pamphlet. 1884.
35. William Morris. 'Art', one of series from 'The Socialist Ideal'. In *The New Review.* 1891.
36. William Morris. Article in *The Manchester Examiner.* 14th March 1892.
37. William Morris. 'How I became a Socialist'. In *Justice.* 1894.
38. William Morris. *Manifesto of the Socialist League.* (Socialist League Publications) 1885.
39. William Morris. Article in the News Chronicle. 1893.
40. T. Cobden-Sanderson. *The Arts and Crafts Movement.* (Doves Press) 1905.
41. Eric Gill. *Autobiography.* (Jonathan Cape) 1940.
42. Eric Gill. *Autobiography.* Op. cit.
43. Ironically, this occurred during his most committed socialist period. There is a further irony in the fact that Cobden-Sanderson bound his copy of *Das Kapital* in tooled and gilded leather.
44. William Morris. 'How We Live and How We Might Live'. In *Commonweal.* 1887.
45. W. R. Lethaby. 'The Art of Workmanship'. In *The Imprint.* No. 1. January 1913.
46. T. Cobden-Sanderson. 'On the Revival of Handicraft'. In *The Register.* 1888.
47. C. R. Ashbee. *Where the Great City Stands. A Study in the New Civics.* (Essex House Press and B. T. Batsford Books) 1917.
48. William Benson. 'Elements of Handicraft and Design'. 1893. And *Arts and Crafts Essays by Members of the Arts and Crafts Exhibition Society.* (Rivington, Percival & Co.) 1893.
49. Bernard Leach. *A Potter's Outlook.* (S. Dominic's Press. Ditchling) 1928.
50. Crafts Study Centre Collection and Archive, Farnham, Surrey. 1911–13. 2/7.
51. Edward Johnston. 'Notes on Picture Framing, Frames and Borders I & II'. In *Illustrator.* (The in-house journal of the Sun Engraving Company, 'A Quarterly Magazine devoted to the Craft of Mechanical Reproduction and thereby dealing with Art and Workmanship in Printing Science in Advertising and Commerce. Edited by Gerard Meynell'.) 1919. The title of this journal clearly shows the influence of Johnston. It is reproduced in Edward Johnston. *Lessons in Formal Writing.* Edited by Heather Child and Justin Howes. Pages 209–217. (Lund Humphries) 1986.
52. Edward Johnston. 'Arts and Crafts'. Letter in *The Times.* November 19th 1934. The original is among the papers given to the Bodleian Library, Oxford by Alfred Fairbank. Ref: MSS Eng Lett. C. 581/8. It is reproduced in Edward Johnston. *Lessons in Formal Writing.* Edited by Heather Child and Justin Howes. (page 203). Op. cit.
53. Johnston exhibited his Perpetual Calender, a vellum writing case, a child's reading book ('written on 1720 paper. Made 1917 and after'), and his manuscript of Shakespeare's Sonnet No. 116. The first three, he pointed out, were 'useful objects' (MSS. Eng Lett. 581. Folio 23.)
54. Letter dated 25th March 1935. Bodleian Library. Ref: MSS. Eng Lett. c. 586. Folio 23.
55. Bodleian Library. MSS. Eng. Lett. c. 581. Folio 54.
56. Bodleian Library. MSS. Eng. Lett. c. 581. Folio 55.
57. Bodleian Library. MSS. Eng. Lett. c. 581. Folio 56.
58. Cited from Priscilla Johnston. *Edward Johnston.* (Faber & Faber) 1959.
59. Cited from *Lessons in Formal Writing* edited by Heather Child and Justin Howes (page 208) in which there is a fuller discussion of this issue.
60. Cited from *Lessons in Formal Writing.* Op. cit.
61. Both quotations cited from *Lessons in Formal Writing.* (page 209) Op. cit.
62. Cited from *Lessons in Formal Writing.* Edited by Heather Child and Justin Howes. (page 210) Op. cit. The documents are in the National Archive.

Left: An early teaching sheet by Johnston for his class at the Central School, dated October 1899. Johnston used a copying process known as a jellygraph. He would make up to forty-five of these sheets. From the Central School archive.
(Courtesy of the Central School, the Westminster Institute.)

Right: Johnston's sketch of himself teaching. From a letter, 23rd May 1901.
(Courtesy of Lund Humphries.)

CHAPTER FOUR

JOHNSTON IN HOLBORN 1898–1905 & HAMMERSMITH 1905–1912

It has been seen that Johnston's *annus mirabilis* was 1898. In that year he found himself in a capital city benefiting from the wealth of late-Victorian imperial power. Flowing from this, London enjoyed a certain artistic prowess and with it opportunities lay waiting. Johnston's progress was rapid. Having responded to Lethaby's encouragement to take up lettering he now responded to his offer to teach in two design colleges. He began at the Central School of Arts and Crafts in September 1899, to whose administration Lethaby had been appointed just three years earlier. He began at the Royal College of Art (RCA) in 1901. These positions gave him some financial security and, as important, an entrée to London's craft community. A tradition of teaching was being put into place to which Johnston was philosophically inclined. Johnston the teacher is the focus of the present chapter.

During the time that Johnston was living in Holborn, between 1898–1905, followed by the seven years, to 1912, that he lived in Hammersmith, he met a widening circle of people for whom the skill of penmanship was a valuable asset. Apart from his fellow-calligraphers they included those who commissioned formally-written manuscripts from him and, as significant, others from the publishing and printing world. For the early 1900s saw the development of the private press movement as well as changes in the printing trade more generally. New design concepts were being asserted and appropriate type designs called for. In this way the scope of Johnston's activities expanded from teaching and calligraphy to embrace authorship and the designing of initial letters for printed books. From 1900 the idea of a handbook on lettering was in Johnston's mind. It was intended to serve, among others, the makers of books. Soon it was taken up by the publisher John Hogg. From 1902 Johnston became involved in writing hand-drawn initial letters for some of Cobden-Sanderson's Doves Press books and in titling for the Insel Verlag (Press) in Germany through Count Harry Kessler.

With these burgeoning opportunities not the least of Johnston's concerns was to combine the high ideals of his artistic principles with ways of earning a living. For by 1903 he was married and soon the breadwinner for his first daughter, Bridget. (By 1911 his two other daughters, Barbara and Priscilla, were born.) He was helped in his lettering-design work by the patronage of like-minded connoisseurs of fine printing. But it was his teaching especially that enabled him to develop his ideals for there was no better ambiance in which to nurture them than at the Central School and the RCA.

By 1898 the London County Council could boast, if somewhat belatedly by comparison with other countries, the recent establishment of two schools specialising in the crafts rather than the fine arts. The lesser-known Bolt Court Technical School was devoted entirely to the teaching of printing techniques. It was followed in 1896 by the Central School which offered a wide spectrum of design courses. As an art inspector for the London County Council, it was Lethaby who was the fulcrum of these education reforms – and of others, at the Royal College of Art (RCA) as well as the teaching of art in primary schools. The London County Council appointment was a key one and Lethaby's application had been supported by William Morris and the painter, Sir William Richmond. Lethaby was then appointed codirector (with George Frampton) at the Central School in 1896. In 1902, he was promoted to be its sole principal, a post he held until 1911.[1] Meantime, he had joined the newly named Royal College of Art in 1901 as the professor of its recently formed School of Design and Ornamentation. He remained at the RCA until 1918.

In both institutions Lethaby set out to implement the beliefs implicit in the Arts and Crafts movement. Prior to his arrival at the RCA, the prevailing ethos there derived from theories which had been put forward in the 1850s by Sir Henry Cole, under whom it was believed that an aptitude for design is best acquired through the observation and drawing of exemplars which could then be applied abstractly to new situations. The Government's *First Report*, of 1852, proposed a pedagogy which was concerned with '... precision, exactness, correct application and imitation of form, careful and severe training and the inculcation of right principles'.[2] Lethaby insisted this approach was flawed and, worse, that in practice it was debased. Designing was thus devoid of any sense of the 'necessity' of the job in hand or of the materials used. He considered that design education at the RCA had become visual learning by rote. It was needlessly boxed in, remote from the circumstances of actual jobs.

Through Lethaby programmes were put into place to reverse this prevailing orthodoxy. At the RCA he had influence over just one department. At his Central School he had, effectively, a *tabula rasa*. Teaching was instituted, based on workshop experience. It was empirical rather than bound to rigid theory. In a lecture given to the RCA in 1901 Lethaby stressed that one cannot learn to design as an activity isolated from the doing of the craft itself:

> The true art is the craft itself, to design for the craft one must first of all be a craftsmen in that art .... A retired cook might accurately design a very good plum pudding, but no one who has never made a plum pudding is likely to design improvements in puddings.

The starting point was the practical making of the particular object. With this approach, a designer undertaking real commissions in professional life would be well placed to proceed to more complex work while shunning dilettante distractions of style. It was for this reason that Lethaby advocated the study of the designed artefacts of the past, not as history to be plundered as 'open forgery', but as a repertoire of design problems and solutions enabling one:

> ... to best perceive the centres of several types ... the tableness of tables, the cupboardness of a cupboard: characteristics which are as necessary to their design as homelikeness [*sic*] to a house. Every utility evolved by man should preserve this direct appeal of necessity, a chair should be as ship-shape and as moving to the imagination as a boat or a fiddle.[3]

It followed, therefore, that Lethaby staffed the Central School with practitioners recruited largely from the Art Workers' Guild. Johnston joined a group of older craftsmen-cum-teachers such as the architect, Halsey Ricardo, the silversmith, Augustus Seward, the mason, R. H. Hood, (his specialism was the construction of stone walls), the cabinet-maker, Charles Spooner, the bookbinder, Douglas Cockerell (he was the brother of Sydney Cockerell), and the enameller, Alexander Fisher. Others arrived in the years following. Noel Rooke, (his father was the painter Thomas Rooke who had been an assistant to Burne-Jones) taught illustration from 1905 and wood-engraving from 1912. John H. Mason taught typography from 1905, and in 1909 he became the head of the Day Technical School of Book Production which made the Central School a source of expertise for the British printing industry.

Under Lethaby, the philosophy of practical instruction also began to prevail at the reconstituted Royal College of Art. Following the recommendations made by Walter Crane during his brief principalship there in 1898–99 four new departments were set up under the direction of a Council of Art. Three of them – Architecture, Mural and Decorative Painting, and Sculpture and Modelling – still met the traditional requirements of teacher-training which was the RCA's main function. But the fourth was an entirely new departure. The School of Design and Ornamentation was Walter Crane's creation. His objective, like Lethaby's, was to introduce 'design and handicraft'. Yet, in spite of his efforts, the RCA was still much run-down. Lethaby regarded his appointment as a challenge. Noel Rooke reported him as saying:

> The RCA is the worst school in England, probably in Europe. So I'm going to it. I feel a call like Livingstone to the heart of darkest Africa. They'll probably try to eat me.[4]

Again, Lethaby brought in several craft teachers from the Art Workers' Guild and from the Central School. Joining Johnston were George Jack to teach wood-carving (formerly he had worked as a furniture designer for William Morris), Mrs Archibald (Grace) Christie to teach tapestry and weaving, Charles Wilson to teach silversmithing, and Christopher Whall to teach stained glass. Moreover, each was commissioned by Lethaby during this period to contribute a volume to his *Artistic Craft Series of Technical Handbooks*. (Mrs Archibald Christie also wrote a philosophical book on decoration.)

In his entry in *Who's Who* for 1937 Johnston clearly regarded this as the period when he attained two of the three principal achievements of his life:

> Studied pen shapes of letters in early MSS., British Museum; Teacher of the first classes in formal penmanship and lettering; designed block letter *based on classical Roman capital proportions* (for London Electric Railways).

The first of the classes to which Johnston referred was at the Central School. It was begun on 21st September 1899. At that time the Central School was located in a set of rambling buildings known as Morley Hall in Regents Street. Only in 1908 did it move to a new building in Southampton Row, the architecture of which involved Lethaby. Invoking William Blake, Johnston began his class in 'some fear and trembling', as he put it, for it was instigated by Lethaby and he felt himself utterly ill-equipped. But Johnston took courage from the thought that he was doing something practical. Initially the idea was turned down within the School administration itself. Johnston recalled:

> I remember Mr Lethaby writing to me: 'Dear Mr. Johnston, They have upset our applecart'. I might say, as far as that went, that it was his applecart, not mine, because I was really greatly afraid of having anything to do with it. Just think of teaching anybody else what I had not taught myself. But the next year Mr Lethaby brought it up again, and the idea of illuminated addresses was brought forward. That clinched the matter. I realised that the thing was practical, and there was something in that practical side though it never stirs my interest as what you might call the pure or spiritual side of the thing does: ... the way I put it for myself when I was beginning was something like this: 'If I can improve the shape of the letter A I shall die happy, or words to that effect...'.[5]

The class lasted two-and-a-half hours a week, each Monday evening, and was small in number. It was made up, in essence, of a peer group very much in keeping with the Arts and Crafts movement's notion of a 'spirit of association', for Johnston's role was tutorial rather than professorial. The notice advertising the classes read:

> ILLUMINATION – a class for the study of writing and ornamentation suitable for addresses and other MSS. will be arranged if sufficient applications are received. The class will meet, under the direction of Mr. Johnson on Monday, from 7 to 9.30 in the Embroidery Room.[6]

His students were largely adult and, for the most part, were already craftsmen in their own right. Among the very first were Thomas Cobden-Sanderson, Noel Rooke, and Florence Kingsford, (she later married Sydney Cockerell). On a surviving class instruction sheet for December 1900 Johnston wrote the names of his pupils. They included H. L[aurence] Christie, [Christopher] Whall, Douglas Cockerell – all teachers at the Central School – M[argaret] Cockerell, (the sister of Douglas and Sydney), Dorothy Walker[7] and Margaret Rooke, (daughters of Emery Walker and Noel Rooke), and the priest, Adrian Fortescue. Graily Hewitt and Percy Smith arrived in 1900. Two of the most significant though later pupils were John Mason and Harold Curwen for both were concerned with the production of books. But the most outstanding pupil was undoubtedly Eric Gill. He joined Johnston's class in 1901.

Unlike the majority of Johnston's early pupils Gill's initial training had not been within the mould of the Arts and Crafts movement. Born in Brighton, in 1882, one of ten children, his family soon moved to Chichester where he studied at the art school. He had recently arrived at the architectural practice of W. H. Caroë in Westminster. Twenty years old when he arrived at the Central School, he was some ten years Johnston's junior. Yet, he rapidly became a colleague and perhaps the closest of his professional friends.

While working with W. H. Caroë Gill had already endeavoured to carve letters. The architect C. H. Townsend, for example, commissioned him to carve an inscription into the wooden beams of the lich-gate of St Mary's at Great Warley in Essex. By 1903, he was commissioned by W. H. Smith's to design the fascia of their high-profile bookshop on the Rue de Rivoli, Paris. But it was Johnston's integrity and his teaching of the interaction of the craftsman with his tools and materials which impressed itself particularly on Gill. In his *Autobiography,* which he wrote in the last year of his life in 1940, Gill recalled his first encounter with his teacher in terms of Platonic love.

> I won't say that I owe everything I know about lettering to him (Johnston) – not that it is very much, for I'm no learned person ... but I owe everything to the foundation that he laid. And his influence was much more than that of a teacher of lettering. He profoundly altered the whole course of my life and all my ways of thinking .... He was a man miraculously deliberate of speech, and equally deliberate in thought .... It will have to be sufficient to say that the first time I saw him writing, and saw the writing that came as he wrote, I had that thrill and tremble of the heart which otherwise I can only remember having had when I first touched her body or saw her hair down for the first time, or when I first heard the plain chant of the church .... I did not know that such beauties could exist. I was struck as by lightning or by a sort of enlightenment ... there are many occasions when you seem to pierce the cloud of unknowing and for a brief second seem to know even as God knows.... On that evening I was thus rapt. It was no mere dexterity, that transported me; it was as though a secret of heaven was being revealed.

For his part Johnston seems to have taken a special interest in Gill's potential. His Notebook for 1899–1904 contains pages on the Roman alphabet of the fifteenth-century Venetian writing master, Tagliente. But the section begins with some hastily jotted thoughts, apparently reminders of things to tell Gill about the Roman alphabet:

> Note to E.G.T. 7 Jan. 1901
> [Argument] on the proportions of the Roman Alphabet; in particular of Tagliente's Letters: Thus:
>
> They are the foundation of all other letters: These are magnificent: They have certain characteristic proportions; these were not affected but evolved naturally: unlike mod: degenerate forms they have good reasons for all their variations: <u>such and such seem</u> to me the reasons (some of them): Study will repay you: Head must be soaked in them, Hand trained, and heart learnt to them. They were the finest: They are the finest & bid fair to be the finest while letters last. They are the Archetypes by which we must be guided.[8]

Between May 1902 and the summer of 1903 Gill shared lodgings with Johnston, at 16 Old Buildings in Lincoln's Inn, Holborn, the largest of the legal quarters of London. Johnston had recently rented the three-room attic chambers through Graily Hewitt, his lawyer-pupil who lived at 23 Old Buildings. It was an intensely social period, enriched by the frequent visits of fellow-pupils such as Graily Hewitt himself, Laurence Christie, Noel Rooke, and Ernest Treglown of

Birmingham Municipal School of Art who took private lessons with Johnston. But it was Gill who was especially affected by Johnston, by his discipline of work and study, by his life style of simple furnishings and food – and perhaps by his cat, Pounce, which could climb out on to the roofs.

Gill's gift for carving letters in stone and in wood became a main strand of his versatile career. It criss-crossed Johnston's own, and on one occasion – the design of the Gill Sans typeface, much inspired by Johnston – stole the limelight from the self-effacing master. In time Gill matured and gained a spiritual independence from Johnston. But at that period he was in thrall to him. In a letter written to him in 1936 following the death of Greta Johnston, Gill recalled his diary for 1903:

> Most Dear Master, When you returned from Scotland on or about the 17th September 1903, I was so moved, excited, all of a tremble, that I stood in the middle of the street outside what was then the Central School ... so that I might see you through the lighted window of the room where the writing class was. I was so overwhelmingly in love with my girl and with you. Your marriage was a type of all heavenly fruitious consumations.[*sic*] I had to look at you from a distance, in secret, before I dared to approach ... in my diary Sept. 17, I wrote only: 'Johnston has returned and is married'. [The marriage took place in Scotland in August 1903.] And on Sept. 22nd 'to see Mr. and Mrs. Johnston'.[9]

Following his marriage and his return to London, Johnston moved to new, though still modest, accommodation at 4 Gray's Inn Square, Holborn, another of the Inns of Court. During this period, 1903–05, he was the neighbour of William Lethaby who had his architectural practice at 2 Gray's Inn Square. (Philip Webb, Morris's fellow-designer and architect, also lived in Gray's Inn.) Gill, meantime, remained at Lincoln's Inn with his brother, MacDonald, who was also an artist with an interest in lettering.

With Gill, these early pupils made up the first generation of the Johnstonian tradition. Graily Hewitt learned to become an accomplished gilder as well as developing a successful career as a calligrapher. Following the example of Johnston's exploration of medieval manuscripts, he revived the medieval technique of illuminating. In 1902, Graily Hewitt taught a second class in calligraphy at the Central School and from 1911 he succeeded Johnston there altogether. In a manner not dissimilar to Cobden-Sanderson, he, too, was inspired by the thought of setting up a medieval-style scriptorium. And like Johnston, Graily Hewitt was commissioned to provide calligraphic initials for private press books. In 1902, he worked for St. John Hornby's Ashendene Press on the biblical *Song of Songs*. It is worth mentioning here, too, that Graily Hewitt also designed a typeface for the Gregynog Press and wrote *Lettering*, a book on the practice of calligraphy which was published in 1930. It was second in influence only to Johnston's own *Writing & Illuminating, & Lettering*. The first sentence of its preface acknowledged his debt to Johnston, '... to him, as my first teacher, I owe more than most'.

Percy Smith studied under Johnston during his spell of teaching at the Camberwell School of Arts and Crafts from 1900. A 'brilliant exponent of the Johnstonian principles',[10] Percy Smith in due course returned to Camberwell to teach lettering himself. A comparable figure to Graily Hewitt, he made a significant impact as an inscriptional lettering artist.

Percy Smith occasioned the only serious altercation which Johnston experienced in his entire professional life. In 1908 he published a teaching portfolio entitled *Lettering and Writing*, which Johnston recognised as a plagiarism of his own planned portfolio, *Manuscript and Inscription Letters*. The incident precipitated the publication of the Johnston portfolio in 1909. Relations between them were severely ruptured; only years later did Johnston feel reconciled.

Noel Rooke was another of Lethaby's close friends and colleagues. In 1935 he became Vice-Principal of the Central School. He worked first with Douglas Cockerell on the wood-engraved illustration for his handbook on bookbinding. He then worked with Johnston on his *Writing & Illuminating, & Lettering* project, engraving the wood blocks for many of its illustrations. Johnston appreciated wood-engraving greatly. In all probability he acquired this interest from Emery Walker who was familiar with the medium from early German printed books and from William Morris who used wood-engraved illustrations in his Kelmscott Press books. Along with Gill, Johnston actually experimented with wood-engraving himself.[11] (Fig. 45). His handbook incorporated some of Bewick's engraved vignettes to demonstrate principles of illustration.

Noel Rooke rethought the use of wood-engraving in its own right rather than as a means of reproduction of drawings for book illustration. But the impetus behind this development had actually come from Johnston: 'Inspired by the thought of Johnston's calligraphy, I started in 1905 to make wood engravings on the same basis.'[12]

Thomas Cobden-Sanderson, who was already sixty years old in 1898, had especially close affinities with Johnston. Retired as a lawyer, he had already taken up bookbinding. He was described by Sir William Rothenstein (the Principal of the RCA from 1920) as a man: '... possessed of a demonic spirit of faith in the power of human idealism'. Cobden-Sanderson's convictions helped to inspire Johnston. He affirmed that:

> Good craftsmanship is necessary because it brings to him who passionately desires it the ripe and sound fruits of wisdom and understanding, respect and tolerance.[13]

It was Cobden-Sanderson who awakened in Johnston an interest in typography and printing. In 1900 he was preparing to embark on his printing enterprise, the Doves Press. He engaged Emery Walker as a partner and lettering consultant. In his need to have a suitable typeface for his press he realised that calligraphy was the prerequisite to good type design. He was therefore prompted to join Johnston's 'writing and ornamentation' class, taking his two children along with him. As in the case of Gill, the impact that Johnston had on Cobden-Sanderson in the process of doing calligraphy was mesmeric. He exclaimed to his son during one class: 'It is like watching some strange bird.' So reported Johnston in his tribute to Cobden-Sanderson of 1929.[14]

Johnston, for his part, was deeply influenced at this time by Cobden-Sanderson (Fig. 46). In 1900 he read for the first time Cobden-Sanderson's tract,

Fig 45. Johnston's wood engravings

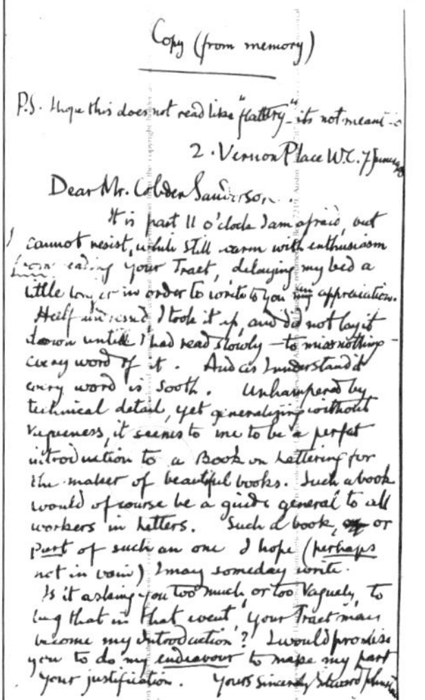

Copy (from memory)

P.S. I hope this does not read like "flattery" – its not meant

2 . Vernon Place W.C. 7 June

Dear Mr. Cobden Sanderson . .

It is past 11 o'clock I am afraid, but I cannot resist, while still warm with enthusiasm from reading your Tract, delaying my bed a little longer in order to write to you an appreciation. Half undressed I took it up, and did not lay it down until I had read slowly – to miss nothing – every word of it. And as I understand it every word is sooth. Unhampered by technical detail, yet generalizing without vagueness, it seems to me to be a perfect introduction to a Book on Lettering for the maker of beautiful books. Such a book would of course be a guide general to all workers in letters. Such a book, or part of such an one I hope (perhaps not in vain) I may someday write.

Is it asking you too much, or too vaguely, to beg that in that event, your Tract may become my introduction? I would promise you to do my endeavour to make my part your justification. Yours sincerely Edward Johnston

Fig. 46. Johnston's copy (from memory) of his letter to Cobden-Sanderson, June 1900, in response to his reading his Tract, *The Ideal Book*. It was printed at the Doves press,1901. Johnston's letters at the Harry Ransom Humanities Research Center. (Courtesy of the University of Texas at Austin, Texas.)

known as *The Ideal Book, or Book Beautiful*. (Cobden-Sanderson was to actually print his seminal tract in February 1901; it was the fourth item on the list of his Doves Press.) In his rush of enthusiasm for its doctrine that calligraphy was the basis of fine printing Johnston wrote immediately to Cobden-Sanderson from his lodgings in Vernon Place. It is in this letter, dated the 7th June 1900, that Johnston indicates for the first time his aspiration to write a handbook on lettering:

> It is past 11 o'clock I am afraid, but I cannot resist, while still warm with enthusiasm from reading your Tract, delaying my bed a little longer in order to write to you an appreciation. Half undressed, I took it up, and did not lay it down until I had read it slowly – to miss nothing – every word of it. And as I understand it every word is sooth. Unhampered by technical detail, yet generalising without vagueness, it seems to be a perfect introduction to a Book on Lettering for the maker of beautiful books. Such a book would of course be a guide general to all workers in Letters. Such a book, or part of such a one I hope (perhaps not in vain) I may someday write.
>
> Is it asking you too much, or too vaguely, to beg that in that event, your Tract may become my introduction? I would promise you to do my endeavour to make my part your justification. Yours sincerely Edward Johnston.[15]

The friendship and partnership between Johnston and Cobden-Sanderson blossomed. The calligraphic work that Johnston, with Eric Gill and Graily Hewitt, were commissioned to do for the Doves Press is better discussed in the context of the private press movement in Chapter Eleven. It was due to Cobden-Sanderson that Johnston at this time seriously toyed with the idea of commercial printing (starting with an edition of the classics), type-designing, and punch-cutting. He was dissuaded from the last by Emery Walker who warned him of its complexity.

Of other early pupils, Laurence Christie later became a teacher of calligraphy at the Central School and, like Johnston, he moved to Ditchling where he became his lifelong friend. Douglas Cockerell had developed great skill as a bookbinder – he had learned the craft at the Doves Bindery – which led to the prestigious commission to bind one of the bibliographical treasures of the British Museum, the eighth-century *Lindisfarne Gospels*.[16] Florence Kingsford was commissioned by St. John Hornby to design initial letters and illumination for the Ashendene Press. For example she worked alongside Graily Hewitt, undertaking the illumination of his calligraphy for the celebrated edition of the *Song of Songs*.

In the longer term, the achievements of John Mason and Harold Curwen are, arguably, among the most significant of all Johnston's pupils from the Central School for through them his standards of excellence passed into the domain of commercial printing and thus benefited a wider public at large. John Mason had been drawn to Johnston's classes through his work as the principal compositor at the Doves Press. Harold Curwen, later a director of the Curwen Press, enrolled in Johnston's calligraphy classes at the Central School in 1907. He was joined shortly after by his colleague, Henry Ball. Johnston's teaching inspired them in the jobbing printing at Curwen's, making it one of the most respected presses of its time.[17]

Johnston's calligraphy classes at the RCA took place from 1901, on Monday afternoons in the Lower Design Room on the ground floor of the building. (It is now part of the Henry Cole Wing of the Victoria & Albert Museum.) Called 'evening classes', they were timetabled for 4.00–6.00 p.m. The classes became an institution of legendary proportions in the minds of the students at the RCA for it was the platform of Johnston's enduring influence as a teacher. All students were required to attend during their time there. The more interested and talented of them were also tutored by Johnston when the formal sessions, packed with fifty people or more, were over. With larger groups of younger students than in his classes at the Central School, Johnston's teaching technique changed to the lecture/ demonstration format. A letter written by Johnston dated the 23rd May 1901 describes the new situation:

> ... at S. Kensington I have a v. big Room with a gt blackboard worked by pulleys, and a platform, where I stand and sit and look down on the ... embryo scribes below.[18]

The blackboard demonstrations were carried out with specially cut chalks which were reported by a pupil, Dorothy Mahoney, to be custom-made, with the dimensions of four-and-a-half inches long, one inch wide, and a half an inch thick.[19] (115 mm x 30 mm x 15 mm) Johnston owned that his students would clap these 'performances', when he left his 'pulpit'.[20]

A number of other records and impressions of the Monday afternoon lectures were made through the years. They are valuable in shedding light on Johnston's methods and manner of teaching. They are therefore worth setting out here though they reach beyond the date of 1905. Among the most treasured are the photographs taken of Johnston's blackboard 'notes' by Violet Hawkes in 1926. (Fig. 47).This photographic archive,[21] together with his handbook and his portfolio *Manuscript and Inscription Letters* of 1909 indicate Johnston's teaching of letter-forms. Violet Hawkes thought Johnston's lectures:

> ... an intellectual delight, gripping the attention of the students throughout. He was expounding profound principles and high ideals, and describing a complex technique; and, because he selected every word and phrase to express precisely what he meant, his English was exact; but it was so perfectly natural; there was no hint of pedantry. He never talked to impress people, but because he wanted to put his meaning across. 'Now, is that clear? Because I want it to be clear'...[22]

One of Johnston's students between 1924–27 was Thomas Swindlehurst. He indicates that Johnston's teaching consisted then of a practical session followed by a lecture and demonstration.[23] In the talk which he gave to the Society of Scribes and Illuminators late in his life, in 1965, he especially recalled the demonstrations:

> He was rather a frail man, slow moving and very slow of speech but every word he spoke was most carefully and thoughtfully chosen to give the exact meaning he wished to convey.... We gained enormously and received most valuable instructions from his blackboard illustration during his weekly lecture, of about one and a half hours duration from four o'clock each Monday. It was an unforgettable experience to see him write with flat white chalk-letters several inches high with absolute precision and unfaltering mastery on the wall blackboard.[24]

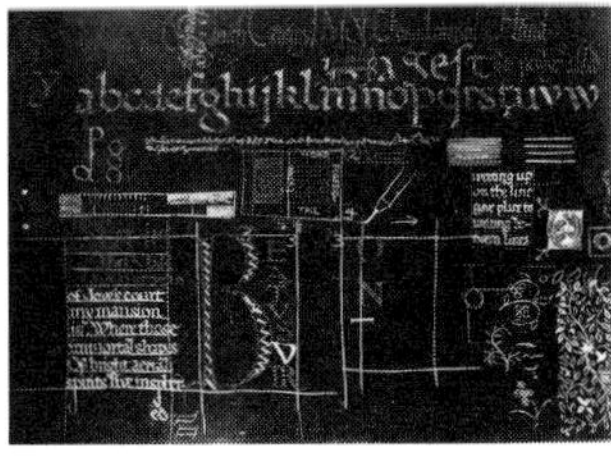

Fig. 47. Johnston's blackboard lesson.

In time, Johnston felt the need of assistants. He was joined by a succession of his more experienced students who were continuing their studies and were devotees of his teaching methods. Bound by the ties of what might be called, with greater or lesser justification, a 'Johnston admiration circle', they included Violet Hawkes, Dorothy Bishop, Irene Wellington, Dorothy Mahoney, Madelyn Walker and the less-known Hilda Gulliver and Margery Raisbeck. Irene Wellington, a contemporary of Swindlehurst between 1925–30, was one of Johnston's most accomplished pupils. She recalled her teacher in an interview with the artist and wood-engraver John Farleigh, made in 1950:

> There was nobody like Johnston. The way he opened up a subject with innumerable apt digressions was most illuminating. He talked about so many things, and with his rare mind he related them to his subject in an extraordinary way. For instance, he compared the ordinary book with a regiment. The small black text would be the privates, other ranks would be represented by capitals, changes of scale and colour, up to the commanding officer.... He taught mainly by talking, although he would show alphabets or a few words for grouping.[25]

Irene Wellington stressed further points about Johnston's teaching which are confirmed by other accounts. He taught a 'traditional standard alphabet as a basic form', that is to say the 'Foundational Hand' based on the tenth-century Ramsey Psalter script. (Johnston also called it a 'later Caroline Minuscule'.) She further stressed the exacting standards Johnston insisted upon. 'If one doesn't set oneself a rigidly high standard, one cannot get very far. That, I think, is the point of the Johnston tradition. He insisted upon absolute pitch.' Priscilla Johnston reported Irene Wellington as having said:

> No pride was left in you after you had sustained his scrutiny, that slow positive remorseless analysis, so unanswerably right. He seemed completely detached, concerned only with the objective truth, not with whether you could take it. He assumed you could.[26]

The advice he gave the novice calligrapher was: 'You are to free to make your statement of what the author is saying, but must never forget his intention; the main point of the writing is that it must be readable'.[27]

Another of Johnston's pupils who wrote down his recollections was Edward Sutton. He attended the RCA probably in the 1930s, when he became Johnston's friend. In a lecture to the British Typographers Guild in 1949 he described him as:

> ... saintly and dignified but without undue reserve. He often appeared to be physically tired. It came as something of a shock to discover he was a very clear and vigorous thinker. He was supremely honest and he had a subtle sense of humour that was never absent. He won and kept the respect of his students all the time. He had the remarkable gift of making friends not merely acquaintances.[28]

It is illuminating, however, to return to one of the very earliest sets of impressions. The young German, Anna Simons, was, with Gill, Johnston's most brilliant pupil from the early 1900s. Coming from Prussia, she found it necessary to study at the RCA from 1896 because the Prussian art schools at that time refused entry to women. She wrote:

> A never-to-be-forgotten event were Mr Johnston's demonstrations on the blackboard. His letters and Initials, freely written with chalk, always bore the mark of original and spontaneous creation. To his Uncial and Half-Uncials he very soon added – much to the chagrin of his first pupils who thought they had learnt all there was to learn – slanted pen forms adapted from a 10th-century Winchester MS., both minuscules and majuscules.[29]

In 1934, Johnston, in turn, wrote an appreciation of her which reveals the qualities which he considered to be a priority:

> Anna Simons was one of the best students (perhaps in some things the best student) I have ever taught. She had the natural aptitudes for the work and a sincerity and directness of outlook which enabled her to master the essential elements very rapidly, and, later, to develop it into her own practical and beautiful work.'[30]

In part, Johnston's tribute was in recognition of Anna Simons' work as the translator of his handbook of 1906. It was published in 1910, as *Schreibschrift, Zierschrift und Angewandte Schrift*. In the following year, 1911–12, she also translated Johnston's *Manuscript and Inscription Letters* as *Hand-und Inschrift Alphabet*. In an article of 1938 she reminisced about the experience of translating Johnston's writings which, again, speaks of the quality of his thinking:

> During the translation of his book I became deeply impressed by its unfaltering thoroughness and clear thinking and the simple and lucid words used to deal with intricate and hitherto unsolved problems .... I have always been grateful and proud to have been a pupil of this great artist and teacher, and favoured that I was instrumental in bringing his methods and principles to my own country.[31]

The substance of Johnston's teaching in this period was presented in *Writing & Illuminating, & Lettering*. It was Johnston's single most important commission during this period and a further demonstration of Lethaby's insight in recognising his gifts. From 1901 Lethaby pursued his idea to make the knowledge of his newly-recruited teachers at the Central School and the RCA available to a wider public by commissioning the ten volumes of the *Artistic Craft Series of Technical Handbooks*. Lethaby believed such handbooks would be a practicable equivalent to the master/apprentice relationship. He intended Johnston's to be the first volume, although Johnston was so long in writing it that Douglas Cockerell's *Bookbinding, and the Care of Books* turned out to be the first.[32] A passage from the preface which Lethaby wrote for the series spelt out his aims. It is couched in the spirit of his reforms at the Central School and at the RCA:

> In the first place, we wish to provide trustworthy text-books of workshop practice, from the points of view of experts who have critically examined the methods current in the shops ... are prepared to say what is good workmanship, and to set up a standard of quality in the crafts which are more especially associated with design. Secondly, ... we hope to treat design an an essential part of good workmanship. During the last century ... there was a tendency to look on 'design' as a mere matter of 'appearance'. Such 'ornamentation' as there was was usually obtained by following in a mechanical way a drawing provided by an artist who often knew little of the technical processes in production. With the critical attention given to the crafts by Ruskin and Morris, it came to be seen that it was impossible to detach design from craft in this way, and

> that true design is an inseparable element of good quality … and that ornamentation itself was rather an exuberance of fine workmanship than a matter of merely abstract lines.… Proper ornamentation may be defined as a language addressed to the eye; it is pleasant thought expressed in the speech of the tool.

Aside from its historical information and technical instruction, Johnston's *Writing & Illuminating, & Lettering* is one of the brightest instances of his involvement with the Arts and Crafts movement. Written between 1902–06, the book was entirely Johnston's concept. The four hundred-odd pages of the loose-leaf draft with its instructions to the printers (Ballantyne's of Edinburgh), which is now held at the V&A, also show Johnston to have been largely responsible for its detailed design.[33] Yet he also planned for contributions from others – from Douglas Cockerell on the binding of manuscripts, from Graily Hewitt on gilding, from Eric Gill on the cutting of inscriptions in stone, and from Noel Rooke who undertook the wood-engraved illustrations. It was intended that Ernest Treglown would also contribute a section on miniatures. In that sense Johnston conceived it in the spirit of cooperative craft work. Additionally, Johnston used extensive quotations from the writings of other lettering experts, notably Emery Walker, Cobden-Sanderson, and Maunde Thompson. In the preface he acknowledged his gratitude to these writers and to William Lethaby for his editor's preface.

Another indication is the wide-ranging scope and practical nature of the handbook, for Johnston was aware of the underlying correspondence between the crafts. Following Cobden-Sanderson's essay, *The Ideal Book or Book Beautiful*, he stressed the value of calligraphy for the design of the printed book. He also recommended its relevance for commercial typography, for lettering artists, and for commercial advertisers. Johnston insisted on reaching the highest standards. His preface ends:

> The production of good work will inevitably create a demand; and finally, the value of Quality is always recognised – sooner or later but inevitably – and whatever practical reasons we may hear in favour of Quantity, the value of Quality is gaining recognition every day in commerce and even in art there sooner or later we shall know we can afford the best.

Another consideration is the interest in historical exemplars which Johnston shared with the Arts and Crafts movement. In the preface he advocates acquiring knowledge of historical letter-forms so as to help cultivate a 'modern and beautiful technique'. Yet he clarified his views concerning the use of past methods and styles in very precise terms. Like Lethaby, he found value in referring to them but eschewed their mere imitation. The preface to *Writing & Illuminating, & Lettering* is inspiring:

> For all things – materials, tools, methods – are waiting to serve us and we have only to find the 'spell' that will act the whole universe a-making for us.

Enlarging on this theme, the preface also cautioned the reader:

> It is as well to recognise at once the fact that mere taking to pieces, or analysing, followed by 'putting together' is only a means of becoming acquainted with the

CALLIGRAPHY
& ILLUMINATION

A paper read before the Society of Arts on the 31st January 1905, with additional matter & illustrations by the Author. 29. Novr. 1905.

The development of the book-hands from the Roman alphabet, shewing the growth of varied letter forms for use or ornament, is the key to the practical study of calligraphy & illumination.

Doubtless the forms of the letters of the fine inscriptions in stone and the forms used in writing, acted and reacted upon each other, so that the pen, the chisel, and the brush all contributed to the development of the perfect forms of the Roman Capitals used in the beginning of the Christian era.

Formal[1] writing may be said to begin with the "Square Capitals": these and kindred forms were used till about the beginning

DVLCIAD
SPIRANS

[1] The formal penmanship here considered

beginning of the fifth century. Though it had not yet become customary to separate the individual words, this writing – 1500 years old – is essentially legible: the vague popular accusation of the old "crabbedness and unreadableness" more truly applies to the hands of ourselves and our friends.

The beautifully rounded Uncial letter of the 5th century is a truer pen-form than the "Sq. Cap.").

CONF
ITEB
DIRE
Fig. 2.

The "Half-Uncial" – or Semi-Uncial – writing of the sixth century is derived from mixed Uncial (see above) & cursive forms (see below. IV).

half uncial
Fig. 3.

The "Cursive" or informal ordinary writing of the Roman capitals, with a stylus, produced the "small letters." These were adopted by the scribes and after 200 years were universally used for books.

Fig. 4.

The

The Roman missionaries brought the Roman "Half-Uncial" writing to IRELAND, and the Irish missionaries brought their writing to ENGLAND in the 7th. century. The "Book of Kells" and the "Durham Book" are the marvellous works of the Irish and English penmen

About this time the thin strokes of the letters became approximately horizontal, but a reversion to the earlier and easier method of holding the pen "slanted" led to the narrow and angular writing of the 12th. and succeeding centuries

"STRAIGHT PEN" "SLANTED PEN"

Thin Stroke

Fig. 5. Fig. 6.

Cut or Held to give approximately horizontal thins, and round, open, highly finished letters.

gives oblique thicks and thins & narrow forms, more freely made.

oinx oinx

The

Fig. 48. One of Johnston's specimen lettering sheets used in his classes at the Central School and the Royal College of Art dated the 27th October 1902. Uncial letter-forms.
(Courtesy of the Crafts Study Centre Collection and Archive, Farnham, Surrey.)

mechanism of construction and will not reproduce the original beauty of a thing: it is an education for work, but all work which is honest and straightforward has a beauty and freshness of its own.

Equally revealing, however, is the handbook's own quiet economy of style. Its Caslon typeface, its format and its binding follow the precedent set by the volume, *Arts and Crafts Essays*. The prose style of Johnston's handbook is a model of plain speaking and its wood-engravings are a model of plain illustration. Following the precedent of Morris, Johnston recommended wood-engraving as the medium for illustration because it combines well with letterpress printing. Without a superfluous flourish of word or image, *Writing & Illuminating, & Lettering* enacts his own – and Lethaby's – strictures against ill-conceived ornamentation.

Although the *Artistic Craft Series of Technical Handbooks* was Lethaby's concept the unsung hero of the overall project was the publisher, John Hogg, who stood to bear the financial risk. The first edition of *Writing & Illuminating, & Lettering*, for example, ran into two thousand copies of which five hundred were issued in USA, where Johnston at this time was wholly unknown. Virtually nothing is known of John Hogg, beyond the fact that he belonged to a line of publishers that goes back into the nineteenth century. His office was at 13 Paternoster Row in the City of London. But clearly he had strong convictions in the Arts and Crafts movement in order to underwrite Lethaby's enthusiasms. He also published some of Lethaby's early lectures.[34]

John Hogg also had an interest in commissioning from Johnston further teaching material dealing with lettering. He published the work *Manuscript and Inscription Letters*, in 1909. The portfolio consisted of sixteen plates showing historical examples of lettering including the alphabet used on Trajan's Column. Ten of these were calligraphed by Johnston 'based on the class-sheets and class-notes given to my students during the past ten years …'. Four others were by Gill showing inscriptional lettering. The sixteenth plate was the Caslon typeface. The portfolio was intended, Johnston said, '… as a working supplement to my Handbook, "Writing & Illuminating, & Lettering", but they form a complete scheme in themselves.' Unlike the handbook, the scale of the specimens was suitable for copying, though in his paragraph 'A Theory of Calligraphy' Johnston cautioned: 'Alphabets wrested from their original places in MSS. and Inscriptions are in danger of becoming mere 'copies', or crystallisations, that may breed literal copies and inscriptions without spirit'. It ends: '… all Rules must give way to Truth and Freedom.'

John Hogg nurtured another proposal that Johnston should write a further handbook, *Formal Penmanship*. It was one of a number of ideas up to about 1916. He was also on the advisory committee behind the publication of the journal, *The Imprint*, in 1913.

In their modesty, Johnston's handbook and portfolio were the distant – and, at five shillings (25p) for the handbook, the affordable – cousins of the restrained typographical style that Emery Walker advised for the Doves Press books. A significant detail that links the two is Johnston's use of the ampersand, as revealed even in his two titles *Writing & Illuminating, & Lettering* and *Manuscript & Inscription Letters*. This convention was common in the medieval period. Its conscious reuse as a typographical device occurred first in Morris's Kelmscott Press books. Emery Walker had advocated its use in lectures and articles written in the late 1890s.[35] It is said that Johnston was particularly fond of the pattern of the ampersand, a sentiment he shared with Morris.

Johnston would certainly have seen printing under way at the Doves Press which, at this time, was located on the ground floor at 1 Hammersmith Terrace. For in 1905 he moved from Gray's Inn Square, to live at house number 3, just next-door-but-one to Cobden-Sanderson's Doves Press.

He moved into his new home at 3 Hammersmith Terrace on the 31st March 1905. He had heard of its availability through Cobden-Sanderson. His landlord was Emery Walker. The house was one of a row of sixteen making up a distinctive Georgian terrace. Narrow-fronted but deep-set, the houses are on three floors with gardens sloping down to the river Thames. At that period Hammersmith Terrace was an appealing enclave in a quarter of West London largely made up by streets of high density housing and small workshops. On the riverside itself were wharfs, factories, and a lead mill. It had, Johnston said, '… the advantages of the country (very nearly) and town combined'. The Terrace connects Upper Mall to Chiswick Mall, which continued as a riverside walk up to Chiswick and Kew, then scarcely more than villages. The Thames meant a great deal to Johnston. He wondered at its varying 'graciousness' but was impressed, too, that it was a natural resource bearing the imprint of man. In a short article he wrote in 1911 for the *RCA Students Magazine* Johnston expressed his sense of place. A bookseller, he said, remembered Hammersmith as a 'country village'. John Ruskin had visited the very house he now occupied: '… he came here (and sat in this very room by the way) and gave the place his benediction of praise'. And then Johnston spoke of:

> … the backs of these houses, into which all their life has crept, look on glorious London River, with its friendly tugs and various barges. The iron tanks so imposing in their cargoes of coal or wood and many curious bales to be guessed at. … We … shall remember thy great water, O Silver River, Oh river, grey or golden, or crimson dyed by the sun, you in all your moods have life. So the neighbours of the Terrace live merry or sad in it, moulding their rooms a little to their liking as its patience and grim graciousness allow; truly, half of each house is the moving river and uninterrupted sky. Perchance they pity those who, having no such River of Life at their doors, nor shiny sky at their windows, live where smoky brick calls to smoky brick – even in such sad houses life holds up its head.[36]

Johnston was well placed in Hammersmith thanks, too, to the company of other craftsmen and artists who were living close by. Many of these he already knew from his circle of friends at the Central School and the RCA. One was Christopher Whall who taught stained glass at both schools and wrote *Stained Glass Work* in 1905. Like Johnston, he was a protégé of Lethaby. He was Johnston's counterpart in that he revived the techniques of medieval 'glass painting'. His daughter, Veronica, became Johnston's pupil at the Central School, aged only thirteen. His wife,

Florence, kept a diary, an entry in which shows Johnston on Boat Race day, March 31st 1900, visiting Hammersmith Terrace and Whall's home nearby, at 19 Ravenscourt Road.

> Invitations from Mr. Spooner & Mr. Cobden-Sanderson. Boat Race – Children & Jessie went to see it from Mr. Spooner's Garden – Allie took Miss Lee & an American lady. Christopher went to Mr. Cobden-Sanderson's to see it – I walked home with Mr. Johnson (*sic*) the gentleman who teaches Veronica at the class for illumination at the Arts and Crafts School. He came in and had tea – and so did Miss Lee and their friends – All stayed some time. Cambridge won.[37]

In the period following his arrival in Hammersmith the craft community there was, by and large, an extension of those existing ones. In turn, it became the springboard for the more cohesive group which began to form in Ditchling from approximately 1912. By this time, now in his mid-thirties, Johnston's contacts with his fellow craftsmen and artists in Hammersmith helped launch him into a period of cooperative development, and this in spite of one of his friends there, Arthur Romney Green, who was moved to say of him '... he had the charm of an obscure and reluctant oracle'.

In the Terrace, Johnston lived next door but one to Cobden-Sanderson, who was at house number 1. (He later lived at River House on the Upper Mall.) The typographer and gravure printer, Emery Walker, was at house number 7.[38] Both had prestigious craft businesses a little distance downstream, on the Upper Mall. In 1893 Cobden-Sanderson located his Doves Bindery at 15 Upper Mall. (It was so-called because it was situated next to the Doves Inn.) One of Cobden-Sanderson's objectives had been to obtain work from Morris's Kelmscott Press, nearby. He also undertook the repair of damaged bindings from Morris's growing private library. He employed Sydney Cockerell's brother, Douglas. In 1900, he merged his newly established Doves Press into this bindery.

Emery Walker had built up a pioneering photogravure business specialising in the printing of pictures, maps, and illustrations for books. It was located in a fine Georgian property, Sussex House, at 12–14 Upper Mall which is virtually opposite the Doves Bindery. With Morris's former home, Kelmscott House, at 26 Upper Mall and with his Kelmscott Press not so long since gone from the premises next door, this stretch of the river embankment at Hammersmith was the Mecca of the Arts and Crafts movement. It had been called the 'most civilised two miles in England'.

There were a number of other residents of Hammersmith Terrace who were friends or acquaintances of Johnston. The most celebrated of these was perhaps Morris's daughter, May Morris, who lived at house number 8. She ran an embroidery workshop there and taught at the Central School until 1908. A closer friend of Johnston was Edward Spencer, a metal craftsmen who lived at house number 10.[39] He belonged to the Artificers' Guild. It had its workshop in Oil Mill Lane, off the Terrace, and a showroom run by Gertrude Spink which was first in Maddox Street and then in Conduit Street, in the West End.

Beyond Hammersmith Terrace other local acquaintances of Johnston included the painter Frank Brangwyn, who was reaching the height of his fame. He lived at Temple Lodge, in Queen Caroline Street, east of Upper Mall just downriver from Hammersmith Bridge (then quite newly-built) in premises somewhat grander than those in Hammersmith Terrace. Like Gill, Johnston, and Pepler, Brangwyn also moved to Ditchling, though not until 1918. Another friend was the painter Sir William Richmond, who lived at Beavor Lodge, in Beavor Lane, another spacious house inset a little from the river just about midway between the Upper Mall and the Terrace.

Yet another well-known Hammersmith craftsman was the metalworker and enamellist, Harold Stabler, who lived with his artist wife, Phoebe, at 36 Upper Mall. Stabler was a colleague with Johnston, teaching in the School of Design at the RCA. In due course he found the tenets of the Arts and Crafts movement too constricting and in 1915 he became a founder member of the Design and Industries Association – the DIA.

A closer friend still of Johnston was the printer Gerard Meynell who, from 1915, lived at 37 St. Peter's Square, Hammersmith. He was from a Catholic family and, like his brother Francis Meynell, he had an interest in fine-quality commercial printing. He owned and ran the Westminster Press. In 1913 Johnston provided Gerard Meynell with a titling alphabet which was used for the printing of initial capitals in the journal, *The Imprint*. In 1915 he printed Johnston's early piece of writing *A Carol and Other Rhymes* as well as an accompanying volume, Hilary Pepler's satirical book *The Devil's Devices or Control versus Service*. Gerard Meynell introduced Johnston to Frank Pick, the publicity manager of the London Electric Railways Company which led to the commission for the block letter alphabet for the London Underground signing system. In the 1920s the Meynells also moved down to Ditching.

Following Johnston, late in 1905, Eric Gill arrived in Hammersmith from his studio in Chelsea. For his new one he made use of a former stable in Terrace Court, a lane which ran off Hammersmith Terrace just opposite number 8. He lived close by, in a small terraced house at 20 Black Lion Lane.[40] His business partner was Laurence Christie, who had been Johnston's pupil at the Central School. Together, in May, 1907, they set up a company called 'Gill and Christie, Inscriptional Carvers and Calligraphers'. Christie appears to have lodged with Gill. Additionally, Gill took on the sixteen-year-old Joseph Cribb as an apprentice lettering carver. His father, Herbert Cribb, was also a Hammersmith resident who worked as a cartographer for Emery Walker. It was Walker who recommended the young Christie to Gill. Both he and Joseph Cribb eventually moved down to Ditchling in order to keep working with Gill.

Aside from Gill, the new resident in Hammersmith who became important in Johnston's life was Douglas Pepler (at that time not yet known by his Catholic name of Hilary). Pepler was a professional social worker and consultant for the London County Council. He had also been a prospective Member of Parliament for the Labour Party for that borough. Involved in social work in Hammersmith (it was through his initiative that meals were introduced into schools in the Hammersmith area) and in writing social tracts, he moved with his family into 14 Hammersmith Terrace in 1907. It was his understanding of social deprivation in Hammersmith, especially child delinquency, unemployment, and poverty, that lay behind his part in setting up the Hampshire House Social Club for Working Men with its associated workshops. It evolved between 1905–16. In this pioneering social experiment, Pepler was joined by his Quaker colleague, the architect Frederick Rowntree. He also lived in Hammersmith Terrace, at numbers 10–11.

At that time Pepler was also a Quaker and therefore shared a common background with Johnston. Moreover, he developed ideas about craft from Johnston and Gill which were broadly parallel to theirs. His new awareness of craft was soon incorporated into his social work project. There, workshop facilities were made available and crafts were encouraged as an essential part of the vision to provide unemployed working men with a sense of fulfilment through making. Part of its interest lies in the way Johnston responded to the project, a reaction which was entirely characteristic of his manner of thought.

While Pepler came progressively into the orbit of Johnston and Gill, he also exerted an influence. Mutually the three absorbed social, political, and aesthetic ideas. Like Pepler, Gill joined the Fabian Society. It was the beginning of a three-way partnership which was further strengthened when they settled in Ditchling.

Their friendship as artists and thinkers was also underpinned by the family ties built up by their wives and infant children who, by keeping open houses, mixed spontaneously. In her biography, Priscilla Johnston wrote of one consequence of their friendship. So preoccupying were the mutual interests of the three husbands that their wives – Greta Johnston, Ethel Gill, and Clare Pepler – dubbed themselves the 'letter box widows' due to the protracted discussions which would ensue when, late in the evening, the three met at the letter box to catch the last collection. It was the same letter box, incidentally, from which Johnston, in the company of Gill, sent off the final printer's galleyproofs of *Writing & Illuminating, & Lettering* on the 21st August 1906. (Possibly it was the old-style one which still exists in Upper Mall.) Pepler, too, has an intimate word-portrait of Johnston at this time which takes its cue from that postbox. It occurs in his reminiscences, *Forty Years Back*, published in the magazine, *The Register*, in 1949:

> Johnston was one of three leavers-to-the-last-minute in posting his mail. He always paused after his script had descended down the pillar (one of those red round variety about four feet high) to roll a cigarette and light it, probably from a match which, having nearly burnt out, he would take by its charred end and succeed in doing so from the last few flickers of its stump. Often, and no less seriously, he would achieve a light from a tinder, set glowing by a flint spark; he carried this flint gadget about him for many years – often, I suspect, that he might be able to entertain the children by playing with fire.... The midnight meetings at the pillar box were slow, however, in leading to these profound intimacies ... the first link to be discovered between us was 'lettering'.... This discovery placed me in the position of a pupil, than which there was no better for getting the best out of Edward Johnston....[41]

In the absence of any memoirs by Johnston himself it is such vignettes which give insights into his life and thought at this period. In this way, yet another newly-arrived to Hammersmith, Arthur Romney Green, is an important source.

Romney Green was a significant if lesser known figure in the fraternity of the Arts and Crafts movement. A furniture designer and maker, he had a particular admiration for the work of Sidney Barnsley and Ernest Gimson. And he evidently held Johnston in considerable awe, coming under his influence during the two years or so, between approximately 1909 and 1911, that he was living off Hammersmith Terrace.

Romney Green arrived in Hammersmith virtually penniless, owing to the breakdown of his marriage. He left his furniture workshop and home behind in Haslemere, in Surrey, where he belonged to a smaller Arts and Crafts movement community. His companion was Bertha Wallace, the estranged wife of the socialist, Harold Wallace. Romney Green had himself been a member of the Independent Labour Party at Haslemere. They lodged in straitened but improving circumstances in the loft of Gill's former workshop until approximately 1911, when they were invited by Gertrude Spink, of the Artificers' Guild, to share her newly acquired home. She had set up home in a building, formerly a pub, called The Ship, on the riverside at Strand-on-the-Green, Kew, some three miles upstream from Hammersmith.

At Ship House, Romney Green led an active intellectual life focused on the Sunday evening soirées held there, which the Oxford social historians G. D. H. Cole and Maurice Reckitt sometimes attended. Both were guild socialists involved in persuading trade unions to take on the functions of medieval guilds. Among them were the metal-worker Edward Spencer, the social theorist, architect, and furniture designer Arthur Penty, and the editor of the journal *New Age*, Alfred Orage. Other socialists who were regular participants defended, on the other hand, the interests of the rural handicrafts movement rather than guild socialism. Additionally, the Irish scholar Francis MacNamara, who was yet another resident of Hammersmith Terrace, and his friend, the painter Augustus John, also made occasional appearances at Ship House.

Romney Green left an autobiography, *Work and Play*, which remains unpublished. Written in approximately 1942, the typescript gives valuable if brief recollections of the Hammersmith period. He was the friend equally of Johnston, Pepler and Gill and on occasions he borrowed Pepler's cottage at Lulworth Cove for holidays – as did Johnston. Of the Johnston family during these years at Hammersmith, Romney Green wrote:

> Among the friends whom we made at Hammersmith before moving to Strand-on-the-Green, Edward Johnston, the calligrapher, had the charm of the rather obscure and reluctant oracle, and was thus adored by Bertha. Greta Johnston had been a pupil of Belloc's at Oxford and now amused herself by reading Greek with Stephen Hobhouse; but she was a most genial and charming person, and Bertha became so intimate with her that she had the honour of acting as sole assistant at the all too sudden birth of Priscilla, whose admirable novel Green Girl we read with great enthusiasm about 20 years later....[42]

> Edward Spencer, also a great friend of Johnston's, was more interested in the social problem, more explicit in his philosophy, extremely witty and therefore rather more attractive to me. But I owe to Johnston for one of those three very sound maxims which I have treasured up together for many years. He said that every artist (though acting instinctively in his great moments) should be able to find three good reasons for everything he does. I compared this with Laurence Binyon's 'art is bettered by hard conditions' – hence the natural hierarchy of the materials – and 'there is great safety in geometry', a remark of Cruickshank's, the Byzantine connoisseur, which was even more congenial to me.[43]

In 1909 Romney Green gave a lecture at the Worshipful Company of Carpenters, which was then printed with the title 'The Influence of Tools on Design' in the volume associated with the architect, R. Weir Schultz, *The Arts Connected with Building* (edited by Raffles Davison). In 1912, he was commissioned by Roger Fry, the editor of the *Burlington Magazine*, to write a series of articles called 'Principles and Evolution of Furniture Making' in which the ideas of the earlier lecture were developed. These articles reflect many influences. They were historically researched and broad-based. In keeping with the thinking of the Arts and Crafts movement, Romney Green referred to writers such as Lethaby and Coomaraswamy. He also relied on the analyses of social writers such as Prince Kropotkin and Harold Rogers.[44]

But the details of his historical approach aside, the articles are also significant in so much as their structure is redolent of Johnston's own thinking. The manner in which Romney Green marshalled his material conforms precisely to Johnston's notion of the triad which so appealed to them both. Romney Green theorised that, in general, design depends upon three basic factors: materials; tools with their associated techniques; and social conditions. To this is added an outline of the notion of guild socialism and rural handicrafts which had a bearing on the formation of the Guild of St. Joseph and St. Dominic, in Ditchling.

Lethaby's thought was always inspiring to Johnston; it therefore merits a closer look. Growing out of Morris's writing, it was socialist in its sense of civic conscience, practical in its view of education, and realist in its distaste for 'pretence' in design. For Lethaby architecture was 'common sense building', the unselfconscious and communual work of craftsmen. During the decade 1910–20 he turned by stages to consider new thinking, thus sowing the seeds – along with many other thinkers – of what he called 'Modernism'.

In her paper, 'Edward Johnston and W. R. Lethaby', Priscilla Johnston wrote: 'Only one man influenced Johnston profoundly and for life: William R. Lethaby'.[45] Uppermost in her mind was Lethaby's impact on the earlier episodes of his career and on those aspects which linked him to the Arts and Crafts movement. However, in addition to their initial collaboration at the Central School, Johnston and Lethaby were neighbours for over two years between 1903–05 in Gray's Inn Square. (Johnston lived at number 4, and Lethaby had his architectural practice at number 2.) Their contact, personal and intellectual, was further enriched by their continuing work at the Central School and then at the RCA. Lethaby's departure as the Principal at the Central School in 1911 partly determined Johnston's own in 1912.

Lethaby's professorship at the RCA lasted into the 1920s, and no doubt it was because of his presence there that little written correspondence took place between them. They both wrote for the journal *Imprint*, in 1913. (Lethaby's article is called 'The Art of Workmanship'.) Although contact diminished – for Johnston eventually became a recluse in Ditchling – theirs was a lasting friendship. Priscilla Johnston recollected her father speaking late in life of '... dear Mr. Lethaby'. She added: 'I do not remember that adjective being accorded in quite that way to anyone else except my mother, after her death.' The progress of Lethaby's ideas beyond the bounds of Morris's is therefore important to an understanding of Johnston.

As a cultural historian,[46] Lethaby was uniquely placed to advance the debate about architectural and design theory. An article of 1910 sees a change setting in: 'We have passed', he claimed, 'into a scientific age ... the old practical arts belong to an entirely different era'. Lethaby began to speak out for 'engineer's architecture', for 'experiment', for a 'research of possibilities', and of 'a time to do something desperate'.[47] The issue hinged on the need for appropriate architectural and industrial design. By 1915, he acknowledged the role the machine could play in the design process. The 'machine aesthetic' joined the more established and familiar idea of functionalism.

In this development, Lethaby took up a dual line of thought which is traceable back to French thought in the eighteenth and nineteenth centuries. The two concepts, the 'machine aesthetic' and functionalism, became so intertwined in the design thinking of the early twentieth century as to appear synonymous. In fact, they are separable strands of the new rationalism which first gained ground in nineteenth-century architectural circles in response to new building techniques. They were then applied by pioneers such as Lethaby to design theory more generally.

One of the more prominent voices of the Rationalist School belonged to Auguste Choisy (1844–1909), a French engineer and historian whose ideas came partly from practical experience and partly from those of his predecessor, the architect and historian Eugène Viollet-le-Duc (1814–1879). Choisy's *Histoire de l'Architecture*, of 1899, was known to Lethaby. Its thesis asserted that architecture needed to divest itself of preoccupations with style alone and to concentrate again on the actual materials and techniques of building. Choisy was concerned that architecture should regain its integrity by following the dictates of structure. Out of this, he claimed, style would emerge of its own accord. He summarised this viewpoint with the startling aphorism:

> ... the logic of method implies the chronology of styles.[48]

Lethaby's own thinking synthesised the two traditions, the 'machine aesthetic' and functionalism. But they themselves shared a number of features. Like the new rationalism they both had their origins in architectural thought before they were applied to design theory in the wider sense. Both, too, had been used as a metaphor for architecture in order to shed light on its essential nature. While the 'machine aesthetic' was used, clearly, as a mechanical metaphor, functionalism was used, less obviously perhaps, as a biological or evolutionary one.

In turn, both were then considered to be appropriate as models to which architecture should aspire. And in a second phase, in the early twentieth century, they became models for designing in general. According to the machine model, it was claimed that the primary criterion of good design was that the artefact should work efficiently, adhering to scientific data, as in the manner of a well-made machine. As importantly, it followed that such an artefact would also be beautiful. In the functionalist model it was thought that the design process should best be guided by the needs to be fulfilled. The optimum solution would flow from the supposed laws of evolution.

The machine has always had a certain appeal as an analogy for human as well as scientific disciplines – for economics or architecture as well as for astronomy or biology. In eighteenth-century France, under the influence of The Enlightenment, Claude-Nicolas Ledoux, architect to King Louis XVI, enthused about the machine, and recommended mechanics and civil engineering as appropriate studies for architects.[49] In 1804 the critic, F. Schlegel, compared Strasbourg Cathedral to the workings of a watch.[50]

A generation before Lethaby was writing in England another French writer and architect, Eugène Viollet-le-Duc, had campaigned to relieve architecture of its historicist burden and to follow, instead, the methods of mechanical and civil engineering. In the tenth of his *Entretiens sur l'Architecture* (*Lectures on Architecture*), of 1863–77, he asked: 'Is the nineteenth century to close without having an architecture of its own?' His response was to suggest that architecture '… should have its own character and style' by expressing the power and energy of engineering just as in the classical era it had expressed the power of religion. The novelty and vitality of Viollet-le-Duc's writings would have affected Lethaby.

Moreover, from about this time, structures such as ships were beginning to be recognised as having aesthetic value by virtue of their mechanical efficiency.[51] Anatole de Baudot, pupil of Viollet-le-Duc, carried such ideas into the twentieth century. In his book, translated as *Architecture Past and Present*, of 1916, he asked:

> The appearance [of ships and steam trains] were deduced from scientific and industrial data. Why therefore … are buildings ... not designed in a similar way?[52]

The functionalist tradition had separate origins from that of the 'machine aesthetic'. It arose out of a theory of evolution which had been developed during the French Enlightenment period of the eighteeth century by the biologist, Jean Baptiste Lamarck (1744–1829) followed by George Cuvier (1769–1832). While believing that evolution was pre-ordained, and exclusive of man, Lamarck also held that the forms of living creatures were determined by their environment and needs.[53] He wrote:

> An animal's habits and manner of life ... has in the course of time fashioned its bodily form.

This idea was taken up by the nineteenth-century evolutionist, Herbert Spencer whose books, in turn, were read by the American architect, Louis Sullivan. Born in

1856, Sullivan's was a generation on from William Morris. It was due in large part to him that design thinking then focused on the notion that modern architectural forms are best determined by their function, rather than by stylistic considerations.

The functionalist model gained an added potency on account of the availability in the late nineteenth century of new building materials – of steel, reinforced concrete, sheet glass, together with new piped energy sources such as gas and electricity, along with water. These new means and techniques went hand-in-hand with new opportunities. (Henceforth, the availability of sheet glass, for example, enabled domestic buildings to take greater advantage of daylight. Accordingly, glass walls began to be incorporated into the architectural canon as a prominent and structural feature.)[54]

This 'truthfulness' to materials had an important corollary: that truth is beauty. It was a familiar cry. The functionalist theorists of the early twentieth century, in looking to contemporary needs, emphasised the very creed implicit in the Arts and Crafts movement. Johnston himself had said:

> If the method is right the work will grow more beautiful.

It was Lethaby's power of critical thought, coupled with a particular analysis of history, that opened the door for him on to these new, industrial, perspectives. Ruskin's humanistic medievalism was now wholly misplaced and Morris's socialist strategies for design were increasingly problematic. Lethaby confronted these outmoded systems of thought afresh. A succession of articles and lectures by him addressed contemporary issues of architecture and design.[55] It was by such means that Lethaby broke through what amounted to an impasse for the Arts and Crafts movement which, increasingly inbred and orthodox, came to be regarded as serving the needs of a wealthy clientele only. So thought Eric Gill, for example, by the time he had moved to Ditchling in 1907.

Lethaby's historical reasoning and his personal convictions related to Johnston's own predispositions during those years, 1910–15. And even earlier, Lethaby's inaugural lecture to the students of the RCA of around 1901[56]might well have provided Johnston with the spur for his and Gill's short-lived Homemaker's Society.

Lethaby's paper, 'Design and Industry', of 1915, summed up a more recently developed set of ideas. He delivered it to the newly formed Design and Industries Association. While good design, he still maintained, was 'the appropriate shaping and finish of the thing required ...'[57] he now urged that 'we should come to closer terms with design in all our industries.' The hub of the problem, he thought, was that '... the designer and the manufacturer have ... largely remained in separate compartments.'

Lethaby's initial interest was to discern sets of meaning – symbolic, mythical, psychological – in the architecture of the ancient world.[58] Early on he undertook a wide-ranging study using many different sources, resulting in his book, *Architecture, Mysticism, and Myth*, of 1891. Over the years he reworked it to be reissued in 1928 in the journal, *The Builder*, and retitled *Architecture, Nature and Magic*. (It became a book in 1956.)

Lethaby's second preoccupation was with the medieval period of European architecture, design, and decoration. Another book, *Mediæval Art*, was published in 1904. These studies enabled him to evaluate the human motives that lay behind the architectural achievements of the past and thereby gave him insights into the dilemmas of design theory in the present. Extrapolating from history in this way was one of Lethaby's outstanding intellectual contributions as the Principal of the Central School and Professor of Design at the RCA. In an appreciation written in 1950, his (and Johnston's) colleague, Noel Rooke, observed:

> Lethaby was a scholar and his knowledge was both extensive and accurate and continually being put to fresh use. He early taught himself to think while he read and so developed his power of relating things to each other. It was this habit of mind probably that gave him his almost uncanny insight ... a poet at heart he not only saw it [Gothic architecture] but was absorbed by its power and pervading mystery.[59]

Thus, Lethaby's concern was not with a typology of the styles of buildings, *per se*, but with architecture as an aspect of cultural history. He read into its history a synthesis, a 'commune of all the crafts', the outpouring of man's will to form, ('kunstwollen'[60]). He set out to interpret the symbolic meanings implicit in architecture's structures, forms, and decoration as the expression of man's understanding of Nature – of the 'known or the imagined facts of the Universe'. He called these meanings 'esoteric principles'. A case in point is Lethaby's book, *The Church of Santa Sophia, Constantinople: a Study of Byzantine Building*, of 1894. Paralleling this holistic approach was the Egyptologist, Flinders Petrie, whom Lethaby readily quoted:

> The demands of each age were its ideals and were the really important things. You may have confidence in the interpretation of mind by the product of art. What, for instance, was there in the writing of the thirteenth century which gave such a perfect picture of the medieval mind as Salisbury cathedral?[61]

Lethaby himself echoed this. In his inaugural lecture on modern design to the RCA in 1901 he described the interiors of medieval and Tudor houses:

> Every piece of furniture, every decoration had a use and a meaning in the economy of the room, the room was a member of the great body of architecture of the time; the architecture was the national thought and aspiration put into stone.[62]

In 1915, he spoke again in the same terms:

> Every architectural frontage is an interior view of the mind that produced it.[63]

Lethaby constructed a synoptic view of architecture as having a wider purpose for the society using it. His claim was that through their particular styles and ornamentation, buildings were infused with ideas of 'magic, ritual rightness and imitations of the order of Nature'. In his *Architecture, Nature and Magic*, of 1928, he maintained:

> All the arts had their origin in the needs of the body and the mind ... the mind was deeply immersed in magic .... The greater buildings were not only for ritual purposes

> but they themselves were embodied magic .... Behind all the minor categories of the styles there is a general unity in ancient architecture of the magic type.[64]

Armed with such insights, Lethaby was able to expose as false the historicism that had gripped much of the architectural profession in the nineteenth century. He regarded the reworking of past styles – whereby the Doric temple, for example, was the model for the form of a railway station or the Baroque church façade that for an hotel – to be culturally barren. He called such a misuse of forms 'whim-works in the sham styles; not even child's play, but the grimaces of grown-ups.'[65] He explained:

> The mere 'look' of the old magic qualities without the awe and wonder that produced them is repulsive, silly and mind-destroying.[66]

Having discerned that a long period of ancient architecture – Lethaby included the medieval period in this category – was the authentic expression of its makers, he made clear the requirements for its renewal. This new phase was to be invigorated by science because the development of science most characterised the times.

> A great gulf is thus set up between ancient magic architecture and modern scientific building .... Wonder for us can only be reawakened by exploration of, and experiment in, realities – in a word, by the scientific method, which is just at this time the most characteristic mode of thinking.[67]

Extending the ideas of Ruskin and Morris, Lethaby loosened architecture – and by implication design philosophy as a whole – from its nineteenth-century entanglement with medievalism. As for historicism, it itself became an anachronism. He stressed the need for design to belong to its time. Yet, Lethaby still maintained the importance of historical continuity, of the vernacular. In this sense, far from belonging to the European avant garde, he represents what has been called a British 'conservative modernism'.

Responding to this challenge, Lethaby was among the earliest in Britain to see the relevance of the 'machine aesthetic'.[68] In fact, the new aesthetic had already occupied the imagination of a post-Morrisian generation of thinkers outside of Britain. Its advocates, of whom the American architects Louis Sullivan (1856–1924) and Frank Lloyd Wright (1867–1959) were key representatives, held the view that the machine was the expressive force for the twentieth century. A 'machine æsthetic' was an entirely fitting idiom for modern living. Achieving this was a matter of re-orientating the education and sensibilities of the designer.

By 1910 the main outline of the 'machine aesthetic' was already firmly in place in the minds of many avant-garde architects, designers, and critics of Lethaby's generation in Europe and the U.S.A. They had all been born in the decades 1850–70.[69] As early as 1901 Frank Lloyd Wright, for instance, had delivered the first of many versions of his lecture, 'The Art and Craft of the Machine'. In the same year Louis Sullivan published his important *Kindergarten Chats*. In 1907, Peter Behrens and Hermann Muthesius had been active in forming the Deutsche Werkbund, which was the first of a growing number of institutions in Europe intended to advance the cause of industrial design, thus superseding the guild organisations within the Arts and Crafts movement.

A second generation of designers, architects and critics built on the manifestos and works of these pioneers, so as to put flesh on the bones of what was becoming recognised as the Modern Movement. The majority of these were born between the 1880s and 1890s.[70] It was Walter Gropius, as the director of the all-important Bauhaus, the school of design established in Weimar, Germany, in 1919, who, above all other writers, articulated the practical aims of the 'machine æsthetic'.[71]

Lethaby was sensitive to the developments pioneered in Europe. He travelled there regularly, particularly to Germany. European design journals like the *Jahrbuch* of the Deutsche Werkbund, (and possibly *L'Esprit Nouveau*, in France), keeping him abreast of the European thinking about the machine aesthetic in Europe. For designers in England itself Lethaby was, at one and the same time, a precursor and a Cassandra. He was astute enough to realise that the pre-eminence in design that Britain had once enjoyed – in the earlier days of the Arts and Crafts Exhibition Society – was slipping away to foreign competition and to Germany in particular. He summed up the dilemma for the Arts and Crafts movement, thus: 'We can't go back but we can't stop where we are'. But rather than locking on to the narrow problem of the machine as had earlier thinkers – Morris included – he took up a much wider brief into which that issue was subsumed.

Much of the strength of Lethaby's new design philosophy lay in his historical grasp of other cultures. But, unlike Morris, he recognised the value of scientific progress. He was keenly influenced, too, by the evolutionist philosopher, Herbert Spencer, though needless to say, entirely because of his methods, and not at all on account of his conservative conclusions about individuality. (The phrase 'the survival of the fittest' is Spencer's.) Such cross-fertilisation of disciplines enriched Lethaby's own convictions about the psychological functions of 'design as making' in society, as well as its utilitarian purposes. Focusing on his specialism of architecture, and using the evolutionary model, Lethaby maintained that architecture, and following it all design, needed to develop its own, quintessential, 'type'.[72] In the concluding passages of his outline survey, *Architecture*, of 1911, he pointed out the need for a relationship between the new scientific age and designing:

> The modern way of building must be possible and vigorous, even smart and hard. We must give up designing the broken picturesque which is part of the ideal of make-believe. The enemy is not science, but vulgarity, a pretence to beauty at second hand.[73]

Lethaby's concern was not to advance a new style but rather a more relevant mode of thinking – a functionalist mode. He sought a new language of forms, a 'type' which was to be founded on what was culturally most significant about industrialised society. He argued from history. For example, he claimed that the architecture of the classical world consisted in part of an 'engineering tradition'. In his paper the 'Architecture of Adventure', of 1910, he spoke of this former 'identity of architects and engineers'. Considering the cultural significance of the twentieth century to lie with the 'scientific method', by 1923, in his article 'The Building Art – Theories and Discussions', Lethaby could insist, as a cry from the heart:

> It is because I want poetry, humanity, and even sacredness in building that I see we must be experimental, courageous, serious, real. Archaeology has taught me: "Modernism" – that is, reality and no pretence.[74]

Lethaby was increasingly struck by the phenomenon of manufactured artefacts which were made expressly for their optimum efficiency. Like Frank Lloyd Wright and Le Corbusier before him, he was impressed by the functional and unselfconscious design of musical instruments, for example, or of the steam engine, or of the ocean-going liner. A design process which used engineering calculations was important to him because the final appearance of the designed artefact was the logical outcome of those calculations, rather than the starting point, or the prime motive. The resulting form was therefore authentic and expressive of its time. In his lecture, 'The Architecture of Adventure', given in 1910, he concluded:

> ... the method of design to a modern mind can only be understood in the scientific or engineer's sense of an analysis of possibilities .... The living stem of building design can only be found by following the scientific method.[75]

Underlying the notion of an 'analysis of possibilities' are rationalist, evolutionist and positivist strands, although Lethaby himself did not point out the connections. In the same paper he is dismissive of late-nineteenth-century architectural practice which, he claimed, 'had been trying to deal with a set of flavours – things that looked like but were not the things themselves'. By 1910–12, Lethaby had pinned his colours to the mast of a new form of functionalism which incorporated 'machine industry'.

In the concluding paragraph of *Architecture, Nature and Magic* (1928) Lethaby returned to this issue and linked it with the necessity for beauty. He was to call it a 'high functional beauty':

> ... men of science naturally and unashamedly confess to enthusiastic appreciation, and make use of the idea of beauty. A solution in mathematics, the result of an experiment, a theory in astronomy still gives a sort of a rapture. In a paper on locomotive engineers by a scientific expert that I saw reported recently, he said: 'England excelled in high speed locomotives of beautiful design and appearance. There was little doubt that in future times men would look back on our really beautiful locomotives in which our practical genius found artistic expression as we now look back on the full-rigged ship.' That is what we have to get back in our building – high functional beauty.[76]

It is also significant for the development of Lethaby's thinking that, for the first time since the eighteenth century, he pointed to a classical architect as an exemplar of architectural practice. Part of his paper, 'The Architecture of Adventure', is an analysis of Christopher Wren, a mathematician and astronomer as well as an architect. Lethaby claimed him to be '... certainly the first in England to apply the methods of scientific investigation to the laws of structure'. (He pointed out, for example, that Wren calculated the Pantheon in Rome to have been built with unnecessarily strong abutments given the weight of its dome. It had been over-designed.) Moreover, Lethaby recognised Wren's work to be symbolically appropriate to its period. Wren himself called it the 'guts of its age'. Lethaby's enthusiasm for St. Paul's is the mirror image of Morris's former aversion, and illustrates the gulf in their thinking by the time of Lethaby's essay of 1913. And it was the self-same order of Graeco-Roman architectural design – controlled and rational, the very canon of classicism – which appealed to other early modernists, among them the architect Le Corbusier.

According to Lethaby's thinking, design needs freedom in order to find its own characteristic 'type', and thereby to express its own modernity. Thus, new materials and techniques must be given their head. The cast-iron and glass construction of the Crystal Palace (1851) was detested by Ruskin; but the steel construction of the Forth Bridge (1889) was praised by Lethaby, just as he enthused about other industrial constructions such as brick-built kilns or Kentish oast-houses, timber-framed barns, or wagons, factory chimneys or lighthouses. Lethaby's intellectual rigour is expressed in an aphorism from his short study, *Architecture*, of 1911:

> A self-conscious aesthetic 'appeal' is likely to become a disease of art, the true appeal is a fact.

Not surprisingly, by 1915, Lethaby was proposing the founding of an organisation which would integrate design into industrial practices. The result was the Design and Industries Association. In his paper, 'Design and Industry', given to the DIA at its outset, he outlined the problem it was established to solve. The unrivalled achievements of the Arts and Crafts movement designers were essentially for wealthy connoisseurs. By its exhibitions the work of the Arts and Crafts movement was influential in continental countries; in Germany, in particular, it had been spectacular. But, Lethaby lamented, in Britain, unlike in Germany, ' … the large manufacturer has not seen what great possibilities there were in adapting these experiments to the larger world of machine industry'.[77] He added ruefully: '… now this is what our foreign competitors have done.'[78]

Lethaby's singular achievement was to think of design not in terms of a style but rather as a methodology, or what he called 'a living stem'. The biological metaphor is richly significant, given the probable influence of the writings of Gottfried Semper. All the nostalgia and the moral indignation which suffused Morris's writings on design was replaced by a rational appraisal of the problem at hand. By careful analysis, the design solution would emerge as 'shipshape', to use Lethaby's down-to-earth term. In his lecture of 1920, 'Architecture as Form in Civilisation', his position became unequivocal:

> The house of the future will be designed as a ship is designed, as an organism which has to function properly in all its parts.[79]

Given the entirely modernist tone of this idea it could well have been Lethaby, rather than Louis Sullivan, who coined the dictum 'form follows function'. But Lethaby did propose a way of thinking that enabled others in England to arrive at exactly that style of restrained ornament which so characterised the designed environment of the first half of the twentieth century. It was a minimalist style which, in architecture, spread across the urbanised world. It is associated with the names of such architects as Le Corbusier, and Mies van der Rohe, and with the

International Style, or International Modernism. (Ironically, within the space of a generation or so International Modernism itself became discredited as merely another preoccupation with style.)

For Lethaby, in the 1910–20s, the functionalist mode was seen increasingly as the valid one for twentieth-century industrial society. Furthermore, in accordance with his reading of history – endorsed by the insights of Sir Charles Petrie – its output was the authentic symbolic expression of its time. In 1918, he had written:

> I have seen much that causes one to look again, in great bridges spanning a valley like a rainbow; in roofs meshed across with thin threads of steel; in tall factory chimneys; great cranes and ships; or even in gasometers …, these things have vital interest for modern people because they are modern and part of life …. There is nothing necessarily evil in modern materials or requirements; it is the spirit that tells.

Something – though by no means all – of Lethaby's 'conservative modernism' came through to Johnston, especially in his role as a letter designer. He was far from being moved to put pen to paper as a 'conservative modernist'. Furthermore, from about 1912 other ways of thinking, traditional and new, were also exerting their influence.

Fig. 49. Hammersmith Terrace and Upper Mall

END NOTES

1. Cited from G. Rubens. 'Lethaby's Lecture on Modern Design (1901)'. In *Craft History One*. Edited by M. Coatts and J. Howes. 1988.
2. W. R. Lethaby. 'Lecture on Modern Design' given in 1901. Cited from *Craft History One*. Op. cit.
3. W. R. Lethaby. 'Lecture on Modern Design' given in 1901. Cited from *Craft History One*. Op. cit.
4. Noel Rooke. 'The Work of Lethaby, Webb, and Morris'. In *RIBA Journal*. Vol. 57. March 1950.
5. From Johnston's 'Lecture IX' given at the RCA on 18th May 1931. Cited from *Lessons in Formal Writing*. Edited by Heather Child and Justin Howes. (Lund Humphries) 1986.
6. See Justin Howes. 'Edward Johnston's First Class at the Central School on 21st September 1899' in *Object Lessons*. Edited by S. Backmayer. (Lund Humphries) 1998.
7. Dorothy Walker's papers at Cheltenham Museum include jellygraphs of lettering made by Johnston. One has a quotation from Ruskin written by him with the message: 'Miss Walker with kind regards from E. Johnston 8 July 1901. (I am sorry the "process" has come out so feebly)'.
8. Johnston's Notebook 1899–04. Harry Ransom Humanities Research Center. University of Texas at Austin, Texas.
9. The letter is dated April 19th Easter Sunday 1936. The remainder of the letter confirms Gill's intense feelings for Johnston over the span of years. Referring to his diary entries Gill writes: '...the only other entry, except for receipts of money and payments is on Oct. 16 "to life class, for the first time". In fact 1903 reads nothing but those life shaking events. I hope I shall be forgiven for this delving into memories of those birthdays. I only want you to know, as I think you had not known before, that, as I think, your marriage meant more to me than to anyone else in the whole world except you and your wife and so it is impossible for me to say even the perfectly good and truthful things which other friends and lovers might say. Though at a distance and separated by sundering floods and strange mists, your wedded life and mine have run parallel and now they both draw to their earthly close. On this Sunday morning you may rejoice more than I who have not yet suffered. Again, I look

as it was from the dark street in through a lighted window … bearing palms in their hands and crying Hosanna to the son of David. With great love and devotion, Eric Gill.' Johnston archive at the Crafts Study Centre Collection and Archive, Farnham, Surrey.
10. See Frank Sedwick. 'The Typographical Work of Percy Smith'. In *The Fleuron*. Vol. 4. 1925.
11. Johnston's *Work Diary* for 1906 mentions these experiments. See M. Renton. 'Edward Johnston and Wood Engraving'. In *Sharpness Unity and Freedom*. (Cambridge Enterprises) 1994.
12. See Justin Howes. 'Noel Rooke: the Early Years'. In *Matrix*. Vol. 3. 1983. In 1920, Noel Rooke, together with Robert Gibbings, Eric Gill, Lucien Pissarro, Philip Hagreen (and others) founded the Society of Wood Engravers. It ushered in a renaissance of wood engraving in England which in its turn extended the repertoire of English book illustration. Other artists associated with this development were Gertrude Hermes, John Farleigh, Gordon Craig, Gwen Raverat, Sturge Moore, Paul and John Nash – and David Jones and Ralph John Beedham both of whom lived for a time in Ditchling. Ralph Beedham's book *Wood Engraving* was published by Hilary Pepler at his S. Dominic's Press at Ditchling in 1921. In the 1920s Hagreen joined the Catholic community of craftsmen living in Ditchling.
13. William Rothenstein. 'T. Cobden-Sanderson'. In *The Fleuron*. Vol. 1. 1923. Cobden-Sanderson was prompted to do bookbinding by the wife of Sir William Richmond, also Johnston's friend.
14. Edward Johnston. 'The Character of the man set forth by his faithful Scribe'. In H. J. Nash. *Cobden-Sanderson and the Doves Press*. San Francisco. 1929.
15. Harry Ransom Humanities Research Center. University of Texas at Austin, Texas.
16. Douglas Cockerell had a son, also named Douglas Cockerell. Known as Sandy, he was a bookbinder who, like his father, had his studio in Letchworth Garden City.
17. See Herbert Simon. *A History of the Curwen Press*. (George Allen & Unwin Ltd) 1956.
18. Cited from Christopher Frayling. *Royal College of Art. One Hundred and Fifty Years of Art and Design*. (Barrie and Jenkins) 1987. Also in Priscilla Johnston. *Edward Johnston*. Op. cit.
19. Dorothy Mahoney. 'Edward Johnston. A Personal Account.' In *The Craft of Calligraphy*. (Pelham) 1981.
20. Priscilla Johnston. *Edward Johnston*. Op. cit.
21. This portfolio is in the N A L at the V&A. Violet Hawkes tried to get Johnston's second, unfinished handbook, *Formal Penmanship*, published by Francis Meynell at the Nonesuch Press after Johnston's death. This was to no avail. See her letter signed Mrs. O. E. Jackson (née Hawkes) to Sir F. Meynell dated the 10th August 1959. Cambridge University Library. (Stanley Morison Room.)
22. V. Hawkes. 'Edward Johnston at the Royal College of Art'. In *Alphabet and Image*. No. 1. 1946.
23. T. Swindlehurst. 'Edward Johnston'. Lecture to the Society of Scribes and Illuminators. 1965.
24. T. Swindlehurst. 'Edward Johnston'. Lecture to the Society of Scribes and Illuminators. 1965.
25. Cited from John Farleigh. *The Creative Craftsman*. Op. cit.
26. Priscilla Johnston. *Edward Johnston*. Op. cit.
27. Cited from Priscilla Johnston. 'So Completely Himself'. Talk to the Society of Scribes and Illuminators. October 1979 and printed in *The Scribe*. No. 38. Winter. 1986.
28. Edward Sutton. 'Johnston and his Influence'. Lecture to the British Typographers Guild. Printed in the *British and Colonial Printer*. January 28th 1949.
29. Anna Simons. 'Tribute to Johnston'. In Sir Sydney Cockerell. *Various printed items relating to E. Johnston*. National Art Library at the V&A. (Ref: 86. QQ. 27.)
30. In *Anna Simons*. Corona VIII. (Oldenbourg Verlag. Verlag der Coruna) Zurich 1934.
31. Anna Simons. 'Tribute to Johnston'. In Sir Sydney Cockerell. Op. cit.
32. The other titles – nine in all – in the series are: Douglas Cockerell. *Book Binding*. 1901; George Jack. *Woodcarving: Design and Workmanship*, 1903; Henry Wilson. *Silversmithing and Jewellery*, 1903; St. John Hope. *Heraldry*, 1903; C. W. Whall. *Stained Glass Work*, 1905; Mrs Archibald Christie. *Embroidery and Tapestry Weaving*, 1910; Luther Hooper. *Handloom Weaving*, 1910; Talbot Hughes. *Dress Design*, 1913; Frank Morley Fletcher. *Woodblock Printing*, 1916. An eleventh volume, *Cabinet Making and Designing*, was planned to be written by Charles Spooner.
33. National Art Library at the V&A. Reference: Box II. 86 ee.

34. Including Lethaby's lecture 'Morris as Work-Master', given at the Birmingham Municipal School of Art in 1901, and his article, 'Education for Industry', in *Handicraft and Reconstruction: Notes by Members of the Arts and Crafts Exhibition Society*. 1919.

35. Emery Walker's articles include: 'The Art of Printing'. (The British & Colonial Printer) 1892; 'Printing'. In *Arts and Crafts Essays*. (Arts and Crafts Exhibition Society) 1893. 'Letterpress Printing as an Art.' (British and Colonial Printer) Vol. XLII. 1898; 'A Brief History of Printing'. (Central School) 1911; 'Printing'. (Central School printed by J. Mason) 1911.

36. Edward Johnston. 'On Other People's Houses' in *The RCA Students Magazine*. II. No. XII. March 1913. It was first written for the *Westminster Gazette* in 1911 but was never printed there in full.

37. From the diary of Mrs Florence Whall. Courtesy of the William Morris Gallery, Walthamstow.

38. A ring of changes had enabled Johnston to move into Hammersmith Terrace. From 1901, Cobden-Sanderson occupied house number 7, which, incidentally, had once been the home of the eighteenth-century landscape artist, Philip de Loutherbourg (said to have been associated with Casanova). In 1903, Cobden-Sanderson moved into house number 1, where his Doves Press was first located. In 1903, Emery Walker, who owned and lived at house number 3, moved into the vacated house number 7. This left house number 3 empty for Johnston to rent on a seven-year lease, at £60 per annum, until 1912.

39. Other residents forming a craft community of Hammersmith Terrace included the elderly Pre-Raphaelite painter, Frederick George Stephens, who lived at house number 9. Stephens was primarily a critic and writer with a book entitled *Artists at Home* (1884) and others on Rossetti and Lord Leighton. He wrote for *The Germ* and became the editor of the *Athæneum*. He was succeeded there in 1907 by the architect and furniture designer, Charles Spooner, who, like Johnston, taught at the Central School of Arts and Crafts and was a member of the Art Workers' Guild. Spooner had been a close associate of William Morris and was to become a colleague of Pepler at his Hampshire House Social Club. (Spooner's earlier home was at Eyot Cottage, on Chiswick Mall, which he shared briefly in 1907 with his cousin, Fr. Adrian Fortescue, one of Johnston's first pupils at the Central School.) Warwick Draper, a Barrister-at-law but also a colleague of Pepler's at the Workshops, was at number 13. Later, Warwick Draper became the incumbant of Morris's Kelmscott House. The genealogist and herald Oswald Barron lived at number 16. He was also a journalist writing *The Londoner* column for the *Evening News*. In an obituary of Johnston in the *Times Literary Supplement* in 1944, the (unnamed) correspondent wrote that Johnston punned about his friend: 'Barron, you remind me of Simeon Stylites. Why, Johnston? Because you live on a column.'

40. The house was situated just south of St. Peter's Church. On Gill's departure, his colleague and lodger, Laurence Christie, lived there. (The house was demolished to make way for Westway.)

41. H. D. C. Pepler. 'Forty Years Back'. In *The Register*. 1949. (A copy exists in the British Library.)

42. Priscilla Johnston was born on the 16th September 1911.

43. A. Romney Green. Autobiography: *Work and Play*. N. A. L. V&A Museum. (Ref: 86. X.67.)

44. One instance of this influence running through the articles is an historical interpretation. Romney Green shares the assumption developed by radical writers from Cobbett to Morris that the alienation experienced by the artisan class was heightened by the introduction of machinery but had its origins much earlier in history, in the periods of the Classical Renaissance and the Protestant Reformation. Cobbett's seminal text, *The History of the Protestant 'Reformation' in England and Ireland. And how that event has impoverished the main body of the people in those countries*, of 1824, well known to Morris and others, was a powerful study suppporting this theory. Romney Green took up Cobbett's proposal that these movements had brought about a fundamental change in the status of the craftsman, the most favoured minority of whom were elevated and esteemed as 'artist', and the rest disregarded as anonymous artisans. Equally pernicious, according to Cobbett's view, were

the Protestant enclosure of the common land and the reform of the Catholic poor laws. These had given rise to a dispossessed, a rootless, and as a consequence a cheap labour force.

45. Priscilla Johnston. 'Edward Johnston and W. R. Lethaby'. In *Lessons in Formal Writing*. Edited by Heather Child and Justin Howes. (Lund Humphries) 1978.

46. The bibliography in G. Ruben's study *W. R. Lethaby, his Life and Work 1857–1931* (The Architectural Press) 1986, lists over three hundred scholarly articles by Lethaby, appearing in *The Burlington Magazine, The Builder, Archealogia, Athenaeum, the Journal of the RIBA,* et al. He also wrote some fourteen major books on art, architecture, and archeology.

47. The phrases come from Lethaby's seminal paper, *The Architecture of Adventure.* (RIBA) 1910.

48. Cited from R. Banham. *Theory and Design in the First Machine Age.* (Architectural Press) 1960.

49. Ledoux has been labelled a Romantic Classicist. Imprisoned during the French Revolution, he spoke of an expressive architecture – 'une architecture parlante'.

50. Cited from Peter Collins. *Changing Ideals in Modern Architecture.* (Faber and Faber) 1965.

51. This led, in due course, to the radical analysis of the Swiss architect, Le Corbusier. In his seminal *Vers une Architecture* (Editions Crès) of 1923, [English translation *Towards a New Architecture.* (John Rodker) 1927] which was compiled from articles written for *L'Esprit Nouveau,* he spoke approvingly of the 'engineer's æsthetic', and uttered the celebrated, if now chilling, phrase: 'The house is a machine to live in'. Lethaby interpreted this phrase benignly as: 'A house is a machine *to live in*'. (W. Lethaby. 'Architecture and Engineering'. In *The Builder.* Vol 140. 1931.) The impact of the machine as both metaphor and model affected – intoxicated, even – a number of art and design movements of the early twentieth century. The equating of efficiency and beauty was central to the 'machine aesthetic'. The German architect, Bruno Taut, said, in 1919: 'The aim of architecture is the creation of a perfect and therefore a beautiful efficiency.' Theo van Doesburg, an architect and leader of the Dutch de Stijl movement, claimed in 1921, in the magazine of the same name:

> Since culture in its widest sense means independence from Nature, we must not wonder that the machine stands in the forefront of our cultural 'will-to-style' ... the new possibilities of the machine have created an aesthetic expressive of our time, that I once called the 'mechanical aesthetic'. (Theo van Doesburg. In *de Stijl.* 1921.)

52. Anatole de Baudot. Published posthumously in English as *Architecture Past and Present.* 1916.

53. It is of some interest to note (as surely Johnston would have done, given his interest in etymology) that the history of the word 'evolution' derives from calligraphy. Its literal meaning was to unroll a scroll. Its metaphorical use in the eighteenth century was, therefore, the revealing of a parchment on which the text – that is, the history of man – had already been written.

54. The buildings of Le Corbusier and Frank Lloyd Wright are classic examples. The use of reinforced concrete, as an overt structural feature, dates from Auguste Perret's Trocadero flats in Paris of 1903. The use of cast-iron as a structural feature dates from Labrouste's Bibliothèque San Geneviève, in Paris, in 1860.

55. A number of these lectures were given to the Design and Industries Association, established in 1915, and some to the Arts and Crafts Society. The article 'Art and Workmanship', of 1913, was printed in *The Imprint.* It was also included in the first publication of the DIA, in 1916, and reprinted by the Deutsche Werkbund.

56. The lecture is reconstructed and discussed by G. Rubens. 'Lethaby's Lecture on Modern Design (1901)'. In *Craft History One.* Edited M. Coatts & Justin Howes. 1988.

57. W. R. Lethaby's paper, 'Design and Industry', read to the DIA. 1915.

58. Two of his sources were Sir James Frazer's *The Golden Bough,* of 1890, and Jane Harrison's *Ancient Art and Ritual,* of 1911. Both studied the function of religion in society. Lethaby realised their value for his thesis that 'the development of building practice and ideas of the world structure acted and reacted upon one another ... at the inner heart of ancient building

were wonder, worship, magic and symbolism.... I do see that science has a new magic wonder of its own'.

59. Noel Rooke. RIBA *Journal*. March 1950. Reprinted in *Architecture, Nature and Magic*. 1956.

60. The 'will to form' is an expressionist concept developed by the German art historian Riegl and then brought to bear by Wilhelm Worringer in his *Formproblem der Gotik,* of 1912, to explain art as a 'psychic spiritual activity of will'. The book was translated as *Form in Gothic*. (Alex Tiranti) in 1927. Paralleling this, Lethaby used the word 'expressionist' in the 1890s. Lethaby read Worringer. Supporting the use of modern materials he wrote, in 1918, '...it is the spirit that tells'.

61. The quotation accompanies the frontispiece to Lethaby's *Form in Civilisation*. (OUP) 1922.

62. G. Rubens. 'W. R. Lethaby's Lecture on Modern Design. (1901)'. In *Craft History One*. Op. cit.

63. W. R. Lethaby. Pamphlet *Design and Industry*. (Design and Industries Association) 1915.

64. W. R. Lethaby. 'Architecture, Nature and Magic'. In *The Builder*. 1928. (Reprinted by Duckworth in 1956.)

65. W. R. Lethaby. *Form in Civilisation*. (OUP) 1922.

66. W. R. Lethaby. *Form in Civilisation*. Op. cit.

67. W. R. Lethaby. *Architecture, Nature and Magic*. (Duckworth) 1956.

68. Other voices in Britain included those of architects like John Sedding and designers like Arthur MacMurdo who spoke out in the congresses of the National Association for the Advancement of Art and its Application to Industry. For this insight I am indebted to advice from Gillian Naylor. See G. Naylor. *The Arts and Crafts movement*. (Trefoil Publications) 1971.

69. Other figures of this pioneering generation included the Austrian, Adolf Loos b.1870, the Dutchman, Hendrik Berlage b.1856, The Belgian, Henry van de Velde b.1863.

70. They included, among others, Gerrit Rietveld, b.1888 in Holland; Siegfried Giedion, b.1883, in Switzerland; Le Corbusier, b.1887 in Switzerland, who worked in France; Ambrose Heal, b.1872; Frank Pick, b.1878; and Herbert Read, b.1893, all in England; Nikolaus Pevsner, b.1902 in Germany, who worked in England; Lazlo Moholy Nagy, b.1895 in Hungary, who worked in Germany and USA; Jan Tschichold, b.1902 in Czechoslovakia, who worked in Germany, Switzerland and England; Vladimir Tatlin, b.1885; El Lissitzky, b.1890; Aleksandr Rodchenko, b.1891, all in Russia; Mies van der Rohe, b.1886 in Germany.

71. In a lecture given to the Design and Industries Association (DIA), following his departure from Germany in 1933, Gropius stressed that, at the very outset, the Bauhaus had: '... accepted the machine as the essentially modern vehicle of form and sought to come to terms with it ... so as to create type forms to meet every commercial, technical and aesthetic requirement'.

72. The term 'type' was of recent currency. It was used but never fully defined by Lethaby. Its provenance probably goes back to a figure whose influence on Lethaby, while almost certainly felt, was not openly acknowledged by him. (Nor has it ever been fully investigated.) This was the German architect, designer and historian, Gottfried Semper (1803–73), who had been active in Britain between 1851–54 and who had contributed to the classification of exhibits for the Great Exhibition of 1851 and the exhibiting policy – using the notion of materials rather than a topology of artefacts or place – at Marlborough House, and then, at the Victoria and Albert Museum, under Sir Henry Cole. Semper was also an evolutionist. In his book, *Der Stil* (1878), he had sought to identify basic archetypes – or 'types', to use Semper's own term – of design, isolated from their specific cultural and historical variations. (Ref. W. Herrmann & H. F. Mulgrave: *Gottfried Semper. The Four Elements of Architecture and other Writings*. CUP. 1989. Also: H. F. Mulgrave. *Gottfried Semper. Architect of the 19th Century*. 1996.) Semper, in turn, had been inspired by the French evolutionist, Cuvier, whose biological scheme at the Jardin des Plantes, in Paris, Semper wrote about. It is likely that an intermediary between Semper and Lethaby was the architect, Viollet-le-Duc, who had done prodigious work in France in restoring medieval buildings and in writing about the value of the engineering tradition. He formed part of the Gothic Rationalist School in company with

Choisy. [A fuller exploration of this theme appears in: Gillian Naylor: 'Lethaby and the Myth of Modernism', included in: *William Lethaby 1857–1931 Architecture, Design and Education*. Edited by S. Backemayer & T. Gronberg. (Lund Humphries) 1984.]

73. W. R. Lethaby. *Architecture: an Introduction to the History and Theory of the Art of Building*. (Home University Library.) 1911.

74. W. R. Lethaby. 'The Building Art: theories and discussions'. In *The Builder*. Vol. 124. 1923.

75. W. R. Lethaby. 'The Architecture of Adventure'. In *Journal of the RIBA*. 1910. Reprinted in *Form in Civilisation* (OUP) 1922.

76. W. R. Lethaby. 'Architecture, Nature and Magic'. In *The Builder* 1928, and by Duckworth, 1956.

77. In fact it was as early as 1907 that the Deutsche Werkbund had given credence to the 'machine æsthetic'. One aim of its founders Hermann Muthesius and Peter Behrens was: '... the improvement of industrial products through the combined efforts of artists, industrialists, craftsmen'.

78. It was as late as 1915 that the organisation, the Design and Industries Association, was formed largely by the efforts of Ambrose Heal, (of Heal's of Tottenham Court Road, and formerly a member of the Art Workers' Guild). Frank Pick was its first President. England was among the last countries in Europe to take such a step. (In 1930, the DIA gave way to the Society of Industrial Artists, and in 1933 to the Council for Art and Industry. In 1944 this was replaced by the Design Council for Industrial Design, or the Design Council, which was finally wound down in 1994.) Lethaby's concerns were met by new aesthetic considerations. In England, in a comparatively late but important contribution, the design and art critic Herbert Read advocated that the new industrial design make use of the same formal properties – proportion, colour relationships, tension and calm within the overall frame – as did non-representational, or abstract, art. In this sense, Read argued, designed artefacts like ceramics, furniture, fabrics, and automobiles appeal to the same aesthetic mechanisms as the fine arts. They were to be regarded as a subset of the fine arts. In the same way as the theorists of the Arts and Crafts movement before him, Herbert Read wished to widen the definition of art to include the industrialised crafts. He campaigned for industry to employ more artists in its design departments. His seminal book, *Art and Industry*, (Faber and Faber) appeared in 1934.

79. W. R. Lethaby. 'Architecture as Form in Civilisation'. Lecture. In *The London Mercury*.

Ditchling Village

CHAPTER FIVE

JOHNSTON AND THE CRAFT COMMUNITIES IN DITCHLING PART I

Edward Johnston's creative work – his 'things' – arose from the interplay between his calligraphy skills, his beliefs and his interactions with friends, with colleagues and with patrons. These interactions were varied: collaborative, challenging, endorsing. They stimulated Johnston into exploring new directions, they confirmed those he had already taken, they provided his bread and butter.

Now, however, the setting was Ditchling, in Sussex, an out-of-the-way and quintessentially English village. Artisanal trade crafts were its essential economy but, increasingly, artist-craftsmen came to live and work there. An ambience grew up among this new group of people, a philosophical sureness prevailed. It was as if the village was an acoustic providing the resonance by which the work of its new craftsmen could be heard.

The details of Johnston's move can be pieced together from his correspondence with Eric Gill and Hilary Pepler and from their diaries. The idea to leave London was inspired by Gill's own rustication, though it lay dormant for some years. Gill himself had been guided largely by memories of his boyhood when he used to tramp from his home in Brighton across the Downs to Ditchling. He moved there in the summer of 1907, buying a modestly-sized Georgian house, Sopers, in High Street. He was attracted to the village as a 'cell of good living' – though this phrase was written at the end of his life, in his autobiography. For both Gill and Johnston Ditchling was a wholesome refuge after the daily bother of life in Hammersmith. While the stretch of the riverside at Hammersmith Terrace was residential, some industrial plants were located nearby, including a lead mill, and it was flanked by an area of closely-packed terraced housing. (Even William Morris, in his day, complained about the noise of urchins playing on the doorstep of Kelmscott House.) Moreover, each now had a family with daughters – Gill with Betty and Petra; Johnston with Bridget, aged eight, Barbara, aged six, and Priscilla, newly-born in 1911.

Gill's contact with the Terrace was far from lost, however. He had kept on his workshop there until his new one at Sopers was ready, in April 1908. Through his work he kept in touch with his colleagues in the Hammersmith craft community. A diary entry for 12th March, 1908 detailing on going life in his workshop is indicative:

> Cribb and I worked all day. May Morris, Epstein, Cobden-Sanderson, Mrs E[dward]. J[ohnston], E[van Gill], T .M, and N[oel] R[ooke] called in noon.

But it was with Johnston that Gill was especially close. The professional interests they shared brought Johnston closer into Gill's widening circle. Numerous entries in Gill's diary for 1907–08 mention their continuing work for Count Kessler, for example, on the 'sub' (the half titles) for the Insel Verlag editions of the writings of Faust, Schopenhauer, and Balzac. Entries for February and March 1908, record another Kessler commission requiring lettering or calligraphy:

> To E. J. in eve re. Kessler Address
> E. J and I made Kessler Address.[1]

Another interest they shared continued to be the activities of the Art Workers' Guild. On 24th January 1908 Johnston and Gill went there to hear a talk on Impressionism. They met up with William Rothenstein, Roger Fry, and the craftsman, Charles Spencer.[2] Yet another was Johnston's Society of Calligraphers. In February 1908 Gill was planning with Johnston a lecture to the Society. Gill noted in his diary:

> Went through lantern slides with E. J. in eve. Sorted slides alone from 9.0-12.0.
> E. J. was out until 12.30.
> Cal. Society in eve. I lectured on 'revival of good lettering' with lantern slides.[3]

There was also Gill's involvement in Johnston's own work. The 28th October 1910 saw Gill working with Johnston preparing the third edition of *Writing & Illuminating, & Lettering*. On numerous other occasions Gill simply visited Johnston socially, coming up from Ditchling and often staying overnight. During 1908 entries in his diary include:

> To E. J. in eve. Til 2.0. argued re. Beardsley and all that gave rise to! To Johnstons to dinner and then stayed with them until Monday.

> E. J. promised to come for weekend but wired to say he couldn't. ce la va [*sic*]
> To Franco-British Exhib. with E. J. and Max [Gill's brother].[4]

In 1910 Gill took some lessons in French with Greta Johnston in preparation for his trip to see Aristide Maillol in France.[5]

It was early in 1912 that Johnston was drawn to visit Gill in Ditchling. The move was made imperative by Greta's ill-health. In 1912 she was diagnosed as suffering from tuberculosis. Johnston found Gill's new life inspiring. He saw in the rural way of life an embodiment of the Morrisian ideal of craft practice. Then, in March 1912, he stayed for a week with Gill, who helped him look for a suitable house. Gill's precisely-written diary conveys a vivid picture of their search:

> E. J. & Aus [?] & B.B & P [Johnston's children] came for weekend 3.46 at Hassocks. E[thel] & I met them there.
> Walked to Wivelsfield and Jacob's Post [on Ditchling Common] with E. J. to inspect possible houses (the rest in pony trap).
> Walked with E. J. in morning to Coombewood. Took shelter from the rain in barn, as Wick Farm in the midst of lambing.
> Walk with E. J. and Max [Gill's brother] in hills. Mirrorscope after supper.[6]

A novice to the countryside, Johnston noted these incidents in his own diary in more romantic terms. The barn at Coombewood becomes 'Noah's Ark', and through the 'v. wet rain (wind)' engulfing them they saw 'a rainbow'.[7] Priscilla Johnston understood this sensibility in her father. She writes of him coming:

> … to look longingly at the country scene, to listen ... to tales of home-brewed ale and home-cured bacon and all the country ways with which the Gills were so enthusiastically experimenting.

A week later Gill wrote to Johnston to say:

> I'm making some enquiries about the Burnt House. I've found out interesting facts relating to it, but I'm not yet in touch with the owners. I hope to be so soon. Yours sincerely, Gill.[8]

Johnston's letter to Gill of the 4th May 1912 shows his interest in moving:

> I hope you will keep a bright outlook for a possible home without taking undue trouble. We shall probably be able to put in a day or two about Michaelmas (in Ditchling) and I think we should be prepared to take a suitable house, if the chance offered, then, tho' we do not give up our lease till [sic] Ladyday next. If something particularly good turned up I might take it sooner. Tho' there is so much to fit in this summer that I don't expect to be able to inspect anything myself before the end of Septr.
>
> (We are off to Lulworth Cove next week probably for about a month into wh. pleasant distraction I must fit work and classes. About the beginning of Aug. we are expected in Scotland at Greta's home for 5 or 6 weeks and a day or two (I dream of one night at least) in the R[oyal] Observatory in Edinburgh. About the 12th–20th. Aug. I have to make a trip to Germany to speak or rather chalk on a blackboard at the Internat[ional] Art Teachers or Drawing Congress (I can't ever remember their name) at Dresden. It suggests rather a giddy time tho' I hope to manage a few solid things in it. Of course, if we hear of anything, or see our way to taking a likely look round we would probably manage to get back from Scotland a little earlier.

> Anyhow we are keen to move to the country soon, and even if it were a temporary house it might be worth our while as an experiment in position climate etc. Ditchling & the Downs have rather captivated our fancy we want to be better acquainted with the fact ... Yrs E. J.[9]

Gill's reply of 15th May ends: 'We shall certainly continue to hunt houses for you.'[10] Another letter of 25th July 1912 mentions the possibility of two properties, one Coombewood House and the other a farm house in East End Lane.[11] Later entries in Gill's diary up to August 1912 read:

> Johnston came in noon to look for home. Stayed the night. We talked until 2.00 am. Househunting with E. J. all morning and noon. E. J. and Mrs J. came down for day to see home.[12]

Johnston actually moved on the 30th September 1912. In the event, he found a house on the Lewes Road named Downsview, making him Gill's close neighbour. On 10th October 1912 Gill noted: 'To supper at Johnston's, with E[thel].' Just after Christmas (the 28th December 1912) Johnston noted: 'Gills to tea, Xmas tree, dance and song'.

Still living in Hammersmith, Pepler's feelings about the loss of Johnston's company are revealed in a number of letters he sent to him in Ditchling. One is dated 24th October 1912:

> Dear Johnston, I reply to say that the 6.30 [postal collection] has escaped me of late that I have saved my half-pennies for the 'New Age' in which for the moment I am interested. But we miss you. It is bad for me to have no one to revise my creeds, and no one with whom to consume the last precious moments of the night. I wonder if we go to bed any earlier? Do you?[13]

In a second, dated 4th December 1912, there is the first indication of Pepler himself wishing to move to Ditchling.

> Dear Johnston, Please answer by return. Could you and Mrs Johnston (one or both) come to a Terrace Xmas supper here on Thursday Dec. 15th. We await your answer before summoning the host.
>
> Can you think of any work which I could do at Ditchling? We want an excuse to follow the prophet (you) into the wilds. Your friend, H. Douglas C. Pepler.[14]

In a third, written on New Year's Eve 1912 from his cottage at Lulworth Cove, Pepler appreciated having once shared Johnston's company:

> My dear Johnston, I send the doggerel which I wrote on receipt of your beautiful verses – but you will be able to see through the poor collection of my words how much we do value yours. I wish you were here in front of our fire (logs and blue flame) so that we might take in the New Year about which I am trying to be cheerful. This year now in its last hours has been a curious one; in many ways the most unhappy I have known but with such fierce glimpses of wonder and light that I cannot be ungrateful for it. I count some of the hours we spent together, and these verses to David, among the joys which has [sic] enclosed in its gloomy folds. That fortnight we had here together was not to be despised. I hope that 1913 will have some replica. Clare and David are here, we have left Stephen and Mark with their grandparents. Your friend Douglas Pepler.[15]

The meaning of this new phase of Johnston's life is varied, for there was both quiet continuity and fundamental change. Up into the mid-1920s Ditchling became home to a growing number of artist craftsmen, of whom the first arrivals, aside from Eric Gill (with his assistant, Joseph Cribb, from 1908) were Johnston himself and Hilary Pepler. Others who arrived in the mid-20s were Joseph Cribb's brother, Lawrie Cribb, the painters Louis Ginnett and Frank Brangwyn, the hand-weaver Ethel Mairet (she wrote the seminal handbook, *A Book of Vegetable Dyes,* 1917) and those in her train – including her husband, the actor and writer Philip Mairet, and her brother, the jeweller Frederick Partridge. Along with Gill's former partner, Laurence Christie, they lived in the village itself.

Others settled on Ditchling Common, some two miles to the north. They included Gill's protégés, the sculptor Desmond Chute and the painter-poet David Jones. Ethel Mairet's assistant, the weaver Valentine KilBride, came in the mid-1920s. Other fellow Catholics who settled there were the artist Philip Hagreen and the loom-builder George Maxwell. They became the nucleus of the Roman Catholic Guild of S. Joseph and S. Dominic.

In the later 1920s, the potter Bernard Leach enabled his Japanese fellow potter Hamada Shoji and his friend, the philosopher of craft Yanagi Soetsu, to make brief but significant visits to Ditchling, where they met Ethel Mairet, Johnston, and Valentine KilBride. Their ideas were closely related to Johnston's own, based on their reading of Morris and Ruskin. In 1936, Bernard Leach stayed for a long summer in Ditchling.

On account of this migration Ditchling was home to a thriving and latter-day outpost of the, by then, diminishing Arts and Crafts movement. It became a 'mansion' of artist-craftsmen, comprising two wings – one, centred in the village, was religiously more diverse; the other, devoutly Roman Catholic, was on the Common. Despite this distinction of religious emphasis, they shared a broadly similar aesthetic regarding craft. In this sense, an overall harmony of purpose prevailed in Ditchling.

However, along with these newcomers there also filtered into this remote village two further strands of thought. One was a form of English modernism. So diverse as to defy precise definition, modernism was nevertheless a tangible force affecting all the arts in the period of the 1910s–30s. Its origins were eclectic and international, its arena was largely urban. Inspired by secular, socialist, and even anarchistic thought, its frame of mind was experimental. Critical in outlook and often ironic in mood, it wished to reinstate the individual in an industrialised impersonal world. In countering this, it was much inspired by notions of the 'primitive'. Yet it looked well beyond the horizons that encompassed William Morris. Based on the craft values he had established, it searched for authentic forms of expression for the new materials and techniques made available by technology. Such issues underpinned a philosophy of design which, in England, found its belated, if moderate, voice in William Lethaby. (Fig. 50).

Not surprisingly, the forms that modernism took in Ditchling were specific – and muted. Johnston was affected differently from other craftsmen there, such as

Fig. 50. Portrait bust of William Lethaby from the Art Workers' Guild

Ethel Mairet, or David Jones. The figures of modernist complexion who impinged on Johnston were Lethaby and his followers, Gerard Meynell and Frank Pick. Lethaby provided insights into the need for design to be of its time which was to inform Johnston's sans serif block letter alphabet for the London Underground. The other figure was Gill, who through his artistic innovations (in carved sculpture, for example) and his wide-ranging contacts, made Johnston more aware than he might otherwise have been that a different artistic consciousness was evolving. Gill became, in effect, Johnston's *avant-coureur*. It is partly for this reason that he features so prominently in this chapter.

The second and, in Ditchling's case, more powerful strand was Roman Catholicism and the radical social thought emanating from its policy-makers. Catholic social policy originated in Italy in the 1880s. It was one of the instruments by which Pope Leo XIII (1878–1903) sought renewed authority for the papacy in the wake of the secular liberal movements in Europe, described as the 'New Order'. The Vatican was particularly exercised by the unification of Italy in 1870 and the consequent annexation of the Papal States, which had left the Pope – at that time Pius IX – 'a prisoner in the Vatican'. Of equal concern were tensions arising from the unification of Germany in 1871 and from developments in the Third Republic of France, also from 1871. Directly threatening were the appeal of socialism and the organisation of trade unions. The politics of the Vatican formed part of a concerted front of Roman Catholic reaction. The spiritual inspiration for this lay in the writings of the thirteenth-century philosopher, St. Thomas Aquinas. The return to the Scholasticism of St. Thomas Aquinas, newly named Neo-Thomism, buttressed a crusading Catholicism which, while caring and inspired, was also theological and prescriptive.

The keystone of Pope Leo XIII's social policy was his Encyclical Letter, *The Condition of the Working Classes* (known as *Rerum Novarum*) of 1891.[16] Adhering to the ideas of St. Thomas Aquinas, this Letter spoke of the need for individual responsibility and the widespread ownership of land. Property, the Letter claimed, is a natural right, enshrined in law. It was a Catholic response to Socialism. Neo-Thomism came to be associated, therefore, with the right wing of the political spectrum of the time, and more so in the late 1920–30s when it had become a bulwark against Communist doctrine. An earlier Encyclical Letter of 1878, entitled *Socialism, Communism, Nihilism,* had dealt expressly with what it called 'these barbarous terms and titles'. It had identified such revolutionary movements as '... a deadly plague tainting society to its core'.

Fig. 51. Photograph of Father Vincent McNabb (photographer and date unknown).

Neo-Thomism, as a set of texts to guide the moral regeneration of society, was taken up and adapted for England by a charismatic Dominican priest, Father Vincent McNabb. (Fig. 51). His leadership was crucial in the setting up, with Gill and Pepler, of a Dominican guild on Ditchling Common. To him can be ascribed Gill's involvement with Father John O'Connor and Pepler, in 1922, in the reading and translation of Jacques Maritain's seminal book based on Thomist thought, *Art et Scholastique*. Pepler printed their translation as *The Philosophy of Art* in 1923.

In a sense, therefore, Father McNabb, the Roman Catholic social thinker, was the counterpart to William Lethaby. His impact was immediate and convulsive.

From 1917, he communed with Gill and Pepler, who by that time were engaged in small-scale farming on Ditchling Common. He officiated in the progress of their increasingly devout Catholic practices. In June 1918, he received them as Novices into the Tertiary Order of Dominicans (an Order for lay artisans). From July 1920, he helped them constitute their own Guild of St. Joseph and St. Dominic. Together, joined by other Roman Catholics, they became a closely knit community, perceived as clannish and enclosed, forming that 'northern wing' in Ditchling, to which Johnston and the craftmen living in the village – and the villagers themselves – had to relate. Winifride Denyer, the daughter of the guildsman George Maxwell, spoke of them (with a smile) as 'intellectual gypsies'.[17]

In this matter, Johnston needed to be clear. One fundamental change, which became apparent from 1917, was the theological issue implicit in land ownership. Belonging formally to the Church of England, Johnston's Christian spirituality had always illuminated his life and thought. His short but moving book, *A Carol and other Rhymes,* of 1915, is a testament to religious faith, *per se*, rather than to dogma. In it craft work was comprehended in a religious light, not unlike a form of spiritual exercise. But it was at Ditchling that the theological substance of his belief came to be tested. According to the Dominican view, as set out by Father McNabb, the sanctity of work extended to include the owning and care of one's tools and implements, where 'tools' also embraced workshops and the land. For Father McNabb, working the land was a 'Primary thing'.

For Johnston, however, land was not subsumed into a religious issue. He also experimented with farming, albeit on the scale of a tiny homestead, consisting of just one field, spurred on by its novelty and the food shortages of wartime. From 1917 to early in 1920 he shared Halletts Farm, on Ditchling Common, with Pepler. For Johnston, however, the working of the land had a practical rather than a religious purpose. Placed in this quandary, he had to clarify his position regarding Roman Catholic doctrine and the role of land. His wife Greta played a crucial role in steering him away from Roman Catholic orthodoxy. Her problem was with the very culture of Roman Catholicism, having been brought up in a Scottish Presbyterian home.

The issue of the absolute authority of the pope finally brought the matter to a head, overlaying any issue about land. Johnston could not accept the notion of papal exclusivity. As a result, there occurred what Hilary Pepler's second son, Stephen (ordained in 1932 as Father Conrad) chose to call a 'quiet and gentle schism'. By February 1920, when Johnston moved with his family back to Ditchling village, his differences with Pepler and Gill, while never acrimonious, were essentially permanent.

Johnston, therefore, steered his own course through various systems of thought. The older foundation of the Arts and Crafts movement was overlaid by both modernist tendencies and by the Roman Catholic resurgence. In a complex manner, some of the ideas propagated by these movements were connected, yet in other ways they were opposed. Johnston adapted his views according to the convictions he had already formed. Their effect on his work as a calligrapher and on the nature of the commissions he took up deserves a specialist study that is beyond the scope of the present chapter.

Fig. 52. View of Ditchling village, wood-engraving by Laurence Christie, 1923.

This will focus instead on Johnston's life in Ditchling and on his links with the craft groups which developed there, informed by these new modes of thought. The initial group of craftsmen comprised, unmistakably, Eric Gill, Edward Johnston and Hilary Pepler. Until about 1918 theirs was a dynamic partnership, combining the energetic, if volatile, inspirations of Gill, the analytical qualities of Johnston, and the initiatives of Pepler, who was so frequently their catalyst.

Johnston thrived on discourse. Contact was made with fellow craftsmen, even if it was not always sustained. He also responded to village life with its convivial gatherings and its chance encounters of the day. (Priscilla Johnston records, for instance, that he would philosophise with a Mr. Cox, a bricklayer in Ditchling, who sometimes did work at his house.) Johnston was especially sensitive to the correspondence between the crafts, to what Ethel Mairet called, with insight, the 'general unity of inspiration'.[18] Yet, he was also entirely self-contained.

However, there is scant anecdotal comment about these friendships in Johnston's otherwise precise and detailed diaries and workbooks. Few of Pepler's papers are in the public domain. Information comes largely, therefore, from Gill's diaries. Their brief but meticulously-kept records of his work and meetings reveal his richly varied life and interests, even though a critical section of them (August 1908 to January 1910) is missing. In them, Johnston is for ever being mentioned. For a further reason, therefore, Gill has a necessary prominence in this account.

Johnston had lived much of his life in towns though the countryside had always appealed to him. Spells in his youth were spent with his cousins, the McInneses, at Rickerby House near Carlisle and family holidays were spent at Laurencekirk, near Aberdeen, in Scotland (with Greta's family) and at Lulworth Cove, in Dorset (with the Pepler family).[19] Now aged forty, he was to settle permanently in a rural environment. Ditchling village (Fig. 52), in the lee of the South Downs and immediately below the Ditchling Beacon, was at that time surrounded by untrammelled countryside. Just to its north lies the open land of Ditchling Common.

Gill was particularly attracted to the Downs – or the 'hills', as he called them – exploring their length as far as Beachy Head to the east, and Shoreham and beyond, to the west. On Coronation Day, 22nd June 1911, his diary reads:

> To Lodge Hill to see Beacon fires grand sight, in wind and mist. Torch light procession to the Beacon.

Gill communicated his enthusiasm for the rural life – and the drama of the weather – to friends and notably to Johnston and Pepler. Aside from the healing effect of the countryside on Greta Johnston (she suffered from tuberculosis and spent time in 1912 in a sanatorium in nearby Midhurst), Ditchling was also congenial to Johnston's family life. Especially important to them were the spacious gardens of both of Johnston's homes in the village – Downsview, until 1916, and Cleves, from 1920 and the South Downs, open to view beyond. Both houses looked on to this ribbon of rounded, scooped hills with the Beacon its high point over eight hundred feet above sea level. They ran from east to west, giving the village protection from the sea winds. Their light changing with the moods of the sun, cloud and rain, the Downs provided a backdrop to their daily lives rather as the River Thames had done, earlier on, at their Hammersmith home. On the western side of the Downs there still thrive two windmills, 'Jack and Jill', which were dear to the Johnstons. His diary for the 9th January 1913 records:

> G. E. Bt. Ba [Greta, Edward, Bridget, Barbara] to windmill. Gathered primroses.

The Mill Book (Fig. 53) was a childhood project written and illustrated in 1917 by the six-year-old Priscilla at the suggestion of her father, who taught her that learning is best achieved doing 'real things'. For them the Downs were a place of spiritual stimulation; the space and light there would have brought an emotional calm.

Priscilla Johnston's biography of her father speaks of the flora of the Downs and their ploughed fields, the substrata of chalk with flint showing through. Recalling the picnics and explorations she enjoyed there as a small girl with her father and sisters, she wrote:

> ... at the top of the Downs one's climb was rewarded not only by the immense view, but by a beautiful dew pond, very large and perfectly circular ... like a small lake, reflecting the sky. Johnston made matchbox boats to sail on it .... We would set the little boat on the pond and watch it sail away.

Noel Rooke, Johnston's constant friend from the Central School, noticed his healthy appearance. Gill's diary records for the last weekend of March 1913:

> Noel Rooke came in noon for the weekend; To E. J. with N. R. to dinner. Met Gerard Meynell there. Home 1.20 a.m. To Patcham on the hills by Standean with E. J. & N. R. & Meynell. N. R. returned to London from Preston. Home via the Beacon. 9.0.

Further recollections from this period were recorded by Hilary Pepler's daughter, Susan (now Falkner) and also by her brother, Stephen (Father Conrad), both of whom were friends of Priscilla. Susan was an acute observer. She was drawn to and recalled the Downs with a child's intensity. She spoke of:

> ... knowing where to find bee orchids on the Downs and the woods where butterfly orchids grow ... My brother Stephen ... was the one for butterflies and, because the Downs were great places for butterflies and orchids of all kinds, he had quite a collection of rarities.[20]

Stephen Pepler, looking back some forty years, and more, recalled:

> One of the grand figures of that time was the old farmer with smock and beard who rode into the village in a pony trap with an enormous umbrella attached to it; he was the Reeve of Ditchling Common, held for life after election by the Common lease-holders, and one which had, apparently, existed since the Elizabethan age.[21]

Aside from the anxiety over Greta's poor health, these were among the most contented in Johnston's life. Moreover, his so-called lassitude also appears to have dissipated. It is the case that in the earlier Ditching years Johnston was extraordinarily productive. Noel Rooke's letter to Bridget Johnston, written in the context of the tributes paid to Johnston in 1945, seeks to confirm this:

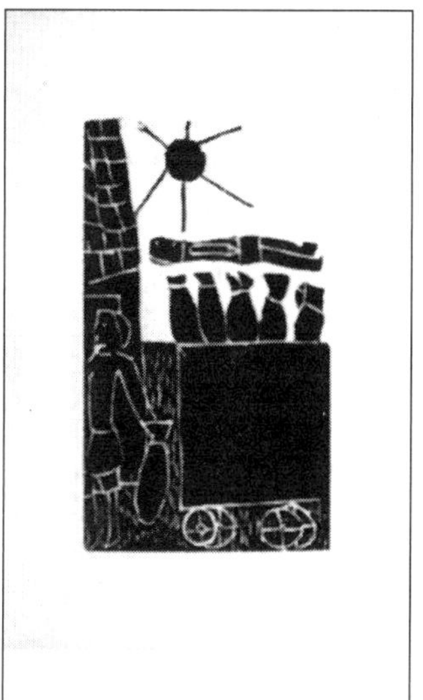

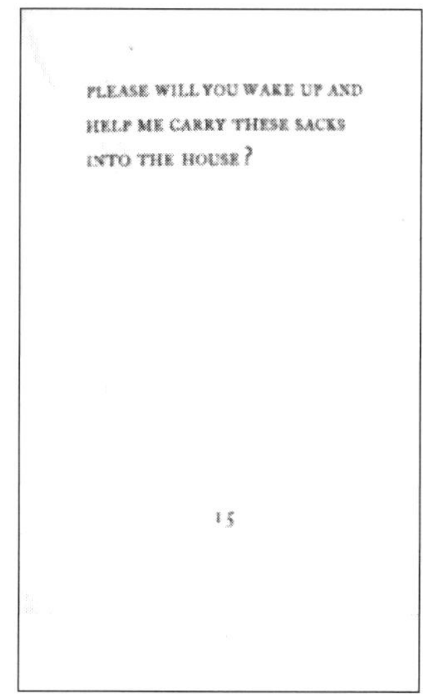
PLEASE WILL YOU WAKE UP AND HELP ME CARRY THESE SACKS INTO THE HOUSE?

15

Fig. 53. *The Mill Book*

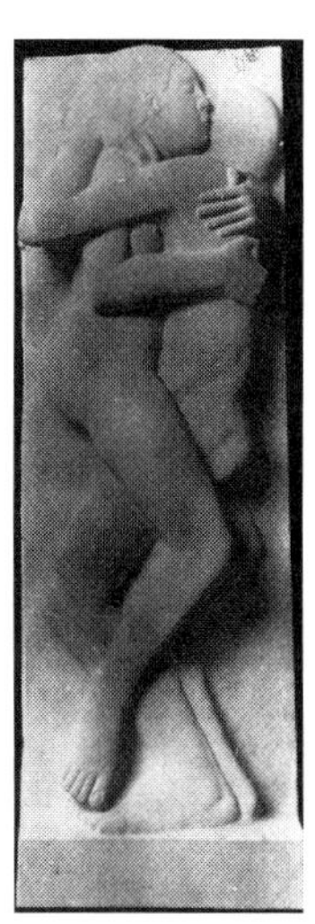

Figs. 54–56. Eric Gill's earliest sculptures: *Crucifixion, Estin Thalassa* (There is the Sea'), *Ecstasy*; made in Ditchling village between 1909–11.

> The move to Ditchling appears to be a great stimulus to his health.... That stimulus appears to me to last six years. Those would have been the years in which you [Bridget] noticed such things and began to remember them.[22]

These years were brightened, too, by the games, the childlike pranks, the magical – and the scientific – play he invented for his children, together with the toys and booklets he made for them. Johnston shared with Gill a fascination for the mirrorscope (a form of epidiascope) and for the telescope. Just after Christmas (28th December) 1912, Gill's diary reads:

> Johnston came to tea and helped me arrange the m'scope. After tea we had the m'scope show of Christmas pictures in the workshop. The children sang carols very nicely. Including Miss Sawyer, who came to see the pictures. We had 25 people in the house. Johnstons came to tea. Mirrorscope after.

There is a similar entry for 12th September 1915:

> To Ditchling to E. J.'s. Looked at Jupiter and his moons thro' telescope.

In 1989 an exhibition was held at the Gillian Jason Gallery in London entitled 'The Lost Idyll'. It showed art works from the Guild of St. Joseph and St. Dominic on its demise in that year. While ignoring the rigours of the Guild's semi monastic life, the title was aptly chosen. The period between the mid-1850s to the 1920s was characterised by a restlessness with the art establishments of the metropolitan centres. In a sense, Gill, Johnston, and Pepler belonged to a wider European phenomenon in reaching out to what Lethaby appositely called 'inherited wisdoms'.[23] A search for spiritual renewal led to an awareness – a nostaglia, even – of cultures more distant in place or more remote in time. Indicative of this malaise were the Post-Impressionists' settlement at Le Poldu in Brittany or Gauguin's sojourn in Tahiti or Mamontov's art colony at Abramtsevo in Russia. Gill and Pepler were exhilarated by their trip in 1919 to the remoter parts of Ireland. At Claddagh, in Galway, they witnessed an unchanged village society whose women were still hand-spinning and hand-weaving clothes dyed in most brilliant colours.[24] This idealist escapism belongs to the modernist sensibility.

Moreover, from 1909, at Sopers, Gill began a major departure: he took up carving in stone. Of his first piece, *Estin Thalassa*, (Figs. 54–56), he said in his autobiography:

> My first erotic drawing was not on the back of an envelope but a week or so's work on a decent piece of hard stone.

Sculpted in relief, with a Greek inscription taken from Aeschylus' *Agamemnon*, it was exhibited at the Whitechapel Art Gallery and sold to Count Harry Kessler. Other early examples are the *Crucifixion* and *Ecstasy*, of 1910–11 and the monumental *Mulier*, a virgin Mother figure. This development led to an intense, if brief, friendship with Jacob Epstein, based on their mutual interest in reviving the art of carving in stone. Epstein came to Ditchling to visit Gill, staying at The Sandrock Inn, next door to Sopers. Gill's lettering for Epstein's monument to Oscar Wilde, in the Père Lachaise Cemetery in Paris, was worked out at Sopers.

The appeal of the ancient was an underlying need which took various forms. Gill's reawakening to Byzantine and Romanesque carved sculpture, Pepler's use of the simplest of printing equipment, and Johnston's extolling the value of medieval pen techniques, exemplified the urge to return to earlier forms, perceived to have a spiritual immediacy. Johnston expressed this necessity in one of the stanzas of his beguilingly simple set of verses included in *A Carol and other Rhymes*:

Let ancient way
Be guide to NEW
And coming DAY
Pick out the true[25]

The Ditchling experiments also involved farming on the Common. It had a certain affinity with the farming initiatives of one of the major figures of the Arts and Crafts movement, C. R. Ashbee, at his Guild of Handicraft at Chipping Campden, in 1908. It also links with the American transcendentist communes of the 1840s, for example, at Brook Farm associated with Ralph Waldo Emerson, a founding father of American individualism. One recalls how Emerson's writings had impressed Johnston in his preface to *Writing & Illuminating, & Lettering.*

There was also a strong Catholic identification with such pastoral idealism. Stephen Pepler, for instance, remembered his days in the Dominican Guild 'with joy' – 'Memories of it bring tears. It was the Third Order in its perfection.' In another piece of writing about his childhood memories there is present the sense of Ditchling being a 'Bethlehem'.[26] The idea may well have come to him from Fr. Vincent McNabb. For Fr. McNabb, this feeling was especially acute. His spiritual quest was '... to go back with Dominic and Francis of Assisi to Jesus of Nazareth'. Ditchling, in his imagination, was held up as the promise and the symbol of his much-hoped-for 'exodus' from the towns, many of them crowded with poor Catholic Irish immigrants – McNabb, too, was Irish – to the Catholic village, the traditional home of the Catholic family subsisting on small-holding husbandry and on handcraft work. In letters he wrote to Hilary Pepler in the 1940s two passages read:

> Your gift of Whitsun cream was more than welcome! It was, of course, one of the best things Ditchling could give. But it had memories in its gift. How irresistibly it brought back the Ditchling I first knew, and loved with the intensity of a first love. I can imagine that many a man marries the girl he loves not merely because he loves her ... but because his love of her has saved him from some fall ....
>
> There was an unforgettable time when 'Ditchling' was like music to my ears. Perhaps through my own fault – and assuredly to my own pain – I idealised it. I had never urged it to any path of sacrifice. But when I found it doing, as well as preaching, the things I could only preach to be done, I gave it something of the love I never gave a woman.[27]

Like all these figures – and like Morris and Lethaby in their historical imaginations – the craftsmen at Ditchling found a spiritual regeneration in withdrawing from an increasingly urbanised society into a form of rural 'primitivism'.

Fig. 57. Photograph of Amy Sawyer.

The earliest signs of Ditchling as the home of artist-craftsmen pre-date Gill's arrival. Gill himself wrote:

> ... you must not put it about that we were the first of the horrid army of arts and crafts people to arrive at and corrupt that ancient village. The good work had begun long before by Miss Amy Sawyer and her friends the Spongs.[28]

Amy Sawyer (Fig. 57), a painter and playwright, lived there as early as 1897. Of a Sussex family from East Grinstead, she had been a prize-winning pupil at the Herkomer Art School and had exhibited at the Royal Academy and at the Paris Salon. Her painting *The Swineherd* is illustrated in Hubert von Herkomer's book *My School and my Gospel* of 1908. Single and reclusive, eccentric in dress and manner, she lived at Russell House at the north end of the village. In 1904 she renamed it The Blue House painting it a striking 'Reckitt's' blue (this colour was the deep ultramarine blue wrapper of a laundry whitener). She also designed the fireplace surrounds in ceramic, built on a studio, and laid out a garden with artistry. Amy Sawyer had a captivating personality. Her young artistic helper Joanna Bourne wrote that she held 'in thrall' those who met her – including Gill – and that she was 'irresistible to men'. She described her as having:

> ... a quicksilver quality – something of the proud secretive gypsy, something of the white witch – perhaps a changeling, with her lissom beauty and her impish sense of humour, at times verging on the macabre.[29]

The fact that she had a withered right hand (afflicted by poisoning by lead paint lodged under the finger nails while painting) prompted her to take up the theatre. Her interest in realistic scenery and costumes was stimulated by her teacher, Herkomer, who enlisted his students to put on 'theatrical experiments' at his school. This, with an ear for the Sussex dialect, led to her writing her *Sussex Plays*. Some were put on in her garden, which lent itself as a natural stage set. She had her own troupe, the Ditchling Village Players, whom, like Herkomer, she enlisted from local people, including children.[30] Her *Sussex Tipteerers' Play* revived the medieval tradition of Mummer plays, understood by her to express the renewal of the Earth in Spring.

In an intuitive way Amy Sawyer was exploring the English folk tradition with the sensibility of Cecil Sharp, the pioneer of the English folk-song revival, whose work was prominent in the 1920s when Amy Saywer was active. Johnston, and no doubt Pepler, were responsive to her plays. Johnston's friends Gerard and Esther Meynell and their two daughters, Rosemary and Joanna, acted in some of them as did Philip Mairet and Joanna and Hilary Bourne. Given that Pepler created mime theatre (his *Plays for Puppets* was published by the S. Dominic's Press in 1929), it is possible that he – even if not Johnston – took part in her celebrated Ditchling Pageant of 1924 for, as Priscilla Johnston wrote '... at least half the village did'. Johnston, however, disapproved of the ethics of her best-known play, *The Brown Pot*. Joanna Bourne remembered his reaction:

> ... the public presentation of an appealing and successful murderess, however tragically provoked to crime, showed a lack of social responsibility.[31]

Let me not to the marriage of true mindes
Admit impediments, loue is not loue
Which alters when it alteration findes.
Or bends with the remouer to remoue.
O no, it is an euer fixed marke
That lookes on tempests and is neuer shaken:
It is the star to euery wandring barke
Whose worths unknowne, although his highth be taken.
not Times foole, though rosie lips and cheekes
Within his bending sickles compasse come.
Loue alters not with his breefe houres and weekes.
But beares it out euen to the edge of doome:
If this be error and vpon me proued.
I neuer writ, nor no man euer loued.

Fig. 58. Johnston's manuscript of 'Shakespeare's Sonnet No 116'. See also page 195.

Gill's diary shows her to have been part of the circle of Gill, Johnston, Meynell. On 10th May 1912, Gill 'took a cast of Miss Sawyer's foot and Ethel's head'. On Sunday 13th October 1912 'The Johnston's and Miss Sawyer came to tea.' At Christmas 1913 Gill gave her the Gladys panel, a figure incised into Hopton-wood stone.[32] Amy Sawyer became a venerated figure in Ditchling. In 1943 Johnston signed the Address given to her on her eightieth birthday. Bridget and Barbara Johnston, with some hundred others, attended her funeral in 1945.

Johnston's closer acquaintance, however, was with Louis Ginnett, a painter who showed at the Royal Academy. He first lived at Russell House in Ditchling as early as 1913. Employed as a war artist, in 1919 he bought (at auction) Chichester House, which is diagonally across the High Street from Sopers. Ginnett had a traditional training at the Académie Julien, Paris, and became a long-established teacher at Brighton School of Art. Two portraits of Johnston were drawn by him. One, dated 1913 when Johnston was forty-one years old, shows him to be robust-looking, of warm personality, with thick hair low on the nape of the neck (page 30). A second, probably done at the the same time, shows him asleep (page 208). (They are in dramatic contrast to William Rothenstein's distinctly dour portrait of Johnston, drawn at the Royal College following one of Johnston's gruellingly-long teaching sessions.) The two were lifelong friends. In 1927 Johnston gave Ginnett's daughter, Mary, his manuscript of Shakespeare's Sonnet No 116 as a wedding gift (Figs. 58 AND 106). It was written, he said, in his 'Black Letter' script, '... indirectly to delay the reader (so that each word would sink in.)'[33]

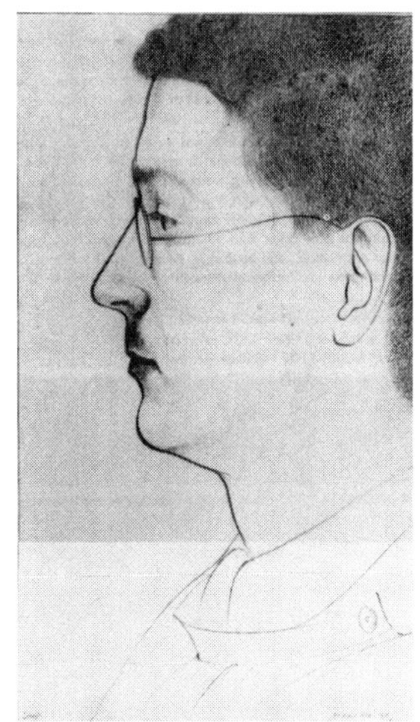

The first of Gill's associates to arrive in Ditchling was the fifteen year-old Joseph Cribb (Fig. 59), who came in 1908. He was born in Hammersmith and had become Gill's first apprentice the year before through his father, Herbert Cribb, who was a highly skilled trade engraver and cartographer and who did work for Emery Walker's photo-engraving business. Initially, Joseph Cribb lodged at The Sandrock Inn in the High Street, and then at a house called Little Cheals. In 1912 Gill sent him to Paris, to attend to the installation of Gill's lettering for the Oscar Wilde memorial in the Cimetière Père Lachaise. On his return from the Great War, in 1919, Joseph Cribb followed Gill to the Common, living at St. Anthony's and then at St. Rose Cottage. A craftsman very much in his own right, with his own practice and workshop, he was Gill's long-serving colleague, responsible for carving most of his lettering designs.[34] Joseph Cribb became the longest-established craftsman resident in Ditchling, with his practice as a stone carver and letter cutter. Yet, as far as their diaries show, he does not appear to have had a close friendship with Johnston. Johnston is wholly reticent about Cribb. His brother, Lawrie Cribb (Fig. 60), became another of Gill's assistants at Ditchling. Having also served in the Great War, he arrived in Ditchling in 1920, aged twenty-two, and lodged with his brother.[35]

Figs. 59–60.
Portrait drawing of Jo Cribb by Eric Gill. Portrait of Lawrie Cribb, silhouette. (courtesy of J. Cribb.)

Another letter craftsman who came to live at Ditchling was Laurence Christie, Gill's former partner in Hammersmith and who had also been Johnston's pupil at the Central School. In March 1914 he visited Johnston while looking for a house in Ditchling. By late 1914 he was living at Rowles Croft. Johnston's diary records for the 29th December: 'G & E dined Christie's 7.35–10.10'. They met up

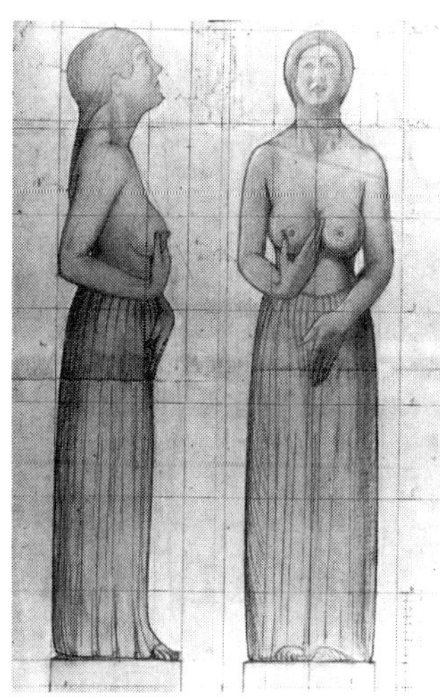

Fig. 61. Studies by Gill for his sculpture, *Mulier*, (Virgin Mother figure) commissioned by Roger Fry for the garden of his house outside Guildford, in 1911.

again on New Year's Day 1915. Sometime later he moved to Gatlands, at the south-west corner of the village crossroads. Laurence Christie appears to have had a low-key career as a lettering artist and decorator of ceramics. A fellow Quaker, worshipping with the Pepler family (at this point, in 1915, Pepler was not yet Catholic), he kept up his friendship with Johnston, and was clearly remembered by Priscilla Johnston as a person who would 'drop in' to Downsland or Cleves. Gill's diary, too, records occasional visits from Christie – he referred to him by his initials, H. L. C. – for tea, or for a tennis party. Johnston also records playing tennis with him, in May 1915. On Johnston's retirement from the Central School in 1912 Christie taught there as a colleague of Graily Hewitt, also Johnston's pupil.

There is contrary sense, however, in which this new life in Ditchling was stimulated by widening contacts rather than narrowed by rural isolation, that Ditchling was a continuum with Hammersmith. The village was not an enforced retreat. Change was evolutionary rather than radical. The London to Brighton railway line ran through nearby Hassocks and Burgess Hill. Accessible at that time by horse-drawn bus, these rail stations enabled Gill and Johnston to maintain their many and important contacts in London. They would often meet in London to have supper with mutual friends. And Johnston continued with his Monday afternoon lectures at the Royal College of Art in Kensington, a college he now preferred to the Central School – with an added advantage that he kept in touch with Lethaby. He would on occasions stay overnight with the Peplers in Hammersmith Terrace. Similarly, London friends and notably Noel Rooke, who was still teaching at the Central School, would visit Ditchling in the years up to about 1920. For example, Noel Rooke spent Christmas 1913 with Johnston and Gill. Johnston's diary records for 31st December:

> G[reta]. B[ridge]t. Ba[rbara], Noel, E. J up to Downs … went over Beacon to dewpond and home by Bostal.

Nor was Johnston to be detached from his basic convictions, built up so securely during the previous decade. Unlike Gill, he was not prone to sudden enthusiasms for *avant garde* departures. For Johnston, influences worked their way through quietly and new ideas took root imperceptibly, well-grounded in the old.

While Gill may have opted for a rural life, he also enjoyed a routine of almost weekly trips to London, combining appointments related to his commissions with an active social life. This aspect of Gill's life had an enlightening effect on Johnston. More reclusive by nature, it was through Gill that he kept abreast not only with those artistic departures that engaged Gill so passionately, but with the London art scene itself. Needless to say, however, Johnston was too self-sufficient to be actually drawn into these new developments.

Gill's trips to London took place mainly on account of his work as a sculptor. He had pieces exhibited in the Grafton Gallery, in the Goupil Gallery, and in the Chenil Galleries, organised largely through Roger Fry. Gill often had invitations to dine, sometimes with patrons in their homes, and sometimes with friends such as the sculptor Jacob Epstein, or Roger Fry or William Rothenstein. Dinner might be at a number of high class restaurants.[36] Gill's diary for 10th November 1910 records:

> To Exhib. of Post-Impressionism at Grafton Gallery in morning with Jacob and to British Museum after.'

The quickening of artistic activity in Ditchling from 1910 was sensed by these London friends, who took a keen interest in Gill's purpose there. This centred on his discovery of archaic, preclassical art. Gill had become possessed with the notion of a 'New Religion'. He proposed the construction of a monumental Temple on the Downs – inspired by Stonehenge and conceived as a kind of Valhalla. He swept along with him in this scheme none less than Jacob Epstein, Roger Fry, who had a key role in London's art world as the editor of *The Burlington Magazine*, and William Rothenstein, the Director of the Royal College of Art. The painter Augustus John also showed interest. In June 1910, Epstein spent the weekend with Gill at Ditchling, and then again in September, with more auspicious consequences.[37]

Gill's contact with Roger Fry was especially fruitful during this period, up to 1912. Fry published Gill's pioneer article 'Inscriptions' for *The Burlington Magazine* in 1910, the same year as he commissioned Gill to sculpt the *Madonna* figure (Fig. 61). He came down to Ditchling on 19th June 1911 to approve of it. Gill's diary for 18th September 1912 records: 'Roger Fry and Clive Bell came in noon to see what I had to exhibit for the forthcoming Grafton Gallery exhibition.' It was the *Golden Calf* sculpture.

Epstein had become aware of African sculpture. Gill, in turn, was awakened to Indian Hindu and Buddhist sculpture. Their sensual forms demonstrated to him the necessary fusion of the religious and the erotic. He began to associate with the Anglo-Singhalese scholar Ananda Coomaraswamy and attended as a founder-member the inaugural meeting of the India Society on the 15th June 1910. (Other founder-members were William Lethaby, Roger Fry, and William Rothenstein – at whose home Gill was able to listen to Indian music.)

Ananda Coomaraswamy is important for Ditchling not because he ever stayed there, but because of his influence over those who did. First and foremost was Ethel Mairet; he was her first husband. But earlier, Gill had met and collaborated with Coomarswamy in a number of ways:

> To Coomaraswamy to dinner. Discuss my contribution to 'Post-Industrialism'. C's mistress sang some beautiful Indian songs.
> Coomeraswamy and A & C cover.
> Coomaraswamy. Design for cover of Myths of the Hindus.[38]

In 1914, Coomaraswamy invited Gill to write the preface for *Visvakarma*, a book of photographs he compiled of Indian sculpture, and so-named because Visvakarma is the 'revealer' of craft and architecture in the Hindu pantheon.[39] In it Gill claimed that Greek classical art of the time of Phidias was:

> … specious and inferior to its archaic predecessors .... Primitive or archaic art are the works of men seeking the Real ....

Realism was defined by Gill as ' ... the imaging of the essential quality of things....', an aim that was distinct, he continued, from the 'commercial atheism of today'. Gill appealed to what, in essence, was a modernist theory of expression. It accorded with the ideas of Epstein and Coomaraswamy and also those of Roger Fry. At this time, Fry, who was already known for his ideas of an aesthetic of 'significant form' and for his evaluation of Cézanne, began to write essays on African art in the same vein as Gill.

These new directions were not lost on Johnston. Through Gill, Johnston would have been conversant with the ideas of Coomaraswamy, Fry and Rothenstein. Once settled in Ditchling, he would often travel to or from London with Gill. On Monday 20th January 1913 Johnston recorded:

> Taxi to Meynells + on with Gill to Grafton Gallery (12.50–1.00)[40]

Evidently, Johnston wanted to see Gill's sculpture there. During these journeys, clearly, they shared news and opinions. Johnston was Gill's confidant and invited critic. Gill's essay on Post-Industrialism is a case in point. During this period the two shared a typewriter. Four entries in Gill's diary in May and June 1913, read:

> E. J. and Mrs E. J. came to supper. I went home with E. J. and read my essay to him. He appeared to approve of it. Essay on Post Industrialism in evening. Typewriting with E. J. and supper with him. E. J. and Gerard Meynell [of the Westminster Press] came to supper & we went kite flying on Lodge Hill at midnight.
>
> To E. J. to supper and to typewrite essay after.[41]

Another entry from the same period in Johnston's diary corroborates this:

> Gill supper and typing til abt. 12.40 talked till 3.25.[42]

Gill passed soon enough through his 'New Religion' phase. On 22nd February 1913, some four months after Johnston had moved to Ditchling, he converted to Roman Catholicism. Then, on 27th October 1913, his diary has the dramatic entry:

> Home alone with keys. Groomed pony for the first time. To Brighton to complete purchase of Hopkin's Crank.

A month later he moved in. Hopkin's Crank, his new house, like Sopers, was Georgian but this time it was situated on Ditchling Common some two miles to the north of the village. Although the house itself was small, it came with two acres of land. Gill proceeded to extend it, building workshops on the plan of a quadrangle In all probability this design looked back to the layout of Lincoln's Inn in Holborn, where he had shared Johnston's tiny flat.

From 1918, one of Gill's closest Roman Catholic friends was his fellow-sculptor, the young Desmond Chute. Writing in 1950, Chute recalled his first stay at Hopkin's Crank, in 1918. Like Pepler's children, he saw it as a kind of 'idyll':

Fig. 62. Hopkin's Crank, a drawing by Moira Hodell.

> Hopkin's Crank was at that time a neat square of a house on the western fringe of the Common, an untouched Georgian squatter's cottage, preceded by a porch and a diminutive fenced garden. Here amid sweet william, honesty and marigolds there grew two rose bushes, which, on stems furry with prickles, bears amid many deep-

grooved leaves, large flat single blooms, white or magenta ... The morning view out of my bedroom faced south: pigeons around the dovecote in the midst of a yard lined with workshops ... an opening [between Gill's and Joseph Cribb's workshop] led the eye through a meadow to the top of Bull's Brow and thence across the hidden Weald to the Downs and the open sky. Quince, apple and medlar bloomed in the orchard behind the house. Grey in the shadow of the workshops, sudden as a monolith on Easter Island, stood Gill's colossal carved figure – Mulier.[43]

The friendship between Johnston and Gill was undiminished by Gill's moving away from the village. Gill felt the need for greater isolation and a growing spiritual involvement in living from the land; yet, he kept Sopers on and used the workshop there for a few months while his new ones were being constructed. His diary reveals a regular routine during this period, 1913–15, of work on his first large-scale sculpture commission, The Stations of the Cross for Westminster Cathedral but also of almost daily trips down to the village, mainly to visit Johnston.

Their collaboration on the books for Count Harry Kessler also continued. From February 1913 to January 1914, they were working on the Cranach Presse edition of the *Eclogues* of Virgil. Gill's design of capital letters to match the Jenson types that were being using for the *Eclogues*, are mentioned in his diary. These confirm the closeness of their partnership:

Kessler alphabet 2 lines for his Jenson type. Kessler re Virgil. tea and dinner with him and E. J. at the Cecil, met Prince [Kessler's punch cutter].
To E. J. after breakfast re Kessler Virgil.
To lunch with Kessler at the Cecil. E. J. and D.[ouglas] Cockerell also there. V jolly time. Re. Virgil.
To Goupil Gallery and finished arranging show after. Home with E. J. 7.15 from V. [Victoria Railway Station].[44]

Another of Gill's letters to Johnston, written from Hopkin's Crank on 13th February 1914, shows his need for Johnston's continued support:

I'm getting ahead with the the carving of the Stations of the Cross now, so if you can come you'd confer a great favour on me by your criticisms. I've also got a particularly beautiful inscription here to show you, a regular snorker. I hope your invalids are now better and your anxieties are over ...[45]

Gill's daily routine is shown by diary entries for 22nd January and 31st March 1914 which show him consulting Johnston again about his Stations of the Cross:

To Ditchling in morn. To lunch E. J's. To tea Miss Sawyer's. Kessler's Virgil. Touching up blocks. Home 10.0.
To E. J's. in noon re gold powder for the haloes.

Johnston and Gill's lives were intertwined in many other ways during this period. Advice was sought mutually. Gill visited Johnston about his life-insurance policy and for loans (for unspecified amounts). Gill, likewise, discussed Johnston's commission for the *Brierley Address* manuscript. Sometimes Gill's brother, Max, accompanied him and sometimes his wife, Ethel, and his children. In all his to-ing and fro-ing from Hopkin's Crank down to the village, Gill depended largely upon his new bicycle and on occasions used a pony and trap.

Johnston, similarly, made frequent visits up to Hopkin's Crank, for tea, for supper, or at Christmas time to see their Christmas tree. His young sister, Olof, also visited. In March, 1915, Johnston was accompanied by some wounded soldiers recently returned from the 'front' (Gill's inverted commas), to amuse themselves with Gill's newly-acquired rifle, which he had bought for rabbit shooting.

Aside from the stimulation of Gill's circle in London, Johnston cultivated his own roots there, too. Like Gill, he was dependent on his contacts for his commissioned work. In this regard the appearance of Gerard Meynell in their diaries for 1913 is one of the most significant pointers in the development of Johnston's work.

Gerard Meynell became a key figure at this point in Johnston's life. He was an energetic go-getter, gifted with powers to enthuse. In promoting good design in printing in Britain he has largely been underestimated. His sense of printing probably originated with his passion for amateur photography. He then became interested in commercial book printing through his uncle Wilfrid Meynell, a Catholic who had acquired the Westminster Press from Cardinal Manning. In 1900 Gerard Meynell was able to buy the Westminster Press which he then sought to expand into the field of quality book printing. He aspired to bring his press up to the standards of the Chiswick Press.

His printing works were situated at 411A Harrow Road, Paddington but its offices were at 11 Henrietta Street, Covent Garden, strategically well-placed for the London publishing market. In character with these ambitions in 1911 Gerard Meynell adopted the most recent technology by using the Lanston Monotype composing machines.

A further and crucial development took place when Gerard Meynell … 'met Edward Johnston and … Eric Gill in Ditchling'. This was probably in the latter part of 1912 and is likely to have been through Gerard's wife, Esther (*née* Moorhouse), who had been brought up in Sussex and who became a prominent writer about life in that county. She married Gerard in 1909.[46]

It seems that Gerard Meynell was the main inspiration behind *The Imprint,* a name which he decided upon in mid-1912.[47] The idea grew out of discussions he had as early as 1911 with two craftsmen from the Central School of Art. Ernest Jackson had trained as a painter and become a teacher of lithography at the Central School with a special interest in book-illustration printing techniques. He was a founder-member of the Senefelder Club, devoted to lithography. In 1911 Jackson introduced Gerard Meynell to John Mason, the head of the book printing department at the Central School. Mason had been the principal compositor with the Doves Press and was a scholar of, and translator from, classical Greek. Mason saw *The Imprint* as the spearhead for the improvement of printing standards in the periodical field. Mason then invited Johnston, whose calligraphy classes he had followed, to become the 'lettering editor'. (At some later date the four editors also became financial directors of *The Imprint.*) The widespread support which the venture received is signalled by the thirty-three prominent figures who were enlisted as members of an advisory board, including Robert Bridges, John Hogg, William Lethaby, Benjamin Fletcher,

Douglas Cockerell – all Johnston's associates. Theodore de Vinne gave *The Imprint* an American dimension. It had an ambitious print run of ten thousand and sold for one shilling. But the venture turned out to be short-lived with nine issues appearing monthly between January and November 1913 (with a lapse in September and October).

The four purist editors aspired to apply the values of the Private Press movement to industrial printing. A competition for good commercial printing was set up. William Blake's 'Glad Dawn' was proclaimed *The Imprint*'s motto – 'an earnest of our ideals'. In the opening 'Notes' the editors laid out their objectives:

> ... we care for our trade and wish to raise it to a worthy place among the crafts.... We are in sympathy with attempts to get improved conditions of [the printer's] life.... We shall aim at improving and spreading technical knowledge .... We wish to bring cheerfulness and gaity into our pages.... Our judgements will be critical and exacting .... The artistic possibilities of lithograhy are scarcely realised.... The revival in wood-engraving has our sympathy and encouragement.

The articles in *The Imprint* were to cover matters of design, illustration and printing techniques. Lethaby led the way with his introductory article entitled 'Art and Workmanship' in which he allayed the apprehensions of readers inhibited by 'art'. He affirmed the Morrisian notion of art as simply the 'well-doing of what needs doing'. In this regard, *The Imprint*'s own typography was possibly its best voicepiece. The work of John Mason, it was informed by his experience with the Doves Press but related, newly, to mechanised printing. Its quality was characterised by the anonymous author of the article in the *Monotype Newsletter* in 1963 as 'a typographical gem of purity and intellectual honesty'. In all this *The Imprint* contrasted with the long-established but wholly traditional trade journal, *Penrose's Process Year Book.*

One of the lasting achievements of *The Imprint* was its typeface. (Fig. 63). Named Imprint Old Style, it was designed by John Mason who based it on an 18 point Caslon Old Face. It was the first type to be developed by the Lanston Monotype Corporation for their mechanical composing machines. But it was also specific for modern printing machines which used dry rather than the dampened paper associated with hand presses. It was in the spirit of *The Imprint* that this essentially industrial design was made available to printers generally. It seems that Johnston's advice about the design was not called upon, nor did Johnston comment on it.

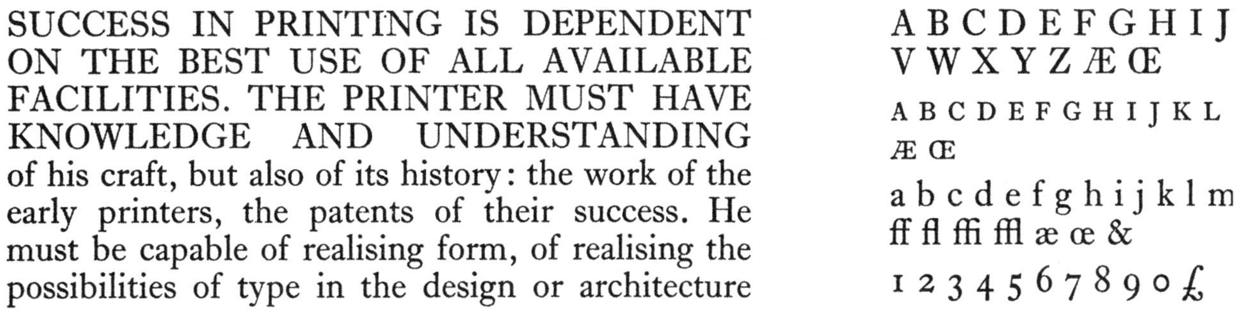

Fig. 63.
The Imprint book type as shown in the Westminster Press Specimen book.

SUCCESS IN PRINTING IS DEPENDENT ON THE BEST USE OF ALL AVAILABLE FACILITIES. THE PRINTER MUST HAVE KNOWLEDGE AND UNDERSTANDING of his craft, but also of its history: the work of the early printers, the patents of their success. He must be capable of realising form, of realising the possibilities of type in the design or architecture

A B C D E F G H I J
V W X Y Z Æ Œ
A B C D E F G H I J K L
Æ Œ
a b c d e f g h i j k l m
ff fl ffi ffl æ œ &
1 2 3 4 5 6 7 8 9 0 £

Figs. 64–66.
Johnston's lettering work for *The Imprint,* including the capital letters used for the openings of articles.

But Johnston's hand in *The Imprint* is evident in other respects. (Figs. 64–66). The calligraphed decorative borders, including the one which frames the quotation from Ruskin, is Johnston's work – as is surely the choice of the Ruskin quotation itself. Johnston pinpointed in his Errata paragraphs on page vii that he calligraphed a number of items. One was the lettering of 'Imprint' itself, which Johnston pointed out 'represents the ancestral type of writing to which all modern printers owe their lower case types'. A second was the lettering of 'Glad Dawn' for the Blake image, used as a frontispiece, which he regretted was reproduced by zincography. A third was the set of initials A, D, P, T, W which begin the articles and which were drawn by brush and, again, reproduced by zincography (regrettably, says Johnston, as the intention was to engrave them in wood). It was surely Johnston's decision, too, to use the wood-engraved Bewick vignettes as tailpieces to the articles.

Given that Johnston wrote the seven articles 'Decoration and Its Uses', his contribution was the most sustained of his fellow-editors. These chapters are a concise – and challenging – reiteration of ideas conveyed in *Writing & Illuminating, & Lettering* but now retold with the printer in mind:

> It is not too much to hope that modern printers … may profit from a study of the methods and principles of that penmanship on which their art is founded.

At the outset Johnston ascribes to the printer the role of 'decorator', conveying the sense that his work should have 'comeliness and grace' – words, he says, which are 'akin to decent'. Later he claimed: '… one of the uses of decoration is to make a thing pleasant to read'. The bedrock of Johnston's discussion is the tradition of formal writing and its dependency on the broad-nibbed pen. In his Chapter One he gives the historical context: formal writing was the medium of the manuscript book and became the model for the types of the early printed book. The printer-'decorator' is then asked to consider a technical principle concerning the 'weight' of letter-forms. Its 'actual weight', he observes, is a factor of the ratio of the thickness of the broad-nibbed pen to the height of the drawn letter, best demonstrated by the letter I:

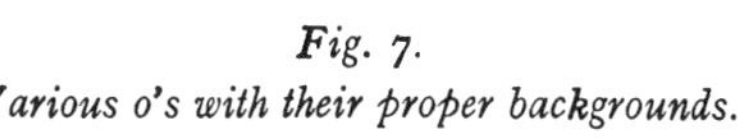

Fig. 67.
Apparent and actual weights of letters according to Johnston's *Writing & Illuminating, & Lettering.*

> … a letter of a height below 4½ nib-widths inclines to be heavy while one above 5½ nib widths tends to be light.

The heavier letters 'incline to the Gothic character', (the Black Letter scripts), while the lighter 'incline to the Roman Small-letter'. Johnston then goes one stage further to consider the concept of the 'apparent weight' of a letter, which is made up by the space between its counters or bowls and its immediate background, best demonstrated by the letter O. He sums up these concepts axiomatically:

> … the 'actual weight' of a written letter may very well be expressed in the ratio of nib-width to height …
>
> We may say, then, that the 'apparent weight' of a writing, other things being equal, depends on the relation of the total area covered by the pen strokes of the letters, to the total area of their internal and external spaces.

Clearly, compressed letters have a heavier 'apparent weight' than regularly written lettters even though they may have the same 'actual weight'.

A further instance of Johnston's ability to get to the essence of a problem occurs in his Chapter Two. This is devoted to the 'ancestral type' – 'the Roman Capital from which all our letters descend'. Johnston points to the Trajan Column where the letters of the inscription vary in thickness according to their horizontal, vertical and 'tilted' curved strokes. Given that they were first outlined on the stone in paint – 'commonly red-lead' – he then claims:

> It is reasonable to suppose that the use of the pen may have strongly influenced the finished Roman characters.

Fig. 10. Outline sketch of letters from the Trajan Column inscription. Scale ¼th. original height.

Fig. 11. Characterization of skeleton capitals by a broad-nibbed pen.

Medieval scripts show the same features, having been formed in the same way. Johnston then returns to the critical principle of holding the broad-edged pen and its effects: there is 'Straight-pen' writing and 'Slanted-pen' writing. But these terms are now substituted by the more explicit 'Horizontal-nib' writing and 'Oblique-nib' writing.

'Horizontal-nib' writing produces a 'slow, formal, upright and elegant letter' as in Roman Square Capitals. This, Johnston argues, tends to give way to 'Oblique-nib writing', which produces 'a comparatively rapid, angular, compressed, heavy-shouldered and strong letter'. With speed of writing it tends to become more ornamental, as in the Roman Rustic Capitals, a script to which the medieval Black Letter script is comparable.

SQ.CAPITALS R.CAPITALS

Square Capitals. Rustic Capitals.

In Chapter Three Johnston presents a schematic survey of scripts from Greek times to those of the fifteenth century, the forms of which then migrate into the earliest printers' types. His Chapter Four is the counterpart: a survey of the four principal kinds of early printing types whose forms were inherited from the scribe: the Black Letter, the intermediary fere ['almost']-Humanistica, the Roman and the Italic.

In Chapter Five Johnston reaches the crux of the discussion: the desirability of good letters. The only reasonable guide, he argues, is 'readableness'. While the printer-'decorator' cannot but accept the force of tradition and use the 'ROMAN CAPITAL, the Roman Small-letter, and the *Italic*' types given him, he can cultivate those letter-forms which display best the qualities of 'simplicity, distinctiveness and proportion'. These criteria, Johnston claims, are to be found in the Foundational Hand written with the broad-edged nib:

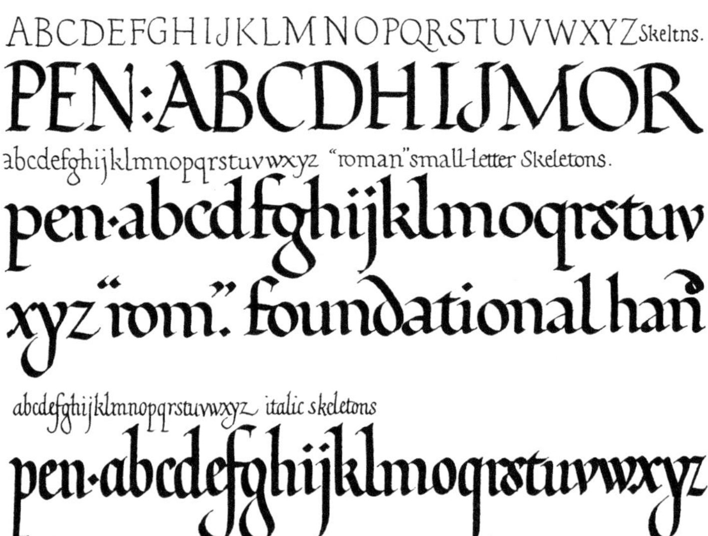

heavier and more "gothic"
&
"black-letter" development

Fig. 24. " Gothic " and " black-letter " developments of the " foundational " hand.

> It forms an excellent general basis for further development, and I would strongly recommend its acquisition by craftsmen generally.

Johnston proposes this as a standard from which other forms can be developed, such as capital letters and even the Black Letter ('this can be used occasionally to good effect'). Johnston's remaining two chapters are devoted to the *mise en page* of the book – to the arrangement of the text, margins and page proportions.

The Imprint's last issue was November 1913 and was dissolved legally in 1915.[48] The ideas which the four editors injected into *The Imprint* presage those which Lethaby's advocated for the Design and Industries Association (DIA), whose first exhibition in 1915 (at the Whitechapel Art Gallery) was to feature British printing prominently. In a sense, in *The Imprint* they enacted Lethaby's intentions. In 'Art and Workmanship', Lethaby's opening article in *The Imprint* in January 1913, he stressed the importance of industrial design to face up to the necessity of an honesty of purpose:

> ... machine work should show quite frankly that it is the child of the machine.

And while not articulating this point precisely, Johnston's notion of the printer as 'decorator' nevertheless approached Lethaby's new thinking. This, in a crucial sense, was partly through the influence of Gerard Meynell.[49]

Although Johnston's contacts with Jackson and Mason appear to have petered out at this time those with Gerard Meynell continued. He became in effect Johnston's agent which led to an even more propitious development for British design.

Another key figure for Johnston was Sir Sydney Cockerell. Cockerell had become the Director of the Fitzwilliam Museum in Cambridge in 1906 but had kept in touch with Johnston intermittently. Once his mentor, he now became Johnston's watchful friend. Johnston's letters to Cockerell were among the first and last of his professional life. Bridget Johnston called Cockerell her father's 'oldest and most revered friend'.[50]

Johnston's manuscript, *The House of David, his Inheritance: A book of sample scripts A.D. 1914* is both a masterpiece of his calligraphy and a key document in his repertoire of scripts. Its catalyst was Sydney Cockerell. Additionally, Cockerell had a curator's sense of Johnston's historical importance. (He was the prime mover in setting up the memorial exhibition of Johnston's work at the Victoria & Albert Museum in 1945.)[51] By giving Johnston complete freedom Cockerell succeeded in persuading him to calligraph a set of scripts without raising the spectre of this being an arid exercise in mere specimens. Cockerell first suggested that Johnston might do this commission early in 1913. Johnston's letter to Cockerell late that year gives an insight into his crowded working life often blocked by his self-confessed dilatoriness:

> 15th December 1913. Dear Cockerell, I have to thank you for your extremely kind letter a fortnight ago. I hope that you have not expected an answer until you got the book itself sometime after Christmas. We did not fix anytime and so I venture to bind myself to Lady Day 1914. If you feel that that is too far off, you may fix an earlier date and let me know. I must let you into a secret, not generally known, at any rate, namely, that when I have promised work for a given date, I have generally been fortunate enough to keep my promise (indeed without boasting I may say that during my 14 years of work I have not been later than my promise more than 5 or 6 times). When I have taken commissions to do for an indefinite date, I have been very remiss and have even quite failed – as you know not even under the offer of 'as soon as possible' has my sense of honour always been able to cope with my native casuistry and the cares of this world. I am at present completing the designs for a second fount of type for Count Kessler. The story of how I was led and persuaded by this extraordinarily persevering 'patron' to do work that to which I had conscientious objections is too long to tell, but actually and with great pains, I have drawn for him an Italic and a 'Black Letter' fount (from early printed books found by Mr Walker) and the punches for the former have been admirably cut by Mr. Prince. These will take me into January or later and I will also have to prepare for a course of ten L. C. C. [London County Council] lectures beginnng on the 20th prox, so that Lady Day will only give me about 8 weeks to deal with your book in, however, under pressure or persuasion that may be cut down by half and a date be fixed for February. To return to your letter – which I shall put with treasured papers – the terms of your commission are very flattering – I shall do my best, though without the stimulus of difficult conditions.[52]

The combination of Cockerell's patient concern and Johnston's willingness to please ultimately bore fruit when, on 23rd March 1914, Johnston finished the manuscript of *A book of sample scripts* and sent it to Charles McLeish, the book-binder who had worked at Cobden-Sanderson's Doves Bindery and had then moved to Swallow Street, Piccadilly. The following day Johnston added the folio numbers and the colophon. His postcard to Cockerell, sent that day, contains his customary and gracious offer to undertake something different should the manuscript not please:

> Dear Cockerell, (written in the train) The MSS book is now posted to you and I hope you will receive it on Lady Day [25th March]. I have not had time to read it over properly (& there may be a lot of mistakes besides the ones noted).
>
> You perhaps have had no notion how difficult a task it is to make a collection of suitable quotations when you are given a free hand – and I fear you may take objection to my choice. I thought over the matter for weeks and finding no comfort in your phrase 'unadulterated Johnston' I at length was held and helped by your direction 'written primarily for your own pleasure and only incidentally for mine'. I thought then that it should be a story with other quotations related coherently. But as you did not bargain for a religious treatise, nor for any erasures* will you please consider it

> carefully, and if you would prefer something else I should be delighted to do it instead (I know a man who would almost certainly take over the present MS.).* You would not believe the number of trials made and of vellum abandoned but I am rather out of practice & apparently constitutionally careless. Yours sincerely E. Johnston.[53]

The trials and tribulations that Johnston hinted at in his postcard are recorded in his diary. His efforts to fulfill his promise and complete the manuscript by Lady Day led him into the drama of the final hours of concentrated work stretching right through the night:

> 12 Feby SCC planned larger page chose vellums cut 4 skins into 14 book sheets (+pieces).
>
> 25 Feby SCC say 3½ hours experiments with vellum discovery of gum. cut 5 sheets p. goat.
>
> 5 March planned book contents about 3½ hours SCC trying age kid Spoilt 2. thought of reverting to large calf sheets (prepared one).
>
> 19 March Wrote p. 26, prepared and wrote Dignus es etc. Cut new sheet, prepared and wrote p. 7 Greek (finishing by about 7.40 by lamplight). Began again about 9.45. Wrote pp 28 29, p. 30 (Et Ostendit) and p. 5 (Title) about 6.30 am. Went to bed at 6.45, got up at 10. Pencil numbered pages, packed book and took it to 12.44 train.[54]

The manuscript occupies thirty-six vellum pages with four numbered blank pages in the front and four at the back.[55] The 'religious treatise' Johnston chose has as its centre piece the story of David and Goliath (taken from Samuel, Book 1). Accompanying this are Psalm 23, a sermon (from Acts 7, v. 44–50), a vision (from

This Book contains 36 pp. of vellum & 2 parchment ends.
The Sample Scripts used in it are —
pp. 8–21. The "foundational hand" based on 10. Century English MS.
pp. 22, 23, 5. "Black Italic" } formal from the above.
pp. 26–29. "Small roman" }
pp. 24–25 { "Modern half-uncial" } based on round skeleton forms
{ "Uncials" to match. } approximated to Uncial Character
used by the Writer as an educational hand since 1900 A.D.
p. 30. "Roman Capital MS." based on Sq. Caps. of 3. or. 4. or 5. Centy.
There are also various pen-made Roman Capitals
in the Title Page and in other places.
EJ, the Writer, I record with regret erasures occurring on pp. 17.23.27.31.
these pp. should have been rewritten but I promised

Revelation 4 and 5, v. 1–9), and a postscript (Revelation 22, v. 1–2). The texts are presented in Greek, Latin, and English and are calligraphed in black and red ink. The principal interest here, however, is in the scripts Johnston presented. He names these in the colophon (together with his customary apologies for erasures and mistakes). (See page 141)

The new feature in this list is the 'Black Italic' script which Johnston points out in the colophon is 'formed from the above', that is, from the Foundational Hand. Its significance is as the precursor of the 'heavy' or 'compressed' italic script which Johnston developed in the mid-1920s. Priscilla Johnston concluded from her father's own comments that this later script was '… the second major change of his career',

A Psalm of David. xxiij.
The LORD is my shepherd;
I shall not want.
He maketh me to lie down
in green pastures:
He leadeth me beside
the [1]still waters. 1. Heb. waters of rest.
He restoreth my soul:
He guideth me in the paths of
righteousness for his name's sake.
Yea, though I walk through the
valley of [2]the shadow of death,
I will fear no evil; 2. Or, deep darkness.

the first being the evolution of his Foundational Hand.[56]

Johnston's 'Black Italic', meanwhile, conforms to the description of the Italic that he gave in Chapter xv of *Writing & Illuminating, & Lettering* ('The Roman Alphabet and its Derivatives'). There the Italic is seen as:

> … closely resembling Roman small-letters (the universally recognised type in which the majority of books and papers are printed), but are slightly narrowed, slightly sloped to the right, and very freely written (commonly with a 'slanted-pen') … the *lines* of writing are generally widely spaced – allowing for long stems: the bodies of the letters being narrow are generally rather closely packed ….

Johnston illustrated this with a manuscript of a poem by Cardinal Bembo written by an unknown Italian Renaissance scribe. (his Plate XXI.) It was lent to him by Sydney Cockerell.[57] Johnston's notes point out that it is:

> … a fine example of the cursive writing perfected in Italy in the first half of the sixteenth century…. This mode is very suitable for a book of poems …. THE WRITING

Tal, ch'a noia et disdegno hebb
Et se non fuſſe che maggior pau
Freno l'ardir; con morte acerba
A la qual fui molte fiate preſſo,

> is very beautiful, clear and rapid – made with a 'slanted-pen' Note the *slightness* of the slope of the letters and the length of the stems and the wide [interline] spacing.

Johnston's own example in *A book of sample scripts* adheres to these strictures. The text he used as its vehicle is Psalm 23. (see opposite).

END NOTES

1. Eric Gill. Diary for 29th February and 8th and 11th March 1908.
2. Crafts Study Centre Collection and Archive. Farnham, Surrey. Johnston archive. (Diary. 2 Loan 5.)
3. Eric Gill. Diary for 14th February 1908; 11th April 1908.
4. Eric Gill. Diary for 12th February, 15th May, 4th July 1908.
5. Eric Gill. Diary for 11th and 18th January 1910.
6. Eric. Gill. Diary for 15th, 16th, 19th, and 21st March 1912.
7. Crafts Study Centre Collection and Archive. Farnham, Surrey. Johnston archive. (Diary. 2. Loan 7.)
8. Crafts Study Centre Collection and Archive. Farnham, Surrey. Johnston archive. (Letters 2/Loan 22.2.)
9. Cambridge Univ. Library. Rare Books Room. (Stanley Morison Papers XXX 111/25.)
10. Crafts Study Collection and Archive. Farnham, Surrey. Johnston archive. (Letters 2/Loan 23.)
11. Ibid. (Ref: Letters 2/Loan. 27.)
12. Gill's diary for the 22nd, 23rd July and the 3rd August 1912.
13. Crafts Study Centre Collection and Archive. Farnham, Surrey. Johnston archive. (Letters 2/Loan 34.)
14. Crafts Study Centre Collection and Archive. Farnham, Surrey. Johnston archive. (Letters 2/Loan 35.)
15. Crafts Study Centre Collection and Archive. Farnham, Surrey. Johnston archive. (Letters 2/Loan 36.)
16. Rev. J. J. Wynne. *Encyclical Letters of Pope Leo XIII.* Benziger Bros: New York. 1903.
17. In a conversation with Peter Holliday in 1999.
18. Philippe and Ethel Mairet. *Essay on Crafts and Obedience.* (S. Dominic's Press 1918).
19. A companion of the Johnstons' to Lulworth Cove was Elisabeth Webb, an American student who took private lessons from Johnston. Her 'epistle' written to the family in 1922 gives a glimpse of the times spent at Lulworth Cove:

> ... write an epistle to the dearly beloved friends, Greta and Edward Johnston and their three lovely daughters .... Also of the days of Priscilla and sister Olaf and of the pleasure thou hadst in them at Lulworth Cove .... Of the shingle beach and the Chapel, the garden and the flowers therein, the kind hospitality and the pleasant hours in talk of poetry and other lovely things.

The letter continues in the same sweet terms about Ditchling. Johnston archive. Newberry Library, Chicago. (Wing MS 2W 983.w 382).

20. Susan Falkner. *A Ditchling Childhood.* (Iceni Publications, 1992).

21. Fr. Conrad Pepler. 'Ditchling. A Community of Craftsmen'. In: *The Dublin Review.* No. 482 (Winter 1959/60).

22. Letter to Bridget Johnston. 29th October 1945. Crafts Study Centre Collection and Archive. Farnham, Surrey. Johnston archive. (Letters 2/255)

23. W. R. Lethaby. 'Village Arts and Crafts'. In *Home and Country Arts* (1922).

24. An article by Gill on his trip to Ireland appeared in *The Game.* Vol. III. No. 2. (1919).

25. Edward Johnston. *A Carol and other Rhymes.* (Hampshire House Workshops. Hampshire Hog Lane. Hammersmith .W (6].) 1915.

26. Fr. Conrad Pepler. 'Memories of Father McNabb's Day'. In *The Chesterton Review.* Vol. XXII. Nos. 1 & 2. 1996.

27. H. D. C. Pepler. 'Handwork or Landwork'. In *Blackfriars.* August 1943.

28. Letter to Priscilla Johnston dated 10th November 1936. Archives. Ditchling Museum.

29. Joanna Bourne. 'Amy Sawyer and her Ditching Players'. Unpublished typescript. Archives of Ditchling Museum.

30. Amy Sawyer. *Sussex Village Plays, and others.* (Hove: Combridges, 1934). See also *The Seasons: Pictured by Amy Sawyer.* (London: Sands and Co., 1905.)

31. Joanna Bourne. Memoir in typescript held at Ditchling Museum.

32. The model was his sister, Gladys. See J. Collins. *Eric Gill. The Sculptures.* (Herbert Press) 1998. It survives at The Blue House set into the wall of her old studio. See: P. Holliday. *Eric Gill in Ditchling: Four Essays* (Delaware: Oak Knoll Press, 2002).

33. Johnston wrote about making this manuscript in his 'Paper on the Labelling of Exhibits', with which he addessed the Arts and Crafts Exhibition Society in June 1935. It was printed in *Four Papers* (Longmans Green & Co. 39 Paternoster Row, London E.C. 4) 1935.

34. Cribb carved Gill's very first sculpture, *La Joie de Vivre*, and helped him substantially with the Stations of the Cross at Westminster Cathedral. The War Memorial in the village was also cut by him in 1919–20, and possibly also designed by him. Much of this information comes from the talk on Joseph Cribb given by his grandson, Joe Cribb, at Ditchling Museum in April 2002. The vexed question as to who designed the Ditchling War Memorial is also treated in T. McCann's 'Gill's Inscriptional Work in Ditchling' in *Eric Gill in Ditchling: Four Essays*, edited by P. Holliday. (Delaware: Oak Knoll Press, 2002.)

35. He also accompanied Gill when he left Ditchling for Capel-y-ffin, in Breconshire, Wales, in 1924 and when again when Gill moved to Pigotts, in Hertfordshire. He ultimately settled in Tremadog in North Wales. This information was kindly provided by Lawrie Cribb's grandson, Kevin Cribb.

36. Some mentioned in Gill's diary include: The Café Royal, The Cock, The Cecil, Pagnini's, Le Tour Eiffel, The Trocadero, the Café Dieppe. The Chelsea Arts Club and the Savile Club were also on Gill's circuit, as were the homes of Jacob Epstein and William Rothenstein and, in turn, those of their friends.

37. Together, they travelled down to see Stonehenge on 12th September. They became interested, too, in the purchase of Asheham House, to the east of Ditchling near the village of Firle, as a location for an artistic community. On 14th and 17th September Epstein and Gill visited Asheham. Gill drew up plans and saw about repairs. On 24th November, Epstein again came down to Ditchling in regard to the house, this time with Augustus John. In December, 1910, he again stayed with Gill in Ditchling, in the company of Francis Cornford, Gill's poet friend from Cambridge. After the improbable Ashenam venture floundered the house was acquired by Virginia Woolf in 1911. Her sister, Vanessa Bell and her Bloomsbury entourage – among them Clive Bell and Duncan Grant – lived in the nearby Charleston

Farmhouse where they furthered the decorative work associated with Roger Fry's Omega Workshops. Little, if any, connection is known to have taken place between the Ditchling and Charleston Farmhouse communities, although Charleston may have given Gill food for thought when he was setting up the Guild. However, Gill visited the Omega Workshops in London, and Pepler used the ceramic dinner plates designed by Roger Fry for use at home, when he moved into Hopkin's Crank on Ditchling Common in 1924. (Fig. 62).

38. Eric Gill. Diary. 22nd January and 3rd, 7th, 11th March 1913.

39. Visvakarma. *Examples of Indian architecture, sculpture, painting, handicraft, chosen by A. K. Coomaraswamy.* Introduction by Eric Gill. (London: The author. 1914.)

40. Crafts Study Centre Collection and Archive. Farnham, Surrey. Johnston archive. (Diary 2/Loan 7.)

41. Eric Gill. Diary. 2nd May, 6th, 7th, and 13th June 1913.

42. Crafts Study Centre Collection and Archive. Farnham, Surrey. Johnston archive. (Diary 2/Loan 7.)

43. Desmond Chute. 'Eric Gill: A Retrospect'. In *Blackfriars.* Vol XXXI (December 1950).

44. Eric Gill. Diary. 19th Feb, 6th, 9th, March 1913, and 8th January 1914.

45. Crafts Study Centre Collection and Archive. Farnham, Surrey. Johnston archive. Letters 2/Loan 26.) Johnston must have been especially interested in Gill's sculpture commission. Priscilla Johnston quotes his letter from their Lincoln's Inn period of 1903 concerning their visit to the cathedral. Characteristic of his writing, it bears re-citing here:

> It is a magnificent building and the size and breadth of its conception is vastly impressive, especially in the dusk which darkened the walls and hid the roof. Far up the windows faintly lit by the evening sky, or London's light perhaps, shone out of the blackness. We stumbled about and examined and felt what we could not see. Far away a party of people were being shown about by a man wth a lantern – a picturesque group in a spot light.

Priscilla Johnston. *Edward Johnston.* (London: Faber and Faber, 1959): page 200.

46. John Dreyfus. 'Gerard Meynell and the Westminster Press'. In *Matrix* 10. (1990).

59. They had two daughters, Joanna and Rosemary. As Gill's diary shows, the Meynells started visiting Ditchling from at least 1913 – coming down from their home in Colville Square, Paddington (though by 1918 they were living at 37 St. Peter's Square, Hammersmith). Esther Meynell's diary shows them staying in Ditchling during the summer of 1918. On the 4th April she:

> Took the 3.40 to Hassocks [local station] and found tea and Greta (Johnston) waiting for us at Amy Sawyer's home. Unpacked and got straight. Gerard went out to Halletts [Johnston's home on Ditchling Common].

They possibly stayed at Amy Sawyer's Blue House, they then rented Bean Acre in Underhill Lane and then Manor Cottage at nearby Keymer. They eventually bought Conds Cottage, in High Street, Ditchling. The Meynell and Johnston families were very close. Esther's diary for the 5th April, 1918, reads, typically:

> Gerard walked out to Halletts with Joanna [the Meynell's first daughter] and didn't return for lunch. So Nanny and I went to Halletts. Nanny returned with Baby and we stayed to tea with the Johnstons.

47. The story of *The Imprint* has been well documented in a number of publications. See: Priscilla Johnston. *Edward Johnston* (London: Faber and Faber, 1959); 'Fifty years on' *Monotype Newsletter* No. 71 (October 1963*);* 'The Imprint Articles' in Edward Johnston *Formal Penmanship,* edited by Heather Child (London: Lund Humphries, 1971); Francis Meynell 'Introduction' in *The Imprint.* Facsimile edition (London: The Curwen Press for the Wynkyn de Worde Society, 1972). N. Barker. *Stanley Morison* (London: MacMillan, 1972); L. T. Owens *J. H. Mason* (London: Frederick Muller Ltd, 1976); John Dreyfus 'Gerard Meynell and the Westminster Press'. In *Matrix* No. 10. (1990). Justin Howes. *Johnston's Underground*

Type (Harrow Weald; Capital Transport Publishing, 2000). A further valuable source is J. Mason's notebooks, made available to L. T. Owens and to the anonymous writer of 'Fifty years on' in the *Monotype Newsletter*.
48. The business side of *The Imprint* was finally wound down in 1915. However, financial problems set in very early on. Gerard Meynell's letter to Johnston dated the 9th May 1913 shows that:

> Mason is particularly anxious to be paid his salary; so we must raise some money to pay them all as we can't pay only one. This means issuing ordinary shares, and we will have to give up our right to bonuses. or at any rate very much modify the present agreements. If you agree to this being done please let me know at once. Many thanks for your articles. Has Mrs Johnston gone away yet and how are all the children? I'll come down and see you if you like any time .... Yours ever Gerard Meynell

Johnston sent off what read as somewhat curt notes to Meynell and to Mason in November 1913 regarding meetings and financial loose-ends. One letter from Gerard Meynell to Johnston dated 3rd December 1913 reads:

> A meeting of the directors of the Imprint Publishing Company will be held at the offices of Field Roscoe & Co., 36 Lincolns Inn Fields, W. at 11.30 a.m. on Saturday December 6th to consoider the advisability of calling an extraordinary General meeting to pass a resolution for the winding up of the Company. Yours faithfully, Gerard T. Meynell. Secretary.

Johnson's letters during March 1915 show his concern to tie up the legal implications of the resignation of the four editor-directors. One, to Meynell, dated 10th March 1915 reads:

> Dear Meynell, I desire to resign my position as a director of the Imprint and do hereby resign it. Please acknowledge this, Yours sincerely E. J.

A further letter from Gerard Meynell to Johnston, dated 30th June 1914 deals with copyright:

> I am sending you all the originals of yours I am able to trace, and if any are missing please let me know. I should like to state on behalf of the Company that all you wrote for us, and all the drawings you made for us are entirely your copyright, and you are at liberty to make whatever use of them you may think fit; also that the originals returned herewith and any that we may still have are also entirely your property. Gerard Meynell Managing Director. For 'The Imprint' Publishing Coy Ltd.

On the 15th March 1915 Johnston wrote to Mason:

> Dear Mason, I have read your letter of the 13th inst. in wh. you intimate that you have resigned your positions of editorship and directorship of the Imprint. I sent my resignation of directorship to Meynell on the 10th inst.so I can only acknowledge your note of resignation as an ex-director but I should imagine it is sufficient that you have communicated it to Jackson and to me. Will you please forward enclosed to Jackson as I have forgotten his address. Do send me a p.c. acknowledging this. E. J.

(These letters are in the archives of the HRHRC, University of Texas at Austin, Texas.) However, Johnston's continued interest in the idea of *The Imprint* is indicated by his favourable response to the letters from Gerard Meynell in 1926 proposing to revive the journal. (See the Elkin Mathews catalogue 56 (Part 1), 1971, item 75: 'A group of three letters in 1926 are concerned almost exclusively with a project to revive Imprint with Meynell and Morison as joint editors. Johnston evidently favoured the idea and was to contribute a "monthly letter or review criticising all manner of things." Unfortunately this came to nothing.' These letters are now in the Newberry Library. Chicago. Johnston archive.)
49. Gerard Meynell's influence on promoting modern design has been under-appreciated.

In 1917 he met the Vorticist poster artist E. McKnight Kauffer and shortly afterwards appointed him to be his director of Poster and Pictorial Advertising at the Westminster Press. In 1924 he printed Kauffer's book, *The Art of the Poster*. (See John Dreyfus 'Gerard Meynell and the Westminster Press'. In *Matrix* 10 (1990).) In 1927 he succeeded in getting Johnston to design a neon sign for Shell, which was not realised but which is illustrated in Justin Howes *Johnston's Underground Type* (Capital Transport Publishing, 2000). This surely makes Gerard Meynell a significant figure in the British design avant garde, anticipating the direction taken by others, like the printer Harold Curwen and later by Herbert Read.

50. One of the earliest letters Johnston wrote to Cockerell, dated 17th October 1900, is a description of the vellum available from a Mr Band, who was one of Morris's suppliers. One of his last letters is the celebrated unfinished one dated 1943, which was posted to Cockerell after Johnston's death. (Ref: V&A Box 86 KK III (xxxi)

This is referred to in Sydney Cockerell's letter to Bridget Johnston, 22nd December 1944. In the same letter Cockerell expands on his friendship:

> I was greatly attached to him [Johnston] but at Cambridge and Ditchling we were so far apart that we met very seldom, and as he did not encourage correspondence not many letters passed between us ....

Crafts Study Centre Collection and Archive. Farnham, Surrey. Johnston archive. Letters 2/51.

51. Cockerell's congratulatory letter to Johnston in 1939 on Johnston being awarded the CBE indicates this awareness: '

> How delightful that your pioneer work and your undisputed preeminence in the world of calligraphers that owes its very existence to your teaching should at last have public recognition! It has been my privilege to watch your career with admiration from its very beginnings – never once have you swerved from the high ideal that you set yourself.... There will be rejoicing far and wide .... What I long to see is a catalogue of all that you have done ... the two examples that I own are among my most treasured possessions ... have you not compiled a chronological list and description?

This was the letter to which Johnston ultimately replied with his unfinished and unposted cypher letter in 1944.

Cockerell realised the necessity for a catalogue of Johnston's calligraphy – a task he urged on Johnston and then on Bridget Johnston after her father's death on 24th November 1944. Cockerell began, if perfunctorily, to compile a catalogue himself (the document is in the NAL at the V&A. Ref: 86 QQ 24). This primary task has still not been thoroughly carried out. In his letter of the 29th November 1944 to Bridget Johnston, Cockerell returned to the historical importance of a catalogue:

> When you are rested a bit I want you to gather together every scrap of your father's calligraphy you can find, finished or unfinished. It has now become very precious and if you care to dispose of anything please consult me beforehand – I am sure the Victoria and Albert Museum would be eager to make a purchase – and pay a good price .... You probably know that I bullied him from time to time to make an authoratitive catalogue of all his calligraphy – was this ever done?'

Crafts Study Centre Collection and Archive. Farnham, Surrey. Johnston archive. Letters 2/49. His letter to Bridget of the 22nd December 1944 reiterates the point:

> I have thought of him a great deal and have sung his praises to many people ... this reputation, already tremendous with a small and specialised group, will spread far and wide ....When the war is over we must get together an exhibition of his work at the Victoria and Albert Museum. (Crafts Study Centre. Johnston archive. Letters 2/51.)

52. Letter, 15th December 1913 (V&A 86 KK Box III (xxxi).
53. NAL at the V&A. 86 KK Box III (xxxi)

54. Cited from the Justin Howes catalogue: Notes on item C 86.59.i, a trial for page seven. Crafts Study Centre Collection and Archive. Farnham, Surrey. 1987: page 52.
55. It was given to the National Art Library at the V&A Museum in 1959 by Sir Sydney Cockerell (L. 4931–1959) Johnston's mock-up of it is also in the V&A. (K. 4315.23. XI. 1966).
56. Johnston calligraphed some of his most expressive manuscripts in his 'heavy' italic, notably the 'Keighley Roll of Honour', in 1924, his manuscript 'Saying of Artists on Art', in 1925, (commissioned by Frank Rinder and now in the National Gallery of Victoria, in Melbourne), Psalm CXXIX, in 1926 (see Priscilla Johnston's *Edward Johnston*: page 249) and the 'Shakespeare Sonnet No. 116', in 1927. Rinder became Johnston's client in 1918. A friendship then developed between them. Rinder found himself in much the same waiting role as Cockerell had had to play. Cockerell hints at Johnston's development of the Italic in his tribute of 1945:

> It is worthwhile to observe that his development as a scribe followed rather closely that of professional handwriting from the eleventh to the fifteenth century. Starting with an open rounded hand, inspired by the early Winchester School, his calligraphy tended to become more and more Gothic and compressed – it may be that an inexorable law prescribed this evolution.

(*Tributes to Edward Johnston, Calligrapher*. Edward Charles Pickering through the Society of Scribes and Illuminators. (Maidstone: Maidstone College of Art, 1945.)
57. It is now known to have been written in 1563. It is now in the V&A.

Drawing by Louis Ginnett, November 1913.
By kind permission of Jeremy Carden.

CHAPTER SIX

JOHNSTON AND THE CRAFT COMMUNITIES IN DITCHLING PART 2

The publication *The Imprint* was but one strand of the new design thinking that was beginning to supersede the Arts and Crafts movement. From 1913 Gerard Meynell, now joined by his colleague Frank Pick of the London Electric Railway Co., helped set in motion two other ventures in the domain of industrial design. One led to the formation in 1915 of the Design and Industries Association (DIA) (Fig. 68), a movement that appealed to a wide spectrum of craftsmen and manufacturers. The other, narrower in scope, was Johnston's sanserif block alphabet, the first phase of which was completed in mid-1916. The two ventures were separate but sprang from the same impetus: that good design should also be applied to industry. Johnston's commission is better understood, therefore, in the light of the development of the DIA.

The commercial failure of the Tenth Exhibition of the Arts and Crafts Exhibition Society, held at the Grosvenor Gallery in 1912, prompted Gerard Meynell to link up with others who felt also disquiet. They were Ernest Jackson and John Mason of *The Imprint* together with the furniture designers Ambrose Heal (of Heal's of Tottenham Court Road), Hamilton Smith (later a director of Heal's) and Harry Peach (of the Dryad Cane Works, Leicester). The initiative, however, was taken by Harold Stabler, a craftsman of metalware (whom Johnston knew and taught with at the RCA). They formed a committee to discuss how the artist-craftsman could better serve mass-produced manufacturing. Their principal starting point was the success that the *Deutsche Werkbund* was enjoying in this respect.[1] The prospect of German 'industrial arts' capturing British markets was alarming for British industrialists.

Fig. 68. Logo of the Design and Industries Association probably designed by John Mason.

In January 1915 a 'Memorandum' was presented to the Board of Trade. In it the committee regretted that in England '... Commerce and Art education remain two separate, unyielding, and opposing activities'.[2] It spoke of the 'stigma of cheap and nasty'. It urged the development of an 'efficiency style' – a phrase which chimed with the aims of Johnston's Housemakers' Society, some seven years earlier, though these had more domestic leanings. Aside from the original committee it was also signed by a number of Johnston's associates including St. John Hornby, the proprietor of W. H. Smith's and adviser to *The Imprint*, Ben J. Fletcher, the principal of the Municipal School of Art, Leicester (the names Ben and Joan Fletcher appear in Johnston's late address book) and H. G. Wells, who, it will be recalled, had belonged to the Housemakers' Society. But there were two other

Figs. 69-72. Early publications by the DIA, 1915–1917, probably designed by John Mason.

signatories, more significant still. One was Lethaby, who was regarded as the 'elder statesman' of the movement and who was about to publish his pamphlet, 'Design and Industry: a proposal for the foundation of a Design and Industries Association'. The other was Frank Pick, a younger and dynamic administrator, who was on the point of collaborating with Johnston. In conjunction with the Board of Trade an exhibition of German goods was arranged to be shown at the Goldsmiths' Hall in March 1915.

On the 9th May 1915 this group, with support from industry and art colleges, inaugurated the DIA with ' ... the object of assisting British industry through the cooperation of the manufacturer, the designer and distributor'. It shared the headquarters of the Arts Workers' Guild at 6 Queen Square. Its first publication was the booklet, *A New Body with New Aims*, 1915. (Figs. 69–72). This comprised a set of articles which reinforced this objective. Its distinctive typography shows, in all probability, the hand of John Mason. One of these essays, by Arthur Clutton-Brock, the art critic of *The Times*, is on the 'Industrial Art in Germany' exhibition. He shares the prevailing anxiety about German goods.

> Finely printed books, not quite so good as the very best English, but showing their influence in every letter, are produced and sold in Germany far cheaper than in England. Mr. Edward Johnston, known only to specialists in England, has influenced the whole German artistic typography, and his lettering, or lettering very like his, may be seen upon the cigarette boxes of an enterprising German industrialist.[3]

Those sitting on the DIA council were of a wide mix. Aside from Lethaby and Frank Pick, who became its president between 1932–34, they included several principals of art and design schools.[4] Other founder-members were Joseph Thorp, printer and journalist, Graily Hewitt, 'maker of letters', Noel Rooke, 'designer and illustrator', William Cowlishaw, architect, John Hogg, publisher – all associates of Johnston. The council immediately reprinted the article with which Lethaby had opened *The Imprint* – 'Art and Workmanship' (and again in 1917 with another Lethaby article, 'The Foundation in Labour').

The first exhibition put on by the DIA took place between 13th October and 24th November 1915 at the Whitechapel Art Gallery. Called 'Design and Workmanship in Printing', it was organised by a Printing Exhibitions Committee set up within the DIA. (Its members included Gerard Meynell, Ernest Jackson, Harry Peach, St. John Hornby, Charles Jacobi and Harold Stabler – though not John Mason). Different versions of the exhibition toured towns in the UK and then went to South Africa. A large number of the posters that Pick had commissioned for the Underground were shown. Two other exhibits were highly significant: a specimen of lettering by Eric Gill and a 'lettering poster' by Johnston.[5]

Johnston's and Gill's participation in the Whitechapel exhibition brings them tantalisingly close to the DIA enterprise. This was another sense in which Johnston was on the cusp of the incipient modernism which was beginning to inform British design. As a calligrapher, his imperative was to uphold the integrity of handicraft. His was a naturally-held resistance, therefore, to the mass production of industry. Mason's and Gerard Meynell's views overlapped those of Johnston. Their *métier*, printing, was necessarily mechanical so they were inclined to state outright what Johnston would have quietly conceded. Mason wrote:

> I recognise that the machine not only has a rightful place in modern civilisation but that it is indispensable...

This came as late as 1933 in a paper given to the Arts and Crafts Exhibition Society. But the actual theme of his paper was 'The Place of Hand-Work in Modern Civilisation'. Fundamentally, Mason shared the same viewpoint with Johnston that 'hand-work' brings life to the artisans practising them. 'They [handicrafts] are worthwhile in themselves'. Mason believed that the process of reducing manufacture into its component stages was a 'spiritual starvation'. He claimed that the best training for the industrial printer remained the hand-operated press. As well as promoting the aesthetic standards of the private presses in the printing industry, Mason also wished to humanise it. He went on:

> Those of us who can give guidance to the use of machinery are right to do so.[6]

This, the quiet reformism of *The Imprint*, shaded imperceptibly into the aspiring modernism of the DIA.

Pick's views were nuanced still further. A career manager with a background in law, he was without any formal art or design training. Nevertheless, Pick realised the need for effective visual communication in mass urban travel. In 1909 he was promoted to Traffic Development Officer of the London Electric Railway Co. (which also incorporated the London General Omnibus Co. and its three tramway companies) and in 1912 to its Commercial Manager, roles flexible enough for him to initiate new policies. He started by commissioning posters by a range of artists, including the lithographer Ernest Jackson (of *The Imprint*) and, in 1915, the emerging Vorticist, McKnight Kauffer – an inspired choice. No doubt it was through the printing of these posters that he came into contact with the Westminster Press, which specialised in poster printing and thereby encountered the persuasive enthusiasm of Gerard Meynell.

Furthermore, Pick was receptive to the ideas of other newly-found colleagues in the DIA movement. He soon found a second vocation as a lecturer and educationist. A measure of this is the support he gave to the DIA's touring exhibition on British printing. In October 1916 he lectured in Edinburgh and in April 1917 in Manchester, giving 'An Address on Design and Industry'. His talk was redolent of Lethaby's 'Art and Workmanship' article:

> Everything is made for a use .... The test of the goodness of a thing is its fitness for use. If it fails this first test, no amount of ornamentation or finish will make it any better; it will only make it more expensive, more foolish.[7]

Another of Pick's concerns was with the lettering of his company's posters in the Underground and of its directional signing system. The challenge he encountered was complex. Hitherto, the predominant lettering on the Underground was the Victorian 'grotesque' types, robust sanserif display faces which varied in quality. But this style also proliferated in the Underground's commercial advertising posters. Aside from wishing to avoid this potential confusion, Pick also recognised the 'grotesques' as deficient because, as Pevsner wrote, they had 'no module to regulate depth and width' – the letter strokes often varied in width; they were not strictly monoline.

On the other hand, any new lettering had to avoid a similar confusion with the fascia boards of the W. H. Smith news stands which were also becoming ubiquitious in the Underground precincts. These were largely in the seriffed Roman (or Trajan) lettering that St. John Hornby had commissioned from Gill in 1903 for the branch of W. H. Smith on the Rue de Rivoli, in Paris – the earliest example, perhaps, of a conscious corporate identity. Furthermore, Pick came to understand a subtle perceptual problem about Gill's lettering. It was modelled on the Trajan Column inscription, which had been cut in stone and was read in the bright sunlight in Rome, aided by sharply-cast shadows. Gill's version, however, was painted on to flat surfaces.

Two clues pinpoint the sources of Pick's ideas. Christian Barman was Pick's biographer and successor as Publicity Manager at London Transport. In his paper on 'Public Lettering', given to the Royal Society of Arts in 1955, he indicated that Pick's 'typographic friends' were Gerard Meynell and Harold Curwen, the printer at the Curwen Press.[8] He might have added the important connection with John Mason, too.

Furthermore, in his pioneer article on Frank Pick of 1962, Nikolaus Pevsner explained that he had been guided in his account of Johnston's sanserif block alphabet by the recollections of Gerard Meynell, Harold Curwen and Noel Rooke. It would seem, then, that Pevsner got to the heart of the matter in writing:

> About 1912–13 Pick began to play with compasses and ruler, trying to work out a new typeface. He could not succeed because he was not an artist. But he busied himself sufficiently to know precisely what he wanted. He also discussed his ideas with men who knew more about lettering than he did. It was Gerard Meynell, apparently, who … first suggested Edward Johnston as the right artist to satisfy his wishes.[9]

By 1913, therefore, Pick's interests converged not only with those of Gerard Meynell, John Mason and Harold Curwen – all printer friends who had put their shoulders to the DIA project – but with Johnston's, too. On 14th June Gerard Meynell wrote to Johnston (in his customarily near-illegible hand):

> Dear Johnston, Will you please come by the early train on Monday [16th June] and I will meet you at Victoria [Station] 10.45. We will then see Pick. Yours, Gerard Meynell.[10]

What Pick's concerns were on that occasion are unrecorded but two years later, on 29th October 1915 – just two weeks after the opening of the DIA printing exhibition at the Whitechapel Art Gallery – they met again, this time more purposefully. Again, the meeting was arranged by Gerard Meynell:

> Gill at Vic[toria Station]. bus to M[eynell] (not a meal) with M at inn and back to office, met Hunter – read argument – and then Mr Greenhill. M[eynell] G[ill] and I to Pick's to discuss blockletter.[11]

It seems that by 1915 Pick was armed with a well thought-out, if flexible, design brief although no document exists detailing this. However, in the lecture,

'Public Lettering', Christian Barman referred back to a talk that Pick himself had given at the Municipal College of Art, Leicester in November 1916, in which he (Pick) explained his ideas about the lettering needed for the Underground. Although this took place some months after Johnston had completed his two principal designs (the capital and lower case) it is the closest the records get to Pick's intentions. Barman reported:

> Pick had aimed at letters that would have the bold simplicity of the authentic lettering of the finest periods and yet belong unmistakably to the times in which we lived .... Pick explained to his audience his own approach to the problem.... Each letter in the alphabet must be a strong and unmistakable symbol with a high degree of individuality; its structure must be clear and open.... It must be straightforward and manly, with the character of an official railway sign and that it was not to be mistaken by the people in a hurry for a trader's advertisement.[12]

While reminiscent again of Lethaby's ideas, these thoughts yield nothing specific about Pick's design brief. However, Barman also conjectured:

> I am pretty sure that it was Harold Curwen, the printer, who encouraged Pick to put his faith in the sanserif alphabet.[13]

This idea needs to be related to Johnston's letter to Harry Peach in 1934 in which he says that the commission from Pick had but one stipulation:

> ... (Block letter mono-stroke [was] the only prescribed condition).[14]

It seems that Pick's 'faith' in the sanserif came in the wake of Johnston's design. This would relate to Harry Carter's opinion that '... Mr Pick, with an audacity rare in industrial magnates, gave the designer a free hand'[15]. Justin Howes skirts judiciously round these ambiguities by writing: 'It was at this meeting that Pick asked Johnston and Gill to think about working on the new designs.' With or without prompting from Pick, their solution combined the block letter (monoline) feature with the sanserif one. The subsequent meetings between Johnston and Pick led to Johnston's final versions of the capitals (Fig. 73) and lower case (Fig. 74) alphabets in June and July 1916.

These steps are described in detail by Justin Howes in *Johnston's Underground Type*, as are the technical details of Johnston's letter proportions and the wide application of the type design to create what became London Transport's corporate identity. And other detailed studies precede his.[16] The most succinct and wisest account is Harry Carter's article 'Sanserif Types' of 1931. According to this, the new type expresses a fusion of Pick's commercial good sense, his Lethaby-inspired notion of modernity and Johnston's belief in the Trajan letter-forms. Harry Carter writes that the Underground block letters are:

> ... easily distinguished by the eye from the types used by surrounding advertisements and therefore sort well with the starkly mechanical associations of an electric railway; yet their essentially Roman forms link them with classical culture.

Beyond Harry Carter's article, these discussions engage in a number of aspects. Gill dropped out of the project almost immediately because of his pre-

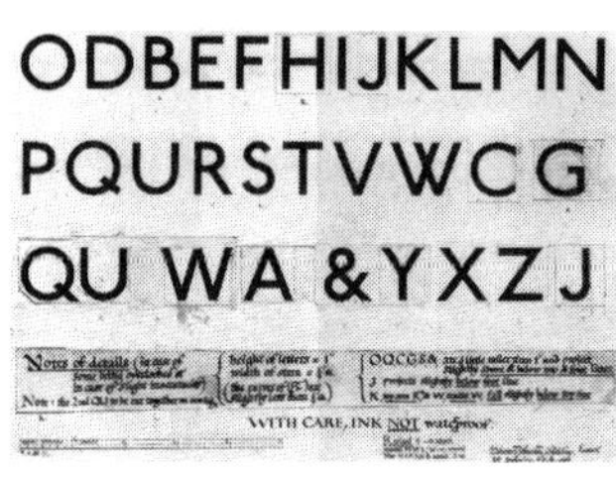

Fig. 73. Johnston's upper case alphabet, completed June 1916. Nominally 1 inch high letters with some variations for optical correction. So:
C, O, Q – 1·2"
I, L, M, N – ·95"
P ·97"
J, D, K, T, U, X, Z – 1".
V&A Museum (Prints and Drawings Dept.) E18–1936.

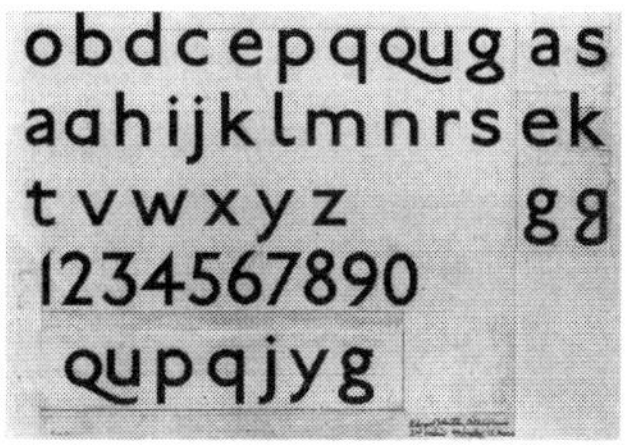

Fig. 74. Johnston's lower case alphabet, completed in July 1915.
V&A Museum (Prints and Drawings Dept.) E47-1936.

occupation with the commission for the Stations of the Cross for Westminster Cathedral. His input was largely advice. Gill's diary for 7th November 1915 says:

> Johnston came to tea (also H. D. C. P[epler]) to discuss Pick (Undergrd. Rly.) lettering.

But Gill's help prompted Johnston to pay him ten percent of the fee of fifty guineas. Johnston's third meeting with Pick (and Gerard Meynell) was on the 8th November 1915.

Johnston was, in a sense, primed to opt for the block letter, sanserif solution. A block letter design had been anticipated in *Writing & Illuminating, & Lettering* in 1906:

> It is quite possible to make a beautiful and characteristic alphabet of equal stroke letters, on the lines of the so-called 'Block Letter' but properly proportioned.[17]

Johnston had also conjectured about a block letter alphabet (Figs. 75–76) in his lecture on signwriting to the Leicester College of Art in September 1909. In it he advocated that the Roman (Trajan) model is the most readable, having the 'utmost simplicity, distinctiveness & proportion'. By contrast, he played down the existing grotesques, '… so commonly used', claiming that 'Ordinary heavy block letters are generally much less readable …'. But then Johnston added:

> These could be developed into a very fine 'block letter' by being made slightly less heavy.[18]

Johnston's alphabet was first intended to be used in the form of sheets which would be traced off and used for posters. The letters were one inch high and Johnston's 1916 designs were made at this nominal size (see the caption for Fig 39). Initially they were reproduced by lithography (undertaken by the Waterlow printing company) – 'by transfers and offsets from his drawings', wrote Noel Rooke. This was a procedure over which Johnston had no control, nor any particular interest, it seems. Noel Rooke continued:

> … But there would be nothing unauthentic for him, who made letters on paper, to provide drawings which would be directly set off on to paper [posters] by lithography.[19]

Only subsequently was the alphabet used for the directional signing system, in the form of enamelled lettering. The alphabet was later produced in wood-letter form for letterpress printing and eventually as metal type.

The letter proportions were based on two models, themselves closely connected. In the *Who's Who* for 1937 Johnston stated the first model:

> … designed block letter based on classical Roman capital proportions (for London Electric Railways).

Justin Howes's insight, however, is that Johnston was also influenced by the Caslon type face which he favoured and which was used in the printing experiments with Hilary Pepler that led to the S. Dominic's Press in Ditchling at this very time, early in 1916. These proportions, Johnston wrote (in 1934 to Harry Peach) were intended to combine:

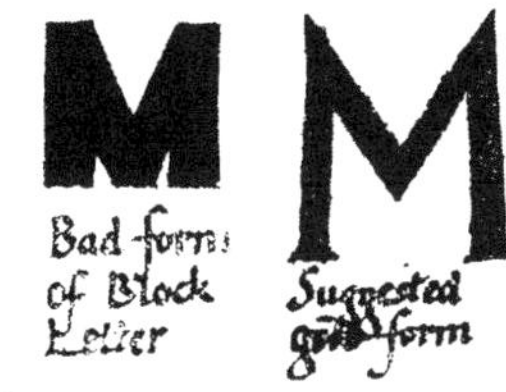

Fig. 75

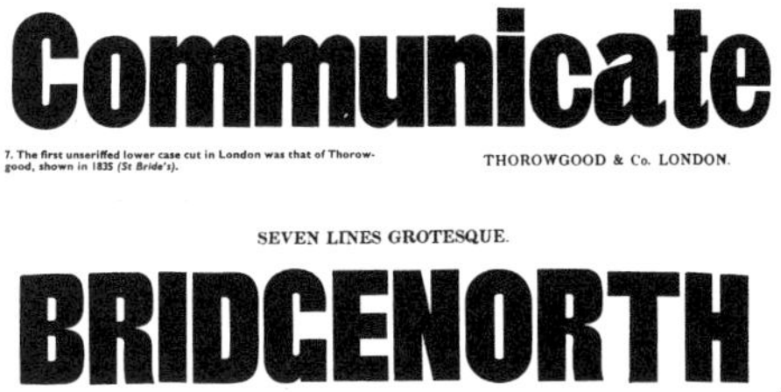

Fig. 76

Figs. 75-76.
75. Johnston's early exploration of the block letter form. From a sheet of lettering used at Leicester College of Art *circa* 1906.
Crafts Study Centre, Johnston archive. 2/418, and courtesy of Justin Howes.

76. Victorian 'Grot' letter design, not strictly monoline, from the specimen book.

… the greatest weight and mass with the greatest clearance of letter shape.[20]

This gave rise to a module where the 'weight' (the width of the stem in relation to the height of the letter) of the lower case letters was 1:4. The ascenders and descenders had a weight of 1:3. Quintessentially, the proportion was therefore 1:7. (Justin Howes points out that there is some variation in the first versions of 1916, but that this proportion is consistent in the Railway Bold version the design of which Johnston oversaw in 1929.)

The application of the design grew apace in subsequent years. In 1919 Johnston finalised the London Underground logo, comprising a rondel with a bar through it supporting the name London Transport – the so-called 'bull's eye' symbol with which the Underground has become synonymous. (Fig. 77)

Fig. 77. Johnston's 'bull's eye' logo for the London Underground.

In late 1919 he also embarked on a condensed version of his alphabet for the London General Omnibus Co.'s destination and route boards. (Fig. 78). This was to answer the problem posed by the requirement for the letters to be between three inches and four-and-a-half inches high to be placed on boards of limited width – a mathematical challenge which Johnston no doubt relished.

ABCDEFGHIJKLMNOPQRSTUVWXYZ&
abcdefghijklmnopqrstuvwxyz
1234567890¼

Fig. 78. Johnston's compressed type used for the bus blinds for London Transport.
(Courtesy of Tim Demuth and London Transport Museum.)

Some ten years later, in 1929, Johnston was commissioned to oversee the designing of the Railway Bold version. (Figs. 79A–B) This has a weight ratio of 1:5. It was needed by London Transport partly in response to the Monotype Corporation's production of the wide range of Gill Sans [serif] type which was becoming very popular in commercial use and which had close similarities to Johnston's design. This was the same problem of confusion which Pick had set out in 1915 to avoid.

In conclusion, it is touching to think that Johnston's venture into the design of public lettering began in his modest workroom in his Downsview house in

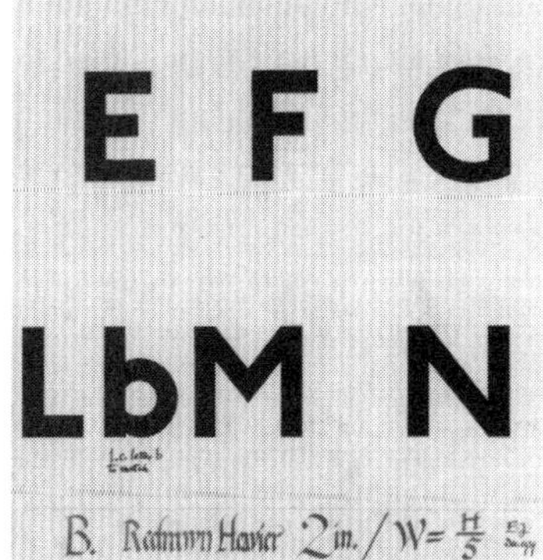

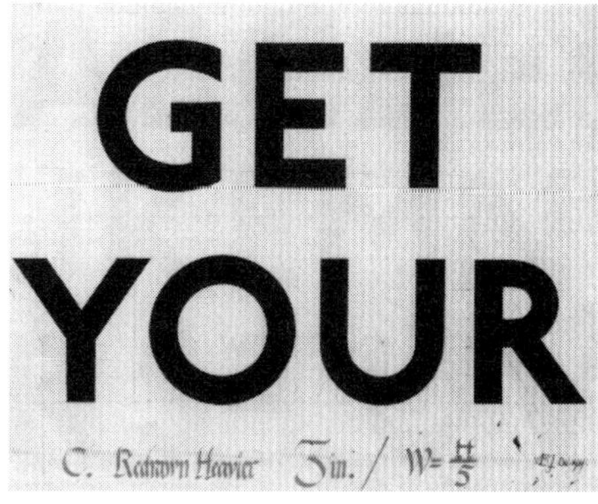

Figs. 79A–B. Johnston's Bold Sans, designed under his supervision in 1929. Two sheets B & C at two and three inches high, giving a weight ratio of 1:5. V&A Museum (Prints and drawings Dept.) E49-1936.

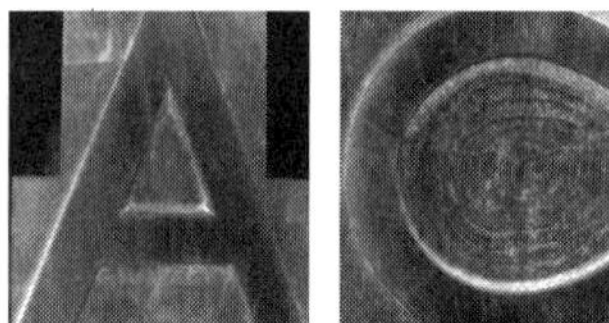

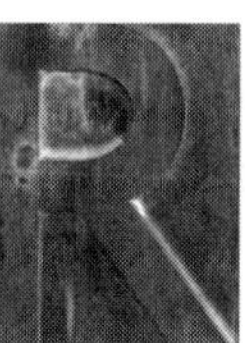

Fig. 80. Some woodletters of Johnston's alphabet. (Courtesy of Ditchling Museum.)

Ditchling village. (Fig. 80) Yet it was the key element of London Transport's corporate identity, and grew into the most comprehensive of its kind at that time and a model for other capital cities. Irrespective of the details of Pick's input, his was a sustained and professional collaboration with Johnston. Johnston remarked in his vellum-bound notebook:

> Peach, Pick and [H.G.] Wells seemed to me to have a real feeling for beauty ...[21]

The last commission which Johnston accepted was from Christian Barman in 1940. It was an address in the form of an inscription on a blotter to honour the retirement of Frank Pick.

Despite Gill's preoccupation with his sculpture, his partnership with Johnston continued to flourish. During the second part of 1915, it broadened to include Hilary Pepler. Gill's diary for March 8th and June 1915, mentions:

> E. J. and Pepler came. Also H. L. C [Laurence Christie] and Gearing. Father Roche called also. Tea on drying ground. Very jolly. E. J. and Pepler came in eve for tennis and all stayed for supper. Duck and g[arden] peas in honour of Jack's [Nye, a Ditchling resident and Gill's early friend there] expected departure for the 'front'. Singing after supper.[22]

While still in Hammersmith Pepler had launched a publishing project which established working links with Johnston and Gill. The collaboration involved a group of three books which Pepler felt compelled to see through the press out of personal conviction. While disparate, each was concerned with the broad theme of craft. Pepler had come to believe that craft should be a form of service undertaken for society out of a sense of religious purpose. The first title was a reprint of Cobbett's *Cottage Economy* of 1822, a classic exposition of the usefulness of craft and the value of thrift as a social and educational process. Pepler's second author was

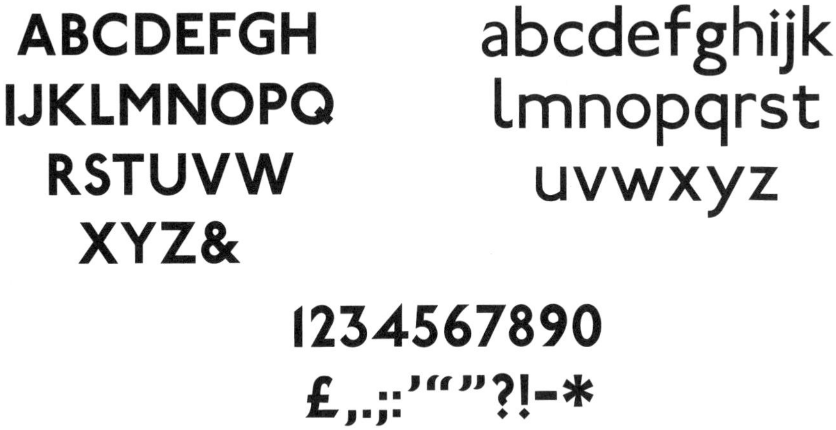

ABCDEFGH
IJKLMNOPQ
RSTUVW
XYZ&

abcdefghijk
lmnopqrst
uvwxyz

1234567890
£,.;:’“”?!-*

Fig. 81. The Johnston sanserif block alphabet, cited from the synopsis printed from surviving fonts by I. M. Imprimit, in 1993.
(Courtesy of I. M. Imprimit.)

Johnston. His little book, *A Carol and other Rhymes*, of 1915, so gentle in tone, speaks of craft in religious terms. *A Carol* has an exacting text which invites close attention. Johnston wrote of Pepler in the preface:

> It was published at the instance of a friend. Responsibility rests with me for consenting, for adding notes and seeing the book through the press.[23]

The third book was Pepler's own. *The Devil's Devices or Control versus Service,* which he completed late in 1915, explored the same themes, though in terms far more acerbic than any Johnston had used. Gill designed its wood-engraved illustrations. These publications brought the three closer together. The strands of contact were being made which would bind them into a small but incipient craft community.

In 1915, Pepler was not yet in a position to print. He relied, instead, on Gerard Meynell whose Westminster Press undertook much Catholic jobbing work. Nevertheless, Pepler published under his own imprint, the 'Hampshire House Workshops, Hammersmith', named after the guild-style community which he established there, in Hampshire Hog Lane, in 1905.

A Carol and other Rhymes provides an insight into Johnston's thinking at this time. His discovery of a medieval carol in the British Museum so interested him that he calligraphed a copy of it. (Fig. 82). It prompted him to trains of thought which are developed in his texts accompanying the carol. They have a religious and even a theological bearing.

Though a short book, *A Carol and other Rhymes* has three distinct parts. In the preface, Johnston submits, with characteristic modesty, that the word 'rhyme' is a more accurate description of his own input than 'poetry' or 'verse'. The middle section consists of the carol itself, followed by a sequence of five of Johnston's own rhymes, some of which had been written earlier during his Hammersmith days. The final part consists of Johnston's explanatory notes on both the carol and his rhymes.

Fig. 82. Examples from *A Carol and Other Rhymes.*

MARY
SAT A-WORKING WITH
HER BABY ON HER ARM:
THE ANGEL CAME TO
BETHLEHEM : TO SEE
THAT SIGHT WITH JOY :
*þerefore Moders preyſe þe Lord
Qui creauit omnia

*Here the Manuscript begins : *vide* foregoing note.

13

His Fader was a Carpenter
Who ymade bothe round and ſquare
And wrought al thing of a borde
Carpenters ſchal preyſe þe Lord
Qui creauit omnia

His makës weren fiſhermen
Taketh þey and tourne agen
And haleth þeir nettes aborde
Fiſhermen alle preyſe þe Lord
Qui creauit omnia

Firſt of men vpon þe erthe
Shepheards dyd admire his byrth
Renning atte þe angel's worde
So lat ſhepherdes preyſe þe Lord
Qui creauit omnia

14

His coſyn was a temple preſte
Serueth ones atte þe hiegh feſte
Hee coude nought ſpeke o worde
Preſtes wyth fere mote preyſe þe Lord
Qui creauit omnia

Thre Kynges were his gyft-bringers
Yfolwed his harbinger
Comen þe brighte ſterre towarde
Ye and Kynges may preyſe þe Lord
Qui creauit omnia

Gretely hee dyd bleſs þe poore
For þe laſſe þey ſchal haue more
Wyth ſynners he dyd acorde
Let poore ſynners preyſe þe Lord
Qui creauit omnia

15 B

ALLE CREATION
GROANED & SWET
Some poore folke do trauaille yet
Waityng for þat bleſſed Worde—
So lat alle creatures preyſe þe Lord
Qui creauit omnia

16

The book is precisely organised with footnotes and references amplifying the texts. Its theme is to realise the importance of seeing human creation in relation to God, who is the creator of all things.

Johnston explains that the carol was written in English on an end leaf of a thirteenth-century chronicle he had studied in the British Museum which concerned the 'Weye of Lyf' of 'workmen' – or craftsmen – of that time.[24] The carol is supposed to have been composed, Johnston continued, by one John Rode, perhaps a hundred years after the chronicle was written when the manuscript was owned by a potter named Nicholas Greenwell, who lived near Chichester. Its eight verses each end with the refrain, written partly in Latin: '... praise ye Lord Qui creavit omnia' – ('... praise the Lord *Who created all things*'). Johnston – in collaboration with Pepler – decided to have the carol itself printed in a 'modern Black Letter type' in order to simulate the Gothic script of the period, rather than reproduce it photographically chiefly because, Johnston says, 'the photo-typographic process destroys the natural quality of the writing'. The refrain 'Qui creavit omnia' ending each verse is printed in red.

In the explanatory notes in part three, Johnston is at pains to urge a deeper sensitivity to God as the ultimate Creator. Part of his notes reads:

> At the time of writing the Carol I had in mind the making-of-Things and the desirability of counting men as craftsmen rather than as 'consumers', in other words, that it would be better if we produced (and consumed) good things than if we consumed (and therefore produced) 'cheap' things. Then I thought of those who had to do with our Lord in the light of craftsmen and workmen, who, knowing something of Creation, would or should praise God the Creator of all things. The craftsmen mentioned are: The Carpenter Joseph ... The Fishermen – Peter, Andrew, James, John, and others ... The Priest Zacharias ... The Shepherds ... The Three Kings or wise men ... The Poor (sinners) ....
>
> It may be noted that the Carol suggests that Mothers – whose craft of Motherhood makes them supreme over all other craftsmen, and who add to this all the crafts of housework – *do* praise The Lord, that Priests *must with fear*, and that Kings *may*.

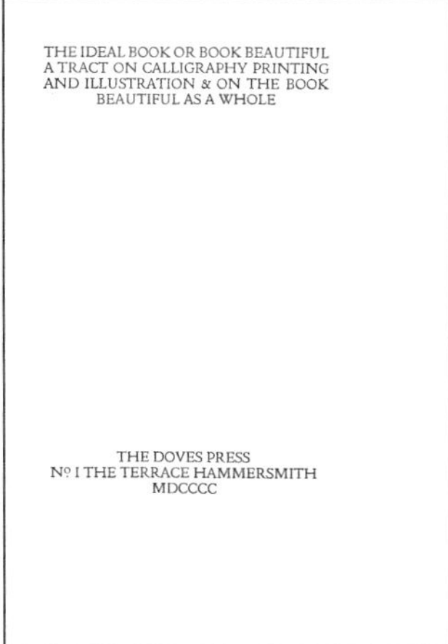
THE IDEAL BOOK OR BOOK BEAUTIFUL
A TRACT ON CALLIGRAPHY PRINTING
AND ILLUSTRATION & ON THE BOOK
BEAUTIFUL AS A WHOLE

THE DOVES PRESS
Nº I THE TERRACE HAMMERSMITH
MDCCCC

Fig. 83. *The Ideal Book or Book Beautiful.*

Two of Johnston's own rhymes take the form of the colophons to manuscripts that he had been commissioned to write. The first one was for Thomas Cobden-Sanderson's essay, *The Ideal Book or Book Beautiful.* (Fig. 83). It concerns the necessity, Johnston argues in his notes, for contrasting extremes. The rhyme '... suggests that the truth is found in *these opposites combined'*. In a footnote Johnston claims: '(Absolute Truth perhaps lies in "all extremes". E. J.)'

The second of his colophons is attached to the manuscript Johnston calligraphed of the *Rubaiyat of Omar Khayyam.*[25] Its main point is to refute Khayyam's own inclination in his poem to criticise the natural scheme of things, and therefore to '... impute blame to the Creator'. By picking up on Khayyam's parable of the broken (and dissatisfied) pots Johnston was able to claim that:

> ... for the finite to blame the infinite shows a false philosophy, for the finite does not possess the data on which to base such adverse criticism. In other words, if one does not know God's object, one is not in a position to criticise the manner in which he attains it.

Instead, for Johnston the pot is a metaphor for creation:

> That Being which cleaves the clay asunder, that Being by which the clay is held together forgets nothing, but holds that rejected or broken Thing – which we call "cast away" – as Part of the Great Universe that can spare nothing; in which Love bears, hopes, believes, and endures All Things.

The three remaining rhymes are also religious. *David was Seven Yesterday* alludes to David, Pepler's eldest son of whom Johnston was especially fond, as well as to the Biblical figure. It deals with the Christian theme of the necessity of having

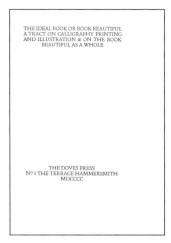

'... the strength of the lion and the quietness of the lamb' in the overcoming of evil. The second rhyme, *The Stars are Seen by God Alone*, is more complex. It touches on the necessity of faith, which Johnston defines as the 'evidence of things not seen'. The explanatory note points out:

> ARGUMENT: We see the light of the stars, not the stars themselves: we see the light reflected from a piece of paper, not the paper itself.

That is to say, we see the outward evidence only. Johnston ends his note:

> In the heart of man there is the shining of all his 'stars' – those 'stars' which he cannot reach or even see with his bodily eyes – but yet he may be in touch with them – Divine Love in his heart sees the stars for him.

The final rhyme is written with the quiet charm that unfailingly emanated from Johnston's pen. *The Thoughts of a Child on Christmas Eve* was first written in December 1910. It speaks of his daughter, Priscilla's, doubts about the existence of Father Christmas. It is of value to quote in full as a profoundly felt, if short, personal testament:

I cannot feel it with my toe,
They haven't filled it yet. I *know*
That Father Christmas is 'pretence'
I think it's Daddy: it's not sense
To think he could take all the toys
Tonight to all the girls and boys
In every house, in every street –
There must be such a lot of feet:
And all their stockings to be filled
And nothing ever lost or spilled.
It *is* the Fathers and the Mothers
Who bring to me, and to the others,
The chocolates, but I don't know
Where all the nuts and apples grow –
It might be magic after all. (Sleeps)

During 1915, Pepler had been busy writing in a very different vein. His project first had the title *Kultur*, but he then changed it to *The Devil's Devices or Control versus Service*.[26] It was the last in the trio of his publishing projects of that year. While Pepler, like Johnston, is concerned with the religious dimension of craft, he enquires more particularly into its social context. The book has the force of an indictment. He commissioned Gill to design a set of twelve wood-engraved illustrations suited to the text, six of which are emblematic images. Their titles are *Dumb-driven Cattle*, *No 27*, *The Moneybag and the Whip*, *The Purchaser*, *The Happy Labourer*, *The Sign and Symbol of Christ, whose Service is perfect Freedom* (Figs. 84–88) An effective graphic counterpart to Pepler's thinking, making them preoccupied Gill throughout November 1915.

The first edition comprised one thousand and three hundred copies, printed at the Westminster Press. Prior to this Gerard Meynell printed two hundred proof copies, signed by Pepler and Gill. (A separate edition of some of the wood engravings was to be hand-printed by Gill in 1919.) One of the proof copies was sent to Johnston at Christmas 1915. It has a handwritten inscription by Pepler acknowledging his debt to Johnston:

> To E. J, i.e., Edward Johnston with my love. The book would not have made much of a show on our own account, but thanks are included in that which is greater. H. D. C. P. 25. xii. 1915.[27]

Without giving any details, the greeting demonstrates Johnston's involvement in Pepler's project. Evidently, Johnston was encouraging, although in all probability he also gave critical insights which were important to Pepler. That the book was the outcome of a partnership is shown by the printed dedication, which is to G. K. Chesterton. Calligraphed by Johnston within the frame of a cartouche, the inscription is signed by Eric Gill, Edward Johnston and Douglas Pepler.

The Devil's Devices, or Control versus Service is undoubtedly a high point in Pepler's literary output. It came after his two sociological tracts, *The Care Committee*, of 1912, *Justice and the Child*, of 1915.[28] It also stands between the two major phases of Pepler's ideological development. In it Pepler casts aside his Fabian sympathies. While religious, he is not yet engrossed in Roman Catholicism. The book's dramatic thrust is different from Johnston's quieter tone. Its underlying message, however, remains the same. Both convey the belief that craft work needs to be respectful of tradition and aspire to the ideal of work as a celebration of divine creation.

Pepler's writing shows remarkable imaginative power. *The Devil's Devices* employs a number of literary and graphic tropes to give an expressive and entertaining force to its ideas. There is dialogue (often in dialect), and rhyme. Additionally, there is adventurous page layout, versatile use of types, printer's tailpieces and Gill's emblematic designs. Chapter One is written as an imaginary silent film – a '*Cinema Comedy*', as Pepler said – and this as early in cinema's history as 1915.

The book is couched in the form of six dialogues between the Narrator and the Devil. Pepler portrays the Devil as a Nietzschean figure who advocates a futuristic world in which the 'old order ... the lumber of tradition' will be consumed in *The Fire of the Future* – this phrase being the title of the last dialogue. An elitist culture will blossom in a necessarily authoritarian society. The Devil exclaims:

> No wonder the world is in chains when so many refuse to open their eyes to the gifts which Science has laid at their feet.

Expediency therefore requires the imposition of '... government from above, downwards'. The Devil argues plausibly; his logic is persuasive. But not all is lost. The Narrator's vision is armed with a deeper form of wisdom:

> No man can be free until he has learnt the limits of his freedom ... craftsmen could not be free in or of their trade until they had mastered their tools. The tradition of any craft or trade is the tradition of respect for limitations not an escape from them.

The Narrator turns to the question of evil. The Devil maintains that:

The Moneybag and the Whip

The Happy Labourer

The Purchaser

Dumb Driven Cattle

Figs. 84–88. Examples of Eric Gill's wood engravings from *The Devil's Devices.*

> ...there is no sin, evil is a delusion, a myth which Science has answered and dispersed .... The battle of the world is not between good and evil but between efficiency or progress and inefficiency or reaction.

The Narrator rejoins, saying that the problem is resolvable not in the Devil's terms of reformed institutions – of social engineering, in effect – but through individual acts:

> Because we can so often hide evil by regulation we are apt to forget that we can only overcome it by good.

Pepler's theme is the absolute requirement of freedom for the individual. He speaks of the necessity for the individual to be responsible to himself and to find his own chosen work as the expression of his love of what is human. He abhors the prospect of state control. He refutes the Devil's notion that:

> ... a wise ruler is not chosen by the people, he choses them.

The first dialogue, to take just one example of Pepler's versatility, is visualised as a silent film called *The Progress of Everyman. The Broad Road to Heaven*. The film relies on a gramophone to provide the dialogue. It progresses with all the stock-in-trade familiar to cinema audiences of the time. The screen titles and the jump cuts, the fades and dissolves, even the chatter of the projector which Pepler introduces are reminiscent of the work of pioneer film-makers such as Lumière or Méliès, which Pepler, with his theatrical interests, is likely to have seen.

The Devil, in the guise of Everyman, is the creator of a '... time, trouble and labour-saving machine', which, he boasts, is '...a solution to all the social and economic problems of the age'. The Narrator then points out: 'Man wants to be wise, to be free, to be good', but 'The Devil sets his snares accordingly.' The Devil's foil, however, is '...a man of Chestertonian girth' who '... whirls a large wideawake hat round on the end of a stick'. He exposes the Devil's 'maudlin sophistry' with a simple but cautionary rhyme. One stanza reads:

> The Devil has a set of slaves
> To watch the cradles, dig the graves,
> To find the home and choose the wife
> To give man an efficient life
> To dope him with an opiate.
> To tolerate the State.

Perhaps with William Morris in mind, Pepler's special insight was to recognise the need of Everyman for a fulfilled life. He is symbolised by two typical English families. One is living in a terraced house – a random address, 'No. 27'. The other lives at the 'village blacksmith's', in Sussex. These choices surely reflect Pepler's experiences as a social worker in Hammersmith and his visits to Johnston and Gill in Ditchling. (The blacksmith was based on a person he had met in a pub – it might it have been in The Sandrock, next door to Sopers, in Ditchling?) In the preface Pepler set out his aim:

> It is because I love these men I write this book. It is their freedom which I see menaced, theirs are the children whom I see driven to useless schools to be taught useless things, it is their money which I see stolen by the rest of us, their work tempted by ignoble aims and their energy prostituted to shameless ends.

'Prostitution', Pepler goes on to explain, in terms rooted in the ideas of Morris and Lethaby, is the only word suitable to describe:

> The transactions in which a man hires himself out to do shoddy, machine-minding work for wages where he could, if he would, become a creator, a master of things bearing the impress of himself.[29]

In due course, in 1915, Sopers became the temporary home for Hilary Pepler and his family. By this time Pepler was thirty-seven years old. Disenchanted by the bureaucratic strictures of his social work with the London County Council in Hammersmith and much enthused by Gill's and Johnston's new lives, he had been anxious for some time to leave London. From 1912 he began visiting Ditchling quite frequently. In his diary for 8th and then the 9th March 1913 Gill recorded:

> The Peplers of Hammersmith called, and in our absence Count Kessler turned up. The Peplers came in the morning.

Pepler also came down to Ditchling late in December 1914 to help organise the art exhibition which was held there for the benefit of Belgian refugees. Gill organised the printing of the catalogues. His diary records for 23rd December 1914:

> E. J. and Peplers came in morning I went over to see the brickyard with them. They stayed to dinner after.[30]

Pepler spent part of 1915 in making the necessary arrangements for his move, including his resignation from the London County Council. He finally moved into Sopers during March. Two entries in Gill's diary, for 23rd March and 21st April 1915, read:

> Pepler called at 5.30 and we went, Ethel and I, down to Ditchling at 8.0 to Sopers for supper, very pleasant evening. Home 10.30.
> To Ditchling in even to supper at Peplers. E. J. also there. Home 11.15.

It was early in 1916 that their craft community effectively came into being in Ditchling – Pepler called themselves a 'triumvirate'. Its first sign was the interest which Gill, Johnston, and Pepler had in experimenting with printing. A glimpse of their artistic life together is given by Pepler in a memoir entitled *Gill in Ditchling*. Their renewed association was regarded by Pepler as an 'unofficial partnership'. In reality, they found again the companionship of their Hammersmith days, though now in a much enhanced form. Pepler explained:

> When we three argued the point in the ampler freedom of Sussex, with the Downs upon which we often walked, the man most often quoted in our talk was W. R. Lethaby .... We were convinced that the workman, craftsman and artist who made anything could not be properly free unless he were master of the material, tools and design so that his work achieved an integrity, a wholeness, in which mind, skill and material were inseparable.[31]

At this point, in 1916, the 'triumvirate' was underpinned by nothing more formal that the idea of religiously inspired craftsmanship. Elsewhere Pepler clarifies this:

> We had never discusssed Faith. We three of us, very much a Triumvirate, were E. J. (calligrapher), Douglas Hilary Pepler (who had just got a printing press) – a Quaker, Eric Gill (who had recently become R.C.); and it seemed to be a sufficient bond between us to believe in the Resurrection and the integrity of the craftsman, especially as a letterer.[32]

In this regard a significant passage is to be found in Gill's essay, *Sculpture* (Pepler printed it in 1918). In it Gill is more definite about how he saw the nature of craft:

> Craft work was a form of devotion, and celebration of God. Beauty ... not merely the lowliness of the earth or of living things, but the absolute entity, which, like Goodness and Truth, is apprehended by conscience.[33]

The main form of collaboration between Johnston, Gill and Pepler continued to be publishing projects. Now, however, the printing was to be done in Ditchling. From 1916 to mid-1918, Pepler continued to use the imprint The Hampshire House Workshops, although the actual printing was now credited to The Ditchling Press, and was 'printed by Douglas Pepler'. His practical involvement in printing dated from early January 1916. He left a number of accounts as to how it began. In his book, *The Hand Press*, written in 1934, Pepler recalled:

> So I left Hammersmith and set up in a Ditchling stable which had recently been used by Eric Gill and Joseph Cribb as a mason's yard. Indeed, I had to wait until Joseph Cribb had finished carving the stone Hog, which marked the site of the Hampshire House Workshops in Hammersmith, London.[34]

The stone slab on which his Stanhope press rested is still to be seen in the former workshop at Sopers (the workshop is now used as a garage).[35] In his article, *Gill in Ditchling*, of 1949, Pepler wrote:

> I had closed with the offer of a hand press, three founts of Caslon Old Face, cases etc, so that a printer and two men of letters found themselves equipped with tempting opportunities for propaganda should they have ideas to propagate.

Practical help was at hand, too, Pepler being '… greatly assisted by the portly, elderly printer, Mr. Dawes'. Gill and Johnston became eager participants. Johnston provided typographic advice, based partly on his experience of Cobden-Sanderson's Doves Press books.[36] In another recollection, *S. Dominic's Press. As to its Founding at Ditchling*, written in 1933, Pepler spoke of Johnston's input:

> S. Dominic's Press was founded in January 1916, after His Majesty's medical advisors had decided that I and a coal-heaver were unsuited to the trade of war. The first of iron presses (a Stanhope), a folio Albion and two founts of Caslon Old Face type, was all the equipment that the stable at my disposal could accommodate. Cobden-Sanderson gave me his blessing but not his type .... In those days I was privileged to have Edward Johnston as guide, and nearly all that is typographically commendable among our subsequent publications is due to his influence, either directly or through his former pupil Eric Gill – H. D. C. P.[37]

Another, lesser known, account is Pepler's short memoir of the press, *Twenty-One Years*, written in 1937.

> On January 16th 1916 a van held up the traffic in Ditchling High Street while twelve cwts of metal which made the *Stanhope Press* were transferred from the same to the stable at the back of 'Sopers' (a stable which had served Gill on his escape from London and was soon to see printed his first wood-cuts.)
>
> Three days later, with Edward Johnston's assistance, we set up, in Latin, the first words of the Fourth gospel 'In principio erat Verbum'. I then printed the bottle labels for the publican next door and quite soon was setting up Mrs Mairet's 'Vegetable Dyes' ....[38]

The very next day, 20th January, Gill's diary reads:

> To Ditchling in evening to see Pepler's printing press. Did my first piece of printing. Supper at Sopers.

Gill quickly made intensive use of the printing facilities. His diary goes on '... printing woodblocks all morning'. Gill was producing on the Stanhope press a separate portfolio of his illustrations for Pepler's *The Devil's Devices*. They were published by Pepler with the title Emblems, under the imprint of the Hampshire House Workshops.[39] Gill was helped by another press-hand, Arthur K. Sabin. As to Johnston's involvement, Priscilla Johnston reconstructed events from his diary:

> ... almost every day he would be round at the press and often they would meet again in the evening.

The first full-scale book that Pepler printed in Ditchling was Ethel Mairet's *A Book of Vegetable Dyes*, though under the imprint of The Hampshire House Workshops, Hammersmith. It was completed on St. John the Baptist's Day (June 24th) 1916. In his catalogue of that year, Pepler defined his publishing aim:

> It is desirable to record what still survives of the tradition of making good things; I shall endeavour to publish the instructions & advice of men and women who still follow these good traditions.[40]

Pepler's second book followed those aims precisely. He issued another edition of Cobbett's *Cottage Economy*. In following years similar craft-based works formed a significant part of the press's output. Otherwise, Pepler always claimed to be a jobbing printer, just as Johnston claimed to be a jobbing scribe.

On January 19th of 1917, Pepler began the tradition of the celebrated Ditchling Press Suppers to commemorate the anniversaries of the 'Foundation of the Ditchling Press'. They were attended by Ditchling friends and became an occasion when the village craft community came together at Halletts. In later years the Press Suppers took place on 14th January, which was the date of Hilary Pepler's birthday. From the names mentioned on the reverse side of an invitation card for 1918, it is clear that Johnston attended. For the 1918 celebrations, Philip Mairet composed a Song of the Evening, which he sang to the tune of a sea shanty, *Sally [or Shallow] Brown,* one of the many songs collected by Cecil Sharp. Although playful, it reflects their own sense of a craft community in Ditchling. The twelve stanzas of the song are, incidentally, so informative about printing and other activities in Ditchling that they should be quoted in full. The second stanza, for instance, shows Pepler to be interested in ordinary jobbing printing, while 'the shop of a tombstone maker' is a reference to Gill's and Joseph Cribb's work on the memorial to Oscar Wilde. The penultimate stanza shows that early in 1918 the press was still located in the workshop at Sopers, in Ditchling village.

We bought a case of Caslon Primer
Way Ho, a-printing we shall go
And set up a press in the village of Ditchling
As the old printers printed printing long ago.

We took the shop of a tombstone maker,
Way Ho, a-printing we will go.
And printed Bills for Mayall the baker,
As the old printers printed printing long ago.

From Africa the learned pressman came,
Way Ho, a-printing we will go.
We printed quite as well – or nearly
As old printers printed printing long ago.

We did a book on dyeing rightly,
Way Ho, a-dyeing we will go.
That taught the art of dyeing brightly,
As the old dyers dyed their dyeing long ago.

The sculptor did the very best he could
Way Ho, a-graving we will go
To grave us pretty pictures upon the wood
As the old gravers graved their graving long ago.

The local scribe we sought and did invite
Way Ho, a-writing we will go.
Some fine capital letters in red to write,
As the old writers wrote their writing long ago.

We printed Latin hymns enormous,
Way Ho, a-printing we will go.
Round them we stand and chant in chorus
As the old chanters chanted chanting long ago.

When work is hard we think it proper,
Way Ho, a-drinking we will go.
To brew us beer in the kitchen copper
As the old brewers brewed their brewage long ago.

But the printer's boy, mind what I'm telling,
Way Ho, a-printing we will go.
Must learn to comp. with better spelling
Than the old compers comp'd their comping long ago.

And when the spring comes and it's nice and warm,
Way Ho, a-carting we will go
We'll cart the Press and ourselves up to Halletts Farm,
As the old carters carted carting long ago.

And now to God, Father, Son, and Holy Ghost,
Way Ho, a-printing we will go.

And Praise His Name whom good works Praise the most,
As the old Printers Praised Him Printing long ago.[41]

From 1918, Pepler's printing enterprise was called the S. Dominic's Press. This second phase of its development, and Johnston's diminishing role in it, is to be discussed shortly.

It is apparent that during this period the close friendship between Johnston, Gill, and Pepler led them into collaborative projects based on an interchange of skills. Their friendship was also cemented by frequent exchanges of gifts. Shortly after his arrival in Ditchling Johnston presented Gill a manuscript of *The Lord's Prayer*[42] written out on vellum. In 1914, Johnston gave Pepler a gift of a similar manuscript, an illuminated religious song-book. In speaking of Gill in his memoir, Pepler recalled that during

> the ten years [1914–24] we shared many things a mutual intimacy and affection.[43]

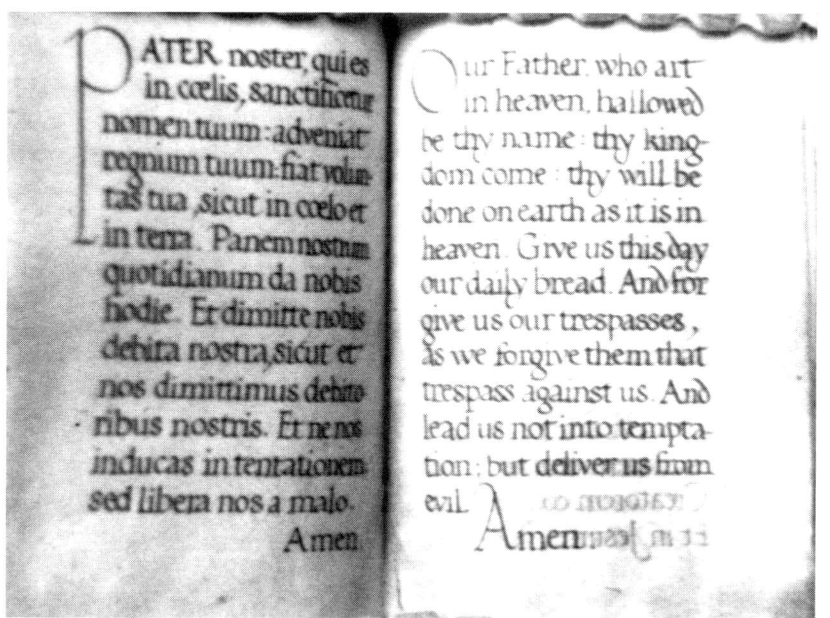

PATER noster, qui es
in coelis, sanctificetur
nomen tuum: adveniat
regnum tuum: fiat volun-
tas tua, sicut in coelo et
in terra. Panem nostrum
quotidianum da nobis
hodie. Et dimitte nobis
debita nostra, sicut et
nos dimittimus debito-
ribus nostris. Et ne nos
inducas in tentationem:
sed libera nos a malo.
Amen

Our Father who art
in heaven, hallowed
be thy name: thy king-
dom come: thy will be
done on earth as it is in
heaven. Give us this day
our daily bread. And for-
give us our trespasses,
as we forgive them that
trespass against us. And
lead us not into tempta-
tion: but deliver us from
evil.
Amen

Fig. 89. Johnston's manuscript of the Lord's Prayer written out on vellum.

Pepler's friendship towards Johnston was equally warm. Like the gift of *The Devil's Devices,* other book gifts were sent to him. Their communality invariably involved the whole family. On Johnston's birthday, 11th February 1916, Pepler gave him a copy of *St. George and the Dragon and other Stories, Children's Series Vol. 1 No. 1.* which includes *Mathew in Greenland* by David Pepler and *A Story* by the three Pepler sons. (Fig. 90). It has one wood engraving by David Pepler and another by the young Ronald Seal, who was taking lessons with Gill. On its wrapper was written:

To Johnston the penman
Mender and maker of toys
From Clare and Douglas
And three obstreperous boys.[44]

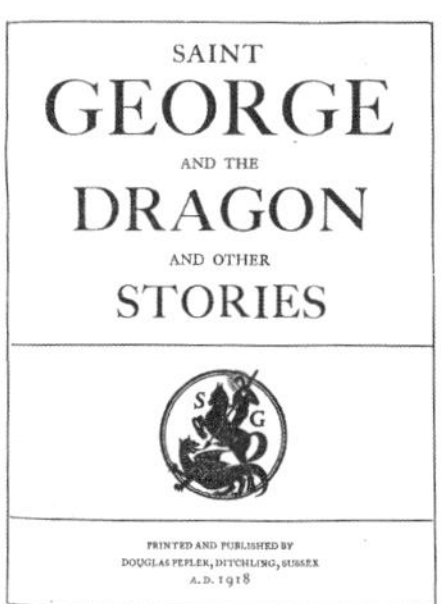

Fig. 90. *St. George and the Dragon and other Stories.*

The tradition flourished. A copy of each of the books Pepler printed was invariably sent to Johnston as it came off the press. One was Pepler's own title *God and the Dragon. A Booklet of Rhymes*, of 1917, with engravings by Gill and Ralph Beedham. It was inscribed: 'with love from H. D. C. P.'[45] Following the death of Johnston's younger sister Olof on 2nd February 1917, Pepler printed an *In Memoriam* for the funeral service. It was accompanied by engraved funeral cards by Gill. (Fig. 91).

As at Hammersmith, their children also intermingled. They were nine in number at this stage: The Gills had three girls – Betty, Petra, and Joan. The Peplers had three boys – David, Stephen, and Mark (his three daughters were yet to be born), matching Johnston's three daughters. Pepler's *St. George and the Dragon and other Stories* was followed by Priscilla Johnston's *The Mill Book*, with wood engravings by Pepler and the young Ronald Seal, and two by Priscilla. In the same spirit, in 1919, Pepler also printed *A Christmas Book*, written by Gill's and Pepler's children, with eighteen illustrations between them. (Fig. 92). A description of these childhood friendships is given in Fr. Conrad Pepler's *In Diebus Illis. Some Memories of Ditchling.*[46] Another collaboration was Pepler's little book, *Concerning Dragons*, of 1924, with five engravings by Gill.

Fig. 91. Gill's engravings for Johnston's younger sister's funeral cards.

Each took an interest in promoting the other's professional work over a wide range of projects, on an *ad hoc* basis, though not necessarily without payment. For instance, between July and September 1912 Gill's diary indicated that he worked on a headstone for a 'Johnston', possibly commissioned by Edward on the death of his father. In 1914, Johnston provided an illustration and the lettering for the cover of the catalogue of an exhibition organised by Pepler at his Hampshire House Workshops in Hammersmith, of the work of English and the Belgian refugee craftsmen. (A similar exhibition of sculpture and paintings was held in Ditchling in December 1914, entitled *Belgian Refugees: The Murder of the Innocents*. Gill arranged to have this catalogue printed locally. (Fig. 93). In March 1914 Gill went:

> To E. J's to see his work for S. C. C[ockerell]'

This was the commission for the celebrated *Book of Sample Scripts*. (Fig. 94). In February 1915 Gill noted in his diary:

> E. J. came to lunch and stayed all 'noon. We discussed Brierley Address MSS.... Walked with E. J. to Ditchling in eve. E[thel] met me on way back.

In September Gill was helping Johnston with a drawing for this manuscript. For almost three weeks, in May and June, 1915, Gill worked on sculpting a crucifix for Pepler. In July, 1915, Pepler commissioned him to sculpt a stone garden roller – with figures intertwined in shallow relief at each end. In September 1915 Gill was working on the wheatsheaf design for Pepler's Hampshire House Workshops' bakery. (Fig. 95).In October 1915, Gill went 'to G. M's [Gerard Meynell] to visit him and to meet Hunter re. £1 note design. Lunch with E. J. and G. M.'. In 1916 Gill engraved Johnston's demonstration of lettering for his *Winchester Formal Writing Sheet, No. 1*, a lettering portfolio based on his teaching sheets, which Pepler then printed. (Fig 96). In September 1916, Gill asked Johnston's advice about the illustrations for the book project proposed by the publisher John Hogg on ship painting.[47] Johnston, in turn, in 1920, designed for Gill an indenture form for his apprentices.[48]

Between mid-1916 to late-1917 Gill helped Pepler by engraving in wood two large-scale titling alphabets (one was one-and-a-half inches high), to go with the Caslon type for the Stanhope press. (Fig. 97). He also designed a watermark for the paper which Pepler was making by hand. Pepler, for his part, was very impressed by Gill's fourteen panels of *The Stations of the Cross* for Westminster Cathedral. Good Friday 1918 found him in the cathedral, on top of a ladder helping Gill with their installation, during the blessing of *The Stations* by the Bishop. In the catalogue of the exhibition on *The Stations*, at the Alpine Gallery, in 1918, Pepler wrote:

> The Stations at Westminster are primarily for use in a workshop – that workshop of praise and prayer called the House of God .... And as if befitting such an extraordinary sign of the love of God, the Stations are out of the hand of a man.[49]

Earlier in 1918, Pepler printed his own book, *The Way of the Cross*. It was illustrated with Gill's engravings based on his designs for *The Stations of the Cross*. Throughout this period from 1912 to 1918 or even to 1919 Gill, Pepler, and Johnston lived harmoniously. Their lives intermingled. They helped and encouraged each other. Characteristic entries in Gill's diary occur in December 1915 and in September 1916:

> To E. J. for breakfast & walk with him and H. D. C. P. via Falmer and Rodmell to Asham. Lunch at Rodmell. Asham was looking perfect'.

> To the Hills with E. and the children and the Peplers for a picnic (a most perfect day).

The three would travel to London, sometimes meeting there to visit exhibitions or dine, or they would meet at Victoria Station to come home together. They had friends in common – Pepler and Gill would stay overnight at Romney Green's home at Strand-on-the-Green, Chiswick. They helped each other on their smallholdings – in haymaking, or in the crisis of swarming bees. They lent each other necessities. They had breakfast, lunch, and supper in each other's houses. They spent Christmas Eves together. They would play tennis in the summer, and in winter would skate on 'the big pond' on the Common 'with Johnston's children'. They sang hymns and plainsong together, though Johnston would not have taken part. Gill gave Pepler's son, David, lessons in wood-engraving. They discussed the war, conscientious objection, aesthetics, and – fatefully, as it turned out – Roman Catholicism. Several evenings were spent in August 1916, discussing the Design and Industries Association. Advice was sought, one from the other and, inevitably, favours were asked and confidences were exchanged. Gill's letter to Johnston, dated 2nd March 1914, speaks of money – and of bicycling up to London as if this effort were a trifle:

> Dear Johnston, Can you possibly lend me some money? I've got to go to London on Wednesday to superintend the erection of the 5th Station [of the Cross] at Westminster Cathedral and can then call on the Goupil Gallery people and see if they can let me have something on account. Meanwhile I haven't even enough money to

A

CHRISTMAS BOOK

BY

E., P. AND J. GILL,
D., S. AND M. PEPLER.

PRINTED AT S. DOMINIC'S PRESS, DITCHLING.
A.D. MCMXIX.

The Stable at Bethlehem

Here is the stable on the hills the sheephairds are coming to see Jesus in the stable who has been born there becours there was no room in the inn Marry and Joseph went

JESUS

Here you see Jesus with his most Sacred Hart although only a little boy he loved us very much and we must try to do the same.

BEDROOM RULES
MARK

RISE 7.30 and DRESS, Wash, Brush Hair and clean Teeth; say Prayers, turn back Bed.

GO TO BED AT 7.30

Bath or Wash well [legs etc.] Brush hair, say Prayers, fold up clothes.

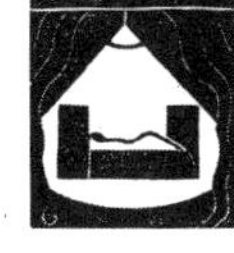

Fig. 92. *A Christmas Book*.

Fig. 93. *Belgian Refugees: The Murder of the Innocents.*

that went to the battle were Eliab the first-born, and next unto him Abinadab, and the third Shammah. And David was the youngest: and the three eldest followed Saul. Now David went to and fro from Saul to feed his father's sheep at Beth-lehem. And the Philistine drew near morning and evening, and presented himself forty days.

AND JESSE SAID UNTO DAVID HIS SON, Take now for thy brethren an ephah of this parched corn, and these ten loaves, and carry *them* quickly to the camp to thy brethren; and bring these ten cheeses unto the captain of their thousand, and look how thy brethren fare, and take their

12

Fig. 94. Page from *Book of sample scripts.*

Fig. 95. Gill's wheatsheaf design for Pepler's bakery.

> pay for the train fare tho' if it weren't for the fact that some amount of cash is always necessary I could easily ride up on the bike and so avoid a train fare. So if you could manage to lend me a fiver I'd be glad indeed, and if you could make it seven so much the better.[50]

Two further entries in Gill's diary, for 22nd January and 18th July 1916, are poignant:

> To D[itchling] after tea to see Pepler and E. J. re. my letter in 'Land and Work'. Supper at Sopers. Walk on hills after with E. J. and Pepler in moonlight. Home 12.30!
>
> To D[itchling] to see Christie, also to Sopers and discussed D. P. love affair with him! Very sad indeed.[51]

Johnston discussed Gill's problem over the controversial Leeds Memorial sculpture with him. The evening of the 20th December, 1918, for instance, saw Gill going:

> To E. J. to supper and later after D. P. had gone discussed L. C. C. certificate affair with E. J. [Johnston's commission] etc until 5.30 am! Then to bed.

In his Memoir, *Gill in Ditchling,* Pepler recalled that although Gill and Johnston were of different religious backgrounds they '...enjoyed a remarkable unity in fundamentals'. At that point, in 1916, Pepler was nominally at least still a Quaker, Gill was a Roman Catholic, and Johnston was of the Church of England. Together, from 28th September 1916, they formed the Latin Club:

> meeting once a week for a Latin class for the reading of the Fourth Gospel in that language with the help of dictionaries and a modicum of grammar from schooldays.

Gill's diary shows that, in fact, they met more spasmodically than that. They would meet in each others' homes, the session invariably being followed by supper. Johnston's interest in Latin was religious but must have arisen, too, from his study of medieval manuscripts in that language. Pepler's interest was to be strengthened by his conversion to Catholicism. Johnston wrote out the conjugation of Latin verbs on to small cards as an *aide-mémoire.*[52] Their routine had, therefore, both a studious and a socialising purpose. (Fig. 99).

During the latter part of 1915, Pepler and Johnston took inspiration from Gill's life on the Common and thought of buying a property together and living from the land. In *Gill in Ditchling* Pepler wrote of the collective belief in what he called a 'back to the land movement'. Gill, Pepler and Johnston were:

> Three Reformers primarily engaged in reforming their own manner of living to the pattern set by Cobbett a hundred years before.

In fact, a fourth friend, Romney Green, thought seriously of joining them. A woodworking craftsman who by this time was living in Chiswick, he and his wife made a number of visits to Gill, Johnston, and Pepler in Ditchling.[53]

In mentioning Cobbett, Pepler was thinking of his book, *Cottage Economy,* which he had recently reprinted.[54] It had a short introduction by G. K. Chesterton who spoke of the need to take up again Cobbett's rural idealism and 'return to freedom'. This was a medieval freedom, needless to say, in which the rural labourer was neither a serf nor even a tenant. Instead, he was a 'cottager', the owner and master of his own cottage and plot of land, who practised a domestic economy comprising the brewing of beer, bee-keeping, bread-making, the rearing of pigs and poultry, and the making of candles. *Cottage Economy* gives hints and recipes for all these practices and other more esoteric ones such as the building of an ice-house. It was a manual for rural self-sufficiency. Its premise was the necessity and virtue of private property and the thrift which is engendered by looking after it. Its aim was to defy what Cobbett saw as the tyranny of a clergy which taught contentment in poverty. It promoted the education of children within the family through the learning of practical skills of home economy. The family, Cobbett believed, was the fundamental unit of society. Gill, Pepler and Johnston wished to re-enact the Cobbett model. Four entries in Gill's diary for February 1916 record their search for a suitable house with land:

> Cycled to Ditchling and went with the Peplers to Plumpton Mills to see the property they want to buy.
>
> To supper at Pepler's. Latin after. Discussed Plumpton Mills project after. Home 3.0 a.m!
>
> To see place called Bankside (north end of Common) with E. J. and Pepler in noon & they came back to tea & supper also. Turkey and Xmas pudding. Songs after. Bed 1.0 a.m.

Fig. 96. Gill's engraving of Johnston's lettering.

ABCDEFGH
IJKLMNO

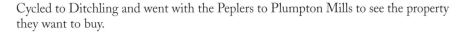

Fig. 97. Gill's large-scale titling alphabet for Pepler.

Fig. 98. St. Margaret's Church in Ditchling

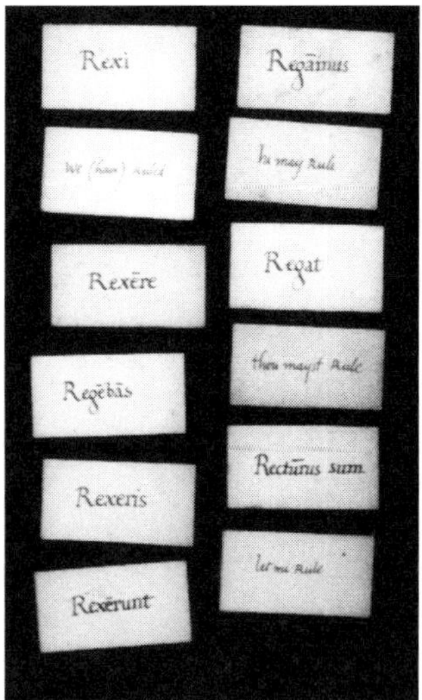

Fig. 99. Johnston's Latin *aide-mémoire.*

> To Ditchling in eve to supper at E.J's. Discussed purchase of Plumpton Mills estate after with E. J. and Pepler. Home 12.0.55.[55]

Of this 'back to the land' project, Pepler wrote in his memoir *Gill in Ditchling*:

> It was not unnatural that we should desire further isolation and look out for a farm or some such place which could be divided into three separate but somewhat interdependent small- holdings. The search for the ideal hamlet we had in mind led us into many attractive corners of the county. These excursions failed but in the end I was able to acquire land and Johnston to buy a house within 500 yards of Gill's homestead.[56]

This house and land was Halletts Farm, of some six acres. It is situated on the main road, Common Lane, leading from the village up to Ditchling Common, a little way south of Hopkin's Crank. The time was August or September 1916. The farmhouse itself was occupied by Johnston. It was then known as Halletts, though Pepler referred to it as the 'old cottage'. (Fig. 100). Priscilla Johnston remembered it as:

> a little, square, brick box with one bow window, in autumn crimson with Virginia creeper. There it stood four-square staring down the road to Ditchling.'[57]

(Nowadays, much enlarged, it is called The Oaks.) Pepler stayed on at Sopers, while farming most of the land at Halletts Farm. Johnston cultivated just one field. Entries in Gill's diary between 1st August and 23rd October 1916, give glimpses of progress:

> E. J. came to supper to tell us the news that D. P. has bought Hallett's Farm. Songs and hymns after supper.

> Romney Green came in noon. Tea at Hallett's with the children and E[thel] & the Peplers and Green. To Sopers to supper. Discussed Green's book on Woodwork after. Home 3.0a.m. To D[itchling] 12.0 to see E.J's nanny goat served by Dumbrell's goat.

> To Fragbarrow with D. P. to take D. P's heifer to bull.

> To Hallett's with D. P. to fetch the cow! I bought her from Pepler for £12. She is 15 months old, approx.[58]

A letter from Pepler to Johnston of 16th September 1916 refers to the forthcoming completion of the purchase, but hints, too, at some slight disagreements between them over Pepler's decision to build on the site:

Fig. 100. Johnstons' house, Halletts.

> Dear Edward, ... I had never thought of not having the 'desirable property', I merely jib at building there. (We made butter this morning) .... Completion (i.e., actually parting with the cash and receiving the land) may not take place until the second week in October but will be some time between St. Michaelmas and St. Luke's (about the same time I expect the Germans to retreat to the Rhine). The Green's came here yesterday [to Sopers]. Green has gone on to see his mother. They will, I think, put up their sleeping hut in the old cottage garden at Halletts and build one room! & give up Strand on the Green. We had a tremendous jaw last night until about 3.a.m chiefly on the point as to whether one material can be more noble in itself (irrespective of use)

than another. Green seems convinced that organic substances are more noble than inorganic ....'[59]

Fig. 101. Cave's Cottage.

In spite of the hesitancy expresssed in that letter, Pepler proceeded early in 1917 to design and have built a two-storey building on land at Halletts Farm, on a site just to the north, but adjacent to Johnston's 'old cottage'. As well as living accommodation it was to incorporate a workshop for his printing press. At this point it was being called Cave's Cottage. (Fig. 101) Gill recorded some of the planning and construction. Entries in Gill's diary between 16th January and 19th December, 1917 read:

> Drawing out of one-eighth scale plans of 'Cave's cottage' etc., at Hallett's for D. P. about 3 hrs in morn.
>
> To tea at Pepler's .... Discussed house plans of Hallett's.
>
> To Hallett's to see water diviner. He didn't turn up.
>
> To Hallett's to see building.'[60]

Its construction continued into 1918. Here was an opportunity for Pepler to give his social ideas an architectural reality. Priscilla Johnston remembered the building as:

> conforming to the ideals of the three men, and having one large living room for all purposes with walls of rough plaster and a huge open fireplace at the end. It smoked and, inevitably, failed to warm the large draughty room.'[61]

Gill diary records for 8th February, 1918: '2.30-3.30 to Halletts with D. P. looking over house.' By May 1918, Pepler was living there. Gill records for 13th May: 'To Hallett's to meet Fr. Austin.' (a priest from Hawkesyard Priory). By July 1918, Pepler had installed his printing equipment, in fact, in an outbuilding.[62] The new house was never known as Cave's Cottage, but simply – and confusingly – as Halletts.

Some eighteen months later, in September 1919, Pepler (with Desmond Chute) bought Fragbarrow Farm, which comprised a large house and some one hundred and sixty acres of land. It was situated on the other side of Common Lane (the main road running up from the village) from Hallett's. It was a only short walk across fields to Hopkin's Crank. The practical side of farming was undertaken by local help, until Pepler's son, David, was old enough to take charge. Pepler made use of a small steam engine with which to mill flour.

It was on a north-eastern portion of this land that the complex of the Guild workshops and a chapel was to be built, from 1920. Meantime, the print workshop of S. Dominic's Press was kept on in the out-house at Pepler's house, Halletts, until 1921, when it was moved into those workshops.

Together, then, from the summer of 1916, Pepler and Johnston followed Gill's lead and launched into the experiment of small-scale family farming. It rather conformed to the Distributist slogan of the time – that each should have 'three acres and a cow'. Pepler's farming activities were more general – pigs, cows, vegetables, and the (illicit) brewing of beer – '... during a brief period of rebellion we worked an illicit still', wrote Pepler in *Twenty-One Years*. Pepler recalled that: 'Home-made bread, bacon, beer appeared on the agenda taken up to help in the feeding of our families.'[63] (In *Twenty-One Years* he also wrote: 'we moved to the edge of the Common – a farm having been acquired as a precaution against the German submarine'.) Gill had been keeping pigs for some time. He recorded in his diary that on October 1st 1914:

> We killed our first pig today. Black Sam the butcher came to do the cutting up. I helped by looking on and supplying the beer.[64]

Johnston's involvement was far more modest. He restricted himself to the growing and (attempted) threshing of wheat for bread.

From 1917, their experiment was joined by Philip Mairet.[65] A writer and the husband of Ethel Mairet, he was soon to become a Ditchling-based craftsman himself. He had worked between 1906–08 as a draughtsman for the designer, C. R. Ashbee, at his Guild of Handicraft, at Chipping Campden, Gloucestershire. Pepler had already met Mairet and, early in 1917, he invited the Mairets to visit Ditchling Common. He subsequently suggested to Mairet, who was a conscientious objector, that he might work on his farm. A passage in Mairet's *Autobiographical Compilation* conveys the ethos of life at Ditchling Common at this, the high tide of their shared convictions:

> The mechanisation of agriculture had not gone very far in Sussex. It was excluded on principle, indeed anathematised by Pepler and his two fellow settlers, Gill and Johnston. For this Ditchling community was, much more thoroughly and comprehensively than the Guild at Chipping Campden had been, an effort to revive and live by pre-industrial values in work. Douglas Pepler was really much more interested in his printing than in farming; but the printing was to be preaching as well as practise of the colleagues' principles ... and he delighted in farming because it was the industry which was still very little corrupted by the technological revolution. On our farm at Ditchling we mowed the hay with the scythe, cut our corn with the swophook; and when it came to the brewing of our harvest beer Cave [a farmhand] thrashed the barley with a flail, winnowed it with a fan, and malted the grain on a piece of sheet-iron over a slow fire .... Some of the old men on neighbouring farms still wore the smock (so beloved by Gill) and so did the shepherds on the Downs, with their crooks, dogs and brollies. It was meat and drink to us to live in such an 'unspoiled' rural economy, and we were sure that nothing could be more pleasing to God than to keep it so.
>
> The craft idealism at Chipping Campden had also been something more than an aesthetic movement, but not much more; the Ditchling colonists wanted to re-create a life based on the living traditions of agriculture and of religion. Eric Gill, for instance, used to speak of 'aht' (art) as an abomination.[66]

A measure of the satisfaction that Pepler and Johnston felt at having found Halletts (and then Fragbarrow) can be gained from another description of village life in Ditchling written by Pepler in 1946. *Village Life* appeared in a guide book, *The Story of Ditchling*. Pepler, whose attachment to the land deepened further on his election as the Reeve of Ditchling Common, believed that the rural community at

Ditchling, sustained by its crafts and embedded in a thousand-year-old Christian culture, was a valuable tradition. Even in the immediate post-war period, he believed – or wished to believe – it to be still intact.

> The 'lay-out' of the village, being based upon different qualities of soil and water supply, will suggest to the reader the diversified life the village has, for centuries, enjoyed. The shepherds, weavers, tanners, brick makers, lime-burners, millers, blacksmiths, sawyers, wheelwrights, carpenters and builders necessary to an agrarian community, lived near their work; over half in the village proper and the rest spread out in holdings among its fields. A number of these tradesmen have disappeared within living memory, there are now no sheep and the forest has but few remaining woods and 'shaws' to remind us of its once close clustered oaks .... But there is still the agrarian pattern of life in the community ... while there is deeper down, another moulding force even more concealed. When the village became a Christian community, its first work was to build a church which ... has remained for a thousand years the focal point of the village and still stands for the inner life from which our craftsmen and farmers have, however unconsciously, obtained their strength and retained their cohesion .... Moreover, the Beacon and its Tenantry Down remain inviolate above us, and the Common may not suffer building without a special Act of Parliament, which is unlikely to be demanded. Ditchling Common (and Down) indeed enjoys pre-Norman Rights and privileges .... It was, and is a part of the life of an organised agricultural community.[67]

Johnston's enthusiasm for a life spent close to the land was, at first, equal to Pepler's. By 1919, though, disillusionment had set in. With the war at an end, and with Gill and Pepler committed more deeply to Catholic Dominican orthodoxy, he was all too ready to give up the drudgery and the risks that went with farming, even on the smallest scale, and to return to Ditchling village. In this he was very much steered by his wife, Greta, who bore the brunt of the hard physical work that was entailed. In February 1920, much relieved, they moved back down to the village.[68] The house they bought there, Cleves, happened to be next door to their first one, Downsview, then occupied by Johnston's brother, Miles.[69]

One further, and all important, aspect of the 'unofficial partnership' of Pepler, Gill and Johnston was their interest in producing a magazine. Gill's diary records:

> E. J. and D. P. came to the Crank for breakfast ... E. J stayed all day. Wrote letters to the Observer with E. J's help. To Hallets in noon & then to D[itchling] to see D. P. re. printing, etc. Began making plans after tea for printing an occasional magazine to be called The Game. Home 8.30.[70]

This name was aptly chosen. From the vantage point of 1949, Pepler recalled:

> Our own view was that we were playing a game and one that gave us considerable enjoyment ... The Game materialised, inter alia, as an occasional magazine in which we three set out to play against all comers by expressing our own particular views upon the meaning of the good life, and it inevitably extended into more precisely defined practice'.[71]

Pepler was referring here to the practices of The Guild of St. Joseph and St. Dominic, since, in due course, *The Game* became its official organ. In 1916, however, they

THE GAME

AN OCCASIONAL MAGAZINE.

Surgant pueri et ludant I. *Reg.* 1. 12.

No. I OCTOBER A.D. 1916 PRICE 6d.

PROLOGUE

IN PRINCIPIO ERAT VERBUM, ET VERBUM ERAT APUD DEUM, ET DEUS ERAT VERBUM. HOC ERAT IN PRINCIPIO APUD DEUM. OMNIA PER IPSUM FACTA SUNT : ET SINE IPSO FACTUM EST NIHIL QUOD FACTUM EST.
ET VERBUM CARO FACTUM EST, ET HABITAVIT IN NOBIS : ET VIDIMUS GLORIAM EJUS, GLORIAM QUASI UNIGENITI A PATRE PLENUM GRATIÆ ET VERITATIS.

• • •

A man having seen the glory of God must thereafter work for the glory of God, the things which he makes he will make for *the glory of God.*

• • •

There are those who do not believe these things, who manitain that such beliefs are irrelevant to the modern problems of industrialism and social order, and that it is possible for Society to organise itself without agreement

Fig. 102. Prologue for the first issue of *The Game.*

... were engaged not with an idea of propaganda ... more a corporate letter-writing to others who were willing to play with us'.[72]

[They] ... did not set out with a programme or even the thought of a constitution. The only point of certain agreement among ourselves is to be found in the first line we set up together in type on the arrival of my hand press: 'in principio erat verbum'. In that beginning we were all agreed but without any precise thinking as to what might follow.[73]

The title, *The Game*, however, belies the high purpose of their writing. It was a modest, small-format publication and as much the result of Pepler's innate sense of good typography as any other item of the S. Dominic's Press. It appeared intermittently and ran through six volumes from October 1916 to January 1923. In all, there were some thirty-four separate issues, some no more than a quarto folded broadsheet, others numbering more than twenty pages. The articles were written for the most part by Gill and Pepler, with contributions by other Catholic writers, for example, Father Vincent McNabb and Stanley Spencer. Pepler recalled that: 'Home-made bread, bacon, beer appeared on the agenda taken up to help in the feeding of our families.'[74] There were extracts reprinted from established texts. One, for example, was Cobbett's advice on brewing beer, taken from his *Cottage Economy*. Another included extracts from the Encyclical Letter, *Rerum Novarum* issued by Pope Leo XIII in 1891. Poems were printed, many written by Hilary Pepler and Gill. Many wood-engraved illustrations were incorporated, initially by Gill, and after 1920, by a number of other Ditchling artist-craftsmen, including David Jones, Desmond Chute, Ralph Beedham, and Harold Purney.

The first issue of *The Game*, in October 1916, (price sixpence, 2½ pence), describes itself as 'An occasional Magazine, published at Ditchling Common, Sussex, and edited by some of the Commoners.' From the outset, the magazine, agrarian in outlook, struck an increasingly religious tone. These two elements – the rural and the religious – are together its ethos and reflect the way of thinking which prompted Gill, Pepler, and Johnston to move up to the Common and to adopt a 'cottage economy'. The two principal articles in this first issue of October 1916, were called *Service* and *The Control of Industry.* They were written by Pepler and Gill, respectively.

Its prologue, however, was written – or at least agreed upon – jointly as an editorial statement. (Fig. 102) In spite of Pepler's view that they were not propagandists, it reads with the zeal of a manifesto. It has an urgency of expression, a sense of mission, and even a certain bravado. This was, one senses, principally Gill's input, for it speaks of 'demands' and 'revolution'. Its ideas, however, are expressed with the precision that points to Johnston. But most probably it was actually written by Hilary Pepler.

Their concern in this editorial was with the importance, in an industrial world, of the handmade artefact. In this sense, this derived from the Arts and Crafts movement. But now craft was considered in terms of religion. The handmade took on an added sanctity. The liberal use of biblical references quoted in Latin is evidence of this new focus. (In fact, henceforth, the magazine was to be dated according to the Christian calendar – Advent, Christmas, Easter, Corpus Christi.) The second to fourth sections of the prologue set out its premises and are important enough to quote at some length:

> A man having seen the glory of God must thereafter work for the glory of God, the things which he makes he will make for the glory of God.
>
> There are those who do not believe these things, who maintain that such beliefs are irrelevant to the modern problems of industrialism and social order, and that it is possible for Society to organise itself without agreement upon or even reference to such beliefs. To such we do not address ourselves ....
>
> In the first place we believe that Religion is the *sine qua non*. We want religion but we do not want religion in order that it may be possible to obtain well made and beautiful things ... these, as by divine accident, shall be added unto us; and these, as by divine Judgment, have not permanence without religion.[75]

The sixth section of the prologue lays down a challenge to the artist-craftsman:

> And as God made things very good, how dares man to make things bad; and having made bad things how dare he pretend they are otherwise?
>
> If in his impiety man has so far muddled his affairs so that bad things are the natural product of his workshop, how is it that he does not see that nothing but a revolution can be a cure and that all other things are palliatives and as such to be condemned?
>
> If a thing is evil – the evil must be driven out. It is permissible to alleviate its consequences but not to hide them. A palliative is a hiding.[76]

The seventh and eighth sections widen the scope from the individual artist to the need for the reform of society at large:

> Generally we maintain that the modern 'movements' which set out to cure the 'impious muddle' will fail ...
>
> We desire that the control of industry shall be in the hands of the workmen and not of their employers. We propose in this magazine to elaborate the distinction between the two.
>
> We desire that machinery and organisation shall be the outcome of the needs and wishes of the workman and not of his employer ...
>
> In brief we demand that work shall be controlled by the workman and the designer, neither the distributor nor the consumer, but the producer paramount. Is this demanding an impossibility? It may be. Yet this is a necessary thing, and the thing we shall try to get ...[77]

The two brief final sections return to the issue of the role of the machine, so fundamental to the Arts and Crafts movement, and, in 1916, still an essential issue for Gill, Pepler and Johnston. The position is stated unequivocally:

Fig. 103. Johnston's Christmas greetings in issue two of *The Game.*

We approve, without reservation, all simple tools; we condemn, without reservation, the factory system.

We affirm that it is and should be within the power of the worker to decide what machines he may or should use.

We cannot make decisions for others; but as workers we can and will decide for ourselves.[78]

It is Pepler's hand which is paramount in the prologue. But, in his aspiration to serve God through good workmanship, he spoke equally for Gill and Johnston. This was the 'unity of fundamentals' of which Pepler spoke in *Gill in Ditchling.*[79] Johnston's single, and concise, contribution in the first number was wholly religious as well:

Man's body desires goods
His soul desires good
and his spirit desires God.

Johnston's involvement in *The Game,* however, did not extend much beyond the second number, Christmas, 1916, after which, he became adverse to its increasingly Roman Catholic bias. This issue, however, has the rare distinction of including the Christmas greetings, handwritten by Johnston in Latin, in red ink: (Fig. 103).

Glory to God in the highest, and on earth peace, goodwill toward men'.[80]

It was restricted to a very few copies, sent out to friends. On the fourth and last page, Johnston, Pepler, and Gill are brought together as craftsmen of the word – the Scribe, the Printer, the Engraver – each writing a poem exalting the Word of God made flesh.[81]

The religious divide became clear on Johnston's resignation from *The Game* in January 1918. It marked what Fr. Conrad described, with infinite tact and regret, as 'the first inevitable schism … – a quiet and gentle one'. It appears to have had other repercussions, too. It is evident, for example, that by 1918 Eric Gill and Ethel Mairet were increasingly engaged in Pepler's publishing projects, whereas Johnston seems to have been left aside. It was on the 29th July of that year, Pepler had joined the Tertiary Order of the Dominicans. At this point he adopted the imprint 'S. Dominic's Press', after the Catholic saint of preaching, although, in fact, the name was used retrospectively to all the items he printed, back to January, 1916. The name was used during the entire period the press was located at Halletts and then at the Guild Workshops on the Common, from 1921.[82] True to his printing aim of '… recording what still exists of the tradition of making good things', Pepler collaborated with Ethel and Philip Mairet as soon as they began to live in Ditchling, in 1918. Their *Essay on Crafts and Obedience* appeared in the S. Dominic's Press catalogue from that year, as did Gill's essay, *Sculpture.* Pepler also published Gill's essay, *Slavery and Freedom,* in 1918, in the form of a Penny Tract.

Unlike Thomas Cobden-Sanderson at the Doves Press, Pepler's purpose was straightforward, modest, and down to earth. In no way did it emulate Cobden-

Sanderson's lofty tract, *The Ideal Book or Book Beautiful.* Pepler was not concerned to publish prestigious editions of classic literature, with handwritten inscriptions and illuminated capitals. His interest was in jobbing printing, including posters, labels, tickets, while keeping a sympathetic eye out, too, for worthy titles on the crafts. In 1918, he printed Romney Green's *Woodwork*, for which Gill provided the woodcut illustrations, and, in 1920, Ralph John Beedham's *Wood Engraving*. Later S. Dominic's Press books on the crafts included Dunstan Pruden's *Silversmithing*, and A. H. Green's *Old English Clocks*. As Pepler explained in his advertising pamphlet of 1933, called *Printing from Saint Dominic's Press*:

> ... with a Stanhope the first of iron presses, a folio Albion, and two founts of Caslon Old Face ... he [Pepler] set out not to insist so much on a high standard of personal achievement, but, to do in the best manner possible what was required of him. And this has been the policy of the Press ever since.[83]

It is indicative, though, that after January 1917 Johnston remained rather outside Pepler's printing activity. Given Pepler's concern with the crafts, it is surprising that Johnston was not invited to write a book on lettering for the S. Dominic's Press. In 1927 Pepler did commission him to design an alphabet for his press. (Fig. 104). Pepler's letter to Johnston is distant and business-like:

> I am sending you the two guineas for the alphabet. It would help me very much to have it this week. If I may say so I hope it will be in the spirit of the original 'sheets' – i.e. not too much of a set piece.

While this tone may have been due in part to Pepler's utilitarian aims, it could also have been because of a divergence that had grown up between them.

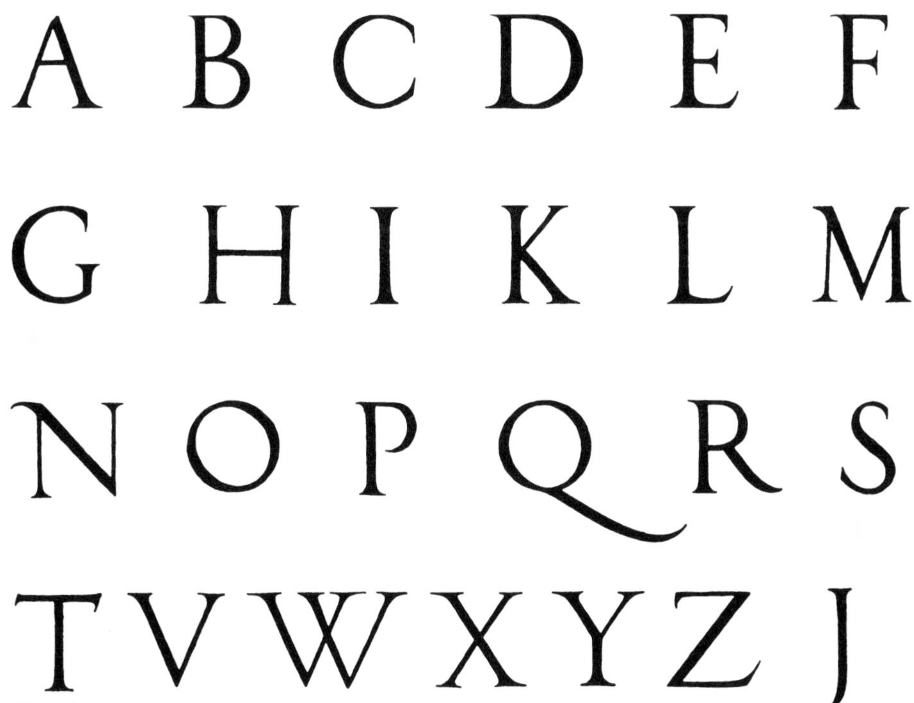

Fig. 104. Johnston's alphabet designed for Pepler.

END NOTES

1. The Deutsche Werkbund was formed in 1907, inspired in part by Hermann Muthesius who, as a trade diplomat in London, had studied contemporary English architecture and design at close quarters. The report which Muthesius wrote and his book *Das Englische Haus* (1904–05) praised English design but urged for Germany the closer cooperation of artists and craftman in the making of industrial products. The Deutsche Werkbund exhibition in Cologne in 1914 was seen by Ambrose Heal and Harry Peach. In later years Harry Peach had a long correspondence with Johnston.

2. Harry Peach. Typescript of his account of the foundation of the DIA. RIBA. In the H. H. Peach archive (DIAP1/3i).

3. 'A New Body with New Aims' (DIA July 1915): page 14. *London's Transport Museum*. Frank Pick archive 2001/55114). Other writers touch the same sentiment: 'The British Arts and Crafts movement has had little effect on the general level of design of ordinary commercial goods .... We cannot get over the notion in England that art is a kind of luxury for the mind .... We are standing still, looking on indifferently .... Surely our somnolent state has lasted long enough. If – and when – we awake we must have an alliance between the artists, the manufacturers, and the traders ....'

Pevsner ascribes the mise-en-page of 'A New Body with New Aims' to '... the Emery Walker-Cobden-Sanderson tradition', which points to John Mason. Another pointer to Mason is the fact that its main contributor was Arthur Clutton-Brock, a Fabian, a Christian, an art critic of *The Times* and a William Morris scholar. In the same year, 1915, Clutton-Brock wrote a satirical poem, 'Simpson's Choice: an Essay of the Future Life', with woodcuts by Roald Kristian. It was published by Roger Fry at the Omega Workshops and, tellingly, was set by John Mason at the Central School.

4. Including Frederick Brangwyn Burridge (Lethaby's successor as principal of the Central School), Morley Fletcher (the Director of Edinburgh College of Art) and W. B. Dalton (Principal of Camberwell School of Art). It was also supported by the director of the V&A, Cecil Harcourt Smith. A number of craftsmen from the Art Workers' Guild also joined, including W. A. S. Benson and Selwyn Image. There was also an impressive list of industrialists, including Charles Jacobi of the Chiswick Press and Charles Pickering of the

Baynard Press. In spite of Gerard Meynell's membership of the committee of 1915, he did not join the DIA until 1918, along with his protégé, the poster artist McKnight Kauffer, his cousin, Francis Meynell of the Nonesuch Press and Simon Oliver of the Curwen Press. These details come from Nicholas Pevsner. 'Patient Progress I. The Life and Work of Frank Pick' *The Architectural Review* Vol. CXXXII (1962) and from the DIA leaflet giving its Aims, Methods and Rules. (Pick archive at the London's Transport Museum.)

5. Two other 'lettering posters' and another 'hand lettered announcement' were also shown. Were these Johnston's too? The merging of interests is shown, too, by the Arts and Crafts Exhibition Society's offer to the DIA of space in its exhibition of 1916 at Burlington House.

6. 'Four Papers' read by Members of the Arts and Crafts Exhibition Society. (London: Longmans, 1935). The typography of this book was set by Mason at the Central School.

7. Quoted from Justin Howes. *Johnston's Underground Type*. (London: 2000): Pages 25–26. A copy of this lecture is in the Frank Pick archive at the London's Transport Museum. Reference: 2001/55368. These phrases so echo the anonymously-written Preface to the catalogue of the Whitechapel Gallery exhibition that it seems possible that Pick wrote it:

> ... good design is tested first and foremost by fitness, secondly by pleasantness in use.... If the first of these ... were generally accepted ... there would be swept out of existence whole battalions of futile, ugly, needlessly complicated (and to that extent necessarily expensive) things ...

8. Christian Barman 'Public Lettering' given on Wednesday 9th February 1955. Journal of the Royal Society of Arts. Vol. 103 (1955): page 289.

9. Pevsner. 'Patient Progress One: The Life and Work of Frank Pick'. *The Architectural Review* CXXXII (1962). Justin Howes's research is more precise. He shows that Pick:

> ... had carried out certain experiments of his own, in which apparently 'certain letters of the alphabet were condensed and certain letters were expanded' – a method which sounds like a sure-fire recipe for disaster!

Cited from *Johnston's Underground Type*. (London: 2000): page 26, footnote 5.

10. Crafts Study Centre Collection and Archive. Farnham, Surrey. Johnston archive. Letters 2/170.

11. Johnston's diary, cited from Justin Howes. *Johnston's Underground Type* (London: 2000): page 28, footnote 2. (The Johnston diaries are now with the Johnston family.)

12. Christian Barman. 'Public Lettering' *Journal of the Royal Society of Arts* Vol. 103 (1954–55): pages 281–293.

13. This is the more likely given that Harold Curwen had designed sanserif letters before Johnston. Curwen said:

> In 1909 I studied lettering under Edward Johnston and Eric Gill at the L.C.C. [London County Council] Central School of Arts and Crafts. In 1912 I drew for myself an address in block letters for private letter paper. As I was studying the basic form of the roman capitals I naturally formed the letters in that way. At about the same time the West Ham Tramline Authority required of my firm a set of large numbers printed on paper to fix on the front of tram-cars to designate the routes. These were drawn by me and lithgraphed in a sans form.

Cited from Denis Megaw. 'Twentieth Century Sanserif Types'. *Typography* No. 7 (1938): page 32. However, Curwen's uppercase sanserif alphabet was not designed until 1924.

14. Cited from Justin Howes. *Johnston's Underground Type* (London: 2000): page 28. Letter to Harry Peach. 6th April 1934. Crafts Study Centre Collection and Archive. Farnham, Surrey. Johnston archive. 2/175–86.

15. Harry Carter. 'Sanserif types'. *Curwen Miscellany* London (1931): page 42.

16. Justin Howes. *Johnston's Underground Type*. (London: 2000.) Other studies make this perhaps the most intensely studied aspect of Johnston's career. They include, chronologically: Harry Carter. *Sanserif types*. Curwen Miscellany London (1931); Denis Megaw 'Twentieth-

Century Sanserif Types'. In *Typography* edited by Robert Harling No. 7 (1938); Nicholas Pevsner. 'Patient Progress: the life and work of Frank Pick'. In *Architectural Review* Vol. XCII. No. 548 (1942): pages 31–48; Christian Barman. 'Public Lettering'. In *Journal of the Royal Society of Arts* Vol. 103 (1954–55): pages 281–293; Priscilla Johnston. *Edward Johnston* (London: Faber and Faber, 1959): pages 198–205; P. M. Handover 'Letters with Serifs'. In *Motif* Vol. 6 (1961); Christian Barman *The Man who Built London Transport.* (London: David and Charles, 1979); Tim Demuth 'Johnston: Part One: the early development'. In *London Bus Magazine* 34 (Autumn 1980); Walter Tracy. *Letters of Credit* (London: Gordon Frazer Gallery Ltd, 1986); Giovanni Lussu. 'Adventure on the Underground'. In *Typographic* (Society of Typographic Designers) issue 45 (1993); Colin Banks. London's Handwriting: *The Development of Edward Johnston's Underground Block-letter.* (London: London Transport Museum, 1994); Colin Banks 'Edward Johnston'. In *Pioneers of Modern Craft* edited by Margot Coatts. (Manchester University Press, 1997). D. Lawrence. *A Logo for London.* The London Transport System. (London: Capital Transport, 2000.)
17. (Cited from C. Banks. *Pioneers of Modern Craft*. Edited M. Coatts. (Manchester: Manchester University Press, 1997): page 44.
18. Edward Johnston. 'The Leicester Lectures' In *Lessons in Formal Writing* edited by Heather Child and Justin Howes (London: Lund Humphries, 1986): pages 92–93.
19. Noel Rooke. 'Paper on Edward Johnston' read before the Double Crown Club. 17th May 1943. Typescript in the Double Crown Club archive, St Bride Printing Library. (The illustrations to this paper were printed separately and privately by Ellic Howe in 1945.)
20. Cited from Justin Howes. *Johnston's Underground Type*. (London: 2000): page 28, footnote 1. (Letter to Harry Peach. 6th April 1934. Crafts Study Centre. Farnham. 2/175–86.)
21. Cited from Justin Howes. *Johnston's Underground Type*. (London: 2000): page 42, footnote 4. (Notebook. Johnston family, formerly Crafts Study Centre. 2 /Loan 13)
22. Eric Gill. Diary. Op. cit. Jack Nye was killed some months later. The Great War does not appear to predominate in the minds of the craftsmen in Ditchling. It is not treated in *The Game*, for instance, nor does Johnston appear to have written about it.
23. Edward Johnston. *A Carol and Other Rhymes.* (Hampshire House Workshops. Hammersmith) 1915.
24. As Johnston explains, the chronicle (Johnston gives it a British Museum reference no., Plato B 100) was based on a medieval encyclopaedia, *De Proprietatibus Rerum* compiled by Bartholomaeus Anglicus, circa 1260, and translated into English by John of Trevisa in 1398. Johnston had in his library a modern compilation of this work, *Medieval Lore*, (Chatto and Windus) 1893, edited by Robert Steele with an introduction by William Morris. It is possible that this modern edition led him to the manuscript of the chronicle in the British Museum.
25. The colophon to the Cobden-Sanderson manuscript reads:

Spurn not FINE GOLD O FOOT-OF-CLAY,
Nor scorn the OLD O FALLEN-AWAY;
Let ANCIENT-WAY
Be aid to NEW,
And coming DAY
Pick out the True:
O happy few,
Whose hearts enfold
HERB-WET-WITH-DEW
And-Wisdom-Old,
Wide-eyed behold
With simple Fay
DECEMBER-COLD
And GLOWING-MAY.

The colophon to the *Rubaiyat of Omar Khayyam* reads:

The Smooth & Fine from force & fire may shrink,

O Brittle unbroke,
O Flawed without a chink,
Ye serve high uses of the Overlord,
Who serve the demigods in meat and drink.
O humble Pots and noble
Amphorae that guess at what has been and what shall be,
THERE IS a Riddle which concerns you *now*
THAT IS even greater than eternity.
THAT IS which cleaves, and *by* which cleaves, the clay,
Counts even the Potsherd which is cast away,
One with the deep blue Bowl that holds the night,
One with the golden Bowl that holds the day.

26. *The Devil's Devices or Control versus Service.* (Hampshire House Workshops, Hammersmith) 1915. A note in Gill's diary for 15th August 1915 reads: 'Read Pepler's book 'Kultur' in noon and in eve he came to supper and we discussed the book and the question of the illustrations to be done by me.'
27. Elkin Mathews Catalogue. 152. Part 1. 1961.
28. *The Care Committee, the Child and the Parent* (London: Constable & Co., 1912), *Justice and the Child* (London: Constable & Co., 1915). Another book which Pepler is said to have written is *His Majesty*, with illustrations by his wife, Clare (publishing details unknown). His venture into play writing came later. The principal titles are: *Judas or the Betrayal*, 1926; and *St. Dominic*, 1929. His pieces for puppet theatre include: *Plays for Puppets*, 1929, *Mimes Sacred and Profane*, 1932, and *The Four Minstrels of Bremen*, 1932.
29. H. D. C. Pepler. *The Devil's Devices*. Op. cit.
30. The 'brickyard' is The Keymer Brick Co Ltd., on Ditchling Common.
31. H. D. C Pepler. Gill in Ditchling in *Print Collector's Quarterly*. Vol. 30. 1949. This reappeared in the form: *A Letter from Sussex about his friend Eric Gill.* (Chicago: Cherryburn Press. Society of Typographic Arts, 1950).
32. Letter from H. Pepler to Fr. V. McNabb cited in F. Valentine: *Fr. Vincent MacNabb.* (Burns & Oates) 1955. (The original MS. was in the possession of Father Brocard Sewell.)
33. Eric Gill. *Sculpture*. (S. Dominic's Press. Ditchling) 1918.
34. H. D. C. Pepler. *The Hand Press*. (S. Dominic's Press) 1934.
35. This information was provided courtesy of Mr. and Mrs. Alic Wheeler.
36. Father Conrad Pepler. 'In Diebus Illis. Some Memories of Ditchling'. In *The Chesterton Review*, Vol. VII. No. 4.(1982).
37. H. D. C. Pepler: *S. Dominic's Press. As to its Founding at Ditchling*. 1933.
38. *Twenty-One Years* was printed in 1937 on the occasion of the St. Dominic's press moving from the Common back down to the village, when it became the Ditchling Press. A copy of this rare item of three pages is at the Newberry Library, Chicago.
39. This edition was of fifteen copies, 'printed in Ditchling by Douglas Pepler and Eric Gill' in February 1916. A second set of thirty-three copies was published also in February 1916.
40. *Catalogue of S. Dominic's Press*. 1916. (Ref: British Library copy.)
41. S. Dominic's Press Supper. 1918. M. Taylor. *Bibliography of the S. Dominic's Press.* (Whittington Press, 1996).
42. This MS. is now in the National Art Library at the V&A. Museum. (Ref: KRP.B 21.)
43. H. D. C. Pepler. 'Gill in Ditchling'. Op. cit. It needs to be borne in mind that this was written years after the bitterness Pepler felt over Gill's rupture with the Guild in 1924 had subsided.
44. Elkin Mathews. Catalogue. No. 152. Part 2. 1961.
45. Elkin Mathews. Catalogue. No. 152. Part 2. 1961.
46. Conrad (Stephen) Pepler In: *Chesterton Review*. Vol. VIII. No. 4. November, 1982.
47. Geo. S. Welch. *The Ship Painter's Handbook*. 3rd edition. (Glasgow Brown) 1916.
48. This commission, it seems, was not realised.
49. A draft of this is at the Pierpont Morgan Library. New York. (Ref: N. 213.)
50. Catalogue. The Stations of the Cross. Alpine Gallery. London. 1918.
51. David Pepler's love affair with Gill's daughter, Betty, of which Gill strongly disapproved.

52 Held at the National Art Library at the V&A.
53. They are recorded for a number of dates in Gill's Diary.
54. W. Cobbett. *Cottage Economy*. (S. Dominic's Press) 2nd. edition.
55. Eric Gill. Diary. Op. cit. February 1916.
56. H. D. C. Pepler. *Gill in Ditchling*. Op. cit.
57. Priscilla Johnston. *Edward Johnston*. 1959.
58. Eric Gill. Diary. Op. cit. 1st, 15th, 20th August, 22nd September, 23rd October. 1916.
59. Crafts Study Centre Collection and Archive. Op. cit., Johnston Archive. (Ref: Letters 2/Loan 42.)
60. Eric Gill. Diary. Op. cit. The 16th January, the 15th April, the 10th June, and the 19th December 1917. A photocopy of the ground plan of the building is in Ditchling Museum.
61. Priscilla Johnston. *Edward Johnston*. Op. cit.
62. This detail is mentioned in a letter from Priscilla Johnston to Robert Speaight in 1966 held in the Archives of the English Province of the Order of Preachers. Edinburgh.
63. H. D. C. Pepler. *Gill in Ditchling*. Op. cit.
64. Eric Gill. Diary. Op. cit.
65. A Swiss by birth, and the son of an eminent watchmaker, he retained the French spelling of his name (Philippe) as an author.
66. Philippe Mairet. *Autobiographical Compilation*. (Carcanet Press) 1981.
67. H. D. C. Pepler. 'Village Life'. In *The Story of Ditchling*. Op. cit.
68. Cleves had recently been built by the Wainwrights, a craft family in Ditchling.
69. Miles Johnston had two children, Gunnar and Isabella. They moved to Ditchling from Coldstream, Ramsgate. Gunnar ran, edited, and largely wrote a small family magazine, *Chatter, A Magazine for Private Circulation*, (The Devonian Press) between 1912–14. There were five issues. Edward Johnston contributed a short story, written with Gunnar, given the name 'The Roothing', for the Spring 1914 issue. (Ref: British Library. X 955/1132.)
70. Eric Gill. Diary. 9th August 1916. Op. cit.
71. H. D. C. Pepler. *Gill in Ditchling*. Op. cit.
72. H. D. C. Pepler. *The Hand Press*. (S. Dominic's Press) 1934.
73. *The Game*. Vol. 1. (S. Dominic's Press. Ditchling) October 1916.
74. *The Game*. Vol. 3. No. 2. (S. Dominic's Press. Ditchling) Advent. 1919.
75. *The Game*. (S. Dominic's Press. Ditchling) October 1916.
76. *The Game*. Op. cit.
77. *The Game*. Op. cit.
78. The Game. Op. cit.
79. H. D. C. Pepler. *Gill in Ditchling*. Op. cit.
80. *The Game*. Christmas 1916. Op. cit.

GLORIA
in altissimus Deo,
et in terra pax ho-
minibus bonae
voluntatis

81. *The Game*. Christmas 1916. Op. cit.

the scribe
The Scribes have sinned and yet do scribes record
The Birth and Death and Rising of our Lord.
May my pen ne'er miss-spell [sic] His Blessed Word.

the printer
The Word of God became flesh on this day
By this word of man do I labour and pray
That God's good Word be not taken away.

the engraver
The Word is God. Now may he give me grace
By wood and stone His Beauty to embrace! -
For they are saved to whom He shows his Face.

82. When, in 1937, his son, Mark, and his manager, Cyril Costick, wished to use a power-operated Arab press it offended other craftsmen of the Guild. The business was then moved back down to the village, and it reverted to the name Ditchling Press. It was at that point that Hilary Pepler retired from printing, leaving the business in the hands of his son, Mark and of his manager. Hilary Pepler remained the proprietor, however.
83. M. Taylor. *Bibliography of S. Dominic's Press*. (Whittington Press) 1995.

Portrait of Johnston in oil by Arthur Henry Knighton-Hammond (1875–1970), painted at Cleves, Ditchling in 1937.
(Courtesy of the National Portrait Gallery.)

CHAPTER SEVEN

JOHNSTON AND THE CRAFT COMMUNITIES IN DITCHLING PART 3

At this time, in 1917–18, the Ditchling community was complemented by the arrival of other craftsmen of great originality. Ethel Mairet was foremost among them. Her contribution to a philosophy of craft is worth attention, not least because it closely parallels Johnston's own. As a pioneer of the revival of hand-loom weaving and natural (or vegetable) dyeing in England, Ethel Mairet's presence in Ditchling enriched immensely the life of the craft community there. Hers was a wealth of experience gained from wide-ranging activities and contacts. She was brought up in the home of a chemist, in Barnstaple – the same town, incidentally, that had nurtured William Lethaby. She had had a long-standing and close friendship with C. R. Ashbee and his wife Janet of the Guild of Handicraft. Ethel was married twice – to Ananda Coomaraswamy in 1902, and to Philip Mairet, in 1913. Both men were philosophers of art and were highly accomplished as thinkers and writers in their own spheres. They amplified Ethel's own interests. She had travelled to Ceylon and India with Coomaraswamy and, like him, was absorbed in the study of the craft artefacts and techniques of those countries.[1]

Ethel Mairet arrived in Ditchling in 1918 accompanied by a family entourage.[2] She rented a cottage, Sundown, in the village. In 1920 she moved into the house she was having built, called Gospels. Helped, possibly, by Philip, she designed its large weaving studio, which was equipped with a gallery and with high ceilings for hanging textiles. They had it built at the lower end of the village, to form a 'southern wing', as it were, of Ditchling's mansion of the latter day Arts and Crafts movement. Her refectory table was made by a prominent cabinet maker, Romney Green. Likewise, her front door was made by Gimson. The wooden sign that advertised the workshops at Gospels was designed by Gill and carved by Joseph Cribb (Fig. 105) According to Gill's diary, in August 1920 the Mairets held a house-warming party.[3] Ethel Mairet was Johnston's close neighbour. While contact was minimal, she regarded him as her spiritual companion.

Fig. 105. Wooden sign outside the workshops at Gospels, designed by Gill and carved by Joseph Cribb.

Ethel Mairet's use of hand-spun yarns and vegetable dyes was at the heart of her artistic endeavour. Some of the plants for dyeing were collected by her and assistants from the chalky Downs, notably Dyer's Rocket (*Reseda Luteola*), yielding yellows. In this, and in many other respects, Ethel Mairet's outlook bears striking parallels with that of the craft community already at Ditchling, and notably with Johnston's and Pepler's. She was initially attracted to Ditchling by its artistic and welcoming ambience. Philip Mairet felt in this reception an 'elective affinity'. The immediate background to their decision to live in Ditchling illuminates this. Ethel had known Pepler from his days in Hammersmith, in 1915. In 1916, Pepler had printed her classic compendium, *A Book of Vegetable Dyes*. Pepler then visited her at her studio, in Shottery, near to Stratford-upon-Avon, and in February 1917 he, in turn, invited the Mairets to Ditchling Common. In his *Autobiographical Compilation*, Philip Mairet evokes the atmosphere of that first outing to the community of Gill, Johnston and Pepler on the Common.

> Ethelmary and I travelled down to Sussex by the old London, Brighton and South Coast Railway, behind one of its old canary-yellow locomotives stained with wartime dirt and neglect. It was a freezing day, the compartment windows were opaque with the travellers' breath; there were long metal boxes of hot water under the seats, which were cooled by the time we got to Haywards Heath and were replaced with new ones too hot to touch. A little horse-drawn bus took us to Ditchling, where we were received by the Peplers, taken in the afternoon to see Johnston the scribe; then shown something of the farm; and finally we were entertained to a tea-party by Eric Gill the sculptor. This was a merry gathering, with children pulling crackers and putting on paper caps, for it was Eric Gill's birthday. This was the kind of company to which we felt we belonged by elective affinity. I think it was on that day that Pepler offered to engage me as one of his farm labourers, a position I accepted with alacrity and took up a very few days later.[4]

As a conscientious objector who had recently resigned from a post with the Red Cross Society in wartime France, Philip Mairet found this a definite step forward. On his release from prison for his beliefs, he returned to Ditchling, staying first at Sopers and then with Ethel at the rented cottage, Sundown.

The Ditchling ambience corresponded with Ethel's earlier and fundamental experiences of craft in Ceylon and India with her first husband Ananda Coomaraswamy. The concern of the Coomaraswamys was to sustain ancient craft techniques in Ceylon, not out of sentimentality but to meet the present and living needs of Singhalese society. This parallelled Johnston's realisation of the need, in England, for a modern script similarly based on medieval craft practice. Although their efforts were not as sustained as Johnston's – they returned to England after only four years, in 1907 – they were the richer for actually witnessing its practice in Ceylon. It was as if Johnston had been enthused by visiting a medieval scriptorium. Moreover, it so happened that the many articles Ethel and Ananda wrote on Singhalese crafts began to appear in 1906, the very year that Johnston completed *Writing & Illuminating, & Lettering*.

When Ethel Coomaraswamy returned to England from Ceylon, in 1907, her interest focused on the traditions of weaving and dyeing which were indigenous to England before the Industrial Revolution. She travelled to the Lake District, for example, to observe hand-weaving at first-hand, and studied dyeing books at the Bodleian Library, at Oxford. The outcome was early experiments at their home, The Norman Chapel, in Chipping Camden, and then further experimentation at her next studio-home (following her divorce) at Shottery. The important (and rare) pamphlet of 1915 followed, with the significant title, *The Future of Dyeing, and the Conflict between Science and Art in the Making of Colour*.[5] It was the prelude to *A Book of Vegetable Dyes*. The preliminary part of this book echoes the proselytising tone of the Ceylon articles:

> Dyeing is an art. The moment science dominates it, it is an art no longer and the craftsman must go back to the time before science touched it and start all over again.[6]

Ethel Mairet was referring to the introduction of the aniline chemical dyes, which she regarded as having a facile artificiality. She quoted William Morris: '... all degradation in art veils itself in the semblance of intellectual advance'. Her analysis continued:

> With chemical dyes it is very easy to produce ugly colours, the beautiful colour is rare; but with traditional dyes it is difficult to make an ugly colour and good colour is the rule. There is a general difference between the results of the two methods – that when a chemical colour fades it becomes a different colour and generally a bad one, when a natural colour fades it becomes a lighter tone of the same colour.

Apart from the aesthetic consequences of industrial technologies, Ethel Mairet also touched on social and philosophical ones:

> The aim of commerce is material gain; the aim of craft is to make life, and no expense must be spared to that end.[7]

With this thought she could have been speaking with Johnston's own voice. The key message of his address to the Teachers' Conference in Dresden in 1912 spoke of the purpose of lettering as being the enhancement of life.

Ethel Mairet's next piece of writing embraced craft in general. Written with Philip, their *Essay on Crafts and Obedience* was printed by S. Dominic's Press in Ditchling early in 1918. It has two main themes, which again have a strong Johnstonian resonance – for its underlying tone is fundamentally Morrisian. It asserts that the great periods of art are founded upon that 'unity of inspiration' which craftsmen draw from a sense of society's religious faith:

> The great characteristic of every period of good art and craftsmanship is a general unity of inspiration.... It is certain that the atmosphere of thought in which [craftsmen] lived made them think in the same forms. At every period when art was great there was a great religious interpretration of the meaning and nature of life. There was a unifying spirit which bound all together and formed, as it were, a common language. It is this which is needed before the gift of universal beauty will permeate again our work. Social order, language and art all have their root in the same reality, and if that reality is felt in the soul of a people, it will find its one fundamental expression in that people's religion. So craftsmen see that no craft can now attain its greatest excellence until some unifying religious spirit is expressed through all of them.[8]

In insisting on religion and on the spirit of an age, the *Essay on Crafts and Obedience* is rooted not just in the *terra firma* of Morrisian thought but also of Lethaby's – in his earlier and more metaphysical mode. In all probability this reflects the input of Philip Mairet, rather than of Ethel.[9]

One major theme emerges, therefore, from the Mairets' disquiet about the lack of a religious basis of contemporary artistic-craft practice. Their essay continues with a plea for its renewal as a form of religiously inspired 'service':

> We know the social necessity of our work, we must feel the divine necessity of our work, transmuting the materials of earth to human uses and to the image of beauty by the *spirit of service* in work, the religious sense of work as worship, as service to mankind.[10]

This idea was also integral to the writings of both Johnston and Pepler at this time, as expressed in *A Carol and other Rhymes*, and in *The Devil's Devices, or Control versus Service*. It is not known whether the Mairets were familiar with these books. Philip Mairet's religion was Church of England and he was also active in the Christian Social Movement. Given that they had a similar religious background, the confluence of thought is very close. The strategy by which Ethel Mairet sought to achieve this higher state of artistic integrity was to return to an apprenticeship system in her workshop. She saw a vital role for herself, therefore, as a master teacher. A second theme, therefore, of their *Essay on Crafts* explores the necessity to foster the craft tradition:

> In all great periods of workmanship craft has been a mystery, the learning of it a kind of initiation requiring long probation, obedience and devotion. But tradition is a living force and we must be fully conscious that we are building tradition, each workshop will add something to it, each pupil will add something.

Again, there is a close affinity with Johnston's outlook. Like Ethel Mairet, Johnston was self-taught and came to recognise the importance of teaching, not only through his work at the Central School and the RCA, but by taking pupils into his home.[11] He also saw it as important to devote much of his time to setting out his ideas in teaching handbooks.

The similarity of their views would suggest that Johnston and Ethel Mairet were continually in touch. The convivial atmosphere at Gospels and the social and musical occasions that took place there would have encouraged such contact. But though living within half a mile of each other, in fact, they saw little of each other.

Ethel Mairet's small community at Gospels included a long succession of assistants and apprentices. (It has been suggested that up to forty young people passed through Gospels during her time in Ditchling). A significant figure was Valentine KilBride, who arrived in 1923.[12] Gill's daughter, Petra, was an apprentice. Another was Margery Kendon, who wrote an informative and vivid memoir of her time at Gospels, from 1922. She recalled Ethel Mairet's sociability and of the visits she organised for her assistants to engender their zest for life.[13]

Margery Kendon's memoir is especially helpful in clarifying the nature of her relationship with Johnston. It confirms that his role in her life was as a largely unseen but powerful presence:

> When she came to Ditchling in 1918, as far as Mrs Mairet was concerned the village might as well not have been there; she admired Edward Johnston tremendously but she never went to see him. Priscilla Johnston bears this out. She knew the Mairets for thirty years and doesn't remember her ever coming to the house. Nor did she ever see Mr and Mrs Mairet together.[14]

Priscilla Johnston does record an occasion when her father gave a talk at Gospels. (It was given on the 7th August, 1935, for a Summer School, on the subject of craftsmanship.). Her mother called it 'a lovely address'. Elsewhere, in her memoir, Margery Kendon returns to the subject:

> Mrs Mairet always felt a close bond with Edward Johnston due to their respective crafts .... Although Pepler was the direct line in bringing Ethel Mairet to Ditchling, it was really Edward Johnston who inspired her over the twenty-odd years that they both lived in the village. They seldom met but it was enough for her to know that he was there.[15]

Johnston's diary reveals that the years of silent understanding were, in fact, punctuated by occasional meetings, usually for afternoon tea, or, as happened in 1922, to meet Ethel's Swedish friends, the Lindquists. It was in this year, too, that Johnston records that his children went to Gospels 'dressed up' for a party. Then, another meatier entry, for 1st June 1933, records Johnston 'abt. 5.35 to Gospels interviewing Mrs Mairet ... ' This activity continued on the 4th June:

> ... Mrs Mairet after tea went over notes with E. J. (& few corrections) and took fair copy.'[16]

The interview was worked up as part of Johnston's *Paper on the Labelling of Exhibits*, which he read to the Arts and Crafts Exhibition Society in June 1935. Johnston's aim in this paper was to promote the use of short explanatory labels to accompany items shown in the exhibitions of the Society in order to help the understanding of the visitor. His original draft reads:

> Mrs Mairet a weaver & dyer & spinner admirably describes her work as 'playing about with raw material'. Her principal materials are silk, wool, & cotton dyed mainly with vegetable dyes and woven plain or in combination of any two or all three together.
>
> Example: Raw cotton is a very different thing from the machined and hardened thread & stuff with which we are familiar. It is v. soft and may be spun by hand with some difficulty into a thickish v. soft somewhat irregular yarn [and] it is spun with silk, wh. facilitates the spinning. It is difficult except in damp parts to make a fine cotton thread. The Indian cotton thread is very good.
>
> Example: A curtain of pure heavy, India-spun cotton thread, hand-woven, hangs beautifully.
>
> Mrs Mairet has some considerable knowledge of how weaving is carried on in other countries, and personal experience of the Weavers methods and conditions particularly in Denmark & Sweden & Jugslavia [*sic*].
>
> A Danish manufacturer told her that all over the continent traditional hand-weaving continues, and contributes valuable ideas to the manufacturers (which, of course, machines cannot give them). In Sweden & Denmark, when threatened by 'Industry', the hand-weavers were not allowed to die out – as they were in England – but were organised and brought up to date to save them from it. Mrs Mairet hopes to help to re-establish Hand-Weaving in England – as it is on the continent – the true source and inspiration of all weaving.

Hand Weaving cannot compete with industry. The hand-weavers should do something much better, and they should not be bound by anything but quality, they cannot be expected to conform to ordinary economic conditions or to compete with them in quantity or price.

Of wools and silks and other raw materials there is a great deal to learn, and our hand weavers have not yet sufficient technical knowledge. Mrs Mairet wants us to improve.

In the meantime this weaver is making innumerable experiments:– making stuffs in all-wool, all-silk, and all-cotton and stuffs which are mixtures of two or more of these (or other raw materials), besides spinning various yarns and dyeing them, and other yarns, in various colours. Various patterns are produced in the home and various things and garments are the most striking & pleasing results.[17]

Clearly, Johnston held Ethel Mairet in high esteem. A letter of 1935 shows him hoping to persuade her to become a member of the Arts and Crafts Exhibition Society.[18] His interest in weaving was enhanced because he saw in the craft a parallel to his own.[19] His letter to Ethel Mairet dated 25th August 1939, following his slow recovery from pneumonia, expands on this idea:

Dear Mrs Mairet, Please forgive me; it is six days since your letter came. My best excuse is that I felt I must refuse and didn't want to; my second best is that I'm trying to write a book (and producing about one moderate sentence a day) and I am surprised by post time every evening.

My energy is rather limited. Tho' I've been 'up' for 15 weeks (after 15 weeks in bed) I'm still slightly groggy and haven't ventured on the road. But perhaps that may be possible ere long, and I shall have to take up walking as an exercise. If that comes about I might drop in at Gospels and do 20 minutes of talking and tricks occasionally.

There are many things in which weaving and writing resemble each other or illustrate each other. My 'Text' was once your 'Texture': my Writing line your Linen thread.

(The line of Writing has important aspects. It is in various ways more of a Unit or Standard than the Page. It gives the width and the texture of the Text column, and the other features of the Page tend to follow. I shdn't wonder if there were some possible parallelisms with weaving, even here.)

I shall look forward to looking in at Gospels (1) where there has always seemed to me an air of Industry and Beauty. (2) Yours always, Edward Johnston.

1. If you see me passing G[ospels] my first promise to call is Mr Mitchel.
2. A somewhat rare conjunction.[20]

Johnston had a more active friendship with Ethel's husband, Philip Mairet. Gill's diary frequently records them arriving together at Sopers during the time Pepler was living there for tea or for supper with discussion ensuing. Mairet was present, for instance, at the 'painful' discussion about Roman Catholicism which occurred between Johnston, Gill and Pepler, in 1917 (to be discussed in the following chapter, 'Johnston and The Guild of St. Dominic and St. Joseph. A Quiet and

Gentle Schism'). Priscilla Johnston, too, touches on their friendship in her biography. She writes of long discussions taking place between the two, which '… threatened to occupy the whole night', ending with Johnston '… walking home with Mairet a distance of about half a mile through the silent, sleeping village.'[21]

Johnston's *Paper on the Labelling of Exhibits* of 1935, shows that the interviews with Ethel Mairet were among a number he undertook during that month. Others were with Ethel's brother, Frederick Partridge, with Gill's former assistant, Joseph Cribb, and with the wood engraver, Philip Hagreen. He invited them to explain about the materials and processes they used for the items they made – a Madonna and Child in rhinoceros horn, a Station of the Cross in Caen stone, and a reading lampstand in wood – and their intentions in making them. From this material he wrote up three 'Technical, Functional and Intentional' labels, which he offered as models to encourage the practice of label-writing. To these he added his own, which he attached to his manuscript of Shakespeare's *Sonnet No. 116*, the item he showed in the exhibition. (Fig. 106)

As with Ethel Mairet, it was Pepler who was the initial link between Frank Brangwyn and the other Ditchling craftsmen – even though this was a somewhat tenuous one. Brangywn settled in Ditchling at about the same time as Ethel Mairet, in 1918, buying a house of Tudor origins with extensive grounds in the centre of the village, called The Jointure. A painter, muralist, etcher and designer, and at that time

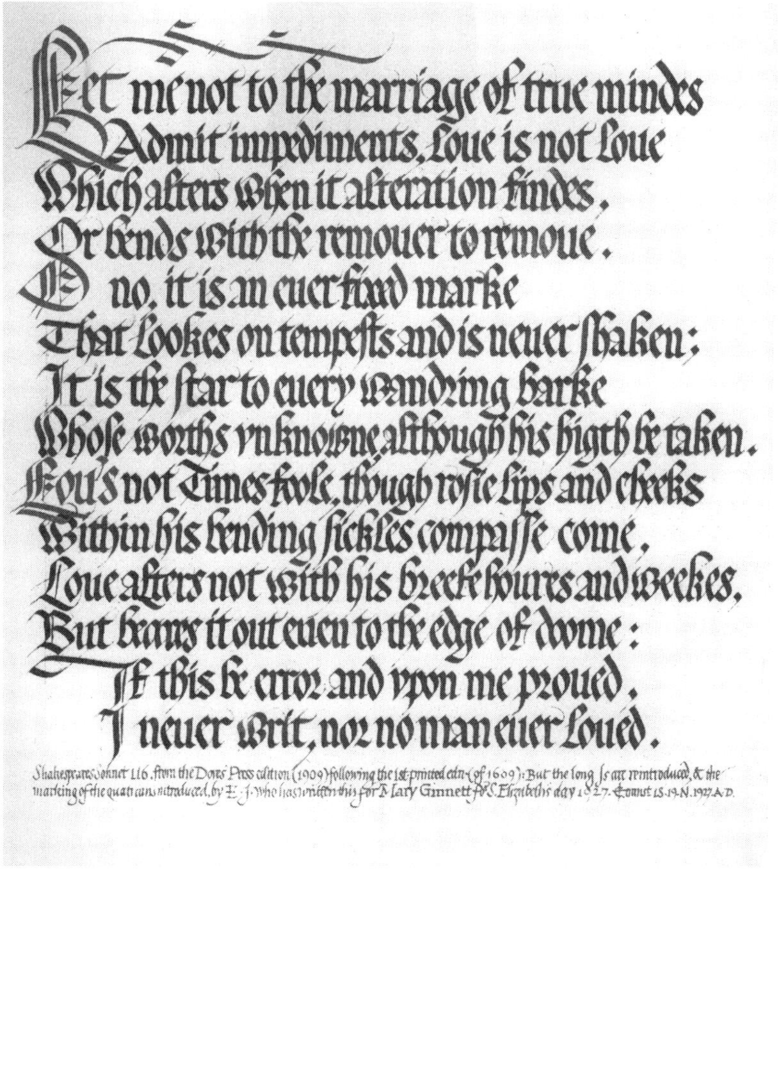

Fig. 106. Johnston's manuscript of 'Shakespeare's Sonnet No 116'.

Fig. 107. Photograph of Sir Frank Brangwyn.

the single most successful artist in England and to be knighted in 1941, he was a powerful force within the wide range of his activities. (Fig. 107). Although reclusive, he contributed enormously to the reputation of Ditchling as an artist-craftsmen's village. And, like Gill, Johnston and Pepler, he had arrived from Hammersmith. (His house there was Temple Lodge, which he had bought in 1900.) While not actively part of the Hammersmith Terrace circle, he had known Pepler there through their mutual friend, the portrait painter, Sir William Richmond. And, like Johnston, he also participated in exhibitions organised by Pepler at his Hampshire House Workshops.

By 1918, Brangwyn was regarded as a grandmaster of the Arts and Crafts movement. He had worked at the age of fifteen as an assistant to William Morris, helping to mark up his fabric and tapestry designs. His decision to move to Ditchling was taken independently of Gill, Johnston and Pepler, though their presence there may have possibly influenced him. He had been visiting Sussex from 1916, as a respite from the war, renting accommodation at Combewood House, just south of Ditchling, and closer to the Downs.[22]

An obsessive worker, Brangwyn was especially celebrated as a painter of large-scale murals, such as those for the House of Lords (now in Swansea) and others at prestigious venues abroad. He employed assistants to help with these commissions. Two cottages were designed by Brangwyn for them within The Jointure grounds. Thus there was a small community in residence there, just as there was a larger one at Gospels. He was also prolific as a designer, with links to the Vienna Secession movement and its periodical *Ver Sacrum*. Notable commissions were for the fittings of the dining room of the liner, the *S.S., Empress of Britain,* and for R. H. Kitson's house, Casa Cuseni, at Taormina, in Sicily. He was preoccupied, too, in the enlarging of his house and in laying out its terraced and walled gardens in the idiom of the Arts and Crafts movement. From childhood, Brangwyn was a Roman Catholic though he never shared the fervour of the newly converted Gill and Pepler. He lived, therefore, independently from other craftsmen in the Ditchling community.

Brangwyn did keep in contact with Pepler, however. He wrote the preface to one of the S. Dominic's Press books, *The Ditchling Drawing Book,* of 1920. He also painted his portrait and drew a separate lithographic portrait of Pepler, with himself in the background. (Fig. 108). A further connection was the study of Brangwyn's murals for the chapel of Christ's Hospital School, at Horsham, Sussex. Written and illustrated by W. R. Macklin, with line drawings of the murals by H. A. Rigby, it was printed by Pepler at the S. Dominic's Press in 1925 with the title *The Decorative Paintings in Christ's Church Hospital. 1913–23.*

Nothing, unfortunately, is known of any contacts between Brangwyn and Johnston or even how they regarded each other. They lived close by to each other, and moved into their new homes within two years of each other. Whatever mutual interest might have been aroused, it subsequently ebbed, as each withdrew into a more reclusive world. No mention is made of Brangwyn in Johnston's diaries or workbooks.

Although isolated, Brangwyn shared the same artistic values as Gill, Pepler and Johnston. True to Morris, he inspired other fellow artist-craftsmen in the precepts of the Arts and Crafts movement. One such figure, who was quintessentially of the Arts and Crafts movement and who had more positive links to the Ditchling craft community and with Johnston in particular, was the potter, Bernard Leach. (Fig. 109).

While Leach's connections with the Ditchling community were somewhat circuitous, they turned out to be highly significant. Through him a link was made between the Ditchling community and his craftsmen friends in Japan. In due course, two of these – Hamada Shoji and Yanagi Soetsu – had the opportunity to visit Ditchling. There, they met Ethel Mairet, whom they knew of because she had exhibited in Japan, Gill, and Johnston. The background to their visit is worth filling in, not least because Johnston, especially, was vividly remembered.

Leach had spent his childhood in the Far East, largely in Japan. He arrived in London in 1906. He was taught by Brangwyn at his London School of Art, in Kensington in 1908, where he followed his course in etching. On his return to Japan in 1909 he, in turn, taught etching before his dramatic conversion, in 1911, to the craft of Japanese *raku* ware under the pottery master Ogata Kenzan. Leach's etchings from Japan and China at this time are strikingly Brangwynesque. An example is his etching of the Chen Mun Gate, Peking, of 1918.

Leach took up and expanded the ideas of his three close Japanese friends. The first was the artist and designer, Tomimoto Kenkicki, whom he met in Japan in 1910. Tomimoto had studied in London where he was much influenced by William Morris's writings, visiting the South Kensington Museum. He took evening classes

Fig. 108. Lithograph of Pepler with Brangwyn in the background.

Fig. 109. Self portrait of Bernard Leach.

in stained glass at the Central School, possibly under Christopher Whall.[23] He visited Morris's home, The Red House, in Bexleyheath, and wrote the first account of Morris in Japanese.[24] He even designed a 'peasant's house' at Ando village, in Japan, along the lines of The Red House. Tomimoto contributed significantly to the building up of interest among the Japanese in the indigenous crafts of the Far East and worked with Leach on various exhibitions.

More important still was the effect Leach had on the philosopher of art, Yanagi Soetsu (or Mineyoshi), and on the potter, Hamada Shoji. Yanagi recalled Leach in reverential terms:

> The first time I met him one evening [in 1910] when he was giving a lecture in his new house in Tokyo, the first lecture ever given in Japan on the art of etching. He demonstrated the process with a big press he had brought from England .... We were drawn to each other silently and irresistibly .... I think we recognised instinctively that our characters were necessary to each other .... From that time on he lived among us as one of us .... Our hope was his hope, our agony his agony .... It is doubtful if any other visitor from the West ever shared our spiritual life so completely.[25]

Yanagi came from an eminent and scholarly family, and had already been the pupil of an expert on Western thought, Dr. Suzuki Daisetsuki. His earlier interest in 'scientific spiritualism',[26] together with the encouragement of Leach, led Yanagi to become a specialist on William Blake and on Western mysticism more generally.[27] He published studies of Western thought in the magazine, *Shirakaba* (*Silver Birch*), which he launched in 1910. The magazine was the voice-piece of the Shirakaba Society, a colony of artist and intellectuals who gathered at his home on the ancestral 'paradisical farmlands' at Abiko.[28] He edited the magazine *Blake and Whitman* between 1929-31. Due largely to Leach, Yanagi became aware of the relevance of William Morris's ideas to the situation in Japan, then in the full throes of its industrialisation. Yanagi was also the channel by which an appreciation of the individualism of Post-Impressionist art arrived in Japan. He related the 'conscious primitiveness',[29] which he identified in Cézanne, Van Gogh, and others, to that of William Blake.

Leach met Hamada Shoji in 1919 through Yanagi, at Abiko, when they became fellow potters. An awareness of the significance of the indigenous craft skill in Japan felt by Tomimoto, Yanagi, Leach and Hamada and their shared regret for its decline parallels exactly the sensibility which Ethel and Ananda Coomaraswamy had developed earlier in respect of the artisan crafts of Ceylon and India. The common source which connects both to the Ditchling community was William Morris.

In 1920, Hamada helped Leach set up the pottery at St. Ives, where he stayed until 1923. On their travels in England, Leach, Hamada (and later, Yanagi) not unnaturally made contact with the artist-craftsmen at Ditchling. Leach was already in indirect contact with Ethel Mairet through shared exhibitions at a number of London art galleries, notably the Three Shields Gallery, in Kensington, which was a long-established outlet for Ethel Mairet. Another was the New Handworkers' Gallery, (see endnote 1) as being set up and partly run by Ethel and Philip Mairet.

A further contact was, as usual, Pepler. In 1928, Pepler published Leach's *A Potter's Outlook,* as one of a series of four *Handworkers' Pamphlets*, issued by that Gallery and printed at the S. Dominic's Press by Pepler.[30] (Fig. 110). Between 1920–23, Leach and Hamada were developing their studio at St. Ives, inspired by the exemplars of Japanese craft-pottery, English medieval pottery, and seventeenth-century Toft slipwares. They saw the divorce between the making and the designing of pottery which had been brought about by Josiah Wedgwood's industrialised methods in the latter part of the eighteenth century as very damaging. This response was identical to both Johnston's and Ethel Mairet's. She had despaired of the effects of the Jacquard loom (also invented in the eighteenth century), with its pre-set designs stored on punched cards, just as Johnston bewailed the arrival of nineteenth-century mechanised type setting and maverick display lettering.

Handworkers' Pamphlets No. 3.
9d.

A
Potter's Outlook

BERNARD LEACH

NEW HANDWORKERS' GALLERY
14, PERCY STREET
W. 1.

Fig. 110. *A Potter's Outlook* by Bernard Leach.

In November 1921, Leach and Hamada travelled down to Ditchling principally to meet Ethel Mairet, who had invited them to visit her studio. They also met Johnston, although no details of the encounter have come to light.[31] Gill noted in his diary for 6th November 1921:

> Mairet brought some friends to see me in eve – Bernard Leach & a Japanese friend Hamada Shojo [*sic*] they stayed for supper.

Interestingly, another entry in Gill's diary mentions a further visit on 11th November, 1923: 'Mairet & Leach & Jap[anese] friend came to tea.' If, as it seems certain, the Japanese friend was Hamada on a second visit,[32] this may well have been the celebrated occasion on which Ethel Mairet gave him a hand-woven (brown tweed) suit which she had already made up for her husband. It is said that, following his return to Japan, he wore it for his wedding in 1924.[33] The sequel to this gesture was that, in return, Hamada sent Ethel Mairet a gift of a Japanese screen.

However, there was another consequence. Hamada's idea to form a community of potters at Mashiko, a village in the region of Abiko, some twenty-five miles north-east of Tokyo, was inspired, he claimed, from his visits to Ditchling. He was struck by the fact that Gill and Ethel Mairet had '...one leg in the city and went there any time they wanted or needed to and participated in the community, yet at the same time they truly and naturally enjoyed living in the country.'[34] (Hamada was based at Mashiko from 1924 where he worked with fellow-potters until his death in 1978.)

In May 1929, Hamada returned to England, this time accompanied by Yanagi Soetsu.[35] They stayed until August or September 1929, visiting, so Yanagi wrote, 'prominent craftsmen' – including Ethel Mairet, Valentine KilBride and Edward Johnston. (They also visited the Skansen Folk Museum, in Stockholm.) Margery Kendon, the apprentice and later the close companion of Ethel Mairet, recorded her impressions of their visit to Ditchling. In her unpublished typescript she recalls witnessing Yanagi buying sixty yards of tweed from Valentine KilBride for £40:

> It was as if they [Valentine KilBride and Bernard Brocklehurst] had made a fortune overnight. But it was Mrs Mairet who really impressed the Japanese. Dr Yanagi, in particular, was interested in her way of life and her work and bought largely of her

stuffs, made copious notes about hand spinning and vegetable dyes, which, in time, were to be incorporated into the folk art movement in Japan.[36]

Less is known of their time spent with Johnston. In an article, *News from London,* which Yanagi submitted to a Japanese newspaper, he indicated that they went to Ditchling within a month of their arrival:

> We visited several places in the countryside at the weekends to stay over for a few nights. Firstly we visited Ditchling being invited by Mrs. Mairet. It was a very nice first trip. Ditchling is a new village for craftsmen. Secondly, we visited Cambridge ....'[37]

Yanagi made no reference to Johnston – in spite of being a prolific writer. Neither does Johnston appear to have mentioned the Japanese visitors. His work diary for 1929 yields little beyond recording that on 19th September he sent Hamada a 'short note and some lines of f.p. [formal penmanship] "scribbled"... ', and on 23rd September he sent him a postcard.[38] A further observation occurs in Johnston's vellum notebook, dating from the later 1920s. On page one hundred and seventy-five appears in microscopic handwriting the sole isolated statement:

> Leach's Japanese friend preferred those shapes. Things wh. were born to those which were made.[39]

Another source of information, however, is Bernard Leach himself, who, with Yanagi's friend Bergen, greeted Yanagi and Hamada on their arrival at Victoria Station, in May 1929. In an appreciation of Johnston, in 1975, Leach wrote that he sent the two Japanese visitors '... to meet this remarkable Scot'. At the end of their stay Leach recalled that they regarded Johnston as '...the most remarkable man we met in England'. Leach added that this was '... because he had no sense of time'. In the same appreciation Leach said that:

> ... to an Oriental this is familiar. They are not tied as we are tied to the passage and the minutes of time. Timelessness is part of their philosophical concept of life.'[40]

In the 1920–30s, Yanagi Soetsu was formulating the aims and aesthetics of the Japanese folk craft movement. He invented the neologism *Mingei* [*min*-folk, *gei*-craft, meaning 'crafts of the people'] to express the hitherto unrecognised aesthetic of the anonymous Japanese craftsman engaged in the straightforward and repetitive work of making everyday artefacts.[41] Yanagi claimed that

> beauty which is not based on everyday life is not true beauty.'[42]

In 1931, Yanagi founded a magazine which exemplified this aesthetic. *Kogei* (*Craft*)[43] was far more ambitious in scope (and it was also far more expensive to produce) than *The Game* ever aspired to be. Hamada's description of his visit to Gill (*Gill Homon*) was published in *Kogei* in 1933.[44] And Gill's early essay, *Sculpture*, was translated into Japanese and printed there, in 1938. (It had been printed years earlier at Ditchling, at the S. Dominic's Press, in 1918.)

Yanagi's folk craft movement had certain affinities to the movement in Ditchling, aside, that is, from the Roman Catholic beliefs of the Guild.[45] On account of Yanagi's efforts, the Japanese movement was uniquely energetic in the collection and conservation of historically important craft works, and it became financially well-endowed. Yanagi's realisation of the 'beautiful truthfulness of [Japanese] domestic hand-made crafts'[46] led him, after many difficulties, to spearhead the setting-up of the Japanese Folk Craft Museum (*Nihon Mingei-kan*) in Tokyo, in 1936.[47]

The Japanese folk craft movement was a broad stream irrigating the practice of craft in Japan. Given that one of its sources was inspirated by Leach, it was fitting that, in 1936, Leach returned to Ditchling where his early teacher, Brangwyn, was then living. For some weeks during that summer he lived with his wife and his dog in a caravan, parked in a disused chalkpit on the Downs. He often visited the Johnston household during this time. Leach wrote in his memoir, *Beyond East and West*:

> Once I called to see him, and his wife Greta came to the door, a finger to her lips. Leading me to the drawing room she whispered: Edward is engaged with his two children in an experiment with light .... I remember when I stayed with them there was peace in that house. Twice I talked with him slowly until the small hours of the morning. Everything he said had meaning.[48]

In a separate reminiscence touching on Johnston, Leach recalled that Cleves:

> Was a house at peace in a kind of timelessness .... When I stayed there at least once for a couple of nights which we spent, Edward Johnston and I, sitting by a skeleton gas heater on which was a covered dish with some food which he could keep warm. .... You could imagine a household without much sense of the usual habits of time in dealing with other people who came with the bread or the milk or whatever it might be, might cause trouble, but in this household, held by some miracle of personality, did not....
>
> What did we talk about? I think the real question is what didn't we talk about. Very quietly, very slowly talking through the hours of the night until dawn broke, and then we went to bed. Time had ceased during that time – during that period.
>
> He never gave an answer to a question which was a commonplace, obvious kind of answer. He did not seek, either, to be extraordinary .... I would say he was in love with perfection and there was never any stopping his search for it, either in his quiet talk or in his pen.[49]

Leach characterised Johnston as a 'half-hidden but penetrating influence'.[50] Like Johnston, Leach spent much time walking on the Downs, attracted by the landscape and flora. There are a number of drawings of the Ditchling landscape by him dating from this time.[51] Leach's genius was to redound to Ditchling for it was during his stay there in 1936 that he began to prepare the text for *A Potter's Book*, the summation of a lifetime's experience and published after much delay by Faber and Faber in 1940. It became a classic of craft literature as did Johnston's *Writing & Illuminating, & Lettering*.

In October 1943 Johnston sent to Bernard Leach one of the very few letters which he exceptionally calligraphed for friends during these last years. (Fig. 111). It incorporated the initials 'B L', intertwined in the manner of a cypher. Johnston said that these unusual and highly expressive cypher-letters:

> ...have features that charm me most and that I have never before seen or written.... I think they are the best I have ever done so far.

Leach himself wrote: 'I gave the original letter, at Johnston's earnest request, to Soetsu Yanagi for his National Craft Museum in Japan.' It was Johnston's last and perhaps his greatest manifestation of this form of his calligraphy. Taken together with its contents, it is a plangent coda to his life and his work among the craftsmen in Ditchling.

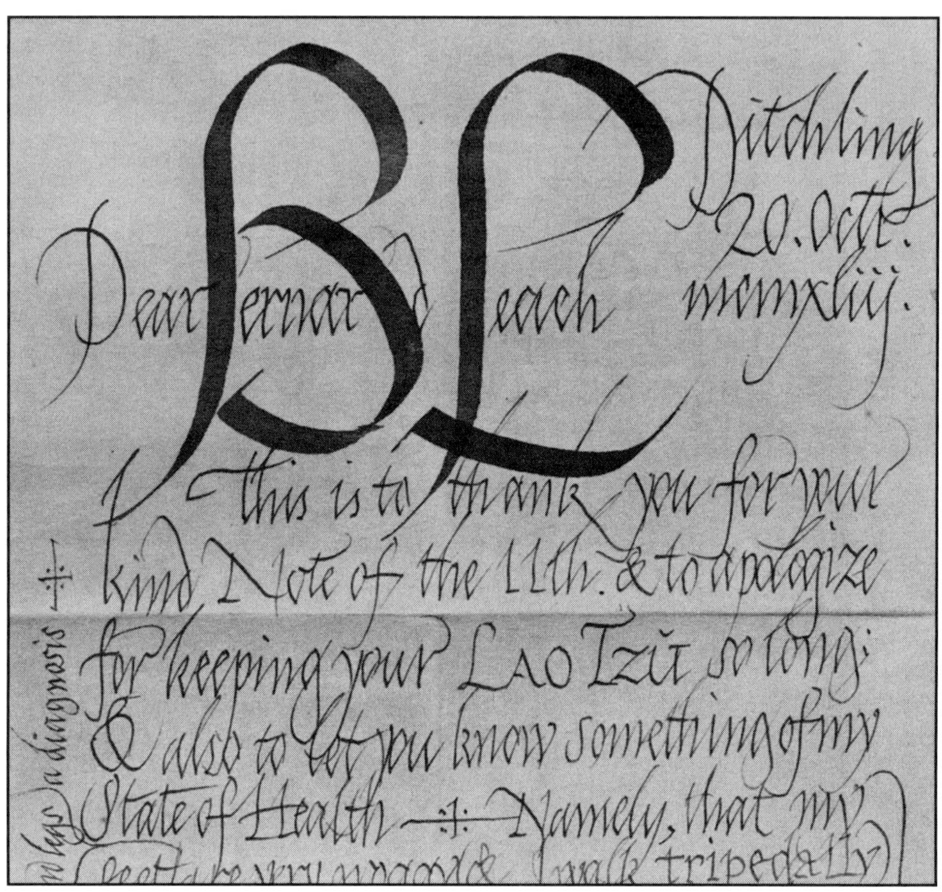

Ditchling
20. Oct.
mcmxliij.

Dear Bernard Leach

this is to thank you for your kind Note of the 11th. & to apologize for keeping your LAO TZU so long; & also to let you know something of my State of Health :: Namely, that my

... diagnosis

Fig. 111. Calligraphed letter from Johnston to Bernard Leach.

END NOTES

1. Ethel's first husband, Ananda Coomaraswamy, was a geologist. During the years 1903–07 she accompanied him on his mineralogical expedition to Ceylon. During this time the Coomaraswamys became aware of the value of Ceylon's own culture, which they saw was being increasingly threatened by the dead weight of two Western influences: colonial dominance and industrial technology.

Ethel took a particular interest in Singhalese textiles and clothes design. Moreover, she understood the relationship between textile design in Ceylon and the ancient, if simple, techniques used. Her enquiry was the more pointed for being made against the background of her husband's committed support for the incipient Singhalese (and Indian) independence movements. It was, no doubt, in this vein that she adopted a Singhalese name – Ratvan Devi.

Their partnership was reciprocal. It was through Ethel that Ananda Coomaraswamy realised the relevance of the writings of Ruskin and Morris to colonialism in Ceylon. He grafted on to his aspirations for a native political consciousness an awareness that Ceylon also needed a cultural renaissance. He began writing polemical articles on such themes as: 'Borrowed plumes, urging the retention of Native Dress and Custom in Ceylon'; 'Singhalese Earthenware; and Notes on Painting, Dyeing, Lace-work, Dumbir Mats, and Paper in Ceylon'. A seminal paper was 'The Colonisation of the East'. It was read to the Ceylon National Reform Society, of which Coomaraswamy was at that time president. It lamented the dominance of the English language and its literature in the Singhalese education system, and the ignoring of two thousand years of Ceylon's pre-colonial history. It pointed out the irony of Singhalese intellectuals learning Greek but ignoring Sanskrit. It also pinpointed the devastation wreaked on the native craft economy by the imposition of free trade policies, letting into Ceylon (and into India) cheap mass-produced, British products. He quoted William Morris:

> So far-reaching is this curse of commercial war that no country is safe from its ravages; the traditions of a thousand years fall before it in a month.

These findings were printed in journals including *Spolia Zeylanica,* and the *Ceylon National Review*, in 1906. Another article appeared in 1907, entitled the *Teaching of Drawing in Ceylon*, in which Coomaraswamy argued for the integration of the ancient system of workshop apprenticeship into schools.

Ethel Coomaraswamy complemented these articles with two of her own. In 'Old Singhalese Embroidery', she argued along historical principles for a re-evaluation of native embroidered textiles and clothing, as opposed to the making of 'fancy' embroidered antimacassars and framed pictures in the manner of early Victorian work then practised in Ceylon. She noted the use of specific techniques. In the second article, 'Music in Ceylon', she urged the use of native musical instruments, such as the tamburi, the vinai, and the sarangi, as opposed to the imitative playing of the piano. Native skills in embroidered stitching or in musical instrument-making had all but died out in Ceylon, suffocated by Western colonial fashions. With the sensibility of an ethnologist Ethel travelled throughout the country, and documented the making of embroidery with photographs.

The concern of the Coomaraswamys to revive ancient craft techniques, not out of hollow sentimentality but to meet the present and living needs of Singhalese society, matched closely the aims of Johnston in his realisation of the need, in England, for a modern script also based on good craft practice. Although their efforts were not as sustained as Johnston's – they returned to England after only four years, in 1907 – they were the richer for actually witnessing its practice in Ceylon. Coincidentally it so happened that their articles began to appear in 1906, the very year that Johnston completed his own manual, *Writing & Illuminating, & Lettering*.

On their return to England the Coomaraswamys returned to Chipping Campden. They had commissioned C. R. Ashbee to restore the Norman Chapel at Broad Campden, nearby, creating a home, a studio and a library for their working partnership. In 1908, Ananda purchased from C. R. Ashbee part of the printing equipment of the Essex House Press (the equipment had originally belonged to William Morris's Kelmscott Press). He issued several tracts in a similar vein to those he wrote in Ceylon, although they were now printed by hand, in limited editions. *The Deeper Meaning of the Struggle Between Englishmen and Indians*, of 1907, was followed by *The Indian Craftsman*, of 1909, and *The Oriental View of Women,* in 1910. This latter pointed to the ancient attitudes in India towards women's emancipation. At this time Ethel was supporting the Women's Suffrage Movement.

Their partnership culminated in *Mediæval Singhalese Art*, Coomaraswamy's masterpiece of printing. He dedicated this book it to 'Ethelmary my comrade in this undertaking'. Published under the imprint of the Essex House Press, Broad Campden, in 1908, 'under the author's care', the book is in the finest tradition of the private press movement and the Arts and Crafts movement. In a run of just four hundred and fifty copies, it is illustrated with fine photographs, many taken by Ethel herself, printed in collotype. It was partly because of her familiarity with printing (and equally with architecture and photography) that Ethel came to have such a rapport with Pepler, in Ditchling. For he had also designed his own workshop at Halletts (as Johnston had done at Downsview and was to do at Cleves) and, just at this point, was printing Ethel's book on the materials of dyeing. They were to collaborate again, in 1927, when Ethel Mairet opened the New Handworkers' Gallery, at 14 Percy Street, Tottenham Court Road, London, where Pepler also exhibited the S. Dominic's Press books. The gallery collaborated with Pepler to produce a series of short publications, the *Hand-workers Pamphlets*, including one by Philip Mairet entitled *The Idea behind Craftsmanship,* written in 1928. The gallery also collaborated with Romney Green, *Instead of a Catalogue*, and Bernard Leach, *A Potter's Outlook*, 1928.

2. Ethel Mairet also brought her relatives with her to Ditchling, in 1918. Her mother and her Aunt Maud lived for a time at Sopers, and then moved on to Sundown, where they ran a teashop. Her brother, Fred Partridge, an accomplished silversmith, who earlier had been at the Guild of Handicraft in Chipping Campden, also had his studio at Sundown where he designed and made, among other things, button accessories for Ethel Mairet's hand-woven clothes. Two other figures of note also came with her in 1918. Elisabeth Peacock, her weaving assistant from Shottery, left Gospels almost at the outset, however, to set up her own studio at Weavers, in Clayton, just a mile or so outside Ditchling. And there was George Chettle,

who had been an architectural assistant and draughtsman with C. R. Ashbee in Chipping Campden, though he worked in Ditchling mainly as a builder.

The link through Ethel and Philip Mairet back to C. R. Ashbee is worth following through in this footnote, though it shifts the story forward to the early 1930s. Apart from being an older key figure in the Arts and Crafts movement, C. R. Ashbee was an important witness of the craft communities at Ditchling, although it seems that he never met Johnston. He visited Ditchling for a few days in 1923. A passage from his *Memoirs* gives a graphic picture of Ethel's 'colony' and of the community of the Guild on the Common:

> Delightful days at Ditchling with Ernest Richmond during his leave. Ethel Mairet and her brother Fred Partridge, her husband P. A. M (now an actor at the Old Vic after an unsuccessful venture into stained glass and concrete building), George Chettle and many others make up a very live and happy colony with lots of the Campden and Essex House spirit in it. Ethel is the centre of it all with her wonderful weaving shops, her looms and carpets and dyed stuffs. She had the soul of oriental colour in her. And always those grey earnest eyes, weighted with tragedy. And one day we visited that other colony – the orthodox – the Roman – Pepler and the S. Dominic's Press. .. You felt that however much they tried to be an isolated community living craftsmanship and medievalism the industrial hat was still there, even though the rim was cut off...

Cited from C. R. Ashbee. *Memoirs*. Typewritten manuscript, (Vol. 10. Pages 95–096.) NAL at the V&A Museum. (Courtesy of Felicity Ashbee.) They were compiled by Ashbee from his Journals, now held at the library of King's College, Cambridge. Ernest Richmond was the architect son of Sir William Richmond, Pepler's and Johnston's friend in Hammersmith. Ernest also settled in Ditchling. He bought Fragbarrow Farm from Pepler in 1924, when Pepler moved into Hopkin's Crank. He became the architect in charge of religious buildings in Jerusalem under the British Mandate of Palestine.

3. Eric Gill. Diary. Date? Op. cit.
4. Philippe Mairet. *Autobiographical Compilation*. (Carcanet Press) 1985.
5. A copy (possibly unique) is in the Bodleian Library (the copy in the BL is missing).
6. Ethel Mairet. *A Book of Vegetable Dyes*. Op. cit.
7. Ethel Mairet. *A Book of Vegetable Dyes*. Op. cit.
8. Philippe & Ethel Mairet. *Essay on Crafts and Obedience*. (S. Dominic's Press Ditchling) 1918.
9. Philip Mairet, in turn, was influenced by his friend the transcendentalist philosopher, Mitronovic. A Yugoslav based in London, he was a frequent visitor to Ditchling. By all accounts, Mitronovic had a mesmeric effect on his listeners.
10. Philippe and Ethel Mairet. *Essay on Crafts and Obedience*. Op. cit.
11. Notable among these pupils was Marjorie Broadbent, *née* Bourne, the eldest of the three Bourne sisters, who were friends of Johnston's daughters. She was an accomplished calligrapher who designed the greetings card given to Greta and Edward Johnston on their silver wedding anniversary on 20th August 1928. It is a testimony to Johnston's long friendship with colleagues from his time in Holborn (1898–1905) and in Hammersmith (1905–12), including the calligrapher Laurence Christie and Ernest Richmond, both of whom also lived in Ditchling. The others were William Lethaby, Noel Rooke, Count Harry Kessler and Emery Walker. They presented Johnston with sufficient funds to take a holiday near Lake Como, in Italy. It is testimony, too, to the continuity of the spirit of that community.
12. Valentine KilBride was particularly struck by the fresh, saturated colours that Ethel Mairet achieved with natural dyes. Initially, he lived in a caravan parked in Gospels Farm, adjacent. He ultimately became a member of the Guild, with his workshops on the Common.
13. Margery Kendon mentions, too, that Philip Mairet's actor friends from the Old Vic visited Ditchling. The philosopher Mitronovic was another person who was invited by Philip Mairet, accompanied by members of his society.
14. This recollection is endorsed by two other assistants, Hilary Bourne and Marjorie Kenny.

15. Margery Kendon. Unpublished manuscript. (Courtesy of the Trusteees of Ditchling Museum.)
16. Crafts Study Centre Collection and Archive, Farnham, Surrey. Op. cit. (Ref: Johnston Work Diaries 2/1.)
17. Crafts Study Centre Collection and Archive. Op. cit., Johnston Archive. (Ref: 2/360.)
18. A letter to A. Fairbank. Bodleian Library. MSS. Eng Lett. 351. Folio 23.
19. His interest must not be over-estimated, however. The pages of his copy of Ethel Mairet's book, *A Book of Vegetable Dyes* remain uncut! It is now in the Edward Clark Library at Napier University, Edinburgh.
20. Crafts Study Centre Collection and Archive Op. cit., Johnston Archive. (Ref: 2/167.)
21. Priscilla Johnston. *Edward Johnston*. Op. cit.
22. Its owner was Marcus Huish, of the Fine Art Society, in New Bond Street, London, and evidently a friend of Brangwyn's. Johnston, himself, had considered buying the house in 1912.
23. C. Whall's handbook *Stained Glass Work* was published by John Hogg as one of the Artistic Craft Series of Technical Handbooks, (John Hogg) 1911, the series to which Johnston's handbook belonged.
24. Tomimoto Kenkicki. 'Wiriamu Morisu' (William Morris). In: Tomimoto Kenkicki *Chosakukshu*. (Satsuki Shobo) Tokyo. 1981. Cited by Yuko Kikucki in *Crafts*. July, August, September 1997.
25. Yanagi. Preface to Bernard Leach. *A Potter's Book*. (Faber and Faber) 1940.
26. Yanagi read the works of Oliver Lodge and other English writers on spiritualism.
27. Yanagi's study, *Triamu Breku* (William Blake), of some seven hundred and fifty pages, was published in 1914. (Ref: *The Great Encounter. Soetsu Yanagi and William Blake*. Japanese Folk Craft Museum. 1990.)
28. Nagata Ken'ichi: 'Hamada Shoji and the Genealogies of Artists Colonies', in the catalogue *The English Arts and Crafts Movement & Hamada Shoji*. Mashiko Ceramic Center. 1997.
29. S. Yanagi. 'The Art of Bernard Leach'. In *Collected Works*. Vol. 14. (Shikumo Shomo) 1980–92.
30. This essay was Leach's first attempt to formulate his ideas about pottery and the forerunner of his more comprehensive and enduring work, *A Potter's Book*, published by Faber & Faber, 1940.
31 Hamada's memoirs (Kama-ni-Makasete), which may contain details, remain unpublished. A summary exists in Japanese. Ref: Mizuo Hiroshi *Hamada Shoji*. (Kodansha) 1992.
32. Given that Gill was so meticulous in keeping his diary, it is odd that he mentioned Hamada by name in 1921, but not in 1923. A possibility, therefore, is that the Japanese visitor was Leach's other assistant, Matsubayashi, who arrived in St. Ives in 1922.
33. In this story the likelihood of Hamada wearing Philip Mairet's suit, given their different sizes, is passed over.
34. Bernard Leach. *Hamada, Potter*. (Kodansha International Ltd.) 1976.
35. Hamada and Yanagi arrived in England on the 10th May 1929, following 'a long monotonous yet impressive journey through Manchuria and Siberia'. Yanagi was en route to the Fogg Museum, Harvard University, USA, where he was invited by its curator, Langdon Warner, to give a series of lectures during 1929–30. (Ref: Letter from Yanagi to Langdon Warner. May 22nd 1929. In Yanagi Soetsu. Collected Works. Vol 21. Pt. 1. Page 95. [Shikuma Shobo] 1980–92.) Hamada came to London partly because of his exhibition at Paterson's Gallery, which opened on the 22nd May 1929. (That of his fellow potter, Kawai, was to follow, shortly.)
36. Margery Kendon. *Memoir*. Unpublished typescript. Ditchling Museum. 142. Yanagi Muneyoshi. *Collected Works*. (Ref: Vol 5. Page. 365.) Op. cit. Translation courtesy of Yoshie Nakayama, provided from Kobe, Japan on the 15th May 1998.
37. Yanagi's prime interest was in Ethel Mairet's weaving. He had already written an appreciation of her work (she exhibited at the Kyukyodo Gallery, Tokyo, 8–12th Dec. 1927). Whether he acquired any Johnston manuscripts at this stage is unknown. He did buy a Johnston manuscript on his visit to the International Craft Conference at Dartington Hall

in 1952. (This latter information is kindly provided by Hilary Bourne.)

38. Crafts Study Centre Collection and Archive. Op. cit., Johnston Archive. (Ref: Diaries. 2/4. 1929.)

39. Idem. (Ref: Vellum Notebook 2/Loan 13. Part III. Page 175.)

40. Bernard Leach. 'Edward Johnston and his Family'. Recorded by Margaret Alexander, cited in *Edward Johnson. Lessons in Formal Writing*. Ed. Heather Child & Justin Howes. (Lund Humphries) 1986.

41. In 1921, Yanagi founded the Korean Folk Craft Museum (he collected material in Korea). In 1926, he established the Japanese Folk Craft Society, the organisation from which the Japanese Folk Craft Museum developed in the late 1930s.

42. Yanagi. Craft-Culture. Cited from Shuichi Nakayama. The Impact of William Morris in Japan, 1904 to the Present. (Ref: Journal of Design History. Vol. 9, No 4. 1996.) In the last of his lectures given at Harvard, in 1930, Yanagi struck the imagination of his audience by saying: 'In the long run, a history of art without heroes is the very one I should like to write.' (Ref: Yanagi. Letter to Bernard Leach. May 23rd. 1930. In Collected Works. Vol 2/a. Op. cit.)

43. Kogei published articles on the entire gamut of Japanese crafts, on paper-making, pottery, spinning, textiles, even on traditional Japanese time-keeping pieces. It was printed in a run of a thousand copies per issue, on handmade paper. Incorporated into its pages are original photographs, samples of hand-woven textiles, vegetable-dyed colour swatches, and paper samples. Its covers and title-pages used hand-painted designs and calligraphy. (Some copies are held by the NAL at the V&A Museum, others are in the library of the School of Oriental and African Studies, University of London.)

44. Hamada Shoji. 'Gill Homon' (A Visit to Gill) In *Kogei*. No 31. 1933. Cited by Yuko Kikuchi. 'Hamada and the Mingei Movement'. In *Shoji Hamada. Master Potter*. Exhibition catalogue. (Lund Humphries) 1998.

45. See Nagata Ken'ichi. *Hamada Shoji & the Genealogies of Artists' Colonies*. Op. cit.

46. Yanagi Soetsu. *The Unknown Craftsman*. (Kodansha International) 1972.

47. The craft movement in Ditchling had to wait as long as 1985 before a related, though more narrowly focused and modest, collection found a home in the form of the Ditchling Museum. It was founded by Joanna and Hilary Bourne on the strength of their personal resources and vision, helped by many benfactors. Johnston's writing desk, for example, was donated by the Cook family. Other substantive gifts have come from Jeremy Carden and Heather Child.

48. Bernard Leach. *Beyond East and West*. (Faber & Faber) 1978.

49. Recording made in 1975 by M. Alexander, printed in *Lessons in Formal Writing*. Op. cit.

50. Bernard Leach. *Hamada, Potter*. (Kodansha International) 1985.

51. Bernard Leach. *Drawings Verse & Belief.* (Jupiter Books) 1973.

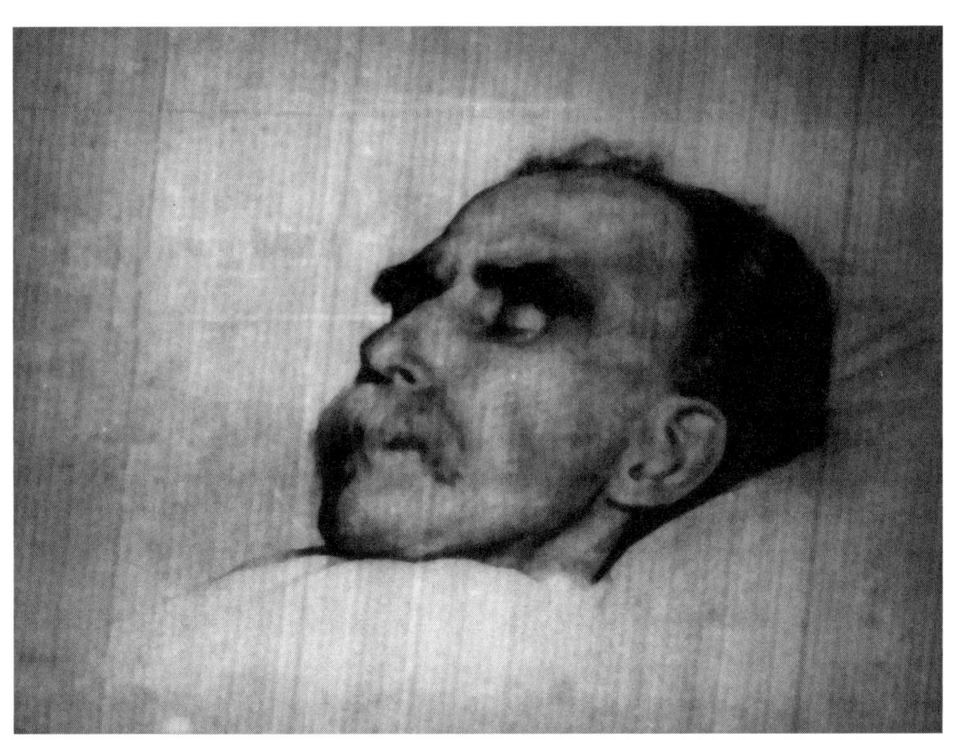

Drawing by Louis Ginnett.
By kind permissions of Jeremy Carden.

CHAPTER EIGHT

JOHNSTON AND THE GUILD OF ST. JOSEPH & ST. DOMINIC. A 'QUIET AND GENTLE SCHISM'

It is now appropriate to turn to those developments on Ditchling Common which took place from 1917 into the 1920s. They led to Johnston's dissociation from his erstwhile partners and his return in February 1920 to Ditchling village where he found a new home, Cleves.

Ditchling Common came to have an attraction for artist-craftsmen equal to that of the village itself. The nucleus of the Catholic community which grew there consisted of Gill, Pepler, and a third figure, Desmond Chute. According to a Memorandum which was almost certainly written by Gill and dated 1922, there were by that year, 'counting all the children and single adults ... forty-one Catholics living and working in this corner of the Common not one of whom was there in the beginning of 1913'.[1] A simple chapel and an incomplete quadrangle of workshops were their focus. An outline of these guildsmen and their crafts will be given in a later section of this chapter.

The formation of their Guild of St. Joseph and St. Dominic took place in a number of distinct phases, each adding to the sense of unease which underlay what Fr. Conrad Pepler was to call Johnston's 'quiet and gentle schism'.[2] There were three main elements in this process pertinent to Johnston and Greta. Roman Catholic dogma and the authority of the Pope was the fundamental and the most decisive issue. Notwithstanding Johnston's religious tolerance – he accepted that his sister, Olof, was a Catholic convert and on occasions he attended Mass with Gill – the very culture of Catholicism with its liturgy and rituals was very probably a contributing factor. So, too, was the Roman Catholic view on land ownership.

The documents from this period convey the palpable excitement with which Pepler, Gill and other new converts took to the Catholic Mass, and then became caught up with a sense of ownership of the real estate of their new Guild. They were absorbed, even to the point of obsession. This was recognised by members of the Guild of St. Joseph and St.Dominic itself. On the 7th March 1924 Father Vincent McNabb wrote to George Maxwell, a Catholic of long-standing and a builder of looms for the Guild:

> You ask me 'Why Ditchling does not seem to attract any but converts?' For the moment your question is pertinent. But the question may become irrelevant sooner or later. Yet, it often happens that converts are keener than are old Catholics on certain external matters of activity. I think the reason is that Catholics have been 'born with a

> silver spoon in their mouths'; whereas converts have had to work in order to buy their silver. Catholics are often like fat cattle in long meadow grass. They lie down in it. Converts are often like oxen in a plough. They drew [sic] it. God reward you. My blessing on your wife and family. Pray for me. Yours affably, Fr. Vincent McNabb. O.P.'[3]

The beginnings of this process can be traced to the period 1917–18, when Gill invited to the Common two forceful and intellectually brilliant Catholics. The first was the Dominican priest, Father Vincent McNabb. The second was the young artist, Desmond Chute. Though Father McNabb later encountered difficulties in his friendship with Gill, he developed a close rapport with Pepler. Gill maintained his deep attachment to Desmond Chute. At the outset, however, the four Catholics formed a new configuration, devout and intellectual, by which, in effect, Johnston was displaced. Johnston's own reactions to Father McNabb and Desmond Chute have not been recorded. He witnessed a creative force set in train which swiftly led to the forming of a group of lay Dominicans belonging to the Tertiary Order. Neither by religious conviction nor by temperament was Johnston able to associate with it.

Desmond Chute, who was already a Catholic in 1917, was educated at Downside School. Instead of university he chose to study sculpture at the Slade School of Art. He became Gill's fellow sculptor and companion, aged just twenty-three. Their first meeting had been in Westminster Cathedral, in April 1918, the outcome of Chute's interest in Gill's *Stations of the Cross* there. By mid-1918, Chute was congenially settled on the Common as Gill's guest, being instructed by him in stone-carving and lettering. In due course he lived at Woodbarton, the small house just to the north of Hopkin's Crank, designed for him by Gill on the site of a former carriage shed.

Chute stayed on at Ditchling Common during the formative years of the Guild, until the autumn of 1921, when his ambition to become a priest prompted him to leave for further study at the Albertinum, at Fribourg, in Switzerland. Gill visited him there in 1922. He returned to England – though not to Ditchling – and was ordained in 1927. Illness ultimately compelled him to live in Rapallo, near to Genoa. He moved in Catholic circles there, meeting with the poet Ezra Pound, and the theatre designer, Gordon Craig. Chute thereby widened the Guild's contacts. It was largely his friendship with Stanley Spencer, for example, which led to Spencer contributing an article to *The Game.*

A more seminal figure still was the Irish priest, Father Vincent McNabb. Born in 1868, in Portaferry, Northern Ireland, he moved as a child to Newcastle-upon-Tyne. His Catholicism was probably the more intense for his having lived in Protestant-dominated lands. He was intensely loyal to the defence of Catholic interests in Europe which was put up by the Papacy.

Having entered the Dominican Order at Woodchester, in Gloucestershire, in 1885, aged 17, McNabb was ordained in 1891. He was then sent to read for a higher degree in sacred theology at the Catholic University of Louvain, in Belgium. Louvain is an ancient seat of Catholic learning where Pope Leo XIII had set up the

Roman Academy of St. Thomas, to revive studies in the life and thought of St. Thomas Aquinas. From 1908 to 1914, McNabb worked as a priest in Leicester. From 1914 to 1917 he was the Prior of St. Thomas's Priory, at Spode House, Hawkesyard, in Staffordshire, where he remained until 1920. He spent the remainder of his life in pastoral work in London. He preached at Tower Hill, on Hampstead Heath, and more famously at Hyde Park Corner.

McNabb chanced to met Gill in Edinburgh, in 1913, through the charismatic figure of André Raffolovich, a Catholic convert and writer whose Russian family had been bankers to the Romanovs. While at Hawkesyard McNabb came to know of Hilary Pepler, having read – and then recommending fellowpriests at Hawkesyard to read – Pepler's *The Devil's Devices*. Impressed with this social tract, he made his first trip to Ditchling Common in June, 1917. The nature of the life which Pepler and Gill were leading on the Common excited him intellectually. It was he who brought to the Guild its affiliations with St. Dominic and St. Joseph, the former saint being associated with poverty and preaching and the latter with craft work.

Father McNabb was a powerful personality, well-suited to his vocation of preacher and writer. He followed a path of poverty. He invariably travelled on foot always ready to sleep on the floor and eat scraps of food, in the manner of St. Dominic whose life he earnestly wished to re-enact. He was a controversial figure, even within the Dominican Order itself. He was seen by many as saintly. Hilaire Belloc said of him: 'I have seen holiness at its full'. G.K. Chesterton thought Father McNabb to be 'one of the few great men I have met in my life. Great in many ways, mentally, morally and practically'.[4] He also recognised his 'democratic, we might almost say demagogic energy ... no man in modern politics has so firmly and even fiercely loved the people.' Bernard Wall remembered him as '... looking like Saint Dominic in Fra Angelico's *Crucifixion* ... ascetic ... angular ... making as little use as possible of any mechanical device.'[5] Hilary Pepler, who was enthralled, called McNabb 'a Pentecostal fire'. Two graphologists, both invited to interpret his handwriting, spoke of his 'spiritual fire' and his 'vital energy'.[6]

For others he was more problematic. A fellow Dominican, Bernard Delaney O.P., saw in him '... a streak of the showman ... a kind of by-product of his apostolic zeal.'[7] By those who were outright antipathetic he was variously labelled as 'a poseur', as 'a charlatan', 'a crank', 'an intellectual bully', and described as being 'proud', 'self-opinionated', 'over-bearing', 'pugnacious', 'eccentric', and 'histrionic'. A later member of the Guild of St. Joseph and St. Dominic, the wood engraver Philip Hagreen, was decidedly sceptical and thought McNabb to be patronising.

In one sense, important to the phenomenon of Ditchling, Father McNabb played out a distinctly Catholic strain of romantic medievalism. His outlook was oddly parallel to William Morris's and, in fact, in his youth he had read Ruskin with whose religious extremism he may have felt a rapport. Unlike Morris though, Father McNabb veered towards the theatrical, dressed in his Ditchling-spun, black and white friars' habit of ' ... coarse black and white material ...'[8] with '... a haversack slung over his shoulder, thick-knitted stockings and a battered shapeless black hat'.

But in another sense – again, in keeping with Morris – Father McNabb faced up to the problems of the modern industrialised world he had seen at first hand, initially in Leicester, where he was chaplain to the prison. He also saw the impact of industrialism in Belgium, and in London's East End. The Encyclical Letter, *The Condition of the Working Classes, (Rerum Novarum)* of 1891 – the very year McNabb went to Louvain – had tangible meaning for him. Catholic social policy was the practical counterpart to the indictment that Hilary Pepler was to make against industrialisation in his book, *The Devil's Devices. Control versus Service.* Comfortably for Father McNabb, the Encyclical Letter was based on theological notions integral to his Dominican Order, and emphasised by the Thomist thought with which he was imbued. Essentially, these were the Catholic strictures of Poverty, Chastity and Obedience.

The Encyclical Letters, therefore, were the basis of McNabb's social thought. In all there were more than thirty such Letters issued by Pope Leo XIII between 1878 and 1891, functioning as policy documents to shape an active though reactionary pontificate. They followed in the same crusading manner as the celebrated *Syllabus of Errors* which had been set out by Pope Pius IX, in 1865, although they were somewhat more conciliatory. The *Syllabus of Errors* had confronted the 'New Order' of the liberalism which gained ground in nineteenth-century Europe. It was met by the staunch reaction of a papal power whose authority rested on the notion of Divine Origin. While most of Leo XIII's Encyclical Letters dealt with spiritual and theological matters, other crucial ones deal with political and social problems. (Two, for example, endorsed the abolition of slavery in Brazil.) Among these there were four which especially affected the young and zealous Father Vincent McNabb.

The first was *Socialism, Communism, Nihilism, ('Quod Apostolici Muneris')*, of 1878. It countered in adversarial tones the perceived threat to Catholic stability from the socialist thought that was developing in Europe. Thus, Pope Leo XIII wrote:

> We allude to that sect of men who, under the motley and barbarous terms and titles of Socialists, Communists and Nihilists, are spread abroad throughout the world and, bound intimately together in baneful alliance, no longer look for support in secret meetings held in darksome places, but standing forth openly in the light of day, strive to carry out the purpose long resolved upon, of uprooting the foundations of civilised society at large.
>
> ... these sectaries withhold obedience and preach up the perfect equality of all men in regard to rights alike and duties. The natural union of man and woman, which is held sacred even among barbarous nations they hold in scorn, and its bond, whereby family life is chiefly maintained, they slacken, or else yield up to the sway of lust.... In short they attack the right of property, sanctioned by the law of nature, and with signal depravity, while pretending to feel solicitous about the needs, and anxious to satisfy the requirements of all, they strain every effort to seize upon and hold in common all that has been individually acquired by title of lawful inheritance, through intellectual or manual labour, or economy in living ... evil-minded traitors, spurning all control, have many a time within a recent period boldly raised impious hands against even the very heads of States.[9]

Pope Leo XIII emphasised, therefore, the Catholic primacy of private property and the family unit. ('Private ownership ... is the natural right of man and to exercise that right … is not only lawful but absolutely necessary. No one ought to live other than becoming ….') Their importance in Catholic doctrine was justified by the counter-balancing principle of charitable works. ('For the happy result we all long for must chiefly be brought about by the plenteous outpouring of charity ... man's first antidote against worldly pride. …')

The second Letter of 1879, *The Study of Scholastic Philosophy, ('Aeterni Patris')* established the validity of philosophical reasoning to support the truth of faith. Where reason contradicted faith, it was no longer valid. On this theme Pope Leo XIII wrote:

> The duty of religiously defending the truths divinely delivered, and of resisting those who dare oppose them, pertains to philosophic pursuits. Wherefore it is the glory of philosophy to be esteemed as the bulwark of faith and the strong defence of religion ... the Catholic philosopher will know that he violates at once faith and the laws of reason if he accepts any conclusion which he understands to be opposed to revealed doctrine.[10]

The Papacy therefore sought to return to the very sources of Catholicism. Of all philosophical writings those regarded with the greatest reverence belonged to the pre-Reformation thinker, St. Thomas Aquinas (1225–74):

> His testimony above that of others … enjoys such … a truth of proposition that those who hold to it are never found swerving from the path of truth, and he who dares assail it will always be suspected of error.[11]

In a later paragraph, the Letter expands on its adherence to St. Aquinas:

> … Our first and most cherished idea is that you should all furnish a generous and copious supply to studious youth of those crystal rills of wisdom flowing in a never ending and fertilising stream from the fountain-head of the Angelic Doctor …. Domestic and civil society even, which as we all see is exposed to great danger from this plague of perverse opinions, would enjoy a far more peaceful and secure existence if a more wholesome doctrine were taught in the academies and schools … such is contained in the works of St. Thomas Aquinas…. The teachings of Thomas … have great and invincible force to overturn those principles of the new order which are well known to be dangerous to the peaceful order of things and to public safety …. We exhort you, Venerable Brethren, in all earnestness to restore the golden wisdom of St. Thomas, and to spread it far and wide for the defence and beauty of the Catholic faith , for the good of society, and for the advantage of all the sciences…. But lest the false for the true or the corrupt for the pure be drunk in, be ye watchful that the doctrines of St. Thomas be drawn from his own fountains; … be careful to guard the minds of youth from those which are said to flow thence, but in reality are gathered from strange and unwholesome streams.[12]

The third Letter, *Working Men's Clubs and Associations ('C'est avec particulière satisfaction')*, of 1885, addressed the development of socialist trade unions. Looking back to the model of medieval guilds, which 'flourished under the inspiring influence of the church', the Letter established the need to reinstitute some form of group organisation among the working classes. Part of it reads:

> We have exhorted the Catholic Faithful in all countries to revive anew the wise Institutions or Corporations of Working Men .... These Institutions ... assure to the working man the education and suitable training of his children, assistance and

> charitable aid in case of sickness or distress, and support in old age. They implant love in the heart of all, instead of hate, which but too often separates the employed from their employers. As regards working men they inspire them with respect and obedience, and loyalty and devotion in their toil.[13]

These three documents prepared the way for one of the most influential of Leo XIII's Encyclical Letters, *The Condition of the Working Classes*, of 1891. Named *Rerum Novarum*, after the first words of the Letter, it came towards the end of Leo XIII's Pontificate, as a long-awaited papal response to the Communist Manifesto which had been published by Marx and Engels over forty years previously, in 1848. It was thought of as a 'Catholic manifesto' or as a '*Magna Carta*' of Christian sociology. Two passages essential to its message read:

> There is general agreement that some opportune remedy must be found quickly for the misery and wretchedness pressing so unjustly on the majority of the working class; for the ancient working-man's [sic] guilds were abolished in the last century and no other protective organisation took their place... Hence, by degrees, it has come to pass that working men have been surrendered isolated and helpless, to the hard-heartedness of employers and the greed of unchecked competition ... so that a small number of very rich men have been able to lay upon the teeming masses of the labouring poor a yoke little better than slavery itself.

> The law should therefore favour ownership and its policy should be to induce as many as possible of the people to become owners. Many excellent results will follow from this, and in the first place property will be more equitably distributed.... If working people can be encouraged to look forward to obtaining a share in the land, the consequences will be that the gulf between vast wealth and sheer poverty will be bridged over and the respective classes will be brought closer to one another. A further consequence will result in the greater abundance of the fruits of the earth to them. Men will always work harder and more readily on that which belongs to them.[14]

Reduced to essentials, these four Encyclical Letters outlined a Catholic remedy for the social evils of urban industrialised life based on capital and usury. The family, as the basic unit of society, should become property- and land-owning, settled on small estates. This is natural and enshrined in law. The restructuring of people's lives, based on the cultivation of the land and organised in 'associations', would provide a much-needed counterweight to the massive imbalance in ownership and power which prevailed. This imbalance is the root cause of class division and social distress. However, 'in God's sight poverty is no disgrace'. The poor must, in the last resort, depend upon charity. Charity is the ethical pillar of society.

Father McNabb took up this message with conviction. At the Hawkesyard Priory estate itself farming was begun. It was prompted by the emergencies of the First World War. Father McNabb took part in organising this new venture. His experience of lifting the soil was revelatory. Father McNabb had discovered that his mission began with the land. Man's rightful place was on the land, with God; towns were only man-made. 'Man', he said, 'was made to plough reap and sow.' A biographical study of Father McNabb is entitled *A Saint in Hyde Park.*[15] The reference is to Speakers' Corner where, from the 1920s, McNabb could be heard preaching fervently, entreating people to leave the city for the land. The rallying cry he used was 'Exodus'.[16]

In a letter to Gill, McNabb answered the pertinent question as to whether 'Ditchling is practicable?'. He set out an appealing, if simplistic, economic equation, which he later developed in his book, *The Church and the Land*, of 1926.[17] The high unemployment suffered in the towns was matched by the depopulation and the under-utilisation of the countryside. From this he concluded:

> There is no hope for England's salvation except on the land. But it must be the land cultivated on a land basis not on an industrial basis. Nothing but religion will solve the land question. And nothing but a religious order seeking not wealth but God will pioneer the movement from town to land. O that I could make religious men and women see what I can see.[18]

From 1917, McNabb began visiting Gill and Pepler on Ditchling Common, staying there from time to time for days at a stretch. Nothing is known of any acquaintance with Johnston. But given that he visited Pepler's farm at Halletts, where Johnston was living, the two surely must have met and presumably engaged in sparring discussion.

McNabb recognised in the developments that had already taken place on the Common the embryo of his vision to enact the *Rerum Novarum* across England, that is to say, the spread of the Catholic village and the Catholic family based on 'landwork and handwork', and guided by the three Dominican criteria of Poverty, Chastity and Obedience.

In principle, at least, these three requirements were already being adhered to on the Common. Holy Obedience was implicit in the vows taken by new converts to Catholicism. In writing on Obedience, Father McNabb held it to be the greatest of the moral virtues: 'Obedience, as part of justice, gives to the superior what is due to the superior, because it is due.'[19]

A holy poverty also existed there, based not on capital investment risked against predicted markets, but on small-scale handwork. More importantly for McNabb, it was discernible in their cultivation of the land. He held that smallholdings should be worked by families to make them self-sufficient, rather than to make a profit. This was what he called a 'Primary thing', though he accepted other ancient activities, like 'clothing, spinning, weaving' to be 'primary', too. An indication of the holiness of such work is given in a letter he wrote to Hilary Pepler:

> Even community spinning (such as exists in many primitive societies) would be perhaps as holy a representation of Nazareth as a Mystery Play. Has Ditchling thought so?[20]

Starting from Thomist principles, Father McNabb discerned only reluctantly a similar holy poverty in the stone-carving workshops run by Gill, Cribb and Chute at Hopkin's Crank and in Pepler's printing-press workshop and, outside of Catholicism, presumably in Johnston's scribal workshop at Halletts.

Chastity was implicit, too, in the familial basis of life on the Common – Gill's special pleading aside. (In 1923, McNabb had a serious difference with Gill over what he considered to be a lewd wood engraving illustrating 'The Nuptials of God', which appeared in *The Game*, in January, 1923.) At this point, in 1917, four families were in place on Ditchling Common, and their collective children already numerous. Between them, Gill, Pepler, Johnston and Joseph Cribb were to have seventeen children.

In 1919, McNabb prepared a summary of the *Rerum Novarum* for the Catholic Truth Society to serve as an English edition. It was printed in *The Game*, later that year,[21] under the title 'Does The Catholic Church Protect Work People?'. It thereby became the accepted position of the Guild of St. Joseph and St. Dominic. Articles written by Father McNabb himself also began to appear in *The Game*. One was the contentious *The Nuptials of God*.[22]

Father McNabb was the pivotal force which moved Gill and Pepler to a more devout form of Catholicism. Through personal contact and more intense discussion, developed over a relatively short period of time, McNabb seems to have become a truly paternal figure – a role which earlier had been fulfilled by Johnston. In March, 1917, McNabb invited Gill and Pepler to lecture on art at Hawkesyard Priory. Gill's diary for 22nd and 23rd March 1917, gives something of the atmosphere of this, their first visit:

> To Birmingham in morn. To Rugeley 12.15 fr. Birmingham and then on to Hawksyard Priory. Walked in park with McNabb and the sub-Prior in morn, and at 4.30 gave lecture on 'art' etc in the library to the fathers and students – discussion after. To Compline after and Benediction. Then supper. Then talk around fire in the Common Room. (22nd. March 1917)
>
> At Hawksyard. Walk around park with D.P. and McNabb in morn.
>
> At 4.30 D.P and self gave second lecture on 'art' and printing etc. Discussion after. (23rd March 1917)
>
> Father McNabb then came to spend the weekend of the 2nd–3rd June, 1917 with Pepler, at Ditchling, spending time at both Sopers and at Hopkin's Crank.[23]

Gill's and Pepler's second visit and lecture at Hawkesyard took place on the 4–7th October 1917. It was on the 6th October that Pepler was received into the Catholic Church. Gill's diary conveys the intensity of their stay:

> With D.P to Hawksyard. Tea in the refectory and to Compline after then to supper and talk in the Fathers' Common Room.
>
> At 9.30 D.P and I began retreat [*sic*] under Father McNabb's guidance.
>
> In retreat [sic] all day. Walked to Rugeley in noon. To confession to Fr. Vincent in eve.
>
> D.P. and I discussed our project of a religious order of artists with Fr. V. in eve.
>
> Douglas Pepler was received into the church by Fr. Vincent at 3.30. Deo Gratias! and we both received the Papal blessing at the end of our retreat [sic] at 6.0. Father Vincent also blessed my Rosary.

> Talked with Fr. Vincent in my room about Beauty & Work etc. etc. Talked in Fathers' Common Room in noon – again chiefly with Fr. Vincent. D.P. and I gave joint lecture to the Prior and Community in the Library at 4.30 on the Factory system.[24]

It was as a direct consequence of their visit that Pepler, under the guidance of Father McNabb, was baptised a Catholic. It was at this point that he took the name Hilary. A description by Pepler, gives an insight into that day, 6th October 1917. It is cited by Brocard Sewell, one of his assistants at the S. Dominic's Press.

> ... I was immediately impressed by the manner of discussion which followed E[ric] G[ill]'s paper – there was much difference of opinion, but all speakers supported their opinion by reference either to the Gospels or St. Thomas Aquinas. [The subject under discussion was Industrialism.] Objective truth was seen to be primary, and sought for in order to form a right opinion. Next day I went for a long walk with Father Vincent; at the end I capitulated without a shot.[25]

Two years later, on the 21st December 1919, Pepler, with a family friend, the youthful Ronald Seal, was confirmed in Westminster Cathedral. Wilfrid Meynell was his witness and godfather.[26] His wife, Clare, together with Greta Johnston, had considerable difficulty in accepting Catholicism. A letter written by Priscilla Johnston to Robert Speaight in 1960 discusses this. (It is referred to in endnote 30.)

The 5th October, 1917, is the first recorded mention of Pepler and Gill thinking in terms of a 'religious order of artists' at Ditchling. In their accounts of the evolution of the Guild both Gill and Pepler stressed, quite separately, that at the outset, when they first arrived on the Common, neither had any notion of joining a religious order. In his *Autobiography*, Gill wrote:

> I hadn't theory about all this domestic and farmyard development … . But it was entirely in line with all our other notions of life and work, so that I couldn't but see that it was good.[27]

In the draft of a letter to the bishop asking for his approval of the Spoil Bank Association Ltd., Pepler expressed much the same idea:

> My Lord, We are often required to explain ourselves to those who imagine Ditchling Common to have originated in an attempt to bring about a kind of mediæval revival in Arts and Crafts upon a basis of Catholic communism. Hence this history to show you that we set out with no 'platform' except to live our own lives as we liked to live them.
>
> Mr Gill secured a holding as near a church as he could. I bought mine before I had any idea that I should become a Catholic – hence our grouping here without the normal facilities of a Parish organisation and difficulties (absence of Catholic schools and catechism) which other Catholic neighbourhoods do not experience to the same degree.This natural isolation has perhaps led us towards the idea of a working Catholic Community and the actual formation of a Guild of Workmen – which brings me to the point of this letter. For we would ask your Lordship's recognition and approbation of probably the smallest Catholic organisation the Guild of SS. Joseph and Dominic which exists in the diocese ....[28]

In these two respects – Pepler's conversion and the idea of a religious order – their sojourn at Hawkesyard, under the direction of Father McNabb, led to a number of irrevocable steps being taken in the following year, 1918.

The question of Johnston's religious beliefs, long dormant, finally came to the surface during this period, three years or more before the formation of the Guild, itself. It was following Fr. McNabb's visit to Ditchling on the 2nd–3rd June 1917 that the exclusivity of Catholic doctrine appears to have first erupted as a problem dividing Gill and Pepler from the Johnstons. It seems likely that Johnston met McNabb during that time. Given that McNabb's particular interest was the land, clearly, he visited Halletts, where Johnston was living. A little later on he actually worked on it, wielding the scythe. Gill's diary records a discussion about Catholicism taking place with Johnston on the 12th June and the 3rd July 1917. Given that Johnston entirely accepted Gill's conversion to Catholicism in 1913 and that these discussions were some four months before Pepler's own conversion, it is probable that they arose during McNabb's visits.

> D. P., Mairet and E. J. came to supper in eve. D.P. M. and self sang plainsong hymns for an hour and when E. J turned up he and D.P. & self discussed question of R.C ch[urch] in relation with Mrs. J[ohnston]. and Mrs P[epler]. V. painful subject![29]

'Painful and disturbing' – not least to Johnston. Evidently, the discussions concerned the position of Greta Johnston, a staunch Presbyterian, and of Clare Pepler, who was also resistant to Catholicism.[30] Pepler's letter to Johnston (12th June 1917) indicates the seriousness of their differences and their effect on Greta Johnston.

> Dear Edward.The fat is in the fire, but what I do not exactly know. Greta tells Clare [that] Gill and I are never to set foot in your house again. I hope you can come up to the Crank early to comfort us with better news. Yrs, H. D. C. P.[31]

One week later, on the 17th June, 1917, another letter from Pepler to Johnston mentions:

> ... Talking of Gill, he refuses to come to Hallett's or Sopers for Latin or anything else as he does not wish to impose himself where he is not wanted.[32]

On the 19th June, 1917, Gill wrote to Johnston from Hopkin's Crank giving, somewhat enigmatically, his own reactions to the acrimony of the previous week:

> Here is another Tuesday that I have not seen you so have had no opportunity of telling you, as I told D. P. [Douglas Pepler], that I have decided to stay away from Hallett's & Sopers for the present. I am sorry if this shd. cause you any displeasure (but it is nice to know that it may for that is evidence in my favour) but it is obviously not desirable that an unwelcome guest shd. be inflicted on people's wives. So long as the unwelcomeness is more or less hidden and only suspected, appearances may be kept up, but when the fact becomes public knowledge it is no longer possible to pretend.
>
> D.P. says 'we must go on with the Latin' & of course we must. He says he will come up here and continue it & if you will come too – so much the better. But I shall quite understand if you think the peace may best be kept by your absence from the domain of vice. There are other aspects of the matter which we have not discussed, I think, if a proper understanding is to be arrived at between you & D. P. and me. We don't want a continuance of misunderstanding. Hunger may well be put up as an excuse for the theft of a loaf of bread but we cannot be [?] an excuse for that of a mug of beer. We

have not yet discussed the beer! I mean that things are in the indictment against us wh. were not discussed last Tuesday or even mentioned & wh. shd. be discussed. But don't worry. Any time will do. Yours with devotion, Eric Gill.[33]

In fact, that Tuesday evening, the 19th June 1917, saw the three meeting together at Hopkin's Crank, though perhaps somewhat guardedly. Gill's diary records:

E. J. and D. P. came in eve. D. P. and self did some plainsong & Latin but E J. came too late. Supper and talk until 11.30 p.m.

By early July relationships seem to have become more stable. On the 3rd July Gill records his going:

To tea at Hallett's and to Sopers after Latin and supper. Discussed Catholicism after with D. P., Mairet and E. J. Home 3.0 a.m!

The position which Johnston maintained in these discussions has not been recorded – at least not in any documents in the public domain. However, it can be inferred with some certainty from the letter he wrote to his sister, Olof, prior to her conversion to Catholicism. Priscilla Johnston mentions this as having taken place a few years previously. In his letter Johnston hoped to 'show clearly' that:

The R.C. 'Church' is no freer of faulty men than other 'churches' (I suppose) but these men by virtue of their office may control one's will (or action at least) more strongly than saints without that authority. That God does use the 'faulty' is obvious in their existence alone. I have only warned you how I think one might stumble over that step.... If in that search you are led to join another (or The) church, I will pray with you, if I may.[34]

Clare Pepler was ultimately received into the Catholic Church, along with the Pepler children, on the 1st May 1923, at St. George's Retreat.[35]

Johnston's cautious tone in writing to his sister about priests 'controlling one's will' was evident, too, in the position he was to take in dissociating himself, as an editor, from *The Game*, in January, 1918. This, the 'Revolution' number, (Volume 2. No.1) carried four articles, two by Pepler, one by Gill and one, significantly for the growing schism, by McNabb. Pepler, in crusading tone, led off with a number of affirmations :

REVOLUTION
We believe that the revolution needed in England is one in which the aim of the revolutionaries will be to replace the worship of mammon with
THE WORSHIP OF GOD

Pepler laid down the need for religious obedience. Couched in the Neo-Thomist language of Father McNabb, a section entitled *The Authority of the Church* reads, in part:

As a Trade Unionist accepts the authority of his Union, so should the Christian accept the authority of the Church, and with even more certain acceptance as The Church has Her authority from God.

> *Note.* The only organised community of Christians in England claiming this authority is that which is usually called the *Roman Catholic Church* .... It must therefore be understood that when we refer to The Church we refer to The Church under the authority of the Bishop of Rome, the Pope.[36]

The following section, 'IN CONCLUSION', reinforces the notion of obedience:

> The programme of revolution which is suggested is not a collective but a personal programme. Thus:
>
> *As an individual* the revolutionist will seek first the authority of the Church of God. *As a member of his family* he will uphold the honour and integrity of his family. *As a workman* he will make things and not money, he will recognise the authority of his craft or trade rather than the dominion of the Capitalist.[37]

Johnston's response – the defining statement of his 'schism' – was cogent. It was placed in a Postscript in the same issue of *The Game*:

> With reference to the editorial 'we' on pp. 8 and 12 (lines 14 and 18): I believe there are other 'churches' than the Roman Catholic which are comprehended in the Church of Christ. E. J.[38]

This was the beginning of the parting of the ways. From January 1918, Johnston began to withdraw from their 'partnership' as Gill's and Pepler's Catholic interests quickened. Their joint Latin classes continued, though more spasmodically – Johnston sometimes missed them by arriving too late – right through to the point when Gill left Ditchling Common to undertake his military service in 1919. Johnston did attend the S. Dominic Press Supper, on the 14th January 1919, and Gill's birthday party, on the 22nd February 1919. But, according to Gill's diary, to cite a key source of information, the collaboration and the socialising – the popping in for tea, for supper – henceforth took place less and less frequently.

Preparations for one of the more fundamental steps in the formation of the Guild of St. Joseph and St. Dominic were taken on the 29th–30th May 1918, when Gill, with Pepler and Desmond Chute, were at Hawkesyard on their third visit. Father McNabb advised them of the existence of the Tertiary Order for lay Dominicans. (The most celebrated Tertiary had been the daughter of a dyer craftswoman – St. Katerina Benicasa – in the thirteenth century.) Gill's diary entries for the 29th and the 30th May record for the first time their discussing the idea of joining such a Tertiary Rule.

> At Hawksyard.
>
> Corpus Christi to High Mass. 9.0. Talked with Fr. Vincent & Fr. Austin re Tertiary Rule and other things. Walked in park in noon with Desmond [Chute] and Frs V & A. Talked to Fr. Vincent re Human and Divine love. Talked in Fathers' Common Room til midnight re Beauty & Truth etc. Br. Vance opposing me and Frs. V. & Austin supporting.[39]

Two months later, from the 27th July 1918, Father McNabb was in Ditchling for a 'few days', when he officiated over the novices' entry into the Tertiary Order of

Dominicans. This was undertaken against the background of Gill's imminent call-up for war service. There was intense Catholic worship, both at St. George's Retreat and at the Oratory at Halletts. Gill's diary records the events but conveys, too, something of the frisson of those few days in the summer when his religious convictions were a way of confronting the anxieties that he must have felt about the future.

> Fr. V. McNabb came midday. He is to stay with us for a few days. To Hallett's & Fr. Vincent blessed the new Oratory. To Hallett's 7.30 for Compline. Home 9.30. Supper and bed.
>
> To Mass and Communion at St. George's Retreat To see Fr [?] and Fr. O'Meara after about our reception as Dominican Tertiaries. It is to take place in the church tomorrow. Sat on lawn in noon talking with Fr. Vincent. Miss Sawyer and Mrs Siddall came to tea and all the Pepler's.
>
> To Mass at Hallett's 7.30. Fr. Vincent said Mass for our intentions. All the family came & Albert. Talked with Fr. Vincent most of day. To St. George's 3.30 & Fr. Vincent received us, Mary, Hilary, Desmond and me as Novices [on probation] of the Third Order of Dominicans. Laus Deo. I took the name Joseph. Sports on the lawn after tea splendid.
>
> Fr. Vincent acted as time keeper. Praise be to God and our Lady & St. Dominic.
>
> Mass at Hallett's.[40]

By July 1918, a Dominican community of craftsmen was instituted. Guided by Father McNabb, they were now committed to its Rule. Springing from a tradition of medieval monasticism, the Rule wedded them to a life that was ascetic, disciplined, and proselytising, Gill was now renamed Joseph. On January 1st 1920 they were 'professed' by Father McNabb at St. George's Retreat. They passed out of 'probation', and were entitled to wear the Dominican habit. As yet, however, no guild formally existed.

Concurrently, another step was taken by Pepler early in July 1918. Hitherto, they had relied for worship on the Catholic chapel in the St. George's Retreat,[41] (a mile to the north, still on the Common), or on the Catholic church at Burgess Hill. Clearly, a chapel was needed on site. Pepler furnished a private Oratory, which was remembered by Fr. Conrad [Stephen] Pepler as having been 'a small stable' close by his new house, at Halletts.[42] Gill's diary for the 8th July 1918, records: 'To tea at Halletts with E[thel] & children & we say Compline there after in the new Oratory.' The Oratory was blessed by Father McNabb on the 27th July 1918, His first mass was on Sunday 18th July.

The Oratory was therefore situated close to the Johnstons' own house at Halletts. The reaction of the Johnstons to the fervent Catholic liturgical activity there over the next twenty months or so, from July 1918, is unknown. But given Greta's extreme discomfort with Catholicism and Johnston's more philosophical objections, it can be fairly surmised. The constant comings and goings, the communal singing, the occasional presence of Father McNabb, and other visiting priests, such as Father Austin, (also from Hawksyard), dressed in their ecclesiastical robes about to say Mass, are very likely to have caused them some disquiet, notwithstanding Johnston's tolerant temperament.The tone of Priscilla Johnston's reconstruction of events in her letter to Robert Speaight, (the surviving pages of the letter are quoted in footnote No. 30), would tend to support this. By February, 1920 the Johnstons had left. A letter from Gill to Johnston four months later, in June 28th 1920, rather shows that their departure was unmarked by ceremony.

> …Thank you for your kind words about my illness. I am now quite well again and hope to see you soon. It is very difficult to find time for calling. It is a pity the Latin lessons had to come to an end. …. You must have had a bad time with all that moving. I am very glad to hear that you are getting straight and I really do intend to come to see you soon. Yours affectionately, Eric Gill.[43]

The last two occasions 'E.J.' is mentioned in Gill's diary are for the 3rd August 1920, when he came with Philip Mairet to a supper party held in Desmond Chute's workshop on the Common ('E.J ... coming home with us after and stayed til midnight.') and three years later, on the 27th October 1923 ('To tea at E.J's.')

Subsequent developments in the Guild included expansion and consolidation. Early in April 1919, Pepler and Gill together bought some land adjacent to Hopkin's Crank, which included the Spoil Bank. This plot was so named on account of the soil heaped up by the engineering earthworks for the railway line, which ran through this spot to Lewes.

Then, on the 19th September 1919, Gill, Pepler, (with Desmond Chute), acquired a further one hundred and sixty three acres of farmland, next to Hopkin's Crank, including Fragbarrow Farm House.[44] Pepler moved into the house, probably in October 1920, a date suggested by an entry in Gill's diary for the 10th November 1920: 'To Fragbarrow to supper to discuss ... business with T. S. and H. P[epler].'[45] It was on the parcel of land in the north-west corner of the Fragbarrow site that the Guild workshops, houses, and the chapel were to be built. The acquisition of land necessitated the formation of the means by which to manage, finance, and develop it. The outcome was the Spoil Bank Association. Two meetings held on the 10th and 20th June, 1920, and recorded in Gill's diary, show its formation:

> Meeting in Desmond Chute's workshop to discuss problem of land and community finances. All present and Dr. Discussion with D. P; T. S; D.C re statement of community aims to be printed and sent to those who might lend money and buy the land.[46]

Pepler prepared and then printed a statement entitled The Spoil Bank Association (For Private Use only). It sheds considerable light on the underlying assumptions, based on Catholic social policy, which guided Gill, Pepler, and Chute in the purchase of the Fragbarrow Farm estate. Land ownership, it seems, became the key to the consolidation of their existence as a Catholic community.

But it is the tenor of the writing which is also important. It hints, perhaps, at a quite separate motive, working, on a more unconscious level. Pepler, its author, appears to be warming to the culture of land ownership, *per se*. A key phrase in the document reads '... the project seemed in itself desirable ....' Sanctioned by the Neo-Thomist values of individual responsibility, of property, and of usury with profit, it becomes evident – along with other indicators, such as his position as Reeve of the Common (to be discussed later) – that Pepler, at least, was on the path to a higher though still spiritually charged level of material respectability. His motivation is in marked contrast to Johnston's.

It is of interest, therefore, to relate the sub-texts of the Spoil Bank Association document to Johnston's own thinking. By the date of the purchase of the Fragbarrow Farm estate – September 1919 – Johnston was already prepared to give up his attachments to land and was contemplating returning to the village. The document is of value, therefore, in exploring the specific issue of land, which together with the question of Catholic authority, came between Johnston and his colleagues when they became Catholics. For these issues also underlay the 'quiet and gentle schism'. Pepler's document reads:

> Desiring to live an openly Catholic life on the lines laid down by Popes Leo XIII and Pius X a number of Catholics living on Ditchling Common have formed themselves into an Association for the purpose of acquiring land and building houses and for other things which may be required.
>
> The first two families of those promoting this Association, settled on the Common in order to stabilise the monies [sic] derived from their trades of stone carving and printing by the ownership of land and the production of home grown and home made food and to avoid the insecurity and dependence of those who are merely tenants of their houses and who have to purchase every necessary [sic] of life from the shops. In these objects they have been successful and in the course of a few years a corner of waste land, known as the Spoilbank, was bought for the purposes of erecting a crucifix partly as a proclamation of faith and partly as a memorial of Catholic sailors and soldiers of Sussex who fell in the war.+ A few months later, [September 1919] the adjoining farm of about 160 acres was bought * in order that 15 acres might be added to their independent holdings thus rendering them more complete security, and it was proposed to dispose of the remaining 150 acres by resale. Pending such disposition the farmland had to be worked and it was agreed that the interest due to the bank on the loan (½ above B.R.) should be paid out of the income derived from working it.
>
> + This is about to be put in hand. Sufficient money has not yet been subscribed to complete the work, but enough has been given to start it.
>
> * The purchase money, £7,000 was obtained on a loan from the bank, on the personal guarantee of a friend. The guarantee is for the term of one year.
>
> Of the original 650 acres, 8 acres (approx) and 7 acres (approx) were taken by the purchasers as individuals, the remainder as joint tenants; and of this remainder 8 acres (approx) have been sold to other Catholics. One of these [Gill] has agreed to hold his land in trust for the erection of workshops by the general use of a body of Dominican Tertiaries who are about to form themselves into a Guild of Catholic workmen. [This took place in July 1920.] When the land was purchased in 1919 it was proposed to sell that portion not required to anyone who would buy; but before long, partly remembering the words of Leo XIII 'The law should therefore favour ownership, and

> its policy should be to induce as many as possible of the humbler classes to become owners' (Encyclical Letter *Rerum Novarum* para. 50.) The project seemed in itself desirable and partly because their own assistant and fellow workmen desire to acquire small portions of land on which to build their homes, the idea was formed to hold the land for gradual disposal in small portions to Catholic workmen likely to be without capital except for the margin they can put by as savings, a more permanent arrangement than is afforded by a loan from a bank at a high rate of interest and a year's guarantee given by a non-Catholic friend.[47]

The remaining text deals with the need to acquire capital in order to finance the down payments of mortgages to be raised on the land, portioned out in small one-and-a-half acre plots, to interested Catholics. A subsequent step, to be discussed shortly, concerned the legalising of these aims and arrangements into a registered company – the Spoil Bank Association Ltd, in October, 1921.

As early as April, 1919, Gill was writing in his diary of his intention to build a chapel and install workshop huts on the first parcel of land, the Spoil Bank. He also wrote of erecting a monumental crucifix on it. On 16th April, 1919, the land was blessed by Father McNabb, and then measured by Gill and Desmond Chute with a view to the intended chapel and workshops.

While the chapel and workshops did not materialise on this site, the Spoil Bank Crucifix went ahead as a paid commission. Gill worked on it intermittently over the next three years. On November 14th–15th, 1919, he was making preparatory drawings for it; during October 1922, he was working concentratedly on carving and painting it. On the 18th November 1922, his diary speaks of 'fixing the figure on Spoil Bank Crucifix'. It was constructed from thick wooden planks, some 15 feet high and with an arm span of six feet – a gesture, no doubt, to Gill's former interest in monumental sculpture for a 'New Religion' at Ashenam. For it, too, was intended to be seen from a distance. It was painted white, with the loincloth in blue, and dedicated to Catholic servicemen of Sussex who had given their lives in the War.

The vital final step, however, took place as the result of a meeting held on Sunday 18th July, 1920 when a draft constitution was drawn up by Pepler, Gill and Chute, proposing such a Guild. It was then submitted to Father McNabb for 'criticisms and approval'. Although this was not yet made public, it is from July 1920, therefore, that the Guild can be said to have existed. However, on account of the deliberations taken by the Catholic authorities, including the bishop of the diocese, this Constitution was not printed in *The Game* until the issue for September, 1921.[48]

It was from mid-1920, too, that construction was started on the workshops. On the 18th and 19th March 1921, Gill noted in his diary that he was 'moving all day' into his new workshop. Pepler's printshop for S. Dominic's Press was also among the first. On 3rd–4th April 1921, visitors were invited to view 'the new Printing Office of S. Dominic's Press'. Both workshops were built of brick, having being laid by the local bricklayer, Mr. Chisholme. The ground plan of the workshop site was a quadrangle, reminiscent of Gill's days at Lincoln's Inn, with Johnston.

On February 19th 1920, Gill drew a scaled plan of the chapel he had in mind, to be built on that portion of land reserved for the Guild complex. By early 1921 it was up, constructed by Mr. Chisholme. During those first months of 1921, Gill was preoccupied in the fitting-out of the chapel, working before breakfast on the seating, the carving of capitals, and the stone for the floor of the predella. An entry in Joseph Cribb's diary for Sunday 6th March 1921 reads: 'Father O'Meara came and blessed the new chapel at 2.45 pm. Persons present: E. Gill, H. Pepler, Susan Pepler, Mary Cohen, Mrs Gill, Gordian Gill, Betty, Petra, Greta, Joe Cribb.'[49] On the 8th March 1921, Mass was said in the chapel for the first time. From the 9th March Gill was again busy, carving and colouring the wooden Rood Crucifix ready for the chapel's consecration. Good Friday, 25th March 1921, saw Mass being said again. On the 10th April 1921, Gill refers in his diary to his serving at the Mass held in 'St. Dom[inic's] Chapel'.

The history of the chapel merits separate discussion beyond the scope of this study. It would include discussion of those priests from Hawkesyard, such as Father McNabb and Father Austin, and Father O'Connor (from Bradford), who officiated there, and the legendary engagement betrothal of David Jones to Petra Gill. Suffice it here to mention the involvement of other Guild craftsmen in its decoration, including a Madonna and Child carved in stone by Desmond Chute and a Joseph carved in stone by Joseph Cribb. Gill also designed in contrasting brick colours for the exterior wall the initials: J. M. J. D. A further inscription taken from Ecclesiastes was carved by Gill in Latin and placed into the chapel's exterior north wall. It reads:

> Homines divites in virtute, pulchritudinis studium habentes: pacificantes in domibus suis. [Men rich in virtue, studying beauty, dwelling at peace in their homes.]

This number of *The Game* consisted of some seven pages of text which formally announced the establishment of the Guild under the patronage of the Saints Joseph and Dominic. *The Game* became its official organ. In a closely reasoned text, the Guild's existence was set out as being a '... society of which the members shall have the same faith and the same or cognate trades, and for this reason: that faith and works may go hand in hand.' This is further developed in the key concept: '*Actus sequitur esse*':

> *Actus sequitur esse.* Doing follows being. This is, indeed, the counterblast to the modern heresy that there is no being behind doing, and being is not behind but before.[50]

One of the arguments which follows upon this premise – being is the prerequisite to doing – was to place it within an expressly religious context, in order that 'all things made might find a place in the nurseries of Heaven':

> The Guild of SS. Joseph and Dominic is a craft Guild, but it is not primarily a craft Guild. It is primarily a religious fraternity for those who make things with their hands. As a guild it aims only at the sanctification of the brethren, and holds that the love of God is the only source of good.
>
> The Guild holds that all work is ordained to God and should be Divine worship. As human life is ordained to God so must human work be. We cannot serve God and Mammon, but we can love God and our neighbour. The love of God means that work must be done according to an absolute standard of form; the love of our neighbour means that work must be done according to an absolute standard of serviceability. Good quality is, therefore, twofold: work must be good in itself and good for use.

> The Guild holds that work being ordained to God should be true and good, and therefore beautiful, for the *nature* of work and the *object* of work combine to determine the *manner* of work, inasmuch as beauty proceeds from truth and goodness as the Holy Ghost proceeds from the Father and the Son ....[51]

This far, there is nothing with which Johnston is likely to have disagreed. The coupled notions that beauty is inherent in what has been well and truthfully made, and that work should be a form of 'Divine Worship' were fundamental to his own thinking. The substance of Johnston's text, *A Carol*, of 1915, embodies this.

However, Pepler and Gill developed their thinking by tying these ideas to specifically Catholic dogma. Whether on account of the direct influence of Father McNabb or not they also introduced the requirement of ownership. In tones reminiscent of the Papal Encyclicals – the *Rerum Novarum* is actually quoted – their text continues:

> The Guild holds that the principle of individual human responsibility being a fundamental of Catholic doctrine, and this principle involving the principle of ownership, workmen should own* their tools, their workshops and the product of their work.
>
> **Leo XIII, Rerum Novarum.* 'It is just and right that the results of labour should belong to those who have bestowed their labour.' (II) 'The law therefore should favour ownership; and its policy should be to induce as many as possible of the humbler classes to become owners.'[52]

Having set the Catholic context, the papal quote affirms the absolute requirement of prayer, and the recitation of the Office. These are the criteria of obedience:

> The life of prayer is not only of primary importance to the brothers of the Guild, but it is of primary importance to the Church, for it is a means not only to the sanctification of the brothers but to the sanctification of our land. Loyalty to the office is, therefore, the first test of our life as Tertiaries and as Brothers of the Guild.[53]

At this point, in September 1921, Johnston was living in the village. But it is reasonable to assume that, with Greta, he would not have been prepared to go that far in accepting Catholic dogma *per se*.

The final stage in the formation of the Guild took place in October 1921, with the formation of the Spoil Bank Association Ltd., as set out in a Memorandum of Association. This was a strictly practical measure designed to safeguard the independence of the Guild's operations.[54] Had it sought charitable status it would have come under the jurisdiction of the Charity Commission. Instead, a private company was registered to 'own and administer the property on behalf of the Guild members'. The financial device of debentures was adopted whereby the value of the land, workshops, and chapel were surrendered by the individual members who, *in lieu*, received the value of their respective portions in terms of debentures – or shares. A capital sum was thereby created, in the form of a bank mortgage, with the debentures redeemable if necessary.

The initial seven members of the Spoil Bank Association Ltd, as cited in the legal Memorandum of Association, dated the 27th October 1921, were Herbert

Joseph Cribb (Carver and Letter carver); Eric Rowton Gill (Carver in stone); W. David Jones; George Maxwell (Builder); H. Douglas C. Pepler (Printer); Wm. John Tull (Printer); Charles L. Waters (Clerk).[55]

The continuing history of the Guild of St. Joseph and St. Dominic is of relevance in this study in so far as it can shed light retrospectively on the events which concerned Johnston. For the later schisms which beset the Guild reveal much about the personalities and underlying partnerships of those involved, notably those of Gill and Pepler, and therefore go some way towards explaining the personal background to Johnston's departure in 1920. It is rewarding, in this regard, to give them some attention.

The first of these schisms concerned Gill. From January, 1923, he was taken by the idea of leaving Ditchling for the remote and ruined Benedictine monastery of Capel-y-ffin. It was situated near to the larger and also disused priory of Llanthony, in Breconshire, mid-Wales. The discovery of such a suitable location, back-of-beyond, was made through the priest, Donald Attwater, on Gill's visit to the Benedictine community on Caldey Island off the Pembrokeshire coast of Wales, in January 1923. An entry in Gill's diary for 24th June 1924 reads that it 'emerged that E.G[ill] must sever his connection with the Guild.' On the 22nd July 1924, he resigned from the Guild. He left for Capel-y-ffin on the 13th August 1924.[56]

A number of factors had a bearing on Gill's departure. His biographers point to the disapproval Gill felt, as a possessive father, towards the liaison which had developed between his daughter Betty and Pepler's son David. Another factor was the increasing publicity which the guild community was attracting, especially from the wider Catholic community, and others. In June 1919, for instance, Gill noted the arrival on the Common of his former acquaintance, the mystic philosopher, Mitrinovic and 'his party' – evidently a group of onlookers, curious about the phenomenon of a 'back to the land' Catholic colony.

Gill's initiative appears to have generated a new dynamism in his religious life. A key role in his move to Capel-y-ffin was played by an entirely new acquaintance, Donald Attwater. It was Attwater who urged that he resettle at Capel-y-ffin with him. This new partnership – Gill had been adroit at striking new allegiances in the past, his friendship with Desmond Chute is but one example – may have challenged the established and dominant one at Ditchling Common between Pepler and Father McNabb. It is reported that Pepler, on inspecting Capel-y-ffin for himself (on the 7th–10th March 1924), was morose and taciturn. It is also known that Father McNabb was adamantly against any move away from Ditchling.[57]

More decisive than these earlier reasons, however, was Gill's growing dissatisfaction with Pepler. The issue was the Guild's finances. His diary for the 18th June 1924 speaks of a meeting with Pepler, George Maxwell and Father McNabb at the Dominican Priory in London. It concerned Pepler's 'financial methods'. Clearly acrimonious, it nevertheless ended with a 'kiss of peace'. Two other entries, for the 10th and 11th August 1924, show Gill was anxious to leave Ditchling with good relations intact:

> Mass and communion at Chapel. 8.00. Ditto, St. George's 9.30. Walked to Ditchling with G. Flood also P(etra) and D. J[ones]. Tea at Mairet's said goodbye also to E. J[ohnston] and L[awrence] Christie.
>
> Reconciliation with H.P(epler) and G(eorge) M(axwell) very happily.

Perhaps unknown to him at the time, Gill's hasty departure was the cause of deep grief to Pepler, and the more so since Gill also attracted other Guild members to Capel-y-ffin, notably David Jones, Philip Hagreen and Laurie Cribb. The very cohesion of the Guild was endangered. It had a lasting effect on Johnston, too. In 1942 he wrote a calligraphed letter to Mary Gill offering condolence following the death of Eric Gill in 1940. He invoked the comment of William Rothenstein who had said of Gill: 'Never have I seen so swift a line.' Johnston added:

> Swift is a good word for him; he lived swiftly – deciding swiftly – and left swiftly. When that happened I felt very much for you and for those he had left who had so much depended on him and had found him so dependable.[58]

The vacuum left by Gill at Ditchling Common was filled, initially, by the Peplers, who moved into Gill's former home, Hopkin's Crank.[59] Then, there was a new arrival. In 1925, the hand-weaver, Valentine KilBride, who had met Gill in 1922, joined the Guild. In due course he became a major figure in the Guild's affairs as the Secretary to the Spoil Bank Association Ltd. In the second 'schism', which began in 1934 and which came to a head in 1937, it was Pepler who found himself at variance. There is an irony in the fact that the dispute which unfolded between Pepler and the other guildsmen, headed by Valentine KilBride, turned on the strict application of protocol and the rules and constitution of the Guild. The first sticking point was the resignation of his two assistants (his son, Mark and Cyril Costick) from the Guild which barred him, strictly speaking, from exhibiting S. Dominic's Press material as *bon fide* work of the Guild at the Liturgical Art Exhibition at Westminster Cathedral, in 1934. Moreover, Pepler was also accused of 'delinquency' by Valentine KilBride for failing to declare his employment of a non-Catholic assistant in his printshop. The quarrel was confounded by a second undercurrent which concerned the confusion over financial dues owed by Pepler to the Spoil Bank Association Ltd, as against the interest due to him from his debentures. A court case almost ensued. Pepler fired off angry letters, and then withdrew them, to be substituted by others from his solicitor. At one point he threatened to remove the altar stone in the St. Dominic Chapel, which had originally belonged to him. One of Pepler's letters to Valentine KilBride, dated 30th December 1937, reads, tersely:

> We can either amicate, arbitrate or litigate. I accept whatever method you choose and shall respond with good will.[60]

The final split between Pepler and the Guild came in 1937 over the quite separate issue of the use of electricity to power the printing presses. Machinery was anathema to the Dominican community. By that date, Mark, and his partner Cyril Costick, wished to upgrade the printing equipment to make it more commercially viable. The outcome, in 1937, was the removal of the S. Dominic's Press to Ditchling village, where it was renamed The Ditchling Press. A brief note signed by Valentine KilBride's son, John, records the collection of the Stanhope and Albion printing presses from Ditchling Common workshop on the 9th February 1937:

> ... a local carrier removed two platen printing presses and some miscellaneous apparatus from Mr. H.D.C. Pepler's Printing Workshop this afternoon.[61]

Pepler then resigned from running the Press and became absorbed instead in his long-standing interest in dramatics, in mime and in his puppets. He remained at Hopkin's Crank, without recriminations, until his death in 1951, although he also had a London residence (4 Horbury Crescent, Notting Hill, W.11). His funeral was the occasion for a genuine display of reconciliation by the guild members.[62] George Maxwell and Valentine KilBride made and furnished his coffin, and joined the funeral procession down from the Common to Ditchling village churchyard.

To probe beneath the surface of these seemingly unresolvable disputes is to conclude tentatively with Father Conrad Pepler who, in referring to Johnston's departure, said: 'now the ... inevitable schism came'. It is clear that the disputes of both 1924 and 1934–37 were exacerbated by the clash of personalities. On the one hand there stood Hilary Pepler, his patriarchal dignity affronted by the indictments of his fellow guildsmen. Learned, artistically accomplished, and hospitable, he had become very much the senior statesman of the Guild. Moreover, he carried all the authority of the Reeve of Ditchling Common. His assistants at S. Dominic's Press had always referred to him as 'the Boss'. A tall authoritative figure, habitually wearing a black cloak and carrying a staff and the author of many a 'scheme' born-on-the-wing, Pepler may well have been the more impressive because of a slight astigmatism in one eye. He must have appeared quite formidable to the younger Valentine KilBride.

Faced with such a 'tribal chief',[63] Valentine KilBride, on the other hand, stood his ground secure in his position as secretary of the Spoil Bank Association Ltd. He held a meeting in camera, which outraged the excluded Pepler. He issued an ultimatum to Pepler that Pepler obey 'Rule 4', and dismiss the non-Catholic assistant or resign from the Guild. Valentine KilBride took umbrage at what was Pepler's 'haughty manner'. In the taking of sides, only Joseph Cribb remained neutral.[64] Calm, rational, kindly and determined, Valentine KilBride, replete in his ecclesiastical robes, also had his strengths.

The personal nature of these two later 'schisms' reflects back to strengthen the view presented here of Johnston's earlier departure from the Common. It is based upon the three interconnected issues of Catholic orthodoxy, Catholic advocacy of land ownership, and the Catholic office, with its demanding routines and its rituals. It suggests that Johnston was in fundamental disagreement on all three fronts.

The Catholic view of events, as presented by the priest who wrote about it, Father Conrad Pepler, concentrates on the question of Catholic orthodoxy only. It is a restricted view which bears closer examination. Father Conrad, who, as Pepler's son Stephen, had lived through some of the events of the period, and been taught calligraphy by Johnston, wood engraving by Gill, and printing by his father, was deeply respectful of Johnston. He regarded him as having been at the very source of the partnership. As a priest, he no doubt viewed Johnston, so distanced from Catholicism, as a soul lost. In an article printed in *The Dublin Review*,[65] Father Conrad wrote:

> Johnston, though never a Catholic himself, was one of the principal thinkers in that brilliant set of men who eventually produced the community of 'simple lives' which is known in many circles simply as 'Ditchling'.... It is very good to think that Johnston retained to the end the ideals which were the inspiration of the Community on the Common.

In developing his theme, Father Conrad went on, however, to take issue with the view of Johnston's departure held by Priscilla Johnston in her biography. There, she stressed the intractability of the problem of Catholic orthodoxy.

> It is hard to believe that so intractable an individual [as Johnston] could have been persuaded to accept a ready-made scheme of things as to allow his own philosophical speculations to be overruled by a priest.[66]

Without her being specific, the 'priest' is, clearly, a reference to Father McNabb. Reading between the lines, her comment may well indicate an attitude of scepticism towards McNabb in the Johnston household. Father Conrad, however, put a different gloss on Priscilla Johnston's view. He developed an essentially conciliatory line. Having established that: '... now the first inevitable schism came – a quiet and gentle one, because Johnston himself was so gentle and undemonstrative', he maintained that Johnston:

> ... had been moving towards not only acquiring a watermill and farm but also towards the Church. Priscilla confirms what my Father always told me: that Edward would certainly have followed his companions into the fold, only his wife was a staunch Presbyterian ... Johnston would I think at that time have been more alive to the whole truth than his daughter wrote.[67]

Father Conrad, however, seems to have ignored the harsh realities of the day-to-day management of a small holding. Priscilla Johnston, in her biography, clearly recognised how welcome the return to the village was:

> For Greta Cleves was paradise. For Johnston it was different. He had made a bid for the Good Life as he saw it and the retreat to civilisation must have been a sort of defeat. He realised, however, that what had happened was inevitable. Neither he, nor Greta, had the strength to battle with that hard life any more.[68]

The down-to-earth practicalities of the management of land aside, the Catholic attachment to land ownership reveals a deeper divide, still, between Johnston and the Catholic community on the Common. The religious significance with which land was imbued for the Catholics at Ditchling is revealed by two articles which Pepler wrote over a wide time-span. The first article deals with the theme of the spiritual paucity of urban living as opposed to the religious fulfilment of country living. It has the curious title 'Missions. I. Sheepfolds and Shambles. II. A Goat in a Sheepfold or a Sheep in the Shambles'. Written in 1921, during the period when the chapel and the workshops were being built on the Common, it was printed by S. Dominic's Press in 1922, as No 9. of the *Welfare Hand-books*. It conveys the passion of Pepler's religious zeal.

Professing those intertwined Catholic values of faith and land ownership, the piece reads as an echo of Father McNabb's utterances. In fact, at its starting point the author describes how he makes his way from Hyde Park, having listened to a speech given there by McNabb. Pepler rues the existence of urban life as a form of living death. Witnessing the urban crowds he wrote:

> I cannot count the number of men and women I pass upon my way, more than I see in ten years by my home. A kind of life, indeed, is on his tongue but step and gesture both belong to Death, and men go by me as those who are about to die and have not tasted life .... For it is townward that men march to their doom, it is in the town where for pleasure and profit they would spend their lives close to the end of all God's commandments, near to the beginning of all the Devil's allurements, with the irresponsibility of the lodger, owning neither the house they live in ... hired for a wage … that Shareholders may have dividends, and they wages, football news, pictures and canned food .... We have seen our sons leave for the town to die, and our daughters do not always marry into butter-making homes ... but choose the gayer clothes and the less responsible existence which brings them death .... Man makes a kind of marriage with the land and has his share of woe as well as weal, but factory work is whoredom ... men and their work united for a wage .... Man's end, as God designed it, is TO GIVE, TO GIVE GOD THE PRAISE, THE LOVE AND SERVICE.[69]

While Pepler's essay was predicated on Father McNabb's own writing, it is right to point out, too, that Father McNabb, in his turn, incorporated into his religious beliefs a sense of the spiritual value of handmade artefacts based on what he saw being produced in the Guild. Like Pepler, he also bemoaned the '... dismal routine of office and factory, the incubus of industrialism ....' claiming that being: '... in a field when the earth is still sparkling with the morning dew is to see God's earth.' The town dweller, he wrote, in 'Landwork and Handwork' should:

> Go out from the town which man has made and meditate on the land as God made it ... to a farmhouse (belonging) to their kindred ... to good Catholic stock .... In such a homestead there is a chance of seeing in full life some of the old hand crafts which once made a farmhouse ....[70]

Pepler's second article, entitled 'The Reeve', was written as late as 1941. It shows his views on land ownership to have become more deeply entrenched over the years. The article deals with the functions of the the Office of Reeve of Ditchling Common in protecting the rights and interests of all land owners. Pepler, himself, held the elected post of Reeve until his death in 1951. The first part of the article establishes the necessity for such an office:

> The Reeve is not only a needful link between landlord and tenant, owner and owner, tenant and tenant, but one who makes individual ownership and particularly small ownership possible.[71]

Pepler then makes a comparison as a man with passionately held Catholic beliefs. He describes the role of the Reeve as being equivalent to that of a Catholic priest:

> The parish priest on the spiritual plane is comparable to the Reeve on the material. His flock is surrounded by a chaos of half-belief and gross ignorance. The Office of priest is necessary to prevent this chaos .... The priest is the bond between the many and the One. In all human activities there is the same need, in the affairs of the land we shall do well to recreate the Reeve ....[72]

Pepler continues by identifying the prerequisite in that re-creation:

> The first need is for lovers of the land precisely as the first need of the Church is for lovers of our Lord.[73]

In a further section, Pepler identifies the dual 'love' as being embodied in the figure of Father McNabb himself. Equally revealing is his invocation of the 'lost idyll' from the years 1917–21:

> I still have vividly in my mind the picture of one at work in the fields who combined both loves. We were harvesting oats with the old-fashioned sickle ... because we had decided that that was the best and happiest way of working. The women and children had made the bonds, following the men as they made their way forward with their reaping hooks into the crop. In the forefront of the battle the even then venerable figure of Father Vincent McNabb sweated with the best of us. Scapular and Rosary tucked into his belt, his bald head unmindful of the sun, the ascetic, allowing himself a rare glass of home-brewed ale, set a pace which the ex-poacher on his right was not ashamed to follow .... The preacher of the love of God, and of the land He has given us, harvested those oats as he would harvest human souls for heaven ....[74]

The article concludes with that vision acquired from, and shared with, Father McNabb: a vision of the Catholic village society, free of centralised bureaucratic interference, fundamentally democratic, expressed in terms invoking the politics of the Middle Ages: 'in Parish units, with a Priest at the altar and an ancient with his Reeve as the only court.' It seems to be the case, readily recognised by Pepler's own children, that in these latter years he had become somewhat over-imbued with a sense of land as property. Susan Falkner, in her *A Ditchling Childhood*, remembers him as a tough guardian who, on occasions, was involved in altercations with gypsies.

The zeal with which Gill, Pepler and Chute, carried out their Office as members of the Tertiary Order of Dominicans was characteristic of the newly converted '...full on new wine'.[75] Moreover, Gill and Pepler, at least, were keen to assist in serving at the Mass. Gill had been instructed in this while working at Westminster Cathedral. Pepler served at Masses held by Father McNabb at St. George's Retreat and St. Dominic's Chapel. The intensity of their commitment is indicated in the memoir presented by Father Conrad Pepler on the occasion of the Centenary Celebrations of the birth of Gill, held at Spode House, in 1982. There, he described the religious routine of daily life on Ditchling Common:

> I cannot remember at all precisely the daily hororium, but I think we began the day with the Office of Prime, and the reading of the martyrdom at about 7.00 a.m. My father and I would then return to Fragbarrow to prepare breakfast, while Mother saw that the girls got up. After breakfast we went off to the printing shop; and I guess it must have been at about nine o'clock when the Guildsmen met in the Chapel for Terce. For the seniors this meant quite a long absence from their workshops as the time following immediately on the short act of worship proved extremely convenient for

> discussing philosophy, theology, or the evils of machinery, and allied questions. We youmger members returned to our work more rapidly. I think the office of Nones must have been said before we went off to lunch. The Angelus was rung – a small bell was hung outside Mr. Gill's workshop – and said at noon, and at 6 p.m. Vespers were said after the evening Angelus, if I remember rightly.[76]

Gill's diary confirms the intensity of this routine. For instance, between 21st and 28th July 1921, he attended Mass and Communion every day either at Halletts or St. George's Retreat.

It was an exacting regime. In her biography Priscilla Johnston made a cogent response to the notion of her father's possible conversion to Catholicism:

> Anyway he'd never get up in time to go to Mass.

It's hardly credible that Johnston, the notoriously late riser, could ever have been fired as were Gill and Pepler by the rigours and the rituals of the Dominican Tertiary Office.

Behind the everyday practicalities, which were so evident to Priscilla Johnston in her understanding of Johnston's life, lay the more fundamental considerations touching on his temperament and his intellectual formation. This is best illustrated, perhaps, by returning to the contrast between Johnston's and Pepler's temperaments.

During the period 1913–1918, they shared the basic values of the Arts and Crafts movement, combined with their more specific viewpoint that craft activity needs to be undertaken – as Gill said – 'in collaboration with God'. The opinion of Philip Mairet is helpful here, especially since he lived both in the Pepler household at Halletts, and then at Gospels, in Ditchling village, where he developed a close friendship with Johnston.

> I would say that the unanimity which had inspired them to migrate to Ditchling had had its origins in – more than anything else – the example of Edward Johnston ... in a certain pure sense he already <u>was</u> what they had set out to preach and practice.[77]

In the years after 1918, however, the deeper-seated differences which underlay the immediate circumstances of the 'schism' began to emerge. Thus, while Johnston was guided by rationalism, Pepler, by contrast, found himself driven by flights of the imagination. While Johnston remained the philosopher, informed by sceptical enquiry, Pepler, was impassioned by belief. While Johnston warmed to the logical and mathematical disciplines, Pepler was inspired by the drama of the symbolic. While Johnston was intrigued by things made – from the techniques of writing medieval letter-forms to the workings of instruments and gadgets, both mechanical and electrical – Pepler was entranced by a religion which claimed the infallibility of its leader. It seems that by temperament, Pepler was absolute in his enthusiasms whereas Johnston, while deeply religious, remained detached. An element of the whimsical lightened the things he believed in and liked to do. Pepler's and Gill's predicament was cogently put by the Dominican archivist in Edinburgh, Father Bede Bailey: 'They took themselves far too seriously'.[78] (The priest serving Ditchling is quoted as having once remarked: 'I don't go there very often, but whenever I do go there Pepler is ordaining Gill or Gill is consecrating Pepler'.[79])

It followed, therefore, that Pepler was more naturally inclined to the ritualistic and the dramatic aspects of the Catholic liturgy, even though he claimed (for example in his play *Missions*, of 1922) that Catholic ritual was the result of belief rather than its cause. In fact, it was Gill who recognised both himself and Pepler, to be 'born Catholic'. The drama of the Mass was one of a piece with Pepler's growing interest in the theatre and in the masks and puppets he began to make, and even put to the service of religious symbolism. In *A Ditchling Childhood*, Susan Falkner writes revealingly about her father in this regard:

> The two great influences in my father's life were religion and the stage, and one can see how the drama of the Catholic ritual and liturgy must have appealed to him. Indeed, he often told me that he regarded the rites of the Mass as a formalised dance. Perhaps the building up of a small Catholic community appealed to his sense of drama ....[80]

Pepler himself wrote on this precise theme. His essay, 'Liturgical Drama', of 1934, made a plea for the return into local churches of dramatic forms such as the procession, mime and the medieval Mystery Play. He considered his own theatre craft – *The Oxford Movement* was one such piece – to be a continuum with the medieval tradition. 'The sanctuary is the ecclesiastical stage ...; the Church is the theatre', were his claims in this article. He ended:

> Drama began in the Church. So for our beginnings we have to turn to the divine crib with St. Francis and to the human crib with the Grimms, the Andersens and the Carrolls of this world ... surely a pleasant company of teachers.[81]

Given Johnston's and Pepler's contrasting dispositions – the rational as against the intuitive, the scientific as against the ritualistic, the measured as against the demonstrative – it was not just coincidental that they tended to gravitate towards two figures who were diametrically opposed. Johnston, it can be said, inherited the mantle of William Lethaby, while Pepler inherited, perhaps, the mantle of Father McNabb.

Lethaby pared away the anachronisms of earlier systems of thought in order to face the challenge of industrialisation. Far from leading a retreat into what Pepler called the 'Parish', Lethaby advocated the authentic expresssion of the 'scientific age', in the sense that the Gothic had been an authentic expression of a theological one. His view of design incorporated the value of tradition, of human equity and individual fulfilment. It advocated not a style, as such, but appropriate forms for design which would arise from the very materiality of the new society. While Johnston remained committed to the Arts and Crafts movement's rejection of industrialism, *per se*, his openness of mind predisposed him towards Lethaby's embryonic modernism.

In the years following Johnston's departure from the Common, two antithetical centres of thought co-existed in Ditchling, albeit in neighbourly civility, each with their corresponding links. The ethos of Johnston-Lethaby prevailed in the village, where Philip Mairet (himself a social scientist with an interest in psychoanalysis) replaced Gill and Pepler as Johnston's close companion, and where

Ethel Mairet found, in Johnston, a little-seen mentor. Two miles to the north, on the Common, there prevailed, at least until the late 'twenties, an axis of allegiance between Pepler and Father McNabb. Together, they made up the religious core of the Guild, and more so on the departure of Gill for Capel-y-ffin and Desmond Chute for Fribourg, Swizerland.

The contrast between Pepler and Johnston can also be sensed, to some degree, by distinctions between their respective craftwork. Concerning his developing interest in theatre, for example, Pepler spoke of the need to return to his own 'theatre storehouse', rather than be inspired by the new forms which he was aware of around him. In his article, 'The Liturgical Drama', he mentions – and plays down – the development of the new (formalist) Soviet cinema. His own theatrecraft returned, to 'the divine crib with St. Francis'. Nor is it insignificant that in his former interest, the S. Dominic Press, Pepler remained unchanging in his faith in the Caslon types and in what was, essentially, an eighteenth-century typography, influenced, no doubt, by the purism of Cobden-Sanderson's Doves Press which he knew from Hammersmith. From this perspective it is significant that Pepler never thought to develop the expressive layouts with which he had once toyed so promisingly in first book, *The Devil's Devices*.

Johnston's Block Letter alphabet, (Fig. 112) by contrast, while not without precedent in the history of letter-forms, was informed, even if unconsciously, by the all-pervading influence of Lethaby.

It is now appropriate to take this line of thought forward and suggest in greater detail the manner in which Johnston's temperament was expressed in his work as a lettering artist during his years at Ditchling.

ABCDEFG
HIJKLMNO
PQRSTUV
WXYZABCD
EFGHIJKLMNOP
QRSTUVWXYZ
abcdefghijklmn
opqrstuvwxyz

Fig. 112. Johnston's 'Railway' block alphabet.
(Reproduced with the courtesy of The Transport Museum. London.)

END NOTES

1 Archives of The Guild of St. Joseph & St. Dominic. NAAD archives. V&A Museum. (Ref: AAD 1989).

2 Father Conrad Pepler. 'A Community of Craftsmen'. In *The Dublin Review*. Winter. 1959. No. 482.

3 Archives of the English Province of the Order of Preachers. Blackfriars. 25 George Square. Edinburgh. (Ref: Ditchling Box 1.)

4. G. K. Chesterton. Preface to Fr Vincent McNabb, *Francis Thompson and other Essays*. (Pepler and Sewell. Ditchling Common) 1935.

5. Bernard Wall. *Headlong into Change: an autobiography and memoir of ideas since the Thirties*. (London Harvill) 1969.

6. Marianne Jacoby and P. Marshall, respectively, cited from Ferdinand Valentine's biography, *Father Vincent McNabb. O.P. The Portrait of a great Dominican*. (Burns & Oates. London) 1955.

7. Cited from F. Valentine. Op. cit.

8. Cited from E. A. Siderman. *With Father McNabb at Marble Arch*. (Blackfriars) 1947.

9. *Encyclical Letters of Pope Leo XIII*. Op. cit.

10. *Encyclical Letters of Pope Leo XIII*. Op. cit.

11. *Encyclical Letters of Pope Leo XIII*. Op. cit.

12. *Encyclical Letters of Pope Leo XIII*. Op. cit.

13. *Encyclical Letters of Pope Leo XIII*. Op. cit.

14. *Encyclical Letters of Pope Leo XIII*. Op. cit.

15. E. A. Siderman. *A Saint in Hyde Park. Memories of Father Vincent McNabb*. (Geoffrey Bles. London) 1950.

16. E. A. Siderman. *A Saint in Hyde Park. Memories of Father Vincent McNabb*. Op. cit. Siderman was McNabb's long-standing heckler. His graphic and sympathetic account of Father Vincent McNabb's Sunday afternoon preaching from the Catholic Evidence Guild's pitch at Marble Arch is given in an earlier study, *With Father McNabb at Marble Arch*. (Blackfriars Publications) 1947.

17. Father Vincent McNabb. *The Church and the Land*. (Burns Oates and Washbourne)

1926.
18. Donald Attwater. *A Cell of Good Living*. (London. Geoffrey Chapman) 1969.
19. Father Vincent McNabb. 'Religious Obedience'. In *Blackfriars*. October. 1930.
20. Cited by A. Cunningham. 'The Nature of Work in the Thought of Eric Gill and Vincent McNabb'. In *The Chesterton Review*. Vol. XI. No. 3. August 1985.
21. *The Game*. No 2. Vol. 4. 1919.
22. A further indication of the impact of Father McNabb's teaching of the *Rerum Novarum* on the Guild on Ditchling Common is the pamphlet which Pepler printed in 1937, some ten years after McNabb's connections with Ditchling ceased. It is called *Notes on Rerum Novarum compiled by a student from talks of Fr. Vincent McNabb*. (Ditchling. Ditchling Press) 1937.
23. Eric Gill. *Diary*. William Andrews Clark Library. UCLA. Microfiche at the Tate Gallery.
24. Eric Gill. *Diary*. 4th, 5th, 6th, and 7th October. 1917. Op. cit.
25. Pepler's manuscript recollections cited by Brocard Sewell 'Hilary Pepler 1878–1951'. In *The Aylesford Review*. Spring 1965.
26. The Meynells were a large and closely integrated Catholic family; Wilfrid and his wife, the poet Alice Meynell, had long been Gill's friends; they were the uncle and aunt of Gerard Meynell, who was Johnston's friend.
27. Eric Gill. *Autobiography*. (Jonathan Cape). 1940.
28. Archive of the Guild of St. Joseph and St. Dominic. NAAD archives at the V&A Museum. (Ref: ADD/1989/2/2/3/7.)
29. Eric Gill. *Diary*. 12th June 1917. Op.cit.
30. A fragment of a letter written by Priscilla Johnston to Robert Speaight on the occasion of the publication of his biography of Gill, in 1966, and now held in the archives of the Order of Preachers, in Edinburgh, is illuminating about the position of Clare Pepler. It reads:

> As you have clearly recognised for yourself, [Robert Speaight] Mr. Pepler was a powerful character, and, in fact, a somewhat overbearing man. He was absolutely determined that his wife was to become Catholic, but her religion was important to her and she could not change it just to please him. – (How Mary Gill made this difficult transition with apparently no trouble? – I have always wanted to know.) In Mrs. Pepler's case the struggle was long and really agonising. We knew later something of her difficulties because my mother was her chief confidant at the time. The children were all baptised into the Catholic Church and she felt they were being taken away from her. The house was filled with priests and Catholic enthusiasts and she must have felt they were conspiring against her. Worst of all, her husband gave her no peace. Who wouldn't be petulant? I wish now I had dealt with this point in my own book. I think I felt at the time it was not essential and might be distressing to the Peplers. I don't know how much they knew about it ....

(Archives of the English Province of the Order of Preachers. Edinburgh. Ditchling Box 1.102.)
31. Crafts Study Centre Collection and Archive. Farnham, Surrey. Johnston archive. (Ref: Letters. 2/Loan 44.)
32. Idem. (Ref: Letters 2/Loan 45.)
33. Idem. (Ref: Letters 2/Loan 28.)
34. Cited by Priscilla Johnston. *Edward Johnston*. 1959.
35. A letter from McNabb to Clare Pepler dated the very same day, 1st May 1923, clearly alludes to her conversion: 'My dear child. Thank you for the butter. It was a good offering. I can't say how much I have been touched by your thinking you will be nearer to Douglas than ever – in the love and life of God. May God love and bless you both. Pray for me. Yours sincerely in J.C. Fr. Vincent McNabb.O.P. From the Archives of the

Order of Preachers. Edinburgh. (Ref. Ditchling Box 1.)
36. *The Game.* Vol. 2. No. 1. 1918. University of Cambridge Library. Rare Books Room.
37. *The Game.* Vol. 2. No. 1. Op. cit.
38. Edward Johnston in *The Game.* Vol. 2. No. 1. Op. cit.
39. Eric Gill. *Diary.* Op. cit.
40. Eric Gill. *Diary.* Entries for 27th, 28th, 29th, 30th, and 31st July 1918. Op. cit.
41. A retreat for mentally ill Catholics. It was established and built by Belgian sisters. Father Vincent McNabb's connections with Louvain, Belgium, warmed him to the St. George's Retreat.
42. Father Conrad Pepler. 'In Diebus Illis'. In *The Chesterton Review.* Nov. 1982.
43. Gill's letter, which primarily concerned any enquiry by Robert Bridges about engraving, was passed on to him by Johnston. Bodleian Library. Dep Bridges. III Fols 36–84. MS.61.
44. A document held in the Archives of the Order of Preachers, in Edinburgh, states: 'Sold to Eric Gill and Douglas Pepler ... and remaining lands of Bull's Barn Farm, with the erections thereon. An area of 163 acres, 1 rood and 33 poles or thereabouts. For the sum of seven thousand pounds to be completed on the 19th September 1919. (Ref: Gill/Pepler correspondence.). Another source records: 'land owned by Brs. E. G. and D. P. in trust for the community (ie Fragbarrow farm)'. See: Minutes Book of the Tertiaries of S. Dominic of Ditchling Common. July 1919–Dec. 1922. (Meeting of the 10th July 1920). NAAD, V&A at Blythe House. (Ref. AAD/1989/2/2/2/1.)
45. Eric Gill. *Diary.* Op. cit.
46. Eric Gill. *Diary.* Op. cit. The minutes of the meetings of the Tertiaries of S. Dominic on Ditchling Common for 10th June 1920 record that "D.P, D.C, T. Shove, and Sr. M.G, 'agreed that to free ourselves from the loan to the bank, by which the land was purchased, a number of mortgages shd. be affected 1. upon the security of the farmland and 2. upon the security of several plots of building land. Agreed that Bro. D.P. shd prepare and print a statement of our purpose and intentions and that this statement shd be sent to those who might be willing to lend us money upon personal security thus enabling us to obtain the margin of difference between the total value of the land and the sum obtained on mortgage (this is estimated to be about £2000, the total value being about £5000.) NAAD. V&A at Blythe House. (Ref. AAD/1989/2/2/2/1.)
47. The Spoil Bank Association document. NAAD of the V&A at Blythe House.
48. *The Game.* Vol. IV. No. 9. (S. Dominic's Press. Ditchling) 1921.
49. Joseph Cribb's manuscript diary. (1921–1930). Photocopy held in the Archives, Edinburgh.
50. *The Game.* (S. Dominic's Press. Ditchling) Vol. IV. No. 9. September 1921.
51. *The Game.* Op. cit.
52. *The Game.* Op. cit.
53. *The Game.* Op. cit.
54. The Spoil Bank Association Ltd was

> 'to be formed for the purpose of creating a "leagl' person to hold and administer the property of the Guild for the Guild and that all Guild members to be members of the Company and vice versa'.

Minute Book of the Tertiaries of St. Dominic of Ditchling Common. 1919–22. The Archive of the Guild of St. Joseph and St. Dominic. NAAD archives at the V&A at Blythe House. (Ref. AAD 1989 2/2/2/1.)
55. The Memorandum of Association. Clause 3 (1) of the document specified the 'sale of freehold lands and buildings to the Company by: Desmond Chute (£1,500); Mr Pepler (£650); Gill and Pepler (£1400) paid in the form of debentures to the Vendors. Interest on the debentures at 6% redeemable on the 29th September 1926, or earlier.' NAAD of the V&A, at Blythe House. (Ref. AAD/1989 2/1/1/2.)
56. However, the idea of removing to a more remote location was in Gill's mind earlier than this. Gill's minute of a meeting with Pepler and Cribb in 1921, records: '...

the question of Crappagh Island [Galway, Ireland] and the possible removal thereto of some or all of the brothers of the Guild .... It was agreed that there was nothing in the Guild's constitution to imply that all the Brothers shd live and work on Ditchling Common'. Minute Book of the Tertiaries of St. Dominic of Ditchling Common. (1919–22). NAAD of the V&A at Blythe House. (Ref. AAD/1989/2/2/2/1.)
57. McNabb's letter of the 24th June 1924, to Pepler, comforting Pepler at the split with Gill and the break-up of the Guild, reveals McNabb's sympathies: 'The crisis was inevitable. A work which aimed so simply at the worship of God was surely to be the object of a deep-laid and lasting plot of the enemy of God. The Devil's success with Judas has heartened him for all time. Archives of the English Province of the Order of Preachers. Edinburgh. (Ref: Ditchling Box 1.)
58. Letter at the Harry Ranson Humanities Research Center. University of Texas, at Austin. Texas.
59. The vacant Fragbarrow Farmhouse was then sold to Ernest Richmond, who was the son of the portrait painter, Sir William Richmond, himself a close neighbour of Pepler and Johnston in Hammersmith. This is another instance of a link between Hammersmith and Ditchling. Miss Hilary Bourne recalls a portrait of Edward Johnston by William Richmond hanging in Ernest Richmond's home, Fragbarrow Farmhouse.
60. Archive of the Guild of SS. Joseph and Dominic. NAAD archives at the V&A Museum (Blythe House). (Ref: AAD. 1989/2/141–207) Also for the next quotation.
61. Pepler's own explanation should be noted here. In an undated letter to Father McNabb he explained:

> '... Another point. The Press never earned my living, that was partly due to incompetence and partly to do with the condition of society. I should still be a printer had I been able to make ends meet by hand work. I could not be interested in any other kind. So, in a sense, it conveys the wrong impression to say that I left the Press, it would be more true to say that the Press left me.'

Archives of the English Province of the Order of Preachers. Edinburgh.
62. A description of the funeral written in all likelihood by Joseph Cribb is held in the Archives of the English Province of the Order of Preachers, at Edinburgh.
63. The phrase was used by a participant following a lecture on Pepler, written by Winefride Pruden, and given by Mr. and Mrs. Ian Clayton at Ditchling Museum, 5th November 1997.
64. However, a letter from Joseph Cribb to Pepler, sent to his London address, shows a marked change in this position. Archives of the English Province of the Order of Preachers. Edinburgh.
65. Father Conrad Pepler. 'Ditchling. A Community of Craftsmen'. In *The Dublin Review*. Spring 1959.
66. Priscilla Johnston. *Edward Johnston*. Op. cit.
67. Father Conrad Pepler. 'Ditchling. A Community of Craftsmen'. In *The Dublin Review*. Spring 1959.
68. Priscilla Johnston. *Edward Johnston*. Op. cit.
69. H. Pepler. *Sheepfolds and Shambles. Welfare Handbooks, No 9*. (S. Dominic's Press) 1922.
70. Father V. McNabb. 'Landwork and Handwork'. In *Blackfriars*. August 1943.
71. H. D. C. Pepler. The Reeve. In Blackfriars. 1941.
72. H. D. C. Pepler. *The Reeve*. Op. cit.
73. H. D. C. Pepler. *The Reeve*. Op. cit.
74. H. D. C. Pepler. *The Reeve*. Op. cit.
75. The comment is Father Valentine's, in his *Father Vincent McNabb. O.P. The portrait of a Great Dominican*. (London. Burns and Oates) 1955.
76. Father Conrad Pepler. 'In Diebus Illis: Some Memories of Ditchling'. In *Chesterton*

Review.Vol. VIII. No. 4. November 1982.
77. Philippe Mairet. *Autobiographical Compilation.* (Carcanet Publications) 1985.
78. In a conversation with Father Bede Bailey, archivist for the English Province of the Order of Preachers, at Blackfriars, 25 George Square, Edinburgh on 16th October 1998.
79. Antony Heath. The Guild of St. Joseph and St. Dominic. NAAD of the V&A at Blythe House. (Ref. AAD/1989/2/2/6/2–4.
80. Susan Falkner. *A Ditchling Childhood.* (Iceni Publications) 1994.
81. H. D. C. Pepler 'The Liturgical Drama'. In *Blackfriars* May 1934. Vol. XV. No. 170.

Robert Bridges 1912.

Mary Monica Bridges.

CHAPTER NINE

EDWARD JOHNSTON & ROBERT BRIDGES 1901–1926: A PHONETIC ALPHABET IN THE HALF-UNCIAL SCRIPT

Edward Johnston enjoyed a lasting friendship with the poet Robert Bridges and his wife, Mary Monica. They exchanged letters intermittently from 1901–26. In one Johnston wanted, he said, 'to send his love to Mrs Bridges but (lest that is a presumption) send my kind regards'. Priscilla Johnston wrote in the biography of her father that he 'retained a great affection and esteem' for Robert Bridges 'all his life'.

Much of their correspondence survives in the Bodleian Library[1] and provides information about the two projects which underpinned their friendship.

The earlier of these was the scheme Robert Bridges devised from 1901 for a phonetic script by which he sought to get over the vagaries of English spelling. (He lamented for example, that the sound *i* – as in *dye* – has, he counted, twenty-one variant spellings.) He asked Johnston to help design the new symbols he needed. Furthermore, both he and Mary Monica Bridges saw beauty in fine writing. They had introduced Johnston to the Half-Uncial hand and now, with the aid of his skill, they visualised their own alphabet dressed in it. The three worked at perfecting the letter-forms at intervals between 1901 and 1913. The result has been called, usefully, the 'Yattendon' script after the village in Berkshire where the Bridges first lived.[2] More information about the scheme comes from Bridges' letters to friends other than Johnston. Yet another source is a portfolio of fifteen manuscript sheets known as 'Calligraphy in Phonetic Script', which were once among Johnston's papers and are now in the V&A Museum (where they are numbered arbitrarily).[3] They show specimens of the symbols devised by Johnston and Bridges. Only two of the sheets are dated. The chronology of the rest and their significance can be deduced by correlating the symbols they show with what is said about them in the Bodleian correspondence. This chapter sets out to make that correlation. Johnston's letters also show his preference for his Foundational Hand over the Half-Uncial, a shift which the Bridges came to accept as the project developed. Not published before, Johnston's letters are valuable, too, for their philosophical asides and for their occasional insights into his domestic life. For these reasons they are quoted in full in this chapter.

The later and shorter project is the portfolio called *English Handwriting* which Bridges compiled as Tract No. XXIII of the Society for Pure English in 1926. Johnston contributed to it a specimen of his Foundational Hand which is illustrated in the frontispiece of the tract.

For Bridges the phonetic symbols used in dictionaries would not do. They were too remote from existing spelling to be useful and had little aesthetic appeal. He explained his intentions for his own system in a letter to his friend Lionel Muirhead. Accompanying it was a specimen demonstrating the script. (Fig 113). Though written in his own hand, as yet untrained, it nevertheless bears the clear influence of Mary Monica. She was a reformer of handwriting who proposed the adoption of the Italic hand in schools. Her knowledge and support in developing the phonetic letter-forms were indispensable: The letter discusses his writing a pamphlet; it reads:

> When ... left a little leisure I fell into my old scheme of phonetics, and Monica and I spent a bit of every evening writing out something in the new script.... The scheme however really works well, and the next thing that I do will be to bring out a pamphlet on it. The object of it is to have a script which shall be 1) purely phonetics. 2) more beautiful than the present script. 3) plainly intelligible to the eye, i.e., not much differing from our present mode of spelling. The reasons for it are 1) the absolute absurdity and inconvenience of present spelling 2) the certainty that some [other] phonetic system must eventually obtain – that it will be phonetically brutal, and horribly ugly. The rationale and justification are that I have imagined a lot of tricks which will get over the difficulties which have baffled etymologists, and believe that I can make a beautiful script.
>
> I have great encouragement in this, that I surprise and convince the learned sceptic. I do not think that a specimen would be of much interest without a few explanations but here is one.[4]

Just three days later, on 30th August 1901, Mary Monica Bridges wrote to Johnston. She broached the subject of his designing just such a 'beautiful script':

> ... I write to ask you when you think we might have the pleasure of seeing you here; we want to talk about a new scheme with you – a notion for a modified and beautiful phonetics wh. we are interesting ourselves in now – it will require some new forms, and these we hoped you wd. assist in contriving.

Miusic when soft voices dį
Vibrats in the memory –
Odurs, when swet vjolets sicken
Liv within the sens they quicken;
Ros-levs when the ros is ded [ded]
Ar hep'd for the belvved's bed:
And so thj thauts when thou art gon,
Luv itself shal slumber on.

In this short extract there are 14 of my tricks. | Ꞇh and th (dh & th) | ü (for iu) | ḭ the new sign for the i sound in die- | R and r distinguished. | C for the ee sound- | E and e distinguished | ş = z | ơ and o distinguished (this last needs some explanation being the short o of horrid, which is short in or when or is before a vowel long when terminal or before a consonant as for and ford) | *a* and ɑ distinguished. and | ɇ the new sign for = ey = eh = a in fate [fɇt may be

Fig. 113. Continuation of Bridges' letter to Lionel Muirhead showing his first version of the phonetic symbols.
(Courtesy of University of Delaware Press. Newark.)

> If you wd. care to come down for a night or so (or a Saturday to Monday) will you let us know when you are likely to be free to come & I should hope that it wd. fit in with our plans wh. are not very definite after mid-September. With kind regards. Yours sincerely M. Monica Bridges.[5]

In the event Bridges' pamphlet did not materialise for some years. Nor immediately did Johnston's letter-forms. The year 1902 saw the Bridges constantly at work on the scheme (Fig. 114). Bridges' letters to friends indicate Johnston's involvement. One, written on the 15th June 1902 to Samuel Gee, claims: 'We have perfected our calligraphic phonetic writing and I hope I might get my book on it done by Christmas.'[6] On the 11th August he informed Henry Bradley: 'I think we have rubbed all the corners off the phonetic writing now. There were one or two symbols that made the script look a little obscure – these we have got rid of.'[7] Another of the 3rd October 1902 to Lionel Muirhead refers, if obliquely, to Johnston's involvement and implies how reassuring this was for Bridges:

> Our phonetic system is I think receiving its final touches and has been patronised in a quarter which will ensure its making its appearance in public ere very long. It meets with great favour.[8]

As to Bridges' own efforts he added: 'I have no practice in writing it yet and make many mistakes'. Although ultimately Bridges became proficient at Johnston's Half-Uncial hand, his struggle to master the craft was one of a number of problems which beset the project.

A more intractable problem still was the necessity to have printing types cut and cast in order for the script to be published. On the 9th October 1902 Bridges wrote to Henry Newbolt, the editor of the *Monthly Review,* the journal in which he now hoped his scheme would be launched:

> I have just written to Johnston, and sent him the new letters required to complete our alphabet. I expect that when he returns me he will have some suggestions about type.[9]

The same day – the 9th October 1902 – Bridges wrote to Johnston, sending him a revised alphabet – 'I enclose you a copy of it as it now stands revised'. There is little doubt that this 'copy' comprises the three small sheets which are now in the *Calligraphy in Phonetic Script* portfolio, Nos. 11–13:

> Henry Newbolt tells me he has seen you, and told you of his notion of bringing out the new phonetics in 'The Monthly Review'.
>
> This will have many advantages. He thought even that he might get a type cast by his printer, and tells me you thought that the type in which the Review is printed wd. do very well for a basis, using the letters which are common to the old and new systems out of that fount, and designing the new symbols to suit.
>
> This will require a good deal of consideration, for the fount is not really very good in all its forms, and if the new symbols are as good as they should be, they might not agree very well.
>
> But today I am writing about some necessary preliminary matters. Experience and criticism have led us to make a few alterations in this alphabet, but I think that its present state (I enclose you a copy of it as it stands revised) will be final.

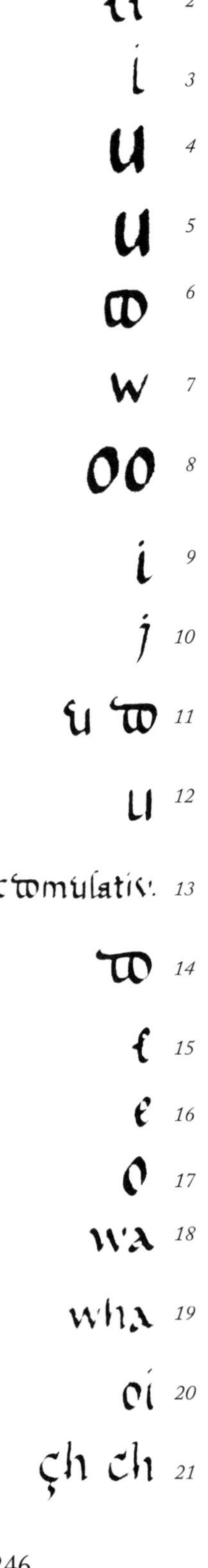

By comparing this new alphabet with your old one you will see what the alterations are: but I shall go through them one by one, with remarks about each new letter. What we want you to do is perfect these new forms so as to make them of a piece with the rest. [Numbers in text relate to numbers and letter-forms shown on the left.]

---

1. The first change is that we have given up our old symbols for the english e and ee (in the and green) the new one I want like this **e** (*1*) and **ee** (*2*) The cursive form wd be the old e written the and green, but the typical (Half-Uncial) shd be more like an **i** (*3*) somewhat as I have drawn it.

---

2. We have entirely revised the **U** s (*4*). The new forms are **U** (*5*) like the common u and **W** (*6*) which may look like **W** (*7*) or **O O** (*8*) as various words will suggest. Both these forms must have some initial kind of twiddle to represent the initial **i** (*9*) or **j** (*10*) sound when that occurs, say something like **U W** (*11*) These are the **U** (*12*) as in cumulative which will be written: . **CWMULATIV.** (*13*)

It will be necessary to design these twiddles so that they not only look well on the letter, but do not make the preceding letter stand away. You will have some fun in designing this **W** (*14*)(This initial sound will in writing be represented sometimes by the foregoing **e** (*15*) (i.e., where **e** (*16*) occurs in the present spelling in beautiful and few).

---

3. We have some most intelligent admirers, who like all the script except in one or two details – and we have given way to an objection against writing quality, was, what, wander, want with short **ò** (*17*) i.e., as quolity, wos, whot, wonder, wont.

Examination of all the words in which qua – wa – occur, shows that we can easily rely on a simple rule that qua, & wa are pronounced in a certain manner when written in ligature. So we want a ligature for qua and **wa** (*18*) and **wha** (*19*) as you will see in the revised alphabet. This task ought also to delight you.

---

4. The ligature **oi** (*20*) is an addition. It is for the eye – it has the same sound as oy.

---

5. We distinguish now between the soft and hard ch i.e., **çh ch** (*21*)
We hope you will have time to attend to these matters. As soon as you have done them we will get to work on the question of type. I hope that Mr. Newbolt was interested in your productions on vellum. Yours truly, Robert Bridges.[10]

Johnston's reply came on the 16th October 1902. Although he did not address the revisions that Bridges proposed, the letter does shows that Johnston shared Bridges' reservations about casting types from the Baskerville type face. (It shows, too, that his thinking had been influenced by Emery Walker's legendary lecture of 1888 in which he spoke of the usefulness of enlarging the letters photographically as an aid to their design):

Mr. Newbolt came a week or so ago and I told him that I should be able to devise the new forms in keeping with the 'Bodoni' type which is used in the Monthly Review. Of course it is a degraded type, and the natural pen letters would have to pass through a process of degradation. But it would be fairly easy to make them match by having enlarged photographs of the 'Bodoni' type to work from. This plan has the one – and great – advantage of letting the 'blow fall' less startlingly. But I think it would be as well at the same time to reproduce a small piece of writing to enforce the aesthetic value of the new phonetics. I have not had time to go over the new alphabets but I hope to do so on Sunday. When Newbolt came I was about to leave for Dinner (before a class) and there was no time to show him anything. I trust he did not think me

> discourteous, as I was somewhat distracted by the thought of the possibility of a meal rapidly vanishing.
>
> Tomorrow I have to demonstrate (for the second time) to sign writers, lithographers and others at the School 'of Art' Leicester: a 'course' of three demonstrations. With kind regards to Mrs Bridges. PS. Two 'sheets' of this session enclosed.[11]

Little progress took place with Henry Newbolt, editor of the *Monthly Review*. The Half-Uncial letter-forms that Johnston practised at that time were assimilated by Bridges into his own handwritten script. He wrote it with increasing competence even though at first he used a steel pen while seated in 'an armchair by the fire'.[12]

The phonetic script had an immediate application to Bridges' work for during 1902 he was completing his poem 'Now in Wintry Delights (Epistle I to L.M)'. This, the first poem in his volume entitled *Poems in Classical Prosody*, was written in classical hexameters. Appropriately enough, therefore, Bridges then set about transcribing 'Now in Wintry Delights' into the phonetic script by hand, for throughout he was frustrated in his desire to print it in this way by the impracticality of casting the types. It was therefore settled that the poem would be printed conventionally by his friend Henry Daniel at his private Daniel Press in Oxford and that a facsimile of a handwritten extract would be included as a demonstration.[13] Clearly, Johnston was the best-qualified person to write such a specimen. A further problem, however, was to keep Johnston motivated. On 11th October 1902 Bridges wrote to Henry Newbolt, still hopeful he might publish his article.

> I would never expect that you would find you could go in for type casting. Perhaps when some facsimiles are out I may find a millionaire who would like to do it. I think I shall get Daniel to print my Epistle in plain English with a facsimile page of phonetic MS. Meanwhile I shall try to get Johnston to work. Please go to see him sometimes – and make him show you his MSS. of various kinds.[14]

The urgency he felt comes through in another letter Bridges wrote on the 15th November 1902, this time to his friend, the Oxford classicist Henry Bradley:

> Before I left home I finished my hexameter Epistle. It ran into 430 odd lines.... I am now amuzing [*sic*] myself by transcribing it in my phonetic. I shall ... go on translating into phonetics for 2 or 3 weeks.... Daniel will print my poem in newspaper spelling, but I should like to have one page of phonetics facsimiled and bound with his text, but I may not have got the whole alphabet in final order in time for him.[15]

On 17th December 1902 he wrote again to Henry Newbolt. The last, and by now terse, sentence speaks volumes:

> I have written out a passage of my phonetic script and sent it to Clarendon press [*sic*] to be facsimiled and bound up with the volume. It looks very well, and I think it will launch the phonetics most favourably.
>
> I could not get any work out of Johnston: so I did it myself.[16]

But Bridges kept on at Johnston. Not unlike his other clients, Bridges was, by turns, encouraging, cajoling, suppliant. His letter of the 2nd February 1903 reads:

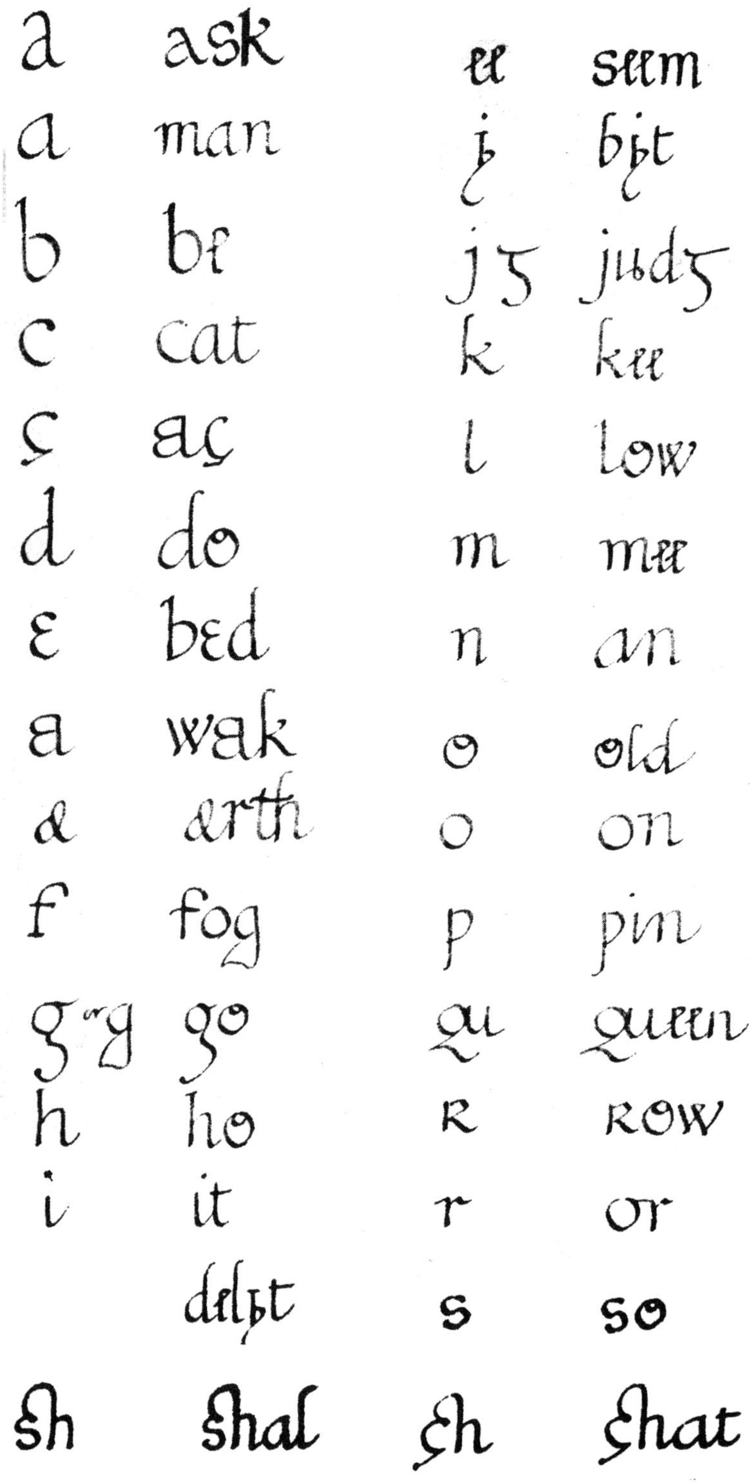

Fig. 114A. Robert Bridges' phonetic alphabet in its initial version as sent to Edward Johnston in October 1902.
(Courtesy of the NAL at the V&A. MSL 24/11–13–1982.)

We were very sorry not to get anything from you about Xmastime, but I hope that means you were usefully occupied.

We brought the phonetic script to a definite stage of perfection, to be I hope further perfected. I have written so much in it that I find it difficult to spell improperly.

Mr Daniel is bringing out a poem of mine written in Greek prosody – and as it does not look as if it scanned at all in the ordinary spelling, I wrote a page of it out in the new script, & I have had this facsimiled, and it will be bound up with the poem.

I am writing now to send you a proof of this page, which will be the first publication of the script. I shall be very curious to see what friends it gets.

I wish that we could have got you to do the writing for us, but it is perhaps as well to have shown that an ordinary mortal can write in it. I find it makes a very good cursive and does not look very odd.

Of course people will laugh at me – but I have written a note, printed with the poem, which will show them that the laugh is not all on their side.

We hope that we shall have your assistance in any future developments. Yours truly. Robert Bridges.

You must regard me as a sort of pupil – for you showed me how to make a pen and many of the forms are yours.[17]

Johnston acknowledged receiving the proof print (it is now in the *Calligraphy in Phonetic Script* portfolio),[18] though his actual letter (or post card, perhaps) does not appear to have survived. Bridges wrote again to Johnston on the 24th February 1903 entreating him further and giving details of improvements to his characters:

I was very glad to hear from you, I was afraid that you might be ill – also very glad you liked the MS. Of course I know how very far superior your writing is to mine – and I have been very sorry to be without your advice on matters of form of letters. The script goes on developing improvements – and I shd like to tell you what are the points on which I shd be glad of your assistance. [Numbers in text relate to numbers and letter-forms shown on p.250.]

First of all I have discarded the old shape **W** (*1*) which we decided on for the vowel of <u>but</u> and <u>come</u>. I found it near very messy in cursive writing, and did not look well unless it was very well made. Also it had an elaborate appearance which was needless and misleading. The forms which I adopted for it **V** (*2*) has the advantage that it might later degenerate into an imperfect **a** (*3*) thus **v** (*4*) – which is its true sound. But if you will look at the facsimile you will see whether you can improve it.

Also I think that the form which I used for the **U** (*5*) of union i.e., yu was a makeshift. I want a mark to suggest something pronounced before the common **U** (*6*). I made it something like this **U** (*7*). It is important that the hook should not keep other letters off. Also it shd be if possible a sign which might be put in front of the big **U** = **W** (*8*). I like some of those you sent very much and will try them..

The chief latest change which I have made is in the **i** (*9*) (ee) sounds. I have them now thus –

i of hit (*10*)

e of **the**	**delight**
ee of **thee**	these two are the same – the **ee** (11) (is merely double **e** (*12*) of
ei of **evil**	the, which I want as much like an **i** (*13*) as an **e** (*14*) can be made and the **ee** (*15*) is meant to be a shortened form of the double **e** (*16*) (of the)

It is very convenient to have both forms, and I think we can very well contrive a single long **é** (= **í**) (*17*) **ee** (*18*) to look like **ee**.(*19*) Can you make anything of this? The original shd have as small a head as possible.

You asked a question about seint. – That is the old English spelling. Their and They are quite correctly spelt. Of their vowel combination I make **ei** = **a** (*20*) as in **slavery** (*21*) for **sleivery** (*22*) and **ey ey** (*23*) as **day** (*24*) for **dey** (*25*) – They are identical in sound. (**i** = **y**).(*26*)

I have encircled with red the letters with which I am in most need of assistance to make – The **W** (*27*) with the hook (as in beauty **bWty**) (*28*) is not at present needed, as I write it with the **e** (*29*) of the. Thus **beWty**, (*30*) **feW**. (*31*)

Glad to hear good news of your fiancee [*sic*]. Margaret [Bridges' daughter] is deeply touched by your remembrance of her magazine. Yours sincerely, R. Bridges.

Excuse my hasty writing & very bad. Any Sunday that you cd come down we shd be of course delighted and cd do a deal of work.

It seems that these entreaties were not heeded. *Now in Wintry Delights* was printed at the Daniel Press in March 1903.[19] The illustration used was Bridges' own specimen in which he achieved a good Johnstonian Half-Uncial hand. (Fig. 115). He was to include the same specimen in his tract *English Handwriting* in 1926.

Though contacts between Bridges and Johnston tailed off after March 1903, they revived in 1910 again – at Bridges' initiative. His paper on his scheme had not materialised in Newbolt's *Monthly Review* and by 1904 the journal had in any case folded. Bridges' ambition was only realised in 1910 when his paper *On The Present State of English Pronunciation* was printed in the volume *Essays and Studies by the Members of the English Association*.[20] This was his opportunity to acknowledge the work Johnston had done for him. Just as he had included a facsimile of his phonetic script in his own hand in the volume *Now in Wintry Delights* of 1903, he now inserted a facsimile of the specimen calligraphed by Johnston (dating from 1902) in his paper of 1910. It transcribes the first of Bridges' *Epitaphs*.[21] (Fig 116).

When thou, my belovèd diedst, I saw Heaven open,

And all earthly delight inhabiting Paradise.

Evidently, Bridges had written to Johnston asking him to make available this specimen which was written in tenth-century minuscule hand. While Bridges' letter has not come to light, Johnston's reply came on the 5th July 1910:

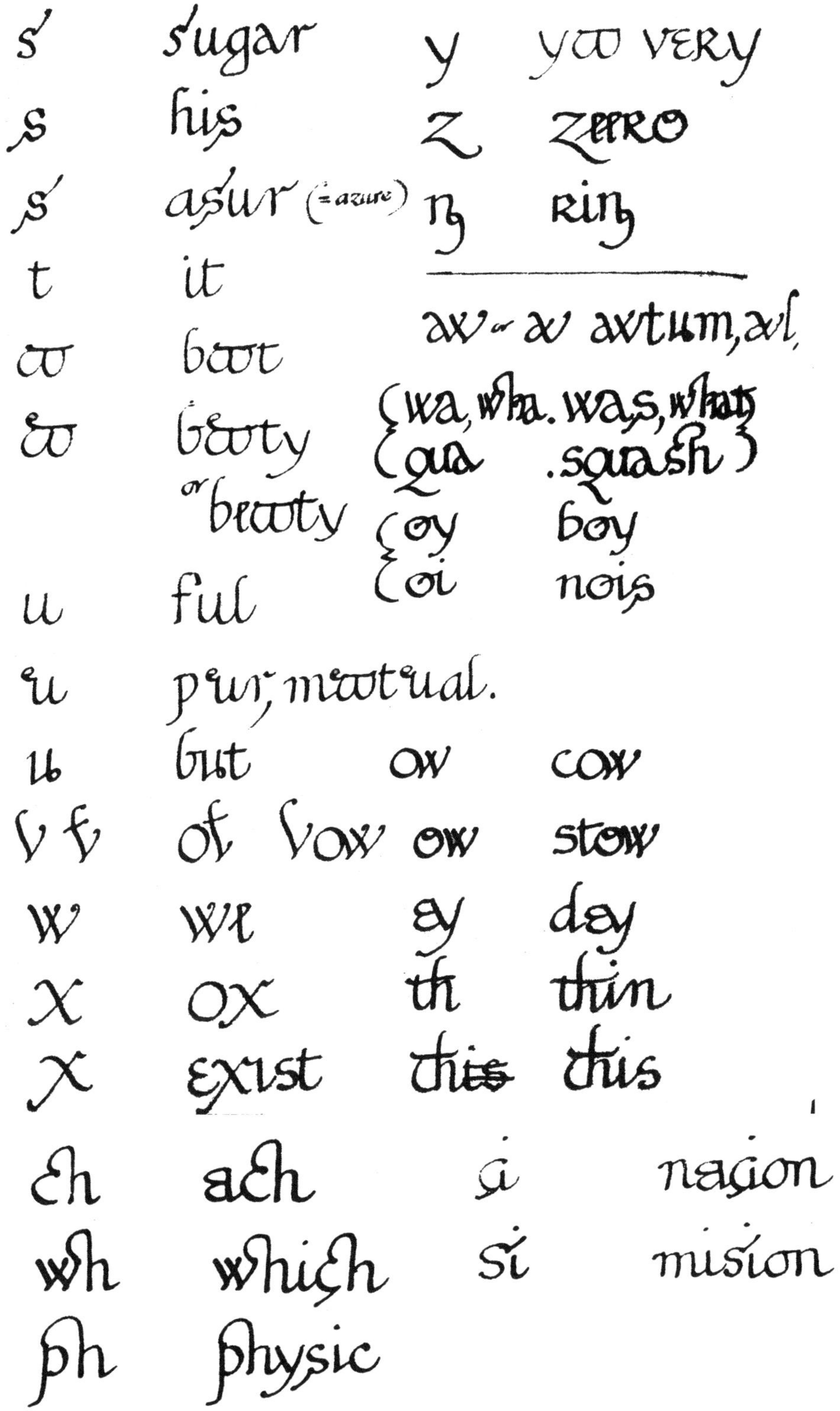

Fig. 114B. Robert Bridges' phonetic alphabet in its initial version as sent to Edward Johnston in October 1902.
(Courtesy of the NAL at the V&A. MSL 24/11-13-1982.)

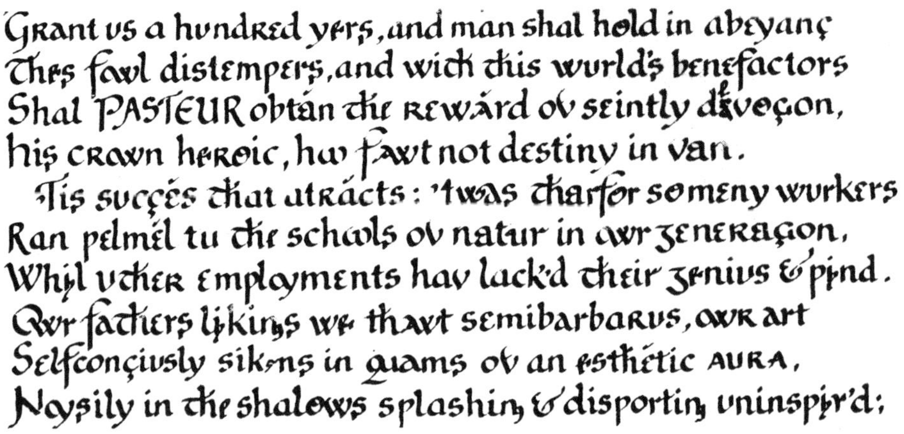

Fig. 115. Extract from the poem by Robert Bridges, 'Now in Wintry Delights', printed at the Daniel Press in 1903. The specimen was written by Bridges in his Half-Uncial script to demonstrate his phonetic system.

Grant us a hundred yers, and man shal hold in abeyanç
Thes fowl distempers, and with this wurld's benefactors
Shal PASTEUR obtán the reward ov seintly devoçon,
his crown heroic, haw fawt not destiny in van.
'Tis succés that atrácts: 'twas therfor so meny wurkers
Ran pelmél tu the schools ov natur in owr generaçon,
Whil uther employments hav lack'd their genius & pind.
Owr fathers likings we thawt semibarbarus, owr art
Selfconçiusly sikens in guams ov an esthétic AURA,
Noysily in the shalows splashin & disportin uninspir'd;

It is very kind of you to write to me about the phonetics: of course I should be proud to see one of those experiments in your article. It is obtainable, I hope, by an outsider? This sounds so like asking – please let me have the name of the publication only – & I shall try to get a copy.

Only two days ago I came across the proof you gave me of part of your poem on Pasteur [*Now on Wintry Delights*] wh. is a great favourite of mine and looks much better than any scribbling wh. I did.

I have often thought of your scheme and wondered what you would do with it and whether it might ever take practical shape – its 'shape' and knowing it seeming to me so good that I feared it was too good ever to be used. But general literacy appears to be fixing things checking changes in sounds perhaps, and giving new literal pronunciation to Names (such as Cirencester, Theobald's & many others*) so the materialistic reformers will very soon be wreaking themselves on spelling – and anything which may turn their hearts – or other people's – may be invaluable.

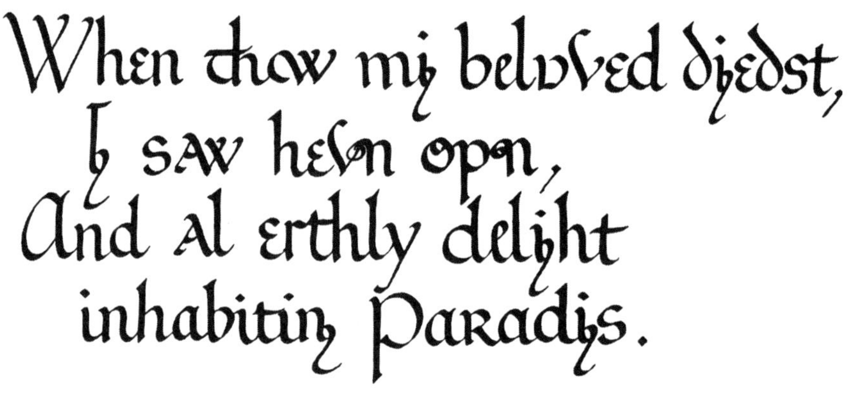

Fig. 116. 'Epitaph', poem by Robert Bridges'. Specimen written by Edward Johnston in 1902 showing Bridges' phonetic system. It was facsimiled by collotype at the OUP for Bridges' article 'On the Present State of English Pronunciation of 1910', in *Studies and Essays by the Members of the English Association*.
(Courtesy of the OUP.)

When thow mi beluved diedst,
I saw hevn opn,
And al erthly delight
inhabitin Paradis.

> I doubt whether the present tendency to literal pronunciation is a healthy one and don't suppose for a moment that it will save the old spelling – but rather the reverse.* also 'Two-pence' 'Three-pence' etc in some of the Board Schools.[22]

With his article in the press, Bridges replied to Johnston on July 7th (1910), from his new home, 'Chilswell House', at Boar's Hill, Oxford:

> Thank you for your kind letter. I send you a copy of the reproduction which I hope will appear in my article. I shall try to get some copies given me, and if I am successful will send you one: the paper may amuze [*sic*] you, and I shall appreciate your general approval. Our phonetic has been produced at the Clarendon Press, but not in the style in which it was designed. I found an old Anglo Saxon fount there, which seemed to be good enough to go on, and adapted my symbols to it, and borrowed from other founts, which does not sound well, and we do not think it very satisfactory, but it is not bad, and it has cost nothing; whereas the making of a type was entirely beyond our means. What we have done will seem very well for an experiment – and the facsimile of your lovely penmanship will show how beautiful it all might have been.... I hope you will have a pleasant holiday. I am so sorry to hear so little of you that you have become almost impossible to reckon with: any domestic details that you think well to favour me with will be acceptable. We are all well, and quite settled down in our new home. I am ashamed to write so badly, but Michel Angelo could write worse if he was pressed. My wife joins in warm remembrances. Yours sincerely, Robert Bridges.[23]

The 'copy' is No. 8 in the V&A portfolio. A footnote to Bridges' article says:

> The facsimile is of the penmanship of Mr. E. Johnston, written when he was assisting me many years ago in my experiments on the forms of new letters, etc. It shows perfectly the artistic effect that was aimed at, but differs in several details from my present alphabet.

Up to 1910, this was the sole occasion when Johnston's 'experiments' were used by Bridges. They were superseded because of Johnston's dilatoriness and because he resolved the problem of the types. As he explained in his letter, Bridges used an Anglo Saxon fount known as the 'Elstob types' which Hart had discovered for him among the 'Fell types'. The extensive adaptations made by Mary Monica Bridges to this fount answered adequately Bridges' needs.[24] (Figs. 117–119).

In his 1910 paper Bridges warned of the '... condition of advanced decay of the pronunciation of English', especially with its unaccented vowels. He argued that the remedy was to fix English pronunciation by replacing current spelling with a phonetic alphabet, thereby '... removing the pronunciation from the spelling'. He advocated that his system should be taught in schools. He opposed a rival system that had been developed by Daniel Jones in his book *Phonetic Transcriptions of English Prose*, of 1907. With an eye evidently still on Johnston, Bridges looked forward to a 'good-looking phonetic alphabet'. He thought that an 'æsthetic phonetics would be easily intelligible'.

Subsequent correspondence shows Johnston to have indeed worked further to this end. By 1912 Bridges was preparing a second and enlarged edition of his essay of 1910. He intended to illustrate it with more facsimiles of specimens of his phonetics, handwritten in the Half-Uncial style. A letter to Johnston, undated but which was evidently written early in 1912, tried to get Johnston interested again:

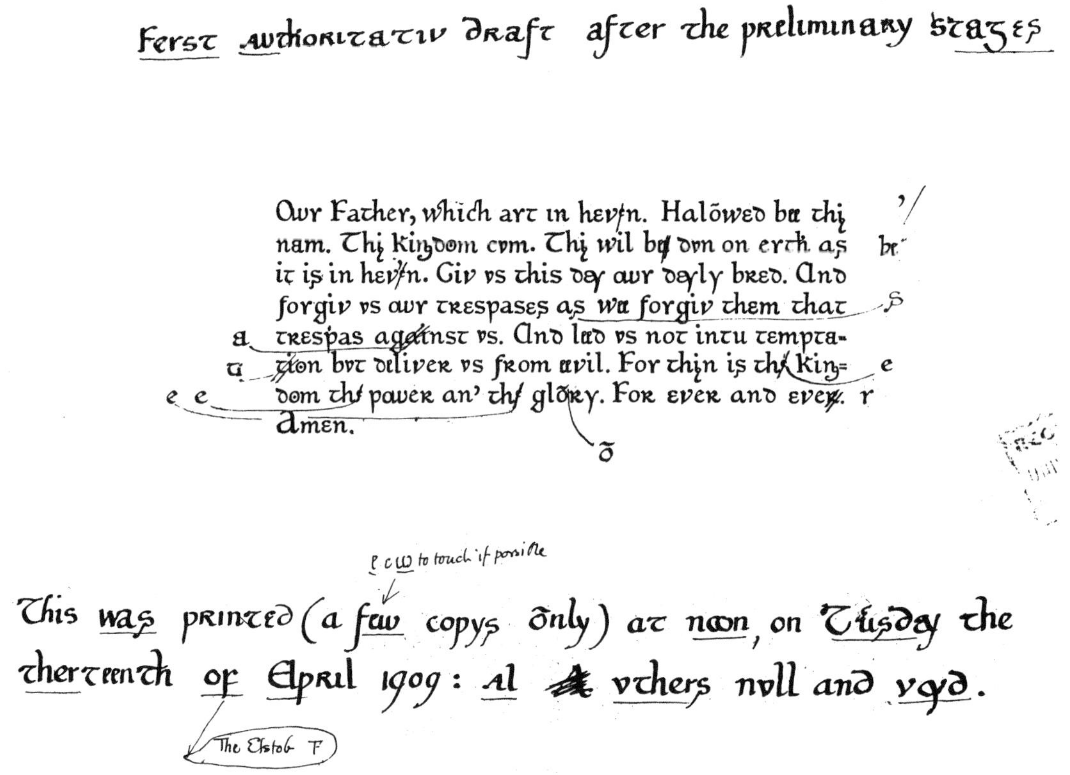

Ferst authoritativ draft after the preliminary stages

Our Father, which art in hevn. Halowed be thi nam. Thi kingdom com. Thi wil be don on erth as it is in hevn. Giv us this dey our deyly bred. And forgiv us our trespases as we forgiv them that trespas against us. And led us not intu temptation but deliver us from evil. For thin is the kingdom thi power an' thi glory. For ever and ever. Amen.

This was printed (a few copys only) at noon, on Tuesday the therteenth of April 1909: al others null and void.

Fig. 117. Monica Bridges' amendments to a proof page of the Elstob typeface with the additional phonetic characters, printed by Horace Hart at the OUP in 1909.

> I am getting ready a new edition of my essay on Phonetics and I shall have several pages of facsimiles of my way of writing it adapted to practical use. I want also to show it in its best form, and I am writing to you to ask whether you wd. have the leisure to write me one 8vo page. As I shd. wish the letters to be as big as they were in the specimen that I gave in the original issue there wd. not be much to write, and it wd. only be a question of a reed pen and I would send you a copy of the sentences that I wanted you to write carefully showing all of the final forms of the letters.
>
> If you are at home, & will undertake this I will write it out for you and send it. I shd. wish you to write 'Copied by Ed Johnston' in the corner and you can charge your proper fee.
>
> Any chance of seeing you here this year? I hope the children are well and Mrs Johnston, to whom my kindest regards in which salutations to yourself my wife joins. Yours truly, Robt. Bridges.[25]

Bridges' next letter came on the 3rd June 1912. It had three enclosures: the 'old copy', 'my [new] copy', and 'letter-forms on another page to remind you of the old

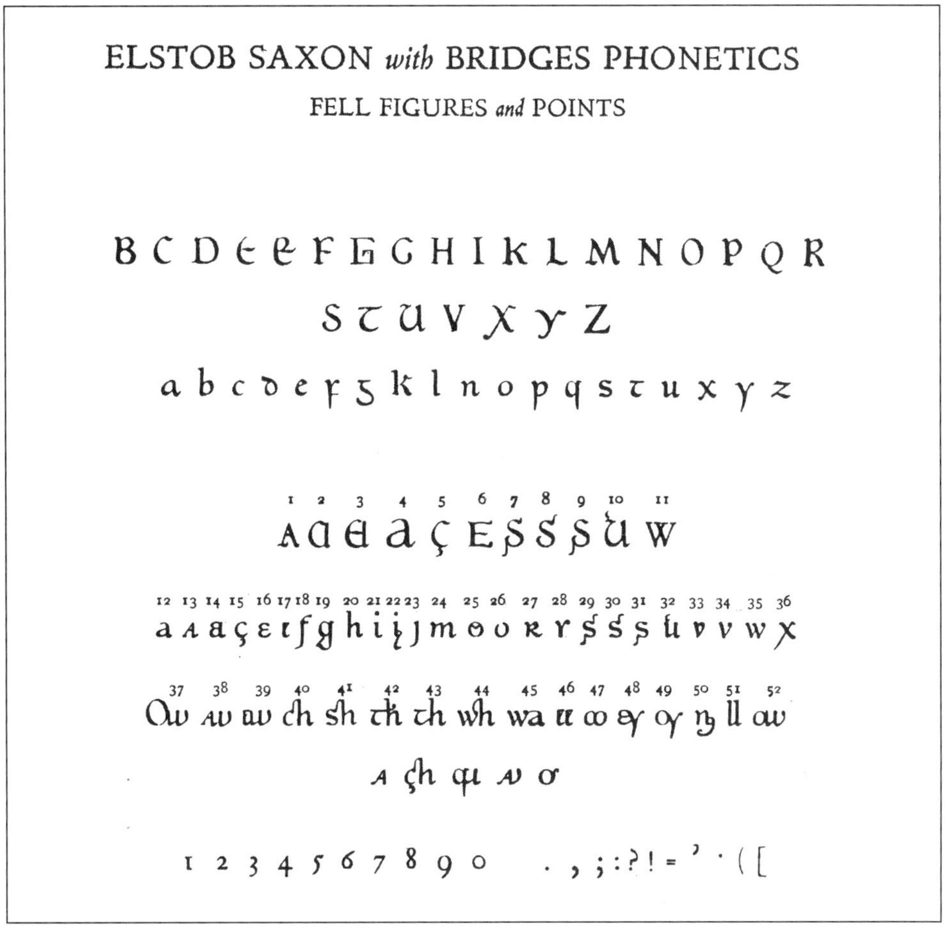

ELSTOB SAXON *with* BRIDGES PHONETICS

FELL FIGURES *and* POINTS

Fig. 118. The characters designed by Monica Bridges between 1908–10 added to the Elstob fount.

alphabet'. The first item corresponds to sheet No. 9 in the V&A portfolio, where the character '·' is a new one. Of it Bridges wrote: 'I write battle **bat·l**.' The second item corresponds to sheet No. 7. Bridges still wanted the script to be in Half-Uncial. He was also concerned how the facsimiles might be incorporated into the octavo format of the forthcoming book. He did not wish to repeat the folded sheet he used in 1903 for the facsimile in the Daniel Press volume, *Now in Wintry Delights*.

> I send you a copy of the old page. The alphabet has changed a little since you wrote that early experiment, and I will show you the differences that you will have to make in forms of letters.
>
> I want the new facsimile to show the script in Half-Uncial (I am going to write other specimens of its court hand and cursive).
>
> For this purpose I think the tails above the line are rather too long in the old facsimile and you wd. no doubt make them shorter without this criticism.

al the world's a stag,
and al the men and wimen merly players:
They hav their exits and their entrances;
and on man in his tim plays many parts,
His acts bein sev'n ages. At ferst the infant,
Müling and püking in the nurses arms.
Then the whining skoolboy, with his satchel,
and shining morning fac, creeping lik snail

Fig. 119. Extract from Shakespeare printed in Bridges' essay of 1912 as a specimen of the phonetic alphabet set in the Elstob fount.
(Courtesy of OUP and The English Association.)

> I wish you to follow your own bent – and if it is easier to get soft effect with big work it might be well to write your 'copy' large and have it photographed down. But you must do what you think best.
>
> What I cannot make up my mind about is the size of the page. I do not like a folded sheet, but it will be necessary to have a folded sheet unless you think the effect of the writing will not be lost by being reduced.
>
> It seems to me that it wd. be best to make your copy the shape of the single 8vo. page, and then consider if it shall be reduced to that size in reproduction, or presented on a folding page double that size.
>
> I have just now written out my copy. I hope you will be able to work from it. I send some letter-forms on another page to remind you of the old alphabet. I think you might as well make a rough draft for us to see, as mistakes are possible after so long an interval to say nothing of new devices.
>
> Of course I will answer any questions. Yours sincerely, Robert Bridges.[26]

Johnston then sent Bridges some trial specimens, including the 'rough draft'. It seems these, too, are among the undated sheets in the *Calligraphy in Phonetic Script* portfolio. Sheet No. 4 shows the entire specimen page (not illustrated). It is a transcript of the seven lines that Bridges intended to have facsimiled as an extract from his poem 'Ibant Obscuri'. This poem is a paraphrase which Bridges made in

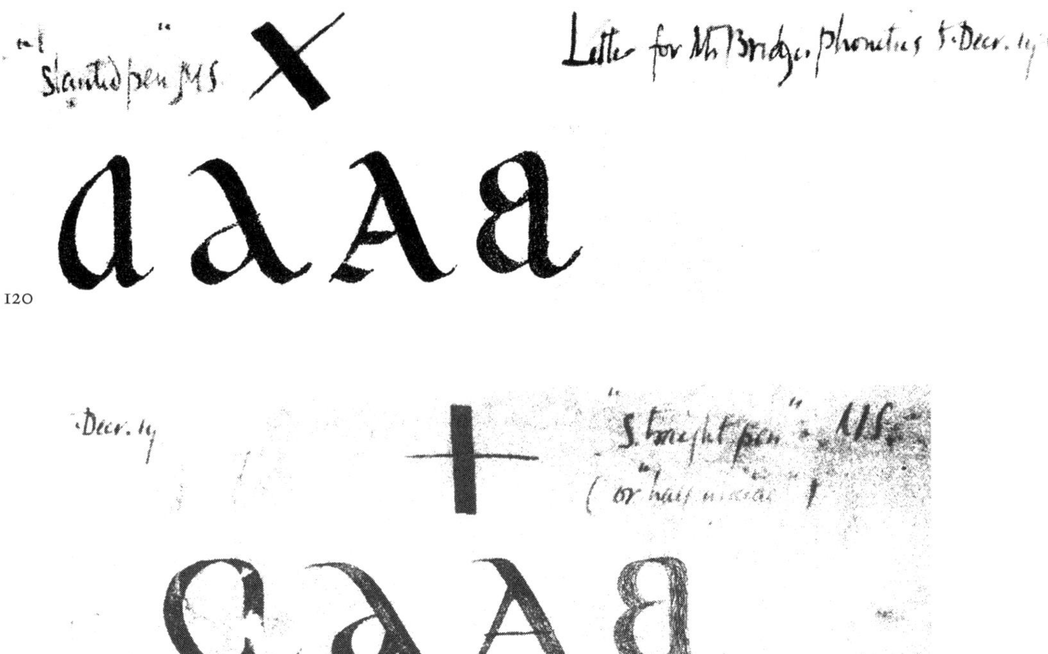

Figs. 120–121. Two details from Johnston's trial letter-forms showing the 'straight pen' Half-Uncial forms and the 'slanted pen' tenth-century minuscule forms of the capital A.
Sheets Nos. 5 & 6 (December 1912) from the *Calligraphy in Phonetic Script* portfolio in the V&A Museum.

1905 of part of Book VI of Virgil's *Aeneid*.[27] Below this Johnston placed the two 'Epitaph' poems which also appear in the facsimile. The specimen is 'in the shape of the single 8vo. page' and is in the Half-Uncial script that Bridges wanted – with characteristic thick vertical and thin horizontal strokes. Bridges corrected a number of Johnston's letter-forms by crossing them through with pen. For example, to the character A he added a curly serif to the base of its right-hand stroke.

Another sheet in the V&A portfolio that Johnston may have sent at this time is No. 3 (unillustrated). It is not annotated by Johnston. It shows alternative ligature letter-forms, for example, for the ç. Bridges returned these sheets with faintly pencilled corrections and the chosen alternatives.

Evidently, Johnston worked promptly. Bridges' next letter is dated the 16th June (1912). It shows that Johnston's preference for the tenth-century minuscule form was gaining ground. It also refers to Bridges' sheet of eight criticisms which is now in the *Calligraphy in Phonetic Script* portfolio (it is sheet No. 2).[28]

> We are very pleased with the sample. I have made corrections of one or two errors in the letters in your MS. We have appended a page of detailed criticism on some shapes. Now as for your general question as to whether this Half-Uncial is preferable to the minuscule that you used before … Monica prefers the old MS., but we should like you

to follow your judgement in this matter. You will be writing again when you send us sample of revised cow symbol. You can write on a p. card.

I return all papers. Yours truly, Robert Bridges.

We think the size you have written, and the shape of the page, will be very convenient whether reduced or no – we will take your advice about reduction – are ourselves rather inclined to reduce, as folded pages are such a bore.[29]

The next stage in the development of Johnston's letter-forms occurred in December 1912 indicated by sheets nos. 14, 5, and 6 in the *Calligraphy in Phonetic Script* portfolio. No. 14 is dated 5th Dec. 1912. (It is not illustrated here.) It shows five lines from the *Aeneid* only. It is also annotated by Johnston: 'Example of MS. in "Slanted pen" X hand [(contr]ast "straight pen" + or "Half-Uncial" MS. of last May)'. Here Johnston shows the slanted pen, minuscule (Foundational) script only. It is written very large.

But on sheets 5 and 6 Johnston demonstrates the alternative letter-forms (i.e., the tenth-century script and the Half-Uncial script) contrasting them side by side (Figs. 120–121). Evidently, Johnston was trying to clarify Bridges' uncertainty. No. 5 shows lower case letter-forms. It is annotated by Johnston: 'Letter for Mr Bridges Phonetics 5th Dec' [1912]. The spot on the paper where the year was indicated is now torn, but the reasonable deduction is the year 1912. It shows the two script styles. On the left-hand side is a set of letters in an 'X "slanted pen" MS.' (i.e., tenth-century minuscules). On the right-hand side is another set in a '+ "straight pen" MS. (or "Half-Uncial")'. Below these are two sets of **a**'s (illustrated). Sheet No. 6 shows trial capital letters in the same arrangement as No. 5. Using the same paper and with almost the same size, it is clearly twinned with it.[30]

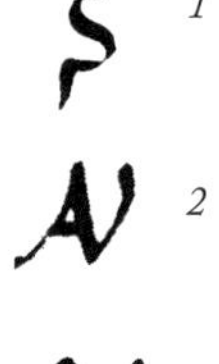

Bridges' next letter is dated the 18th December [1912]. He now accepted Johnston's preference – 'Of course we accept the 10th century minuscule' – and highlighted the remaining problems with some of the letter-forms and the format:

My dear Johnston, I send you a new copy. I think you will be able to follow it and recognise my imitations of your forms. They are lovely and excellent.

I have marked the alternatives that you sent me in red ink as you requested.

In my copy some of the S (= Z) form of S have their tails exaggerated for sake of identification thus S (*1*) not of course for copy of form. [Numbers in text relate to numbers and letter-forms shown on the left.]

The AV (*2*) is very good now.

In deciding your V (*3*) consider the word beloved in which a V (*4*) and a V (*5*) come together. They need that V (*6*) shd be in a form which [one cannot] confuse with the U (*7*) of but (V).(*8*) Now I think it is alright.

About the size. I don't think it will go into an 8vo page. Therefore it must be folded – but I won't fold it at the top or the bottom – Therefore the depth of the MS. is the

> only important thing. It must be reduced so as to be no deeper from top to bottom than the pages of the essay of the book. [Therefore] if necessary omit last epitaph.
>
> Of course we accept the '10th century minuscule'.
>
> I shall be glad to do anything to help IMPRINT and you may put my name on advisory committee. I see that you include "illumination" in your department. That is an indefinite term. Pray let me exhort you to keep yourself quite clear of anything in the way of "pictures" – Don't be led on to that – not on any pretext. R. B.[31]

Johnston then sent Bridges the final manuscript of the three specimens to be facsimiled. It was paid for and presumably kept by Bridges. (However, it has not survived in the Bodleian papers nor in the *Calligraphy in Phonetic Script* portfolio.) On the 23rd January 1913 Johnston replied to a note from Bridges (the note is also missing):

> Thank you for your note of the 21st [January 1913]. I am indeed pleased to hear that you like the MS. (in spite of its faults). It is very difficult to fix a price for it but I think that since it was first begun in the Spring [1912] I must have spent about four days over it (hatching it) so perhaps four guineas would be fair. It seems a great deal for the MS. itself – for which I have been keeping you waiting for so long – but I hope you won't be afraid to order another, should you ever want one, as the actual writing would cost very much less.
>
> I have been wondering whether you will try the spelling on other languages than English? I suppose German would read very well in it – with another [?]. I know no languages, but imagine that the learned might be amused, or, rather, entertained, if you printed, say, a short piece of Latin in it. Have you abandoned the single e?
>
> May I add I feel very much the consideration you have shown me – and that you have not even been justly impatient with me? Solomon ought to have said, also – A soft question bendeth the will.
>
> I have never been so beautifully reproached as by your letter. My wife said 'whose is that writing?' And I said 'It's Mr. Bridges', and I'm afraid to look at it!' But in fact it not only compelled me but helped me to write for you. Yours sincerely, E. Johnston.[32]

Bridges' paper finally appeared in the autumn of 1913 with the amended title *Tract on the Present State of English Pronunciation with Notes and Explanations*. Again it was printed by Horace Hart at the Oxford University Press. It has three plates of illustrations of the phonetic script, one of which shows the three specimens by Johnston. Bridges' accompanying notes point out that Plate No. 2 is a specimen written by himself in 'a careful court'. Plate No. 3 is the same specimen 'written in a quick flowing cursive' … 'obtained by making three copies quickly with different pens'. His specimens are in a simplified version of the phonetic spelling. (Bridges' specimens are not illustrated here.)

Plate No. 1, however, shows the 'full phonetic alphabet' in Johnston's three specimens. The first is the seven-line extract from 'Ibant Obscuri', (the *Aeneid*) (Fig. 122) though reproduced at a smaller scale than the sheet No. 4 trial specimen. Below

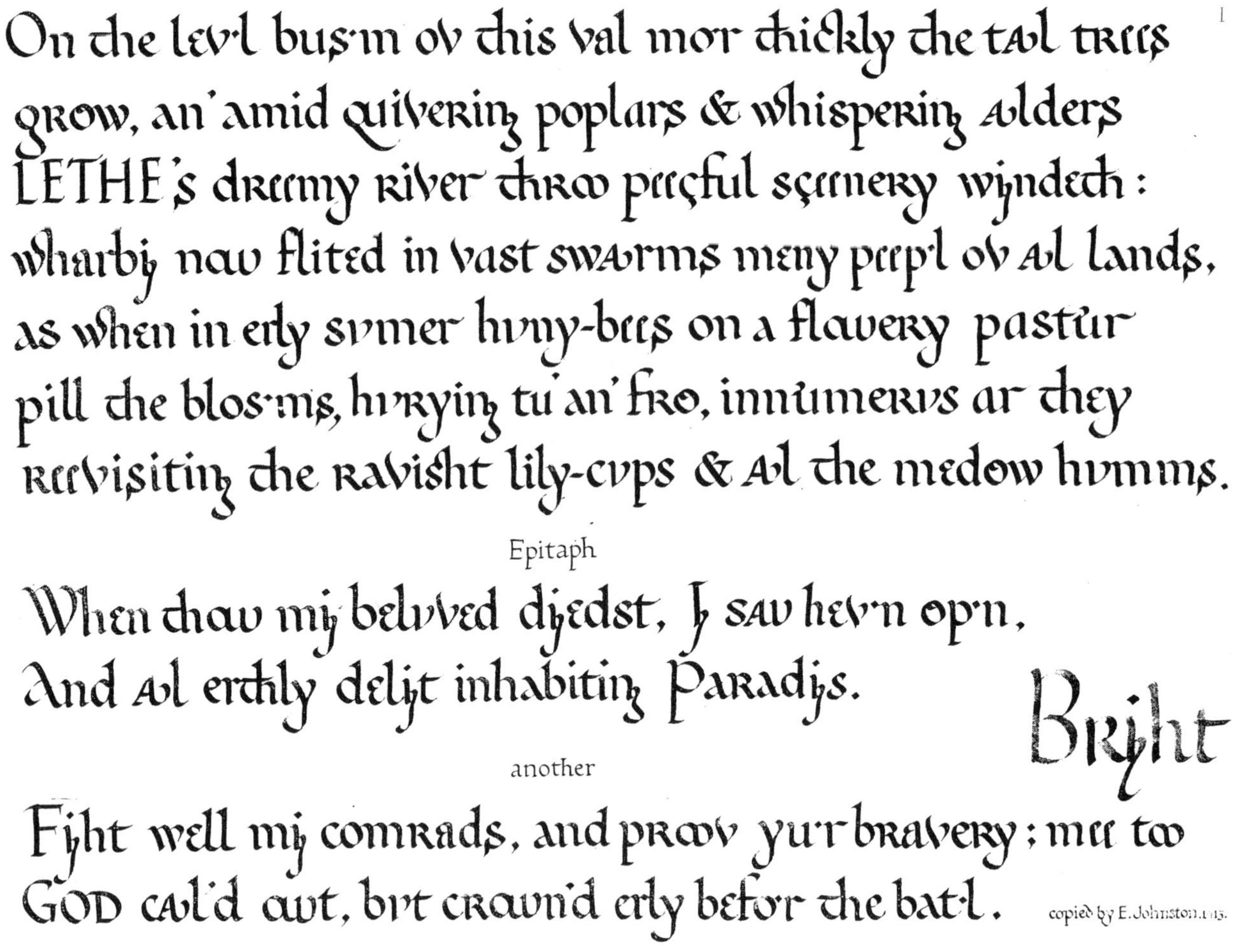

1

On the lev·l bus·m ov this val mor thickly the tal trees
grow, an' amid quiverin poplars & whisperin alders
LETHE's dreemy river thro peeceful scenery windeth:
wharbi nau flited in vast swarms meny peep·l ov al lands,
as when in erly sumer huny-bees on a flavery pastur
fill the blos·ms, huryin tu an' fro, innumerus ar they
reevisitin the ravisht lily-cups & al the medow humms.

Epitaph

When thau mi beluved diedst, I sau hev·n op·n,
And al erthly delit inhabitin Paradis.

Bright

another

Fiht well mi comrads, and proov yur bravery: mee too
GOD cal'd aut, but craun'd erly befor the bat·l.

copied by E. Johnston. 1913.

Fig. 122. Extract from Bridges' poem 'Ibant Obscuri' (Virgil's *Aeneid* Book VI). Specimen of the phonetic script written by Edward Johnston in the '10th c. minuscule' hand used in Bridges' essay 'On The Present State of English Pronunciation, with Notes and Explanations' in the 1913 edition. This specimen incorporates the curly serif to the character *A* ('*tal*') and the '·' character (*lev·l*) which Bridges marked on sheets Nos. 4 and 14 in the *Calligraphy in Phonetic Script* portfolio. Bridges' correction of Johnston's earlier version of the curly-tailed *i* is written in on the right. (Courtesy of OUP.)

this are the two 'Epitaph' poems. Perhaps wearying somewhat of Bridges' constant revisions Johnston managed to get the tail curve of the **i** the wrong way round. Bridges compensated for this by adding the word '*Bright*' with the tail of the new form of the **i** curving correctly to the right.

The Great War and the death of Horace Hart of the Oxford University Press spelt the end of Bridges' phonetic scheme for some time and marked the end of Johnston's involvement in it definitively.[33] A silence of seven years then ensued between them. In 1920 Bridges enquired of Johnston about the engraving of some letter-forms. Johnston referred him to Eric Gill. His note of 2nd July 1920 forwards Gill's reply.[34] Johnston's work diary states that he spent the weekend of 15–17th December with the Bridges in Boar's Hill. His thank you letter of the 20th December bestows on his hosts his customary thoughtfulness and gentle charm:

> Dear Mrs. Bridges, This is a rather belated letter to thank you and Mr. Bridges for your kindness – first in letting me stay with you and then in making me feel welcome. It is difficult to write, because I feel so much more than I can – or would venture, if I could – put into words. (That does not sound very grammatical somehow but there isn't time to put it right).
>
> It has been a great pleasure to see you both again and a wonderful experience to see and to hear your husband. I shall not forget his showing me some of his works, and though even now the words of them are slipping away from my untrained memory, the feeling of inspiration which they gave me will remain. Experience has come slowly to me (partly because I go to meet it so slowly) but I am beginning to understand a little of what it means to suffer fools gently.
>
> The writing, or scribbling for which Mr. Bridges insisted on paying me wasn't work at all but a sort of pleasant pasttime [*sic*] like an 'object' for a walk, of which the real point & enjoyment is the walk itself.
>
> With kind regards to yourself, Edward Johnston
>
> PS. It might interest Mr. Masefield to hear the following testimonial from our second daughter (now just back from school) who thinking that perhaps I might see him at Boar's Hill, says in a p.c. to her mother: 'How thrilling for Daddy to see J. M. I wish I'd sent him my love & most heartfelt thanks. I do love him for writing such wonderful stuff'. (That largely refers to R. the Fox, I think.) I envy Barbara's vocabulary in writing this letter to you.[35]

Johnston evidently returned home with a commission for a manuscript in Greek from Bridges. It is the subject of his next letter written on the 2nd February 1924.

> 3 enclosures
>
> Dear Mr Bridges, Here is the copy – I am sorry to have kept you waiting so long.
>
> I fear you will not like the Greek so well. It was impossible quite to recapture such free and rough writing (with different paper, ink & nib & in a different mood, also with spectacles on). – It might have been a little nearer in some details. But I think that the engraver, if he is any good at all, can use the original sketch (or photograph of it) & consult this copy if in doubt.
>
> On closer examination, it does not look to me as if the photographer had 'fooled' with the original sketch but that the blue-black ink has 'run' on the blue ruled lines of the f'cap – where the ink crossed them. I noticed that the f'cap was a little absorbent, but presumably we did not notice their crossing lines that Sunday evening partly because the daylight had gone and partly because the blue-black ink had not had time to darken.
>
> The present copy is written in stick Indian ink (for safety) – it is semi-waterproof.

> Enclosed also are original sketch and the photo. If you like I can try blotting out the wrong marks on the latter. Please let me know if I can do anything. I shall be really glad to. Yours sincerely, Edward Johnston.
>
> I should like to send my love to Mrs. Bridges but (lest that is a presumption) send my kind regards.[36]

The next batch of letters was written in 1926 and concerned Bridges' Tract XXIII of the Society for Pure English, called *English Handwriting*.[37] It consisted of a portfolio of thirty-four specimens with introductory essays by Roger Fry and the palaeographer E. A. Lowe. Johnston contributed to it a specimen in his Foundational Hand. (Frontispiece). His letter to Bridges of the 3rd January 1926 is evidently a reply to Bridges' request for a specimen of handwriting. It reads:

> Dear Mr. Bridges, Please forgive my not replying sooner to your letter (wh. has been delivered by exceptional post last Sunday morning). My wife and I have just got over a 3 week bout of influenza wh. has left me rather more dilatory and feckless than usual. I trust you will be able to extract from this some kind of defence for my neglect of the opportunity which you offered.
>
> I have nothing suitable to send you but will try to write a small piece this week and will hope to be in time.
>
> Mr. Rothenstein (my 'boss' at the Royal College of Art) asked me some time ago if I could find any handwriting for you – the doctors having ordered him to rest in bed for six weeks. I have heard lately that he is in better condition now & intends to go to Italy shortly. His wife asked me for one of his own letters (for you) & I sent one to her, but not a v. good one. Encld. envelope is a better example (as is often the case with envelopes – on wh. people write with greater boldness).
>
> I do not know many good hands and some, like S. Morison's, are known to you.
>
> For my part (& in that small acquaintance) I should 'bracket' Mrs Bridges and your own at the top = tho' in slightly different categories.
>
> With good wishes to you both and in (my usual [tho' you might not believe it]) haste. Yours sincerely. Edward Johnston.[38]

Apparently dissatisfied, Bridges wrote to Johnston a more insistent note. Johnston's reply of the 14th January 1926 accompanied the promised manuscript:

> Dear Mr. Bridges, I cannot resist your appeal to send you 'at once' an old MS. (of which part can be screened off as suggested). It cannot be cut because it is not exactly my property (i.e., one of my customers has a claim on it).
>
> This is the best piece of writing in my hands & probably better than anything I could write now. For my part I should prefer to be represented by this to any other MS. wh. I may have written. It did not occur to me to use it til the other day or you shd. have had it earlier.

The MS. is based on a 10th century English Psalter in the B. M. (Harley MS. 2904) and is what I have brought my students up on for the last 15 years or so.

I shall try to write further tomorrow.[39]

This 'hurried note' was indeed quickly followed by a longer letter dated the 18th January 1926. It is the most expansive of all Johnston's letters to the Bridges and one in which he looked back on their friendship to acknowledge the influence the couple had had on his formation as a teacher:

> Written in the train. There hasn't been a proper opportunity to write a sequel to my hurried note of 14th January. The 'weekend' produced a number of interruptions – including the unfreezing of bath pipes (with hot water hot bricks and hot pokers). The note (and pencil notes) perhaps said all that was necessary but I wished to go over your letter again & make sure of the matter.
>
> In your second letter you specify the sort of script wh. you would like to have, Q from B to EJ 'viz. a fair specimen of your Half-Uncial script wherewith you exalted the emotions of your London classes'.
>
> You and Mrs Bridges put me on the track of the Half-Uncial as you may remember, long ago, when you gave me a copy of Maunde Thompson's 'Greek and Latin Palæography'. I have always been most grateful to you for that assistance and it (the ½ U.) made a sound foundation for my own work, and for about 10 years I used it as the foundation for my students' work. I found, however, that the average student could not give sufficient time to writing to permit of such thoroughness and therefore, about 15 or 16 years ago I took them from roman Caps hurrying through Uncials to the 10th centy. Winchester MS. (on wh. the MS. I sent you was based). This Winchester MS., which I frequently refer to as 'the Foundational Hand', might I suppose be accurately described as a <u>late Caroline Minuscule</u>. It has considerably advanced from the Half-Uncial, &, tho. it does not give such good discipline as that, it has the advantages of identity – in all good points at least – with our modern printed letter. Only four archaisms had to be replaced: **a e s t** by a e s t. If you have a copy of my book you will find a plate and descriptive note of it.
>
> Students who have not had a good grounding in the Half-U. have to be carefully watched or they will fail to acquire the true form of this Winchester letter (even in my own case, particularly in my book I made a partial failure in reproducing its character.)
>
> The MS. wh. I sent you had been put aside as doubtful because the writing 'went off' towards the end of it. But the piece screened off is as good as most of my best MSS. & better than anything wh. I could do at present. Its chief fault is that the lines of the MS. are a little too close together. But on the whole it is representative of anything of mine wh. you could have had. And that, I presume, is what you wanted.
>
> Mr. Sydney Cockerell, the Curator of the FitzWilliam Museum Camb. has a book wh. I wrote for him entitled 'Sample Scripts'.* I don't know whether he wd. lend it but he might give a photograph. It has some of my best MSS. in it of various sorts. (*writ. c. 1915). Of late I have been experimenting with a sort of Italic in wh. I write most of my present work. Yours sincerely Edward Johnston.

> PS. You said it wd. take me 'only half an hour'. On reading this I said to my daughter 'I wd. give half of my substance to any man who wd. teach me to do anything in ½ an hour.'
>
> PSS. As to facsimile size you doubtless appreciate the importance of this. It is v. specially important in MSS. reproduction because the camera changes the scale of thicks and thins equally but this is not the case in the compression of large and small MSS..[40]

With hindsight this letter of 1926 can be seen as the swan song of Johnston's friendship with the Bridges for their correspondence ends at this point. Robert Bridges died in 1930 and Mary Monica Bridges in 1949.

END NOTES

1. MSS. Eng. Lett. Dep. Bridges III. Albums 2 & 3. Folios 44–70. There are nineteen letters in these albums.
2. By Simon Nowell-Smith after the precedent of the 'Chilswell' type face made for Bridges in the 1920s. See his 'The Phonotypes of Robert Bridges'. In *Alphabet & Image.* Vol. 2. No. 5. 1947.
3. *Calligraphy in Phonetic Script.* NAL. V&A. Ref: MSL 24/15/1982. The portfolio was a gift from Priscilla Roworth (née Johnston), made in 1982 (at the suggestion of Justin Howes).
4. 27th August 1901. *Selected Letters by Robert Bridges.* Edited by D. Stanford. (Newark) 1983. Bridges explained further the need for his phonetic system elsewhere: 'If English were spelt as it is or should be pronounced, then the syllables would scan according to Greek prosody. The adoption of the Greek rules was made by William Stone in an essay now published with my *Milton's Prosody* at the OUP'. (Preface to 'A Peace Ode' in *The Monthly Review*, June 1903. No. 33. XI. 3.)
5. 30th August 1901. Bodleian Library. MSS. Eng. Lett. Dep. Bridges. III Album 2. Folio 44.
6. *Selected Letters by Robert Bridges.* Edited by D. Stanford. (Newark) 1983.
7. *Selected Letters by Robert Bridges.* Edited by D. Stanford. (Newark) 1983.
8. *Selected Letters by Robert Bridges.* Edited by D. Stanford. (Newark) 1983.
9. *Selected Letters by Robert Bridges.* Edited by D. Stanford. (Newark) 1983.
10. Bodleian Library. MSS. Eng. Lett. Dep. Bridges III. Album 2. Folios 47–48. If the 'copy' Bridges refers to does, in fact, correspond to the three sheets showing the phonetic alphabet which are now in the *Calligraphy in Phonetic Script* portfolio (MSL 24/11–13/1982), they can be dated circa October 1902.
11. Bodleian Library. MSS. Eng. Lett. Dep. Bridges III. Album 2. Folios 49–50.
12. Letter to Lionel Muirhead, 27th November 1902. *Selected Letters by Robert Bridges.* Edited by Donald Stanford. (Newark) 1983.
13. His preface to the volume published in 1903 begins: 'These experiments in quantitive verse were made in fulfilment of a promise to William Johnson Stone that I would some day test his theory.' It then continues: 'The poem is an experiment in obedience to a consistently

thought-out body of phonetic rules, and its principles are explained in the 'Note' on pp 19–24. For the typography and dæmonography of English, my friend the printer cannot be held responsible.' See Falconer Madan. *Memorials of C. H. O. Daniel with a Bibliography of the press*, (Daniel Press) Oxford. 1912.

14. *Selected Letters of Robert Bridges*. Edited by D. Stanford. (Newark) 1983.

15. *Selected Letters of Robert Bridges*. Edited by D. Stanford. (Newark) 1983.

16. *Selected Letters of Robert Bridges*. Edited by D. Stanford. (Newark) 1983.

17. Bodleian Library. MSS. Eng. Lett. Dep. Bridges. III. Album 2. Folios 54. The dates of this and the following letter, (Album 2. Folio 52–53) seem to have been inadvertently substituted in the typed transcripts of some of the letters in the Bridges papers.

18. *Calligraphy in Phonetic Script*. NAL at the V&A. MS L. 24/1/1982.

19. It was printed in a run of 300 copies in a small pica Roman type face taken from the Fell types on handmade paper with a J. Whatman watermark. A folding plate showing a facsimile of Bridges' phonetic script, printed in red, is tipped-in. This facsimile was printed by Horace Hart at the Clarendon Press in collotype on to semi-transparent paper. It is likely that the manuscript which is now in the portfolio *Calligraphy in Phonetic Script* (shown in Fig. 115) is Bridges' original. (V&A Museum. NAL. MSL. 24/1/1982).

20. It was published by the Oxford University Press, edited by A. C. Bradley. Bradley was Bridges' friend and a co-founder in 1910 of the Society for Pure English.

21. A print of Johnston's specimen is now in the portfolio *Calligraphy in Phonetic Script* in the V&A. MSL. 24/8/1982. The two-line poem 'Epitaph' was incorporated into the collection *Poems in Classical Prosody* as No. 19. The volume was published in 1912.

22. Bodleian Library. MSS. Eng. Lett. Bridges Dep. III. Album 2. Folio 55.

23. In the *Calligraphy in Phonetic Script* Portfolio in the NAL at the V&A. MSL 24/15/1982.

24. Elisabeth Elstob (1683–1756) was a scholar of Anglo-Saxon who had had the fount cast in 1712. Destroyed by fire, a second version was cut and manufactured by the typefounder Robert Andrews. It was finally deposited by William Bower (the younger) at the Sheldonian Press Oxford in 1764. See T. B. Reed, revised by A. F. Johnson *The History of the Old English Letter Foundries*. (Dawson of Pall Mall) 1974. The additional characters designed by Monica Bridges date from 1908–10. Working with Horace Hart, some fifty-seven characters were added to the original Elstob fount. Finally there were sixty-four characters in the lower case and thirty-seven capitals. Documentation for Monica's work is in the archives of the OUP. See the article by Simon Nowell-Smith: 'The Phonotypes of Robert Bridges' in *Alphabet & Image* (Vol. 2. No. 5. 1947).

25. Bodleian Library. MSS. Eng. Lett. Dep. Bridges III. Album 3. Folio 71.

26. Bodleian Library. Dep. Bridges III. Album 3. Folios 56.

27. It was first published in *New Quarterly* in 1909 and became No. 21 of the collection, *Poems in Classical Prosody*, published in 1912.

28. *Calligraphy in Phonetic Script*. NAL at the V&A. MSL 24/2/1982.

29. Bodleian Library. MSS. Eng. Lett. Dep. Bridges III Album 3. Folio 57.

30. *Calligraphy in Phonetic Script*. NAL at the V&A. MSL 24/5-6/1982.

31. Bodleian Library. MSS. Eng. Lett. Dep. Bridges 111. Album 2 Folio 51. It was possibly as a *quid pro quo* that Bridges' essay was reviewed in *Imprint* (September 1913) by E. H. Mason.

32. Bodleian Library. MSS. Eng. Lett. Dep. Bridges III. Album 3 Folios 58–59.

33. Bridges' phonetic project did not come to fruition because of Johnston's input but rather because the types were not cast. However, in 1923 Bridges struck up a partnership with Stanley Morison to print his poem 'The Tapestry' using a newly-cut typeface based on Arrighi's Italic which was devised by Stanley Morison and Frederick Warde and cut by hand in Paris. Following this, Morison organised the manufacture of Monotype Blado Italic (also based on Arrighi) for machine printing. Types for the twenty-eight extra symbols were designed by Alfred Fairbank and were then cast. The new typeface was christened 'Chilswell'. Bridges' *Collected Essays* were printed in it between 1927–32 at the OUP, edited by Monica Bridges. See Nicolas Barker: *The Printer and the Poet*. (Cambridge) 1970 and Simon Nowell-Smith: 'The Phonotypes of Robert Bridges' in *Alphabet and Image* (Vol. 2. No. 5. 1947).

34. It reads: 'I thought Gill would write directly to you. The enclosed came from him yesterday = I am sorry I could not attend to it until today. I am asking him to send G. Friend's address to you. Enclos. lithograph of the letters wh. he refers to as "free from art nonsense" may amuse you.' (i.e., the railway block lettering.) Bodleian Library. Dep. Bridges III. Album 3. Folio 60.
35. Bodleian Library. MSS. Eng. Lett. Dep. Bridges III. Album 3. Folios 62–63.
36. Bodleian Library. MSS. Eng. Lett. Dep. Bridges III. Album 3. Folio 64.
37. It was printed at the Oxford University Press, edited by A. C. Bradley. Bradley was Bridges' friend and a co-founder in 1910 of the Society for Pure English. A second Tract, No XXVIII, 1927, had an extra thirty-one plates devoted to Italic handwriting with a paper by Alfred Fairbank called 'Notes on Penmanship'.
38. Bodleian Library. MSS. Eng. Lett. Dep. Bridges III. Album 3. Folios 65–66.
39. Bodleian Library. MSS. Eng. Lett. Dep. Bridges III. Album 3. Folio 67.
40. Bodleian Library. Bridges Papers. MSS. Eng. Lett. Album 3. Folios 68–70.

Johnston at Cleves in Ditchling aged 58.
(Photographer unknown. Courtesy of the Edward Johnston estate.)

CHAPTER TEN

THE TRADITION AND STUDY OF JOHNSTON IN BRITAIN

By all accounts to be present at Johnston's lecture-demonstrations on the blackboard was to witness a teacher reaching the heart of the matter. Violet Hawkes wrote that they were 'an intellectual delight … gripping the students' attention throughout'. Irene Wellington said of them '… it was like living through a miracle'. Johnston's revival of Roman Humanist lettering at the Central School and at the Royal College of Art broadened out into a mainstream tradition. It is now instilled into a fourth, even a fifth, generation of lettering artists. It displaced much of Britain's vernacular lettering from what has been called the 'vessel of culture' – that is, that tradition of commercial lettering which derived from the English Roundhand/Copperplate script and of display types which derived from the Baskerville-'modern' designs. It also profoundly influenced lettering practice elsewhere, notably in the USA, Germany, and Holland. One of Johnston's most admiring friends was the calligrapher, Alfred Fairbank. 'I was not taught by Edward Johnston', he wrote, 'though I was very much a disciple of his.'[1] In his article 'Mr. Edward Johnston and English Calligraphy', written in 1931 for the German periodical *Schrift und Schreiben*, he suggests one of the ways in which the ascendancy of Johnston's lettering took place:

> Many of the students on gaining the diploma of the Royal College receive appointments as masters of schools of Arts and Crafts throughout the country and have spread Mr. Johnston's teaching, so that scripts that are related recognisably to Mr. Johnston's models are to be found everywhere.

How the penmanship of individual lettering artists in Britain has fared in the spirit of Johnston since the 1900s is a topic entirely beyond the scope of this chapter. So, too, is the parallel revival of Italic handwriting (known originally as Chancery Cursive or *Cancelleresca*), which was spearheaded by Alfred Fairbank and others but which grew out of and co-existed with Johnston's own teaching.

The main purpose here is to establish the connection of teacher and pupil of Johnston's lettering. The pattern of such relationships in a widening network of colleges, workshops, and private studios is the very stuff of a craft tradition and evokes the older pattern of master-scribe and novice in the scriptorium. Crucial to understanding this tradition are the views and methods of teachers as reflected in the recollections of their pupils. Through them a vista is opened up right back to Johnston's own. In this respect especially valuable are the insights of Ann Hechle, Donald Jackson, and Ann Camp.

Other developments have helped to swell the Johnstonian tradition. Paramount is the publication of his own writings. *Writing & Illuminating, & Lettering,* which he revised in 1929, and has gone through as many as forty reprints (under the imprints of John Hogg, Pitman, A & C Black, Taplinger, Dover, also Macmillan, 1908, 1911 and 1939) making it a 'Scribe's Bible', and surely the most widely read of all craft manuals. Important, as well, are the commemorative exhibitions to Johnston, the accumulation of public collections of his work, the growth of calligraphy societies and journals, and the presence of good workaday civic lettering. They are its evidence, the raw material of its study. Particular attention will be paid to Stanley Morison and Johnston. As a leading scholar of lettering in the following generation, Morison was able to implement views which advanced matters beyond Johnston's thinking. The chapter's conclusion will return to Fairbank's observations.

The acceptance of Johnston's edged-pen method is comparable to that enjoyed by the pointed nib in the eighteenth and nineteenth centuries. It was employed by a wide spectrum of designers trained in the design schools. An index would be its use by, say, ceramicists or stained-glass artists. Furthermore, his Roman Humanist revival has been resilient against other lettering. It has effectively blocked the impact of seminal teachers such as Rudolf Larisch, for example, who was Johnston's counterpart in Germany and Austria. By contrast, Larisch had an influence in the United States although even there his handbooks have remained largely untranslated. It also forestalled the progress of the Black Letter scripts such as Fraktur in Britain where the expressionist overtones of the Rudolf Koch/Berthold Wolpe school have been a minor though significant development. Similarly with typography, Johnston's Humanist block letter alphabet and its successor, Gill Sans, eclipsed the 'constructed' sanserifs, designed by Germans such Peter Behrens, or Jacob Erbar or Paul Renner, or those conceived with modernist bravura by Jan Tschichold or Herbert Bayer. Johnston's reforms are a story of success – providing grist to the mill of theorists of cultural diffusion.

Two related but distinct traditions flow from Johnston's notion of the 'Freedom' of calligraphic expression which he envisaged could be achieved through the individual's development of his scripts (largely the Foundational Hand) guided by the concepts of 'Sharpness' and 'Unity'. One of these is inscriptional lettering, applied either on to a surface, as in signwriting, or engraved, as in stone. The concepts are also apparent in the work of the type punch-cutter. Although not exclusively so, inscriptions are more associated with the capital letters. The other tradition is calligraphy itself, i.e., formal writing with illumination. It is more associated with the minuscule letters. The combined body of work shows not so much a homogeneous style of lettering – though in Britain this is discernible[2] – but, rather, the imprint of Johnston's holistic approach. Underlying this, particularly as far as calligraphy is concerned, are his three guide-lines concerning the technique of the writing tool. They teach that it must be the broad-nibbed pen (or edged pen) used with minimum pressure, and that it must be kept at a constant angle to the horizontal line of writing. (A standard of thirty degrees was adopted by Johnston from the tenth-century *Ramsey Psalter* or *Harley MSS. 2904*, and forty-five degrees for Italic).[3] Lastly, the fact is realised that it is the width of the pen's nib which determines the maximum width of the strokes of the letters. These principles, with Johnston's step-by-step analysis of the individual pen strokes and lifts which make up the letter-form, are adhered to in the calligraphy handbooks written by his pupils and followers.[4] Graily Hewitt's manual *Lettering*, for example, attributes to the 'edged tool' alone (Fig. 123):

> ... the contrast of thick and thins and the gradations automatically provided. This feature is ever the essential of penmanship, the pleasure deeply instinctive ...

Inscriptional lettering includes both written and engraved forms, the latter most often in stone and wood but also in metal and glass and, very importantly, in type design. In Johnston's mind, the exemplar was the Roman *Capitalis Quadrata* letters, as on the Trajan Column.[5] The model became virtually synonymous with the capital letters per se. (Fig. 124). That assumption was made by Johnston's two early pupils who took up inscriptional careers: Eric Gill at the Central School of Art and Percy Smith at the Camberwell School of Arts and Crafts. While Gill says in his

Fig. 123. Graily Hewitt. Title page of *Lettering for Students and Craftsmen* (reduced). (Courtesy of Seeley, Service Ltd.) 1954.

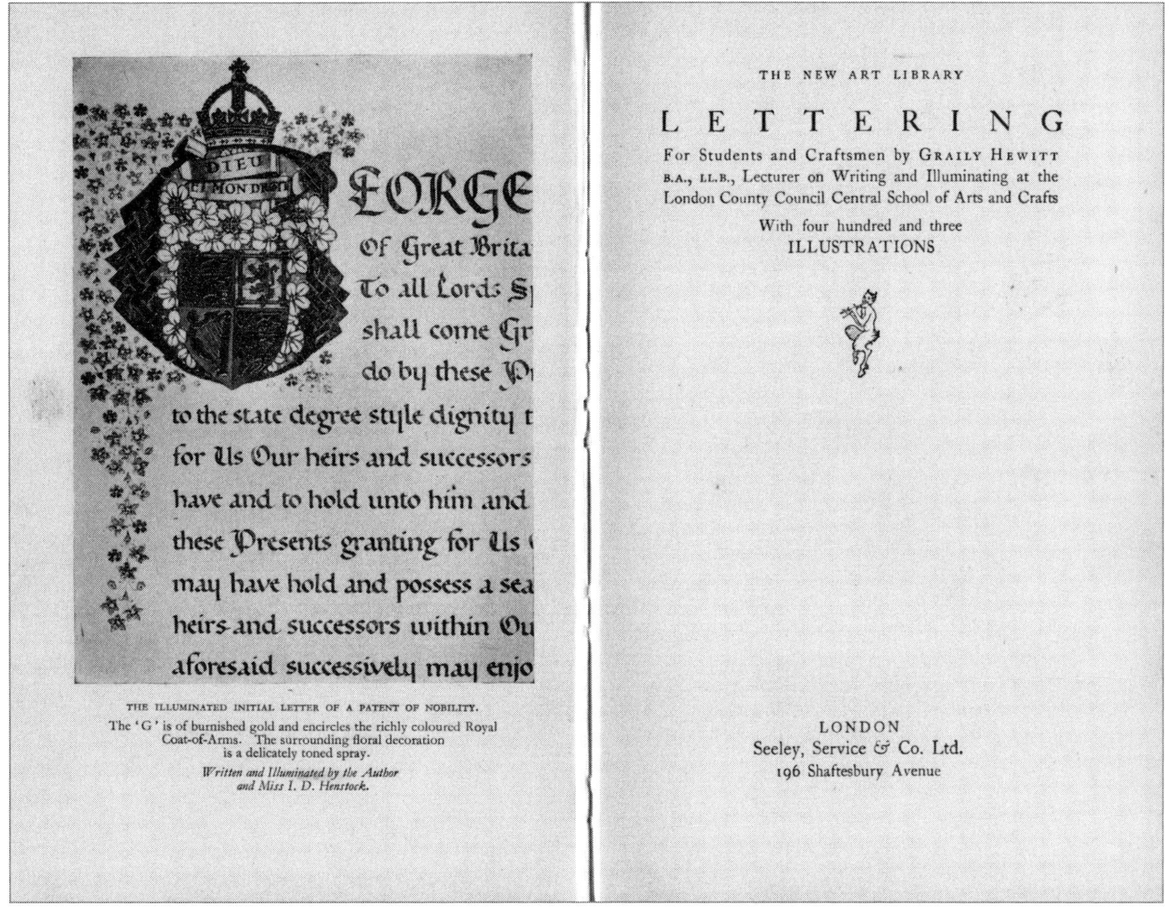

THE ILLUMINATED INITIAL LETTER OF A PATENT OF NOBILITY.
The 'G' is of burnished gold and encircles the richly coloured Royal Coat-of-Arms. The surrounding floral decoration is a delicately toned spray.
Written and Illuminated by the Author and Miss I. D. Henstock.

THE NEW ART LIBRARY

LETTERING

For Students and Craftsmen by GRAILY HEWITT
B.A., LL.B., Lecturer on Writing and Illuminating at the London County Council Central School of Arts and Crafts

With four hundred and three ILLUSTRATIONS

LONDON
Seeley, Service & Co. Ltd.
196 Shaftesbury Avenue

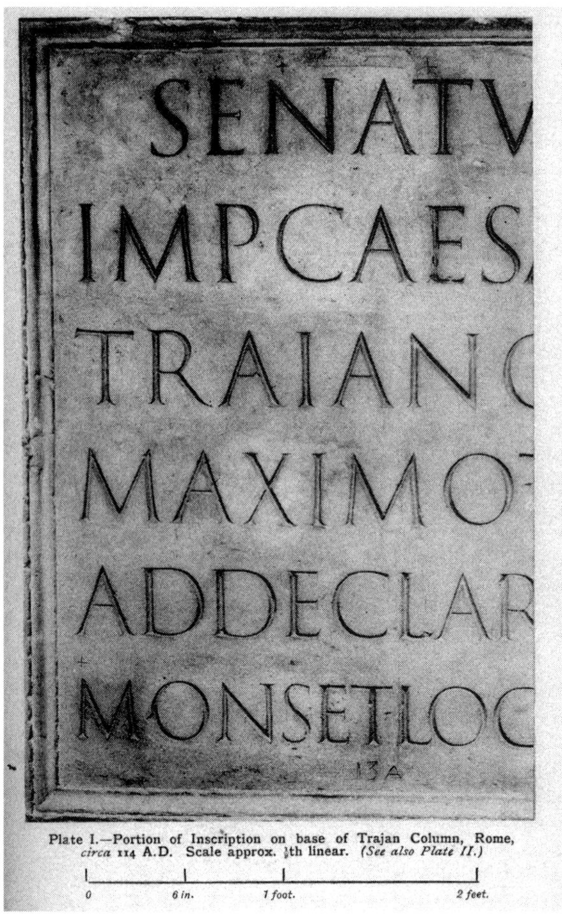

Plate I.—Portion of Inscription on base of Trajan Column, Rome, *circa* 114 A.D. Scale approx. $\frac{1}{8}$th linear. *(See also Plate II.)*

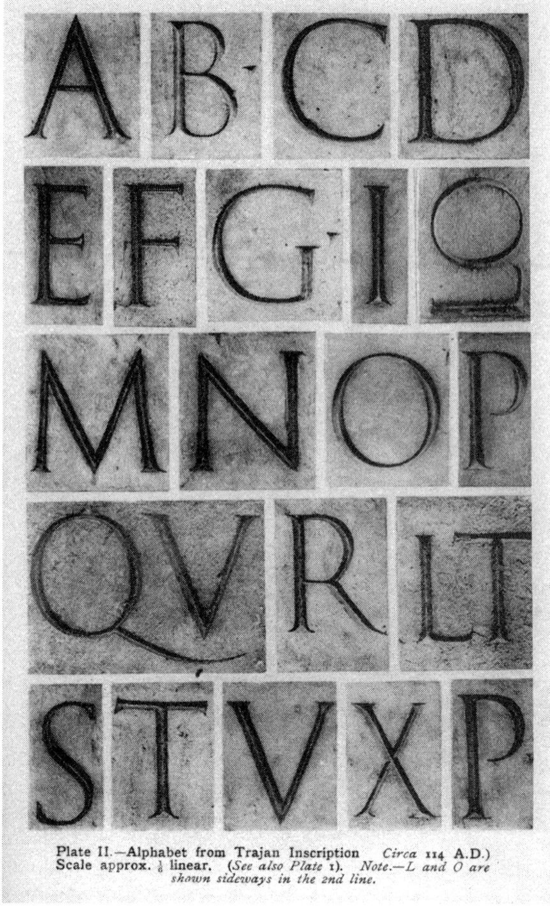

Plate II.—Alphabet from Trajan Inscription *Circa* 114 A.D.) Scale approx. $\frac{1}{6}$ linear. (*See also Plate* 1). *Note.—L and O are shown sideways in the 2nd line.*

Notes on the Collotype Plates

THE BORDERS.—The lettering practically fills the panel (see p. 352): the surrounding moulding is approx. 4 inches wide.

THE LETTERS (*for their forms* see next note).

Approximate heights		
	First two lines:	$4\frac{1}{2}$ inches high.
	Second two lines:	$4\frac{3}{8}$ „ „
	Fifth line:	$4\frac{1}{8}$ „ „
	Last line:	$3\frac{7}{8}$ „ „

THE SPACES (between Lines) decrease from 3 inches to $2\frac{3}{4}$ inches. A decrease in the height of the letters from the top to the foot line is common in early inscriptions (see figs. 203–205). Several reasons for this suggest themselves: (*a*) (Sometimes the beginning words, being farther from the reader, may require to be larger). (*b*) The architectural beauty of a large heading (comp. *stem heads*, p. 288). (*c*) The importance of *beginnings* generally (there is very often a marked difference between the upper lines containing important words and the rest of the inscription: comp. figs. 197, 91).

NOTE.—The WORDS are separated by triangular points (p. 384).

PLATE II.—Alphabet from Trajan Inscription. (*Circa* 114 A.D.) *Scale approx.* $\frac{1}{6}$*th linear.* (See note above.)

THE "TRAJAN" ALPHABET.—Very fine letters for inscriptions in stone: possibly painted before incision (see p. 292); see also remarks on Roman Capitals, pp. 268–296, and note:—

SERIFS.—Small and carefully curved.

THIN PARTS about half the width of the *thick stems* (pp. 375, 285).

A (M and N), *pointed* (p. 280).
B—a very beautiful form, with large lower *bow* (p. 278).
C, G, and (D)—Upper parts rather straight (p. 281).
E and F—*mid arm* slightly shorter than upper arm.
E and L—*lower serif* pointed out (p. 282).

410

Notes on the Collotype Plates

LO (shown sideways in collotype) and LT show L's *arm* projecting under next letter.

M—*pointed:* slightly spread (p. 284), distance apart of points above equal to *inside* distance of stems below.

N—*pointed:* practically no difference in thickness of vertical and oblique parts (p. 285).

O—very beautiful: *width slightly less than height* (p. 270); slightly *tilted* (as are all the other curved letters: see p. 285).

P—*Bow* not joined to stem below (first P rounder topped).

Q—*tail* carried under V (U).

R—large *bow:* straight *tail*, with finishing-curve (p. 291).

S—leans forward slightly (p. 286).

Proportions of widths to heights (comp. with pp. 269–273)		
	OCDGMNQ	width slightly *less* than height.
	ARTV	width approx. $\frac{1}{6}$th *less* than height.
	BX	width rather more than *half* height.
	P	width approx. equal half height.
	LS	width slightly *less* than half height.
	EF	width approx. $\frac{3}{7}$ths of height.

H, (J), K, (U), W, Y, Z are not present in the inscription. A rough diagram (fig. 219) is given below showing approximately suitable forms for these (*Re junction of* U in *stone;* see p. 400, & fig. 215).

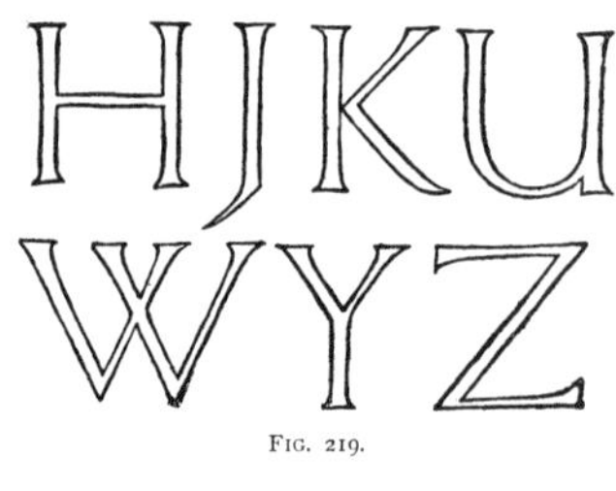

FIG. 219.

411

Fig. 124. Illustrations and text from Johnston's *Writing & Illuminating, & Lettering* devoted to the capital letters at base of the Trajan Column. First edition. (John Hogg) 1906.

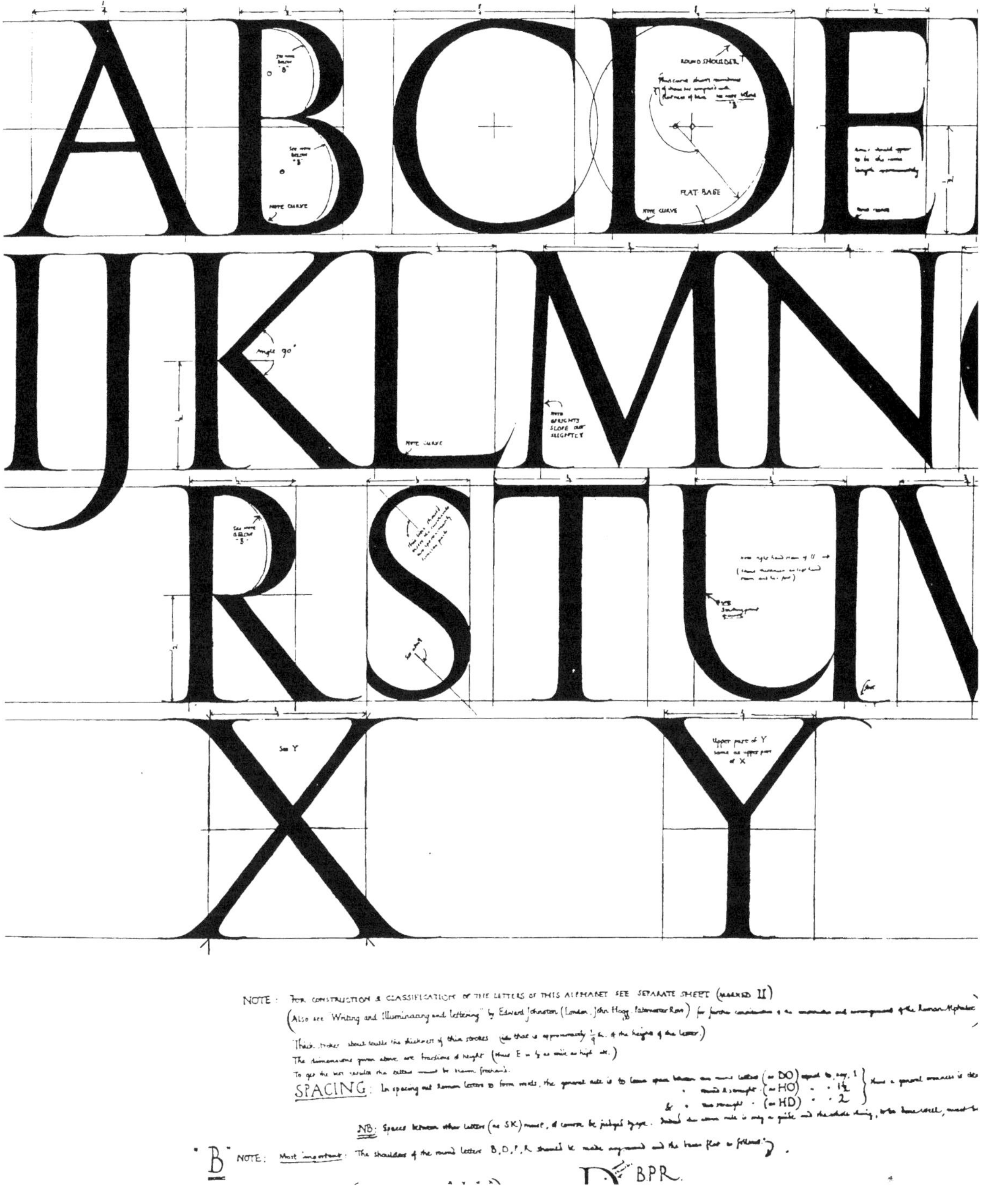

Fig. 125. First of four sheets of letter-forms drawn by Eric Gill in 1907 at Hammersmith Terrace with a note referring to Edward Johnston's *Writing & Illuminating, & Lettering.*
Cited from Robert Harding. *The Letter Forms of Eric Gill.* 1979.
(Courtesy of Eva Svensson.)

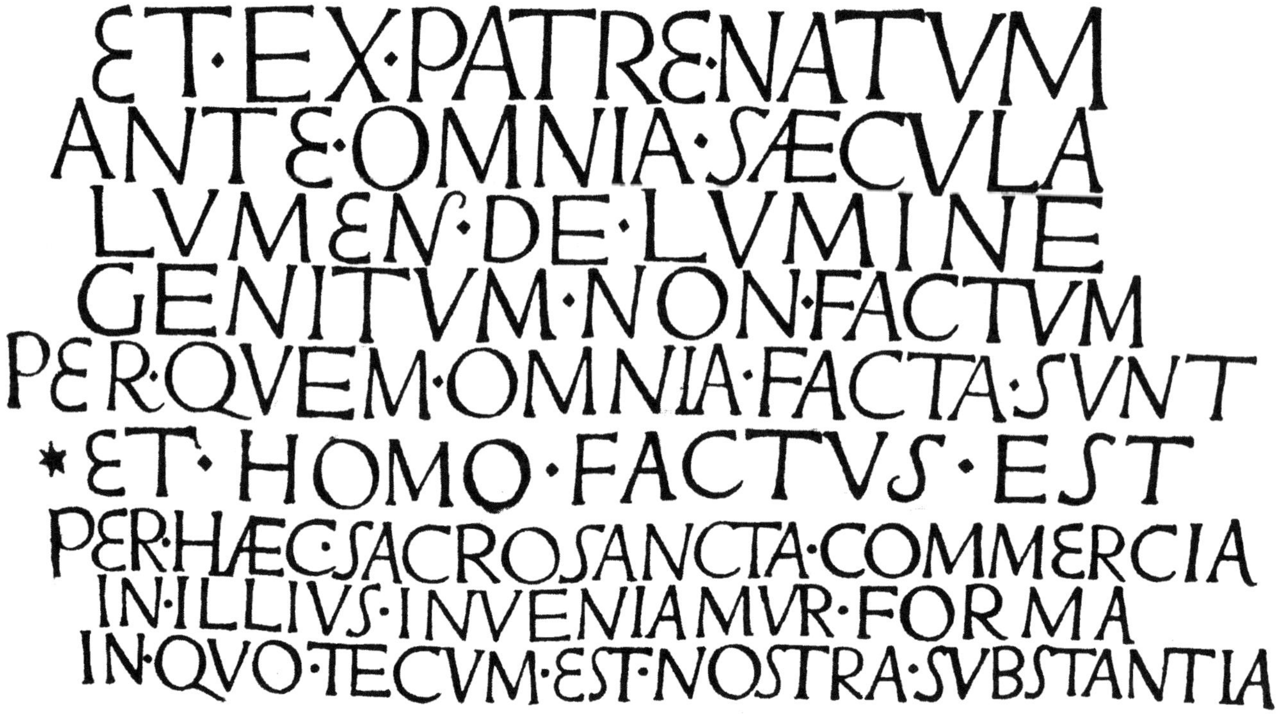

ET·EX·PATRE·NATVM
ANTE·OMNIA·SÆCVLA
LVMEN·DE·LVMINE
GENITVM·NON·FACTVM
PER·QVEM·OMNIA·FACTA·SVNT
*ET·HOMO·FACTVS·EST
PER·HÆC·SACROSANCTA·COMMERCIA
IN·ILLIVS·INVENIAMVR·FORMA
IN·QVO·TECVM·EST·NOSTRA·SVBSTANTIA

Fig. 126. Inscription by David Jones. Part of the *Creed* and part of the *Secret for the Midnight Mass of the Nativity*. c. 1953. Cited from *Agenda*. Summer 1967.
(Courtesy of the editors of *Agenda*.)

diary that he eventually abandoned the Trajan model, Johnston remained avowedly his mentor throughout his life. The set of four drawings of letter-forms Gill drew up in Hammersmith in 1907 show his continued allegiance to Johnston's methods of construction. The note on Gill's Plate I refers the reader to Johnston's handbook. (Fig. 125). Gill was not a teacher of regular classes of students in art schools but rather of a succession of apprentices in his workshops at Hammersmith, at Ditchling, at Capel-y-ffin, in mid-Wales and at Pigotts (near High Wycombe in Buckinghamshire).

Immediately connected with Gill are the two Cribb brothers. Joseph Cribb worked closely with Gill at Hammersmith and Ditchling until 1924 and continued his career as a lettering artist in Ditchling until his death, in 1967. The younger and lesser-known Lawence Cribb was also with Gill, both in Ditchling and in Capel-y-ffin. He then became his principal assistant at Pigotts until Gill's death in 1940.

There have been a number of other exceptional inscriptional lettering artists who can be linked back to Johnston, albeit indirectly through Gill. Among them,

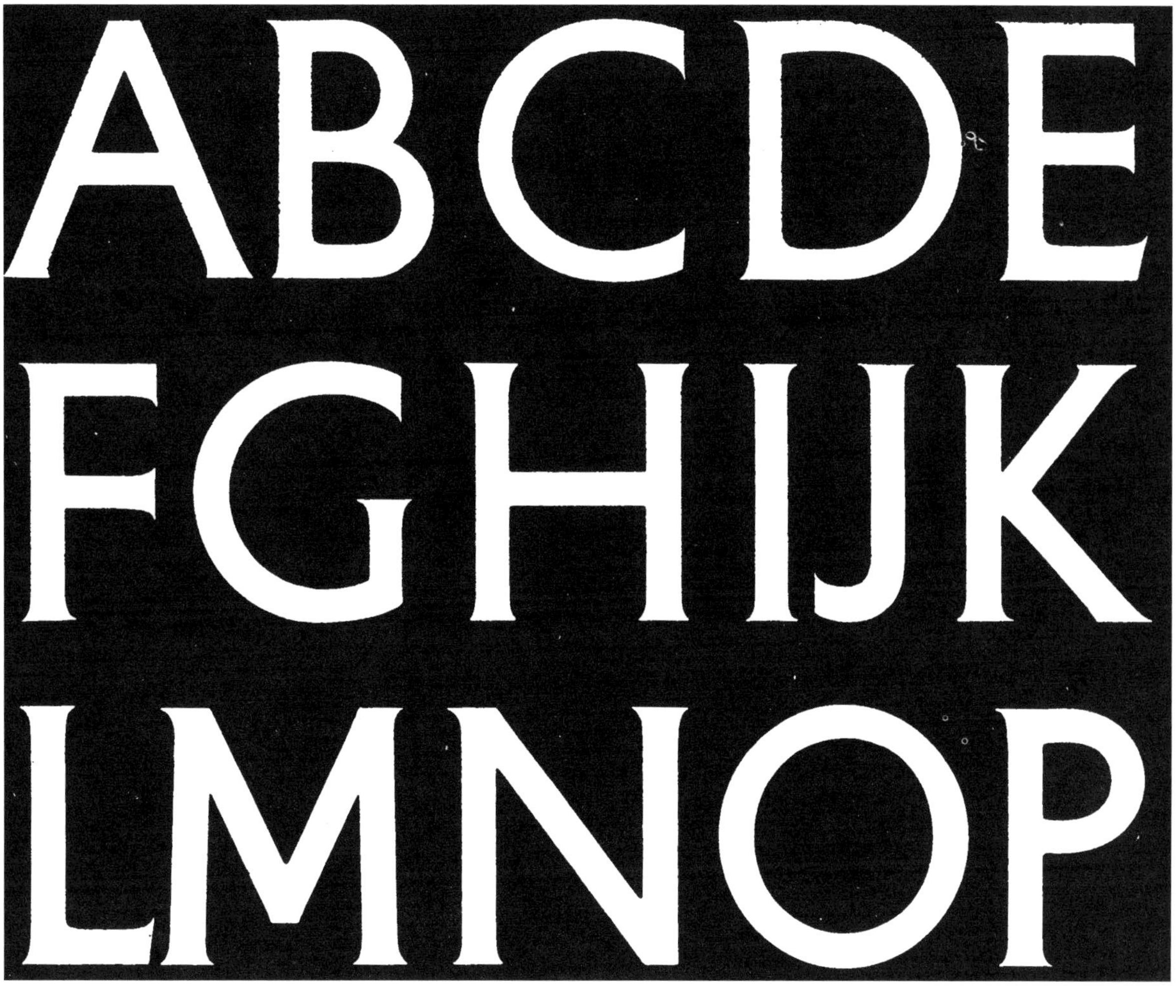

Fig. 127. 'Petit Sans Serif' designed by Percy Smith for the headquarters of London Transport. (Courtesy of A. & C. Black)

the artist-poet David Jones is prominent. He was especially close to Gill at Ditchling between 1919 and 1924 then briefly at Capel-y-ffin and more spasmodically at Pigotts into the 1940s. Esoteric in style and arcane in meaning, David Jones's painted inscriptions may appear far removed from any origin in Johnston's appeal to the Trajan Column. Yet, the connection between Johnston and Gill was the prerequisite of his development. (Fig. 126).

In the mid-1930s other lettering artists came under Gill's influence at Pigotts and so can be associated with Johnston in the same way as David Jones. Reynolds Stone, who practised wood-engraving, printing, and the design of medals and type, spent just two formative weeks with Gill in 1932.[6] Gill's biographer, Fiona MacCarthy, considers that he was 'in many ways … Gill's closest disciple, in that English tradition of typographic reticence'.[7] Another was Gill's nephew, John Skelton, whose career as a lettering artist and sculptor continued at Streat, near Ditchling, until 1999. Yet another was David Kindersley who worked with Gill on a number of projects including the stone-cut lettering for the fascia of the store

Bentalls (Kingston-upon-Thames), and then later the sculptures for the block of flats known as Dorset House, in Gloucester Place, London, and the design of the fat founts of the Gill Sans typeface.[8] Kindersley set up his own workshop in Cambridge which become influential. The German refugee Ralph Beyer, who earlier had been at Piggots, practised there – his lettering at Coventry Cathedral dates from 1956. So, too, did David Kindersley's son, Richard, who then trained Tom Perkins.

Percy Smith represents a parallel line of development in inscriptional lettering. He set up his own lettering business, the Dorno Workshop and Studio, (later Dorian). His book *Civil and Memorial Lettering*, was published in 1945. In it Smith points out that his 'petit-serif' alphabet, which was commissioned by the London Passenger Transport Board for their head office building at St. James's Park Station, was directly based on Johnston's own block letter alphabet and maybe also influenced by Gill's work, both perhaps stemming from Johnston's earlier teaching. (Fig. 127). Other lettering by Smith, for example, at London University's Senate House, is equally Roman Humanist. That Smith was marked by Johnston's teaching shows, too, in his search for the origins of letter-forms. His article 'Initial Letters in the Printed Book', in Vol. I of *The Fleuron* in 1923, echoes the historical method Johnston adopted in his handbook; its very ethos is Johnstonian:

> The duty of an initial, as of all art is to serve. Service lives while assertiveness is ultimately ignored or rejected.

Smith also trained a number of assistants who, in turn, practised independently, developing the much overlooked craft of sign writing. This has been brought to light by John Nash in the exhibition catalogue, *Sharpness, Unity & Freedom.*[9] Himself a lettering artist, he has written of William Sharpington, who taught at the City and Guilds of London Art School, of Kenneth Breese, and of Bob Cuvier, as being '… as living a part of the Johnston tradition as any illuminated manuscript'. Also discussed is the wood engraver Michael Renton. He was introduced to lettering by George Mansell (an assistant of Percy Smith) and was trained by William Sharpington. Renton is also the author of a pioneering article, 'Edward Johnston and Wood Engraving', in the same catalogue.

Of the other tributary flowing from Johnston – formal calligraphy – its source is to be found principally in Graily Hewitt. In company with Gill and with Anna Simons in Germany he was surely Johnston's most influential pupil-teacher. He taught a second class at the Central School from 1901 and then succeeded Johnston altogether in 1912, and continued teaching into the 1930s. He also taught at Camberwell School of Arts and Crafts. His particular contribution was in the field of gilding and illuminating and these skills were passed on to a number of his students, notably Florence Kingsford (she became Lady Sydney Cockerell), Louise Powell (née Lessore), Vera Law, and Dorothy Hutton. Hewitt published several works on lettering: *Lettering for Students and Craftsmen* in 1930; the *Treyford Writing Cards* in 1932; and *Handwriting: Everyman's Craft* in 1938. He was a founder-member of the Society of Scribes and Illuminators (the SSI), to be discussed below.

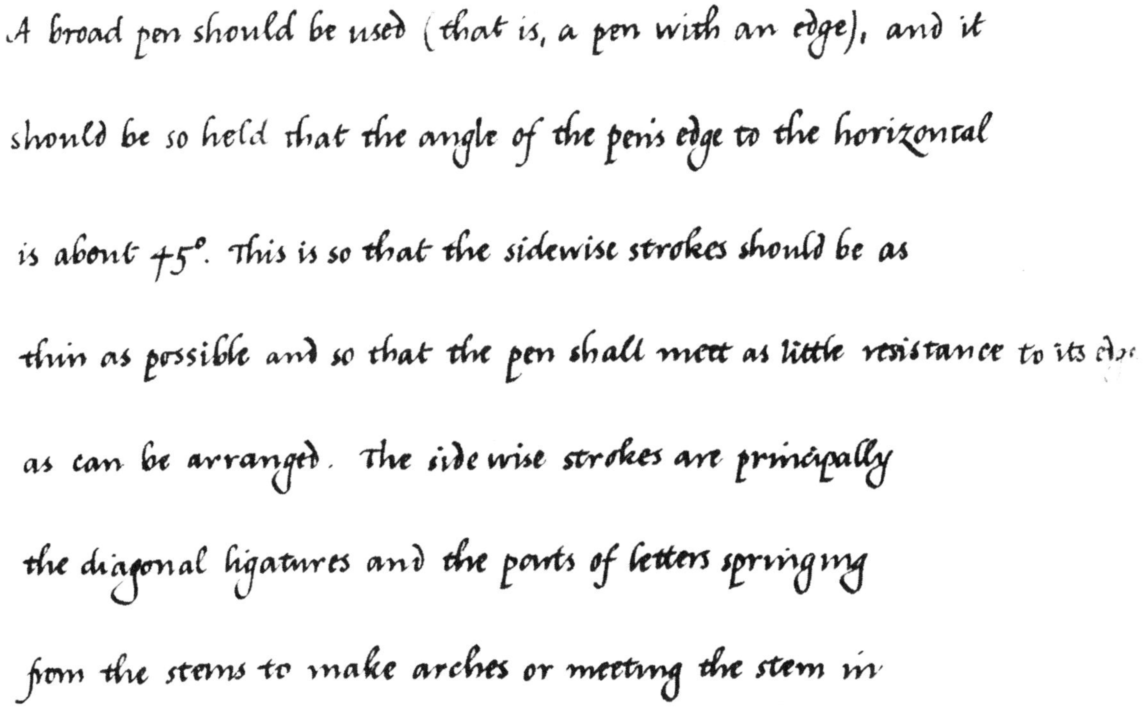

A broad pen should be used (that is, a pen with an edge), and it
should be so held that the angle of the pen's edge to the horizontal
is about 45°. This is so that the sidewise strokes should be as
thin as possible and so that the pen shall meet as little resistance to its
as can be arranged. The sidewise strokes are principally
the diagonal ligatures and the parts of letters springing
from the stems to make arches or meeting the stem in

Fig. 128. A page from Alfred Fairbank's manuscript copy book. 1926. Cited from the exhibition catalogue *Calligraphy*. 1958. Portland Art Association. Oregon.
(Courtesy of the Pierpont Morgan Library.)

Later on Graily Hewitt discounted Johnston's block letter alphabet. The text of a letter to Sydney Cockerell reads:

> In Johnston I have lost confidence. Despite all he did for us at the beginning of this century he has undone too much by forsaking his standard of the Classical Roman alphabet – giving the world, without safeguard or explanation, his block letters which disfigure our modern life. His prestige has obscured their commercialism and vulgarity. And latterly he has given us the calligraphic firework of the panel, which is the modern equivalent of the seventeenth century writing-master's tour de force; beautiful, no doubt, but not the true business of the scribe – which to me has remained, as I learnt it at first, that of the *scriptor librarius*, not the conjurer.[10]

Hewitt was joined in the SSI venture by Alfred Fairbank. A professional civil servant, Fairbank's training began part-time in 1920 at the Central School under Graily Hewitt and Lawrence Cribb. His inspiration, however, was to revive the Italic script as a book hand and for handwriting. 'I believe as strongly in ordinary handwriting as in formal calligraphy', he said. He had first marvelled at the illustrations of the Italian sixteenth-century Italic script in *Writing & Illuminating, & Lettering*. (One example is Plate XXI and Figs. 178–81 showing a manuscript devoted to the poems of Cardinal Bembo which Johnston calls 'cursive' or 'Italic'.)

Although Fairbank was the president of the SSI from 1951–63 it was partly due to him that the Society for Italic Handwriting was established in 1952. Fairbank's earliest utterance on the Italic script came in 1927, in the Tract no. XXVIII of the Society for Pure English, an issue devoted to Italic handwriting, compiled by Robert Bridges. In developing the Italic script, Fairbank's teaching method (the edged pen, the pen angle, the analysis of the strokes of the letter-forms) is entirely Johnstonian. (Fig. 128). Fairbank acknowledged the role of Johnston's 'print script' in the reform of handwriting in his paper *The Teaching of Handwriting: A Suggested Reform* given to the Royal Society of Arts in 1932. The outcome was his own book, *A Handwriting Manual*, of 1932 (with a reprint in 1965 and a revised edition in 1975) and the instructional *Barking Writing Cards* of 1935, later named the *Dryad Writing Cards* (Both were published in house by the Dryad Press, in Leicester, whose proprietor, Harry Peach, was an important force in rethinking the role of crafts in England.) A later series, for schools, is the *Beacon Writing Books* of 1957–6. Fairbank was its editor and author of volumes five and six. His best-known book, however, is an historical survey, *A Book of Scripts*, a delectable King Penguin volume designed by Jan Tschichold in 1949 with five later editions, one in French. His affinity with Johnston is shown in his letter of 1932. It informs Johnston, who remained rather beyond Fairbank's reach in Ditchling, with an air of modest caution about his German article 'Mr. Johnston and English Calligraphy':

> I send you a copy of Schrift und Schreiben and also a copy of the article I sent in English. I cannot read German, but from the errors in the English words I fear the translation is not good. As to the article as I wrote it, may I say that I have not had the opportunity to study under you and learn your methods as I shd. have liked, but I hope I have understood or appreciated you rightly in what I have said.[11]

Another seminal teacher in the Johnston mode from the 1930s was Mervyn C. Oliver. A craftsman of wide talents, he had earlier practised metalwork, drawing, and engraving, and was an assistant to Harold Stabler (Johnston's near neighbour) on the Upper Mall, in Hammersmith. He gained a free scholarship to the RCA in 1911 at which point he came under Johnston's influence, though not exclusively so. He took up calligraphy professionally from 1922, learning yet more from Graily Hewitt, at the Central School and then from Percy Smith. In turn, M. C. Oliver taught at Chelsea School of Art and at St. Martin's School of Art, in London.[12] He also established calligraphy at the then relatively obscure but later significant outpost, the Hampstead Garden Suburb Institute. (Fig. 129).

In September 1921 the hall of the Art Workers' Guild in Queen Square, Holborn, saw the first meeting of the Society of Scribes and Illuminators (SSI). It was a brainchild of a number of Johnstonian calligraphers – from the older generation were Lawrence Cribb, Graily Hewitt, and Alfred Fairbank. From the younger were Louisa Puller and Dorothy Hutton. With the long demise of Johnston's own Society of Calligraphers in mind, its aims embraced the principle of the '… advancement of the crafts of writing and illuminating by the practice of them for themselves alone, without any necessary consideration of reproduction or commercial advantage.' Closer still to Johnston, another of its aims was to '… foster

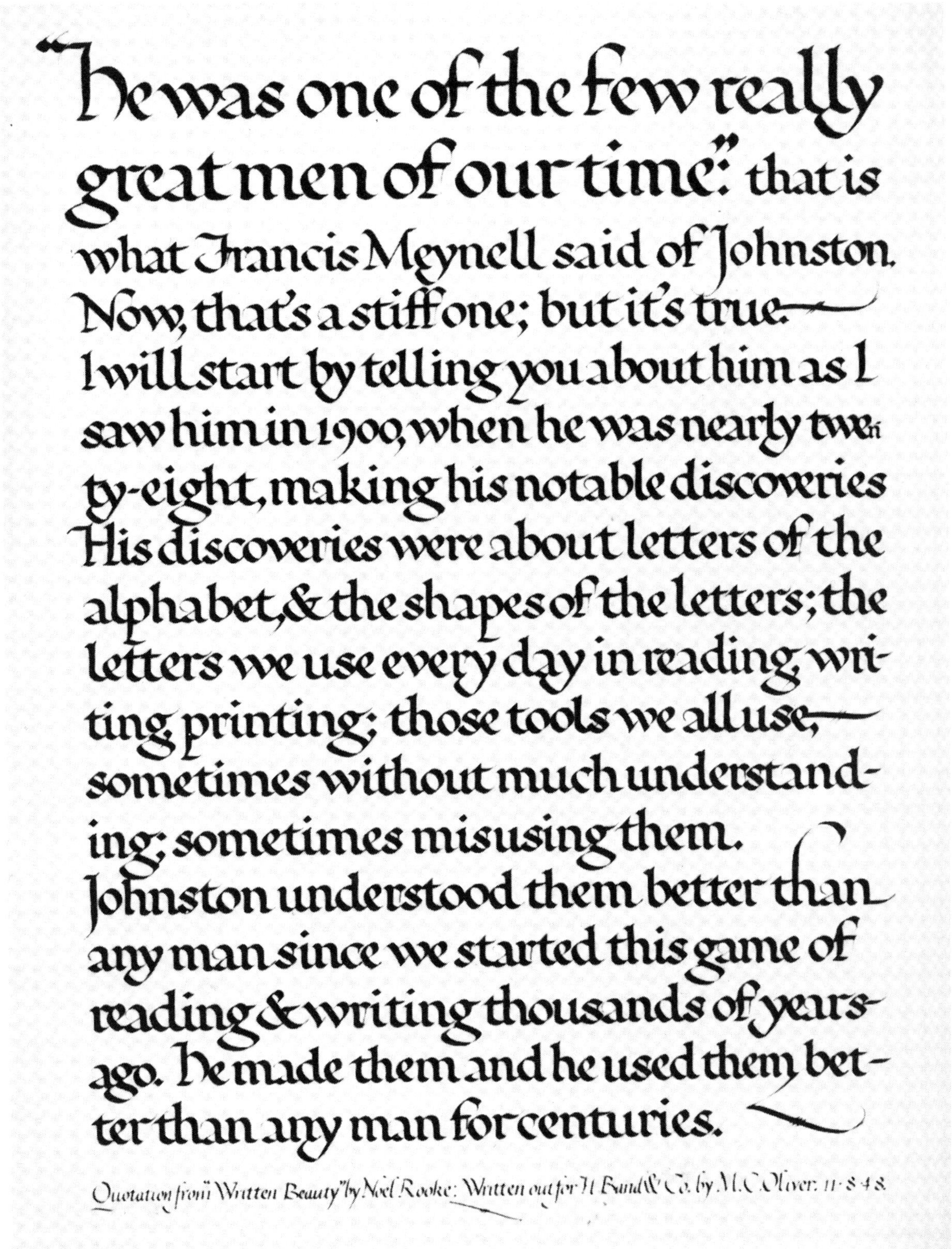

"He was one of the few really
great men of our time": that is
what Francis Meynell said of Johnston.
Now, that's a stiff one; but it's true.—
I will start by telling you about him as I
saw him in 1900, when he was nearly twenty-eight, making his notable discoveries
His discoveries were about letters of the
alphabet, & the shapes of the letters; the
letters we use every day in reading, writing, printing; those tools we all use,—
sometimes without much understanding; sometimes misusing them.
Johnston understood them better than
any man since we started this game of
reading & writing thousands of years
ago. He made them and he used them better than any man for centuries.

Quotation from "Written Beauty" by Noel Rooke: Written out for H Band & Co. by M.C. Oliver: 11·8·48.

Fig. 129. From *Written Beauty* by Noel Rooke 1948. Written by Mervyn C. Oliver in the Foundational Hand. Cited from *Calligraphy Today*. 1988.
(Courtesy of A & C Black.)

The Foundational Hand Fig. 1

abcdefghijklmnopqr
stuvwxyz

Three essentials of form
① Angle of thin stroke of each letter shd be constant at about 30 degrees to the horizontal writing line
② whole alphabet is based on a circle

abcdefghijklm

③ good average height 4½ times the width of nib
"l" has foot
"l" and "t" have round limb

nopqrstuvwxyz

note springing of arches
Notice inside shapes of letters
Exception v and w pen held more steeply

ABCDEFGHIJKLMNNOPQRSTUVWXYZ

Fig. a
ear
here the pen is held with the thin stroke horizontal giving a beautiful writing but remote from present day use.

Fig. b
ear
here the pen is held with the thin stroke at 30 degrees giving good form - greater speed in writing and more legibility. It is nearer to the printed Roman that our eye is used to.

Fig. c
earth
here the pen is held too steeply giving heavy shoulders & feet. This is to be avoided as ugly

Fig. 2
oblique nib

Fig. 3
pad
paper
writing
level
guard

Fig. 4
writing board at angle of about 45°

Of wealth and fame and power
These masons did not know:
'Let's build,' they said, 'a tower,
Square to the winds that blow;
We are not men of culture,
Yet we are here to build
Room for a king's sepulture
And worthy of our guild.'

So came each beam and rafter;
Each winged flight of stone.
Their deathless work lives after,
Their names were never known:
For beauty did they plead not,
Yet beauty they did win,
And, like a child you heed not,
The grace of heaven crept in.

Footnote concerning the diagrams:-
Since the Foundational Hand is stated as being based on a circle, this form should be repeated in the arched letters as well as in the round ones. So the letter 'p' is similar to a reversed 'q' in form, or an inverted 'd'; an 'n' is like an inverted 'u' in shape and the 'h' and 'm' have the same unity and contain part of an 'o', as does the top arch and bottom loop of an 'a'. The diagram does not strictly carry out this essential unity of form. Irene Wellington 26 November 1947.

Borne out in:-
benediction
prebendary
illuminate

Fig. 130. Page from *Copybook No. I* written by Irene Wellington. Cited from Irene Wellington. *More than Fine Writing*. 1996. (Courtesy of Overlook Press. Woodstock. New York.)

a body of sincere and vital endeavour rather than mere technical ability.' Yet another was '… [to] be zealously directed towards the production of books and documents wholly hand-made, regarding other application of the work as preliminary or subordinate, but not excluding it from its scope.'[13] In order to perpetuate high standards the SSI set up an honorary membership by invitation based on merit. Early members given this distinction were Mildred Ratcliffe and Daisy Alcock. (In 1952 the SSI admitted lay members.) Johnston was its first honorary member and Fairbank its secretary and then its first (and only) president. A forum for discussion, one of its earliest lectures was given on heraldry by Johnston's lifelong friend from Hammersmith Terrace, Oswald Barron. The SSI also organised exhibitions. The first was called 'Writing and Civilisation', with an introduction by William Lethaby. Another, held at the V&A in 1931, was called 'Three Centuries of Illuminated Addresses, Diplomas and Honorary Freedom Scrolls'. It showed five pieces Johnston calligraphed for the livery companies of the City of London. Other exhibitions were sent abroad. One, also in 1931, went to the Livre d'Art exhibition in Paris and another, in 1938, to the Institute of Graphic Arts in the USA (to New York, Boston, Chicago, New Haven), where it inspired Johnstonian ideas.

The advent of the SSI underscored the work of a second generation of Johnston's pupils/teachers. Important among those were his assistants at the RCA from the 1920s to the late 1930s. A number of them are mentioned by Johnston. Madelyn Walker is

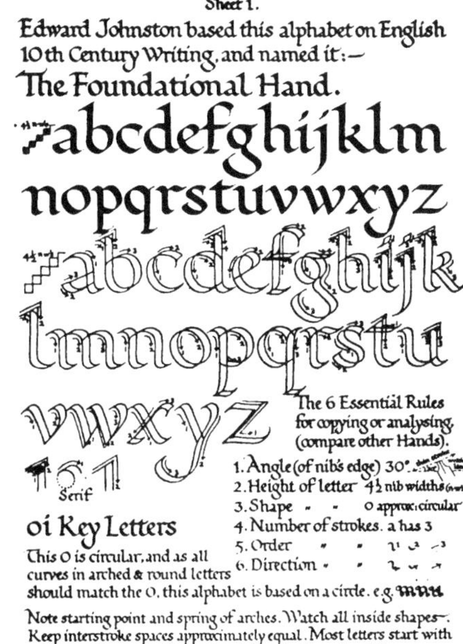

Fig. 131. Writing Sheets based on Johnston's Foundational Hand written by Margaret Alexander.
Cited from *Calligraphy Today*. 1963.
(Courtesy of Studio Books.)

the best known. She taught at Sheffield Technical College of Art. She was with Graily Hewitt at the Central School between 1922–24 and also worked with him (as did another Johnston student, Ida Henstock) in Hampshire, before retiring to a convent.

Perhaps the most revered of all these assistants/pioneers is Irene Wellington (née Base, her first married name was Sutton), who was at the Royal College of Art between 1925–30 assisting Johnston there from 1928. She taught at the Edinburgh School of Art between 1932–43 and then at the Central School between 1944–60, where her approach was the wholly Johnstonian one of concentrating on the item of work rather than on exercises. She published her series of *Wellington Copybooks I–III* in 1957 (Fig. 130). An omnibus edition was published by Pentalic in 1977 which included a fourth *Copybook*. And, as in Johnston's case, another more expansive handbook remained unfinished. A biographical study, *More Than Fine Writing*, was published about Irene Wellington in 1986, with a new edition in 1998. Its contributors were Heather Child, Heather Collins, Ann Hechle, and Donald Jackson.[14] These last two were outstanding pupils of hers at the Central School. Donald Jackson stresses the reality that by no means all of Johnston's pupils 'stayed the course' and that his 'monkish' aura deterred some who were motivated more by commercial pressures. Yet through Jackson's account one senses the sequence of generations enacting Johnston's notion of 'freedom':

> Irene was always proud to acknowledge her debt to Johnston but she was able to admire him without abdicating responsibility for her own ideas.... She was able to take him [Johnston] at his own word: 'Rules are there to be used as a spring board for right and lively work, not rigidity but liberation'....
>
> By chance we were just far enough removed in time from Johnston to be able to admire the spirit and form of his work without feeling tempted to copy his 'style'.

In Ann Hechle's comments one reads a nearly identical set of reflections. She reports Irene Wellington's thoughts about Johnston and then her own about Wellington:

> To think of Johnston is to think of Truth; it was, I believe, his unswerving insistence on truth that made his teaching so alive and so deeply fixed in those who stayed the course.

> In her working life she [Irene Wellington] stretched the whole concept of calligraphy from the formal roots of Johnston's teaching (itself embedded in the historical tradition) to the freedom of personal expression.

It was Irene Wellington whom Johnston wished to come to Ditchling in 1944 to write the celebrated manuscript commissioned by Winston Churchill which he was too frail to undertake. It was to be presented to Harry Hopkins, the personal assistant of President Roosevelt.

Another of Johnston's assistants was Dorothy Mahoney (née Bishop). She became Johnston's successor at the RCA on his retirement in 1939 until 1953. A vital line runs from her to her pupil, Ann Camp. She also taught at the Central School and wrote a manual, *The Craft of Calligraphy*, which was published with support from the Society of Scribes and Illuminators in 1981. One of Johnston's private pupils in the 1930s was Margaret Alexander. Her vivid impressions of three visits to Cleves (two in April 1932 and one in November 1934) were recorded in a series of accounts[15] which have not been published to date. She did, however, publish a series of writing sheets. (Fig. 131).

Another significant figure whose career began in the prewar period was William Gardner, trained first by M. C. Oliver at Hampstead Garden Suburb Institute and then by Johnston (and by a Johnston-trained designer, Professor Tristam) at the RCA. He also learnt about metal engraving and die-casting at the Central School from the punch-cutter George Friend who had been Johnston's punch-cutter in his type design work for the Cranach Presse.[16] Gardner developed a long and eminent career as a calligrapher, as a medallist working for the Royal Mint, and as a designer of heraldry and type. He wrote many articles. His first handbook, *Alphabet at Work*, appeared in 1982 and his second, *William Gardner's Book of Calligraphy*, in 1988. (Fig. 132).

To the period spanning the years between the wars belong the achievements of a number of typographers and printer-scholars. Notable are J. H. Mason, Francis Meynell, and Harold Curwen. Curwen was Johnston's pupil at the Central School but as his followers they all carried his convictions into the domain of commercial printing and, thence, to a reading public at large. In this sense their work is of wider significance than that of the lettering artists. Mason was a compositor at the Doves Press. He then became head of the School of Book Production at the Central School. Harold Curwen, of the Curwen Press, along with his colleague, Henry Ball, followed Johnstonian precepts which inspired them in the day-to-day production at Curwen's from about 1911, making it one of the most respected presses of its time. In 1913, Harold Curwen designed a sanserif typeface which happened to precede,

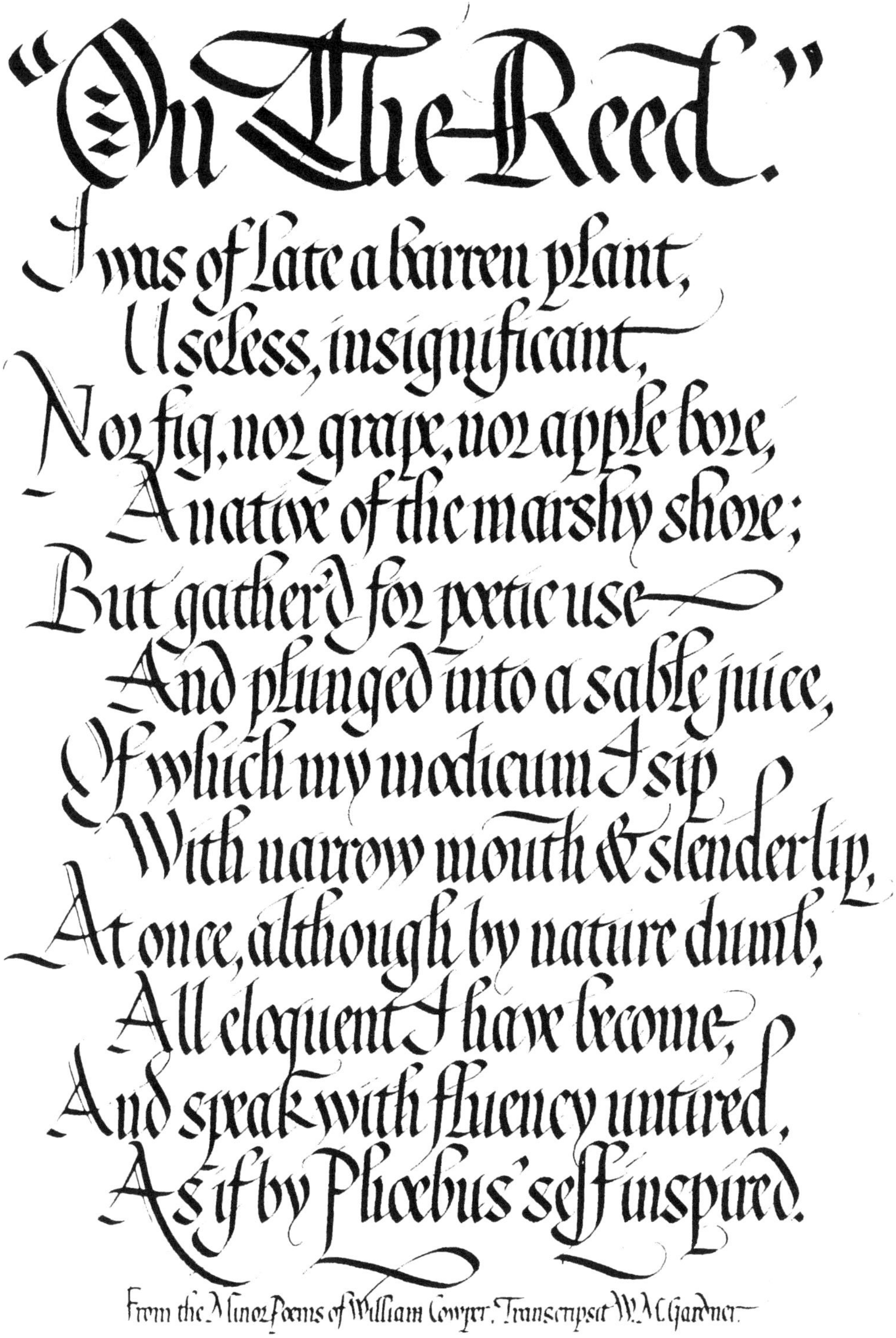

"On The Reed."

I was of late a barren plant,
Useless, insignificant,
Nor fig, nor grape, nor apple bore,
A native of the marshy shore;
But gather'd for poetic use
And plunged into a sable juice,
Of which my modicum I sip
With narrow mouth & slender lip,
At once, although by nature dumb,
All eloquent I have become,
And speak with fluency untired,
As if by Phœbus' self inspired.

From the Minor Poems of William Cowper. Transcripsit W. M. C. Gardner.

Fig. 132. Transcription of a poem by William Cowper written out by William Gardner. Cited from *Lettering Today*. 1937.
(Courtesy of *The Studio*.)

ABCDEFGHIJKLMNO
PQRSTUVWXYZ
abcdefghijklmnopqrst
uvwxyz

CURWEN SANSERIF TYPE
DESIGNED BY HAROLD CURWEN

Fig. 133. Letters from Johnston's block letter alphabet compared with Harold Curwen's sanserif alphabet based on the Trajan Column. Cited from Harry Carter in *Curwen Miscellany*. 1931.
(Courtesy of the Curwen Press.)

though did not rival, Johnston's own Railway block alphabet. (Fig. 133). In his article 'Sanserif Types', in the *Curwen Miscellany* in 1931, the scholar Harry Carter pointed out that '... it was conceived at a time when Mr. Curwen was studying lettering under Edward Johnston. It was quite natural that they should both solve the problem of a simplified Roman letter in the same way, for both took the Trajan Column as a model of good lettering.'

Francis Meynell belonged to a celebrated Catholic and literary family headed by the poet and writer, Alice Meynell. He had been a 'private press' man who, with youthful enthusiasm, had borrowed a fount of the pre-Caslon Fell types[17] from the Oxford University Press intending to reinstate a high degree of typographic purity in printing. In 1916 he set up his small-scale private Pelican Press and, in 1923, the Nonesuch Press. At the latter his objective was to depart from an indulgent attachment to private printing and, instead, apply its craft values to commercial book-printing. In his account, *The Nonesuch Century*, of 1936, he reminisced about:

> ... the theory that mechanised means could be made to serve fine ends, that the machine in printing was a controllable tool. Therefore we set out to be ... architects of books rather than builders.[18]

This raises related questions about Johnston. Might he have approved of the notion of a book designer as an 'architect' rather than as a 'craftsman-builder'?

Bernard Newdigate was another printer-typographer of influence who faced up to the same issues. Scholarly, Catholic, and conservative, yet he was forward-looking for the needs of book-printing. He, too, valued the Johnstonian tradition. Moreover, Newdigate was a practising printer who managed the family's Arden Press until 1914. He owed much to Emery Walker for practical advice and employed Joseph Thorp as an associate. In 1907, the Press moved to Letchworth, the first Garden City, bringing with it some thirty Catholic workers. (In 1908 it was taken over by W. H. Smith.) There he met Adrian Fortescue, a priest and a scholar of oriental languages who had been an early recruit to Johnston's lettering classes – he joined the Thursday evening course at the Central School in December 1899, staying for six months.[19] Newdigate was inspired by Fortescue's library of antiquarian books and manuscripts (said by the local paper, *The Citizen*, to number some ten thousand volumes[20]) and gained an appreciation of Morris, of calligraphy, and of printing history. He was devoted to the use of the Caslon typeface. *The Collected Works of William Morris, 1910–15*, for example, was set by him in Caslon. In 1913 he printed for Fortescue his translation, *Latin Hymns sung at the Church of St. Hugh Letchworth,* using an Albion handpress with the help of his sister, Katherine (Mary) Newdigate, the work being done at her home, Astley Cottage, and supervised by Fortescue himself. From 1920 Newdigate was the typographer at the Shakespeare Head Press which was at Stratford-upon-Avon and from 1930 at Oxford. In his article, 'Lettering and the Printer', in Vol. XXXIV of *Penrose's Annual* in 1932, he acknowledged Johnston's classes at the Central School to be '… the starting point of a movement which has spread far beyond England'. In one of the 'Book Production Notes' written for *The London Mercury* between 1920–37[21] he remembered Johnston's handbook:

> … there is one treasured volume whose well thumbed cover and pages always give satisfaction: and its grime is evidence of the delight it has given to scores of readers and students. I bought Mr. Johnston's *Writing, & Illuminating & Lettering* [sic] soon after its first publication early this century. Since then, I have lent it more than any of my books.… No other is so good, because no other is so fundamentally sound.

Newdigate's particular contribution was to recommend a basic education in calligraphy for compositors in the printing industry. In another of his 'Book Production Notes', entitled *Type*, his advice resembles that made by Stanley Morison:

> 'What we need most is not the revival of old types, however great their historical, aesthetic, or technical interest. We need instead a modern school of type designers who shall be trained in calligraphy … and shall practise it with an eye to the requirements of the printed letter. And they must not ignore the conditions which rule in typefounding and modern printing. The future of type-design is with the calligrapher.'[22]

Newdigate commissioned a number of calligraphers who had been Johnston's pupils. One was Anna Simons who designed for him the initial letters for the edition of Milton's *Paradise Lost* and *Paradise Regained* published by the Cresset Press (Fig. 134). Another was Joscelyne Gaskin. She calligraphed the titling in a

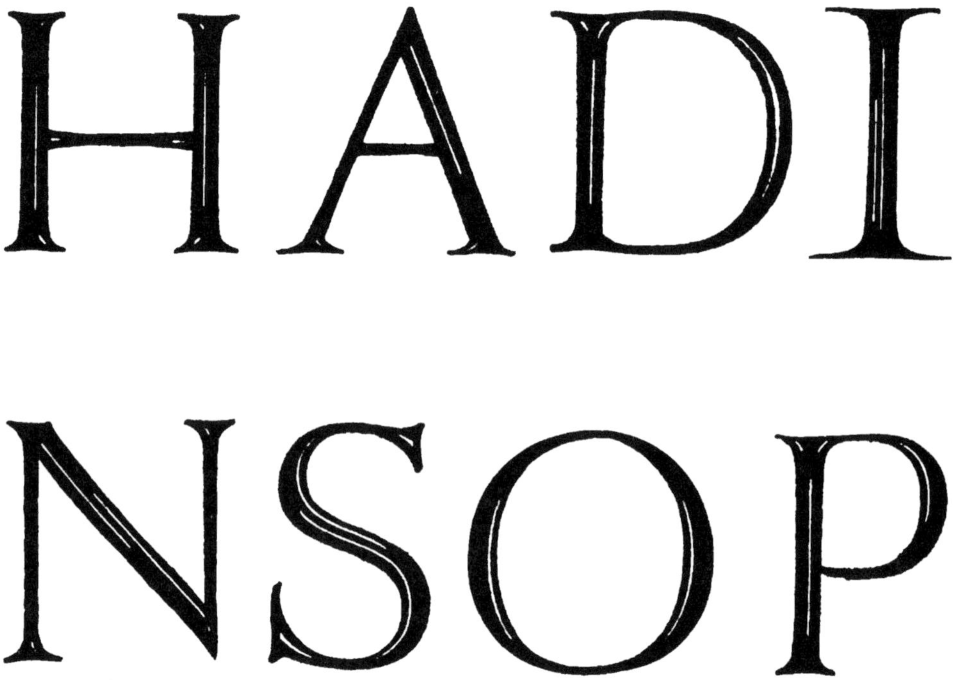

Fig. 134. Anna Simons' initial letters used in Milton's *Paradise Lost* and *Paradise Regained*. 1931. Cresset Press edition. Cited from *Penrose's Annual*. Vol. XXXIV. 1932. (Courtesy of Lund Humphries Ltd.)

HADI

NSOP

variant of the Uncial style for an edition of Spenser's *The Faerie Queene* and for Bacon's *Essays*, both of which were also published by Cresset. (Fig. 135). Of special interest, however, is the lesser known Eleni Zompolides who had been at the RCA from 1896 under Walter Crane, studying design and embroidery. She then studied under Johnston at the RCA, where she was a contemporary of Anna Simons. She continued her studies under Johnston and Graily Hewitt at the Central School where, in 1904, she met the bookbinder, Douglas Cockerell. From 1906 she became his design assistant at W. H. Smith. In 1907 Johnston, Graily Hewitt and Lethaby provided Eleni Zompolides with references to teach at Putney School of Art.[23] At this time Eleni Zompolides moved in a circle of artistic friends which included Noel Rooke's sister, Margaret, and Anna Simons. It was probably her introduction that later enabled Newdigate to meet Anna Simons.[24] In 1908 Zompolides' work with Douglas Cockerell took her to Letchworth where he was Controller of W. H. Smith's bindery. She also worked for Newdigate at the Arden Press. She provided the decorative initial lettering for the prestigious Arden folio books, *The Gold and Silver of Windsor Castle* of 1911 and *Old Silver of American Churches* of 1913. It is likely that she designed the woodcut initials inset into a Latin edition of *De Imitatione* by Thomas à Kempis, with an introduction in Latin by Fortescue, printed in 1919. She also did design work on the bindings of the Everyman books published by J. M. Dent, a company which was based at Letchworth. One early and major calligraphic commission was the *Eton College Memorial Book* done in 1903 with the binding by Douglas Cockerell. It commemorates the pupils who were victims to the Boer War.

To those whose ideas were influenced by Johnston's teaching must be added the name of Stanley Morison, one of the most outstanding figures in British typography in the twentieth century. Morison's interest in typographic matters

THE FOURTH BOOKE OF THE FAERIE QUEENE

Fig. 135. Lettering by Joselyne Gaskin for the Cresset Press edition of Spenser's *The Faerie Queene*.
(Courtesy of the Cresset Press.)

developed on account of two early experiences. In September 1912 he came across *The Times Printing Number* of that year, a wide-ranging survey which introduced to him many facets of the subject, both historical and contemporary. Count Harry Kessler, for example, wrote about modern German printing stressing the roles of Gill and Johnston. Then, in 1913, Morison met Johnston in person – this was his first encounter – and read his *Writing & Illuminating, & Lettering.* His interest in the history of scripts was aroused. By the time of his death in 1967 he had written some fifty books and one-hundred-and-twenty articles on lettering topics. The scholar was emboldened to become a typographer and a type designer. Morison is especially known for the major part he played in designing the Times New Roman typeface for *The Times* newspaper, which was first printed in it on the 3rd October 1932. However, many other typefaces were initiated by him previously. Like Johnston before him, Morison brought his knowledge of the history of scripts and types to bear on the problems and the needs of the present. And like Harold Curwen and Francis Meynell, he had a fundamental impact on the aesthetic standards of British book- and jobbing-printing.

For these reasons the extent to which Morison took up Johnston's ideas and then developed others in response to the need to adapt to mechanisation is of particular interest. It was through Johnston that Morison first realised the relevance of calligraphy to type forms. But in due course this was to give way to an awareness of the tradition of engraving rather than pen-based calligraphy, as an equal influence on type designing.

Morison's views on typography, together with his Catholicism, his conscientious objections to the Great War, and his socialist convictions, combined to make him enlightened and forward-looking, tradition being to trace forward as well as to trace backwards. Yet, in matters typographical, he remained convinced of the value of tradition. His rational conservatism found its mature voice in his article *First Principles of Typography.* Amounting to a distillation of his faith in continuity, it was first printed in the *Encyclopaedia Britannica* in 1929 (though formulated earlier) and was revised for *The Fleuron* No. 7 in 1930 and eleven other editions (including a translation in French by Fernard Baudin, in Dutch by Jan van Krimpen and in German). At the heart of what he called his 'doctrine' is the notion of 'public service':

> It is of the essence of typography and the nature of the printed book that it provides a public service.... Experiment was possible at printing's infancy ... nowadays ... literate society is greater in mass and correspondingly slower in movement.... No printer should admit typographical distraction ... doing violence to logic and lucidity in the supposed interests of decoration.[25]

Some twenty-five years later Morison, in 1953, wrote one of his last books, *A Tally of Types*. Couched in an almost valedictory tone, Morison gave an historical anchorage to the thoroughly Johnstonian restraint of *First Principles of Typography*. He looked back on a career as a creator of typefaces and acknowledged their pedigree:

> ... it was to Morris, Walker, Cockerell, Lethaby, Johnston we owe the right making of letters in both calligraphy and typography.[26]

From the very outset Morison was favoured by the friendship of socially well-placed Catholics, among them Father Herbert Thurston and the literary Meynells, a family headed by the poet Alice Meynell. He was equipped with scholarly knowledge, written in a faultless and at times colourful, if acerbic, prose style. Furthermore, he was endowed with formidable powers of persuasion, invariably delivered in the form of critical reports. Morison rose quickly through the hierarchy of the printing industry. In early 1913 he was appointed an assistant to *The Imprint*, for which post he was interviewed by its editors, including Johnston. Late in 1913, through Gerard Meynell, he joined the Catholic publishers Burns and Oates, and there gained a friend in Gerard's cousin, Francis Meynell, who was fast developing as a book designer. In 1916 Morison joined Francis Meynell in his celebrated excursion into private printing at 67 Romney Street, Westminster, assisting him in the printing of *Ten Poems by Alice Meynell*. The ten initials of this slim volume were 'rubricated by Edward Johnston in November 1915' – this was probably Morison's second encounter. (Fig. 136). In 1919 he replaced Francis Meynell as 'the designer of printed matter' at the Pelican Press which, owned by Francis, they together made famous by using decorated initials and printer's flowers.[27]

In 1922 Morison joined with Oliver Simon and others to launch the typographic journal, *The Fleuron*. As with *The Imprint*, it aimed to demonstrate the artistic potential of books typeset by machine. Morison contributed articles and reviews. In 1923 Morison became 'typographic adviser' to the Lanston Monotype Corporation, destined to become Britain's leading typefoundry, working with two successive managing directors, Harold Duncan and William Burch, and with the sceptical works manager, Frank Pierpont. In the same year, 1923, he designed Vol. XXV of *Penrose's Annual*, setting it in Monotype's new Garamond typeface. In 1925 he gained the typographic consultancy to the Cambridge University Press under its

TEN POEMS
BY ALICE MEYNELL
1913—1915

WESTMINSTER
THE ROMNEY STREET PRESS
1915

ALL NIGHT had shout of men, & cry
Of woeful women filled His way;
Until that noon of sombre sky
On Friday, clamour and display
  Smote Him; no solitude had He,
  No silence, since Gethsemane.

¶EASTER NIGHT

Public was Death; but power, but might,
But Life again, but victory,
Were hushed within the dead of night,
The piteous dark, the secrecy.
  And all alone, alone, alone
  He rose again behind the stone.

Fig. 136. Double page from book printed by Francis Meynell and Stanley Morison. *Ten Poems of Alice Meynell,* 1922, with initial letters written in colour by Edward Johnston.

Printer, Walter Lewis. In 1925 he also succeeded Oliver Simon as the editor of *The Fleuron*, seeing to the issue No. 5 in 1926. He remained editor until its demise with No. 7 in 1930. In 1929, Morison was appointed typographic consultant to *The Times* newspaper under its editor, Geofrey Dawson.

Morison's positions at *The Fleuron*, at Monotype (together with its journal *The Monotype Recorder*), and at CUP gave him a platform. *The Fleuron* enabled Morison to undertake the writing and publishing of monographs under its imprint. Such was his book *Type Designs Past and Present*, of 1927. Two other projects under its ægis directly concerned Johnston. One, conceived in the autumn of 1922, was Morison's plan for a study of sixteenth-century Italian writing books, for which Johnston was drawn in to provide twelve panels to be printed by collotype. Another was an article for *The Fleuron* No. 5, 1926, on 'Edward Johnston and Calligraphy in England'. It was to be written by William Lethaby. While Morison and Oliver Simon made *The Fleuron* the leading typographic journal of its day, these particular ideas did not materialise.

Morison's work for Monotype was another beneficiary of his forceful convictions. In his *A Tally of Types* he claimed to have initiated for Monotype a '… programme of typographic [i.e., type] design, rational, systematic, and corresponding effectively to the foreseeable needs of printing'. The claim to have drafted the programme in advance of his appointment as a lapse of memory have been challenged, however, by James Moran in his study *Stanley Morison: his Typographic Achievement* of 1971.

Putting the controversy about Morison to one side, the period of reconstruction after the Great War saw the need for book-printing to adapt to technological change, as had the newspaper industry. Morison invoked the spirit of the Design and Industries Association in his account, stating his programme to be a '… new or repeated application of the Lethaby doctrine'. In this sense, the creation of new typefaces by and for machinery went far beyond Johnston's typographical horizons. For it meant not just the application but also the integration of two inventions: the Lanston Monotype automated type-composing machine, which eliminated typesetting type by hand, and the Benton mechanical type-engraving machine, which made the role of the punch-cutter equally redundant.

Inspired by a sense of purpose, Morison took on, as it were, the mantle of knight errant. The outcome was the marriage of the interests of the Monotype Corporation, now festooned with Morison's newly commissioned typefaces, to those of the Cambridge University Press, whose use of them would stimulate a widening demand. (The Curwen Press under Harold Curwen and the Westminster Press under Gerard Meynell were among the first to take up the new typefaces.) Morison's programme was not one of innovation, however, but of the 'revival of historic design', as he put it. In this sense Morison and Monotype were following the precedent of the English private press movement except that Morison rejected an aesthetic based on the fifteenth-century Jenson types. He considered such designs to be too self-conscious. Morris's Golden type, Rickett's Vale Press type, Lucien Pissarro's Brook type (for his Eragny Press), St. John Hornby's Subiaco type (for his Ashendene Press), and their counterparts in America, were unacceptable to the doctrine of *First Principles of Typography*. Morison even spoke of a '… private press gang rating themselves a little too seriously'.[28] Unacceptable, too, was the recent wave of Antiqua, or Roman, designs in Germany. Only Emil Weiss's Antiqua was innocent of being overly individualistic. And, anyway, in his scepticism of modernism, Morison regarded Germany as the 'land of heresy'. 'The German has naturally a greater love for experiment than we. Much of his present-day architecture is so novel as to be fantastic to our taste.' So he wrote in *A Tally of Types*.

To the word 'rational' Morison might well have added 'refined'. A trend was developing with which he identified. It flew in the face of the time-honoured Caslon typeface which was first shown in 1734, but used earlier, and was so praised by Johnston and so relied upon by others of his generation. (In designing the Imprint typeface, Gerard Meynell and John Mason were inspired by Caslon. Hilary Pepler at the S. Dominic's Press believed in nothing else.) Morison, by contrast, agreed with the American typographer Bruce Rogers that Caslon was not without its rivals. Rogers, who had preceded Morison as typographic adviser at the Cambridge University Press from 1918–20, had spoken of '… many other old models nobler in proportion and finer in drawing than Caslon'.

Through his own researches (and through those of others, notably by the American scholars Daniel Updike and Beatrice Warde),[29] Morison recognised the merit of the Aldine-Garamond types – that group of 'Old Style' designs which had superseded the Jenson, or 'Venetian', ones of the 1460s–70s. (Fig. 137). They originated in the books printed by Aldus Manutius (still at Venice) a generation later than Jenson, from 1495. It was to the Aldine-Garamond style that the Caslon design was distantly related. Morison saw the advantage of the more refined and bracketed serifs of the Aldus types and their shorter capital letters. He argued that they relate better to the lower case letters than do the 'solid horizontal and unbracketed' Jenson capitals, thus making for a more even page of text. In his article 'Towards an Ideal Type' (later renamed 'Towards an Ideal Roman Type') printed in Vol. 2 of *The Fleuron* for 1924, Morison pointed to the history of calligraphy: first to the Carolingian School of Tours where '… the height of the capitals occurring in the text is considerably lower than the ascenders' and then to Renaissance Humanist manuscripts in which, he claimed, '… reduced capitals tend to predominate in number but normally occur in the best specimens'. Aldus's types (notably his edition of Cardinal Bembo's *De Ætna* of 1495) were used by the French punch-cutter Claude Garamond as his model in the 1530s, for Garamond was inspired by the humanist Geofroy Tory who had returned to France from Italy. He was then joined by others such as Antoine Augereau. Morison claimed that the Garamond design was '… preferable in its weight and thickness of line, in the openness and generous width of its letters'. Of Claude Garamond himself he wrote praising his punch-cutting skills:

> … he was incomparably the finest engraver of romans among the first great generation of French renaissance printers and publishers who led the movement away from Gothic and towards Roman.

THE FIRST ROMAN USED BY ALDUS MANUTIUS SHOWN IN THE DIALOGUE 'DE AETNA' BY PIETRO BEMBO, VENICE 1495. FIRST RECUT IN 1929 BY THE MONOTYPE CORPORATION

Of the several romans used by Aldus the most noble is the roman whose trade name is Bembo. It arrives in order of historic precedence next to the roman of Jenson, which is separated from it by an interval of twenty-five years. Neither the Bembo roman nor the press for which it was cut enjoys anything like the

THE THIRD ROMAN USED BY ALDUS MANUTIUS AND FIRST SHOWN IN THE HYPNEROTOMACHIA POLIPHILI VENICE 1499. FIRST RECUT IN 1923 BY THE MONOTYPE CORPORATION

ATIN was not the abiding love of Teobaldo Manucci, better known as Aldo Manuzio or Aldus Manutius. He early became a devotee of Greek, talked Greek in his household, staffed his office

THE 'GARAMOND' ROMAN

CUT BY THE MONOTYPE CORPORATION IN 1922

N the new programme of type-design adopted by the Monotype Corporation in 1922 a face of French renaissance origin was given first place. It was necessary in the early stages of the new Monotype effort, which included the Polifilo roman

Fig. 137. Stanley Morison's commissioning of new type designs for the Monotype Corporation based on the Aldine/Garamond group of Old Face designs. *Above*: Bembo 1929. *Centre*: Poliphilus 1923. *Below*: Garamond 1922. Cited from *A Tally of Types*.
(Courtesy of Cambridge University Press.)

THE FIRST ROMAN USED BY ALDUS MANUTIUS SHOWN IN THE DIALOGUE 'DE AETNA' BY PIETRO BEMBO, VENICE 1495. FIRST RECUT IN 1929 BY THE MONOTYPE CORPORATION

To which is added a cutting of an italic designed by Alfred Fairbank and another italic, made standard for the fount, originally designed by Giovantonio Tagliente, Venice 1524.

Of the several romans used by Aldus the most noble is the roman whose trade name is Bembo. It arrives in order of historic precedence next to the roman of Jenson, which is separated from it by an interval of twenty-five years. Neither the Bembo roman nor the press for which it was cut enjoys anything like the praise given to the *Eusebius* roman and the press of Nicolas Jenson. Few indeed have found anything to admire in the romans (save one) of Aldus Manutius, and everybody has condemned his greeks. According to Morris, the types of 'the famous family of Aldus' were 'artistically on a much lower level than Jenson's, and in fact they must be considered to have ended the age of fine printing in Italy'. Updike was less severe, and prepared to admit one of the Aldine romans as

30

Fig. 138. Cited from *A Tally of Types*. Aldus Manutius' edition of Bembo's *De Ætna*.

Fig. 139. *Writing & Illuminating, & Lettering*, Fig. 180 Italian manuscript.

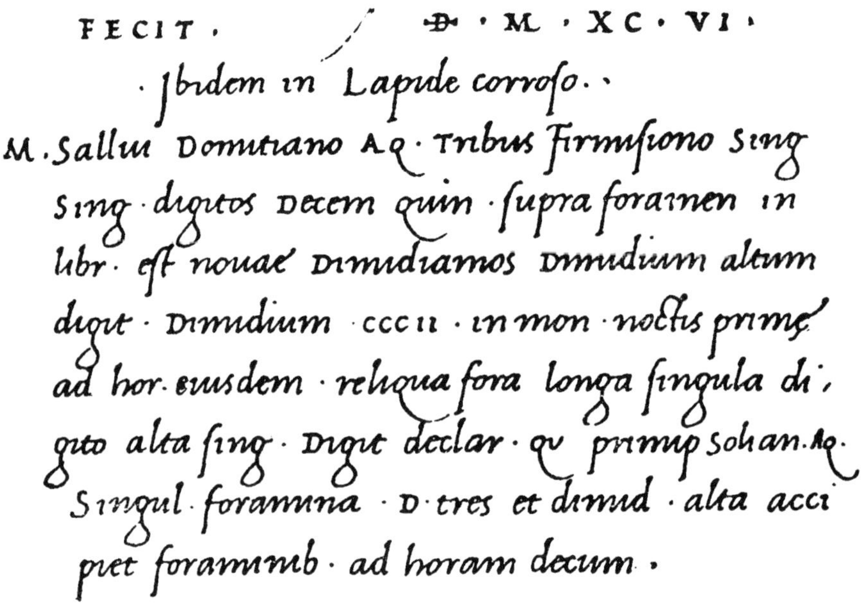

FECIT . ·D· · M · XC · VI ·
· Ibidem in Lapide corroso. ·
M. Sallui Domitiano Aq · Tribus Firmisiono sing
sing · digitos Decem quin · supra foramen in
libr · est nouae Dimidiamos Dimidium altum
digit · Dimidium · cccii · in mon · noctis prime
ad hor. eiusdem · reliqua fora longa singula di,
gito alta sing · Digit declar · qu primip soli an. Aq.
Singul. foramina · D · tres et dimid · alta acci
piet foraminib · ad horam decum ·

FIG. 180.

The designs of Garamond were developed by his successors of the next generation, principally the punch-cutter Robert Granjon. These designs, in turn, passed on to Christophe Plantin who had his main printing office in Antwerp. (Some passed on again to the Oxford University Press through the efforts of Bishop Fell and his agent in Holland, Thomas Marshall, as the Fell types, in 1668.)

The new typefaces Morison helped organise for Monotype between 1922 and the early 1930s were largely taken, therefore, from the classic Aldine/Garamond designs first used by the Italian and French Renaissance printers. They were given appropriate names. One was Poliphilus Roman. Produced in 1923, it was taken from a copy of Aldus's edition of Francesco Colonna's bizarre though alluring novel, *Hypnerotomachia Poliphili,* of 1499. Its cutting was achieved, wrote Morison in his *A Tally of Types*, by '… conscientious photography, exact tracing and efficient engraving'. Another was Bembo Roman, of 1929, based on Aldus Manutius's edition of Bembo's *De Ætna* of 1495. (Fig. 138). There were also two designs very close to the Garamond, one by Granjon and another by Jannon. Morison also revived for Monotype some of the transitional Roman typefaces of the eighteenth century whose letter-forms anticipated the modern type designs. Among these were re-cut versions of Baskerville, Fournier, and Bell.[30]

Important, too, were the Italic type designs which Morison added to Monotype's repertoire to accompany the Humanist Romans. The Italic letter-form had its origin as a cursive variant of the upright Humanist script. Compact and usually sloping, it was being practised by the Humanist Niccolò Niccoli as early as 1410. Its use was categorised by Morison as a 'second-class book-script'. It then passed to the papal chancery in Rome, a move probably initiated by the Humanist Cardinal

Dear Mr. Bridges. Your letter recalls me to a sense of duty. I have been for several weeks on the point of writing about writing. First I wanted to send you the enclosed pieces written by a friend, Adrian Fortescue of Letchworth: I wonder if you wd think it gd. enough for the projected little book on handwriting, i.e. the series of cursive (Fortescue's is hardly that) hands used, not by professional calligraphers but by mere human beings. I think this book wd be a power for good & very much hope that you will bear it in mind. I think Fortescue's church notice sheet an admirable piece – he did this writing habitually, never used any other & was very rapid.

& to

Mrs. Bridges I send one or two arrangements of flowers in proof stage. Any evolutions from her cunning hand wd. be very welcome to

Yours
& hers: Stanley Morison

Fig. 140. Stanley Morison's Italic handwriting. Letter mentioning Adrian Fortescue to Robert Bridges. 1923. Cited from *S. P. E. Tract No. XXIII.* (Courtesy of the Oxford at the Clarendon Press 1926.)

Piccolomini who was a papal secretary. In the mid-fifteenth century it was being used in diplomatic for the writing of a category of letters in the papal chancery. This is indicated by its Italian name, *Cancelleresca Corsiva*, or Chancery Cursive; the papal letters were written *Brevi Manu*, in a 'quick hand', hence their name, *Breve*, or Briefs. The term 'Italic' applies to type. The design was pioneered by Aldus Manutius from 1500 for the production of cheaper, small format books. He referred to this Italic type as *Cancelleresco Italico,* thus differentiating it from Roman types which derived from the Humanist *Littera Antica* script. (The adjective *Italico* designated things Italian as opposed to things of ancient Rome, or Roman.)

Morison's involvement with the Italic – both scripts and types – is of particular interest to this chapter because it had its starting point in his own handwriting which was firmly grounded in Johnston's teaching. It was truly a case of the acorn becoming the mighty oak. His awareness of the Italic was first stimulated by an illustration in Johnston's *Writing & Illuminating, & Lettering* (Fig. 180 in that book and Fig. 139 in this). In his notes on this text illustration, Johnston did not identify the manuscript he reproduced, but wrote that it had been ' … taken from a sixteenth-century Italian manuscript [of inscriptions] written in a semi-formal cursive hand on one-hundred-and-fifty pages of fine paper'.[31] In his *Tally of Types* Morison wrote that he had recognised Fig. 180 to be:

> … the most rational and speedy of all the current [cursive] Humanist scripts and made to serve as a model for my own hand. This was in 1913 when the writer [Morison] first met Johnston. (Fig. 139).

The handwriting of a letter which Morison wrote to Johnston in 1913 shows certain 'Italic traits'. (Fig. 140). It is possible that he also used Monica Bridges' manual, *The New Handwriting,* a copy of which he bought in 1916. Consolidation

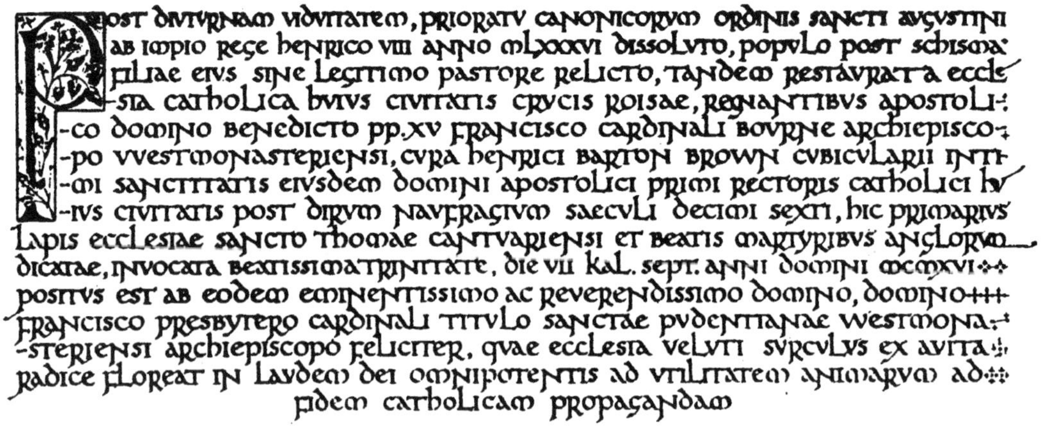

Post diuturnam viduitatem, prioratu canonicorum ordinis sancti augustini ab impio rege henrico viii anno mlxxxvi dissoluto, populo post schisma filiae eius sine legitimo pastore relicto, tandem restaurata eccle-sia catholica huius civitatis crucis roisae, regnantibus apostoli-co domino benedicto pp. xv francisco cardinali bourne archiepisco-po westmonasteriensi, cura henrici barton brown cubicularii inti-mi sanctitatis eiusdem domini apostolici primi rectoris catholici hu-ius civitatis post dirum naufragium saeculi decimi sexti, hic primarius lapis ecclesiae sancto thomae cantuariensi et beatis martyribus anglorum dicatae, invocata beatissima trinitate, die vii kal. sept. anni domini mcmxvi positus est ab eodem eminentissimo ac reverendissimo domino, domino francisco presbytero cardinali titulo sanctae pudentianae westmona-steriensi archiepiscopo feliciter. quae ecclesia veluti surculus ex avita radice floreat in laudem dei omnipotentis ad utilitatem animarum ad fidem catholicam propagandam

Fig. 141. An example of Father Adrian Fortescue's Half-Uncial hand.
(Courtesy of Mr. Michael Davies.)

came in 1919 when he '… regularised the details of the lettering' and '… achieved a greater degree of precision'.[32] Clearly, the Italic script won out over the other influence on Morison's handwriting, the more formal (Half-Uncial) hand practised by Adrian Fortescue which also stemmed from Johnston's early teaching at the Central School. (Fig. 141).

Morison's personal enthusiasm for the Italic clearly played its part when, he co-authored (with A. F. Johnson) a profound study of the development of the earliest Italic type designs. 'The Chancery Types of Italy and France' appeared in *The Fleuron*, No. 2, in 1924. It focuses on the Italic types of Ludovico degli Arrighi, a writing-master and printer based in Rome, who described himself as a scribe in the Apostolic Chancery there. In it Morison reproduces a page from a book printed by Arrighi in 1524, set in his Italic typeface. Called *Coryciana* (it is a collection of poems in Latin), Morison probably had it reproduced from his own personal copy. He highlighted the significance of Arrighi as the first to have published a writing

A chiunque uole imparare scriuere lra
corsiua, o sia cancellaresca conuiene
osseruare la sottoscritta norma
&
Primieramente imparerai di fare que=

Fig. 142. Arrighi's type design, cut by the goldsmith Lautitio Perugino.

book which employed printed models of the Italic, or *Cancelleresca,* script. Called *La Operina* ('The little work' – it has only thirty-two pages), its colophon stamps it as being printed in Rome in 1522, though the correct date is probably 1523–24. It was printed by woodblocks engraved by Ugo da Carpi, the artist who also developed a technique of colour printing by super-imposed woodblocks called *chiaroscuro.* Arrighi's second writing manual, *Il Modo di Temperare le Penne*, ('The method of cutting quills') was printed in Venice in 1524. It is of greater interest still because in addition to the woodblocks for the models of the scripts it also used Italic type for the nine pages of text. The blocks were engraved by Eustachio Celebrino, who possibly cut the types, too. Apart from this first type for *Il Modo*, Arrighi designed a second and a third type, with a number of variants. They were cut by the goldsmith, Lautitio Perugino, who is mentioned by Cellini in his autobiography. They are a larger size than Aldus', more gracious, decorative, with swash capitals and small letters with curved ascenders. The third is somewhat more utilitarian than the second. They were used for printing more spaciously designed books. (Fig. 142).

As an outcome of this knowledge, in 1924 Morison brought out the first Monotype Italic design, which he intended should accompany the Poliphilus Roman of 1923. This was the Blado Italic, so-called because the book on which it was based (*Vita Sfortiae* by P. Giovio) was printed by Antonio Blado in 1539. An associate of Arrighi, Blado was a printer working in Rome with close connections to the papal chancery. Morison stated that Blado's typeface 'originated in Rome in 1526' and was based on the 'third fount of Arrighi'. In effect, Morison, with Monotype, created an Arrighi Italic facsimile. Morison explained in *A Tally of Types* that: 'Like the Polifilo Roman, it [the Blado Italic] was reproduced direct from the page without drawing or allowance for the spread of ink'.

From the outset, Morison's programme for Monotype amounted to a counter-current to the Morrisian aesthetic based on Jenson and – more to the point of the discussion here – to a Johnstonian aesthetic based on English Caroline Minuscule. His involvement with both the Humanist Roman and the Chancery Italic types correlates precisely with his deepening reservations about Johnston's Foundational Hand as a basis for type design. In *Towards an Ideal [Roman] Type,* of 1924, he wrote:

> Mr. Johnston's unique contribution to calligraphy has also laid many printers under a great sense of obligation.... His influence is to be found in the books of the Bremer Presse [via Anna Simons in Munich to be discussed in the following chapter] and indeed the new German calligraphic movement derives directly from Johnston.... It must be admitted, however, that Mr. Johnston's influence creates the danger of archaism which renders the use of calligraphy unsuitable for the printer. Mr. Johnston himself, and certainly, I think, his school, has eyed almost too lovingly and too exclusively the pre-Humanist MSS. Mr. Johnston's school would tend to carry calligraphers, architects, and with them printers, back to the eighth century and the pure Carolingian minuscule.... It is safe to say that they will not develop a type-form of which we could make anything like general use today.[33]

He followed this up in 1926 in his book *Type Designs of the Past and Present* observing that 'Mr. Johnston's school' has:

> … the unfortunate tendency to confine their interest and practice to formal hands. Rather than include within their repertoire easy, running, cursive hands which might be learnt by anybody in a couple of hours, they tend to scare the birds with horrible words like 'Uncial' and 'Lombardic' and rum texts from Ruskin written in Runes. Perhaps Mr. Johnston will one day give us weaker brethren of the laity a new copy-book to teach us hands which we can write without recourse to quill and Indian ink. Until he does so, type-design and interest in it is likely to remain within a narrow groove.

During the 1920s, Morison was to remain closely involved with the Chancery Italics. An unceasing flow of scholarship underpinned his ideas for Monotype. From 1922 his book on sixteenth-century Italian writing books concerning the development of the chancery script/types (already mentioned as having involved Johnston) was an on going idea, though it was finally dropped. Associated articles did materialise, however. In 1924 'Note on the Italic of Antonio Blado' appeared in *The Monotype Recorder* (No. 199). In 1926 his article 'Towards an Ideal Italic' appeared in *The Fleuron*. No. 5. In 1926, too, he published a facsimile edition of Arrighi's *La Operina* with an introduction called 'The Calligraphic Models of Ludovico degli Arrighi named Vicentino'. It was printed by his friend, Hans Mardersteig, at his private press, the Officina Bodoni, at Montagnola, Italy and set in the Arrighi Italic typeface initiated by Morison with his American friend, Frederick Warde. They had it cut by hand in Paris in 1925 by the punch-cutter Georges Plumet. In 1927 his article 'The Italic Types of Antonio Blado and Ludovico Arrighi' appeared in *The Monotype Recorder* (No. 217). In 1929 his books *Eustachio Celebrino da Udene. Calligrapher Engraver and Writer for the Venetian Press* and *Andreas Brun, Calligrapher of Saragossa* were published at the Pegasus Press in Paris.[34]

In 1928–29, Morison brought to fruition a second Italic for Monotype, this time intended to accompany the Bembo Roman. This was based on a still more florid Italic typeface than Arrighi's. Garnished with ligatures, kerned ascenders, and swash letters, it was designed by the writing-master Giovanantonio Tagliente who was Arrighi's counterpart (and rival) in Venice. Tagliente adapted it from his own script as the typeface for the eight pages of text of his writing book, *Lo Presente Libro Insegna La Vera Arte*, which was printed in Venice in 1524. Like Arrighi's *Il Modo*, the actual writing models were printed by woodblocks engraved by Eustachio Celebrino. It is uncertain who cut the types. Morison states in his *A Tally of Types* that the Monotype Bembo Italic was severely adapted from Tagliente, with seriffed ascenders and 'roman capitals mechanically slanted'. It replaced an alternative one that Morison had commissioned from Alfred Fairbank based on Fairbank's own Italic hand.

It is of interest to note that William Morris owned a copy of the 1525 edition of Tagliente's *Lo Presente Libro*, which was bound up with three other sixteenth-century Italian writing books (the two by Arrighi and the *Thesauro de Scrittori* by Ugo da Carpi). The Tagliente typeface was chosen by Emery Walker, perhaps as early as 1910, as the model for the Cranach Presse Italic for Count Harry Kessler, which Johnston then redesigned from 1914. It appeared in book form (in Rilke's

Duineser Elegien) in 1931.[35] Ironically, Morison was unaware of Johnston's design, let alone of the shared model, hearing about it later through Count Harry Kessler. Later still, as is mentioned in *A Tally of Types*, he borrowed Johnston's drawings from Johnston's punch-cutter, George Friend.

It was in February 1929, too, that Morison brought out his third Italic for Monotype, called Arrighi Italic. It was based on drawings provided by Frederick Warde made from his hand-cut Arrighi Italic of 1925. It was intended to accompany the Centaur Roman which had been designed by Bruce Rogers in 1925 inspired by Jenson Roman. Centaur, too, was adapted through Morison's help for Monotype in 1929.

Morison's knowledge of the chancery scripts/Italic types was the basis of his conviction that the Italic was suited to work in tandem with Romans for modern book work. Thus, in a later study still, *Notes on the Development of the Latin Script*, (started in 1949 but left unfinished), he again saw fit to bewail Johnston's formal (he calls it a 'ceremonial') hand. Alluding to the Italic writing books of Graily Hewitt (the *Treyford Copy Books*) and of Alfred Fairbank (*A Manual of Handwriting*) he affirmed:

> In England today there exists an influential group which considers that Johnston's handwriting is highly artificial, too formal for workaday use... there is a tendency to revert to the best i.e. the earliest type of Humanistic Cursive.[36]

There is a further aspect to Morison's aspiration to create a Roman text type truly of its time which relates to Johnston. This concerned the role of inscriptional lettering. In effect, Morison challenged Emery Walker, Cobden-Sanderson, and Johnston for having elevated the link between calligraphy and typography into an orthodoxy. He counter-claimed that engraved lettering was as important an influence on type design. He pointed, for example, to the part played by Renaissance engraved medals and by lettering cut in stone. In *Towards an Ideal [Roman] Type* of 1924 he affirms:

> The Roman type will not be based immediately on writing, however fine....The relationship between calligraphy and typography is certainly close, for both crafts live by applying the alphabet to paper and vellum. But the alphabet was not developed only by the pen of the calligrapher. The graver and the brush also played a part in determining the details of the forms which the printing trade unleashed in the fifteenth century.

In his work for Monotype, Morison thus found it appropriate to commission the most outstanding inscriptional lettering artist of the day, Eric Gill, whom he first met through the Meynells at the publishers Burns and Oates. Due to Morison's initiative Gill produced three typefaces: the Roman Perpetua; the Italic Felicity; the sanserif Gill Sans. Regarding Perpetua, Morison planned for an entirely new Roman text face rather than a revival. He focused on the necessity for it to be finely seriffed for this, he considered, was the key to legibility. Looking back in *A Tally of Types* he explained:

ABCDEFGHIJKLMN
OPQRSTUVWXYZ
abcdefghijklmnopqrs

Fig. 143. Gill Sans alphabet: capitals (above).
Fig. 144. Gill Sans alphabet: minuscules (below).

ABCDEFG
HIJKLMN
OPQRSTU

Fig. 145. Gill's Perpetua, titling alphabet. Cited from Robert Harling. *The Letter Forms and Type Designs of Eric Gill*. 1979.
(Courtesy of Eva Svensson.)

> The fine serif is not in origin calligraphic but epigraphic; not written but sculptured. It followed that … a finely seriffed face could best be made by an engraver … or preferably a sculptor on stone or slate. On this analysis the problem became soluble, and Gill was the obvious man to solve it. He was asked to make drawings of the letters he had long been habitually carving.

Gill worked on the Perpetua between November 1925–30. Morison's plan was that it should first be cut by hand before being passed over to mechanical cutting at Monotype, thus 'fusing the talents' – to cite Nicolas Barker's phrase – of the type designer and the punch-cutter. He engaged the services of the Parisian craftsman, Charles Malin. The accompanying Italic, Felicity, appeared in 1930. During the same period Gill also worked on the Gill Sans which finally appeared in 1932. (Fig. 144).

Arguably, the commissioning of Gill rather brought Morison back into the Johnston fold. For the Gill Sans is a 'graceful reworking' of Johnston's Humanist block letter alphabet though, unlike Johnston's, its lower case is not 'truly monoline'.[37] And Gill, anyway, took part in preliminary meetings in October and November 1915 with Johnston, Pick, and Gerard Meynell about the Railway alphabet. Furthermore, Perpetua relates to the Gill Sans. (Fig. 145). In his study of Gill's lettering, Robert Harling claimed that the two designs ' ... have profound similarities of structure'.[38]

In a contrary sense, though, Morison's subsequent pursuit of the inscriptional tradition led him further still from Johnston. In his paper 'Calligraphy and Typography', of 1934, he again claimed that:

> ... the relation of calligraphy to typography never was as intimate as is taken for granted by modern scribes and by those printers who seek calligraphical inspiration.[39]

This was somewhat provocative, given that it appeared in a *Festschrift* to none other than the calligrapher Anna Simons, one of Johnston's most accomplished pupils.[40] Morison's point focused on the formation of the serifs of the Aldine types, an issue he had already explored in *Towards an Ideal Type.* He developed his argument historically. He adduced, firstly, that Roman inscriptions are the work of 'scriptors' (i.e., letter carvers) rather than calligraphers and, secondly, that through Alcuin of York the Carolingian period had revived those Roman inscriptions. He concluded:

> It is not just [correct] to say that the printer owes everything to the scribe, when the scribes themselves are indebted to the engravers. Since, moreover, the humanistic Renaissance depended upon the Carolingian Renaissance, printers should be conscious of a debt to the same stone engravers. It should be pointed out here that when the humanistic printers, particularly Aldus, established the lower case ... known as Old Face ... they copied the serif formation from the capitals, thus bringing both the capitals and the lower case into harmony. And these serifs were directly derived from the old inscriptional capitals. They were adapted first by engravers of medals. Thus, as far as Roman typography is concerned, printers are immediately indebted to stone carvers and metal engravers.

In this respect, Morison distanced himself from 'Mr. Johnston's school'. In a letter to the typographer Jan van Krimpen in 1956, Morison established himself:

> ... to have been at great pains to maintain the engraving craft in the service of typography; to graft the old tree of the hand-engraver upon the young sapling of the machine punch-cutter.... Typography has been made to bear the weight of all sorts of calligraphic experiments many of which went far to break down the true ... standards of type-cutting.[41]

Overall, Morison's views about typography had some affinity with the progressive outlook of men associated with the DIA, like Lethaby or Frank Pick. Morison had once said of Morris: 'I feel it almost *lèse-majesté* that Morris was an anachronism'. In his mind, Johnston must have mellowed much the same, aided perhaps by a sense of resignation. Replying to Morison's letter about the panels for his project on 'sixteenth-century Italian handwriting' (i.e., writing books) Johnston wrote in December 1923:

> It is absurd for you who can write so well to be seeking my assistance. I *have* an impression there is a letter and a pattern book [Morison called it a 'copy-book'] of yours buried somewhere on my desk. I hope it will not pain you to know that they will probably not be answered until – or rather, before – next January (if then), but it will be best really to avoid having to answer, by fixing a meeting for some day next year. I should be both proud and pleased to meet you and a Mr. J(enkinson?) at lunch some Monday.[47]

In July 1924, Morison again wrote to Johnston, threatening penalties should his promise for the 'copy-book' not be forthcoming – '… if the plates be not delivered by the right time you be boiled in oil until your ligatures melt & you suffer the loss of your majuscules'. The panels never materialised.[42] Morison's discussions with Johnston about the Cambridge University Press publishing *Formal Penmanship* ended desultorily: 'I did not have much hope that he would ever finish the book in his lifetime. Nor did he ….'

Yet Morison's recognition of Johnston's achievement remained solid. He gave to the Johnston support fund organised by Noel Rooke in 1943 and he responded to the 'summons to Ditchling' in aid of the publication of 'Johnston's *reliquae*'.[43] While Morison's thinking went well beyond Johnston's, like him, Morison enhanced profoundly the broad tradition of Roman-Humanist lettering.

Apart from these developments in type design, a number of others in the immediate postwar period were additional milestones of the Johnston calligraphic tradition. In 1945 the National Art Library at the V&A Museum put on its 'Memorial Exhibition to Edward Johnston, Calligrapher' and published a catalogue to commemorate his death in the previous year. It was curated by James Wardrop who undertook fundamental research into Renaissance Humanist Scripts (especially on Arrighi and acquired the Johnston). Although the library had been presented pieces of Johnston's calligraphy by the SSI as early as 1934 (via the V&A's Circulation Department), this signalled the active interest of a national institution to conserve his work – and that by other calligraphers. By 1946 the National Art Library had also acquired two other important Johnston manuscripts: the early *Order of the Communion* of 1902, and a later piece, *Of Gardens*, a text transcribed from Francis Bacon.[44]

While the exhibition was still on, in December 1945, the SSI held a gathering at the Art Workers' Guild to pay tribute to Johnston. The addresses were given by Sydney Cockerell, Noel Rooke, Alfred Fairbank, Irene Wellington, Bridget Johnston, and James Wardrop. They were published as *Tributes to Edward Johnston* in 1948 and printed privately in a limited edition by the School of Printing of Maidstone College of Art by the design educationist and Johnston devotee, Charles Pickering.

Another tribute was prompted by the V&A's memorial exhibition. In 1946 the *Studio* magazine published an article, 'Edward Johnston. A Retrospect', written by James Wardrop.[45] In mentioning Wardrop in her biography, Priscilla Johnston reported that he was '… a devoted admirer of *Writing & Illuminating, & Lettering* since his boyhood and that [it] had largely influenced his choice of career.' This was a career devoted to the Italic script. His induction, like Morison's, was through Johnston. Wardrop would sometimes lunch with Johnston in the William Morris Room at the V&A on the Mondays he was teaching at the Royal College. With Fairbank's article, 'A Retrospect' is one of the earliest appraisals of Johnston's achievements.

A major initiative by the SSI led to the publication in 1956 of the first of two editions of the *Calligrapher's Handbook*.[46] Intended to be a supplement to and a celebration of the fiftieth year of Johnston's own *Writing & Illuminating, & Lettering*, it contains an anthology of essays on the practicalities of the craft. Some are written by members of the prewar generation – M. C. Oliver, Sydney Cockerell, Alfred Fairbank, William Gardner. Others were written by the younger 'second' generation – John Woodcock, Dorothy Hutton, Irene Wellington, and William Bishop. Its editor was the Reverend C. M. Lamb.

Of this 'second' generation, other noteworthy calligraphers in the Johnston mould should be mentioned in this brief survey. One was Thomas Swindlehurst, who studied under Johnston between 1924–27. He then became a very influential teacher at Leeds College of Art. Another was Joan Pilsbury who studied under M. C. Oliver also at the Central School. Another was Ida Henstock, who became an assistant to Graily Hewitt.

In 1959 a further development strengthened the Johnston tradition. The V&A Museum acquired significant pieces of calligraphy from Sir Sydney Cockerell,

Fig. 146. Book jacket by Irene Wellington of *Edward Johnston*.
(Courtesy of Barrie & Jenkins.).

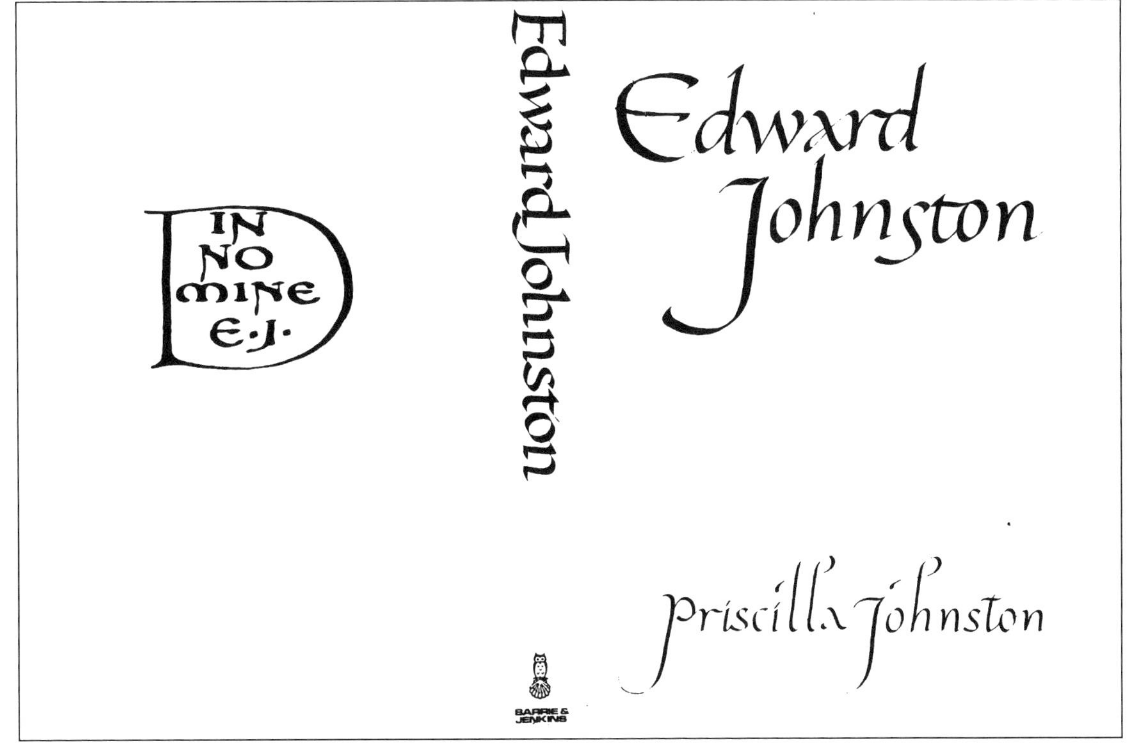

including one of Johnston's most prestigious manuscripts, *A Book of Sample Scripts* (it had been commissioned by Cockerell in 1913). In 1966 it issued a facsimile edition with an introduction by Johnathan Harthan, the keeper of the library. Other items acquired by the library include Johnston's printer's proof of his handbook, his annotated editions, and an archive of photographs of his lettering classes in chalk on the blackboard.

Cockerell played a vital role in preserving Johnston's legacy. But so, too, have the publishers, Faber and Faber because their chief designer, B. Wolpe, who had been a pupil of Koch, had read *Writing & Illuminating, & Lettering*. The company had already issued the *Calligrapher's Handbook* and in 1959 it published Priscilla Johnston's biography *Edward Johnston*. Cockerell linked up with Faber and Faber to write the foreword. For its factual detail, its evocative descriptions, and its knowledge of Johnston's day-to-day life this study remains a principal source for his life. The book went into a second edition in 1976 when its cover and end-papers were designed by Irene Wellington. (Fig. 146).

Between 1957 and 1961 there also appeared the catalogues of Johnston material issued for sale by the antiquarian booksellers, Elkins Mathews. One of its senior partners was Percy Muir who contributed scholarly annotations.[47] On the winding-up of Johnston's estate Elkin Mathews was appointed to dispose of Johnston's collection of manuscripts, holographs, his book library and other material. It was largely from these sales that American institutions acquired their holdings of Johnston material. Among these was the John M. Wing Foundation at the Newberry Library in Chicago, which had been looked after first by Ernst Detterer and at that time by James Wells. (Detterer was one of Johnston's private pupils in Ditchling, in 1913, and became a notable teacher of calligraphy himself. He thus opened the door for Johnston's influence in USA.) Another was the Pierpont Morgan Library in New York, and a third the Harry Ransom Humanities Research Center at the University of Texas at Austin. A purchaser in Edinburgh was the Edward Clark Library, whose founding purpose was to benefit printing apprentices. It acquired books from Johnston's library, some of then annotated by him. Two examples are Lewis F. Day's *Alphabets old and new* and Percy Smith's *Lettering and Writing*. The library is now part of Napier University (as is the former library of Bernard Newdigate). Other Johnston papers passed into private hands, to resurface into the public domain later on.

In this period, too, a 'third' generation – those who had been the pupils of Johnston's pupils and themselves had become teachers – took calligraphy into the late 1950s and beyond. Marie Angel was a student of Irene Wellington and Dorothy Mahoney at the RCA. Ann Hechle studied under Irene Wellington at the Central School where she, in turn, taught until the demise of the calligraphy courses there in 1963. Prominent, too, was Ann Camp. She was taught by M. C. Oliver at Hampstead Garden Suburb Institute and by Dorothy Mahoney at the RCA. She, in turn, initially taught at the Byam Shaw School of Art, in London. Her teaching is especially significant, given that the calligraphy course at the RCA was phased out in 1953 by the new principal, Robin Darwin. Darwin was convinced that the priority then lay with the newly respected discipline of typography. For two decades, calligraphy education was overshadowed by these developments, for the pattern was repeated in art and design colleges throughout Britain. In 1965, however, Ann Camp initiated a calligraphy course at Digby Stuart College, a teacher-training college which in 1975 became incorporated into the Roehampton Institute (and now part of the University of Surrey). In 1979 it became a full diploma course in calligraphy and bookbinding. Faced in the 1980s with the prospect that too free an approach to calligraphy was being let loose, Ann Camp wrote her paper, 'Changing Views and Educational Opportunities'. Taking a liberal traditionalist line, she defended the Johnstonian precepts:

> Johnston's work was rooted in very thorough historical research and then moved on to a highly personal style of writing.[48]

She supported innovation in principle but held to Johnston's dictum that '... one may lawfully follow a method without imitating a style'. Building on Ann Camp's twenty-five years of teaching at Roehampton, the courses in calligraphy and the book-binding there in the 1990s became the springboard for a renewed working of the Johnston tradition.[48a]

Another of this generation is John Woodcock. He was taught by Dorothy Mahoney at the RCA and he then taught at the Central School and later at Roehampton. Yet another is Tom Gourdie who was taught by Irene Wellington at Edinburgh. He introduced Italic handwriting into Scottish schools. His first book was *Italic Handwriting*, of 1955, which includes examples of the Italic hand which he collected for an international exhibition in Edinburgh. In it he says that his own Italic alphabet 'has been devised from the teaching and hand of Mrs Irene Wellington but it also owes a lot to Arrighi.' His other handbook is *Simple Modern Hand*, of 1965. He also produced the *Puffin Book of Lettering* in 1961 and *Calligraphy for the Beginner*, in 1983. The texts of both of these are written in Gourdie's own calligraphic hand. In 1962 Gourdie became an adviser to E. S. Perry Ltd, the makers of the Osmiroid calligraphic pens.

There are two other seminal figures from the period of the 1960s–70s. Heather Child was a student of M. C. Oliver at Chelsea School of Art and became an eminent freelancer specialising in decorated maps. She was active on the committees of the Society of Scribes and Illuminators where she worked for its reorganisation following the retirement of Alfred Fairbank. Heather Child also did invaluable work co-editing (with the Johnston scholar, Justin Howes) two volumes of Johnston studies: *Formal Penmanship and other papers*, of 1971, and *Lessons in Formal Writing*, of 1986. The former is Johnston's unfinished handbook and the latter a collection of documents by, or relating to, him. Together with Priscilla Johnston's biography, they are the second major foundation for the study of Johnston. Heather Child also edited a second edition of the *The Calligrapher's Handbook*, published in 1985, and compiled three editions of *Calligraphy Today*, published in 1963, 1976, and 1988. They are surveys of postwar calligraphy which also covers developments in the USA and Europe.

Donald Jackson has already been mentioned. He is linked back to Johnston, for he was taught by Lonsdale Boner, at Bolton, who, in turn, had been taught by Thomas Swindlehurst, one of Johnston's earliest students.[49] He then studied at the Central School, under both Irene Wellington and M. C. Oliver. The doyen, perhaps, of the calligraphy fraternity in the 1970s and 80s, Donald Jackson has been a major force in calligraphy education in Britain and the USA. His *The Story of Writing* of 1981 has been widely read. It was the basis of a television broadcast in the mid-1980s.

Other developments in the 1970s have enabled the Johnston tradition to flourish. In 1972 the journal of the Society of Scribes and Illuminators, *The Scribe*, superseded its *Newsletter*. It was set up under its first editor, the calligrapher-scholar Stan Knight. It has become a venue for a continuing debate about the Johnston canon, his life and work, carrying articles of an analytical, descriptive, and anecdotal nature.[50]

The centenary of Johnston's birth was commemorated in 1972 by a major exhibition at the Royal College of Art. Its catalogue, *Edward Johnston (1872–1944)*, was written and designed by the typographer, Herbert Spencer – with belated irony, given that typography had displaced calligraphy at the RCA in the mid-1950s.

In 1985 the museum at Ditchling was set up with the most slender of resources by Hilary and Joanna Bourne. Part of its brief is to collect and conserve the work of the Ditchling craftsmen. Johnston is well represented in the Hilary Bourne Gallery which is dedicated to this period of Ditchling's history with items mostly donated by Ditchling residents, by relatives of the Ditchling craftsmen, and by friends of the museum. One is the door from his studio at Cleves which, characteristically, he equipped with an adjustable draught flap; another is his desk.

In this respect, the Ditchling Museum complements the Crafts Study Centre, Farnham Campus, which replaced the Crafts Study Centre at the Holburne Museum in Bath which, in 1985 was donated a major collection of Johnston's work from his nephew, Andrew Johnston, and his family. In 1987, the centre issued the indispensable volume *Edward Johnston. A Catalogue of the Craft Study Centre Collection and Archive.* Compiled by Justin Howes, this work lists and annotates the entire Johnston archive there, including finished manuscripts, trial pieces of calligraphy, diaries, work-books, letters, class teaching-sheets, and lecture notes. Alongside the Johnston archive itself, this catalogue is the third great foundation for his study. Other resources include the archives at the RCA and at the former Central School (now reorganised as Central St. Martin's). Other resources, relating to Johnston, are the Alfred Fairbank papers at the Bodleian Library, in Oxford, and the Stanley Morison papers, which includes the Kessler correspondence with Johnston, Emery Walker and Edward Prince, at the University Library, Cambridge.

The half-centenary of Johnston's death was celebrated in 1994 by an exhibition held at Ditchling Museum entitled 'Sharpness Unity and Freedom. Edward Johnston and the Continuing Tradition in Calligraphy'. Its prime movers were the calligraphers of a 'fourth' generation, Ewan Clayton, Gerald Fleuss, and Patricia Gidney, all students of Ann Camp at the Digby Stuart College/Roehampton Institute. It was accompanied by a catalogue of the same title carrying significant articles including Ewan Clayton's 'Edward Johnston and the Continuing Tradition in Calligraphy'. Ewan Clayton's interest as to how the history of letter-forms might serve calligraphy today is grounded in Johnston's approach. He has written other seminal articles on Johnston. Referred by him as a 'series of preliminary essays' they explore the spiritual dimension of Johnston's thought and work and are based on Johnston's private notebook, devoted to the years 1934–37.[51] An additional benefit of the Ditchling Museum exhibition is the greater awareness it has engendered of Ditchling as the home of modern British calligraphy.

Just prior to the exhibition at Ditchling the same group of calligraphers established the Edward Johnston Foundation. Its honorary president is Hermann Zapf who gives the foundation an international link. It is based in Ditchling and works closely with the museum there. A key phrase of its mission statement is '... to forward calligraphy and lettering as a central expression in cultural creativity'.[52] To this end it has organised exhibitions exploring aspects of contemporary lettering. Another aspect of its mission is to acquire, catalogue and display an archive of twentieth-century British lettering arts. Material directly relevant to the Johnston tradition has been acquired for its study archive; for example from the estate of Heather Child and from Johnston's pupil, Daisy Alcock. Both donations were made in 1997. It is important to add that the Heather Child bequest also donated items by Johnston and other material belonging to his tradition to Ditchling Museum itself and to the Craft Study Centre, Farnham Campus.

More recently, in 1999, the National Art Library at the V&A Museum acquired an important collection of Johnston documents. It consists of some seventy-six items, including his calligraphy, a number of his class instruction sheets, important items of correspondence, the original typescript for his short story, *The Roothing* of 1924. Most valuable, perhaps, are his few and fragile experiments in wood engraving and woodcuts. These pieces were originally sold

Fig. 147. ITC's Johnston typeface, designed by Dave Farey and Richard Dawson.

ABCDEFGHIJKLMNO
PQRSTUVWXYZ
abcdefghijklmnopqrst

from the Elkins Mathews catalogues.[53] They are contained in an album titled *Edward Johnston 1872–1944* which was assembled, and mounted, and bound by Garth While. While was a pupil of Dorothy Mahoney who became a bookbinder, calligrapher, and artist.

The year 1999 saw, too, the International Typeface Corporation issue for the first time (and long overdue perhaps) the typeface, 'Johnston Sans'. (Fig. 147.).Dcsigned by Dave Farey and Richard Dawson, it is closely based on Johnston's block letter alphabet. (Fig. 133). The booklet advertising its launch carries a valuable essay by Justin Howes on the origin of Johnston's block letter alphabet. This, it suggests, lies less in the lettering of the Trajan Column and more in the titling founts of Caslon (a Two-line English, or 28 point, and a Two-line Great Primer, or 36 point)[54] which Hilary Pepler acquired for his printing press in Ditchling – called in due course the S. Dominic's Press. Johnston would have known the fount well having helped Pepler during the earliest stages, in January 1916.

These varying activities – inscriptional, calligraphic, scholarly – have worked together since Johnston's death in 1944 to preserve and strengthen his scripts and the philosophy which gives them a context. This raises the question as to how new scripts gain momentum and become integrated with living custom. Some of the reasons for Johnston's *succès d'estime* within Anglo-Saxon culture can be quickly teased out. They were taught in colleges throughout the country which were already shaped by the Arts and Crafts movement. Not so dissimilar, arguably, to the spread of the Carolingian script there was a bureaucratic authority to promote them, inspired by the administrative genius of Lethaby's achievements at the Central School. Others reasons remain more elusive. Certainly, Johnston himself was not a forceful propagator, although much has been hinted concerning his saintly appeal to a succession of lady pupil-assistants who, in turn, passed on their sense of devotion to others.[55] In fact Johnston's faint efforts at devising a print script for schools gave way before the appeal of the Italic introduced by Alfred Fairbank. It cannot be said that commercial factors were working in their favour, as occurred with the spread of the English Roundhand/Copperplate script throughout the mercantile world. Yet certain commercial factors – albeit genteel ones – did operate. It was Heather Child who pointed out that Britain, with its tradition-laden institutions, has a built-in need for ceremonial and therefore for formal writing.[56] The City of London's livery companies for which Johnston undertook commissions are such an instance. Then, in the aftermath of the two world wars the widespread requirement for war memorials of all kinds, from the calligrapher and the mason, made the need more urgent. Johnstonian lettering, coeval with the Arts and Crafts movement's more general sweeping of the stables of Victorian eclectisism, could respond with appropriately dignified work. Lettering artists were offered many such commissions.

A convincing line of thought, too, is Morison's notion of the 'authority of tradition'.[57] A certain paradox seems to underlie the acceptance of new scripts and typefaces. Whether they evolve or are devised, they invariably have a appeal of a new wave – even the whim of fashion can be at work. One thinks of the intellectual frisson that Poggio Bracciolini's barely-formed Humanist script is said to have caused in the fifteenth century. But invariably their novelty also answers a need. A case in point is Morison's Times New Roman, which swept all before it. Its letter-forms are cleverly compressed with sharpened serifs.[58] It responded to the needs of the reform of newspaper design, taking in paper quality, fast and lightly-inked presses, and the width of the column – and thereby it gained sales. Yet, Morison's design was strictly traditional. Based on the Garamond-Granjon-Plantin family of types first drawn up in the sixteenth century, it was backed by the 'authority of tradition'. (In all probability it was redrawn from the type known as the Gros Cicero designed by Robert Granjon in 1568).[59]

On the other hand, the Foundational Hand evolved from origins in the tenth-century Carolingian hand. In the history of scripts arguably a cyclical process of renewal and reform of outworn usage is anyway at work. Morison's First Principles of Typography, redolent with Johnstonian precepts and anchored to his own kind of English conservatism, withstood the modernist doctrines from Europe.[60]

END NOTES

1. Cited from J. A. Cole. 'A Scholar Penman in Calligraphy and Palæography'. *Essays Presented to Alfred Fairbank.* Edited by A. S. Osley. (Faber and Faber) 1965.
2. See Rowan Watson. 'The Modern Calligraphy Collection of the National Art Library at the Victoria and Albert Museum'. In *Calligraphy Review.* Vol. 5. No. 1. Fall 1986. The writer makes the useful distinction between a modern tradition of British and the 'exciting foil' of German calligraphy.
3. For an analysis of the geometry of the pen angle see the article by Richard Middleton, 'Thirty Degrees', in *The Scribe.* Winter 1986. No. 38.
4. Among these are: Graily Hewitt. *Lettering for Students and Craftsmen* (Frederick Warne) 1930; Ann Camp, *Pen Lettering* (Dryad Press Leicester) 1958; Marie Angel, *The Craft of Calligraphy* (Robert Hale, London) 1977; Alfred Fairbank. *A Roman Script for Schools* (Ginn & Co) 1970; Dorothy Mahoney, *The Craft of Calligraphy* (Pelham Books) 1981; William Gardner. *Alphabet at Work* (A. C. Black) 1982; John Nash and Gerald Fleuss, *Practical Calligraphy* (Hamlyn) 1992; Gaynor Goffe, *Calligraphy Made Easy* (Parragon Book Services) 1994. These handbooks necessarily simplify Johnston's more thorough discussions in *Writing & Illuminating, & Lettering* and in *Formal Penmanship.* For example, concerning the weight of the letters (i.e., the relationship between the width and the height of the letter's strokes), they recommend as basic practice a ratio between the nib's width and the *x*-height (or body) of the letter to be 7:1 for the capital Roman letters, 4·5:1 for the small Roman letters (although more recently this has been reduced to 4:1), and 5:1 for the small letters of the Italic script. Another handbook characterised by Johnstonian teaching is *Practical Lettering and Layout* by F. J. Mitchell. (Adams and Charles Black) in seven editions between 1935 and 1960. An Associate of the Royal College, Mitchell taught lettering at Hornsey College of Art.
5. See James Mosley. 'Trajan Revived' in the periodical *Alphabet.* (Kynoch Press) 1964.
6. See the catalogue of the exhibition *Reynolds Stone. 1909–1979* at the V&A, 1982, and Reynolds Stone. *A Book of Lettering.* (A & C Black) 1935.
7. Fiona MacCarthy. *Eric Gill. A Lover's Quest for Art and God.* (E. P. Dutton. N.Y.) 1989.
8. See David Kindersley's article 'Mr Gill' in *The Life and Works of Eric Gill.* (William

Andrews Clark Memorial Library Symposium). 22nd April 1967. See also his two articles, 'My Apprenticeship to Mr Eric Gill' in *Craft*. Nos 39 and 40. July/August and September/October 1979.

9. John Nash. 'The Johnston/Gill Tradition in English Brush Lettering' in the catalogue *Sharpness Unity and Freedom*. Edited by G. Fleuss. (Calligraphic Enterprises Cambridge). 1985.

10. Cited from *Cockerell* by Wilfrid Blunt. (Hamish Hamilton) 1964.

11. From the typescript of the article 'Mr. Edward Johnston & English Calligraphy'. A copy of the typescript is at the Craft Study Centre. Farnham Campus. Reference Johnston Archive 2/70.

12. An essay by M. C. Oliver entitled 'Writing and Lettering' appears in *Fifteen Craftsmen on their Craft,* edited by the wood-engraver, John Farleigh. (Sylvan Press) 1945. An essay on M. C. Oliver is included in John Farleigh's *The Creative Craftsman.* (G. L. Bell and Sons Limited London) 1950. A further study by M. C. Oliver is the address, 'Revival of Writing and Lettering', published in the *Journal of the Royal Society of Arts*, September 1950.

13. Cited from C. M. Lamb. 'Notes on the History of the Society of Scribes and Illuminators' in *Calligraphy and Palæography. Essays presented to Alfred Fairbank.* (Faber and Faber) 1965.

14. *More Than Fine Writing: The Life and Calligraphy of Irene Wellington.* (The Overlook Press) N.Y. 1987.

15. A typescript copy is in the Ditchling Museum.

16. See William Gardner's article 'Reminiscences' in *The Scribe.* Winter 1994. No. 62.

17. The Fell types are discussed in Horace Hart. *Notes on a Century of Typography at the University Press Oxford 1693–1794. A Facsimile Edited by Harry Carter.* (Oxford. Clarendon Press) 1970.

18. Francis Meynell. *The Nonesuch Century*. With bibliography by Desmond Flower and appraisal by A. J. A. Symons. (Nonesuch Press) 1936. Another edition (English Printed Books) 1947.

19. See Justin Howes. 'Edward Johnston's First Class at the Central School on 21 September 1899'. In *Object Lessons.* Edited by Sylvia Backmayer. (Lund Humphries) 1996.

20. It included Kelmscott Press books. In 1911 he catalogued those books he intended to sell. See *Fortescue's diary in Latin* translated by Edith Codell. Westminster Cathedral archives.

21. Bernard Newdigate. *Book Production Notes for the London Mercury. 1920-25.* (The Tabard Private Press) 1986. See J. Scuby's articles on Newdigate in *Albion*, 24. Winter 1984 and 33 Oct. 1987.

22. Cited from Joseph Thorp. *B. H. Newdigate Scholar-Printer.* (Basil Blackwell Oxford) 1950.

23. This information is courtesy of Eleni Zompolides' daughter, Mrs Margaret Payne.

24. See the article by John Scuby. 'Eleni Zompolides' in *Albion*. Vol. 33. October 1987.

25. Stanley Morison. *First Principles of Typography*. (Cambridge University Press) 1951.

26. Stanley Morison. *A Tally of Types*. (Christmas Book. Cambridge University Press.) 1953.

27. See F. Meynell and Stanley Morison. 'Printers' Flowers and Arabesques' in *The Fleuron*. Vol. I. 1923.

28. The 'historicist' typefaces, which are designed in the tradition of the private presses and based largely on fifteenth- and sixteenth-century types, are prolific. Morison's achievement was all the greater in superseding this weighty tradition.

29. See Beatrice Warde (pseudonym Paul Beaujon). 'The 'Garamond' Types' in *The Fleuron*. No. 4. 1925 and D. Updike. *Printing Types. Their History, Forms, and Use.* (Merrymount Press) 1922.

30. In spite of Morison's preferences, Monotype also acquired a Jenson design, in 1929, called Centaur. Designed by the American, Bruce Rogers, it is a refined version of Jenson. Its Monotype serial number is 252. (Other serial numbers are: Bembo, No. 270; Poliphilus, No. 170; Garamond, No. 156; Baskerville, No. 169; Fournier, No. 185; Bell, No. 341; Perpetua, No. 239; Felicity, No. 262; Times New Roman, No. 327.)

31. Stanley Morison. *A Tally of Types.* Page 43. (CUP) 1953. This manuscript passed into the hands of James Wardrop and is now in the V&A. This information is received, courtesy of Mr. Nicolas Barker.

32. The quotations are cited from Nicolas Barker. *Stanley Morison*. Page 83. (Macmillan) 1972.
33. Stanley Morison. 'Towards an Ideal Type' in *The Fleuron*. No 2. 1924.
34. Morison also wrote articles on the Roman Humanist scripts and types during this period. In 1924 'The Type of the Aldine Polyphilus' appeared in *The Monotype Recorder* No. 199. In 1925 two other articles on the Aldus Roman appeared: 'The Polyphilus Type' for the *Monotype Recorder* and 'The Type of the Hypnerotomachia Polyphili' for the *Gutenberg-Festschrift*, in Mainz. Morison also wrote the introduction to *A Newly Discovered Treatise on Classical Letter Design by Damianus Moylus, circa 1480,* which was published by the Pegasus Press in Paris in 1927.
35. See John Dreyfus. 'Emery Walker: A Victorian Champion of Chancery Italic' in *Calligraphy and Palaeography. Essays presented to Alfred Fairbank*. Edited by A. S. Osley. (Faber and Faber) 1945.
36. Stanley Morison. 'Notes on the Development of the Latin Script'. In *Letter-Forms in Manuscript and Print*. Vol. I. (C. U. P) 1981.
37. The phrase is James Mosley's. See J. Mosley. 'On Type. Eric Gill's Perpetua Type' in *Fine Print*. Vol. 8. No. 3. 1982. (See also John Dreyfus. 'Stanley Morison as Typographer' in *Signature*. New Series. 3. 1947, and A. Hutt. 'Times Roman: A Re-assessment' in *The Journal of Typographic Research*. Vol IV. Summer. 1970.)
38. Robert Harling. *The Letter Forms and Type Designs of Eric Gill*. (Eva Svensson) 1976. Gill's designs were further modified by the Drawing Office of the Monotype Corporation.
39. In *Anna Simons*. Coronna VIII. (R. Oldenbourg Verlag) München-Berlin. 1934.
40. Cited from Nicolas Barker. *Stanley Morison*. P. 462. (Macmillan) 1972.
41. Stanley Morison papers. Cambridge University Library. Morison's draft is now in the Newberry Library, Edinburgh.
42. The quotations are cited from Nicolas Barker. *Stanley Morison*. Pages 447, 518. (Macmillan) 1972. Nor did Morison's actual book materialise. The material was edited later by Nicolas Barker and published as *Early Italian Writing-Books Renaissance to Baroque* (David R. Godine, Boston) in 1990.
43. Cited from Nicolas Barker. *Stanley Morison*. (Macmillan) 1972.
44. See Rowan Watson. 'The Modern Calligraphy Collection of the NAL at the V&A'. Op. cit.
45. James Wardrop. 'Edward Johnston: a Retrospect' in *The Studio*. Vol. 32. 1945. See also James Wardrop. 'Arrighi Revived' in *Signature*. No. 12. 1939. and *The Script of Humanism*. (Oxford at the Clarendon Press) 1963.
46. *The Calligrapher's Handbook*. Edited by C. M. Lamb. (Faber and Faber) 1956.
47. There is no single collection of the catalogues for public reference.
48. See Heather Child. *Calligraphy Today*. (A. & C. Black) 1988.
48a The course became a degree course, but has since closed.
49. A lecture on Johnston by Thomas Swindlehurst was read by the Rev. Stanley Knight to the SSI in November 1965.
50. E.g. Priscilla Johnston, the transcript of her lecture on her father, 'So Completely Himself', given to the SSI in 1979. See *The Scribe*. No. 38. Winter 1986.
51. See Ewan Clayton. 'An Edward Johnston Notebook' in *The Scribe*. No. 32. Summer 1984.
52. Edward Johnston Foundation. *Newsletter*. (Ditchling) Autumn 1999.
53. This information was kindly provided by George Ramsden of Stone Trough Books, York. The album was exhibited by Rupert Otten at Wolseley Fine Arts, in London in 1997.
54. See 'Johnston's Sans: a context' by Justin Howes in *Johnston's Cat* (Cloister Press) Cambridge 1999.
55. The somewhat star-struck Violet Hawkes – she invariably wrote to Johnston as 'Dear Father Scribe' – has done much to aid this air of reverence. It is due to her, however, that the invaluable sets of photographs of Johnston's blackboard lettering were taken. (But even a most cursory view would show that British calligraphy, while conservative, is far from being a female-dominated and, presumably, a middle-class preoccupation.)
56. Heather Child. *Calligraphy Today. Twentieth-century Tradition and Practice*. (A & C Black) 1988.
57. See Stanley Morison's *Politics and Script*. Edited and compiled by Nicolas Barker. (Oxford) 1972.

58. See Peggy Lang. 'Times Roman: A Revaluation' in *Alphabet and Image*. 2. September 1946.
59. A specimen of the Gros Cicero typeface was published in the book, *Index Characterum 1905*, which was complied by Max Rooses in 1905 to list the archive of types held by the ancient Plantin Moretus Printing Office that had become a museum in 1875. Rooses also used the Gros Cicero as the text type for his introduction. There are a number of accounts which discuss in what respect the Gros Cicero was the model for the Times New Roman and how it, and the Times New Roman itself, relate to the earlier Monotype typeface, called Plantin (Series 110), which was cut in 1913. See: Alan Hutt. 'Times Roman: a re-assessment 'in *The Journal of Typographic Research*. Vol. 3. (Cleveland) 1970; J. Moran. *Stanley Morison: his Typographic Achievement*. (Lund Humphries) 1971; Nicolas Barker. *Stanley Morison*. (Macmillan) 1972; W. Tracy. *Letters of Credit*. (Gordon Frazer) 1986; and 'The Art and Craft of Lettering', a book review by the editor of *The Book Collector*. Vol. 36. No. 2. Summer 1987. There are early articles on Times New Roman in *The Monotype Recorder* Vol. 36. No. 4. 1932 and Vol. 38. No. 4, 1942. Other articles include: P. Lang. 'Times Roman: a revaluation' in *Alphabet and Image*. Vol. 2. 1946; John Dreyfus. 'The Evolution of Times New Roman' in *The Penrose Annual*. Vol. 66. 1973.
60. Morison's scepticism of the typographic *avant garde* in Europe comes through in a review of a trade magazine almost certainly written by him in *The Fleuron* Vol. 6. 1928: '...as a depressing anti-climax comes the *Craftsman Number* of *The American Printer* (N.Y. May 1927) from which it would seem that a large section of the western typographic world has Gone Modern. The style, indeed, is not so much of Mr. Ivin's "Here and Now" [referring to the previous notice] as Vienna and Five Years Ago; but on the measles principle that the later you have them the harder you have them, "modernism" may have a new and exciting lease of life in America.' In his Introduction to Cyril Burt's *The Psychology of Typography* (CUP) 1959, Morison writes: ' "Leftist" or "coterie" styles in typography are likely to remain with us. There can be no objection to that. Indeed, so long as they are not regarded too seriously, they are to be welcomed.' See also the chapter, 'Morison and the Modern Movement' in Herbert Jones's *Stanley Morison Displayed*. (F. Muller) London 1976.

Johnston in old age (1940). Drawn by Edmond Xavier Kapp, 1890–1978.
(Courtesy of the National Portrait Gallery, London.)

CHAPTER ELEVEN

THE INFLUENCE OF JOHNSTON IN GERMANY

Edward Johnston's influence was wide ranging not only in England but in Germany. In April–May 1905, an exhibition was held in Weimar, in Germany, devoted to a subject of considerable originality for Germany at that time. Its title was 'Austellung von Werken der Modernen Druck und Schreibkunst' – 'An Exhibition of the Work of Modern Printing and Calligraphy'. It was put on by Count Harry Kessler at the Grossherzogliches Museum für Kunst und Kunstgewerbe, the Archducal Museum of Arts and Crafts. Kessler was the museum's Honorary Chairman. Its catalogue, which had a cover designed by Gill, discussed the integrity of craftsmanship. Its scope reflected the same interests that were being cultivated by bibliophiles in England, including the view that calligraphy was a prerequisite for good type and book design. Early Italian printing (including Jenson from Venice), were shown alongside the range of the English private press movement, including the Doves *Bible* and *Paradise Lost,* to which Johnston had contributed. Also shown were the Insel Verlag series of German classics for which Johnston had designed the lettering for the sub-title page. His work was therefore prominent, though English calligraphy was represented by Graily Hewitt rather than Johnston.

The 1905 exhibition was an outcome of Count Harry Kessler's aesthetic and Anglophile preoccupations. He had carried the ideas of the English Arts and Crafts movement into the equivalent German circles. He was on the committee of the Deutsche Kunstlerbund, and from 1896 was a co-editor of the avant-garde magazine, *Pan*, which for the first time in Germany had enthused about the Kelmscott Press and other artistic developments in Britain, such as the drawings of Aubrey Beardsley. Both were shown in the 1905 Weimar exhibition. Born in France of an Irish mother and a German banker and schooled in England (where his companion was Roger Fry), Kessler was a man of many roles. Aristocrat and diplomat, Anglophile and cosmopolitan, writer and librettist, his diary records him equally at home discussing music with Strauss, science with Einstein, choreography with Isadora Duncan, and dance with Josephine Baker. Importantly, Kessler was a republican with socialist leanings. He may have been, quite literally, the first political emigrant to leave Germany on the election of Hitler in 1933. He was compelled to flee – it was said within the hour – because of his sympathetic biography of the Jewish poet and foreign minister, Walter Rathenau, who had been assassinated in 1922. Kessler himself died in France, in 1937.

It was as consultant to the prestigious publishers, Insel Verlag, that Kessler had turned to England in 1902 seeking advice about typography from Emery Walker. Through him, he had been put in touch with the Central School, that is with Cobden-Sanderson, John Mason, Eric Gill, Graily Hewitt – and Johnston. All, in due course, helped him with his book production. Their shared outlook on matters of design strengthened the design links between England and Germany.

But it was Johnston in particular who impressed Kessler. In 1907 he asked Johnston to design the titling for an edition of a Shakespeare play. Precisely which one is uncertain. The project came to nothing, although the work may have been the first stirring of activity connected with Kessler's eventual printing of *Hamlet* published as late as 1929. In 1912 Kessler, through Muthesius, also wanted Johnston to teach in Germany. Instead, Johnston recommended Anna Simons, thus launching her career and, through her, enhancing his own reputation in Germany.

Following the example of the Doves Press, from 1909, Kessler established by fits and starts his own private press, the Cranach Presse. To a large extent this turned out to be an Anglo-German enterprise. A Roman type face was designed by Emery Walker, using as a model the same sixteenth-century types by the printer Jenson that he had used for the types of the Kelsmcott Press. By 1911 it had been cut by Edward Prince, ready for casting. The technical back-up for the press work was provided in 1914 by the compositor J. H. Mason. The links with England continued. From 1925–31, H. Gage-Cole, who had once been Morris's pressman, also worked for Count Harry Kessler.

What was Johnston's contribution to the Cranach Presse? From 1912 Kessler wished him to design a series of typefaces: an Italic, a Black Letter and a Greek face, which arose from his request in 1911 that Johnston transcribe a text from Plato. But the more pressing need was for an Italic face that would complement Walker's Cranach Presse Roman. Walker's own attempt at an Italic was based on the writing manual of the sixteenth-century Renaissance scribe and writing master, Tagliente (Tagliente's book *Lo presente libro insegna* was printed partly from wood blocks and partly in an Italic typeface in 1524). Walker's work had not been a success. As a calligrapher, Johnston understood better the pitfalls of the cursive script. He had made notes about Tagliente's lettering based on the copy he studied in the British Museum at the outset of his career. From mid-1912, he became involved in protracted discussions and trials to bring about a satisfactory design based, still, on Tagliente. But quite different viewpoints were held respectively by Kessler as the patron, by Johnston as the designer, and by Prince as the punch-cutter. Moreover, the three were each in a different location, their correspondence by letter took time, and they were pressured by other commitments. Kessler was over-demanding, Johnston was painstakingly slow, and Prince took umbrage.

All the problems of transcription from one craft to another which made Johnston so chary indeed surfaced during the realisation of this Italic design. Johnston had drawn no more than what he called 'character sketches' from the Tagliente manuscript (Fig. 148). His expectation of Prince was that he should make his own sensitive interpretation. He wished Prince to be 'given as free a hand as possible'.[1] Johnston's ideas about design are expressed in a letter, dated the 10th September 1912:

> Now the whole of the Arts and Crafts movement in England (and incidentally of my own work as a craftsman) has been based on the belief that DESIGN and

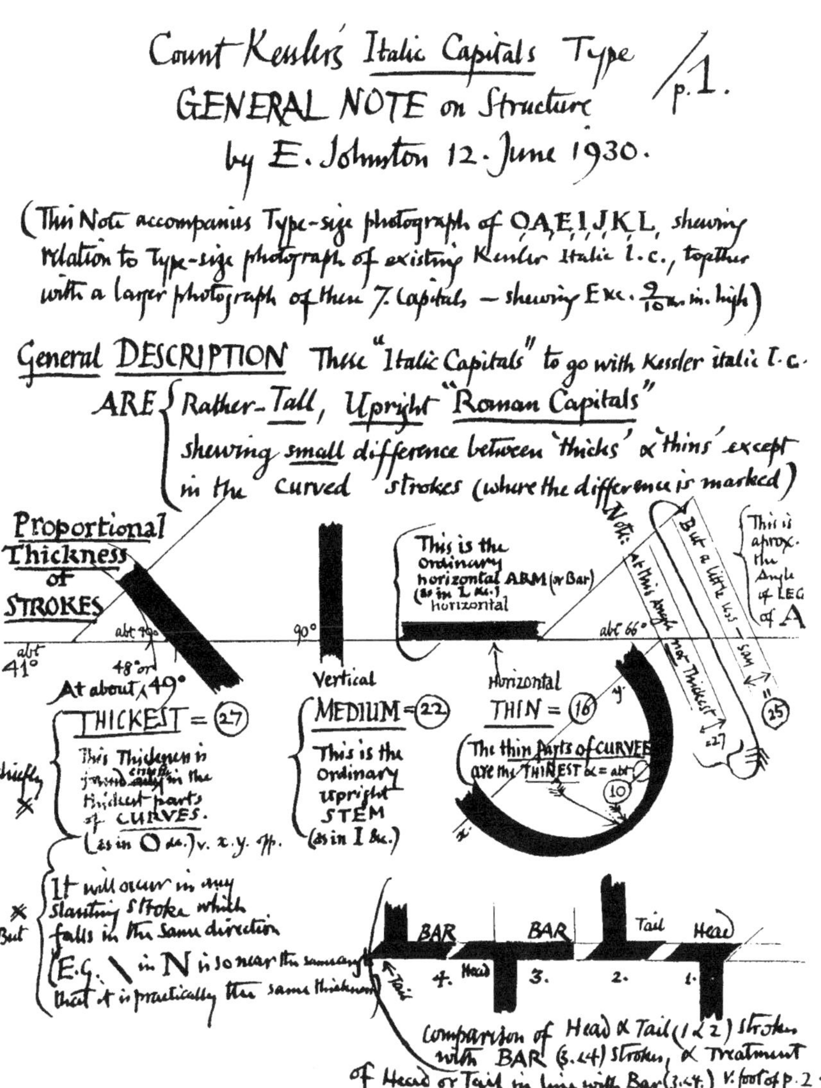

Auenduti scritto cotante uarie sorte de lettere, hora e necessario a duiui lo amaestrumento dello imparare & prima,

Fig. 148. *Above*: Johnston's 'General Note on Structure' of the capital Italic alphabet for the Cranach Presse, 1913. From 'Illustrations to a paper on Edward Johnston read before the Double Crown Club', by Noel Rooke, 17th May 1945.
(Courtesy of the V&A Museum.)
Below: enlarged detail of the Italic script of Tagliente's *Il Modo de Temperare le Penne*, 1531, which Johnston used as a model.

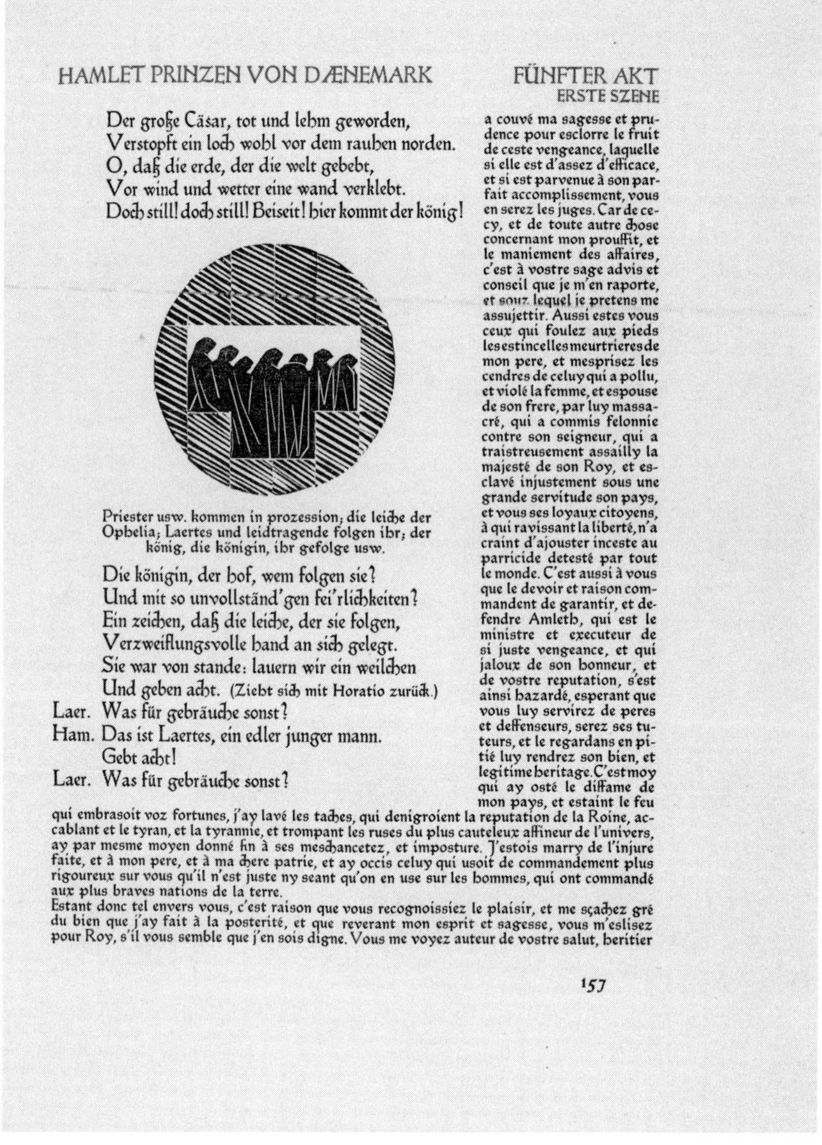

HAMLET PRINZEN VON DÆNEMARK

FÜNFTER AKT
ERSTE SZENE

Der große Cäsar, tot und lehm geworden,
Verstopft ein loch wohl vor dem rauhen norden.
O, daß die erde, der die welt gebebt,
Vor wind und wetter eine wand verklebt.
Doch still! doch still! Beiseit! hier kommt der könig!

Priester usw. kommen in prozession; die leiche der Ophelia; Laertes und leidtragende folgen ihr; der könig, die königin, ihr gefolge usw.

Die königin, der hof, wem folgen sie?
Und mit so unvollständ'gen fei'rlichkeiten?
Ein zeichen, daß die leiche, der sie folgen,
Verzweiflungsvolle hand an sich gelegt.
Sie war von stande: lauern wir ein weilchen
Und geben acht. (Ziebt sich mit Horatio zurück.)
Laer. Was für gebräuche sonst?
Ham. Das ist Laertes, ein edler junger mann.
Gebt acht!
Laer. Was für gebräuche sonst?

a couvé ma sagesse et prudence pour esclorre le fruit de ceste vengeance, laquelle si elle est d'assez d'efficace, et si est parvenue à son parfait accomplissement, vous en serez les juges. Car de cecy, et de toute autre chose concernant mon prouffit, et le maniement des affaires, c'est à vostre sage advis et conseil que je m'en raporte, et souz lequel je pretens me assujettir. Aussi estes vous ceux qui foulez aux pieds les estincelles meurtrieres de mon pere, et mesprisez les cendres de celuy qui a pollu, et violé la femme, et espouse de son frere, par luy massacré, qui a commis felonnie contre son seigneur, qui a traistreusement assailly la majesté de son Roy, et esclavé injustement sous une grande servitude son pays, et vous ses loyaux citoyens, à qui ravissant la liberté, n'a craint d'ajouster inceste au parricide detesté par tout le monde. C'est aussi à vous que le devoir et raison commandent de garantir, et defendre Amleth, qui est le ministre et executeur de si juste vengeance, et qui jaloux de son honneur, et de vostre reputation, s'est ainsi hazardé, esperant que vous luy servirez de peres et deffenseurs, serez ses tuteurs, et le regardans en pitié luy rendrez son bien, et legitime heritage. C'est moy qui ay osté le diffame de mon pays, et estaint le feu qui embrasoit voz fortunes, j'ay lavé les taches, qui denigroient la reputation de la Roine, accablant et le tyran, et la tyrannie, et trompant les ruses du plus cauteleux affineur de l'univers, ay par mesme moyen donné fin à ses meschancetez, et imposture. J'estois marry de l'injure faite, et à mon pere, et à ma chere patrie, et ay occis celuy qui usoit de commandement plus rigoureux sur vous qu'il n'est juste ny seant qu'on en use sur les hommes, qui ont commandé aux plus braves nations de la terre.

Estant donc tel envers vous, c'est raison que vous recognoissiez le plaisir, et me sçachez gré du bien que j'ay fait à la posterité, et que reverant mon esprit et sagesse, vous m'eslisez pour Roy, s'il vous semble que j'en sois digne. Vous me voyez auteur de vostre salut, heritier

157

Fig. 149. *The Tragedie of Hamlet Prince of Denmarke*, Cranach Presse, Three sizes were cut – eighteen point, twelve point, and ten point – by Edward Prince in 1914 and were cast by Shanks and Co. of London.

EXECUTION ARE INSEPARABLE, that the pure designer not being familiar with the working part, cannot design a thing suitably for its execution, and that the 'operative' attempting to obey such a designer's design is led astray and does bad work.[2]

Prince, on the other hand, wished merely to be given clear and undeviating instructions in order to execute the 'point' made by the designer. Kessler, who was caught between the two, was by turns insistent and then conciliatory. Johnston's Cranach Italic was finally completed in December 1913.

The second type design with which Johnston provided Kessler was commissioned in 1914. This was the Cranach Presse Black Letter, or Gothic design, which was an essential resource in any German press's repertoire of types. Like Morris's designing of his Troy type for the Kelmscott Press, Johnston worked from photographic enlargements made by Walker, probably from the edition of Gratiani's

fuerit·ar·i·q·i·ventū·io·qd verū credo·b. :la electione nō ↄsequi
Electio·ↄsueuit istud induci ꝗ ex so: tur aliquis ius·ut de
di·lxiij·di·quanto· ·in agro damasceno·
Illud aūt·padisū·: ꝗ racōe loci vel nobilitatis vel digtatis
hec loci·ar· p aliquo nō ꝑsumitur ·ut·xij·q·ij·gloria·
ar·ↄtra·xxiiij·di·qū·et certe p nobilitꝰ dꝫ ꝑsumi in hijs q̄ spectāt
ad nobilitatē·ar·
·ff·de fide instru.
·l·fi·io·
Q dibet·oc
cidta·ar·ↄtra be:
remitas.
Eratibꝰ·id ē
peccatis.
Peruersa ciui:
tate·ar·ꝗ nō no:
cet bono maloꝝ
ↄuersatio vel co:
habitatio.
m In mōte·xv·
·q·i·inebriauerit.
Cecidit·nā ex
varietate locoꝝ
nullū discrimen in
ducitur·C·de tē·in
integ·rest·l·ul·ar·
ↄtra·xxxij·q·v·q̄
viderit.
n Cecidit·et h̄ ē
cā quare nos ꝑse
quitur·qꝛ nos il·
luc debemus ascē
dere vñ ip̄e descē

peccando cecidit. Itē· De eodē.
Adam ꝑmus homo p pctō eie
ctus ē de paradiso ·qꝛ nobili
tatem dei a se eiecit nobilitate loci
priuatur. Itē iohānes crisosto:
mus. Nō est vere sacdos oīs q̄ vo:
Multi sacerdotes catur sacdos
et pauci sacerdotes·multi no
mine pauci in ope· Videte ergo q̄:
modo sedeatis sup cathedrā qꝛ ca:
thedra non facit sacerdotē·sed sac:
dos facit cathedrā. Non locus san
ctificat hominē s; homo locū. Nō
oīs sacerdos ē sanctus·sed oīs
sanctus ē sacerdos. Qui bñ sede:
rit sup cathedrā honorē accipit ca
thedre·qui male sederit iniuriā fa
cit cathedre. Ideoq; malus sacer:

agit̄. ut huana diuinis tribuāt auctoritatē: cū potius humanis diuina de-
buerint. Quę nūc sane omittamus. ne nihil apud istos agamus. et i infinitū
materia pcedat. Ea igr̄ quęramus testimonia. q̄bus illi possint aut credere:
aut certe non repugnare. Sibillas plurimi et maximi auctores tradiderūt
grecoꝝ: Aristoricus. et Appollodorus· Erithreus: nostroꝝ Varro et Fenestella. Hi oēs pcipuam et nobilem pręter cęteras. Erithream fuisse cō-
memorat. Appollodorus q̄de ut de ciui ac populari sua gloriat. Fenestella
uero etiā legatos Erithreos a senatu ee missos refert. ut huius Sibille car-
mina Romā deportarent̄. et ea consules Curio et Octauianus i capitolio

Fig. 150. Above: page from the *Decretum* by Gratianus, printed in 1472, which was the principal model for Johnston's Black Letter lower case type design and for Kessler's page layout.
(Courtesy of The British Library.)
Below: a page of the Subiaco type design from Cicero's *De Oratore* printed by Sweyenheim and Pannartz at the Benedictine monastery at Subiaco in 1464, being the model Johnston used for the capitals.

Decretum printed by Peter Schoeffer in 1472. Kessler had examined this book in the British Museum and was enthusiastic about both its type design and its *mise en page*. The device of surrounding the text with glosses printed in a smaller type was adopted by him as the format of *Hamlet*. The progress of the punch-cutting went much more smoothly than the italic. Three sizes were cut – eighteen point, twelve point, and ten point – by Edward Prince in 1914 and were cast by Shanks and Co. of London. (Fig 149).

The capital letters were modelled, however, on an early Roman type design, known as Subiaco. It was designed by the first printers in Italy, the two Germans from Mainz, Sweyenheim and Pannartz, for their edition of Cicero's *De Oratore* of 1464. They had established their press at the Benedictine monastery at Subiaco in 1463. (Fig. 150).

In the third type design, Johnston returned to the Greek types project. Only a small number of letters were designed and cast, and remained unused. (Fig. 151).

Johnston's types were used in a very limited number of the Cranach Presse books, although they were major ones. The earliest was Virgil's *Eclogues*, which finally appeared in 1927. It was printed in the Cranach Roman, with Gill's lettering used in the titles and with the inclusion of forty-three wood-engraved illustrations by the French sculptor, Aristide Maillol. Johnston's Cranach Italic appeared in the colophon only although it was also used in a separate Prospectus advertising the *Eclogues*. Kessler intended it to be used, too, for an edition of Horace's *Odes*, an unfinished project. There are some eight other titles printed by the Cranach Presse which use Johnston's Italic. It was also used to set the entire text of the English translation edition of Rainer Maria Rilke's *Elegien* done by Vita and E. Sackville-West as *Elegies of the Castle of Duino*. This was printed by Kessler but published by the Leonard and Virginia Woolf's Hogarth Press in 1931. (Fig. 152).

The second book was *The Tragedie of Hamlet Prince of Denmarke* in a German and an English edition. It was the last item from the Cranach Presse and is its masterpiece. Its design and printing were undertaken by Kessler, with the close collaboration of the theatre director-designer Edward Gordon Craig, whose idea it originally was. Craig was the son of the actress Ellen Terry and the architect Edward W. Godwin, and was Johnston's exact contemporary. He had first thought to print an edition of *Hamlet* which would explain his ideas for its production. A notice had appeared to that effect in 1908 in the periodical which he founded (and largely wrote) in Florence called *The Mask*:

> HAMLET We have the pleasure of announcing the publication of an Edition of "Hamlet" which we believe will be without parallel in the History of the European Stage. This edition will be printed on hand-made paper, the text of the first folio will be adopted, and the De Vinne type used. This edition will contain Text of the Play, Descriptions and Designs for each Scene, each costume, each piece of Furniture used. It will also contain ground plans of each scene and full directions as to how to light the play. Every movement of the Actors will be noted at the side of the Text, and at times a design will help the student to the full significance of the movements. The designs will be engraved upon wood, and in some cases otherwise reproduced, if not injurious to the beauty of the book as a whole. …

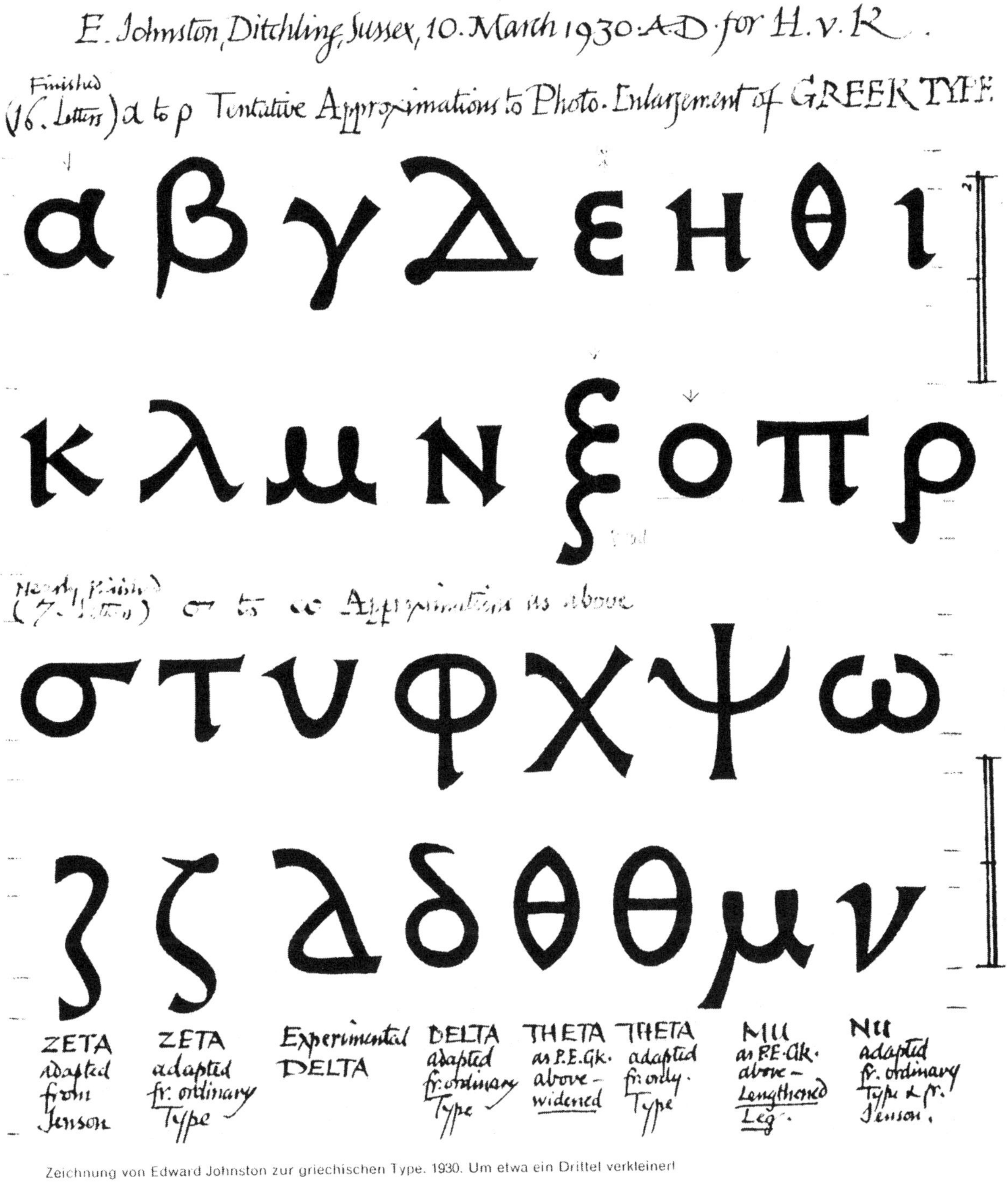

E. Johnston, Ditchling, Sussex, 10. March 1930 A.D. for H.v.R.

Finished (16. Letters) α to ρ Tentative Approximations to Photo. Enlargement of GREEK TYPE

α β γ Δ ε Η θ ι

κ λ μ Ν ξ ο π ρ

Nearly finished (7. Letters) σ to ω Approximations as above

σ τ υ φ χ ψ ω

ζ ζ δ δ θ θ μ ν

ZETA adapted from Jenson

ZETA adapted fr. ordinary Type

Experimental DELTA

DELTA adapted fr. ordinary Type

THETA as P.E. Gk. above – widened

THETA adapted fr. ordy. Type

MU as P.E. Gk. above – Lengthened Leg.

NU adapted fr. ordinary Type & fr. Jenson.

Zeichnung von Edward Johnston zur griechischen Type. 1930. Um etwa ein Drittel verkleinert

Fig. 151. The Greek types project; only a small number of letters were designed and cast, and remained unused.

DIE FÜNFTE ELEGIE

Frau Hertha Koenig zugeeignet

er aber sind sie, sag mir, die fahrenden, diese ein wenig
Flüchtigern noch als wir selbst, die dringend von früh an
Wringt ein wem — wem zuliebe
Niemals zufriedener wille? sondern er wringt sie,
Biegt sie, schlingt sie und schwingt sie,
Wirft sie und fängt sie zurück; wie aus geölter,
Glatterer luft kommen sie nieder
Auf dem verzehrten, von ihrem ewigen
Aufsprung dünneren teppich, diesem verlorenen
Teppich im weltall.
Aufgelegt wie ein pflaster, als hätte der vorstadt-
Himmel der erde dort wehegetan.
Und kaum dort,
Aufrecht, da und gezeigt: des dastehns
Grosser anfangsbuchstab . . ., schon auch, die stärksten
Männer, rollt sie wieder, zum scherz, der immer
Kommende griff, wie August der Starke bei tisch
Einen zinnenen teller.

55

er, wenn ich schriee, hörte mich denn aus der engel
Ordnungen? und gesetzt selbst, es nähme
Einer mich plötzlich ans herz: ich verginge von seinem
Stärkeren dasein. denn das schöne ist nichts

Fig. 152. *Above*: Johnston's Italic typeface as used for the Hogarth Press edition of Rainer Maria Rilke's *Duineser Elegien, Elegies from The Castle of Duino*, 1931. The book was designed by Count Harry Kessler who also supervised the type composition and printing.

Below: enlarged detail of the Italic type.

Craig first met Kessler in 1903 through William Rothenstein and again in 1912 in Moscow where he was putting on a production of *Hamlet* for the Moscow Art Theatre, the company built up by Stanislavsky. An *enfant terrible* of the theatre of his day, Craig developed the concept of 'noble artificiality'. His vision was that 'realism' in the theatre should give way to a form of constructivism. Thus, mimetics in acting was to be replaced by stylisation and dialogue and text by means such as gesture and sounds. Craig revived the expressive use of masks and symbolic costume. Rather than scenery, the *mise en scene* was suggested by screens illuminated by projected lights. His screens idea was explored in his book *Scene,* of 1923. He was inspired by the theatre of ritual and festival, by marionettes and the *commedia dell'arte.* One of his key essays is titled 'The Actor and the Über-Marionette'. The notion of the de-personalised actor is a major theme of his first book *The Art of the Theatre,* of 1905, and its expanded versions, *On the Art of the Theatre,* of 1911, and *Towards a New Theatre*, of 1913. These tracts, together with *The Mask* and two other periodicals, *The Page* and *The Marionette,* had a decisive impact on pioneers of modern theatre as diverse as Berthold Brecht, Oscar Schlemmer, Sergei Eisenstein, Vsevolod Meierkhol'd, and the French director Jacques Copeau. W. B. Yeats wrote for *The Mask.* 'I wish to rebuild on old truths', Craig wrote in *The Mask.* In returning to the primal sources of stage craft, Craig's overall aims relate to Johnston's own.

Given that Craig lived much of his life in semi-retirement in Florence, Paris, and Rapallo, he never met, or even corresponded, with Johnston. Their mutual focus was Count Harry Kessler through whom Craig was aware of Johnston's designs. (With Kessler, he disapproved of Johnston's trial design of the capital H.) Their respective work on the Cranach *Hamlet* is one of the most fortuitous yet distended partnerships in the history of the book. Kessler described Craig as 'an island exile'. He might well have thought the same of Johnston whom he found reclusive and ponderous. Craig had been struck by the fact that Shakespeare left no stage directions for the players of *Hamlet.* This reinforced his antipathy to the customary rhetoric of the actor, ever encumbered by personality, for Craig's aim was to rid the stage of such distractions. Thus his idea for *Hamlet* found its ultimate form in the silent reading of a book. 'Hamlet was finished ... when Shakespeare wrote the last word of his blank verse, and for us to add to it by gesture, scene, costume, or dance, is to hint that it is incomplete and needs these additions', Craig wrote in *The Art of the Theatre.*

From an early stage Craig had experimented with wood-engraving, taught him by the 'Beggerstaff Brothers'. (Three hundred-odd appear in *The Page* between 1898–1900.) This led in 1912 to his obtaining, quite by chance, impressions from the side grain of blocks of printing 'furniture' – those strips of oak used by printers to wedge in the lines of type in the forme. They had been brought to him in Paris by Kessler. Craig's eighty wood-engraved illustrations for the Cranach *Hamlet* were developed from this encounter. The slated-screen effect of the grain of the 'furniture' accompanied the silhouetted figures he cut and printed from holly wood. These, in turn, had evolved from the wooden cut-outs which he had originally made to guide the Russian actors in his production of *Hamlet* in Moscow in 1912. (From them he

HAMLET PRINZEN VON DÆNEMARK

FÜNFTER AKT
ERSTE SZENE

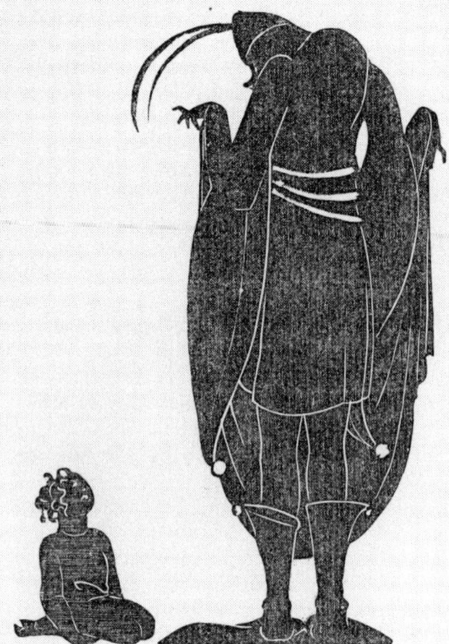

Erster totengr. Ja, ja, eben der.

Ham. Ach, armer Yorik! - Ich kannt ihn, Horatio, ein bursche von unendlichem humor, voll von den herrlichsten einfällen. Er hat mich tausendmal auf dem rücken getragen und jetzt, wie schaudert meiner einbildungskraft davor! mir wird ganz übel. Hier hingen diese lippen, die ich geküßt habe, ich weiß nicht wie oft. Wo sind nun deine schwänke, deine sprünge? deine

et soucis, en tout miserables. Combien de fois, faignant l'insensé, vous ay-je ouy plaindre mon desastre, et vous lamenter en secret de me veoir desherité, et sans aucun, qui vengeast la mort de mon pere, ou punist le forfait de mon incestueux oncle, et beau pere plein de meurtres, et massacres? Ceste charité me donnoit coeur, et ces voz affectionnees complaintes me faisoient veoir evidemment vostre bon vouloir, qui aviez presente la calamité de vostre Prince, et engravé en vostre coeur le desir de vengeance de la mort de celuy, qui meritoit de vivre plus longuement. Et quel sera le coeur si dur et peu maniable, ny l'esprit tant severe, cruel, et rigoureux qui ne s'amollisse par la souvenance de mes passions, et angoisses, et n'aye pitié d'un enfant orphelin, et ainsi abandonné de tout le monde? Quels seront les yeux si taris et sans humeur, qui encor ne destillent quelques larmes, voyans un pauvre Prince assailly des siens, trahy par sa mere, poursuivy par son oncle, et si fort accablé, que le peuple qui l'ayme n'ayt osé luy monstrer les effects de sa charité, et devotion bien affectionee? Ah! messieurs, ayez compassion de celuy que vous avez nourry, et que vostre coeur sente quelque elancement pour la memoire de mes infortunes. Je parle à vous, qui estes innocens de toute trahison, et ne souillastes onc ny voz mains, ny vostre esprit, ou desir du sang du grand et vertueux Roy Horwendille. Ayez pitié de la Royne jadis vostre Dame, et ma treshonoree mere, forcee par le tyran, et soyez joyeux de veoir finy, et esteint l'object de son deshonneur, et lequel la contraignoit à estre peu pitoyable à l'endroit de son mesme sang, voire d'embrasser le meurtrier de son cher espoux, portant sur elle un double fardeau d'infamie, et d'inceste, et de souffrance, pour l'avilissement de sa moytié, et ruine de sa race. Ç'a esté l'occasion, Messieurs, pour laquelle j'ay fainte ceste sottise, et ay voilé mes desseins souz le fard d'une grande folie, laquelle

Die verdeutschung des Saxo Grammaticus ist mit freundlicher erlaubnis der buchhandlung von Johann Ambrosius Barth in Leipzig der in ihrer ausgabe von „Shakespeares Hamlet-Quellen" von Max Moltke und Robert Gericke (Leipzig 1881) enthaltenen übersetzung nachgedruckt. Die auszüge aus François de Belleforest und der Hystorie of Hamblet sind zum ersten male für diese ausgabe übersetzt von HARRY GRAF KESSLER. Dieser leitete auch satz und druck des bandes. Die schrift des haupttitels schnitt in holz ERIC GILL. Die typen entwarf im auftrage der Cranachpresse EDWARD JOHNSTON in anlehnung an die schrift, die Fust und Schœffer in ihrem 1457 gedruckten Mainzer Psalter verwendeten. Edward Prince und nach seinem tode G. T. Friend schnitten die stempel. Das papier der gewöhnlichen ausgabe ist nach dem besonderen, von Harry Graf Kessler und Aristide Maillol ausgebildeten verfahren unter leitung von Gaspard Maillol hergestellt. Der druck wurde 1927 bis 1929 auf den handpressen der CRANACHPRESSE in WEIMAR durchgeführt und zu Weihnachten 1929 beendet. Die textkorrektur besorgte H. Wengler-Dresden, an der satzleitung waren beteiligt J. H. Mason und Max Goertz; als setzer waren tätig Walter Tanz und Hans Schulze, als drucker H. Gage-Cole und Max Kopp, als hilfsarbeiter Hugo Bergmann und Franz Hornik. Die ausgabe erfolgt durch den INSEL-VERLAG in LEIPZIG und S. FISCHER in BERLIN.

Fig. 153. *Above*: Page from the Cranach Presse *Hamlet* 1928–29, showing Johnston's Black Letter typeface, used in two sizes, 12 pt and 10 pt. Reduced.
(Courtesy of St. Bride Printing Library.)

Below: the colophon of the German edition of *Hamlet* (reduced).

had printed his 'black figures'.) The grey grained tones and black silhouettes on the pages of *Hamlet* combine with Johnston's dense Black Letter typeface and the running titles in capitals, printed in red. (Fig. 153).

But there were other contributors to the Cranach *Hamlet* ensuring its success. Henry Gage-Cole was brought to Weimar especially to undertake the printing. He developed a particular technique of a preliminary 'blind' printing for the Craig illustrations which rendered the paper harder and smoother. Otherwise the printing would not have impressed sufficiently on its uneven, soft, surface. It was handmade by Gaspard Maillol, the nephew of the sculptor Aristide Maillol, at Montval in France.[3]

The Great War and a long illness which Kessler suffered impeded the work on *Hamlet*. The two hundred and thirty copies of the German edition were finally printed in 1928–29 and the three hundred copies of its English edition in 1930. It was printed throughout in the three sizes of Johnston's Black Letter. The eighteen point was used for the text of the play itself. The twelve point was used to print the older versions of the Hamlet story in the form of a gloss surrounding the main text. They were incorporated because they were Shakespeare's own sources and consisted of the *Historie of Hamlet* translated from Belleforest and the *Histoire Danica* in the *Saxo Grammaticus*. The ten point was used for titles in the margins of the English edition.[4]

The impact of Johnston's lettering in Germany is better understood when seen in its wider context. One consideration is the general influence there from the 1890s of the English Arts and Crafts movement, to which Johnston was seen to belong. Another is the development of lettering in Germany itself where two categories of script, the Gothic (or Black Letter) and the Roman (or Antiqua), coexisted in a shifting partnership. A debate had been under way since the impact of Humanism in the sixteenth century as to which should prevail. It intensified in the twentieth century into the so called *Schriftstreit*, or battle of the scripts, in which Johnston's revival of the Roman-Humanist tradition of lettering clearly carried weight. Knowledge of Johnston's ideas in Germany were largely spread by his pupil, Anna Simons. A German herself, she was highly gifted and, of all his pupils, his *alter ego*. Forming part of the debate was the drive to simplify the overwrought forms of the blackletter scripts, especially the Fraktur. In this sense lettering artists – the *Schriftkünstler* – such as Otto Eckmann, Peter Behrens, and Jacob Erbar were pursuing a rationalist course parallel to Johnston's in England. Joined later by younger designers such as Paul Renner and Jan Tschichold, they took a further step in the process of simplification by designing Grotesk or sans serif type faces. These letter-forms had two features: they were serifless and monoline, relying simply on strokes of equal width. The style, long used for display only, was now advocated for book texts. The new sans serifs carried the glamour of being *unsere Zeit*, or of our time – they signalled modernity. It was a mode in which Johnston's block letter alphabet of 1916, though scarcely known in Germany, can now be seen as a precedent. These complex and evolving developments need to be disentangled and discussed in turn.

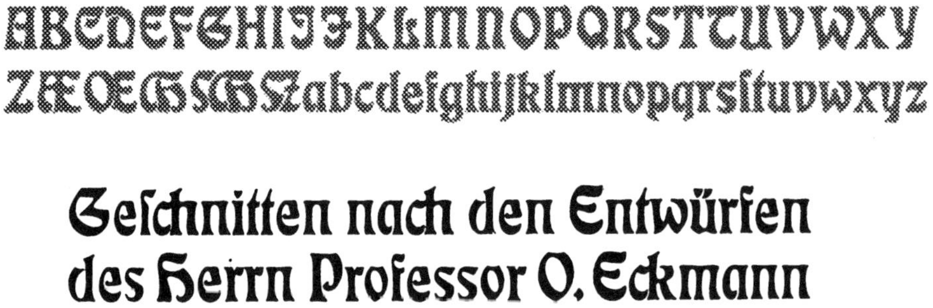

ABCDEFGHIJJKLMNOPQRSTUVWXY
ZÆŒCHSCHSZabcdefghijklmnopqrsſtuvwxyz

Geſchnitten nach den Entwürfen
des Herrn Professor O. Eckmann

Fig. 154. Eckmannschrift, *above*: alphabet (enlarged) and *below*: text, designed by Otto Eckmann in 1899–1900. Produced by the Rudhardsche (later Klingspor) Typefoundry. Offenbach am Main.
(Courtesy of *Fleuron*. Vol. 4. 1925 and courtesy of Verlag von Günther Wagner, from F. H. Ehmcke's *Schrift ihre Gestaltung & Entwicklung in neuerer Zeit*. Hanover. 1925.)

The influence of the English Arts and Crafts movement was widespread in Europe. Germany, however, was particularly receptive. In one sense this was a natural development because the German artist-designer *Werkstätte*, or workshops, had an affinity with English design thinking. The view was held, for example, that craft training should be rooted in workshop practice. A new phenomenon, the workshops were largely set up by enlightened patrons such as Ernst Ludwig II and design educationists such as Hermann Muthesius, who had known Lethaby in England. In another sense these workshops shared the *fin de siècle* reaction against stultified academicism. They were part of a radical stance known in Germany and Austria as the Secession. The movement had its origins in the fine arts. Many of the *Schriftkünstler*, or new lettering artists, in Germany had set out as painters. Peter Behrens, Otto Eckmann, Henry van de Velde, Emil Weiss, Ernst Schneidler, and Rudolf Koch are examples.

But underlying Germany's new-found interest in English design was a hard-bitten commercial self-interest to achieve a competitive position in international trade. One of the earliest *Werkstätte* was the Künstlerkolonie, or the Artists' Colony, set up by Alexander Koch in 1898–99 and patronised by the Grossherzog, or Grand Duke, Ernst Ludwig II von Hessen. It was situated on the Mathildenhöhe in Darmstadt. Ernst Ludwig was the grandson of Queen Victoria (his mother, Princess Alice, was Queen Victoria's second and favourite daughter) and, as such, was said to combine the roles of the English gentleman with the German patriot.[5] Ernst Ludwig II was a close friend of the Anglophile Count Harry Kessler and he commissioned the English architects, C. R. Ashbee and Baillie Scott, to design furniture for his palace at Darmstadt.[6] Both visited him there, as did Queen Victoria. The Künstlerkolonie was modelled, in part, on Ashbee's Guild of Handicraft although it was much smaller. At the outset it had only seven artists and craftsmen. Among them were the important painters, and architect-designers, Otto Eckmann and Peter Behrens. Behrens stayed at Darmstadt between 1899–04. During this period both designed radically new typefaces, Eckmannschrift in 1899 and Behrensschrift in 1900. (Figs. 154–155.) These designs are significant to the history of lettering because they were the first attempts to simplify the Fraktur

ABCDEFGHIJKLMNOPQRSTUVWXYZÆ
abcdefghijklmnopqrsſtuvwxyzchckſchflſtſi

DER heutige Tag, an dem Sie auf eine 25jährige Tätigkeit als Chef der Firma Feld zurückblicken, darf Sie mit froher Genugtuung erfüllen. Wohl waren dieſe 25 Jahre eine Zeit der Mühe und Arbeit, aber auch des Erfolges. Und wenn heute Ihre Firma zu den vornehmſten und beſten Buchdruckereien im Reiche zählt, ſo verdankt ſie dieſen Umſtand in erſter Linie Ihnen, der Sie ihr alle Zeit Ihre ganze Kraft, Ihr reiches Wiſſen und Können widmeten. Nie

Fig. 155. Behrensschrift, alphabet and text, designed by Peter Behrens in 1900. (Courtesy of *Fleuron*. Vol. 4. 1925, & Verlegt von Günther Wagner. Op. cit.)

script, to be truly of their time. Eckmannschrift was drawn by brushstroke and modified by the rounder calligraphic element of *Jugendstil,* or *Art Nouveau* (the German term comes from the periodical, *Jugend*, which was established in 1894 and was itself part of the jigsaw of pre-modernism), and by Eckmann's leanings towards *Japonaiserie*. Behrens' design was the more advanced, being architectural and even severe. Later he was influenced by Anna Simons. To a greater extent than Ashbee's community, the Künstlerkolonie aspired to economic self-reliance. In its philosophical outlook it was a precursor of the Deutsche Werkbund (the German Society of Work), of 1907, which sought the integration of artistic-craft design into industrial production and commerce.

Another design workshop organised on the same lines had been set up a year earlier, in 1897, in Munich, by the artist-designers Hermann Obrist, Richard Riemerschmid and others. The ever ubiquitous Peter Behrens was also involved. Significantly named the Vereinigte Werkstätte für Kunst und Handwerk (United Workshops for Art and Handwork) its organisers aimed at a level of commercial viability which was far in advance of Ashbee's Guild of Handicraft.

Another pointer to future developments in Germany was the Applied Arts Seminar organised by the architect-designer, Henry van de Velde, at Weimar in

1902, at the instigation of the Grand Duke of Saxe-Weimar. Initially van de Velde was much inspired by William Morris and the architecture of Charles Rennie Mackintosh, later to be regarded as *Art Nouveau*. Traces of this influence can be seen in the apartment van de Velde designed for Count Harry Kessler in Weimar. His Applied Arts Seminar led to the establishment of the Kunstgewerbeschule – School of Applied Arts – there in 1905–06 and then to his designing its building. This school evolved into the celebrated Bauhaus, which was established in 1919 following the end of the Great War.[7]

Other lesser-known craft enterprises which paralleled English developments rather than being directly inspired by them included the Stiglitzer Werkstätt of 1900, run by the designers Fritz Ehmcke, Friedrich Wilhelm Kleukens, and Georg Belwe in Munich. It was especially active in printing and alert to new developments. Its prospectus, for example, was set in the *avant-garde* Eckmannschrift typeface.

Workshops were also set up by Fritz Ehmcke at the Kunstgewerbeschule at Düsseldorf from 1903 and later at Munich. Ehmcke designed a number of typefaces and was interested in the teaching of handwriting. He was also a prolific writer. In 1925 he published his masterfully designed *Schrift: ihre Gestaltung und Entwicklung in neuerer Zeit* (Lettering. Its Formation and Evolution in Modern Times). Ehmcke is considered to have adhered to the teaching of the Austrian lettering artist, Rudolf von Larisch, who will be discussed shortly in contradistinction to Johnston.

Following the First World War, in 1918, a craft workshop was organised by the best known lettering artist of this time, Rudolf Koch. Called the Offenbacher Schreiber, or the Offenbach Penmen, it evolved into his wider-based Wertstattgemeinschaft, or Workshop Community at the Kunstgewerbeschule in Offenbach am Main, in 1921. Like Johnston, Koch held deep religious convictions although his sympathy towards the industrially made artefact was greater than Johnston's, partly, no doubt, because of the influence of his father who was the Inspektor of the Bavarian Museum of Handicrafts at Nûrnberg. Unlike Johnston, Koch was very active as a type designer working at the Klingspor typefoundry, where he eventually produced some thirty different typefaces. However, like Johnston, a down-to-earth practical regime was the counterpart to the spiritual basis of his workshops. Of this Koch wrote:

> … we are craftsmen and we have to work for everyday life and everyday needs. The noise of the typefoundry and the printing press takes us each day from our secluded dreams into the living working day. We love our work and we believe that it will be of value in the future in spite of the seeming insignificance of the things which we produce.[8]

In believing that the purpose of his skills was to serve his religion, Koch's workshop resembles the earlier years of the community which Johnston enjoyed in Ditchling with Hilary Pepler and Eric Gill. Koch also took up weaving and produced one of his most celebrated works, the seven great tapestry hangings, in the early 1920s. They explored religious themes and incorporated woven lettering.

William Morris's ideas aroused intense interest in Germany (as they did in other industrialising countries, such as the USA and Japan). Some of his writings soon appeared in German. The utopian *News From Nowhere,* for example, which came out in England in 1896, was translated by August Bebel and published 1898 by W. Liebknecht in the social democratic journal, *Die Neue Zeit.* His *The Dream of John Ball* was published in Vienna in 1904 as *Ein Traum von John Bull.* Some of Morris's articles on design appeared in German, for example *Ein paar Winke über das Musterzeichnen* in 1902. Morris's designs were discussed in the British periodical, *The Studio*, (e.g., *The Art of the Book*, 1914), which was widely read on the continent. They were also shown in German art periodicals such as J. Meier-Graefe's *Dekorative Kunst.* The presence of this literature prepared the way, in a general sense, for the reception of the Johnston tradition of lettering in Germany.[9]

The interest in modern English design was part of the openness among thinkers in Germany to foreign design theory. Three of these, Henry van de Velde, Hermann Muthesius and Peter Behrens, were architects and designers. Belonging to the same generation – they were born in the 1860s – they were all adherents of Morris and became key figures in the development of design education in Germany. Henry van de Velde remained rooted in the *Jugendstil.* Yet he enthused about Morris's notion of the unity of the arts. He used Morris's wallpapers and fabrics in his lectures on industrial art in Brussels and in 1898 he wrote an article entitled 'William Morris, Artisan et Socialiste'.[10]

Hermann Muthesius was especially active in transmitting Morris's ideas. Trained in philosophy and architecture, he was installed as the cultural and technical *attaché* at the German Embassy in London where he was briefed to investigate the state of English architecture and design. He wrote articles on John Ruskin, William Morris, Philip Webb, and C. R. Ashbee for German periodicals. One, entitled 'Art and the Machine', appeared in *Dekorative Kunst.* In 1904 he published his *magnum opus*, the two-volume *Das Englische Haus*, which evaluated the work of architect-designers of the Arts and Crafts movement such as Philip Webb, Charles Voysey, Baillie Scott, R. S. Lorimer, Edwin Lutyens and others, for example the metal worker, William Benson. Muthesius anticipated the ideas of Lethaby in focusing on the inevitable role of mechanisation in design.[11] Returning to Germany in 1907, he was appointed director of the Handels-hochschule in Berlin from where he campaigned to set up an organisation to bind together commerce, industry, and the artist-designer. This materialised as the Deutsche Werkbund in 1907. It was the watershed in design theory throughout Europe, spawning similar societies. It marked the onset of the modernist era of design.[12]

Peter Behrens was a similar case. Early on he was impressed by the connection between design and the tools and materials of its making as theorised by Morris, taught by Lethaby, and practised by craftsmen such as Johnston. Behrens became an all-round designer. And like Muthesius, he developed the notion of quintessential forms. Standardisation based on these forms would facilitate mechanisation, especially in the building industry. But as well as being an architect, Behrens designed furniture, glass, ceramics, fabrics, books, and he produced other typefaces after his Behrensschrift. The motif of a ship as the logo for the Insel Verlag editions of classics was his. The series was called Insel-Bücherei. Its proprietor, Anton

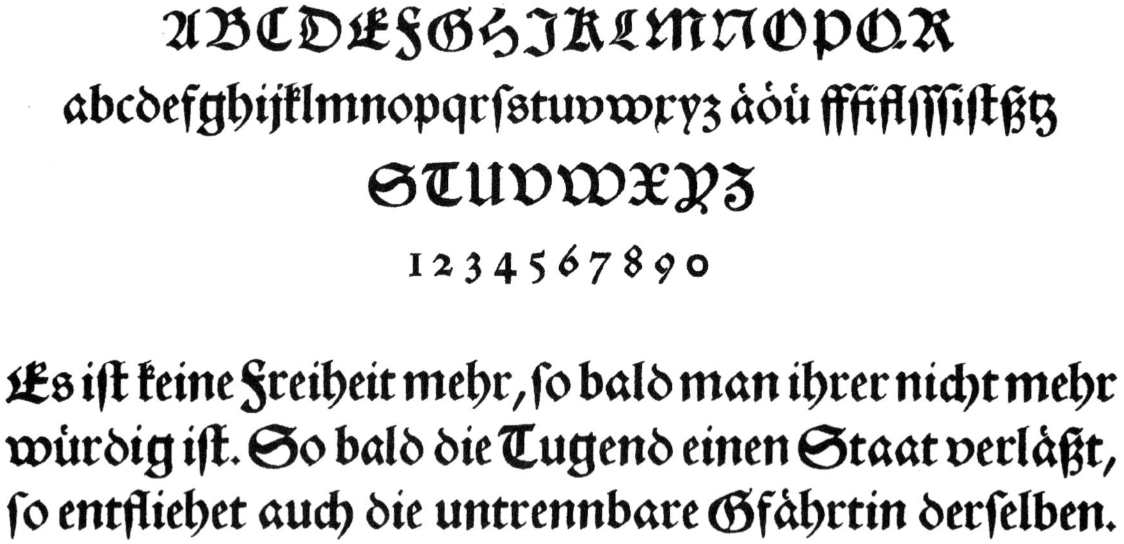

ABCDEFGHIJKLMNOPQR
abcdefghijklmnopqrſstuvwxyz äöü fffiflſſſiſtßtz
STUVWXYZ
1234567890

Es iſt keine Freiheit mehr, ſo bald man ihrer nicht mehr würdig iſt. So bald die Tugend einen Staat verläßt, ſo entfliehet auch die untrennbare Gfährtin derſelben.

Fig. 156. Schwabacher design, alphabet and text. Seventeenth century. (Courtesy of Jan Tschichold. *Gute Schriftformen*. Basel. 1941–46.)

Kippenberg, commissioned Johnston and Gill and others. In 1903, Behrens was appointed through Muthesius as the director of the Kunstgewerbeschule at Düsseldorf where, three years later, he engaged Anna Simons to teach. In 1907, he was a founder member of the Deutsche Werkbund.

There is a contrary sense, however, in which the English influence in Germany is remarkable, at least as far as lettering and typography are concerned. The contrast between the printing traditions of the two countries might well have inhibited contact in the same way that the vernacular traditions in France – that of the *livre d'artist*, for example – left France relatively impervious to other influences. It was the drive to reform lettering in Germany which opened the door, first to the Morrisian view of typography, and then to the Johnstonian tradition.

The tradition of Gothic, or Black Letter, scripts and type designs in Germany was profound. Its origins date from the first period of printing there. As elsewhere in Europe, it followed medieval scribal practices. As a general rule of thumb, different type designs denoted different categories of literature. Religious works were largely printed in Latin in the Gothic Textura design – the *Gutenberg 42-line Bible* setting a precedent – or in Roman. Legal works, also in Latin, were printed in Gothic Rotunda. Humanist works, in Latin or in Italian, were printed in Humanist, i.e., Roman designs. Erasmus, for example, insisted that his books should be set in Roman. Works in the vernacular, however, tended to be printed in the designs based on the Bastarda cursive scripts which had developed for speed of writing in the bureaucratic scriptoria of each country.

In Germany, two cursive scripts were the models for the two principal type designs. Both were written with a broad-edged pen. Schwabacher, (the origin of the name is unknown) was characterised by wide letters and open, mandorla-like, bowls

ABCDEFGHIKLMNOPQRS
TUVWXYZ
abcdefghijklmnopqrſstuvwxyz
äöüchckffſiflllſiſſßſtz
Die Buchdruckerkunſt entreißt alle anderen Künſte und Wiſſenſchaften dem Untergange; ſie unterrichtet in den Grundſätzen der Religion

Fig. 157. Breitkof Fraktur, alphabet and text. Sixteenth century. (Courtesy of Jan Tschichold. *Gute Schriftformen*. Basel. 1941–46.)

of the *a* and *o* letter-forms. (Fig. 156.) In effect, it is a German form of Rotunda. The second was the more elaborate and stressed Fraktur, which originated in a script used in the Chancery of Emperor Maximilian I. (Fig. 157). An early version was calligraphed by the writing master, Johann Neudörffer, in 1522, and cut by Hieronymous Andrae, of Nürnberg. It was used in the printing of the books of the artist, Dürer, in the 1530s. It was a compressed design with 'broken' letter-forms and agitated descenders. It came to have a floriated, Baroque quality, with swirled extensions to the serifs which were named *Schnörkel*, or elephant trunks. In 1523, the newly-translated Luther Bible was printed in Schwabacher and from 1534 in Fraktur, as a gesture of defiance to the Catholic tradition of Latin set in Textura or Roman. Fraktur became the norm in Germany, and was applied on a wider scope than just vernacular texts. It replaced Schwabacher, which took on the role of emphasis, as Italics did with Roman typefaces. (Fig. 158.)

With the impact of the eighteenth-century Enlightenment, however, Roman types took on a new currency in Germany. This was especially the case for natural history and philosophical works and for new literature, whose authors aimed to be read abroad.[13] Of significance is a book dealing with the Temple of the Muses which was translated into German and printed in Roman. Its preface was written by the translator, Christoph Stockmann, in 1733, in which he argued for the wholesale printing of the German language in Roman types.[14] The new mood was also reflected in the design of a neo-classical Fraktur, which was designed by Johann Frederich Gottlieb Unger in 1790. Didot-like, it was elegant even to the point of

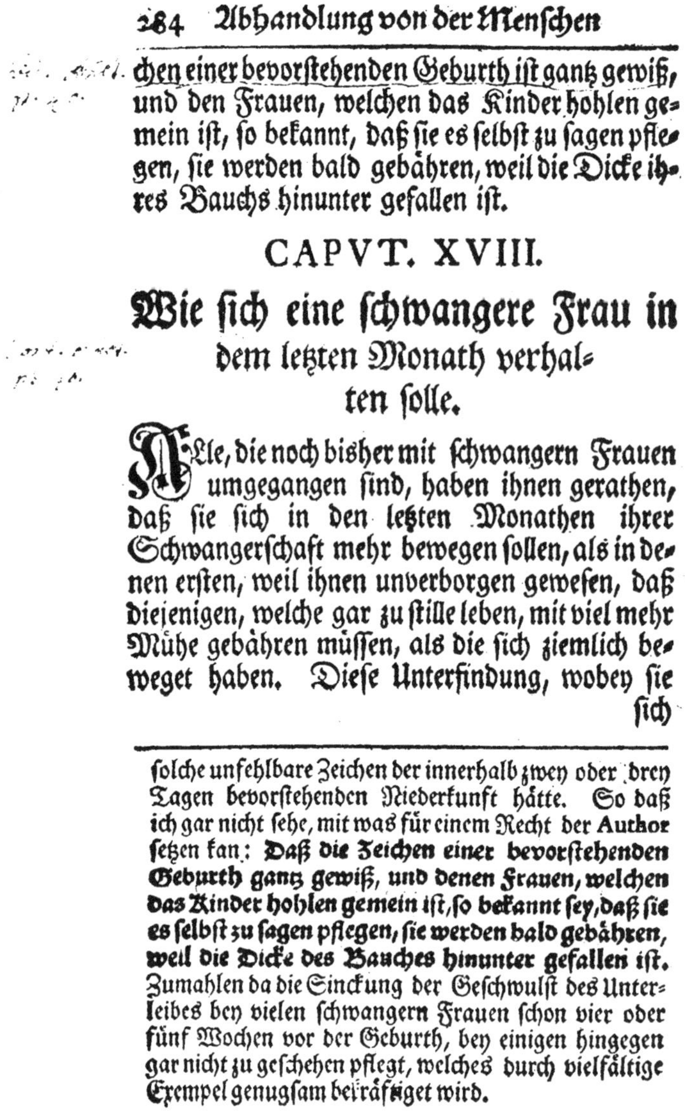

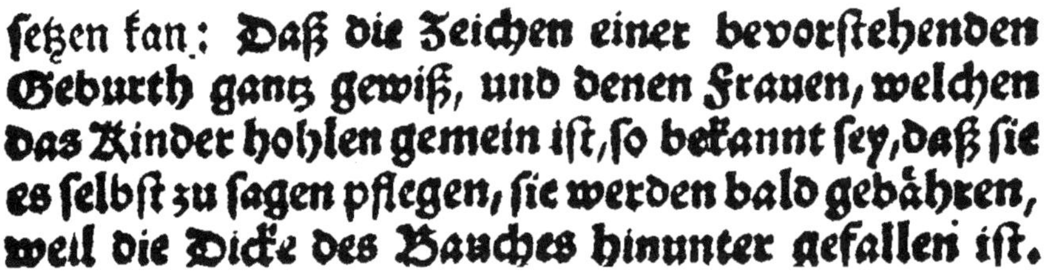

284 Abhandlung von der Menschen

chen einer bevorstehenden Geburth ist gantz gewiß, und den Frauen, welchen das Kinder hohlen gemein ist, so bekannt, daß sie es selbst zu sagen pflegen, sie werden bald gebähren, weil die Dicke ihres Bauchs hinunter gefallen ist.

CAPVT. XVIII.

Wie sich eine schwangere Frau in dem letzten Monath verhalten solle.

Alle, die noch bisher mit schwangern Frauen umgegangen sind, haben ihnen gerathen, daß sie sich in den letzten Monathen ihrer Schwangerschaft mehr bewegen sollen, als in denen ersten, weil ihnen unverborgen gewesen, daß diejenigen, welche gar zu stille leben, mit viel mehr Mühe gebähren müssen, als die sich ziemlich beweget haben. Diese Unterfindung, wobey sie sich

solche unfehlbare Zeichen der innerhalb zwey oder drey Tagen bevorstehenden Niederkunft hätte. So daß ich gar nicht sehe, mit was für einem Recht der **Author** setzen kan: **Daß die Zeichen einer bevorstehenden Geburth gantz gewiß, und denen Frauen, welchen das Kinder hohlen gemein ist, so bekannt sey, daß sie es selbst zu sagen pflegen, sie werden bald gebähren, weil die Dicke des Bauches hinunter gefallen ist.** Zumahlen da die Sinckung der Geschwulst des Unterleibes bey vielen schwangern Frauen schon vier oder fünf Wochen vor der Geburth, bey einigen hingegen gar nicht zu geschehen pflegt, welches durch vielfältige Exempel genugsam bekräfftiget wird.

setzen kan: **Daß die Zeichen einer bevorstehenden Geburth gantz gewiß, und denen Frauen, welchen das Kinder hohlen gemein ist, so bekannt sey, daß sie es selbst zu sagen pflegen, sie werden bald gebähren, weil die Dicke des Bauches hinunter gefallen ist.**

Fig. 158. *Above*: Page from an eighteenth-century medical book, *Abhandlung von dem Menchen*, showing the combination of Fraktur used as the text face and Scwabacher used (in bold) for emphasis- and Roman for the chapter heading and number.

Below: enlargement of the Schwabacher design.

being emasculated. Another indicator was a neo-classical Roman typeface by the typefounder, Justus Erich Walbaum, in 1803. It followed the style of Firmin Didot's Modern Roman, of 1784, with sharp contrasts between thick and thin strokes and with vertical, rather than sloping, rounded bowls. Then, in the early nineteenth century, the influential German grammarian, Jakob Grimm, also campaigned for the adoption of Roman letters, using much the same set of arguments as Stockmann.[15] His *Deutsche Grammatik* of 1819 and his *Deutsche Wörterbuch*, or dictionary, of 1854, were both set in Roman types. More radical still, they also eliminated capital letters for all words except proper nouns, an issue taken up again by the modernists.

But the early- to mid-nineteenth century saw the return of the Fraktur to denote a measure of cultural nationalism. As a reaction to the aggression of the Napoleonic Wars and then of the Franco-Prussian War, 1870–71, Fraktur was upheld and became a strand in the movement towards the unification of Germany. It was endorsed by Bismarck and widely used for newspapers, magazines and for non-German language works, too. Fraktur became known as 'Deutsche Schrift'. Thus, by the turn of the century, German printing assumed the use of variants of the Fraktur and Schwabacher scripts. Scientific works, however, were still printed in Roman types. With all the design innovations in the early-twentieth century, the tension between Fraktur, which was seen as inherently Germanic, and Antiqua (Roman), which was seen as classical and foreign, intensified among the lettering and typographical fraternity. There was passionate engagement on both sides. Unger's Fraktur and Walbaum's Roman came back into currency largely on account of the preferences of Carl Ernst Poeschel, who is regarded as Germany's foremost printer at that time. Paul Renner, who is best known as the designer of the rationalist sanserif typeface, Futura, of 1927, argued historically. He claimed that Roman lettering was the main stem of German writing, having being promoted by Charlemagne, who had his capital at Aachen, in Germany.[16] For Renner, Fraktur was essentially a side branch. Fritz Ehmcke, who is more associated with Rudolf von Larisch and the Black Letter tradition, argued that, in practice, Fraktur was more authentically German. Adopting a more empirical approach, Dr. Gustav Kühl, the author of a perceptive and fair-minded tract, *On the Psychology of Writing*[17] (translated from German in 1905), argued for the 'spirit' of literature, and advocated that German be printed in Fraktur but other literatures in appropriate type designs:

> A medieval Latin author printed in Gothic might suit our taste but we should strongly object to a Caesar or Horace being printed in that style.... We cannot imagine Luther's or Lessing's works written in a Latin script. Goethe returned to the German from the international style.

Interestingly, Kühl's booklet, which was produced by the Ruhard'sche Giesserei or typefoundry (it became the Gebr. Klingspor Giesserei in 1906), was printed in the Behrensschrift typeface. From 1912 the lettering artist Rudolf Koch argued from a religious rather than an historical viewpoint and favoured the expressive force of the Black Letter. Similarly, the art critic, Julius Meier-Graefe, speaking from the heart, claimed that:

> The German 'Fraktur' is the most beautiful printing type existing, unapproachable in its wealth of graphic potentialities'.[18]

As a measure of the progress of the Roman type designs in Germany it has been claimed that '… in 1928 it was recorded that 57% of new book titles were set in Black Letter as compared with 43% in Roman faces'.[19]

The issue had deep roots, too, among those who were concerned with the teaching of handwriting. Among educational circles a lobby movement called the Allgemeiner Verein für Altschrift, (the General Association for Roman Script) petitioned the German parliament in 1911 for the adoption of the Roman letter-forms for handwriting. But the result of this *Schriftstreit*, however, was indecisive. Whether the lobby included Anna Simons, and therefore promoted Johnston's lettering, is unclear.

Quite independently, therefore, of any English developments there was a resurgence of high standards of lettering in Germany from the 1890s on account of the Secession movement. This was the very impetus which spearheaded a return to the Roman letter-forms. Pioneering these changes was a series of literary and art periodicals. The earliest was the influential *Blâtter für die Kunst*, edited by the writer Stefan George in Berlin from 1892. However, it was still printed in Black Letter. Another, was the lavish *Pan*, edited by Julius Meier-Graefe and by Otto Bierbaum in Leipzig from 1894. It carried new writing by authors such as Verlaine, Rimbaud, Novalis, Nietzsche, articles on design by Count Harry Kessler and Peter Behrens, and original lithographs and etchings. As if to demonstrate its modernity, *Pan* was printed in Roman type. A third, rivalling *Blätter für die Kunst*, was *Die Insel*, edited in Leipzig from 1899 by the millionaire Alfred Heymel and the poet Rudolf Alexander Schröder. In 1912 *Die Insel* grew into the publishing house, Insel-Verlag. It proclaimed its modernity, however, by using the new Eckmannschrift. Yet another *avant-garde* periodical was the prestigious *Hyperion* which ran between 1905–08. The creation of Franz Blei and Carl Sternheim, it carried new works by writers including Kafka, Musil, Rilke, Carl Sternheim, Hugo von Hofmannsthal, and by artists such as Klimpt, Nolde, Heckel, Gordon Craig, Aubrey Beardsley, and Hokusai. It was published by the Hans von Weber Verlag and printed in Leipzig by Carl Ernst Poeschel. It was set in a new Roman typeface, Tiemann Schrift, designed by Poeschel's partner, Walter Tiemann. An Austrian periodical was *Ver Sacrum*. The equivalent of the German *Pan*, flourishing a *Jugendstil* style, it was set in a Roman typeface. Similarly, the writers Nietzsche, Stefan George, Hofmannstahl, Dehmel, Schröder chose to have their books set in Roman types.[20] The typographic excellence of all these publications was quite independent of any English influence.

As the new periodicals partly show, *Jugendstil* was still a vital force. Important within this domain was another purely German activity: the ideas of free letter-forms taught by Rudolf von Larisch. A radical lettering artist who was based at the Kunstgewerbeschule in Vienna, Larisch's approach to lettering was diametrically opposed to Johnston's, he saw himself as evolving from the *Jugendstil* tradition. He and Johnston had already met in London, in 1909,[21] and again at the conference on art education in Dresden in 1912 where both gave lectures. Larisch's home address in Vienna is to be found written in tiny writing in Johnston's address book (now kept at the Craft Study Centre in Farnham). The encounter of the two most influential lettering teachers of that period could not have been lost on people in that audience in Dresden: the single-minded Johnston, whose belief was in freedom of expression as the outcome of the discipline of using the broad-edged nib – his concept of Sharpness, Unity and Freedom – and the more expansive Rudolf von

SO FLEHTEN SIE. ES
HUB DA AN ZU KL
GEN DER ARME HI
RICH IN DES HERZ
NOT DER HOFFNU
LIEBER WOLLTE ER
ENTSAGEN ALS SIC

16. 1/2 der Originalgröße. Fragment. Mit der Rohrfeder groß schreiben. Rücksicht auf die Material- und Werkzeugsprache.

der Buchstabenschenkel — kann übrigens leicht zur Folge haben, daß diese Massen für das Auge zusammenfließen, daß aber gleichzeitig

ei einer Beurteilung der graphisch-technischen Leistungen der Staatsdruckerei ist es nur natürlich, wenn dem Buchdruck der breiteste Raum zugewiesen wird. Nicht allein seine kulturelle Bedeutung, welche den Charakter der von uns „Neuzeit" genannten geschichtlichen Epoche weitaus mehr zu beeinflussen bestimmt war, als es die Entdeckung Amerikas vermochte, ist hiefür maßgebend, sondern auch der Umstand, daß der Buchdruck als die Mutterkunst aller übrigen graphischen Fächer anzusehen ist, und endlich die Tatsache, daß ihm vor allem andern der größte Anteil an der Beschaffung der für die verschiedensten Bedürfnisse auf allen Gebieten des staatlichen, gesellschaftlichen und geschäftlichen Lebens notwendigen

Fig. 159. Above: Detail from Rudolf von Larisch's *Unterricht in ornamentaler Schrift*. Vienna 1905.

Below: Detail from the book, *Zur Feier des einhundertjäjrigen Bestandes der k.k Hof-un Statsdruckerei*, 1804–1904, with lettering designed by Rudolf von Larisch. Vienna. 1904 (Courtesy of the Bauer Typefoundry. Cited from *Aventur und Kunst*. Frankfurt am Main. 1940.)

Larisch, whose belief in artistic spontaneity, in experiment with different writing tools, and in a creative leap beyond lettering's history was, within its own terms, equally fruitful. (Fig. 159)

Like Johnston, Larisch also advocated the use of the broad-nibbed pen. He developed his own version, his 'kelemi' pen, made from oriental reeds and fitted with a brass spring to serve as a reservoir. He also worked in cooperation with the Blanckertz's pen company and had an interest in lettering for modern situations like electric signs.[22]

One of those in the Dresden audience was the owner of that company, the entrepreneur Rudolf Blanckertz. He had spent time in Anna Simons' circle in England and also knew the lettering teacher, Robert Howie, in Glasgow. Blanckertz was a publisher and the founder of the Schrift Museum in Berlin. He had organised the Exhibition of Writing and Lettering concurrent with the Dresden conference. Through Anna Simons, Johnston and other members of the Calligraphers' Society contributed exhibits. In his paper, 'Anna Simons and the German Script Movement', of 1937, Blanckertz refers to the conference and makes the point that:

> Johnston delivered an address. The officials from the Ministries and educational departments opened their eyes at the things they saw and heard at this exhibition. This was only equalled when Rudolf von Larisch in a thrilling speech proved that a German art of writing had come into being, a genuine native product, suited to our lives and schools .... I had the privilege of introducing Anna Simons to Rudolf von Larisch.[23]

On account of the growing ascendancy of the Roman letter-forms, English trends were taken up with creative effect in Germany. Although Johnston was the principal voice of the renewed tradition of Roman-Humanist lettering in England, its celebration was already under way. It had began with the recognition of Morris. Count Harry Kessler's Cranach Presse edition of *Virgil,* of 1902, was dedicated to him. The connections continued with Emery Walker and his contribution to the Insel Verlag press and the Cranach Presse. In an article on Emery Walker, Bernard Newdigate, of the Shakespeare Head Press, claimed:

> I think it may be said with truth that the revival of printing in Germany owes more to Emery Walker than to anyone else for its best and finest features'.[24]

Cobden-Sanderson was also influential. His treatise, *Ecce Mundus: Industrial Ideals and the Book Beautiful*, was an important text for the new generation of *Buchkünstler,* or book artists, in Germany. It was translated by Richard Stettiner and printed in periodical form in 1901–02, and in book form in 1921.[25] (Another translation was made in by Jan Tschichold in 1963.) In 1909, the edition of *Faust,* printed in German in Emery Walker's Doves Press type, was very esteemed there. Other figures of influence were St. John Hornby of the Ashendene Press, Douglas Cockerell, the bookbinder, and Johnston's colleagues, Graily Hewitt and Eric Gill.

Numerous German private presses followed in the path of the flowering achievements in England of the Kelmscott, the Ashendene and the Doves Presses.

During the period up to the early 1920s active and well-to-do *Buchkünstler* in Germany set up hand-operated presses and oversaw the design of new typefaces in order to create limited editions, mainly of classic texts often in bespoke bindings. In some cases their interests extended to involve *avant-garde* artistic and literary developments. Count Harry Kessler at the Cranach Presse, for example, published the autobiographical treatise, *Amo*, written by his friend, Henry van de Velde. Likewise, Willy Wiegand at the Bremer Presse published new writings by Hugo von Hofmannsthal, who is also well known as a poet and the librettist of Strauss's opera *Der Rosenkavalier*.[26]

The earliest of the new German private presses dates from 1907 when the partners Carl Ernst Poeschel and Walter Tiemann set up the Janus Presse. Carl Poeschel was the director of his own commercial printing house, Poeschel & Trepte, at Leipzig. He had strong Anglo-Saxon connections having studied printing in America, possibly with Daniel Updike at the Merrymount Press in Boston. It is also suggested that he '... was able to study printing with William Morris and Cobden-Sanderson, in England'.[27] He became an honorary member of the Double Crown Club in London and was a friend of Stanley Morison and of Oliver Simon.[28] Apart from pioneering the use of new typefaces, such as Behrensschrift, Poeschel was responsible for printing the Insel Verlag series of German classics, the Insel Bücherei, which were the forerunner of the King Penguins series in England, and set, interestingly, in Emil Weiss's new Fraktur typeface.

Walter Tiemann was an artist, a calligrapher, and the type designer for the Janus Presse. He became an eminent educationist who, from 1920, was the director of the state-run Akademie für Graphische Künste und Buchgewerbe (Academy for Graphic Arts and Book Production) at Leipzig, a town whose pre-eminence as the centre of German book production was in part sustained by the German private press movement.

The typographic style of the Janus Presse was closely modelled on the Doves Press. Just five books were printed, including a work by Hofmannsthal. Its pages of meticulously-spaced type were lightened by hand-drawn titling and initials. Tiemann's Janus type, like that of the Doves Press, was modelled closely on Venetian letter-forms. His later Roman type designs, the Antiqua and Mediäval, could well have been inspired by Anna Simons's work. Tiemann the type designer was described by Julius Rodenberg as:

> ... reminiscent of a serene sky after a tempest. His art does not rise to the sublime. Instead he possesses grace and elegance of form ... conforming to the new tendency for simplicity as a reaction against the excesses of the Jugendstil. His work resembles nothing so much as the charming melodies of Mozart.[29]

The Ernst Ludwig-Presse of Darmstadt was founded in the same year, 1907, by the two Kleukens brothers. Friedrich Wilhelm Kleukens was a type designer who also taught at the Akademie für Graphische Künst und Buchgewerbe at Leipzig. Christian Heinrich Kleukens was a designer and editor. The press was so named because it was under the patronage of the Grand Duke Ernst-Ludwig of

DURCH UNSERE LETZTE REDE sind mehrere schon in der ersten versprochene Beweise geführt und vollendet worden. Es sei dermalen nur davon die Rede, sagten wir, und dies sei die erste Aufgabe, das Dasein und die Fortdauer des Deutschen schlechtweg zu retten; alle andere Unterschiede seien dem höhern Überblicke verschwunden; und es würde durch jenes den besondern Verbindlichkeiten, die etwa jemand zu haben glaube, kein Eintrag geschehen. Es ist, wenn uns nur der

Fig. 160. German Roman (Antiqua) type design by Willy Wiegand and possibly Anna Simons for the Bremer Presse, with initials calligraphed (and then printed) by Anna Simons in the Johnston mould. Fichte. *Reden an die deutsche Nation*. 1922. (Courtesy of *Fine Print*. Vol. 12. 1986.)

Fig. 161. Initial letters by Anna Simons for the Bremer Presse. *Left:* Dante. *Right*: St. Augustine

Darmstadt. In 1911 Christian Heinrich produced an edition of Shakespeare in sixteen volumes which he dedicated to Cobden-Sanderson. Later, Friedrich Wilhelm set up his own Ratio Presse, while Christian set up his own commercial Mainzer Presse.

Some other presses were significant. The Officina Serpentis was owned by Eduard W. Tieffenbach in 1911 in Berlin. To an extent greater than the Kelmscott Press, the Officina Serpentis was devoted to the use of Gothic types modelled on some fifteenth-century exemplars. Its type has been compared to Ricketts's Vale Press type.[30]

The Rupprecht Presse was established by the lettering artist, Fritz Ehmcke, in 1913. It grew as an extension of his workshops at Munich. Ehmcke used his own types designs, in which activity he was prolific. In 1921, the lettering artist F. H. Ernst Schneidler set up his Juniperus Presse in Stuttgart.

Additionally, typefoundries such as the all-important Klingspor and Bauer also had their own Hausdruckei, or presses, dedicated to specialist publishing with the purpose of demonstrating their typefaces and printing skills. Of particular interest, too, was the Rudolfinische Drucke set up by Rudolf Koch and Rudolf Gerstung, where they were involved in printing handwritten books.

Aside from Count Kessler's Cranach Presse, it was the Bremer Presse which perhaps most closely emulated English models. It was established as an occupation for Ludwig Wolde in Bremen, in 1911. The literary figure, Rudolf Alexander Schroeder (a founder figure of the periodical *Die Insel)* was an inspirational force and Willy Wiegand became the dominant partner and its operational manager. In 1917 the Bremer Presse was moved to Munich. Wiegand came from a family of shipping magnates. (His father, Heinrich Wiegand, was the general manager of the North German Lloyd Lines and commissioned designers to fit out the interiors of luxury liners.) His aim was to regenerate the book as a craft-based activity. In an adddress which he gave to the Grolier Club in New York, in 1929, to open its exhibition of German private press books, he claimed in terms reminiscent of the Arts and Crafts movement that:

> … since the invention of the mechanical press, that is since the beginning of the nineteenth century, the book has lost the spiritualised form which it possessed up til [*sic*] then.… The book, the embodiment of the spirit, this receptacle of the thoughts of all humanity, was apparently inferior to and at the mercy of the machine.[31]

Wiegand is said to have visited Cobden-Sanderson and St. John Hornby of the Ashendene Press in London. Like Cobden-Sanderson, his title list included classical German literature. His principal bookbinder was Frieda Thiersch who had learnt the craft under C. F. McLeish at the Doves Bindery in Hammersmith. Following exactly Emery Walker's approach, in 1912–13, Wiegand designed a Roman type – called Antiqua in the German classification – based on those used by the fifteenth-century German printers, Adolf Rusch (1464), and Da Spira (1469). (Figs. 160 & 161.) This was possibly in collaboration with Anna Simons although Wiegand, in the company of Ludwig Wolde, did make his own study of incunabula in Italy itself.[32] It was cut at the Bauer typefoundry by Louis Hoell.[33] And, like Emery Walker's Doves type, it was large, in sixteen point, and was used throughout the entire Bremer Presse publishing list until 1921. Only then did Wiegand have smaller sizes cut though this was mainly for the machine-printed editions published by his ancillary Verlag Bremer Presse. (There was also a Greek and a 'Biblia' Fraktur-like type used for a Luther Bible.)

Wiegand was a typographic purist emulating Cobden-Sanderson. And just like Johnston at the Doves Press, Anna Simons was commissioned by him to calligraph titling and initial lettering, to be discussed shortly. Speaking of his experience of English printing during the same address to the Grolier Club, Wiegand continued:

Fig. 162. Antiqua by Peter Behrens. 1908.

ABCDEEFGHIKLMNOPQURSTUVW
XYZÆŒ abcdefghijklmnopqrsſtuvwxyzſch

ABCDEFGHIJKLMNOPQRSTUVWXY
ZÆŒabcdefghijklmnopqrsſtuvwxyzchckſch

> We owe indeed an infinite amount of gratitude to the genius and intuition of William Morris for the deliverance of the printed book from this state of neglect and danger. He, and after him Cobden-Sanderson pointed out the new tasks, the new possibilities and, at the same time, the course that should be followed .... On the pattern of the Kelmkott [*sic*] and the Doves Press the German presses were founded about twenty years ago. They are, like their English originals and models, real laboratories of the art of printing .... We examine the manuscripts and the early printed books of the fifteenth century to find the secret of their dignity, of that nobility which awakens in us the feeling of reverence for their spiritual contents and makes us value the possession of the books.[34]

Wiegand's adoption of a Roman type design was not restricted to aesthetics, however. In the same address he touched on issues implicit in the *Schriftstreit*, stressing the importance of the psychological and perceptual laws of the book and of the need to:

> ... penetrate into the relations of type and language, to recognise that each language requires its particular alphabet, its specially shaped type, responding to the structure of the language, its character, its laws, its rhythm, a type which blends with the language, so that perfect correspondence between type and language is created.

While Wiegand adhered to his Antiqua typeface only, activity was ongoing to produce other Roman type designs. Following the German practice whereby typefoundries employed artist-designers, new ones were designed for general commercial use. At the outset they tended to be hybrid forms not dissimilar in spirit to the fifteenth-century 'fere-Humanistica' designs. That is to say they were transitional, preserving traces of the Black Letter. Generically they were called Antiqua and Mediäval. Antiqua refers to the 'Modern' category of Roman design of the eighteenth century associated with Didot. Mediäval refers to Old Style Roman, associated with the printing of Jenson in Venice. It followed the tradition set by William Morris. Morris's Troy type, designed for the Kelmscott Press, was reissued after his death by the American Typefounders Company under the name Satanica.

ABCDEFGHIJKLMN
OPQRSTUVWXYZ

Fig. 163. Mediäval type designs, 1913. (Courtesy of *Fleuron*. Vol. 4. 1925.)

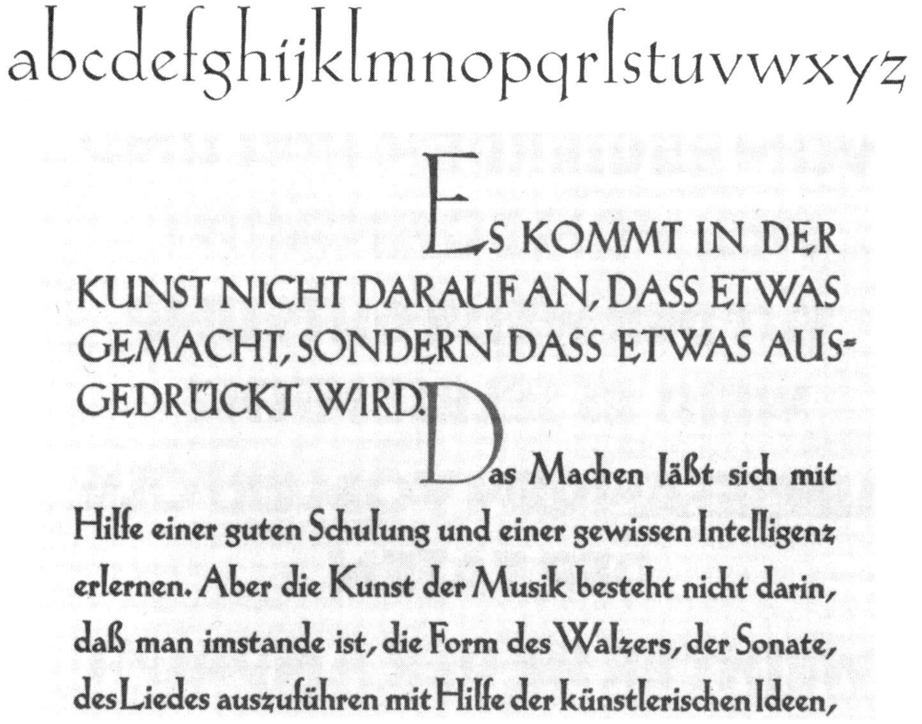

abcdefghijklmnopqrſstuvwxyz

ES KOMMT IN DER KUNST NICHT DARAUF AN, DASS ETWAS GEMACHT, SONDERN DASS ETWAS AUS-GEDRÜCKT WIRD. Das Machen läßt sich mit Hilfe einer guten Schulung und einer gewissen Intelligenz erlernen. Aber die Kunst der Musik besteht nicht darin, daß man imstande ist, die Form des Walzers, der Sonate, des Liedes auszuführen mit Hilfe der künstlerischen Ideen,

Fig. 164. Antiqua Medium by Rodolf Koch. *Above*: alphabet and *below*: sample text. 1924. (Courtesy of *Fleuron*. Vol. 4. 1925.)

It was duly exported to Germany where it helped to stimulate the revival of the Mediäval designs.

One of the earliest Roman designs was from the Klingspor foundry: an Antiqua by Peter Behrens in 1908, in which Uncial traits also feature. (Fig. 162.) His Mediäval followed in 1913. (Fig. 163.) One of the most esteemed is Koch's Antiqua Medium, of 1924.[35] (Fig. 164.) Other Roman typefaces were created by Otto Eckmann, Peter Behrens, E. R. Weiss, F. H. Ehmcke, Otto Hupp, Walter Tiemann, F. H. Ernst Schneidler, and the lesser known Heinz König.

The new designs, Antiqua and Mediäval, form an accomplished and distinctively German development. The impetus behind the investment they cost the typefoundries which manufactured them derived in some measure from the Anglophile connection. In 1905, Count Harry Kessler, who was the embodiment of the phenomenon called Englänterei or 'English mania', imported especially a fount of Caslon Old Style for the printing of the catalogue of the exhibition he mounted in the Archducal Museum in Weimar, showing English book arts. The exhibition included examples of Johnston's work for the Doves Press, along with Eric Gill's and Grailly Hewitt's calligraphy. It toured Dresden, Düsseldorf and Berlin.[36]

It was Hermann Muthesius who suggested in 1905–06 that Johnston be appointed as teacher of summer school courses in calligraphy at the state-run Kunstgewerbeschule at Düsseldorf. It followed a major exhibition on German arts and crafts there.[37] Johnston declined but he recommended that his German pupil, Anna Simons, be appointed instead. Her close colleagues there were Peter Behrens, who was the director of the school, and Fritz Ehmcke, who was her co-teacher.

Anna Simons's memoir, *Edward Johnston and English Lettering*, of 1937 is an indispensable record:

> As Mr. Johnston was unfortunately unable to come [to Düsseldorf] I, as his pupil, was asked to undertake this work in his place. These courses have been continued during the last thirty years in a number of towns. Since 1909, no longer as holiday courses for teachers but for students of Arts and Crafts Schools during some weeks of the term, since 1914 once or twice each year in Munich and on two occasions in Zurich. The course of lectures built up on verbal instructions given to me by Mr. Johnston has been written out on a number of sheets which were first shown at an exhibition held in South London in 1913.... I have always felt grateful and proud to have been a pupil of this great artist and teacher, and favoured that I was instrumental in bringing his methods and principles to my own country. [38]

This was the platform from which Anna Simons crusaded among German calligraphers and the *Buchkünstler* with whom she collaborated for the cause of

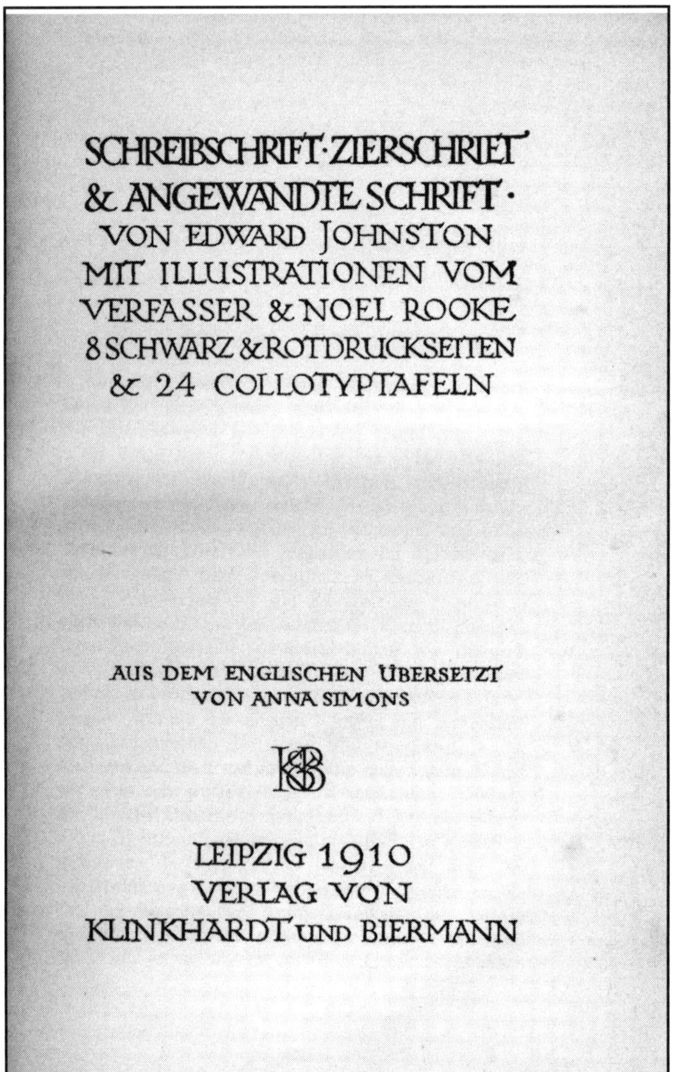

SCHREIBSCHRIFT·ZIERSCHRIFT
& ANGEWANDTE SCHRIFT·
VON EDWARD JOHNSTON
MIT ILLUSTRATIONEN VOM
VERFASSER & NOEL ROOKE
8 SCHWARZ & ROTDRUCKSEITEN
& 24 COLLOTYPTAFELN

AUS DEM ENGLISCHEN ÜBERSETZT
VON ANNA SIMONS

KB

LEIPZIG 1910
VERLAG VON
KLINKHARDT UND BIERMANN

Fig. 165. Title page of the first edition, dated 1910, of Johnston's *Writing and Illuminating, & Lettering*, translated by Anna Simons as *Schreibschrift Zierschrift und angewandte Schrift*.

Roman letter-forms. In the tributes paid to her in 1934, Henry van de Velde called her the ' ... apôtre de la belle lettre'.[39] Anna Simons also organised exhibitions of lettering. One took place in 1908. It was made possible by Johnston's Society of Calligraphers. It toured to Berlin and then to Hamburg, in 1910.

Given this trend, it followed that Johnston's lettering was especially respected. That his achievements were known to the German typographic fraternity was due almost entirely to Anna Simons for she perpetuated his teaching methods, developed her own variants of his Foundational hand, and translated his two lettering manuals, *Writing & Illuminating, & Lettering* (Fig. 165) in 1910 and *Manuscript and Inscription Letters* in 1911. Anna Simons at Düsseldorf became a source of influence in much the same way as Johnston was at the RCA. Her methods were adopted at other schools of the applied arts: at Weimar where she was invited to teach by Henry van de Velde in both 1908 and 1912, and at Hamburg, Halle, Frankfurt, and Nürnberg. In this work her principal assistant was Franziska Kobell, whom she trained. Anna Simons was also involved in policy-making for the teaching of handwriting in German schools.[40]

It was due to Anna Simons, too, that Johnston was invited to address the conference in Congress Hall, Dresden in 1912. (Its full title was the International Congress on Art Education, Drawing, and Art Applied to Industry.) His lecture was translated by Minna Blanckertz for the Report of the Congress from a record which Johnston wrote out subsequently from memory.[41] It took the form of a blackboard demonstration in the manner of his teaching at the RCA. Anna Simons, who stood by his side to interpret, reported that his address '... made a sensation and excited unstinted admiration'.[42]

There were other signs of Johnston's presence in Germany. It is significant that Bernard Newdigate, in visiting the international exhibition of the book and graphic arts (the Internationale Austellung für Buchgewerbe und Graphik, or Bugra) of 1914, at Leipzig, reported his '... seeming to see, in the German pavilions, the hand of Johnston on every stall and on every wall'.[43]

Anna Simons was employed to insert hand-drawn titles and initials into limited editions for some of the new private presses in order to lighten and embellish the pages of type. She also designed letters for wood-cut initials, made to be printed in conjunction with the letter-press process. Sets of work were done for the publications of the Marées Gesellschaft (Society), under the direction of Julius Meier-Graefe and for F. H. Ehmcke's Rupprecht Presse, of which the edition of the writings of Savonarola is an example. But her later and more complete involvement was with Willy Wiegand's Bremer Presse. Its editions of Tacitus' *Germanica*, of a *Chinese Ballad*, of Emerson's *Essays* and of Francis Bacon's *Essays* (printed in English in 1920) display her titling work in Roman lettering. (Fig. 166.) The titling for the Bremer Presse's *Luther Bible* of 1926–29 was also executed by her, though in a Gothic script.[44]

Anna Simons's article, 'Lettering in Book Production', of 1937, credited Johnston for:

ALBII TIBVLLI
ELEGIAE

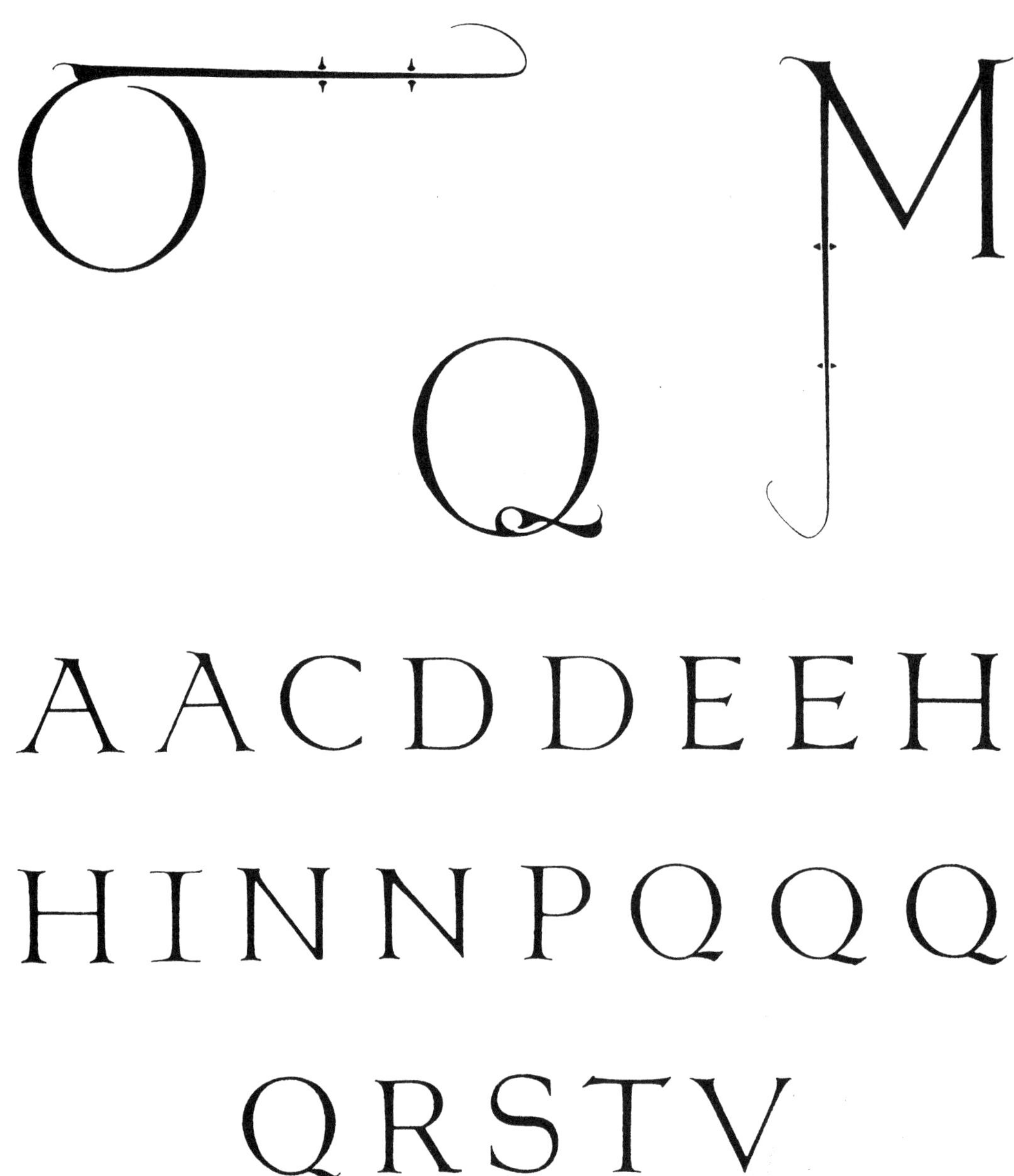

Fig. 166. Examples of lettering, initials and titling by Anna Simons for the Bremer Presse. (Courtesy of Verlag für Schriftkunde. Heintze & Blanckertz. Berlin-Leipzig. Cited from Dr. E. Hölscher. *Anna Simons*. 1937.)

> ... having contributed in no small degree to the high standards found in contemporary book production in England and abroad.... The revival of lettering, initiated by William Morris, aided by Emery Walker, and T. Cobden-Sanderson, and established by Edward Johnston's teaching and his book *Writing & Illuminating, & Lettering*, has exercised a far-reaching influence on general education, book production, typography and other spheres of national life, not only in England but also abroad. Mr. Johnston's early pupils and associates, Mr. Graily Hewitt, Mr. Eric Gill, Mr. Percy Smith and Mr. L. Christie have done their part to widen its range. The progress and development likely to be made in the future will probably arise from new tasks and new requirements. It will always be possible to meet these by adhering to Mr. Johnston's cardinal precepts – to make good letters and arrange them well.[45]

While addressing an English readership, Anna Simons was alluding as well to the shift, already discussed, from the Black Letter designs to Roman ones in Germany, at least for the printing of literature. This was a profound cultural change. For the Black Letter was not only historically entrenched but was also being actively developed by lettering designers and teachers, principally by Emil Rudolf Weiss and Rudolf Koch. Weiss was also a painter, a calligrapher, and a poet. He did much to raise the standard of German book design, his particular *forte* being the design of printer's flowers and vignettes. Like other artist-designers, he designed typefaces for the Bauersche Typefoundry at Frankfurt, most notably his Weiss Fraktur and Antiqua. Rudolf Koch became the most esteemed lettering artist-designer in Germany of this period. His typefaces Neuland and the Black Letter Kochschrift are notable. (Fig 167.) He worked in close harmony with the Klingspor Typefoundry, in Offenbach am Main. But he also taught at the city's Kunstgewerbeschule.

While the distinction between two script traditions is significant, its boundaries were actually blurred. Differences of artistic approach and even ideology did not necessarily divide neatly in the minds of the lettering artists. Skilled in lettering, *per se*, they saw fit to switch between one and the other. In his study of the type designs of the Klingspor foundry Julius Rodenberg, of the Deutsche Bücherei, touched on this issue. The development of the Klingspor types, he wrote,

> ... is specifically German because it started from the dispute about roman *or* black-letter, [*sic*] and after the failure to fuse the two kinds the dispute was renewed and subsequently settled by the answer roman *and* black-letter.[46]

Anna Simons, for example, also practised Black Letter scripts. (In 1935 the English calligrapher Rosemary Ratcliffe went to Munich to study Gothic lettering under her.) In an article on her work with the Bremer Presse, George Abrams maintains that it was she, rather than Willy Wiegand, who was the real designer of the Black Letter *Luther Bible* type – and probably of the Wiegand Antiqua, as well.[47] If this is the case, he argued, her feminine propriety all too modestly precluded her from claiming authorship. And it is the interesting as well as special case, too, that Johnston designed a Fraktur for the Cranach Presse which was used for the edition of *Hamlet*.

In a similar cross-over, Anna Simons introduced the Johnston tradition of broad-edged pen lettering to Emil Rudolf Weiss. That Weiss was receptive to her

Das Evangelium
des Johannes

Das erſte Kapitel

+ Im Anfang war das Wort
und das Wort war bei Gott, und Gott war das
Wort. Daſſelbige war im Anfang bei Gott.
Alle Dinge ſind durch daſſelbige gemacht, und
ohne daſſelbige iſt nichts gemacht, was gemacht iſt. In ihm war das Leben, und das Leben war das Licht der Menſchen. Und das Licht
ſcheinet in der Finſternis, und die Finſternis
hat's nicht begriffen. Es ward ein Menſch von
Gott geſandt, der hieß Johannes. Derſelbige
kam zum Zeugnis, daß er von dem Licht zeug-
te, auf daß ſie alle durch ihn glaubten. Er war
nicht das Licht, ſondern daß er zeugete von
dem Licht. Das war das wahrhaftige Licht,
welches alle Menſchen erleuchtet, die in dieſe
Welt kommen. Es war in der Welt, und die
Welt iſt durch daſſelbige gemacht; und die
Welt kannte es nicht. Er kam in ſein Eigentum
3

GOTT DER OPFRER
GOTT DES ALTARS FLAMME
UND NUR GOTT KANN

Fig. 167. Black Letter designs by Rudolf Koch.
Above: Kochschrift. 1910.
Below: Neuland. 1923.
(Courtesy of *Fleuron*. Vol. 4. 1925.)

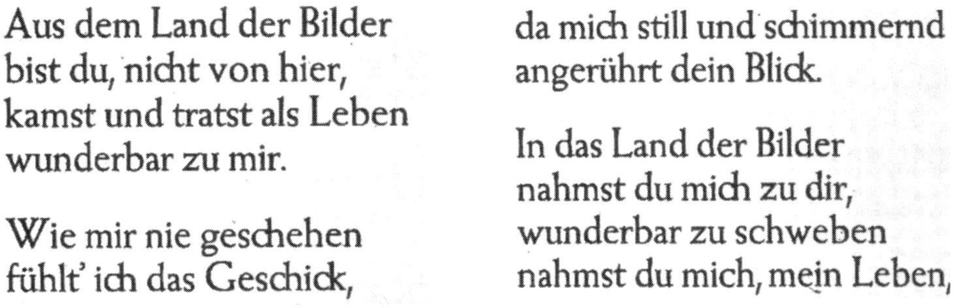

Aus dem Land der Bilder
bist du, nicht von hier,
kamst und tratst als Leben
wunderbar zu mir.

Wie mir nie geschehen
fühlt' ich das Geschick,
da mich still und schimmernd
angerührt dein Blick.

In das Land der Bilder
nahmst du mich zu dir,
wunderbar zu schweben
nahmst du mich, mein Leben,

Fig. 168. Weiss Roman Antiqua type design. 1924. (Courtesy of Schmidt-KünseMiller (?)

English innovations was due in part, perhaps, to his special admiration for William Morris. His Roman typeface, Weiss Antiqua, was designed in 1924. (Fig. 168.)

Johnston's influence is apparent on a number of other type designers, among whom are Peter Behrens, Jacob Erbar, Rudolf Koch and Jan Tschichold. It was Anna Simons's presence at Düsseldorf which may well have influenced the Mediäval type design by Peter Behrens, her colleague there. Produced between 1909–14, it is a purer Roman form than most other German versions. In his account, *Anna Simons as Scribe and Illuminator*, Dr. Eberhard Hölscher mentions that:

> ... so distinguished an artist as Peter Behrens ... who exercised a leading influence on artistic lettering frankly admitted the valuable suggestions which he owed to his collaboration with Anna Simons.[48]

In his own endeavours as a lettering artist Behrens had already followed a methodology remarkably similar to Johnston's. His awareness of the calligraphic tradition of the Black Letter scripts had convinced him that the broad-edged pen was its essential tool. This, combined with his modernist aspiration to find a quintessential design, led to his Behrensschrift of 1900–01. Behrens explained the design rationale of his simplified Fraktur in a preface to the typefoundry's specimen sheet. He affirmed that:

> Just as architecture fully reflects the whole movement of a time and the physical life of a nation, written characters symbolise inner life; they betray the pride and humility, the faith and doubt of a race.... As Gothic was the first solid proclamation of the German spirit, the character of this Gothic letter has survived among the German people until the present day.... When the art of book printing had not yet been discovered, script was written with the quill pen, and, in technical terms, the formation of the letters displayed clear signs of their formation.... The wide vertical stems were clearly differentiated according to the angle of the hand.... With fraktur also, these constructional characteristics became [*sic.* an] aesthetic principle.

Then, like Johnston, Behrens lamented the condition of late nineteenth-century lettering. Of his own design he went on to explain:

> Therefore, having omitted all extraneous features [of Fraktur] so that the constructional principle of the diagonally-held pen might be clearly expressed, I hoped, above all, that the letter would hold together well and that I might capture the aesthetic factor which would make the type suitable for all kinds of text.... In this effort, there is nothing more worthy than the search for a style of letter which is stamped with the spirit of our time.[49]

Fig. 169. Uncial-inspired lettering by Peter Behrens and Anna Simons for the Reichstag Building. Berlin. 1909. (Courtesy of P. Windsor. *Peter Behrens.* [Architectural Press London.])

The Behrensschrift is a manifestation of his aim, expressed in the same preface, that '... all things surrounding us shall be simple, solid and therefore instinctively artistic'. It can be seen as a precursor of the sanserifs which were to come. It is little wonder, therefore, that he related so well to Anna Simons's Schriftkursus, or lettering courses, at the Düsseldorfer Kunstgewerbeschule in the summers of 1906–07. (They also met again when she gave another course, in Berlin, in 1909.) Anna Simons's – and so Johnston's – emphasis on the historical understanding of scripts corresponded to Behrens's own approach. The Behrens Antiqua typeface, of 1908, already mentioned, was hailed as a 'German Roman',[50] though it also had Uncial features. In fact, in an entirely Johnstonian manner the Antiqua was the outcome of his study of a fifth-century manuscript with Uncial lettering, the *Codex Argentus.* Then, Behrens's Mediäval, designed between 1909–13, was a purer form of Roman. Julius Rodenberg wrote that it '... shows his personal interpretation of the Renaissance'.[51]

In 1909 Behrens collaborated with Anna Simons in the design of the lettering for the Reichstag, in Berlin. (Fig. 169) In his tribute to her in 1934 Behrens recounted that:

Fig. 170. Peter Behrens early sanserif for the AEG Electrical Combine in Berlin. 1916. (Courtesy of P. Windsor. Op. cit.)

Allgemeine Elektrizitäts Gesellschaft
PROF. PETER BEHRENS
NEUBABELSBERG
Hamburg Amerika Linie

ÄBCDCEFGHIJKLMNÖ
PRSTÜVWXYZ
abcdefghijklmnöpqrst
úvwxyz +!?".; * &
1234567890 ß

Fig. 171. *Left*: Jacob Erbar's Feder-Grotesk and *right*: Koloss quasi-sanserif designs. 1910. (Courtesy of Architectural Press. Op. cit.)

> This was the time [1906] when Anna Simons, a pupil of Johnston, came from England to Germany. Anna Simons brought with her not only her own talent but great knowledge and technical know-how. Thus it is not astonishing that I considered myself to be most fortunate to have found such a competent assistant and cannot refrain from mentioning that due to her skill with tools a great many variations of characters and letter-forms were created.... I must also emphasise that due to her academic historical background and her practical skills ... I myself gained many new concepts and ideas.
>
> We considered these new indicators as new aspects of form for present-day requirements. As an example I can mention the lettering for the pediment of the Reichstag building in Berlin, *Dem Deutschen Volke*.... This was not an easy task as we had to produce monumental letterforms to suit architectural purposes. Not Antiqua, but an easy to read lettering reflecting the German character. After lengthy discussions we decided on an Uncial lettering and Anna Simons undertook the task to produce the sketches for the individual letters, 1.5 metres high, in preparation for them to be cast in bronze.[52]

In 1916, Behrens designed a sanserif type for the giant electrical combine AEG, the company based in Berlin by which he was retained as artistic advisor and architect. (Fig. 170) The roots of this design are in preliminary drafts which go back to 1906. Given that Johnston's own block letter (sanserif) alphabet was designed in 1913–16, Behrens' AEG block letter shows a confluence of ideas rather than any direct influence from Johnston himself.

There were closer connections still with other lettering artists of importance in the development of the sanserif designs in Germany. One was Jacob Erbar. His earliest sanserif, commissioned by the Ludwig and Mayer typefoundry, appeared in 1910. It was named Feder Grotesk. Meaning feather or quill, 'Feder' is a clear indication of a calligraphic connection. (Fig. 171) Although Erbar was influenced later by Bauhaus thinking, his earlier attachment was to Johnston, through Anna Simons.[53] In a memoir written following his death in 1935, its author, Gunter Beissert, pointed out that:

> At Düsseldorf the Johnston method was taught by his pupil, Anna Simons, with great success. J. Erbar participated in her lessons. He acquired here the foundation of all his later letter-creations. Entirely according to Johnston's own conceptions is the Feather-Sanserif. [*sic*] With it he established, a long time before the Sanserif of the London Underground stations had appeared, the principal forms of his later Sanserif. (As early as 1913 the firm Ludwig and Meyer, Frankfurt on Main made the first suggestions for the later Erbar-Sanserif.) Besides the Feather-Sanserif he created Kanzlei, old style Roman and a modern Roman. This was a necessary preparation for his creation of Sanserif.[54]

But the Feder Grotesk and his later design, Koloss, were not yet pure sanserifs. True, they were without serifs, but they lacked the other essential of being monoline. Different widths were used for uprights and horizontal strokes. Furthermore, the curves of the rounder letter-forms show the distinct trace of the broad-edged quill. It was a quasi-sanserif, a precursor of the fully-fledged classic designs which were to follow in the 1920s: Erbar's own eponymous Grotesk, of 1923, (Fig. 172.) though begun in 1913 (Ludwig and Mayer typefoundry), Paul Renner's Futura, of 1927

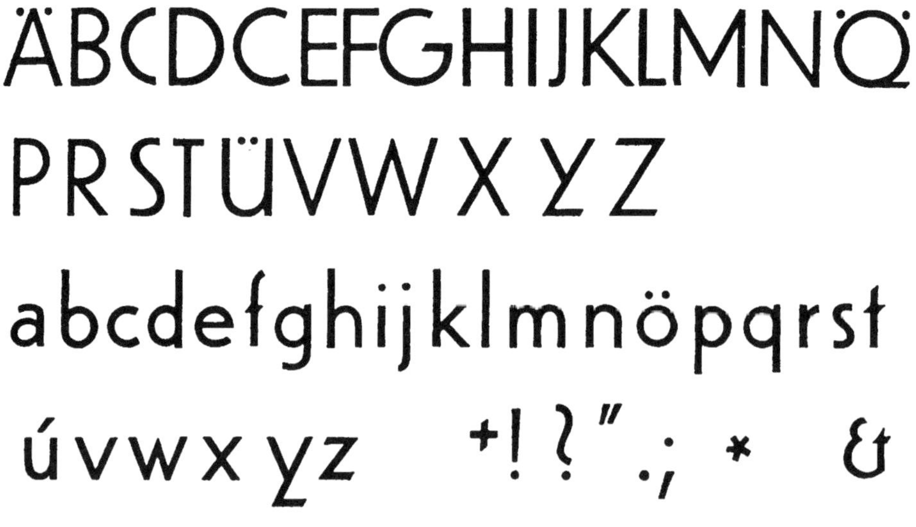

ÄBCDCEFGHIJKLMNÖ
PRSTÜVWXYZ
abcdefghijklmnöpqrst
úvwxyz +!?".; * &

Fig. 172. Erbar's Grotesk (preliminary drawing) of 1922–26.

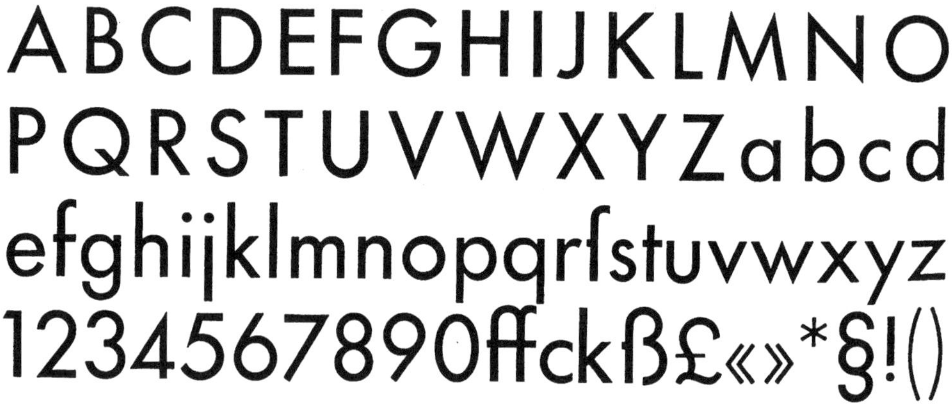

ABCDEFGHIJKLMNO
PQRSTUVWXYZabcd
efghijklmnopqrſstuvwxyz
1234567890ffckß£«»*§!()

Fig. 173. Futura by Paul Renner. 1923–27.

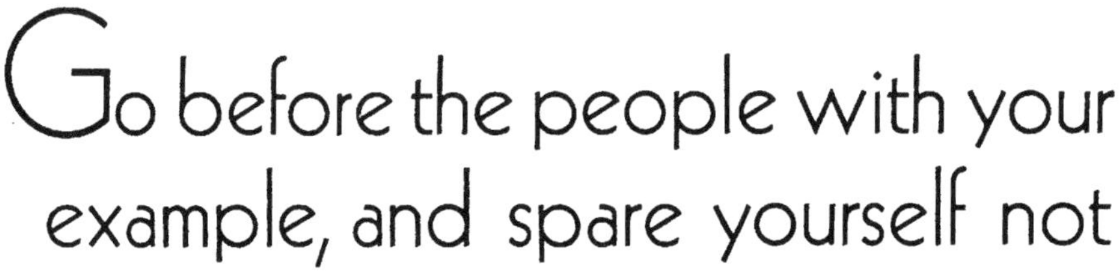

Go before the people with your example, and spare yourself not

Fig. 174. Kabel by Rudolf Koch. 1927.

(Bauer typefoundry), (Fig. 173.) and Rudolf Koch's Kabel, of 1927 (Klingspor typefoundry). (Fig. 174.) While there is no direct influence of Johnston on these important typefaces, the background glow of his presence is nevertheless discernible.

It is the case, for instance, that in 1924 a delegation from the Bund Deutsche Gebrauchgraphiker (German Union of Graphic Designers), visited London in order to take in Johnston's London Transport block letter alphabet, *in situ*. The report claims they were duly impressed.[55] One member was Heinrich Jost, the artistic advisor to the Bauer Typefoundry, who supervised the designs of Paul

Maximilian-Antiqua (Koch) 1914 ABCDEFGHIJKLMNOPQRSTUVWX YZ1234567890

MERCHANTS SOCIE

Fig. 175. Maximilian type design by Rudolf Koch, alphabet and text. 1914. (Courtesy of *Fleuron*. 1925.)

Renner's Futura type leading to its issue in 1927. Jost himself designed a slab-seriffed type called Beton between 1936–39, which was close to Futura.[56]

There was a similar confluence of interests between Johnston and Rudolf Koch. According to an account written about Koch by his pupil, Berthold Wolpe, Koch kept a copy of both the English and the German edition of Johnston's *Writing & Illuminating, & Lettering* at his school at Offenbach. Koch's own handbook on lettering, *Das Schreiben als Kunstfertigkeit*, (Artistic Skill in Penmanship) of 1921 (second edition 1924), refers to Johnston's '... detailed and excellent book'. He applauds Johnston's technical grasp of all aspects of lettering, including his use of gold leaf. And he continues:

Fig. 176. Illustrations from Johnston's *Writing & Illuminating, & Lettering*. (Courtesy of Verlag von Günther Wagner. Hannover. 1925. Cited in F. H. Ehmcke's *Schrift: ihre Gestaltung & Entwicklung in neuerer Zeit*.)

"Durham Book" hand (copy).
abcdefghijklm
nopqrstuvxyz:
Abb. 49. Modernisierte Halbunziale (I).
Grade Federform der Serifen &
Quadratische Endungen
Schräge Federform der Serifen
& abgeschrägte Endungen
Abb. 145.

> It contains so much sound advice that every serious scribe ought to own a copy. One finds in it all that is missing from my book. His understanding of old manuscripts is astounding, and the intensity of his scholarship cannot be surpassed.... Through his infinite dedication and through the purity of his taste and the astonishing skill of his hand, he has resurrected for us the marvels of earlier times .... He has passed on to us ... all the rules, practices and trade secrets of the ancients .... It is a solid foundation to build on well and securely.'[57]

While Koch's achievements are entirely independent of Johnston, it was arguably on account of his influence that Koch then combined the lower case of his Black Letter type designs with Roman capitals, creating effective partnerships which were much more readable than blocks of Gothic capitals. However, it is equally likely that market forces played a deciding role.[58] The capital letters for his Maximilian design, of 1914, are an example. (Fig. 175.)

F. H. Ehmcke also acknowledged the English origin of the revival of calligraphy and its importance to Germany. As early as 1911, Johnston is discussed in his first lettering compilation: *Ziele des Schriftunterrichts. Ein Beitrag zur modernen Schrift.*[59] His later, fuller, and widely read account, *Schrift: Ihre Gestaltung und Entwicklung in neuerer Zeit,*[60] (*Script: its Form and Evolution in Modern Times*) of 1925, begins with a description of the impact of Johnston's achievements in the context of Morris, Cobden-Sanderson, and Walter Crane. The book illustrates Johnston's early calligraphy. (Fig. 176.)

Especially significant was Johnston's influence on Jan Tschichold. This is the more interesting because Tschichold's subsequent development as a modernist thinker, typographer, and type designer helps to highlight the limits of Johnston's own position. It was in approximately 1917 that Tschichold first discovered Johnston's lettering. At that time he was studying drawing at the Grimma teacher-training college, before he continued at the Akademie für Graphische Künst und Buchgewerbe, in Leipzig under Hermann Delitsch. He was then still in his mid-teens. By 1923, aged twenty-one and a freelance designer, he claimed to be pioneering the profession of 'typographic designer'. To his mind this included the new and vital role of preparing proper instructions for the compositor/printer. In that year, too, he was practising the 'new typography'. The phrase was first used by Moholy-Nagy to describe developments at the Bauhaus. By the age of twenty-six Tschichold, with remarkable and radical fervour, had written two seminal tracts on this theme, 'Elementaire Typographie' (1925) and 'Die neue Gestaltung' (1928).

In 1935 Tschichold made his first visit to London. An exhibition of his work was put on by the publishers, Lund Humphries. (He was invited by Eric Humphries to design their printing journal, *The Penrose Annual*, for 1938.) While he never met Johnston, he was to become the close friend of his colleague, the calligrapher Alfred Fairbank. In an article on Fairbank, written in 1946, Tschichold recalled that visit:

> One of the strongest impressions I had during my first visit to England about ten years ago was given by the lettering used for the stations of the Underground in London. The perfectly formed characters of all official inscriptions and notices, their well-thought out and convincingly simple disposition far surpasses anything that is used for

> similar purposes on the continent. (Only in Denmark have I seen a few station noticeboards of similar quality.) I was not very much surprised to hear that Edward Johnston, the master and renewer of the art of writing was the designer of those letters, seeing that the influence of this eminent calligrapher is to be met with in other spheres in England, and especially in London, almost at every step one takes. We may say that nowhere in Europe is there such a high proportion of well-informed characters amongst the usual jumble of ugly street signs. This is due to the work of Edward Johnston and his school in long years of valuable instruction. It is by no means a matter of chance that the finest handwriting in correspondence comes from England today and that too must be put down to the influence that Johnston's activity as a teacher exercised, directly or indirectly, on many generations. Even the high level in the cultured typography of English books owes much to Edward Johnston, seeing that many of the designers of English books sat at his feet and owe their vital understanding of the forms of lettering to his instruction, this being the most important qualification for the formation of fine books.[61]

While Tschichold's vision for lettering and typographic design for the twentieth century went far beyond anything Johnston envisaged, the first steps of their careers were curiously parallel. Tschichold acquired a feeling for lettering as an adolescent from his father, who was a signwriter. It led him – as a similar instinct had led Johnston – to a period of intense study of its history. He used the uniquely rich library of the Master Printers Federation in Leipzig and, like Johnston, he was impressed by Caslon type, seeing there a magazine set in it. He became a self-taught calligrapher. Two published statements by Tschichold recall this period. A letter to Alfred Fairbank of 1949 reads:

> I taught myself calligraphy, by following Johnston and Larisch [*Ornamental Lettering*] and was also taught to some degree, by Professor H. Delitsch. I executed several MSS. and taught, at eighteen, calligraphy in the evening class of the Leipzig Academy.[62]

In the same year Tschichold gave an address to the Royal Society of Arts on receiving their honorary award of Royal Designer for Industry. This was partly in recognition of the work done from 1946 in setting up the compositional rules for the publishers, Penguin Books, where he also designed many individual books and title pages. In it he paid '… tribute to English civilisation to which I owe such a lot'. He continued:

> When I was fifteen years old I had my first contact with English lettering. I became fascinated by my study of Edward Johnston's famous book, *Writing & Illuminating, & Lettering* [using Anna Simon's translation.] For several years I practised calligraphy according to his teaching. My ideas were further influenced by Eric Gill's work, and, as a letterer, I feel and should like to be regarded as belonging to the English school.[63]

In an instance of Tschichold's early lettering, an advertisment for a Leipzig Trade Fair of 1922, there is a line of writing which is remarkably reminiscent of Johnston's own lettering. (Fig. 177.)

The intellectual passion aroused by his early study of printing history led to an initial statement of his beliefs. Much of the typography Tschichold encountered around him was defunct in his eyes. Just as the youthful Johnston had expressed his convictions in his lecture to the Royal Society of Arts in 1905, so Tschichold

LEIPZIGER MESSE

Allgemeine Mustermesse mit Technischer Messe und Baumesse

Die allgemeine internationale Messe Deutschlands

Die erste und größte Messe der Welt. Für Aussteller und Einkäufer gleich wichtig.

BEGINN DER HERBSTMESSE AM 27. AUGUST 1922.

Auskunft erteilt und Anmeldungen nimmt entgegen

MESSAMT FÜR DIE MUSTERMESSEN IN LEIPZIG

Fig. 177. Advertisement for a Leipzig Trade Fair by Jan Tschichold showing Johnstonian features. 1922. (Courtesy of Lund Humphries. Cited from Ruari McLean. *Jan Tschichold*. 1975.)

published what amounted to his manifesto in the form of the article 'Elementare Typographie'. It was prefaced by another, 'Die neue Gestaltung'. They appeared in a special issue of the printing trade journal, *Typographische Mitteilungen* (Leipzig Typographical News), in 1925.[64]

A period of gestation ensued. It resulted in his first handbook of typography, *Die neue Typographie*, published in Berlin in 1928. (It was translated into English as *The New Typography* in 1998.)[65] The title was taken from Moholy-Nagy's article for the Bauhaus exhibition catalogue of 1923. Like Johnston's *Writing & Illuminating, & Lettering,* it is a how-to-do-it manual, the practical application of Tschichold's philosophy of design. As an artefact the book is a *tour de force* of modernist design. It is the more accomplished on account of its historical knowledge, its intellectual insights, its impassioned arguments, and its declamatory, and on occasions even acerbic, tone. Tschichold's starting point was the same dissatisfaction that Johnston had felt for the 'artistic printing' of the late nineteenth century, which was marred by over-ornamented lettering – both Fraktur and Roman – and by senseless pattern-making in layout. But from this point on the similarities between the two lettering masters end.

Unlike Johnston, Tschichold dismissed Morris's notion of craft as the antidote to an encroaching machine culture. A turning point had come in 1923 when he saw the major exhibition of Bauhaus design in Weimar. He also became aware of the Russian Constructivists, notably the graphic designer El Lissitzky. The intellectual excitement even prompted him to russianise his name to Iwan. He also felt the impact of the Dutch de Stijl, notably the abstract painter Piet Mondrian, and of the Italian Futurists. Marinetti's manifesto *Typographic Revolution,* of 1919, is quoted in his own *Die neue Typographie*. An awareness of the need to relate to technology was the key element in Tschichold's philosophy of the new typography. He regarded it as 'a second kind of nature'. In *Die neue Typographie* he wrote:

> Both nature and technology teach us that 'form' is not independent but grows out of function (purpose), out of the materials used (organic or technical), and out of how they are used.

Tschichold, it seems, inherited the biological analogy for the machine which had its origins in the evolutionary theories of the eighteenth century.

Henceforth, Tschichold recognised the 'imitation styles' of the German private press movement to be an anachronism. In *Die neue Typographie* he respectfully claimed that the 'squared-up' typography of such accomplished *Buchkünstler* as E. R. Weiss or Carl Ernst Poeschel belonged to a misguided phase of 'sensitive eclecticism'. He felt an equal disquiet for the Antiqua and Mediäval type designs of *Schriftkünstler* such as Walter Tiemann or F. M. Ehmcke. Of such typefaces he said: 'The eclectic nature of the pre-war period led people to play with typefaces of every period, thus revealing their artistic poverty.' On an ideological plane Tschichold indicted the older generation for the self-consciousness of their designs. He rejected the 'individualism' or the 'handwriting' of the artist-designer in favour of anonymity.

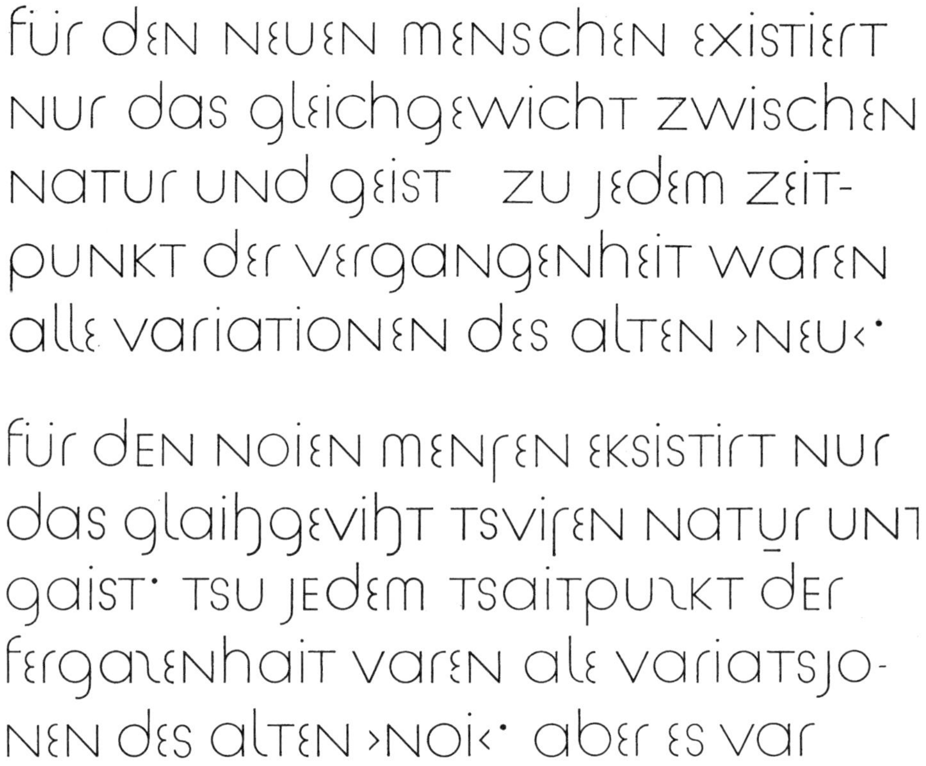

für den neuen menschen existiert nur das gleichgewicht zwischen natur und geist zu jedem zeit-punkt der vergangenheit waren alle variationen des alten ›neu‹·

für den noien menʃen eksistirt nur das glaiçgeviçt tsviʃen natur unt gaist· tsu jedem tsaitpuŋkt der fergaŋenhait varen ale variatsjo-nen des alten ›noi‹· aber es var

Fig. 178. Jan Tschichold's single sanserif alphabet of 1929. *Below* shows the phonetic version. (Courtesy of Lund Humphries. Cited from Ruari McLean. *Jan Tschichold*. 1975.)

In the place of 'personal vanity' and 'private language' Tschichold wished to establish a 'collective culture'. In the introduction to *Die neue Typographie* he observed that:

> The objects in use by the new generation suffer from the fatal compromise between a supposedly 'artistic' intention and the dictates of technical manufacture.

Tschichold also considered the avant-garde *Jugendstil* to have fallen into the same creative dead-end. While it was a pioneering movement,

> … its main aim was seen too simply as new forms, a new line (van de Velde: *La ligne, c'est une force* – a line is power), in other words, an aesthetic renewal, a change in outward shape, instead of the construction of objects in obedience to their purpose, their materials, and their methods of manufacture.

In its place, Tschichold took up a radical position closer to those of Gropius, El Lissitzky, and Le Corbusier – to which can be added Lethaby. In *Die neue Typographie* his design philosophy aspired to a 'spiritual expression of our world view':

> Instead of recognising and designing for the laws of machine production, the previous generation contented itself with trying anxiously to follow a tradition that in any case was only imaginary. Before them stand the works of today, untainted by the past, primary shapes which identify the aspect of our time: Car Aeroplane Telephone Wireless Factory Neon-advertising New York! These objects, designed without reference to the past, have been created by a new kind of man: **the engineer!**

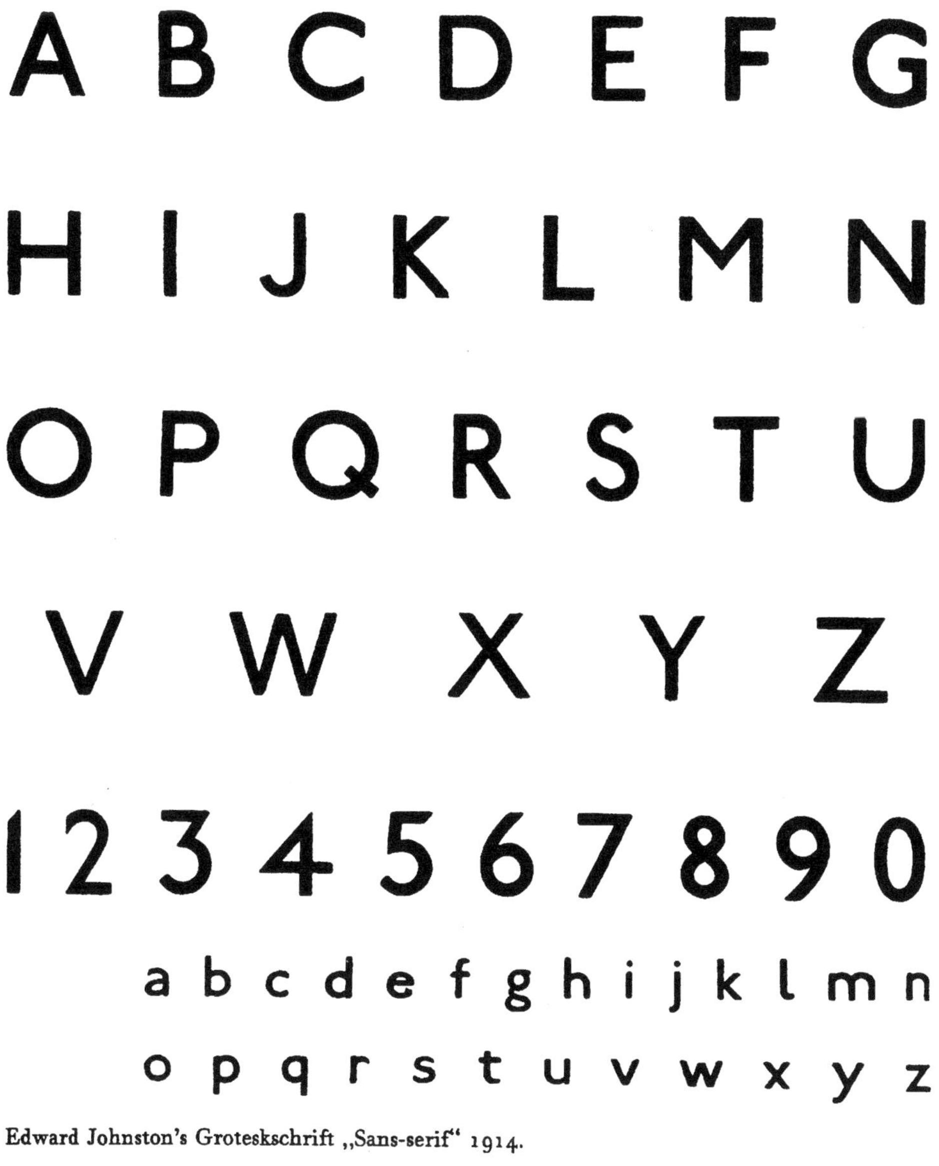

A B C D E F G

H I J K L M N

O P Q R S T U

V W X Y Z

1 2 3 4 5 6 7 8 9 0

a b c d e f g h i j k l m n

o p q r s t u v w x y z

Edward Johnston's Groteskschrift „Sans-serif" 1914.

Fig. 179. Johnston's block letter alphabet of 1913–14, reproduced in Anna Simons's article 'Moderne englische Pressen' in *Imprimatur*, 1931. (Courtesy of *Imprimatur*. Hamburg.)

In his euphoria Tschichold little realised how much the engineer also edges forward by clinging to the handrail of tradition. As a lead-in to the Introduction to *Die neue Typographie* Tschichold quoted from his admired abstract painter, Piet Mondrian:

> At every moment of the past all variations of the old were 'new' – but they were not 'THE' new. We must never forget that we are now at a turning-point of civilisation, at the end of everything old. This parting of the ways is absolute and final.

Tschichold looked beyond the book to other media which were more essentially of the twentieth century: to the poster, the magazine, the newspaper, the advertisement. He claimed that in their design the first objective must be '... to develop [their] visual form out of the functions of the text'. With the proliferation of information, the priority was clarity. It was this need which most characterised the twentieth century. Two principal means to ensure greater clarity were explored in *Die neue Typographie.* Tschichold sought first to replace 'central-axis composition', or symmetrical design. Thereby, he claimed, the contents are subordinated to 'beautiful-line arrangement' which was '...today as pretentious as the tall white collars of Victorian gentlemen.' Instead, typography was to be guided by the demands of the clear expression of the text. This required both the flexibility and the order of asymmetrical page layout: '... asymmetry is the rhythmic expression of functional design', wrote Tschichold.

Secondly, Tschichold wished to replace the 'artistic' Antiqua (and Mediäval) Roman types with the sanserif. Thereby would be achieved '... for the first time the needs of our age for purity, clarity, fitness of purpose and totality'. His concept of a sanserif went beyond Paul Renner's geometrically-inspired Futura design. 'A good typeface has no purpose beyond being of the highest clarity', he wrote in *Die neue Typographie*:

> Like every one else, we must look for a typeface expressive of our own age. Our age is characterised by an all-out search for clarity and truth, for purity of appearance. We require from type plainness, clarity, the rejection of everything that is superfluous. That leads us to a geometric construction of form. In the sans serif we find a type that comes very close to those requirements.

Tschichold also advocated a spelling reform of the German language to rid it of capital letters.[66] This would make it simpler to write and read and less burdensome for school children. Economic benefits would also accrue for the production of type and typewriters, and in the saving of printing costs.[67]

He worked on his own sanserif designs between 1926–29. (Fig. 178) Quite unlike Johnston's, it combined what Tschichold considered to be the most legible of the upper and lower case letters into a single unified alphabet. To accompany it he also designed phonetic alternative letter-forms.[68] It was never taken up by a typefoundry. Between 1933–36, Tschichold also designed a sanserif (among some ten other alphabets) for the Uhertype photo-composing machine. It was called Uhertype-Standard-Grotesk. Sebastian Carter claims it to be very close in style to Gill Sans.[69]

It is wholly unlikely that Johnston's block letter alphabet played any direct role in Tschichold's first, experimental, sanserif design. Johnston's block letter design was illustrated in Germany as late as 1931 in the periodical *Imprimatur.* (Fig. 179.) Its editor, Siegfried Buchenau, had been instrumental in commissioning Paul Renner to design his sanserif Futura. The article in which it appears was written by Anna Simons. Entitled *Moderne englische Pressen*, it is a major study of English modern presses, commercial as well as private, and was expensively illustrated with original offprints of examples from those presses inserted into the text.[70]

In 1936, Germany's recognition of Johnston culminated in a comprehensive exhibition mounted by the Schrift Museum Rudolf Blanckertz, in Berlin, to show the entire range of contemporary English lettering. Given the title *Schrift und*

Formalgestaltung in England/Lettering Design and Script in England, it showed books from the major British private presses – Kelmscott, Doves, Ashendene, Essex House, Eragny, Golden Cockerel, the Shakespeare Head, Gregynog and from the more prestigious commercial presses such as Chiswick, Curwen, and Hammersmith. Johnston's calligraphy was the most prominent with contributions from Graily Hewitt, Thomas Swindlehurst, Louise Powell, Stanley Morison, Alfred Fairbank, Albert Barlow, A. C. Gorham. Work was shown, too, from English design colleges and secondary and primary schools to demonstrate the extent of Johnston's teaching. Assistance was given by Sydney Cockerell and Alfred Fairbank. The exhibition's preface was written by Eberhard Hölscher, was translated in English, and was printed in Fraktur. It grouped all the work as belonging to the Johnston school. It claimed that a new showing of Johnston's achievements was long overdue in Germany following the exhibition which Blanckertz had set up in Dresden in 1912. It suggested that the exhibition was to be compared with the previous one held there, devoted to Rudolf von Larisch.[71]

A full discussion of a later – and darker – chapter in the development of Roman letter-forms in Germany would need to touch on the value of their greater clarity to the National Socialist government in communicating to the outside world. In 1933, the Nazi party had declared that Fraktur was the 'true' and the 'appropriate' script. An exhibition in Leipzig connected with National Culture Week, in 1933, showed Fraktur. Another, in 1934, in Frankfurt, showed Fraktur as 'Die Schöne Schrift', or beautiful writing. New and simplified Fraktur designs were created, the so called 'jackboot Grotesques'. They proclaimed themselves with evocative names such as Tannenburg and Deutschland.[72] In January 1941, however, this policy was reversed. Hitler's deputy, Martin Bormann, issued a directive which declared:

> 'It is wrong to regard or describe the so-called Gothic script as a German script. In reality, [it] consists of Schwabacher Jew letters.... the Jews resident in Germany, on the introduction of printing, possessed themselves of the printing works and thus happened the strong [sic] introduction of the Schwabacher Jew letters in Germany.'[73]

It is pointed out that Bormann was able to sustain this idea by associating the name Schwabacher to that of a Jewish banker of the same name. Henceforth Roman typefaces were referred to as 'Normalschrift' and were to be officially adopted for '... those newspapers and periodicals which already have a circulation abroad'. The ban on Black Letter was also to apply to the teaching of handwriting in schools, to government offices, to street names. And, in fact, Anna Simons was commissioned by the government to undertake associated calligraphy work.[74] The reversal of the policy left those type designers following the Black Letter school – F. H. Ehmcke was among them, Rudolf Koch, however, had died in 1934 – quite isolated since their beliefs had never been politically motivated.

In the post-war period it has been the eminent lettering artist and type designer Hermann Zapf who, above all others, has perpetuated the tradition of Johnston's lettering in Germany. In the preface to *Sharpness Unity and Freedom*, the catalogue of the exhibition of that name held at Ditchling in 1994, Hermann Zapf acknowledged his esteem for Johnston, claiming that it was from Johnston that he '... acquired a basic knowledge of writing and gained access to sources of letter-forms in general'[75]. He bought his copy of *Writing & Illuminating, & Lettering* in 1935, at the outset of his career as a self-taught calligrapher. Of the present day he went on to write:

> What Edward Johnston taught us is that letter-forms have a function to perform. They should convey the message to the reader in a pleasant way; their purpose is to underline the meaning of the text through the artistic expression of the chosen letter-forms, without the calligrapher allowing too much of his personality to obtrude upon the reader.
>
> There are no new rules. Edward Johnston's outline of principles still apply. Although we are accustomed to using letter-forms daily without special attention, they do still have a special meaning for us. That is what Edward Johnston showed us. We owe thanks to him for that. He is still the ideal teacher and his example will continue to be followed far into the future.

END NOTES

1. A full exploration of this episode is given by John Dreyfus in his *Italic Quartet*. Op. cit.
2. Edward Johnston. *Letters*. Cited from John Dreyfus. *Italic Quartet*. Op. cit.
3. An account of this development is given by Craig's son, Edward Craig, in his article: 'Edward Gordon Craig's Hamlet' in *Private Library*. Vol. 10. Spring 1977. See also: L. M. Newman. 'Artist and Printer: a problem of the Cranach Presse' Hamlet resolved'. In *Matrix*. Vol. IV. 1984.
4. See R. Müller-Krumbach. *Harry Graf Kessler und die Cranach-Presse in Weimar.* (Maximilian-Geselleschaft Hamburg) 1969. See also Petra Cerne Oven. *Edward Johnston and the Cranach Presse Hamlet*. M.A. thesis. Department of Typography and Graphic Communication. University of Reading. 1999; and Adela Spindler Roatcap. 'Designing Literature. The Book as Theatre: The Cranach Presse Hamlet' in *Fine Print*. Vol. 145. No. I. January 1988.
5. Alan Windsor. *Peter Behrens*. (Architectural Press) 1981.
6. See *The Werkbund. Studies in the History and Ideology of the Deutscher Werkbund 1907–1933*. Edited by Lucius Burckhardt. (The Design Council) 1980.
7. In Vienna a similar group of workshops, the Wiener Werkstätte, was also inspired by C. R. Ashbee's Guild of Handicraft. It was set up by Koloman Moser and financed by Fritz Wärndorfer in 1903. Unlike the Ernst Ludwig's Künstlerkolonie, however, it developed a membership of up to one hundred craftsmen.
8. Cited from Siegfried Guggenheim. 'Rudolf Koch. His Work and the Offenbach Workshop'. In *Print*. Vol. V. No. 1. New Haven. 1947. It is worth adding that the American calligrapher Warren Chappell worked in Koch's workshop between 1931–32 before returning to the USA. Another, was Berthold Wolpe. Being Jewish, he came to England in 1935 where he developed the Black Letter tradition into a particularly individual idiom. He designed the type face Albertus. Also, see Rudolf Koch's *A Typefoundry in Silhouette.* (The Arion Press) San Francisco. 1982.
9. Articles by German writers up to 1912 include: P. Aronstein. 'William Morris'. In *Magazin für Litteratur*. 1896; G. Swarzenski. 'William Morris und die Entwicklung des modernen dekorativen Stils in England'. In *Neue Deutsche Rundschau*. Vol. 9. 1898; P.

Aronstein. 'William Morris'. In *Die Zukunst*. Vol. 31. 1900; Gustav Bing. 'William Morris als Buchdrucker'. In *Jahresericht der Gutenberg Gesellschaft*. Vol. 8. Mainz. 1909; Ernst Collins. 'Die Künstlerischen Ideale von William Morris'. In *Zeitschrift für Bücherfreunde*. Vol. 4. 1912. Cited from the bibliography in F. A. Schmidt-Künsemüller. *William Morris und die neuere Buchkunst*. (Otto Harrassowitz) Wiesbaden. 1955.
10. Published by Editions de l'avenir social. Brussels. 1898. Cited from the bibliography in K. J. Sembach. *Henry van de Velde*. (Thames and Hudson). 1989.
11. See the bibliography in H. Muthesius. *Style - Architecture and Building Art*. (Getty Center) 1994. The periodicals included *Centralblatt der Bauverwaltung* and *Dekorative Kunst.*
12. Muthesius anticipated Lethaby in other respects, too. His ambitions for the future of design were underpinned by notions deriving from Gottfried Semper to do with 'type' forms. These new, though archetypal, forms were to be expressive of a true modernity and exemplify a true national culture. Design was to arrive at the 'type' forms most suited to the purpose in hand by the rational interplay of materials and techniques. The combination of materiality and concrete practicality was referred to as 'Sachlichkeit'. Moreover, it was to be industry-led. Muthesius had misgivings about the individualistic creations of the artist-designer whom he saw as being all too prone to the vagaries of Jugendstil, then still so prevalent, and the irrelevant by-ways of historicism. While he considered the concept of 'type' form to be a rational one, Muthesius wished to elevate it to the plane of the spiritual. In an address in 1911 he claimed that '… spiritual considerations are more important than material ones, and higher than function, material, and technique stands form'. Implied in this was the notion of the designer as seer, distilling out the ultimate forms best suited to express modern society and best adapted to industrialised processes. Muthesius' artist-critics – the most prominent was Henry van de Velde although he, too, was an original member of the Deutsche Werkbund – were alarmed by what they saw as a popish plot to subvert artistic freedom. For Muthesius was a very powerful administrator within the Prussian Board of Trade. They saw themselves threatened by what was called an 'elevated general standard'. Accounts of Muthesuis and his ideas appear in: Gillian Naylor. *The Bauhaus Reassessed.* (The Herbert Press) 1985; John Heskett. *Design in Germany. 1870–1918.* (Trefoil Design Library) 1986; H. Muthesius. *Style-Architecture and Building Art. Transformations of Architecture in the 19th century and its Present Condition*, translated, with an editorial commentary, from Muthesius' original text, *Stilarchitectur und Baukunst,* of 1902. (The Getty Center) 1994.
13. Outside Germany the Black Letter was also under threat. The Swedish Academy under Linnaeus, for example, decreed the use of Roman types for Swedish books in 1739.
14. See David Paisey. 'Roman Types for German Text: A Proponent in 1733'. In *Gutenberg Jahrbuch.* Vol. 58. 1983. Also see John Flood. 'Nationalist Currents in Early German Typography'. In *The Library*. Vol. 15. No. 2. 1993.
15. See C. Burke. *Paul Renner. The Art of Typography*. (Hyphen Press London) 1998.
16. See C. Burke. *Paul Renner. The Art of Typography*. Op. cit.
17. Gustav Kühl. *The Psychology of Writing*. Translated from the German edition (Klingspor Giesserei) 1907.
18. Julius Rodenberg. 'The Work of Karl Klingspor'. In *Fleuron*. No. 4. 1925.
19. Walter Plata. 'The Present Status of Black Letter in German-speaking Countries'. In *Alphabet. International Annual.* 1964.
20. See 'Fine Printing in Germany'. (Anonymous.) In *The Times Printing Number*. 1912.
21. See F. M. Ehmcke. *Rudolf von Larisch*. (Staatliche Akademie für Graphische Künste und Buchgewerbe) Leipzig 1926.
22. Anna Simons [a memoir] in *Edward Johnston and English Lettering. In Monographien Künstlerischer Schrift.* Band I. (Verlag für Schriftkunde Heintze & Blanckertz) Berlin/Leipzig. 1937. Rudolf von Larisch did not disregard the history of lettering, *per se*. In fact, he was employed as archivist in the Imperial Chancery in Vienna and for the Order of the Toison d'Or and keeper of the Habsburg Records. He compiled an historical work in four volumes, *Beispiele Künstlerischer Schrift* (Examples of Artistic Writing) between 1900 and 1910. (It also illustrated the lettering of Charles Rennie Mackintosh, among examples from many others.) Other writings by Larisch include the pamphlet *Über Zierschriften im Dienste der Kunst*, (Decorative Writing and Lettering in Art) of 1889. His major work was

Unterricht in ornamentaler Schrift (A Manual of Instruction in Decorative Writing and Lettering) of 1906. Rudolf von Larisch also designed an Antiqua or Roman typeface. It was used in a commemorative volume called *Zur Feier des einhundertjährigen Bestandes der k. k. Hof-und Statsdruckerei 1804-1904*, (Vienna 1904) designed by Koloman Moser and Czeschka of the Wiener Werkstätte (The workshops of the Austrian Secession movement). Rudolf von Larisch also taught at two other schools in Vienna: the Graphische Lehr-und Versuchsanstalt and the Akademie der bildenden Künste. A commemorative exhibition called Internationale Ausstellung künstlerischer Schrift (International Exhibition on Lettering Art) devoted to Rudolf von Larisch was held at the Museum für Künst und Industrie in Vienna, in 1926, and an appraisal is Fritz Ehmcke's *Rudolf von Larisch,* printed at the workshop of the Akademie für Graphische Kunst und Buchgewerbe. Leipzig. 1926.

23. R. Blanckertz. 'Anna Simons' [Tributes] in *Monographien Künstlerisher Schrift* Band 2. (Verlag für Schriftkunde Heintze & Blanckertz) Berlin-Leipzig, 1937. In this regard, it is as well to stress that while Anna Simons is presented as being the steadfast exponent of Johnston's lettering, she also came under the influence of Rudolf von Larisch. In her memoir on Johnston (*Monographien künstlerischer Schrift* Band I. 1937) Simons appears to wish to reconcile these polarities, saying that '... although Rudolf von Larisch and Mr. Johnston started from diametrically opposed ends and in spite of their methods being entirely diverse, the final conclusions arrived at by both were fundamentally the same, although achieved absolutely independently.' See the other contributions in the issue of *Monographien Künstlerischer Schrift* (Band II). 1937 by F. H. Ehmcke, Rudolf von Larisch, Peter Behrens, Rudolf Blanckertz, Willy Wiegand, Henry van der Velde, Stanley Morison, Alfred Fairbank, Edward Johnston, and Ortwin Eberle.

24. Bernard Newdigate. 'Contemporary Printers: Emery Walker'. In *Fleuron*, No. 4. 1925.

25. In the periodical *Zeitschrift für Buchfreunde*. Vol. 5. 1901–02 and as the book *Das Idealebuch Das schöne Buch*. (Euphorion Verlag) Berlin (Charlottenburg). 1921.

26. Private presses were also set up in the USA, Italy, Holland, Ireland and elsewhere. They include: Charles Rickett's Vale Press, of 1896; Ashbee's Essex House Press, of 1898; Elizabeth Yeats' Cuala Press, of 1902, in Ireland; W. Goudy's Village Press, of 1903, in the USA; J. F. Royston's Zilverdistel Press, of 1916, in Holland; Hilary Pepler's S. Dominic's Press, of 1916, in Ditchling; Jan van Krimpen's Palladium Press, of 1920, in Holland; G. Mardersteig's Officina Bodoni, of 1922, in Switzerland; R. Koch's Rudolfinische Drucke, in Offenbach, Germany. (other typefoundries in Germany, like Bauer, at Frankfurt, also had their own Hausdruckerei, or presses); R. Maynard's Gregynog Press, of 1922, in Wales; Francis Meynell's Nonesuch Press, of 1923; Dard Hunter's Press, of 1923, in the USA; Robert Gibbing's Golden Cockerell Press, of 1924, in London; De Roos's Heuvel Press, of 1927, in Holland.

27. See Hannah Keil. 'Tendencies in German Book-Printing since 1914'. In *Fleuron*. No 4. 1925. It seems unlikely, but given that Morris died in 1896 when Poeschel was twenty two, the claim may have a germ of truth in it. Hannah Keil was the manager of the Officina Bodoni Press.

28. See Hans Schmoller. 'Carl Ernst Poeschel'. In *Signature*. New Series. Vol 11. 1950.

29. Julius Rodenberg. 'The Work of Karl Klingspor'. In *Fleuron*. No. 4. 1925.

30. See Hannah Keil. 'Tendencies in German Book-Printing since 1914'. In *Fleuron* No. 4. 1924.

31. Willy Wiegand. 'German Private Presses'. An address to the Grolier Club, New York on 11th April 1929 printed in *Imprimatur*. (Hamburg) Vol 1. 1930.

32. George Abrams. 'Twentieth-Century Fine Printing in Germany'. In *Fine Print*. Vol. 12. 1986.

33. See Christopher Burke. 'Luxury and Austerity: Willy Wiegand and the Bremer Presse'. In *Typography Papers* II. (University of Reading) 1997.

34. Willy Wiegand. 'German Private Presses'. An address to the Grolier Club. New York. Op. cit.

35. See: Julius Rodenberg. 'The Work of Karl Klingspor'. In *Fleuron*. No. 4. 1925 and C. Burke. 'German Hybrid Typefaces 1900–1914'. in *Black Letter: Type and National Identity*. (Princeton Architectural Press) 1998.

36. 'Fine Printing in Germany'. Anonymous In *The Times Printing Number*. 1912.
37. 'Fine Printing in Germany'. Op. cit.
38. Anna Simons [memoir] 'Edward Johnston and English Lettering'. In *Monographien Künst-lerischer Schrift*. Band I. (Verlag für Schriftkunde. Heinze & Blanckertz. Berlin-Leipzig). 1937.
39. Henry van de Velde. *Anna Simons* [Tributes]. (R. Oldenbourg Verlag München-BerlinVerlag der Corona. Zürich). 1934.
40. Of interest in this context is the work of the Berlin-based handwriting teacher, Ludwig Sütterlin, and that of E. R. Weiss.
41. Programm. Juli 1912. Hauptbericht, Nov. 1912. Dresden. See C. Burke. *Paul Renner. The Art of Typography*. (Hyphen Press) 1998. In her biography Priscilla Johnston speaks of Johnston giving two lectures but German sources speak of one only.
42. Anna Simons [memoir] in 'Edward Johnston and English Lettering'. Op. cit.
43. Cited from Priscilla Johnston. *Edward Johnston*. Op. cit.
44. See: Anna Simons. 'Titel und Initien'. In: J. Lehnacker. *Die Bremer Presse: Königin der deutschen Privatpressen*. (Typographische Gesellschaft München) 1964.
45. Anna Simons. 'Lettering in Book Production'. In *Lettering Today*. (Studio Publications) 1937.
46. Julius Rodenberg. 'The Work of Karl Klingspor'. In *Fleuron*. No 4. 1925.
47. George Abrams. 'Anna Simons: Calligrapher, Letterer, Teacher, and Type Designer'. In *Fine Print*. No. 2. April 1986. In his article, 'Luxury and Austerity: Willy Wiegand and the Bremer Presse', (*Typography Papers* No. II. 1997) C. Burke doubts the likelihood of this thesis.
48. E. Hölscher. Cited from *Anna Simons*. [Tributes] *Monographien künstlerischer Schrift*.
Band II. (Verlag für Schriftkunde Heinze & Blanckertz) Berlin-Leipzig. 1937.
49. Translation cited from Peter Behrens' *BehrensSchrift und Zierat*. (Ruchard'sche Giesserei. Offenbach am Main) 1902, translated by C. Burke in his article 'Peter Behrens and the German letter: Type design and Architectural Lettering'. In *Journal of Design History*. Vol. 5. No. 1. 1992.
50. C. Burke. *Paul Renner. The Art of Typography*. (Hyphen Press) 1998.
51. Julius Rodenberg. 'The Work of Karl Klingspor'. In *Fleuron*. No. 4. 1925.
52. Peter Behrens. [Tributes] In *Anna Simons* (R. Oldenbourg Verlag) München-Berlin. Verlag der Corona. Zürich) 1934. Translation courtesy of Elisabeth Robinson.
53. See Walter Tracy. *Letters of Credit*. (Faber and Faber) 1986.
54. Gunter Beissert. *Jacob Erbar and the Sanserif. Retrospection. One year after his Death*. Translated by F. Maclean. Frankfurt. 1936.
55. See C. Burke. *Paul Renner. The Art of Typography*. (Hyphen Press London) 1998.
56. See C. Burke. *Paul Renner. The Art of Typography*. (Hyphen Press London) 1998.
57. R. Koch. *Das Schreiben als Kunstfertigkeit*. (Leipzig. Verlag des Deutschen Buchgewerbe-Vereins) 1924. Cited from *Edward Johnston. Lessons in Formal Writing*. Op. cit. 1986.
58. I am indebted to Mr. Gerald Cinamon for this cautionary observation.
59. Fritz Ehmcke. *Ziele des Schriftunterrichts. Ein Beitrag zur modernen Schrift*. 1911.
60. Fritz Ehmcke. *Schrift: Ihre Gestaltung und Entwicklung in neuerer Zeit* (Verlag von Günter Wagner Hannover) 1925.
61. Jan Tschichold. 'Alfred Fairbank, ein englischer Kalligraph und Schreiblehrer/an English Calligrapher and Lettering Teacher'. In *Graphis*. Vol. 2. 1946.
62. Cited from R. McLean. *Jan Tschichold. Typographer*. Appendix 6. (Lund Humphries) 1975.
63. Cited from B. Wolpe. 'A Tribute to Jan Tschichold from London'. In the exhibition catalogue *Jan Tschichold. Typographer and Type Designer 1902–74*. (National Lib. of Scotland) Edinburgh. 1982.
64. Jan Tschichold. 'Die neue Gestaltung and Elementare Typographie'. In *Typographische Mitteilungen*. Sonderheft. Leipzig. 1925.
65. Jan Tschichold. *Die neue Typographie*. (Verlag des Bildungverbandes der deutschen Buch-drucker) Berlin. 1928. It was followed by *Eine Stunde Druckgestaltung* in 1930, the

introductorary text of which was translated as 'New Life in Print', in *Commercial Art.* July 1930. *The New Typography* was translated by Ruari McLean. (University of California Press) 1998.

66. Behind this initiative lay a seminal work, titled *Sprache und Schrift,* by Dr. Walter Porstmann, published in 1920. Much in vogue at the Bauhaus, it advocated the abolition of capital letters and the use of phonetic characters, a 'world alphabet' suited to handwriting and printing, alike.

67. The new typography also exploited vertical composition, montage, overlaying, and shifts in type scale and weights. Its origin has been claimed to lie with the 'visual', or 'concrete', poem by Stéphane Mallarmé called 'Un coup de dés n'abolira jamais le hazard', printed in 1896. It is a visual experiment in which the placing of the poem's words gives symbolic nuance to its meaning. This approach was followed up and institutionalised in design schools such as the Bauhaus and the Vkhutemas, in Soviet Russia. as well as in the shaped poems by Apollinaire, his *Idéogrammes* of 1914. The new tropes were introduced into England in a characteristically late and muted form. But, significantly, they were beckoned through half-opened doors by open-minded printer-publishers who had been at the Central School of Arts – by Harold Curwen of the Curwen Press, by Francis Meynell of the Nonesuch Press, and by Eric Humphries, of Lund Humphries Publishers. Tschichold's design of the 1938 issue of *The Penrose Annual* was among the first instances of asymmetrical design in Britain. (It happened also to carry articles by Harold Curwen and another influential scholar, the American, Beatrice Warde.) See J. R. Tarr. 'What are the Fruits of the New Typography?'. In *The Penrose Annual.* Vol. 37. 1935.

68. Jan Tschichold wrote an explanation of his phonetic spelling reform. His article 'noch eine neue schrift'. In *Typographische Mitteilungen.* Vol. 3. 1930, is referred to in C. Burke's. *Paul Renner. The Art of Typography.* (The Hyphen Press London) 1998.

69. Sebastian Carter. *Twentieth-century type designers.* (Trefoil Publications Ltd) 1987.

70. *Imprimatur.* (Gesellschaft der Bücherfreunde zu Hamburg) Vol. 2. 1931.

71. Schrift und Formalgestaltung/Lettering Design and Script in England at the Rudolf Blanckertz Schrift Museum, Berlin. 43 Georgenkirchstrasse 44, nahe Alexanderplatz. May–August 1936. (A copy of this rare pamphlet is held at the NAL, at the V&A.)

72. See *Black Letter: Type and National Identity.* Edited. by Peter Bain. (Princeton Architectural Press) 1998. and C. Burke. *Paul Renner. The Art of Typography.* (Hyphen Press) 1998.

73. Saul Steinberg. 'Secret Decree Reveals Hitler's Real Attitude to Gothic Type'. In *Printing News.* 9th May 1957.

74. Anna Simons' papers were destroyed during the bombing of Munich during the war.

75. Exhibition catalogue *Sharpness Unity & Freedom.* Edited by Gerald Fleuss. (Cambridge Enterprises) Ditchling Museum. 1994.

Die
zeitgemäße
Schrift

Fig. 180. Front cover of the copy of *Die Zeitgemasse Schrift* for January 1935 carrying Alfred Fairbank's article, *English Calligraphy and Illuminating.* which was sent to Johnston, Christmas 1934, with a covering note.
(Courtesy of Napier University. Edinburgh.)

APPENDIX ONE

JOHNSTON'S BACKGROUND: HIS SCOTTISH & ENGLISH-QUAKER ANCESTRY AND HIS FAMILY TREE

There were indications in Edward Johnston's childhood that he was destined for a contemplative life. His artistic talent, however, was not particularly evident at this time nor was he from an especially artistic family. He was born on February 11th 1872 of Scottish parents, though there were English elements in his ancestry making him only 'three-quarters Scotch', as Priscilla Johnston puts it in her biography.

Fig, 181. Edward Johnston aged three years.

Johnston spent the first two years of his life on a ranch, 'The Arazaty', near to Montevideo in Uruguay. His father, Fowell Buxton Johnston, was an adventurer who had gone to South America in 1866 to take up cattle-rearing. Caught up in the opportunities – and the risks – presented by the expanding British Empire, he had earlier had unsettled and fitful careers including a phase as a commissioned army officer in India which had been brought to a halt by illness. Fowell Buxton Johnston was a younger brother and, it seems, possibly an aggrieved one. Priscilla Johnston describes him as:

> ... an erratically brilliant ne'er-do-well, contrary, original and highly eccentric.[1]

He cultivated an interest in natural history which led him to read Charles Darwin's *The Origin of Species*. This and his robust agnosticism prompted him to correspond with Darwin. A hitherto undiscovered letter shows Fowell Buxton Johnston to have offered to make field observations for Darwin at 'The Arazaty' ranch, though it is not known whether Darwin took up his offer.[2]

Other figures of high profile in Johnston's ancestry included his paternal grandmother, Priscilla Buxton. It was through the Buxtons that Johnston acquired his English 'strain', for they were a family of prominent Quakers from Norfolk and themselves connected through marriage to the Hanburys, another powerful Quaker family long established in Norfolk.

Fig. 182. Edward Johnston aged twelve years.

Priscilla Buxton is most remembered for having participated alongside her father (Johnston's great-grandfather), Thomas Fowell Buxton, in Wilberforce's successful parliamentary campaign of 1834 for the abolition of slavery in the British Empire. Thomas Fowell Buxton pursued this cause out of religious conviction and in the capacity of Member of Parliament (for Weymouth). He had married into the wealthy banking family of Gurney whose seat was Earlham Hall in Norfolk. The Gurneys were thus the third Quaker branch of Johnston's well-endowed and gifted family tree. His wife Hannah Gurney was, Thomas claimed:

> ... constant, steady, invariable, and indefatigable, she sought and found the truth and taught it to me.[3]

A more notable connection still, through the same Gurney line, was with Hannah's sister, Elizabeth, who married the Quaker, Joseph Fry. Elisabeth Fry is wellknown as the redoubtable pioneer of prison reform in the early Victorian period. Born a Gurney in 1780, she was Edward Johnston's great grand-aunt.

Johnston's paternal grandfather was Andrew Johnston, whose family came from Rennyhill near Fife, in Scotland. Following his marriage to Priscilla Buxton he became a banker with the Gurney bank in Norfolk. (The Gurney bank was eventually subsumed into Barclays Bank.) He also became a Member of Parliament (for Aberdeen).

Less is known of Johnston's maternal side. His mother, Alice Douglas, was Scottish. She studied at Edinburgh School of Art before going to Argentina with her father, who was also a rancher. Her sister, Maggie – Johnston's aunt – accompanied her there and became an inseparable part of Fowell Buxton Johnston's household on his marriage to Alice Douglas in 1869.

From the age of three, Johnston lived in England. He had an elder brother, Miles and two younger sisters, Ada and Olof. His was, apparently, a low-key and even an uneventful childhood except that the family were constantly on the move. Places as widely afield as Torquay, Ventnor and Central London (at 25 Regent's Park Road) saw them settling into rented premises only to be uprooted again by a restless and doggedly independent father.[4] Edward Johnston was intensely saddened by the loss of his companion sister, Ada, who died in 1888 aged fourteen, when he himself was sixteen. His father was similarly affected. 'Desolation came upon the house', wrote Priscilla Johnston.

Johnston did not attend school. He was educated at home and, not surprisingly, in a haphazard fashion given the whims of his father – and his own and his brother's enthusiasms. On one occasion a mathematics tutor arrived. Johnston was restricted to the house, bound there by his mother, who was decidedly frail (she died in 1891 when Johnston was nineteen) and his fastidious aunt Maggie, who inflicted her hypochondria on the children.

To judge from Priscilla Johnston's biography, he appears to have been constrained in an enclosed family world which, even so, afforded him real boyhood happiness in the discovery of the countryside. He was absorbed by the adventure stories of Jules Verne, Arthur Conan Doyle and Talbot Baines Reed. (There is a certain irony, given Johnston's later interests, that Talbot Baines Reed was a typographic historian who managed the Fann Street foundry which cast the types for William Morris's Kelmscott Press.) Johnston displayed immense curiosity. He absorbed articles from the popular science magazine, *The Aerial World*. He was intrigued by scientific demonstrations, he was fascinated by the paradoxes of certain number series and he loved gadgets. Curiosity was matched by ingenuity. As a boy

Fig. 183 A–C. Details from Johnston's alphabet book for his sister, Olof. c. 1888. The letters are gold coloured. (William Clark Memorial Library. EG 702.)

he made intricately soldered toys and electrical devices such as bells. Of his childhood he wrote:

> We had a somewhat narrow upbringing and we inherited a great deal of wilfulness.[5]

Looking back on his childhood education, Johnston wrote in 1938:

> Without a classical education, have a fair knowledge of the Bible and L.C.'s [Lewis Carroll] two *Alices* besides a good grounding in folk tales. Possibly a real affection for Bks. 1, 2, 3, and 4 of *Euclid* and for the simple demonstrative virtues of algebra.'[6]

As an adolescent, Johnston also entertained himself by drawing, including renderings of cats to illustrate the stories which he offered his younger sister, Olof. The most elaborate was *Aunt Bull's Dinner Party*. Another was an alphabet book. (Fig. 183) Johnston discovered Ruskin's writings and to some degree noted his observations on drawing. He was also absorbed by the hobby of 'illuminations', which involved the copying-out of texts and homilies in the manner of a medieval illuminated manuscript. This was not an uncommon pastime in Victorian homes.

At the age of seventeen Johnston was given a copy of the book, *Lessons in the Art of Illumination*, by W. J. Loftie. It captured his imagination. First published in 1889, Loftie's *Lessons*, like Frederick Delamotte's *Primer of the Art of Illumination*, was the more popular end of a long line of such works running through the nineteenth century. Others, such as Henry Shaw's *Handbook to the Art of Illumination* (1843), Owen Jones's *1001 Initial Letters* (1854) or Digby Wyatt's *The Art of Illuminating* (1860) are indicative of the serious interest in medieval illuminated manuscripts during that century.[7] Often sumptuously hand-printed (by the expensive and newly developed chromolithographic process) they were a source of motifs for ornamentation as well as of inspiration for copyists. Much knowledge of the techniques of medieval manuscript illumination and painting was resuscitated in these studies. Significantly though, virtually nothing is said in them of the specific techniques behind the writing of letters, a deficiency which Johnston did not yet register. His earliest lettering and illuminations are entirely traditional, in the Victorian mode. One piece, his most ambitious, was done aged eighteen. It was a rendering of the *Magnifiat*. Johnston called these efforts his 'parchments'. Touchingly pursued, they were the vocational preoccupation of an adolescent. But, importantly, it introduced Johnston to the sensuality of making art.

The pleasure derived from calligraphy is not so different, perhaps, from that gained by doing other motory skills, like dancing. And, in fact, in later years one of his more devoted students from the Royal College of Art, Violet Hawkes, recalled the fluency of his lettering demonstrations on the blackboard in exactly those terms:

> The easy swinging rhythm of his strokes was unhurried and unhesitating, like the movements of an accomplished skater, combining perfect control with perfect freedom.[8]

Johnston's own account of the sensation of writing out pen strokes corresponds to Violet Hawkes' description. In a lecture given at the Royal College of Art in 1935, he likened the flourishes of letters to the controlled swings of a golf club and to the

Fig. 184. Detail from a chronogram (an inscription where the letters, M, D, C, L, I, can also be read as Roman numerals and so indicate a date). Rubbing from a slate inscription in Rye, 1655, illustrated in *Writing & Illuminating, & Lettering* (Fig. 207, page 382.)

casting of a line by a fly fisherman. These metaphors relate to another, more charming still, used by Johnston in *Formal Penmanship,* where the scribe:

> Care-free (like the spirit of the stream) ... writes – pen in hand, racing with the text, his mind flying back and forth over the whole –[9]

Johnston's was an exceptionally enclosed childhood, even by the standards of Victorian England. His life continued in the same self-motivated, if sometimes listless, fashion until the age of twenty-one. He was then offered an office job in London by his paternal uncle, Andrew Johnston, who was concerned for the future of his nephew and caring of the family generally after the death of the mother and the remarriage of Johnston's father. Andrew Johnston was an MP – the third in the lineage – as well as a successful businessman, a sheriff, and Chairman of Essex County Council. Following the remarriage of his father, Johnston lived with his sister, Olof, and his aunt, Maggie, at his uncle's home in Woodford, in Essex. They then joined Johnston's brother, Miles, in Edinburgh, living at 3, Merchiston Crescent. In the following year, 1896, Johnston was helped further by his uncle with his medical studies at Edinburgh University.

Johnston suffered constitutionally from what Noel Rooke called his 'lassitude' though, when the agreed deadline for a commission loomed, he could also sustain concentrated bursts of energy. His abandonment of his medical studies after two years was due largely to this problem. On visiting Johnston in Edinburgh, his uncle, Andrew Johnston, realised that he would never cope with the demands put on a medical doctor. Noel Rooke enlarged on this in a letter to Bridget Johnston:

> ... the general impression was of physical vitality reduced to the lowest possible ebb compatible with absence of serious illness. It was quite outside any previous observation or experience.... Then he spoke and the clearness and vigour of his mind came as a shock, as a delight, a bright Alpine flower in blossom on the bare ground, which all around that one spot of colour seemed incapable of producing a blade of grass, or a leaf under the blossom. I am sorry that this sounds lurid. But the contrast was the experience of a lifetime.[10]

In her biography Priscilla Johnston suggests that Johnston's character was entirely formulated early on in boyhood. He had always shown a tendency to be preoccupied in thought, to be independently minded, and to be prepared to wrestle with questions long after others had either given up or fobbed him off with inadequate explanations. Priscilla Johnston alluded to Longfellow's translation from Frederick von Logan: 'Edward's brain was like the mills of God, it ground slowly but it ground exceeding small.' [*sic*] In inferring that Johnston inherited these characteristics, she pointed out, too, that his tenacity and independence of spirit were traits apparent in his father and especially in his great-grandfather, the Quaker, Thomas Fowell Buxton. She quoted the latter as having said that children should be taught:

> habitually to seek the truth whether for or against previous opinions and interests.[11]1

Following Priscilla Johnston, the claim that the temperament of Johnston's Quaker ancestors formed part of his make-up is a convincing one.[12] It was precisely these qualities which enabled Johnston to develop into a painstaking craftsman. His was an instinctive sympathy with those notions about art and design which came to the fore in England during the late 1890s and which found expression in the Arts and Crafts movement. It was as though Johnston was naturally predisposed to that movement's distinctive ethos of simplicity in lifestyle, of straightforward usefulness in the making of things, and of a distaste for the contrived and the meretricious. Johnston lamented in *Writing & Illuminating, & Lettering* that in the:

> last century of calligraphy, illuminators descended to every kind of artifice....

In his preface he made a plea, heartfelt and resounding with optimism, that:

> ... we endeavour that our work should *be effective* rather than have 'a fine effect' – or *be*, rather than appear, good – and following our craft rather than making it follow us. For all things – material, tools, methods – are waiting to serve us and we have only to find the 'spell' that will set the whole universe a-making for us.[13]

Here, he was surely speaking in the tone of traditional Quakerism. This was a plea for quality marked by modesty and restraint, a craftsman's version of those values of 'integrity, conscientiousness, service' considered by Priscilla Johnston to be inherent in Johnston's forebears. While the mode may have been ancestral, the message that Johnston projected was that of the spiritual leaders of the Arts and Crafts movement – of John Ruskin, William Morris and William Lethaby.

END NOTES

1. Priscilla Johnston. *Edward Johnston.* London: Faber and Faber. 1959.
2. Darwin archive. Manuscripts Dept. Cambridge University Library. The letter is dated 9th March 1873. (Calender No. 8803. Dar 88: 183–184.)
3. Cited from Priscilla Johnston. *Edward Johnston.* London: Faber and Faber. 1959: page 13.
4. A fuller list of these places includes: South Norwood, Hastings, Hampstead, Turnham Green, Upper Norwood, Balham, Plymouth, and Okehampton.
5. These details of Johnston's early life are based on his childhood diaries (in the Johnston estate) and are cited from Priscilla Johnston. *Edward Johnston.* Faber and Faber. 1959. These traits persisted. As an adult living at Hammersmith he concocted fireworks and at his home, Cleves, in Ditchling, devised such items as a draught-proof door and a water-clock to open the door of a henhouse; he was adept at carpentry, too. Algebra interested Johnston and he would run through Euclidean theorems to lull himself to sleep. Yet another instance of his playful constructions is the perpetual calendar which he made for his wife, Greta. He was much intrigued by chronograms incorporated into ancient inscriptions.
6. Cited from Priscilla Johnston. *Edward Johnston.* Faber and Faber. 1959. pages 43–44.
7. Other works in this tradition are Edwin Jewitt's *Manual of Illuminated Missal Painting*, published in 1860 and Henry Shaw's *Alphabets*, 1866.
8. Violet Hawkes. 'Johnston at the Royal College of Art'. In *Alphabet and Image*. No. 1. 1946.
9. *Formal Penmanship and other papers*. Edited by Heather Child. London: Lund Humphries. 1971. page 142.
10. Letter dated 29th October 1945. Crafts Study Centre Collection and Archive. Farnham, Surrey. Johnston archive (Letters 2/255).
11. Priscilla Johnston. *Edward Johnston.* Faber and Faber. 1959. pages 33.
12. This interpretation begs the question, of course, of any influences coming from the maternal side of Johnston's background, about which so little is known. It should be mentioned here, too, that Johnston's wife, Greta Greig was also Scottish. Her father, James Greig, was a banker. Her mother was Irish, from County Down. The family, with five daughters, was based in Laurencekirk near Aberdeen, Scotland.
13. Edward Johnston. *Writing & Illuminating, & Lettering*. London: John Hogg. 1906. page xx.

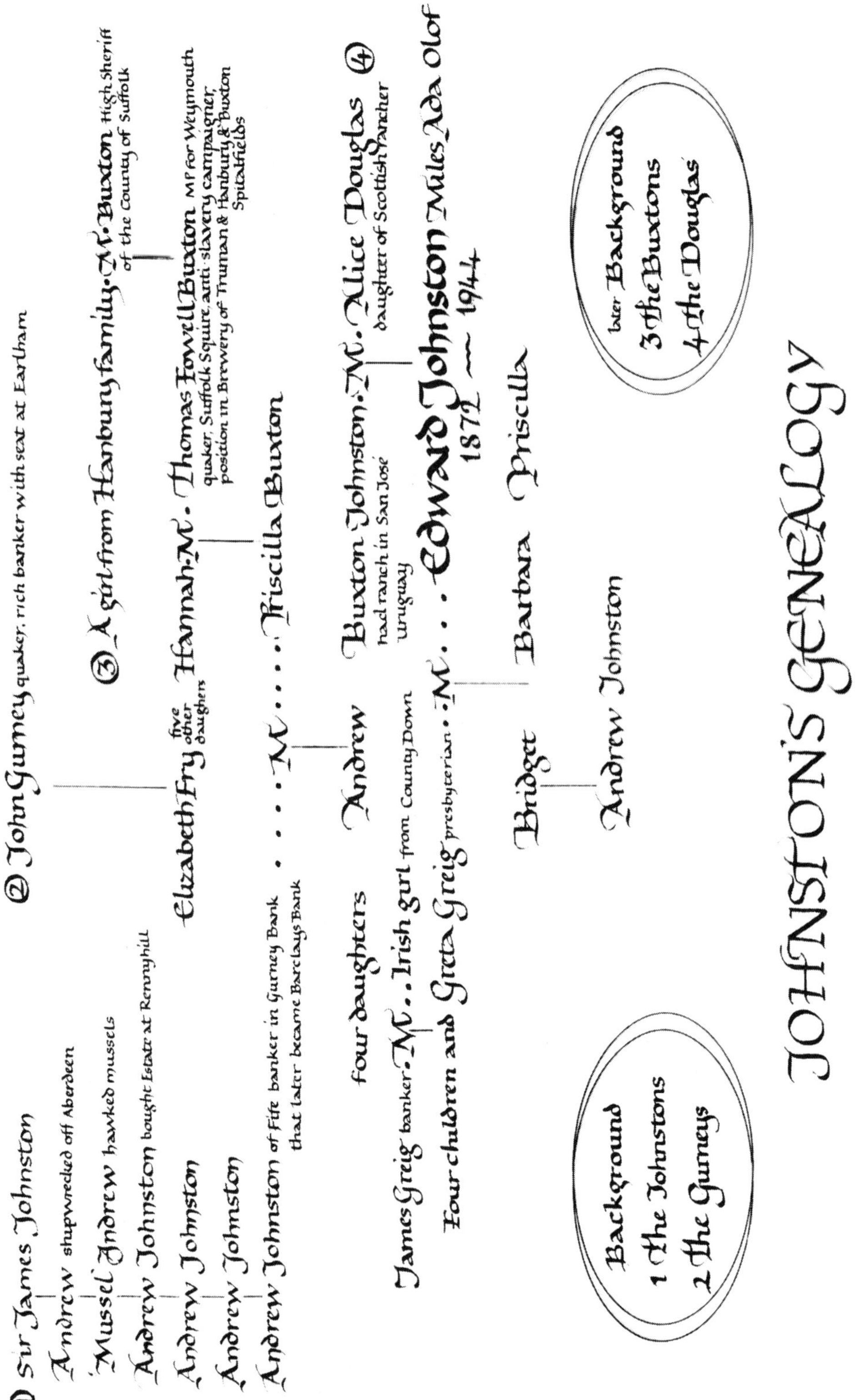

JOHNSTON'S GENEALOGY

1 Sir James Johnston
Andrew shipwrecked off Aberdeen
'Mussel' Andrew hawked mussels
Andrew Johnston bought Estate at Rennyhill
Andrew Johnston
Andrew Johnston
Andrew Johnston of Fife banker in Gurney Bank that later became Barclays Bank . . . . M . . . . Priscilla Buxton

2 John Gurney quaker, rich banker with seat at Earlham
Elizabeth Fry five other daughters
3 A girl from Hanbury family · M · Buxton High Sheriff of the County of Suffolk
Hannah M · Thomas Fowell Buxton MP for Weymouth quaker, Suffolk Squire, anti-slavery campaigner, position in Brewery of Truman & Hanbury & Buxton Spitalfields

Four daughters
Andrew
Buxton Johnston had ranch in San José Uruguay · M · Alice Douglas daughter of Scottish rancher 4

James Greig banker · M . . Irish girl from County Down
Four children and Greta Greig presbyterian · M . . . Edward Johnston 1872 — 1944 Miles Ada Olof

Bridget
Barbara
Priscilla
Andrew Johnston
Andrew Johnston

Background
1 the Johnstons
2 the Gurneys

later Background
3 the Buxtons
4 the Douglas

185

Fig. 185. Johnston's genealogical tree.
(Calligraphy courtesy of Susan Skinner.)

APPENDIX TWO

JOHNSTON AND JOHN RUSKIN: A SOCIAL THEORY OF DESIGN

When Johnston travelled down to London in April 1898, destined to meet Lethaby, he was twenty-six years old and relatively inexperienced in the wider fields of design, architecture, and the fine arts. It is known that while he was living in Edinburgh he was much taken by an exhibition of Burne Jones' paintings and by the caricatures of Phil May. He also read *The Studio,* a magazine of the arts which was seminal at that time.[1] But beyond that he was relatively innocent of the wider questions addressed by theorists such as Ruskin and Morris as to how design related to society, or of William Lethaby's aspirations to introduce workshop practice into design education.

His artistic potential and intellectual honesty were qualities which Lethaby instantly recognised. In describing Lethaby's impact on Johnston, one of their mutual friends, the woodengraver Noel Rooke, wrote: '... Lethaby knew, in some way, what point in the history [of calligraphy] to direct Johnston to, and thanks to that Johnston was able to get started'.[2] And in studying the stylistic and technical aspects of medieval manuscripts, Johnston was also led to reflect on the nature of medieval history itself. Through the views of friends such as Lethaby, Sydney Cockerell, Cobden-Sanderson, and Emery Walker, an awareness of the past and its relevance to the present began to form in his mind.

These friends, in turn, had imbibed a set of values and a sense of mission from earlier writers, notably John Ruskin and William Morris. They were inspired by their discovery of medieval Gothic society. Its culture of guilds of handicraft workmen expressing their religious beliefs by building cathedrals and furnishing them with devotional art inspired them in their own endeavours. They belonged to that loose grouping of like-minded but quietly individualistic people known as the Arts and Crafts movement. Johnston identified with this generation. Through them and the institutions they founded he was linked into the traditions of Ruskin and Morris.

Johnston became familiar with Ruskin's writings early on. In due course he was quoting a passage from Ruskin's *Lecture on Art* (No. 5) to open the chapter in his handbook entitled *The Development of Illumination.* Almost thirty years later, in 1931, he again invoked Ruskin, referring to his 'three primary considerations for a craftsman' in a lecture to students at the Royal College of Art. (They were what Ruskin called the 'position', the 'office' and the 'material' of the object.) Johnston recognised in Ruskin's thought not only the ideas but also a lucidity to which he himself aspired.

One of the most influential thinkers of the nineteenth century, Ruskin became the scourge of Victorian philistinism. His ideas, which he formulated in the early 1850s, largely shaped the aesthetic and the moral values of the period. The son of Scottish Protestant parents, Ruskin was immersed in religion. At the outset, he had wanted to become a clergyman and religious convictions were to remain the basis of his thought. He never lost his evangelical zeal, nor a certain religious nostalgia. Moved by this, he developed a profound disquiet about the materialistic excesses and deprivations of Victorian society. Ruskin had a moral as well as an aesthetic aversion to the industrialisation of Britain. He feared that, if left to itself, rampant and headstrong, it could have only a detrimental, indeed a brutalising, effect on society.

Reinforcing this view of his own times was Ruskin's interpretation of history. In spite of his remaining a Protestant, he espoused the Gothic era of the thirteenth to the fifteenth centuries, a period of high Catholicism, and developed a profound knowledge of its architectural history. In his *The Stones of Venice,* written in three parts between 1851–53, Ruskin concluded that the craftsmen working on the great Gothic cathedrals must have experienced a deep sense of fulfilment. Although they lived within the communal security of the guilds, they felt a personal responsibility for, and a joy in, the process of creation. Life and work were an organic continuum and the architecture they built was, as a consequence, 'an index of religious principle'.

The conviction that Ruskin felt about the medieval world was counterbalanced by his mistrust of the classical one. Like Morris after him, he played down the span of history which included the Classical Renaissance of the fifteenth to the sixteenth centuries, the subsequent scientific revolution, and the Enlightenment of the eighteenth century. His belief was that the revival of classicism coincided with the rise of the patron and the consequent demise of the artist-craftsman, who became a mere executor of the patron's schemes. The artist-craftsman, trapped in a form of social bondage, thereby lost his creative independence.

Moreover, Ruskin believed that the eighteenth-century Enlightenment and its outcome, the French Revolution, had destroyed what he perceived as the wholesome balance between religion and feudal society. While the political upheaval of 1789 gave birth to a bourgeois entrepreneurial class, the scientific revolution gave birth to technology, to the Industrial Revolution and to the philosophy of Positivism. For Ruskin, it followed, for example, that the technologically advanced cast-iron and glass structure of the Crystal Palace of 1851 was anathema. Unacceptable, too, in his view, was the very entrepreneurial spirit of its designer, Joseph Paxton. (It was only later on in the nineteenth century that Paxton was acclaimed as one of Britain's first industrial designers – as it happened, by William Lethaby.)

Based on these religious and historical views, Ruskin developed two lines of thought. They were mutually reinforcing and amounted to a social theory of design. The first focused on the plight of the thing made – the artefact; the second on the plight of the maker – the artisan. In speaking of the artefact, Ruskin made a two-pronged attack. Appalled by the ugliness of unplanned cities and the effects of insanitary conditions, he reserved his most bitter invective for the vulgarity of a culture of indifferently mass-produced goods. The lack of well-considered design shown by their makers, their misapplication of styles to artefacts which, as a consequence, contradicted the functions intended, and their indulgence in applied decoration – especially over-wrought rococo motifs – were particularly irksome for him. The collapse of aesthetic standards was the outcome of historical and social forces, a consequence of modern urban life.

Ruskin's particular concern was the problem of false ornamentation. He approved of ornamentation which was guided entirely by its use in a religious context. Its rationale in ecclesiastical buildings was as a symbolic celebration of God's work. Upholding this, he wrote that 'the highest nobility of a building does not consist of its being well built, but in its being nobly sculptured or painted.' In the competitive and secular market-place of manufactured goods, on the other hand, appropriate and sensitive ornamentation had become virtually unknown.[3]

By the time of Ruskin's *The Stones of Venice* appeals for restraint in ornament had given way, in practice, to flamboyance. The results of such over-designing were displayed at the Great Exhibition of 1851, trumpeted as the very pinnacle of British craftsmanship. The profusion of manufacturing activity in Britain had been facilitated by new techniques – such as electroplating, to name but one – and further complicated by the availability of many design vocabularies. These included all the European styles and others, like Egyptian or Indian, collected from the exotic quarters of the British Empire. There was a glut of styles as a consequence of market over-stimulation. The resulting state of confusion was all too apparent in the Great Exhibition. It was a clear signal to Ruskin of a lack of an organic balance between the designer, the manufacturer, and the consumer of artefacts. Designed artefacts no longer had the fitness of purpose they had once enjoyed in the Gothic-Catholic world of medieval Europe.[4]

Ruskin's second line of thought concentrated on this breakdown of the co-ordination between the designer and the entrepreneur. The making of an artefact was divorced not only from its user but also from its creator. He pointed out that, broadly speaking, the artisan-craftsman, who had once been the designer, was now relegated to being merely the factory employee. He was trapped in the system of the division of labour by the processes of the economies of large-scale production. The intervention of the entrepreneur, whose priority was an ample return on investment and whose market was an undiscerning and under-educated urban middle class, had split the hitherto integrated process of the making and the designing of artefacts. The entrepreneur resorted, increasingly, to the expediency of relying on mere pattern-books. The need was met by such compendia as John Loudon's *Cyclopædia of Cottage, Farm and Villa Architecture and Furniture*, a classic title which was first issued in 1833. It provided a vast anthology of designs from which preferred ones could be chosen regardless of context, need, or suitability. Such pattern-books proliferated.

In Ruskin's view, the demise of the craftsman and the lack of motivation in those who took his place led to a moral rupture. Essentially, Ruskin was constructing a theory of alienation which might well have admitted him across the threshold into Marxism had he not been tied to a religious notion of spiritual degradation. Unlike Morris, it was Ruskin's religious convictions, bolstered by his reactionary High Toryism (for he upheld a rigid class-system), which blocked any such development. Along with earlier reactionaries, like Carlyle and Coleridge, Ruskin believed in the rule of aristocracy rather than democracy. (This was not to be the case, however, in later years with many members of the Arts and Crafts movement who, with Morris, did embrace Socialism.)

Ruskin's social theories are developed in his *The Stones of Venice*. A celebrated and key chapter in this four-volume work has the title 'On the Nature of the Gothic'. It was written in 1853. It is here that Ruskin's historical analysis fused with his social and political analysis of contemporary society. He lambasted Victorian complacency with the whiplash of moral indignation. Two short passages suffice to give the bite of his prose style. It relied on a high-flown rhetoric which, on this occasion, was laced with a cynicism directed largely at Albert, the Prince Consort. The royal address at the opening of the Great Exhibition had extolled 'the great principle of the division of labour ... which may be called the moving power of civilisation'. Ruskin rejoined:

> We have much perfected the great civilised invention of the division of labour, only we give it a false name. It is not, truly speaking, the labour that is divided but the men .... Divided into mere segments of men ... broken into small fragments and units of life ...[5]

The same chapter analyses further the split he saw between labour and the intellect:

> We are always these days endeavouring to separate the two, we want one man to be always thinking and the other to be always working. Now it is only by labour that thought can be made healthy, and only by thought that labour can be made happy; the two cannot be separated with impunity.[6]

The effect of Ruskin's polemics on the generation of the Arts and Crafts movement was almost universally exhilarating. In the case of Johnston's friend, the wealthy and cultivated Cobden-Sanderson, for whose private Doves Press Johnston was commissioned to design lettering, the effect was ecstatic, even verging on the unhinged. In his essay, *The Arts and Crafts movement*, written in 1905, Cobden-Sanderson spoke of Ruskin with an almost biblical fervour:

> ... one of great name, greater than all whom I have named, impels me to pause and praise him, him [*sic*] who begat the begatters, [*sic*] him who was 'as the morning star in the midst of a cloud, as the moon at the full', Ruskin .... To Ruskin, then, all honour all praise, to Ruskin, the Great Dead who, in life, living, begat us.[7]

Such reverence sprang from Cobden-Sanderson's deep attachment to a quasi-mystical view of life.[8]

Johnston, too, was moved to pay tribute to Ruskin, though in more measured terms. Ruskin's thoughts on the beauty of the calligrapher's pen strokes, which he wrote about in his 'Lecture on Art' (No. 5) (mentioned at the outset of this chapter), matched Johnston's own thinking – as did his gift for aphorism. Ruskin's description made a suitable quotation for the opening of Johnston's chapter 'The Development of Illumination' in *Writing & Illumination, & Lettering*. Part of the quotation reads:

> Perfect Illumination is only writing made lovely .... But to make writing itself beautiful – to make the sweep of the pen lovely – is the true art of illumination.[9]

In all likelihood it was Johnston who chose another passage from Ruskin to accompany the frontispiece of the first issue of *The Imprint*, of January 1913, for Johnston was a co-editor of the journal and author of five essays – 'Decoration and its Uses' – which were fundamental to its mission.[10] The religious nature of Ruskin's text also points to Johnston's editorial involvement:

> As the art of life is learned, it will be found at last that all lovely things are also necessary: the wild flower by the wayside, as well as the tended corn; and the wild birds and the creatures of the forest, as well as the tended cattle; because man doth not live by bread only, but also by the desert manna; by every wondrous word and unknowable work of God. Happy, in that he knew them not, nor did his fathers know, and that round about him reaches yet into the infinite, the amazement of his existence.

Profoundly affected by a sense of God as Creator, Johnston's religious outlook brought him closer to Ruskin, perhaps, than to William Morris.

END NOTES

1. *The Studio* was set up in 1893 by Charles Holme. It was read widely in Europe, USA, and in Japan by those interested by new ideas in the applied arts and design.
2. Noel Rooke. 'The Work of Lethaby, Webb, and Morris'. In *The Journal of the RIBA*. Vol. 57. February 1950.
3. Ruskin, however, had not been alone in developing this idea. The issue of ornamentation had already exercised the members of the Henry Cole circle as well as Augustus Pugin, whose Gothic Revival designs graced the interior of the new Palace of Westminster, from the mid-1840s. Pugin, too, recommended severe restraint. In his book, *The True Principles of Christian or Pointed Architecture*, of 1841, he laid down that 'all ornamentation should consist of enrichment of the essential construction.' From his circle Owen Jones, Matthew Wyatt and Richard Redgrave wrote books and provided articles for the *Journal of Design and Manufactures* on the role of ornamentation in design. (Edited by Richard Redgrave, this was a copiously illustrated journal, including bound-in swatches of woven colour and patterned textiles. It ran between 1849–52.) Owen Jones' *The Grammar of Ornament*, of 1856, with its celebrated thirty-seven principles, is considered the most significant of these works
4. Of this situation N. Pevsner wrote in his *Pioneers of the Modern Movement*, of 1936: 'With the extinction of the mediæval craftsman, the shape and appearance of products were left to the uneducated manufacturer. Designers … had not penetrated into industry, artists kept aloof ….'
5. John Ruskin. *The Stones of Venice*. Vol. 42. Chapter 6. Paragraph 16. 'The Nature of Gothic'. 1853. (Everyman) 1907.
6. John Ruskin. *The Stones of Venice*. Op. cit.
7. T. Cobden-Sanderson. *The Arts and Crafts movement*. (Doves Press) 1905.
8. This tendency was to lead Cobden-Sanderson in 1916 to throw the lead types of his Doves Press from Hammersmith Bridge into the Thames. The outcome of a long-standing dispute with his former colleague, Emery Walker, he regarded his action to be a ritualistic reunion of art with its origins in the Earth and God. In his *Journals*, he wrote of his emotions during this episode: 'I stood upon the bridge and walked to and fro and bethought me of the time when I had crossed and recrossed it in wintertime, in the darkness and, as the buses

brought protection, threw the type from the bridge into the river. Then I lifted my thoughts to the wonder of the scene before me, full of an awful beauty, God's Universe and Man's – joint creators. How wonderful! And my Type, the Doves' type part of it.' (There is a precedent for this gesture, if not for the thought which lay behind it. In 1904, Charles Ricketts ended his Vale Press in Chelsea by melting down the lead types and casting the punches and matrices into the Thames.)

9. Edward Johnston. *Writing & Illuminating, & Lettering*. Chapter 12. 'The Development of Illumination'. Page 204 in the first edition. J. Hogg. 1906.

10. Johnston also designed the decorative border for *The Imprint*, setting it around a woodcut illustration by Bewick. He had a particular admiration for the modest effectiveness of Bewick's work, using other woodcuts in *Writing & Illumination, & Lettering* to illustrate principles of illumination. Although he was an eighteenth-century artist Bewick was at the head of a particularly English tradition of book illustration for which Johnston felt an affinity.

Fig. 186 Blackboard flourish by Edward Johnston.

INDEX

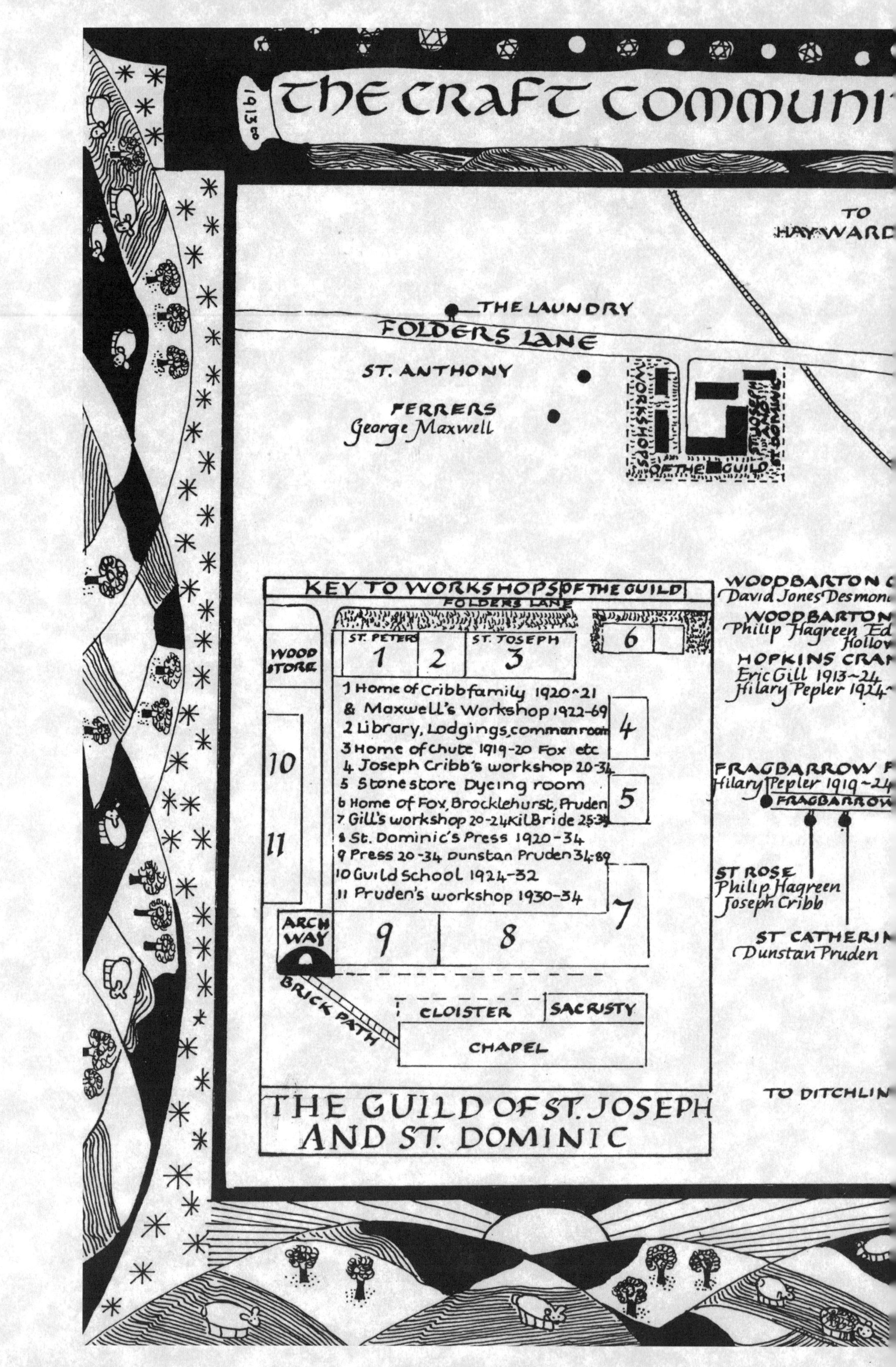

1913 ~ 89
THE CRAFT COMMUNI
TO
HAYWARD
THE LAUNDRY
FOLDERS LANE
ST. ANTHONY
FERRERS
George Maxwell
WORKSHOPS OF THE GUILD
ST JOSEPH AND ST DOMINIC
KEY TO WORKSHOPS OF THE GUILD
FOLDERS LANE
WOOD STORE
ST. PETERS
1
2
ST. JOSEPH
3
6
1 Home of Cribb family 1920~21
& Maxwell's Workshop 1922-69
2 Library, Lodgings, common room
3 Home of Chute 1919-20 Fox etc
4 Joseph Cribb's workshop 20-34
5 Stonestore Dyeing room
6 Home of Fox, Brocklehurst, Pruden
7 Gill's workshop 20-24 KilBride 25-34
8 St. Dominic's Press 1920-34
9 Press 20-34 Dunstan Pruden 34-89
10 Guild School 1924-32
11 Pruden's workshop 1930-34
4
5
10
11
7
ARCH WAY
9
8
BRICK PATH
CLOISTER
SACRISTY
CHAPEL
THE GUILD OF ST. JOSEPH AND ST. DOMINIC
WOODBARTON C
David Jones Desmon
WOODBARTON
Philip Hagreen Ed
Hollow
HOPKINS CRA
Eric Gill 1913~24
Hilary Pepler 1924
FRAGBARROW F
Hilary Pepler 1919~24
FRAGBARROW
ST ROSE
Philip Hagreen
Joseph Cribb
ST CATHERI
Dunstan Pruden
TO DITCHLI